ADVANCES IN
AIRLINE ECONOMICS

Competition Policy and Antitrust

ADVANCES IN AIRLINE ECONOMICS

Competition Policy and Antitrust

VOLUME 1

Edited by

Darin Lee
LECG, LLC
Cambridge, USA

ELSEVIER

AMSTERDAM • BOSTON • HEIDELBERG • LONDON • NEW YORK • OXFORD
PARIS • SAN DIEGO • SAN FRANCISCO • SINGAPORE • SYDNEY • TOKYO

387.71
A244

Elsevier
Radarweg 29, PO Box 211, 1000 AE Amsterdam, The Netherlands
The Boulevard, Langford Lane, Kidlington, Oxford OX5 1GB, UK

First edition 2006

Library of Congress Cataloging-in-Publication Data
A catalog record for this book is available from the Library of Congress

British Library Cataloguing in Publication Data
A catalogue record for this book is available from the British Library

ISBN-13: 978-0-444-51843-9
ISBN-10: 0-444-51843-6

For information on all Elsevier publications
visit our website at books.elsevier.com

Printed and bound in The Netherlands

06 07 08 09 10   10 9 8 7 6 5 4 3 2 1

Contents

Preface

Following the deregulation of the U.S. airline industry in 1978, papers analyzing the industry were a regular feature in prominent economics journals such as the *American Economic Review*, the *Quarterly Journal of Economics* and the *Journal of Political Economy*. While important research on the airline industry continued throughout the mid to late 1990s, the number of academic economists actively pursuing research on the airline industry had clearly waned. After a brief hiatus however, there has been a resurgence in academic research on the airline industry, both in North America and throughout the rest of world. This, no doubt, reflects the dramatic changes sweeping through the industry. Indeed, one could argue that the changes over the past several years—including the growing prominence of "low cost carriers" and their interplay with the "legacy carriers" the advent of the Internet and its affect on industry pricing and the proliferation of international alliances—have resulted in changes that rival those following the passage of the Airline Deregulation Act.

The purpose the *Advances in Airline Economics* series is to provide a comprehensive overview of the current state of economic research on the airline industry. Each volume will consist of several previously unpublished research papers written by an international panel of distinguished academic and industry economists, as well as a select number of reprints of influential papers by prominent researchers in the field.

Volume 1: Competition Policy and Antitrust features sixteen essays, including reprints of important papers by Professors Jan Brueckner (University of California—Irvine) and Steven Morrison (Northeastern University). These essays span four main topics: Predation, Alliances and Codesharing, Airline Competition Issues and Airport Competition Issues.

I hope readers find the essays enlightening and that they help stimulate further debate and research in this continually evolving and fascinating industry.

Darin Lee, Editor

Contributors

O. Armantier	Département de Sciences Economiques, CIRANO, CRT, and CIREQ. Université de Montréal, C.P. 6128, succursale Centre-ville, Montréal QC H3C 3J7.
G.E. Bamberger	Lexecon, 332 S. Michigan Ave., Chicago, IL 60604.
S. Berry	James Burrows Moffatt Professor of Economics, Yale University.
V. Bilotkach	University of California, Irvine, Department of Economics, 3151 Social Science Plaza, Irvine, CA, 92697, USA.
J.K. Brueckner	Department of Economics, University of California, Irvine, 3151 Social Science Plaza, Irvine, CA 92697.
D.W. Carlton	The University of Chicago, Graduate School of Business, 5807 S. Woodlawn Ave., Chicago, IL 60637, NBER and Lexecon.
M. Carnall	Senior Managing Economist, LECG LLC.
Eckert	Department of Economics, University of Alberta, Edmonton, Alberta T6G 2H4.
P. Forsyth	Department of Economics, Clayton Campus, Monash University, Vic, 3800, Australia.
S. Giaume	Lavoisier post-doctoral fellowship at the Centre for Research on Transportation (CRT) at the University of Montreal.
S. Guilloiu	University of Nice-Sophia Antipolis, CNRS.
S.D. Gurrea	Economists Incorporated, Emerystation North, Suite 205, 5980 Horton Street, Emeryville CA 94608.
M.E. Hartmann	Department of Economics, University of St. Thomas, 2215 Summit Avenue, St. Paul, MN 55105, U.S.A.
O. Heimer	ZIM Integrated Shipping Services LTD
H. Ito	NBER
D. Lee	LECG, LLC. 350 Massachusetts Avenue, Suite 300, Cambridge, MA 02139.
M.G. Lijesen	Netherlands Bureau for Economic Policy Analysis (CPB), The Hague and Free University, Amsterdam. CPB, PO Box 80510 2508 GM The Hague, The Netherlands.

A.V. Marques de Oliveira   Center for Studies of Airline Competition and
                              Regulation (NECTAR) Instituto Tecnológico de
                              Aeronáutica, Brazil.

S.A. Morrison   Department of Economics, Northeastern University,
                              Boston, MA 02115.

P. Nijkamp   Free University, Amsterdam

D.H. Owens   Welch Consulting, Silver Spring, Maryland 20910

E. Pels   Free University, Amsterdam

O. Richard   Economic Analysis Group, Antitrust Division,
                              US Department of Justice, 600 E Street N.W., Suite
                              10000, Washington, DC 20530.

P. Rietveld   Free University, Amsterdam

N.G. Rupp   Department of Economics, East Carolina University,
                              Greenville, NC 27858-4353.

O. Shy   WZB – Social Science Research Center,
                              Reichpietschufer 50, D–10785 Berlin, Germany.

P.T. Spiller   Jeffrey A. Jacobs Distinguished Professorship in
                              Business and Technology Chair, Haas Business and
                              Public Policy Group, Haas School of Business,
                              University of California, Berkeley.

D.S. West   Department of Economics, University of Alberta,
                              Edmonton, Alberta T6G 2H4.

T. Whalen   University of Illinois at Urbana-Champagin

Advances in Airline Economics, Vol 1
Darin Lee (Editor)
© 2006 Published by Elsevier B.V.

1

Predation and the Entry and Exit of Low-Fare Carriers[*]

Gustavo E. Bamberger[†] and Dennis W. Carlton[‡]

ABSTRACT

Low-fare airlines grew rapidly in the United States during the first half of the 1990s, but their growth stagnated in the second half of the 1990s. The growth of low-fare airlines resumed after 1999, and by 2003 these carriers accounted for 27 percent of U.S. domestic passengers. The Department of Transportation and others attributed the 1995–99 slowdown, at least in part, to systematic predatory conduct by incumbent carriers. In this paper, we review the history of entry by low-fare carriers, and the price responses to such entry by major carriers. We find that there is no empirical support for claims that predatory pricing conduct against low-fare carriers is a systematic problem that explains their slowdown in growth between 1995 and 1999. Instead, we find that: (1) most low-fare carrier entries were successful; (2) incumbent carriers' average fares typically did not fall substantially after low-fare entry; and (3) incumbent carriers' average fares typically did not increase substantially after low-fare exit. We also find that the success of low-fare carriers since 1999 does not appear to be the result of less aggressive competition from major carriers.

In the first half of the 1990s, several U.S. "low-fare" airline carriers expanded rapidly. By 1995, these carriers – most notably Southwest Airlines – accounted for about 20 percent of domestic U.S. passengers. Over the next several years – a period that includes the crash of a ValuJet Airlines flight in Florida – the growth of these carriers largely

---

[*]This paper is based in part on a study presented to the Department of Transportation on behalf of United Airlines. We thank Lynette Neumann and Dan Stone for their assistance. All opinions in this study are our own and do not necessarily reflect the views of United or any other airline.
[†]Lexecon, 332 S. Michigan Ave., Chicago, IL 60604. E-mail: gbamberger@lexecon.com. Tel: (312) 322-0276.
[‡]The University of Chicago, Graduate School of Business, 5807 S. Woodlawn Ave., Chicago, IL 60637, NBER and Lexecon. E-mail: dennis.carlton@chicagogsb.edu. Tel: (773) 702-6694.

stagnated.[1] Since 1999, however, the growth of low-fare carriers' share of domestic U.S. passengers has resumed, reaching 27 percent in 2003.

During the 1990s, various critics of major airlines' pricing practices claimed that these carriers engaged in systematic predatory conduct against low-fare carriers, and that this conduct explained the slowdown in the growth of these carriers. At least partly in response to these claims and to a U.S. Department of Transportation ("DOT") study, the DOT called for special rules for the airline industry;[2] Congress commissioned a study by the Transportation Research Board ("TRB") of the National Research Council ("NRC"); and the U.S. Department of Justice ("DOJ") sued American Airlines for predatory conduct. Claims of predatory conduct by major carriers against low-fare carriers also have been made in recent years in Canada (against Air Canada); Australia (Qantas); and Germany (Lufthansa).[3]

In this paper, we review the history of entry by low-fare carriers, and the price responses to such entry by major carriers.[4] We find that there is no empirical support for claims that predatory pricing conduct against low-fare carriers is a systematic problem that explains their slowdown in growth between 1995 and 1999. In particular, we find that a "standard" description of predation against low-fare carriers by major carriers – many low-fare entrants are forced to exit by large fare reductions by incumbent major carriers, after which incumbents substantially increase average fares – typically did not occur. Instead, we find that:

- Most low-fare carrier entries were successful;
- Incumbent carriers' average fares typically did not fall substantially after low-fare entry; and
- Incumbent carriers' average fares typically did not increase substantially after low-fare exit.

We also find that the success of low-fare carriers since 1999 does not appear to be the result of less aggressive competition from major carriers.

1   BACKGROUND

Throughout most of the 1990s, several smaller airlines complained to the DOT about allegedly predatory actions taken against them by major carriers.[5] In response to these

---

[1] The Federal Aviation Administration grounded all ValuJet flights on June 17, 1996 (about one month after ValuJet's May 11, 1996 crash). See CNN.com, "ValuJet Grounded," June 17, 1996 (www.cnn.com /US/9606/17/ valujet.grounded/). According to the Department of Transportation ("DOT"), "[w]hile [the DOT] and the FAA began reviewing new entrants' applications for authority more rigorously after the ValuJet crash, that heightened scrutiny of new entrants did not end new entry. The longer time needed to obtain authority from [the DOT] and the FAA would not have discouraged all potential entrants." See DOT, "Findings and Conclusions on the Economic, Policy and Legal Issues," Docket OST-98-3713, January 17, 2001.

[2] See DOT, "Competition in the U.S. Domestic Airline Industry: The Need for a Policy to Prevent Unfair Practices" ("DOT Proposal").

[3] See Ito and Lee (2004), at 2, footnote 2.

[4] For the purposes of the empirical analysis in this study, we define seven "major" carriers: American, Continental, Delta, Northwest, TWA, United and US Airways (TWA is included for the years 1990-2001).

[5] The Transportation Research Board reviewed 32 complaints received by DOT between March 1993 and May 1999 from "new entrant airlines" about "unfair exclusionary practices." See "Entry and Competition in the U.S. Airline Industry: Issues and Opportunities," TRB, NRC, Special Report 225, July 1999 ("TRB Report"), Appendix C.

complaints, the DOT "concluded that unfair exclusionary practices have been a key reason that competition from new low-fare carriers has not been able to penetrate concentrated hubs" and proposed guidelines in April 1998 "as to what constitutes unlawful behavior."[6] In response to criticisms of the proposed guidelines by several carriers, Congress requested a six-month study by the NRC to address competition issues in the airline industry, including the DOT's proposed guidelines. The report, issued in July 1999, criticized the DOT proposals, but it too raised concerns about pricing practices in the airline industry:

> The committee [convened by the NRC] harbors reservations . . . about DOT's proposal for identifying and forbidding predation in the airline industry. Many members are concerned that DOT's proposal could become increasingly regulatory, thus inhibiting genuine competition. . . . However, other members – while sharing the committee's general concerns about regulatory risk – judge the problem serious enough to warrant the more active involvement of DOT, exercising its own independent enforcement authority to prevent unfair methods of competition.[7]

In 2001, the DOT responded to the TRB study:

> Having considered the comments and the TRB's recommendations and having undertaken further investigations, this Administration is reaffirming its initial findings that airlines have responded to new competition with unfair competitive practices, that those practices eliminate or reduce competition, and that this Department has an obligation to prevent unfair competitive conduct since it harms the public.[8]

According to some observers, antitrust laws are inadequate to deal with predatory pricing issues in the airline industry. For example, Alfred Kahn, who oversaw much of the deregulation of the U.S. airline industry, has written that the DOT's proposed guidelines have

> inspired intensified attention to the adequacy of the antitrust laws' proscriptions. There are in fact strong reasons to believe that, at least so far as the airlines business is concerned, the Supreme Court's view that 'predation is rarely attempted and even more rarely successful' is simply incorrect; and also that the dominating Areeda-Turner test provides an inadequate basis for identifying it.[9]

Similarly, a report prepared on behalf of Frontier and Spirit Airlines also suggests that the antitrust laws do not prevent predatory conduct by major airlines. According to this report, a federal statute "authorizes the [DOT] to prohibit conduct that does not amount to a violation of the antitrust laws, but could be considered anticompetitive under antitrust principles."[10]

---

[6] DOT Proposal, p. 7.

[7] TRB Report, p. E-8.

[8] See DOT, "Findings and Conclusions on the Economic, Policy and Legal Issues," Docket OST-98-3713, January 17, 2001.

[9] Alfred Kahn, "How to know airline predatory pricing when you see it," FTC:WATCH, No. 512, December 7, 1998.

[10] John Haring and Jeffrey H. Rohlfs, "Public Policy to Deter Exclusionary Practices in the Airline Industry," Prepared for Frontier Airlines and Spirit Airlines, September 25, 1998.

Notwithstanding these suggestions that the antitrust laws cannot adequately prevent predation in the airline industry, the DOJ sued American Airlines for predatory pricing in May 1999. The DOJ's suit was dismissed by a district court judge in April 2001, and that decision was subsequently affirmed by the 10th Circuit Court of Appeals.[11]

Critics of major carriers' pricing actions appear to be concerned with situations that can be described roughly as follows: (1) a low-fare carrier begins to offer service on certain routes that are served primarily by major carriers; (2) an incumbent major carrier responds by reducing average fares by large amounts; (3) the low-fare carrier fails to capture sufficient traffic to be profitable and is forced to withdraw service; and (4) the incumbent carrier responds to the low-fare carrier's exit by raising fares dramatically (i.e., the incumbent "recoups" losses associated with its predatory conduct). The DOT (and others) suggests that these situations are common in the airline industry.

In this paper, we empirically assess whether the type of conduct with which the DOT and others are concerned is widespread in the airline industry. (We do not address the specific allegations made by the DOJ in the American Airlines lawsuit.) In particular, we examine: (1) entry by low-fare carriers since 1990; (2) the survival rates of low-fare carriers; (3) the fare responses of incumbents to entry by low-fare carriers; and (4) the fare responses of incumbents to exit by low-fare carriers.

As we explain in the remainder of this paper, we find that the empirical evidence fails to support concern that incumbent major carriers systematically engaged in predatory conduct to force low-fare carriers to withdraw service in the mid-1990s.[12] We also find that the growth in low-fare service since 1998 was not associated with less aggressive pricing by major carriers.

2   LOW-FARE SHARE AND ENTRY

2.1   Low-Fare Carriers' Share of Domestic Passengers

Critics of major airlines' responses to low-fare competition claim that their pricing policies reduced entry by low-fare carriers. For example, according to the DOT, there was "a reversal of growth in low-fare competition" since 1996 (DOT Proposal, p. 3). In particular, the DOT explained that

> [f]ollowing the Valujet crash [in May 1996], a number of small new entrants complained to the DOT about unfair competitive practices on the part of large network carriers. The alleged increase in anti-competitive behavior appears to have had a chilling effect on new entry. No new scheduled passenger jet operators have applied to DOT for a certificate and started service since the Valujet crash (DOT Proposal, p. 6).

---

[11] United States v. AMR Corp., 335 F. 3d 1109 (10th Cir. 2003). For discussions of this case, see Edlin (2001); Eckert and West (2002); and Edlin and Farrell (2004).

[12] Our finding does not imply that there can never be isolated instances of predation in the airline industry; instead, we show that there is no evidence to support the claim that successful predation in the airline industry was widespread.

The DOJ, it its case against American, argued that American's conduct during the mid-1990s was designed, in part, to establish a "reputation for predation."

In 1990, seven major carriers – American, Continental, Delta, Northwest, TWA, United and US Airways – accounted for 74.7 percent of U.S. domestic passengers.[13] Southwest accounted for almost all domestic passengers carried by low-fare carriers, with a share of 7.1 percent; other low-fare carriers accounted for only 0.3 percent of total U.S. domestic passengers.[14] A few regional carriers (e.g., Alaska Airlines, Aloha Airlines, America West and Hawaiian Airlines) accounted for most remaining passengers.

Between 1992 and 1993, however, low-fare carriers other than Southwest quadrupled their domestic passenger share, from 0.8 to 3.2 percent. Between 1993 and 1995, low-fare carriers other than Southwest further doubled their domestic passenger share, from 3.2 to 6.4 percent. This increase largely reflected the entry of several new carriers – Airtran Airways; Frontier Airlines; Kiwi International; Midway Air (in reconstituted form); Reno Air; Spirit Airlines; ValuJet Airlines; Vanguard Air; and Western Pacific. During the first half of the 1990s, Southwest's domestic passenger share almost doubled, from 7.1 to 13.7 percent.

Between 1995 and 1998, however, low-fare carriers other than Southwest lost domestic passenger share (from 6.4 to 5.8 percent of domestic U.S. passengers). During the same period, Southwest's domestic passenger share was roughly constant. As a result, low-fare carriers' share fell from 20.1 percent in 1995 to 19.6 percent in 1998. See Figure 1.

Since 1998, low-fare carriers other than Southwest have increased their share of domestic passengers every year through 2003, reaching an aggregate share of 10.1 percent; Southwest's domestic passenger share reached 16.8 percent in 2003; total low-fare carriers' share reached 26.9 percent.[15] The increase in share of low-fare carriers other than Southwest largely reflects the success of four existing low-fare carriers and the entry of a new low-fare carrier. Between 1998 and 2003, four low-fare carriers at least doubled their share of domestic passengers – Airtran (1.2 to 2.5 percent); American Trans Air (1.1 to 2.2 percent); Frontier (0.3 to 1.1 percent); and Spirit (0.4 to 1.1 percent). In addition, Jet Blue – an entrant in 2000 – had a 2.3 percent share of domestic passengers in 2003. Several low-fare carriers – Kiwi, Reno, Tower, Vanguard and Western Pacific – stopped providing service between 1998 and 2003. See Table 1.

2.2   Entry by Low-Fare Carriers

We examine the history of entry by low-fare carriers since 1990. Most of the economic literature treats pairs of airports ("origin and destination pairs," or "O&D pairs") or "city

---

[13] This total includes 3.7 percent from associated commuter carriers. Eastern Airlines accounted for 4.7 percent of U.S. domestic passengers, but exited in 1991. We base our analyses on data compiled by Data Base Products, Inc., a commercial vendor. Data Base Products, Inc. relies on the Department of Transportation's OD1A and Commuter 298C T-1 databases.

[14] For purposes of this study, we define the following as low-fare carriers: Air South, Airtran Airways, American Trans Air, Carnival Air Lines, Jet Blue, Frontier Airlines, Kiwi International, Markair, Midway Air, Midwest Express, Morris Air, National Airlines, Reno Air, Spirit Airlines, Sun Country Air, ValuJet Airlines, Vanguard Air and Western Pacific.

[15] In 2003, the six remaining major carriers (American, Continental, Delta, Northwest, United and US Airways, with associated commuter carriers) had a U.S. domestic passenger share of 64.0 percent.

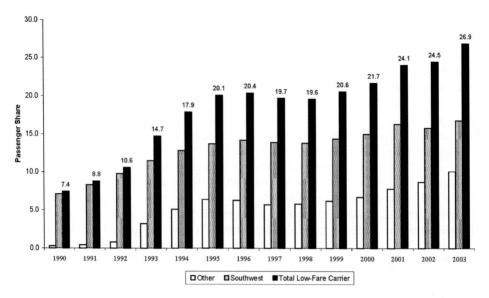

Figure 1   Low-Fare Carriers' Share of Passengers.

Source: Data Base Products, Inc. based on U.S. Department of Transportation OD1A and Commuter 298C T-1 data.

pairs" as separate economic markets.[16] For this reason, we analyze entry since 1990 by determining entry into O&D pairs. That is, we analyze the extent to which carriers (whether new or established) add O&D pairs to their route networks.

2.2.1   Entry on All O&Ds

We define a carrier as an "entrant" on an O&D pair if its share on that O&D was less than one percent in the year prior to entry and at least five percent in the following year. For example, if a carrier had a share of 0.1 percent on an O&D in 1990 and a share of 10.0 percent in 1991, we treat it as an entrant in 1991.

Figure 2 shows that the number of O&Ds entered by low-fare carriers other than Southwest fluctuated substantially during the 1990s.[17] After a rapid increase between

---

[16] See, for example, Borenstein (1989) and Bamberger and Carlton (2003). Our analysis is based on O&D pairs, so that we treat, for example, Chicago O'Hare to San Francisco and Chicago O'Hare to Oakland as different O&Ds. We limit our analysis to O&D pairs with total traffic of at least 10 passengers per day in every year of our analysis (1990-2003); in addition, we exclude O&D pairs where both endpoints are in Hawaii or both endpoints are in Alaska. We also exclude itineraries with more than two coupons in one direction and "open-jaw" itineraries (e.g., Chicago O'Hare to San Francisco to Washington Dulles).

[17] Several mergers (e.g., American's acquisition of TWA) occurred during the period we analyze. If (1) an acquired carrier offered service on a particular O&D in the year prior to its acquisition; (2) the acquiring carrier did not offer service on that O&D in the year prior to the acquisition; and (3) the acquiring carrier offered service on that O&D in the year of the acquisition, we do not treat the acquiring carrier as having entered on that O&D.

Table 1 Low-Fare Carriers' Share of Passengers, By Carrier

Airline	Airline Code	1990	1991	1992	1993	1994	1995	1996	1997	1998	1999	2000	2001	2002	2003
AIR SOUTH	WV					0.0	0.3	0.2	0.1						
AIRTRAN AIRWAYS	FL					0.0	0.1	0.3	0.3	1.2	1.3	1.5	1.6	2.0	2.5
AMERICAN TRANS AIR	TZ	0.1	0.1	0.1	0.4	0.7	1.0	0.9	0.8	1.1	1.2	1.3	1.6	1.9	2.2
CARNIVAL AIR LINES	KW	0.0	0.1	0.1	0.2	0.3	0.4	0.4	0.4	0.0					
FRONTIER	F9					0.0	0.2	0.3	0.3	0.3	0.5	0.6	0.6	0.8	1.1
JET BLUE	B6											0.3	0.8	1.5	2.3
KIWI INTERNATIONAL	KP			0.0	0.2	0.4	0.5	0.4	0.1	0.2	0.0				
MARKAIR	BF	0.0	0.0	0.1	0.3	0.5	0.3	0.0							
MIDWAY AIR	JI				0.0	0.1	0.3	0.4	0.3	0.4	0.4	0.6	0.5	0.1	0.0
MIDWEST EXPRESS	YX	0.2	0.2	0.2	0.3	0.3	0.4	0.4	0.4	0.5	0.5	0.5	0.6	0.6	0.6
MORRIS AIR	KN				1.1	0.9									
NATIONAL AIRLINES	N7										0.1	0.4	0.6	0.5	0.0
RENO AIR	QQ			0.1	0.6	0.9	0.9	1.2	1.2	1.1	0.7				
SPIRIT AIRLINES	NK			0.0	0.1	0.1	0.2	0.2	0.2	0.4	0.6	0.7	0.9	1.0	1.1
SUN COUNTRY AIR	SY										0.2	0.5	0.4	0.1	0.2
TOWER AIR	FF		0.0	0.0	0.1	0.2	0.2	0.2	0.2	0.3	0.3	0.0			
VALUJET AIRLINES	J7				0.0	0.6	1.2	0.7	0.6						
VANGUARD AIR	NJ					0.0	0.2	0.3	0.2	0.3	0.3	0.3	0.3	0.2	
WESTERN PACIFIC	W7							0.5	0.4	0.0					
SUBTOTAL		0.3	0.4	0.8	3.2	5.1	6.4	6.3	5.7	5.8	6.2	6.7	7.8	8.7	10.1
SOUTHWEST	WN	7.1	8.3	9.8	11.5	12.8	13.7	14.2	13.9	13.8	14.4	15.0	16.3	15.8	16.8
TOTAL		7.4	8.8	10.6	14.7	17.9	20.1	20.4	19.7	19.6	20.6	21.7	24.1	24.5	26.9

Note: 0.0 indicates a share smaller than 0.05; a blank indicates no passengers.
Source: Data Base Products, Inc. based on U.S. Department of Transportation OD1A and Commuter 298C T-1 data.

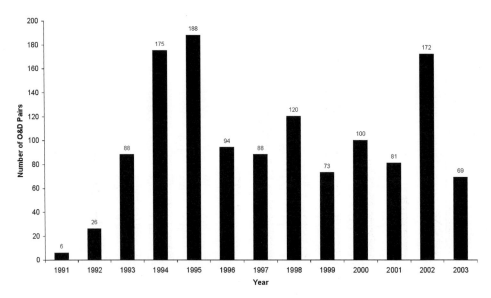

Figure 2 Entry on O&D Pairs by Low-Fare Carriers other than Southwest.

Source: Data Base Products, Inc. based on U.S. Department of Transportation OD1A and Commuter 298C T-1 data.

1990 and 1995 (from six to 188), the number of entries fell by 50 percent between 1995 and 1996, the year of the ValuJet crash.[18] Since 1996, the number of O&Ds entered by low-fare carriers other than Southwest has fluctuated between 69 and 172. Southwest entered relatively few O&Ds in 2002 and 2003.[19] See Figure 3.

Figure 4 shows that the number of O&Ds entered by major carriers also fluctuated substantially during the 1990s. For example, major carriers added relatively few O&Ds in 1997.[20]

2.2.2   Entry on Hub O&Ds vs. Non-Hub O&Ds

As we have discussed, the DOT "concluded that unfair exclusionary practices have been a key reason that competition from new low-fare carriers has not been able to penetrate concentrated hubs." For this reason, we also distinguish entry on O&Ds on which one

---

[18] "Concerns about the safety of startup airlines – particularly after the 1996 crash of a Valujet flight – also might have slowed expansion during the latter half of the 1990s" (TRB Report, at E-5). Furthermore, as we have discussed, additional scrutiny from the DOT and the Federal Aviation Administration may have delayed entry of new carriers after the 1996 ValuJet crash.

[19] However, Southwest began offering service in Philadelphia in 2004 and Pittsburgh in 2005.

[20] The annual number of O&Ds entered by major carriers, low-fare carriers other than Southwest and Southwest are not correlated over time at statistically significant levels (all significance tests we report are at the five percent level).

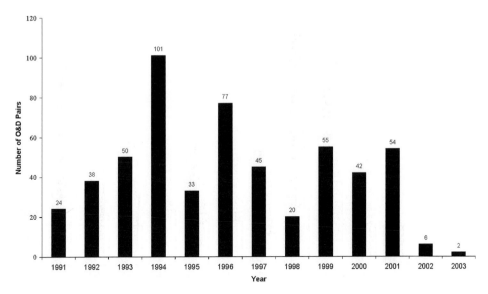

Figure 3 Entry on O&D Pairs by Southwest.

Source: Data Base Products, Inc. based on U.S. Department of Transportation OD1A and Commuter 298C T-1 data.

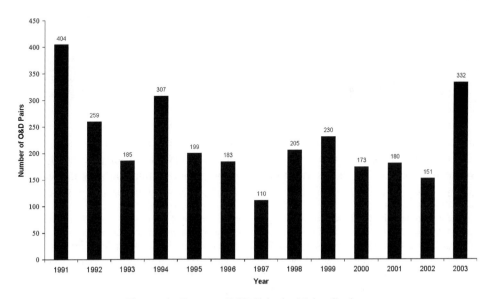

Figure 4 Entry on O&D Pairs by Major Carriers.

Source: Data Base Products, Inc. based on U.S. Department of Transportation OD1A and Commuter 298C T-1 data.

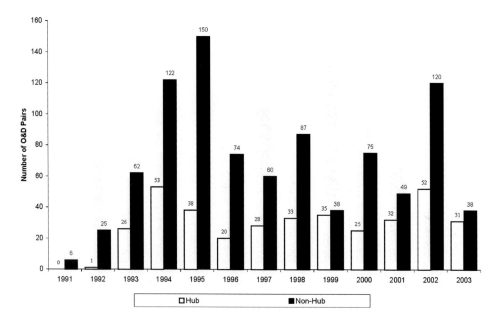

Figure 5   Entry on Hub and Non-Hub O&D Pairs by Low-Fare Carriers other than Southwest.

Source: Data Base Products, Inc. based on U.S. Department of Transportation OD1A and Commuter 298C T-1 data.

endpoint airport is a major carrier's hub – which we refer to as "hub O&Ds" – from entry on other O&Ds – which we refer to as "non-hub O&Ds."[21]

Hub routes account for about 20 to 45 percent of the O&Ds entered by low-fare carriers other than Southwest in every year since 1993. See Figure 5. In contrast, Southwest entered more than three hub routes in a year only in 1994 and 1996.[22] See Figure 6.

Major carriers entered more non-hub O&Ds than hub O&Ds in every year during our period of analysis. Hub O&Ds account for roughly 20 to 35 percent of major airline O&D entries in every year except 2002 (when hub O&Ds are 45 percent of O&D entries). See Figure 7. That is, most entry by both major carriers and low-fare carriers

---

[21] There is no standard definition of a "hub" airport. For the purpose of our analysis, we define a "hub pair" as an O&D pair that has one of the following airports as one or both endpoints: Atlanta; Charlotte; Chicago O'Hare; Dallas/Ft. Worth; Denver; Memphis; Minneapolis; Pittsburgh, St. Louis; and Salt Lake City. (These are the top 30 airports in the United States for which the percentage of passengers changing planes was 50 percent or more in 1990. See Borenstein (1992).) We also have used an alternative definition of a hub airport (including the same airports and an additional five airports). Using this alternative definition does not substantially change the conclusions we discuss later about survival rates on hub vs. non-hub O&Ds.

[22] We determine whether an O&D involves a hub on an airport (instead of city) basis. Southwest often uses secondary airports in major airports (e.g., Midway instead of O'Hare in Chicago) and so serves relatively few hub O&Ds. As we have discussed, Southwest began offering service in Pittsburgh in 2005 (a US Airways hub).

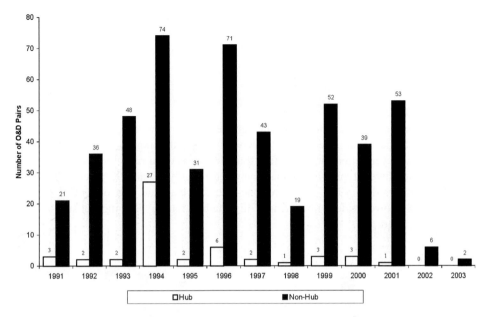

Figure 6 Entry on Hub and Non-Hub O&D Pairs by Southwest.

Source: Data Base Products, Inc. based on U.S. Department of Transportation OD1A and Commuter 298C T-1 data.

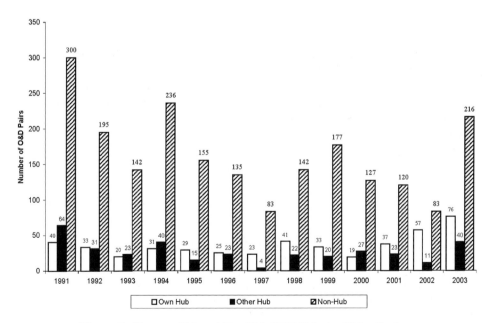

Figure 7 Entry on Hub and Non-Hub O&D Pairs by Major Carriers.

Source: Data Base Products, Inc. based on U.S. Department of Transportation OD1A and Commuter 298C T-1 data.

was on non-hub O&Ds during the period we analyze.[23] Of the hub O&Ds entered by major carriers, about 60 percent (464 out of 807) included the carrier's own hub as an endpoint (i.e., the other hub O&Ds included a different major carrier's hub).[24]

2.3   Entrant Survival Rates

2.3.1   All O&Ds

For each O&D entry, we determine whether the entrant survived on the O&D pair for one year.[25] In particular, we define "survival" as maintaining at least a five percent O&D share one year after entry. We find that annual survival rates for low-fare carriers other than Southwest typically fluctuate between roughly 60 and 90 percent. The only exception occurred in 1997, when the one-year survival rate was only 27.3 percent. See Figure 8. However, low-fare carriers' high failure rate in 1997 did not substantially

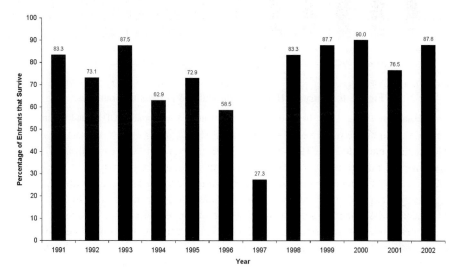

Figure 8   One-Year Survival Rates on O&D Pairs for Low-Fare Carriers Other than Southwest.

Source: Data Base Products, Inc. based on U.S. Department of Transportation OD1A and Commuter 298C T-1 data.

---

[23] The straight-line distance between endpoint airports tended to be somewhat larger for O&Ds entered by low-fare carriers than for O&Ds entered by major carriers during 1991–2003. For example, the median straight-line distance for O&Ds entered by major carriers ranged (on an annual basis) between 464 and 979 miles; median straight-line distance for O&Ds entered by low-fare carriers other than Southwest ranged between 600 and 1,218 miles; and median straight-line distance for O&Ds entered by Southwest ranged between 840 and 1,450 miles.

[24] Atlanta and Salt Lake City are hubs for Delta; Charlotte and Pittsburgh are hubs for US Airways; Chicago O'Hare and Denver are hubs for United (Denver was a hub for Continental for 1990–1995); Chicago O'Hare and Dallas/Ft. Worth are hubs for American; Memphis and Minneapolis are hubs for Northwest; and St. Louis is a hub for TWA (and American after 2001). The database we rely on does not allow us to distinguish individual commuter carriers (e.g., United Express and American Eagle). For the purpose of our analysis, we assume that a commuter carrier entering at a hub airport is associated with that airport's hub carrier and therefore classify the entry as "own hub."

[25] Dresner and Windle (2000) also analyze entrants' survival rates and fare responses to entry.

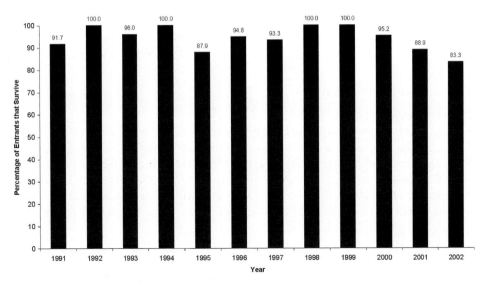

Figure 9 One-Year Survival Rates on O&D Pairs for Southwest.

Source: Data Base Products, Inc. based on U.S. Department of Transportation OD1A and Commuter 298C T-1 data.

reduce entry in subsequent years – as Figure 2 shows, the number of O&Ds entered by these carriers exceeded the 1996 level in 1998, 2000 and 2002. In contrast, Southwest had a survival rate in excess of 83 percent in every year of our analysis.[26] See Figure 9.

Major carriers' one-year survival rates typically fluctuate between 65 and 85 percent; that is, major carriers' one-year survival rates are similar in magnitude to those of low-fare carriers other than Southwest, with the exception of 1997. See Figure 10. In 1997, the one-year survival rate for major carriers (75.5 percent) was almost three times higher than that of low-fare carriers other than Southwest (27.3 percent). We note, however, that major carriers entered only 110 O&Ds in 1997, the lowest number of O&Ds entered by major carriers in any year during the period we analyze (the next lowest number of O&Ds entered by major carriers was 151 in 2002; see Figure 4). That is, major carriers were able to successfully enter only a relatively small number of O&Ds (83) in 1997.[27] Over the entire 1991–2002 period, the weighted (by number of O&Ds) average one-year survival rates was 73.8 percent for low-fare carriers other than Southwest and 76.1 percent for major carriers; the difference between the two averages is not statistically significant at the five percent level (the weighted average for Southwest over the same period is 95.6 percent; Southwest's average one-year survival rate is statistically significantly higher than the other two groups').

---

[26] We find that one-year survival rates and number of O&Ds entered in following year are not correlated at statistically significant levels for low-fare carriers other than Southwest (we also find no statistically significant correlation between changes in survival rates and changes in entry rates for these carriers.) Our findings for Southwest are similar.

[27] We find that one-year survival rates and number of O&Ds entered in following year are not correlated at statistically significant levels for major carriers (we also find no statistically significant correlation between changes in survival rates and changes in entry rates for major carriers.)

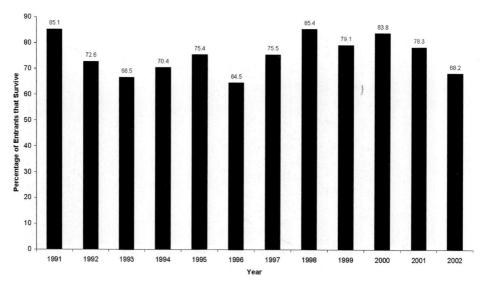

Figure 10 One-Year Survival Rates on O&D Pairs for Major Carriers.

Source: Data Base Products, Inc. based on U.S. Department of Transportation OD1A and Commuter 298C T-1 data.

2.3.2 Hub O&Ds vs. Non-Hub O&Ds

We also analyze one-year survival rates separately for hub O&Ds and non-hub O&Ds. Figure 11 shows that the survival rate of low-fare carriers other than Southwest often was higher on hub O&Ds than on non-hub O&Ds. For example, one-year survival rates by these carriers were higher on hub O&Ds than on non-hub O&Ds in 1993–1996 and 2000–2002. With the exception of 1997, survival rates on hub O&Ds were 70 percent or higher in every year of our analysis.[28]

One-year survival rates for major carriers by hub status also fluctuate substantially over time. For these carriers, we calculate survival rates for own hubs, other carriers' hubs and non-hubs separately. Major carriers' one-year survival rates on other carriers' hub O&Ds were lower than on non-hub O&Ds in nine of the 12 years in our analysis. For entry on carriers' own hubs, one-year survival rates typically were relatively high. See Figure 12.

The weighted average one-year survival rates over the period 1991–2002 for hub O&Ds was 77.8 percent for low-fare carriers other than Southwest; for major carriers, one-year survival rates were 69.3 percent at other carriers' hubs and 80.9 percent at own hubs. For non-hub O&Ds, one-year survival rates were 72.2 percent for low-fare carriers other than Southwest and 76.2 percent for major carriers. (Differences between each of these survival rates are not statistically significant at the five percent level.)

Our analysis shows that: (1) low-fare carriers continued to enter O&Ds throughout the 1990s; (2) low-fare carriers continued to enter both hub and non-hub O&Ds; (3) low-fare carriers' one-year survival rates were typically high and similar to major carriers'

---

[28] Low-fare carriers other than Southwest did not enter any hub O&Ds in 1991 and 1992.

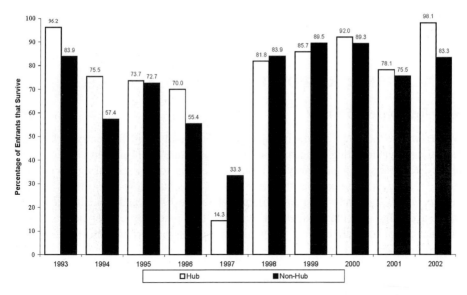

Figure 11 One-Year Survival Rates on Hub and Non-Hub O&D Pairs for Low-Fare Carriers Other than Southwest.

Source: Data Base Products, Inc. based on U.S. Department of Transportation OD1A and Commuter 298C T-1 Data. Note: We Omit 1991 and 1992 Because Low-Fare Carriers other than Southwest did not Enter Hub O&Ds in those Years. One-Year Survival Rates on Non-Hub O&Ds by these Carriers were 83.3 Percent in 1991 and 76.0 Percent in 1992.

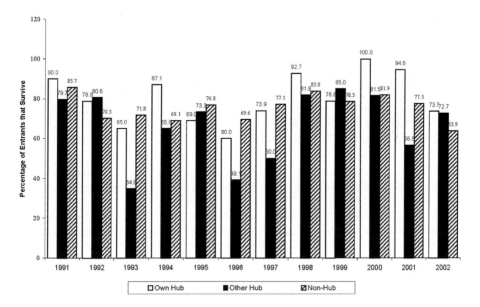

Figure 12 One-Year Survival Rates on Hub and Non-Hub O&D Pairs for Major Carriers.

Source: Data Base Products, Inc. based on U.S. Department of Transportation OD1A and Commuter 298C T-1 data.

one-year survival rates; and (4) low-fare carriers' survival rates on hub O&Ds were typically high and similar to non-hub O&D survival rates.

3   INCUMBENT RESPONSES TO ENTRY AND EXIT

3.1   Responses to Entry

We investigate the extent to which major carriers respond to low-fare entry by large price reductions by calculating the change in the average fare of incumbent carriers on each of the O&D pairs on which entry by a low-fare carrier took place during the period we study.[29] However, we note that the prior section's results – low-fare carriers continued to enter O&Ds (both hub and non-hub) throughout the 1990s, and typically those entries were successful – is the most direct evidence that predation cannot be a systematic explanation for low-fare carriers' growth slowdown in the second half of the 1990s.

In this section, we show that:

- Average fare changes by incumbents after entry by low-fare carriers vary over a wide range;
- Large declines in average fares after entry by low-fare carriers are unusual; and
- Large average fare increases after exit by low-fare carrier also are unusual.

Table 2 shows that the median incumbent average fare change after entry by a low-fare carrier other than Southwest ranged between -14.8 and 8.2 percent during the period 1991–2003.[30] Table 2 also shows that relatively large (e.g., 40 percent) average fare changes after entry by a low-fare carrier were unusual. For example, the 25th percentile incumbent average fare decline after entry by a low-fare carrier other than Southwest was smaller than 25 percent in every year except 2002 (in which the 25th percentile average fare change was -25.6 percent), and the 5th percentile average fare decline was smaller than 40 percent in all but two years. Furthermore, as Table 2 indicates, the incumbent average fare change was positive for a substantial percentage of O&Ds.

The median incumbent average fare change after entry by Southwest ranged between -20.0 and 11.0 percent during the same period, and was substantially more negative than the median fare change after entry by other low-fare carriers for the years 1995–2000. See Tables 2 and 3.

We also compare incumbents' average fare changes after entry by low-fare carriers to incumbents' fare changes after entry by major carriers. In general, incumbents' fare

---

[29] In general, changes in major carriers' average fares reflect changes in individual fares and changes in the mix of tickets sold (e.g., "restricted" vs. "unrestricted" fares). A major carrier may respond to entry by a low-fare carrier by matching the low-fare entrant's lowest fares, but not reducing its higher fares. If it adopts this strategy, the percentage decline in the major carrier's average fare may be less than the percentage decline in its lowest fares. However, if the major carrier also increased the availability of its lowest fare seats, the percentage decline in its average fare may be greater than the percentage decline in its lowest fares. A major carrier's average fare also could change after entry by a low-fare carrier even if the incumbent did not change any fare (e.g., because it lost primarily low-fare passengers to the entrant).

[30] Low-fare carriers other than Southwest entered six O&Ds in 1991, but two of those entries occurred on the same O&D, so we measure incumbent fare responses on only five O&Ds.

Table 2 Incumbent Average Fare Change After Entry by Low-Fare Carrier Other than Southwest

Year	N	1st Percentile	5th Percentile	10th Percentile	25th Percentile	50th Percentile (Median)	75th Percentile
1991	5	1.5	1.5	1.5	2.2	8.2	18.1
1992	26	−41.3	−34.9	−33.2	−20.4	−9.2	−1.8
1993	83	−50.8	−48.0	−35.3	−20.8	−4.2	4.3
1994	167	−43.0	−34.4	−30.7	−20.8	−9.4	0.1
1995	188	−44.9	−23.3	−17.3	−6.8	1.3	8.9
1996	94	−47.3	−38.1	−29.5	−18.0	−8.6	2.9
1997	84	−40.8	−25.6	−21.2	−13.7	−6.4	2.2
1998	119	−40.2	−32.9	−27.7	−16.6	−4.8	5.6
1999	71	−31.9	−24.8	−18.7	−11.6	−0.5	4.5
2000	93	−34.7	−31.0	−20.5	−10.4	−1.6	5.6
2001	80	−41.0	−29.4	−25.6	−17.7	−11.2	−3.6
2002	170	−47.1	−41.6	−34.7	−25.6	−14.8	−5.1
2003	69	−33.7	−29.6	−25.2	−17.1	−8.1	−0.3

Note: Low-Fare Carriers are: Air South, Airtran Airways, American Trans Air, Carnival Air Lines, Frontier, Jet Blue, Kiwi International, Markair, Midway Air, Midwest Express, Morris Air, National Airlines, Reno Air, Sirit Airlines, Sun Country Air, Tower Air, Valuejet Airlines, Vangaurd Air, and Western Pacific.
Source: Data Base Products, Inc. based on U.S. Department of Transportation OD1A and Commuter 298C T-1 data.

Table 3 Incumbent Average Fare Change After Entry by Southwest

Year	N	1st Percentile	5th Percentile	10th Percentile	25th Percentile	50th Percentile (Median)	75th Percentile
1991	24	−41.6	−35.6	−30.7	−19.8	−5.7	−1.0
1992	38	−53.8	−47.8	−25.4	−17.2	−8.8	−2.1
1993	49	−61.3	−20.9	−15.9	−3.6	11.0	17.4
1994	101	−46.4	−37.6	−31.6	−19.4	−8.7	−1.2
1995	33	−44.7	−44.5	−43.1	−26.4	−17.8	−5.2
1996	77	−37.9	−31.7	−27.9	−20.5	−12.8	−6.5
1997	45	−39.1	−32.0	−28.8	−23.6	−15.0	−10.1
1998	20	−65.6	−52.4	−37.1	−26.7	−13.4	−0.3
1999	55	−49.8	−38.8	−32.5	−28.2	−20.0	−7.5
2000	42	−47.4	−44.0	−36.3	−34.3	−12.0	−2.8
2001	54	−39.0	−32.3	−28.7	−20.1	−14.8	−9.6
2002	6	−26.3	−26.3	−26.3	−13.7	−11.5	−8.9
2003	2	−9.9	−9.9	−9.9	−9.9	−6.5	−3.1

Note: Low-Fare Carriers are: Air South, Airtran Airways, American Trans Air, Carnival Air Lines, Frontier, Jet Blue, Kiwi International, Markair, Midway Air, Midwest Express, Morris Air, National Airlines, Reno Air, Sirit Airlines, Sun Country Air, Tower Air, Valuejet Airlines, Vangaurd Air, and Western Pacific.
Source: Data Base Products, Inc. based on U.S. Department of Transportation OD1A and Commuter 298C T-1 data.

changes will depend on the fares offered by entrants. If low-fare carriers tend to enter with relatively lower fares than major carriers, incumbents' fare changes after low-fare carrier entry likely will be larger than incumbents' fare changes after entry by major carriers. Thus, evidence that incumbents' fare changes after entry by low-fare carriers are, on average, larger than fare changes after entry by majors would not be sufficient to establish that such a difference was due to predatory conduct.

We find that average fare changes by incumbents after entry by major carriers also vary over a wide range. See Table 4. In every year since 1991, incumbents typically reduced average fares more (or increased average fares less) after entry by a low-fare carrier than a major carrier.[31] For example, in 1994, the median fare change after entry by a major carrier was −3.8 percent, while the median fare change after entry by a low-fare carrier other than Southwest was −9.4 percent, a difference of −5.6 percent. However, the evidence also shows that major carriers typically continued to respond relatively more aggressively to low-fare carrier entry than to major carrier entry after 1999. For example, in 2002, the median fare change after entry by a major carrier was −8.5 percent, while the median fare change after entry by a low-fare carrier other than Southwest was −14.8 percent, a difference of −6.3 percent. That is, we find no evidence that incumbent fare responses to low-fare carriers were systematically less aggressive after 1999. Over the entire period, the average difference in fare change after entry was −5.8 percent. See Table 5.

Table 4 Incumbent Average Fare Change After Entry by Major Carrier

Year	N	1st Percentile	5th Percentile	10th Percentile	25th Percentile	50th Percentile (Median)	75th Percentile
1991	388	−20.4	−14.3	−10.6	−5.3	3.0	10.4
1992	242	−31.0	−20.4	−16.9	−11.3	−1.3	7.5
1993	177	−28.3	−15.2	−8.8	−2.0	6.7	14.8
1994	302	−48.2	−36.9	−31.1	−17.5	−3.8	3.7
1995	197	−25.9	−14.2	−9.4	−3.0	3.8	12.0
1996	177	−36.3	−21.9	−15.0	−4.6	4.5	11.0
1997	106	−32.0	−21.2	−12.7	−7.1	−2.3	4.1
1998	196	−39.2	−15.7	−11.1	−4.5	2.7	8.0
1999	215	−27.1	−13.1	−9.1	−4.2	0.8	7.2
2000	167	−24.3	−14.9	−10.1	−2.2	2.2	8.8
2001	175	−42.1	−23.3	−19.3	−11.4	−4.4	1.1
2002	149	−39.9	−31.9	−26.5	−15.4	−8.5	0.0
2003	325	−27.2	−19.1	−11.3	−3.1	3.4	10.3

Note: Low-Fare Carriers are: Air South, Airtran Airways, American Trans Air, Carnival Air Lines, Frontier, Jet Blue, Kiwi International, Markair, Midway Air, Midwest Express, Morris Air, National Airlines, Reno Air, Sirit Airlines, Sun Country Air, Tower Air, Valuejet Airlines, Vangaurd Air, and Western Pacific.
Source: Data Base Products, Inc. based on U.S. Department of Transportation OD1A and Commuter 298C T-1 data.

---

[31] We compare average fare changes after entry by major and low-fare carriers other than Southwest on a year-by-year basis to control for common economic factors (e.g., fuel costs).

Table 5   Median Incumbent Average Fare Change After Entry, Low-Fare vs. Major Carriers

Year	Low-Fare Carriers Other Than Southwest	Southwest	Major Carriers	Difference	
				LFC Other Than Southwest Minus Major Carriers	Southwest Minus Major Carriers
1991	8.2	−5.7	3.0	5.2	−8.7
1992	−9.2	−8.8	−1.3	−7.9	−7.5
1993	−4.2	11.0	6.7	−10.9	4.3
1994	−9.4	−8.7	−3.8	−5.6	−4.9
1995	1.3	−17.8	3.8	−2.5	−21.6
1996	−8.6	−12.8	4.5	−13.1	−17.3
1997	−6.4	−15.0	−2.3	−4.1	−12.7
1998	−4.8	−13.4	2.7	−7.5	−16.1
1999	−0.5	−20.0	0.8	−1.3	−20.8
2000	−1.6	−12.0	2.2	−3.8	−14.2
2001	−11.2	−14.8	−4.4	−6.8	−10.4
2002	−14.8	−11.5	−8.5	−6.3	−3.0
2003	−8.1	−6.5	3.4	−11.5	−9.9
Average	−5.3	−10.5	0.5	−5.8	−11.0

Note: Low-Fare Carriers are: Air South, Airtran Airways, American Trans Air, Carnival Air Lines, Frontier, Jet Blue, Kiwi International, Markair, Midway Air, Midwest Express, Morris Air, National Airlines, Reno Air, Sirit Airlines, Sun Country Air, Tower Air, Valuejet Airlines, Vangaurd Air, and Western Pacific.
Source: Data Base Products, Inc. based on U.S. Department of Transportation OD1A and Commuter 298C T-1 data.

3.2   Incumbent Responses to Exit

Discussions of predation also imply that incumbent carriers increase fares substantially after the exit of a low-fare carrier. We investigate the average fare change of incumbents after exit by a low-fare carrier by calculating the change in the average fare of the incumbent carriers on those O&D pairs on which entry by a low-fare carrier was followed by exit by that entrant within one year (that is, we analyze O&Ds where the low-fare entrant did not survive).

As in our analysis of fare changes after entry, we find that fare changes by incumbents after exit by low-fare carriers vary over a wide range. We also find that relatively large (e.g., 40 percent) fare increases after exit by low-fare carriers – which would be predicted by proponents of a predation explanation for such exit – are unusual. For example, the 75th percentile incumbent average fare change after exit by a low-fare carrier other than Southwest was less than 20 percent in every year except 1992 (based on only seven exits), and less than 10 percent in most years. The 75th percentile incumbent average fare change after exit by a low-fare carrier other than Southwest was less than 40 percent in every year except 1992. In a substantial percentage of O&Ds, the incumbent average fare change after exit was negative (i.e., at least 25 percent of O&Ds in every year except 1999). See Table 6.

We find that fare changes by incumbents after exit by major carriers also vary over a wide range. See Table 7. Furthermore, we find that the median average fare change

Table 6   Incumbent Average Fare Change After Exit by Low-Fare Carrier Other than Southwest

Year	N	25th Percentile	50th Percentile (Median)	75th Percentile	90th Percentile	95th Percentile	99th Percentile
1991	1	−0.4	−0.4	−0.4	−0.4	−0.4	−0.4
1992	7	−5.0	6.9	53.0	58.9	58.9	58.9
1993	11	−16.2	−8.2	−0.5	4.4	48.8	48.8
1994	65	−18.6	−6.1	3.6	10.4	19.4	43.6
1995	51	−16.9	−6.6	2.8	13.9	27.7	132.2
1996	39	−6.8	4.5	15.4	26.4	42.8	71.8
1997	62	−9.5	2.9	15.5	26.1	30.6	76.1
1998	20	−4.6	4.4	12.8	18.0	24.1	26.8
1999	9	0.4	5.2	17.3	21.6	21.6	21.6
2000	10	−29.0	−13.2	−6.2	−1.0	0.7	0.7
2001	19	−22.5	−16.9	−3.2	2.7	3.3	3.3
2002	21	−14.6	−4.9	1.2	5.2	5.6	15.1

Note: Low-Fare Carriers are: Air South, Airtran Airways, American Trans Air, Carnival Air Lines, Frontier, Jet Blue, Kiwi International, Markair, Midway Air, Midwest Express, Morris Air, National Airlines, Reno Air, Sirit Airlines, Sun Country Air, Tower Air, Valuejet Airlines, Vangaurd Air, and Western Pacific.
Source: Data Base Products, Inc. based on U.S. Department of Transportation OD1A and Commuter 298C T-1 data.

Table 7   Incumbent Average Fare Change After Exit by Major Carrier

Year	N	25th Percentile	50th Percentile (Median)	75th Percentile	90th Percentile	95th Percentile	99th Percentile
1991	59	−9.6	−2.8	5.4	13.6	21.1	48.4
1992	66	0.8	6.6	16.8	23.1	39.5	108.2
1993	61	−14.2	−4.2	1.4	8.1	12.7	27.1
1994	87	0.5	6.3	17.9	41.8	52.1	91.6
1995	48	−17.8	−1.7	16.2	22.9	25.1	35.8
1996	64	−10.6	−4.1	3.1	17.5	35.1	45.9
1997	26	0.3	5.2	21.1	44.9	62.5	117.5
1998	29	−4.9	1.7	7.2	16.1	29.6	40.6
1999	44	−1.5	3.5	8.0	12.9	15.3	30.3
2000	28	−9.8	−3.3	3.0	9.3	10.4	12.7
2001	39	−18.5	−5.4	1.9	7.4	14.7	25.5
2002	47	−11.2	2.1	7.1	12.9	20.4	40.1

Note: Low-Fare Carriers are: Air South, Airtran Airways, American Trans Air, Carnival Air Lines, Frontier, Jet Blue, Kiwi International, Markair, Midway Air, Midwest Express, Morris Air, National Airlines, Reno Air, Sirit Airlines, Sun Country Air, Tower Air, Valuejet Airlines, Vangaurd Air, and Western Pacific.
Source: Data Base Products, Inc. based on U.S. Department of Transportation OD1A and Commuter 298C T-1 data.

Table 8 Median Incumbent Average Fare Change After Exit, Low-Fare vs. Major Carriers

Year	Low-Fare Carriers Other Than Southwest	Major Carriers	LFC Other Than Southwest Minus Major Carriers
1991	−0.4	−2.8	2.4
1992	6.9	6.6	0.2
1993	−8.2	−4.2	−4.1
1994	−6.1	6.3	−12.4
1995	−6.6	−1.7	−4.9
1996	4.5	−4.1	8.6
1997	2.9	5.2	−2.3
1998	4.4	1.7	2.8
1999	5.2	3.5	1.7
2000	−13.2	−3.3	−9.9
2001	−16.9	−5.4	−11.5
2002	−4.9	2.1	−7.0
Average	−2.7	0.3	−3.0

Note: Low-Fare Carriers are: Air South, Airtran Airways, American Trans Air, Carnival Air Lines, Frontier, Jet Blue, Kiwi International, Markair, Midway Air, Midwest Express, Morris Air, National Airlines, Reno Air, Sirit Airlines, Sun Country Air, Tower Air, Valuejet Airlines, Vangaurd Air, and Western Pacific.
Source: Data Base Products, Inc. based on U.S. Department of Transportation OD1A and Commuter 298C T-1 data.

after exit by a major carrier is larger than the median average fare change after exit by a low-fare carrier other than Southwest in seven of the 12 years in our analysis.[32] See Table 8. These findings also are inconsistent with a systematic predation strategy aimed at low-fare carriers.

Finally, we find that occurrences of the "standard" description of predation – relatively large incumbent fare reduction when a low-fare carrier enters, followed by a relatively large incumbent fare increase when the low-fare carrier later exits – are rare. For example, over the 12-year period we analyze, we find only 16 occurrences (out of 315 total exits) of an incumbent average fare reduction of 20 percent after entry by a low-fare carrier other than Southwest, followed by an incumbent average fare increase of 20 percent or more when that low-fare carrier exits. Furthermore, the average incumbent fare after exit was higher than the average incumbent fare before entry for only six of these 16 O&Ds. In only three of these 16 occurrences was a reduction in incumbent average fare of 40 percent or more after entry by a low-fare carrier other than Southwest followed by an incumbent average increase of 40 percent or more when that low-fare carrier exits (i.e., less than one percent of low-fare carrier exits in our analysis).[33] We find no occurrences of a 50 percent or more incumbent average fare reduction in response to

---

[32] We do not report results for fare responses of incumbents to exit by Southwest because Southwest exited so few routes.
[33] The average incumbent fare after exit was lower than the average incumbent fare before entry on one of these three O&Ds; only two percent higher on one O&D; and 18 percent higher on the third O&D.

low-fare entry followed by a 50 percent or more incumbent average fare increase after low-fare exit.[34]

Our analysis shows that: (1) fare changes by incumbents after entry by low-fare carriers vary over a wide range; (2) relatively large declines (e.g., more than 40 percent) in average fares after entry by low-fare carriers are unusual; (3) fare declines by incumbents after entry by major carriers also vary over a wide range; (4) after 1999, major carriers' average fares generally continued to fall more after entry by a low-fare carrier than by a major carrier; (5) fare changes by incumbents after exit by low-fare carriers vary over a wide range; (6) relatively large fare increases after exit by low-fare carriers are unusual; and (7) fare increases by incumbents after exit by major carriers often exceed those after exit by low-fare carriers.

These findings contradict claims that a standard description of predation against low-fare carriers by major carriers – large fare reductions by incumbent major carriers in response to low-fare entry, followed by large fare increases by incumbents after exit of low-fare carriers – can be a systematic explanation for difficulties faced by low-fare carriers in the mid-1990s. Furthermore, these findings indicate that the renewed growth by low-fare carriers after 1999 was not a result of a reduction in competitive responses to low-fare entry by major carriers.

4   CONCLUSION

Our review finds no evidence that predation by major carriers against low-fare entrants, if it existed, was systematic and successful during the mid-1990s. Indeed, we find that low-fare carriers continued to enter O&Ds throughout the 1990s, and those entries typically were successful. Furthermore, we find that the continued growth of low-fare carriers after 1999 is not associated with less aggressive pricing responses by major carriers to entry than in earlier years. Although our analysis cannot rule out isolated instances of predatory conduct, the evidence shows that the type of fare responses that concern critics of major carriers' pricing practices are relatively rare and also occur in response to entry and exit by major carriers. Thus, the claim that competition in the airline industry was "chilled" in the mid-1990s because major carriers systematically charged predatory prices is inconsistent with the empirical evidence.

REFERENCES

Bamberger, Gustavo E. and Dennis W. Carlton (2003), "Airline Networks and Fares," in *Handbook of Airline Economics*, 2nd ed., Darryl Jenkins, ed.
Borenstein, Severin (1989), "Hubs and High Fares: Dominance and Market Power in the U.S. Airline Industry." *RAND Journal of Economics* 20:344–65.

---

[34] In comparison, the corresponding rates in response to entry by a major carrier are: 22 out of 598 (3.7 percent) for incumbent fare increases of 20 percent of more followed by incumbent fare increases of 20 percent or more after exit; four out of 598 (0.7 percent) for fare increases/reductions of 40 percent; and two out of 598 (0.3 percent) for fare increases/reductions of 50 percent.

Borenstein, Severin (1992), "The Evolution of U.S. Airline Competition," *Journal of Economic Perspectives* 6:45–73.

Dresner, Martin and Robert Windle (2000), "Assessing Competitive Behavior by U.S. Air Carriers," *Journal of the Transportation Research Forum* 39:177–89.

Eckert, Andrew and Douglas S. West (2002), "Predation in the Airline Industry: The Canadian Antitrust Approach," *Antitrust Bulletin* 217–242.

Edlin, Aaron S. (2001), "Stopping Above-Cost Predatory Pricing," *Yale Law Journal* 111:941–991.

Edlin, Aaron S. and Joseph Farrell (2004), "The American Airlines Case: A Chance to Clarify Predation Policy (2001)," in *The Antitrust Revolution: Economics, Competition, and Policy*, John Kwoka and Lawrence White, eds.

Ito, Harumi and Darin Lee (2004), "Incumbent Responses to Lower Cost Entry: Evidence from the U.S. Airline Industry," unpublished working paper.

National Research Council, Transportation Research Board (undated), "Entry and Competition in the U.S. Airline Industry: Issues and Opportunities," Special Report 255.

U.S. Department of Transportation (undated), "Competition in the U.S. Domestic Airline Industry: The Need for a Policy to Prevent Unfair Practices."

U.S. Department of Transportation (2001), "Enforcement Policy Regarding Unfair Exclusionary Conduct in the Air Transportation Industry: Findings and Conclusions on the Economic, Policy, and Legal Issues."

Advances in Airline Economics, Vol 1
Darin Lee (Editor)
© 2006 Published by Elsevier B.V.

2

Predation in Airline Markets:
A Review of Recent Cases

Andrew Eckert and Douglas S. West
Department of Economics[1], University of Alberta, Edmonton,
Alberta T6G 2H4

ABSTRACT

Over the past decade, there has been a substantial expansion of low cost carrier (LCC) services across North America, Europe, and Australia. The network carriers' response to the entry and expansion of LCCs has given rise to numerous complaints of predation by the network carriers, and a number of important antitrust cases. The purpose of this paper is to provide a review of recent airline predation cases that have generated judicial decisions. The objectives of this review are to see whether there is a judicial consensus on the method for carrying out the price/cost predation test and whether there is agreement across jurisdictions on what must be proved to make out an airline predation case. We find that the answer to both questions is essentially no. Rather, there is lack of agreement on: (1) the unit of analysis; (2) the costs that should be included in an avoidable cost test for predation; (3) whether fare matching is a legitimate business justification for below cost pricing; and (4) whether recoupment of predatory losses can be through the creation of a reputation for predation.

1 INTRODUCTION

Over the past decade, there has been a substantial expansion of low cost carrier (LCC) service across North America, Europe, and Australia. Airlines such as Southwest Airlines, WestJet, Ryanair, and Virgin Blue have expanded their route networks and market shares at the expense of the established network carriers.

---

[1] Corresponding author: Douglas West. Email for Andrew Eckert: aeckert@ualberta.ca. Email for Douglas West: douglas.west@ualberta.ca. West served as an economic expert for the Commissioner of Competition in the *Air Canada* case and for the Australian Competition and Consumer Commission in the *Qantas* case. The authors would like to thank Darin Lee and Oliver Richard for helpful comments.

An LCC differs from a network carrier in certain important respects. An LCC attempts to keep its costs low by offering a "no frills" service. This could mean no meal service (or passengers will be asked to pay for a meal), no advanced seat selection, no headsets or movies, no airport lounges, and possibly no frequent flyer plan. The LCC will also seek to have a flexible labor force that is not tightly constrained by union rules, and it will try to achieve rapid turnarounds for its aircraft. An LCC might also operate with one type of aircraft to keep pilot training and maintenance costs down.[2]

When an LCC enters a new route, typically it will charge fares that are substantially lower than those that have traditionally been charged on the route by the network carriers.[3] The network carriers then respond to the LCC entry by lowering fares, perhaps matching the lowest fare charged by the LCC for some subset of seats on each flight. The network carriers might also increase capacity on the route.[4]

The network carrier responses to LCC entry have given rise to numerous complaints from the entering carriers.[5] These complaints suggest that the incumbent network carrier response has at times been predatory. By lowering fares and increasing capacity on a route, the network carriers are alleged to be operating below cost. This type of network carrier response to entry could be designed to drive the LCC from the market, so that higher fares can be restored.

While there have been many complaints regarding network carrier responses to LCC entry, only a few have given rise to major antitrust investigations and subsequent cases. The purpose of this paper is to provide a review of the recent airline predation cases that have generated judicial decisions. One of the objectives of this review is to see whether there is any judicial consensus on the method for carrying out the price/cost predation test. Another objective is to determine whether there is any agreement across jurisdictions on what must be proved to make out an airline predation case.

In the next section, the policy response to concerns regarding airline predation will be summarized. This is followed in Sections 3-6 with reviews of the *Lufthansa*, *American Airlines*, *Air Canada*, and *Qantas* cases, respectively. These reviews will include summaries of the commentaries on the cases and decisions that are available so far. Section 7 then attempts to draw out what can be learned from the recent airline predation litigation to date.

2   AIRLINE PREDATION POLICY

Bolton, Brodley, and Riordan (2000, pp. 2242–2243) have defined predatory pricing as "a price reduction that is profitable only because of the added market power the predator

---

[2] Recently, there has been some blurring of network carrier and LCC service levels. On the one hand, some LCCs are improving the quality of their service by, for example, increasing legroom, putting TV screens in the seatbacks, and installing leather seats. On the other hand, some network carriers have reduced the quality of service by, for example, serving fewer or no meals on flights (or charging for them), reducing frequent flyer mileage for certain fare types, removing blankets, and charging for advance seat selection (again for certain fare types).

[3] See Morrison (2001), Ito and Lee (2004), Dresner, Lin, and Windle (1996), and the Transportation Research Board (1999, pp. 49–61).

[4] Ito and Lee (2004) have studied the incumbent price and capacity response to LCC entry for 370 entry events. Bamberger and Carlton (2006) have also carried out a study of incumbent response to LCC entry, but for a smaller set of markets. See also Alderighi, Cento, Nijkamp, and Rietveld (2004), who examine the pricing response of European network carriers to LCC entry on some European routes.

[5] See, for example, the list of complaints appearing in Appendix C of the Transportation Research Board (1999) report.

gains from eliminating, disciplining, or otherwise inhibiting the competitive conduct of a rival or potential rival. Stated more precisely, a predatory price is a price that is profit-maximizing only because of its exclusionary or other anticompetitive effects." There have been two major streams of literature in economics dealing with predatory behavior: a theoretical stream and one focused on the problem of defining a legal rule for courts to follow in cases of alleged predation.

The modern theory of predation had its first statement in the papers by Kreps and Wilson (1982) and Milgrom and Roberts (1982) that proposed reputation models of predation. Their papers were followed by others that developed both deep pocket and signaling models of predation. Theories of predation are surveyed by Ordover and Saloner (1989). The theoretical predation literature was concerned with showing under what conditions predation would be rational, profit-maximizing conduct for a firm. Its focus was on predation broadly defined, rather than on the subset of behavior usually referred to as predatory pricing.

The law and economics literature on predatory pricing rules was initiated by Areeda and Turner's (1975) classic paper that proposed the "price less than average variable cost" test for predatory pricing. Their paper was followed by a number of others that suggested either alternative legal rules (e.g., Williamson's, 1977, output expansion rule) or an extended version of the Areeda and Turner rule (e.g., the two-stage rule of reason approach of Joskow and Klevorick, 1979). The courts in the U.S. have tended to adopt the Areeda and Turner rule, and the Supreme Court's *Brooke Group* decision in 1993 made it clear that a test for predatory pricing would have to include both a price/cost test and an analysis of the possibility of recovering the cost of the predatory conduct by earning profits that could not have been earned in the absence of predation.[6]

Incumbent airline pricing and capacity responses to new rivals have given rise to numerous complaints of predatory pricing and capacity expansion. The challenge for economists and lawyers has been to design tests for predatory conduct that can distinguish predatory behavior from aggressive competitive conduct in the airline industry. This task is made difficult by problems associated with deciding the appropriate price or revenue measure on the one hand, and measure of cost on the other hand, to be used for purposes of a below-cost pricing test.

A literal interpretation of a price-cost test for airline predation might suggest that one should compare an airline fare with the variable cost of carrying a passenger. However, airlines carry passengers paying a variety of different fares, and only a small number might be charged fares that appear to be unreasonably low. Even then, given that all common costs are excluded by a test for predation at the seat level, it is unlikely that a carrier's pricing would be found to be predatory (even though its low fares might be capable of forcing economic losses on its rivals). As it turns out, cases involving alleged predation do not compare individual fares with per passenger variable costs. Rather, as a minimum, economists have done revenue and cost comparisons at the flight level.

Still, the question remains as to the appropriate measures of revenue and costs to be used for the test. Should a given flight's revenues, for example, include some portion of the revenues of passengers connecting from or to other flights? Should the measure of flight costs include only variable costs, or should it also include fixed costs such as aircraft costs? Clearly, whether a carrier is found to be engaging in predatory conduct will turn on the answers to such questions.

---

[6] See *Brooke Group v. Brown & Williamson Tobacco Corp.*, 509 U.S. 209, 222 (1993).

Another issue that arises in carrying out a predation test in the airline industry is the treatment of product differentiation and price matching. As noted above, most complaints of predatory pricing come from LCCs and are directed at the price/capacity response of network carriers to their entry. Partly, the concern is that network carriers offer a higher quality product and more service than LCCs, and operate with higher costs. If a network carrier matches the fares of an LCC, the LCC views it as effective price undercutting. The network carrier may then be operating below its own costs. The LCC may have to cut its fares even further to attract passengers, and end up operating below its costs as well. The question then is whether fare matching is an absolute defense against allegations of predatory pricing (ignoring quality differences), or whether fare matching is legitimate provided revenues remain above costs.

There are then a number of important issues that need to be addressed in carrying out predation tests for the airline industry. The growing number of predation complaints combined with government's perceived need to provide some guidance on what would be viewed as anti-competitive conduct in the airline industry have led to several important policy responses.

First, in June 1997, Roger Fones, Chief of the Transportation, Energy, and Agricultural Section of the Antitrust Division of the U.S. Department of Justice (DOJ) set out the DOJ's approach to analyzing allegations of predation in the airline industry. Consistent with the Supreme Court's *Brooke Group* decision, Fones acknowledged the requirement to show in a case of alleged predation that the alleged predator will be able to recoup the cost of its predatory strategy.[7] If the recoupment element is satisfied, then the DOJ will proceed to the next stage, where it must be shown that the alleged predator's prices are below an appropriate measure of its costs. The measure of costs to be used is avoidable costs. Fones went on to discuss some of the issues that arise in carrying out an avoidable cost test (e.g., the unit of analysis to use, the time period over which to measure costs and revenues, the treatment of aircraft costs). Fones' speech was made well in advance of the DOJ's predation case brought against AMR Corp., American Airlines Inc., and American Eagle Holding Corp. in May of 1999.

In 1998, the U.S. Department of Transportation (DOT) issued its Statement of Enforcement Policy Regarding Unfair Exclusionary Conduct.[8] The purpose of the statement was to describe what it regarded as potentially anti-competitive conduct of a major carrier that would give rise to a DOT investigation. According to the statement,

> DOT will consider that a major carrier is engaging in unfair exclusionary practices if, in response to entry by a new carrier into one or more of its local hub markets, it pursues a strategy of price cuts or capacity increases, or both, that either (1) causes it to forego more revenue than all of the new entrant's capacity could have diverted from it, or (2) results in substantially lower operating profits—or greater operating losses—in the short run than would a reasonable alternative strategy for competing with the new entrant.

---

[7] *Id.*
[8] See U.S. Department of Transportation, Statement of Enforcement Policy Regarding Unfair Exclusionary Conduct, Docket OST-98-3713. According to the DOT (2001), the U.S. Congress has given the DOT the responsibility of preventing anti-competitive practices in the airline industry. It enabled the DOT to prohibit unfair competitive practices even if they do not violate the antitrust laws.

The DOT's proposed policy would also focus on a comparison of the revenues earned through the adopted strategy and those that could have been earned through a "reasonable" alternative response.

The DOT's proposal represented a serious departure from the usual antitrust approach to investigating allegations of predatory conduct. It was subject to strong criticism from both small and large airlines, and their economic consultants.[9] In January 2001, the DOT announced that it would not be issuing a revised version of the guidelines, but would instead consider allegations of predation on a case-by-case basis.

The DOT's belief that there was a need for a written enforcement policy was probably driven by the growing number of complaints regarding potentially predatory behavior by the network carriers that were being made by entering LCCs. In Appendix C to the Transportation Research Board's special report, "Entry and Competition in the U.S. Airline Industry", there are descriptions of complaints involving low cost and network carriers.[10] In these complaints, there are allegations of incumbent carriers lowering fares in response to entry, and/or increasing capacity.[11] Several of these cases are discussed by Oster and Strong (2001).

At about the same time that the AMR case was being filed and the DOT was receiving submissions regarding its proposed enforcement policy, Canada's largest network carrier, Air Canada, proposed acquiring its failing rival network carrier, Canadian Airlines. The acquisition was expected to give Air Canada close to 90 percent of domestic passenger revenues and in excess of 80 percent of domestic passengers carried.[12] The acquisition was ultimately approved, and as a result, the Government felt it was necessary to strengthen the competition laws pertaining to dominant air carriers. Bill C-26, which came into force on July 5, 2000, authorized the Governor in Council to define by regulation what constitutes anti-competitive acts in the airline industry for the purpose of the abuse of dominance provisions, sections 78 and 79, of the *Competition Act*.

Given the authorization provided by Bill C-26, the Governor in Council approved the *Regulations Respecting Anti-competitive Acts of Persons Operating a Domestic Service* (the "Airline Regulations"), which came into force on August 23, 2000.[13] These regulations, in part, added a set of airline specific anti-competitive acts to the list of anti-competitive acts contained in section 78 of the *Competition Act*. The first three

---

[9] See, for example, the "Statement of Professor Janusz A. Ordover and Professor Robert D. Willig", "Declaration of Professor William J. Baumol", "Statement of Dr. Franklin M. Fisher", and "Statement of Dr. Laura D'Anrea Tyson", appearing under DOT Docket OST-98-3713.

[10] Complaints were filed involving the following air carriers: AccessAir and Northwest Airlines (May 1999), AccessAir and Delta, Northwest, and TWA (March 1999), Kiwi Airlines and Continental Airlines (February 1998), ValuJet Airlines and Northwest Airlines (March 1997), ValuJet Airlines and Delta (February 1997), Frontier Airlines and United Airlines (January 1997), Spirit Airlines and Northwest Airlines (November 1996), Vanguard Airlines and American Airlines (October 1996), Vanguard Airlines and Northwest (August 1995 and June 1995), ValuJet and Delta (December 1993), and Reno Air and Northwest (March 1993). The complaints involving Spirit Airlines and Northwest Airlines (November 1996), Vanguard Airlines and American Airlines (October 1996), and Reno Air and Northwest (March 1993) are specifically mentioned by the DOT (2001) as giving rise to concerns.

[11] See Appendix C, "Informal Complaints to DOT by New Entrant Airlines about Unfair Exclusionary Practices, March 1993 to May 1999", to the report of the Transportation Research Board (1999).

[12] Letter from Konrad von Finckenstein, Commissioner of Competition, to Lawson Hunter, Counsel for Air Canada (December 21, 1999) (available on the Competition Bureau's web site at www.competition.ic.gc.ca).

[13] These regulations are discussed in detail in Eckert and West (2002).

of these acts consist of a dominant air carrier's main line or low-cost second brand
carrier operating or increasing capacity on a route or routes at fares that do not cover
the avoidable cost of providing the service. Possible preemption of airport facilities,
services, or slots is also covered by the Airline Regulations. The first application from
the Commissioner of Competition to the Competition Tribunal citing anti-competitive
practices contained in the Airline Regulations was filed on March 5, 2001.

Thus, at the beginning of a new millenium, the U.S. and Canada were trying to
define new policy and, along with Germany and Australia, bring forward cases with
respect to possible predation in the airline industry.[14] There were cases of alleged airline
predation prior to this time, but not necessarily involving entering LCCs. For example,
in an important case, the case of *Continental Airlines Inc. v. American Airlines, Inc.*[15],
Continental Airlines and Northwest Airlines alleged that the "Value Pricing" policy that
American Airlines first announced in April 1992 represented predatory pricing.[16] Under
this policy, full coach fares were cut initially by 38 percent, and reduced further after
responses by Northwest, Continental, and other airlines. The plaintiffs made additional
allegations, including that American had attempted to convince rival firms to set higher
prices jointly.

With respect to market definition, the plaintiffs argued that both regions and city
pairs could be relevant geographic markets. The plaintiffs took the position that entry
barriers into airline markets included computer reservation systems, frequent flyer plans,
lack of available slots at certain airports, lack of available gates at certain airports,
travel commission overrides, and frequency dominance. One of the plaintiffs' experts
found that American's pricing action cost the plaintiffs approximately $520 million from
April to October 1992, and that prices were below average variable cost during the
second and third quarters of 1992. Costs net of depreciation were found to be around 94
percent variable. The plaintiffs also concluded that American could recoup the cost of
its predatory strategy.[17]

Not surprisingly American Airlines staked out a position quite different from that
of the plaintiffs. First, it was argued that the relevant geographic market was national
in scope. This view was based on the observation that the Value Pricing program was
national in scope, on considerations of supply substitutability, and on the belief that fare
cuts and fare sales spread from one region to another. Second, one of the defendant's
experts argued that there were no barriers to entry into airline markets. Third, it was
concluded that average variable costs constitute about two thirds to three quarters of
total costs, and that American Airlines did not operate with revenues below average
variable costs. (Regarding the cost-based test, one issue of contention was whether and
how aircraft costs should be included in variable costs.) In addition, American argued
that it would not be able to recover its losses from the implementation of a predatory
pricing scheme.[18]

---

[14] A comparison of the elements that need to be proved in predatory pricing cases in various jurisdictions has
been made by Niels and Ten Kate (2000).

[15] *Continental Airlines, Inc. v. American Airlines,* Inc., 824 F. Supp. 689 (S.D. Tex. 1993).

[16] A discussion of this case is given in Clouatre (1995).

[17] This summary of the plaintiffs' position was obtained from a review of various transcripts from the case.

[18] See Clouatre (1995, p. 893).

Stating a position taken in later work (e.g., Baumol, 1996), defendant's expert Professor Baumol listed three necessary components for firm conduct to be predatory: (1) no legitimate business justification, (2) prices so low that they constitute a threat to an equally efficient rival (the Areeda-Turner test would be the test for this), and (3) recoupment of the costs of the predatory strategy. It should also be noted that the defendant argued that price matching was legitimate business conduct, even if American matched the fares of rivals that undercut American's original Value Pricing levels.

In the end, the jury found in favor of American Airlines, and neither Continental nor Northwest appealed the decision.

More recent airline predation cases have concerned the response of a network carrier to the entry and expansion of an LCC in one or more of the markets served by the incumbent network carrier. Below we consider the outcomes of these more recent cases involving alleged airline predation in order to see whether there is any consensus or convergence on an appropriate test.

3   THE LUFTHANSA CASE

3.1   Allegations, German Law, and the Decision

Germania Fluggesellschaft mbH (Germania), previously a German charter airline, began regularly scheduled and ticketed flights between Frankfurt and Berlin on November 12, 2001. (A regularly scheduled flight with approximately the same departure time every day will henceforth be referred to as a schedule flight.)[19] Four schedule flights in each direction were offered each workday. The one-way fare for these flights was 99 Euros, including fees and tax.

Before Germania's service commenced, Deutsche Lufthansa AG (Lufthansa) offered 14 schedule flights in both directions, at a round trip price of 485 Euros. On November 9, 2001, Lufthansa introduced a one-way economy class fare of 100 Euros including fees and tax, for a 200 Euros round trip fare. It appears that no new flights were scheduled. On November 12, 2001, Germania lowered its one-way fare to 55 Euros. In January 2002, Lufthansa replaced its 100 Euros one-way fare with slightly higher fares, which as of February 2002 were approximately 105 Euros. On February 18, 2002, the Decision Division of the Federal Cartel Office decided that Lufthansa's pricing on this route violated the abuse of a dominant position section (section 19) of the *Act Against Restraints of Competition (ARC)*.

Section 19(1) of the *ARC* prohibits "the abusive exploitation of a dominant position by one or several undertakings." The general definition of dominance in section 19(2) of the *ARC* specifies that an undertaking is dominant as a supplier of certain kinds of goods or services if it has no competitors or faces no substantial competition, or "has a paramount market position in relation to its competitors." The *ARC* indicates in section 19(3) that "an undertaking is presumed to be dominant if it has a market share of at least one third." Section 19 of the *ARC* lists certain types of behavior that would be considered abuses

---

[19] See Bundeskartellamt Decision B9-144/01 (available online at http://www.bundeskartellamt.de/wEnglisch/download/pdf/entscheidungen/B9-144-01_e.pdf).

if pursued by a dominant firm, including in paragraph 19(4) behavior that "impairs the ability to compete of other undertakings in a manner affecting competition in the market and without any objective justification. . ."

The Federal Cartel Office argued that the relevant market was all flights between Frankfurt and Berlin, and that Lufthansa had a dominant position on this route. Specific market shares were not given in the decision. The Federal Cartel Office argued that Lufthansa's fare of 100 Euros, and subsequent fare of 105 Euros, represented "cut-price predatory behavior. . . intended and suitable to impede Germania's opportunities to compete and to force it from this route."[20] In particular, it was argued that:

- Lufthansa's product was more attractive to consumers than Germania's product, due to onboard service, the Miles and More air travel miles program, the larger number of flight times, and other advantages. The Federal Cartel Office stated that "Lufthansa's flight price must exceed that of Germania considerably in order to represent a comparable offer in terms of price-performance ratio. Despite all the problems which arise in trying to express Lufthansa's additional services in monetary terms, and allowing for an appropriate security margin, the Decision Division is convinced that a minimum price difference of €35 is necessary."[21]
- A fare of 105 Euros did not cover Lufthansa's average costs per paying customer. Specific numbers are not published in the decision, and it is unclear how the average cost per customer was computed. The Federal Cartel Office noted that whether Lufthansa earned profits or losses on the route is an open question.
- Predatory intent can be inferred from conclusions that Lufthansa's fares were "suitable for squeezing competitors out of the market,"[22] and that "There is no objective justification for Deutsche Lufthansa's low price strategy."[23] It is unclear which specific justifications the Federal Cartel Office considered.
- By engaging in predatory pricing against Germania, "Lufthansa's strategy is sending a signal to other market participants deterring them from entering the market."[24] Hence, it was argued that the alleged predation would create a reputation for predation that would prevent other new entry. No evidence that such a reputation was created was given in the decision.

Based on these findings, the Federal Cartel Office ruled that Lufthansa must, for a period of 2 years, maintain a one-way fare that exceeds Germania's by at least 35 Euros, as long as Germania's fare is no more than 99 Euros. If Germania's fare was between 99 and 133 Euros, Lufthansa was required to set a fare of 134 Euros.

3.2   The Court of Appeal

This case was appealed to the Regional Appeal Court of Dusseldorf, which affirmed the Federal Cartel Office's decision with the exception that the required margin was

---

[20] *Id.* at 15.
[21] *Id.* at 11.
[22] *Id.* at 16.
[23] *Id.* at 20.
[24] *Id.* at 16.

reduced from 35 Euros to 30.5 Euros.[25] It appears from the decision of the Court of Appeal that Lufthansa's appeal was based upon several points. Lufthansa apparently argued that the geographic market definition adopted by the Federal Cartel Office was too narrow, and that the relevant market should include more than a single route and other modes of transportation. The Court of Appeal noted that even if certain "sprinter" trains were included in the relevant market, Lufthansa would be deemed dominant. The Court of Appeal also decided that leisure and business travelers could not be considered separately in determining dominant market position.

According to the Court of Appeal decision, Lufthansa apparently argued that the extra services offered by Lufthansa were not relevant to the analysis, and that Lufthansa's fare in question conformed to the fare of its competitor. The Court of Appeal affirmed that it is appropriate to take into consideration the differences in services offered in determining whether one price effectively undercuts another. Finally, the Court of Appeal considered whether the given fares were sufficient to force Germania from the market and whether these fares could be justified simply as a competitive response to new entry. On these issues, the Court of Appeal affirmed the Federal Cartel Office's conclusions.

3.3   Other Commentary

Subsequent commentary on this case has been limited. Hüschelrath (2003) notes that whether the observed behavior was truly predatory cannot be examined rigorously because of the confidentiality of relevant data, and focuses on whether fixing a price spread between Lufthansa and Germania was an appropriate policy response. Hüschelrath argues that a preferred policy would be to adopt rules (such as those proposed by Baumol, 1979, Williamson, 1977, and Edlin, 2002) that restrict the manner or timing by which the alleged predator can adjust output or price, in order to weaken or remove the incentives to engage in predation.

Morrison (2004) notes that while it may be appropriate to consider differences in service quantity, it is difficult to know precisely what value to place on these differences. Morrison also takes exception to the time horizon of two years for the specified price differential, arguing that if Germania remains a "value-based airline", then Germania will be as vulnerable after two years as when the minimum differential was imposed. Finally, Morrison argues that if other value based airlines and Lufthansa expect the Federal Cartel Office to impose a similar margin in other cases, then this would lead to reduced competition and higher prices.

3.4   Comments

Several features of the Lufthansa decision distinguish it from the approaches taken in other cases (and their decisions) to testing for predation. In contrast to the U.S. Department of Justice case against American Airlines, discussed below, no quantitative evidence was presented regarding the potential for recoupment of the predatory losses. No evidence was presented to establish an abuse of dominance, and such evidence

---

[25] The discussion in this section is based on an unofficial translation of the decision of Regional Appeal Court of Dusseldorf.

appears not to be required by the *ARC*. While the decision claims "the only rational explanation for this pricing strategy is that it is an attempt to force Germania from this route and to recoup resulting losses at a later stage," there is no indication that quantitative evidence was introduced to establish this. A related observation is that while the Federal Cartel Office did make a predation for reputation argument, no further discussion of the appropriate economic theory of rational predation was provided.

Second, while specific cost figures and the exact breakdown of costs are not provided, the "average cost per paying customer" standard appears to differ substantially from the "avoidable costs of a flight or route" standard that has been adopted in other jurisdictions. It does not appear that the Federal Cartel Office considered whether the entire route, or specific flights, were covering the costs of offering those flights, considering all revenues attributable to the flight. Therefore, it remains in considerable doubt whether Lufthansa would have failed an avoidable cost test of the sort being applied in other jurisdictions.

Finally, the Lufthansa decision makes a very strong statement regarding the legitimacy of price matching, by arguing that fares above Germania's fares in fact represented undercutting once product differentials were taken into account, and by providing an estimate of the value to consumers of this product differential. Economically, as mentioned earlier, this is sensible. However, it is unclear whether such a differential can in fact be reliably measured.

4   THE AMERICAN AIRLINES CASE

4.1   Allegations and U.S. Law

On May 13, 1999, the Department of Justice (DOJ) of the United States filed a complaint against AMR Corporation and its subsidiaries American Airlines, Inc. and AMR Eagle Holding Corporation (together, AMR), alleging that AMR had engaged in predatory and monopolistic conduct in violation of Section 2 of the *Sherman Act*.[26] These allegations concerned capacity increases on routes out of Dallas/Fort Worth International Airport (DFW). AMR was granted summary judgment in April 2001.[27] This decision was appealed to the Tenth Circuit of the United States Court of Appeals, which affirmed the order granting summary judgment in July 2003.[28]

According to the initial complaint, AMR engaged in predatory conduct against Vanguard Airlines, Sun Jet, and Western Pacific, all LCCs, who during the 1990s entered or announced plans to enter several routes to or from Dallas/Fort Worth, where AMR had its largest hub. According to the complaint, AMR responded to this entry by expanding capacity through additional flights on the challenged routes, and re-entering a route that it had previously abandoned. At the same time, AMR allegedly lowered fares, in general matching the fares set by the LCCs and making more seats available at lower fares by removing fare restrictions.

---

[26] Department of Justice documents for this case are available at www.usdoj.gov/atr/cases/indx199.htm (last accessed December 15, 2004). AMR documents are available at www.aadoj.com (last accessed December 15, 2004).

[27] *U.S. v. AMR Corp.*, F. Supp. 2d 1141 (D. Kan. 2001).

[28] *U.S. v. AMR Corp.*, 335 F. 3d 1109 (10th Cir. 2003).

Focusing on four routes (Dallas/Fort Worth and Kansas City, Wichita, Long Beach, and Colorado Springs), the DOJ argued in the initial complaint that as a result of AMR's capacity expansion, accompanied by reduced fares, added flights on each route were being operated below their variable costs, total revenues on each route fell below total costs of serving the route, and each route was being operated unprofitably according to AMR's own route profitability indexes. This expansion was allegedly intended to drive Vanguard, Sun Jet, and Western Pacific out of the routes they had entered, and to obtain a reputation for predation that would prevent LCCs from entering other routes to and from Dallas/Fort Worth.

The DOJ alleged in its complaint that AMR violated section 2 of the *Sherman Act*, which prohibits actual or attempted monopolization. Notably, the DOJ did not claim that AMR was engaged in predatory pricing, but rather predatory capacity expansion. Some commentators have suggested that one purpose for this approach was to avoid having to present comparisons of price with marginal cost as the cost-based test of predation, and to focus on whether the alleged capacity expansion involved sacrifice that could only be recouped through subsequent anticompetitive effects.[29]

4.2   AMR's Initial Response

AMR's response to the DOJ's allegations was dated May 13, 1999, and denied the DOJ's main claims. AMR argued that (i) it "simply matched the fares set by the competition and then provided enough seats to meet consumer demand";[30] (ii) it covered variable costs on the routes in question; (iii) because of the presence of Delta and other major and low-cost airlines at Dallas/Fort Worth airport, and the presence of Southwest at nearby Love Field, AMR did not and could not recoup losses from any predatory campaign; (iv) on the Dallas/Fort Worth – Kansas City route, AMR's capacity increases merely replaced the flights cancelled when Delta withdrew from the route, and did not represent a flooding of the market; and (v) Vanguard Airlines survived and posted annual profits of $1.5 million in 1998, predicting a 20 percent increase in revenues in 1999.

4.3   The DOJ's Tests for Predation

The DOJ's economic expert offered four tests comparing AMR's revenues and costs. In the DOJ's Reply Brief for Appellant United States of America, the stated purposes of these tests were to determine:

Test 1: whether incremental cost exceeded incremental revenue;
Test 2: whether long-run (18-month) average variable cost exceeded price;
Test 3: whether price was below American's 18-month cost measure (persistent
        negative profitability); and
Test 4: whether incremental (average avoidable) cost exceeded price.[31]

---

[29] See "Roundtable: Recent Developments in Section 2," *Antitrust*, Fall 2003, pp. 15–25.
[30] *American Airlines' Response to the Department of Justice's Allegations of Predatory Practices, (1999)*, p. 1. Available at http://www.aadoj.com/pdfs/narrative.pdf (last accessed December 15, 2004).
[31] Reply Brief for Appellant United States of America, Public Redacted Version, page 12. Available at http://www.usdoj.gov/atr/cases/f10800/10856.pdf (last accessed December 15, 2004).

Hence, the focus of Tests 1 and 4 was whether the costs of the allegedly predatory increments to capacity were greater or less than the revenues earned by the incremental capacity. In contrast, Tests 2 and 3 examined whether the routes in question were covering long run average variable costs.

In conducting these tests, the DOJ made use of AMR's internal decision measures FAUDNC (Fully Allocated Earnings plus Upline/Downline Contribution Net of Costs), and VAUDNC (Variable Earnings plus Upline/Dowline Contribution Net of Costs). According to the district court decision, the costs included in VAUDNC account for over 72 percent of total costs for the Kansas City, Wichita, Colorado Springs, and Long Beach routes, while FAUDNC accounts for 97 to 99 percent of total costs.

According to the district court decision, Test 1 considered whether VAUDNC, VAUDNC-AC (VAUDNC adjusted to include aircraft costs), and FAUDNC declined with the allegedly predatory capacity changes.[32] Similarly, under Test 4, the costs included in VAUDNC-AC were compared with the estimated revenue from incremental passengers. Tests 2 and 3 made use of FAUDNC, and considered whether the capacity additions rendered FAUDNC negative on particular routes (Test 2) and whether FAUDNC remained negative for longer than 12 months (Test 3). In its Reply Brief, the DOJ noted on page 12 that "American failed each test everywhere it was applicable."

In addition, the DOJ presented evidence intended to support the argument that AMR would likely recoup the losses of the predatory campaign on the routes on which predation was alleged to occur, on routes where expansion of the LCCs was thus prevented, and on a number of routes that would be subsequently protected through the achieved reputation for predation. According to the district court, Professor Berry, expert for the DOJ, provided three tables relating to recoupment.[33] The first table provided estimates of the predatory losses incurred on the four routes in question, and compared these estimates to estimates of recoupment already achieved on these routes through higher prices. According to the district court, the estimated costs of predation were lower than estimated recoupment for Wichita, but were greater than estimated recoupment for Colorado Springs.

Table 2 provided estimates of the increase in profits AMR would realize if its reputation decreased the probability of an LCC establishing a hub at Dallas/Fort Worth within five years by ten percent. Table 3 estimated the increase in profits that would result from delaying the establishment of an LCC hub at Dallas/Fort Worth by two years.

4.4 The District Court Decision

In April 2001, the district court granted AMR summary judgment. First, the district court rejected the four revenue-cost tests presented by the DOJ. The court concluded that "Given the government's relevant market definition, its claim requires proof that American underpriced its services on the entire market/route, not just one particular fraction of those services,"[34] and that average variable cost is "the only appropriate,

---

[32] 140 F. Supp. at 1202–1203.

[33] As Professor Berry's expert report remains under seal, our discussion of the evidence regarding recoupment is based on information provided in the district court decision.

[34] *Id.* at 1202–1203.

credible measure of costs in the present action."[35] Tests 1 and 4 were rejected as being "short-run tests for profit-maximization."[36] The court rejected the inclusion of aircraft costs, stating that "Aircraft ownership costs are properly considered fixed costs in the industry, and are not an avoidable cost of changing capacity in a route."[37] Tests 2 and 3 were rejected as based on average total costs as opposed to average variable costs.

Second, the district court stated that by only matching the fares of the alleged prey, and never undercutting those fares, AMR was simply meeting the prices of the competition and was therefore entitled to summary judgment. Third, the court held that "the uncontroverted evidence establishes that DFW routes are not structurally susceptible to the supra-competitive prices which is prerequisite to a successful predatory scheme,"[38] and that there was not a dangerous likelihood of recoupment. This conclusion was based on a decision that there were no structural barriers to entry, and on the presence and success of a number of low-cost carriers at Dallas/Fort Worth. In addition, the court rejected the argument of recoupment through reputation, stating that "the government's broad-based claims of predation by (subjectively-felt) reputation offer no principled basis for distinguishing between a reputation for predation, and a reputation for lawfully vigorous competition."[39]

4.5 The Appeal

In its Brief for Appellant United States of America, the DOJ first argued that the district court should have focused specifically on the challenged conduct, which was the capacity expansion on the routes in question, and whether this expansion "made business sense apart from its exclusionary effect."[40] Second, the DOJ argued that the district court had been resolving disputed issues of material fact by deciding that the government's evidence did not demonstrate that the added capacity was unprofitable. Next, the DOJ alleged that the district court erred by refusing to consider recoupment in other markets through reputation, and in its conclusion that supracompetitive prices could not be charged by AMR at its Dallas/Fort Worth hub. Finally, the DOJ argued that the meeting competition defense does not apply to section 2 of the *Sherman Act*, and that the district court erred in its claim that summary judgment should be granted because AMR matched fares and did not undercut them.

In its decision affirming the granting of summary judgment, the Tenth Circuit of the United States Court of Appeals stated that market-level average variable cost "may obscure the nature of a particular predatory scheme and, thus, contrary to what is suggested by the district court, we do not favor AVC to the exclusion of other proxies for marginal cost."[41] However, the court rejected all four of the DOJ's proposed tests of predation. It stated that Tests 2 and 3 included costs "that are not, in large part, variable

---

[35] *Id.* at 1196.
[36] *Id.* at 1201.
[37] *Id.* at 1175.
[38] *Id.* at 1209.
[39] *Id.* at 1215.
[40] Brief for Appellant at 29.
[41] 335 F. 3d at 1116.

or avoidable with respect to capacity increases. . ."[42] The court concluded that Test 1 considers only whether a company has maximized short run profits, and would (page 20) "condemn nearly all output expansions."[43]

Test 4 was rejected because it included costs that were allocated arbitrarily across flights or routes, and was not based on average avoidable cost as the DOJ had asserted. In particular, the court lists the costs of airport ticket agents, arrival agents, ramp workers, and security as costs that are arbitrarily allocated.

The court did not comment on whether the creation of a reputation for predation may be considered as part of a demonstration of a dangerous probability of recoupment. As well, the court explicitly declined to rule on whether a meeting the competition defense applies under section 2 of the *Sherman Act*.

4.6   Other Commentary

Edlin and Farrell (2004) base their commentary on the summary judgment and the appeals briefs (the Tenth Circuit decision had not been released at the time of their writing). The authors argue that the question of which cost test to use was really a disagreement over which benchmark should be used to determine whether AMR sacrificed profits. The DOJ's tests considered whether AMR's capacity increases led to a sacrifice compared to profits without the capacity increase, while AMR proposed to consider whether it would have been better off not serving the route in its entirety. The authors argue on page 513 that a test based on route level variable costs or avoidable costs has "shaky underpinnings."

Further, Edlin and Farrell are critical of the practicality and usefulness of meeting the competition defenses, arguing on page 520 that "it is not clear what safe harbor a matching defense would offer to a defendant if the quality difference is hard to quantify," and on page 521 that while price matching need not be anticompetitive, "we see no basis to be sure that it's always pro-competitive." Regarding recoupment, the authors note that whether a reputation argument should only apply when there are linkages across markets (as suggested by the DOJ) is a question for appellate courts.

Another detailed commentary is provided by Werden (2003), who argues that both the district court and appellate court missed the distinction between the AMR case, based on allegedly predatory capacity expansions, and a traditional predatory pricing case. He notes the DOJ's argument that the increased choice of flight times and larger aircraft (which many passengers prefer) that resulted through the capacity expansion were instrumental to the alleged predation, and not, as the district court believed, simply necessary to make AMR's fares available to more passengers. Regarding the appellate court's rejection of the cost tests, and in particular Test 4, Werden conjectures on page 34 that "The Tenth Circuit must have spent months combing the record for even the slightest indication that the Department's experts had overstated true incremental cost." Finally, Werden notes that the appellate court's affirmation based on rejecting the DOJ's cost tests allowed it to avoid commenting on the meeting competition defense and the issue of recoupment through reputation.

---

[42] *Id.* at 1117.
[43] *Id.* at 1119.

4.7   Comments

The AMR decisions of the district court and court of appeals are notable in part because the conclusions reached on several issues differed dramatically from the conclusions of courts or adjudicating bodies in other cases discussed in this survey. As in the Lufthansa case, the question of whether matching fares is permissible was an important issue in AMR. However, while the German court of appeals accepted the claim that price matching by a major carrier constitutes effective undercutting against a low cost carrier, the district court in the AMR case accepted that AMR deserved summary judgment because it was simply meeting the competition. Again in contrast to Lufthansa, where an argument of reputation was accepted, the AMR district court rejected reputation arguments for reasons of practicality.

Finally, while the AMR case raised many important policy issues, as discussed by Edlin and Farrell (2004), ultimately the decision came down to the fact that the court disagreed with the DOJ regarding which costs are avoidable. Notably, as will be discussed in the next section, those costs that the court of appeals considered to be arbitrarily allocated were all costs that were accepted by the Canadian Competition Tribunal as avoidable. Similarly, aircraft costs, which were rejected by the district court as being variable, were accepted by the Canadian Competition Tribunal as avoidable.

5   THE AIR CANADA CASE

5.1   Case History

On March 5, 2001, the Commissioner of Competition filed a Notice of Application with the Competition Tribunal, alleging that Air Canada had violated section 79 (the abuse of dominance provision) of the *Competition Act* by

(a) operating and increasing capacity on a number of eastern Canadian routes at fares that did not cover the avoidable cost of providing the service;

(b) engaging in a policy of 'matching' fares offered by low cost carriers on those routes, and operating capacity at those fares (1) without regard for the effect of such fares on Air Canada's profitability, (2) without regard to the additional benefits associated with the service offered by Air Canada, and (3) with the foreseeable effect of significantly diluting revenues of low cost carriers, rendering their operations unprofitable.

The application to the Competition Tribunal was partly motivated by Air Canada's response to the entry of WestJet, a Canadian LCC, onto the Hamilton/Moncton route. According to the Notice of Application, WestJet announced on February 29, 2000 that it would begin service on the Hamilton/Moncton route with one-way fares at $129. Service commenced on April 19, 2000. The application states that Air Canada responded to this entry by increasing capacity on the Toronto/Moncton route, as well as several other eastern Canadian routes, maintaining the capacity on the Toronto/Moncton route up to the date of the application, introducing substantially lower fares on the aforementioned routes, and, as a consequence, operating capacity on the routes at fares that did not cover the avoidable costs of providing the service. It was stated in the application that by matching WestJet's fares, Air Canada was in fact undercutting them because Air Canada's service was more valuable than that offered by WestJet.

The application to the Competition Tribunal was also motivated by Air Canada's response to the entry of a new carrier, CanJet, on a number of routes out of Halifax. The application states that Air Canada responded to the entry of CanJet by adding and maintaining additional capacity on three Halifax routes, introducing new lower fares on the routes, and consequently operating capacity on the routes at fares that did not cover the avoidable costs of providing the service.

The abuse of dominance case brought against Air Canada was the first to cite anti-competitive acts (specifically, those in (a) above) contained in the Airline Regulations. In order to make out a case under section 79, it must be shown that "(a) one or more persons substantially or completely control, throughout Canada or any area thereof, a class or species of business, (b) that person or those persons have engaged in or are engaging in a practice of anti-competitive acts, and (c) the practice has had, is having or is likely to have the effect of preventing or lessening competition substantially in a market." If these elements are proved, then the Competition Tribunal may make an order prohibiting all or any of those persons from engaging in that practice.[44]

According to the Competition Tribunal, "On May 15, 2001, at the request of both the Commissioner of Competition and Air Canada, the Competition Tribunal (the "Tribunal") ordered that the application be heard in two phases: Phase I, to deal with the application of the avoidable cost test to two sample routes, from the period of April 1, 2000 to March 5, 2001; and Phase II, to deal with the balance of the application."[45] The Tribunal was to consider four questions during Phase I. The four questions were as follows:

  (a) What is the appropriate unit or units of capacity to examine?
  (b) What categories of costs are avoidable and when do they become avoidable?
  (c) What is the appropriate time period or periods to examine?
  (d) What, if any, recognition should be given to "beyond contribution"?

Having answers to these questions provided by the parties, the Tribunal would then consider whether Air Canada had operated or increased capacity at fares that did not cover the avoidable costs of providing the service on the Toronto/Moncton route and the Halifax/Montreal route.

The Tribunal's hearing commenced in September 2001, but was adjourned on September 11 due to the terrorist attacks in the United States. It was adjourned again on October 15, 2001, and the hearing was started anew on November 27, 2002. The hearing lasted for 40 days and the Tribunal's decision was handed down on July 22, 2003, over three years from the date when the alleged anti-competitive conduct against WestJet had commenced. At the time of the release of the Phase I decision, Air Canada was

---

[44] Subsequent to the filing of the Notice of Application in the *Air Canada* case, the *Competition Act* was amended in 2002 to permit the Competition Tribunal to impose administrative monetary penalties of up to $15 million when, after a hearing, it finds that there has been a breach of the abuse of dominance provisions by a dominant air carrier.

[45] See *Commissioner of Competition v. Air Canada* (2003), Comp. Trib. 13, paragraph 3.

in bankruptcy protection (which it had entered in April 2003) under the *Companies' Creditors Arrangements Act* (CCAA). The Tribunal stayed the execution of the decision until Air Canada emerged from CCAA protection, which it did at the end of September 2004.

On October 29, 2004, the Commissioner of Competition announced that the litigation between the Competition Bureau and Air Canada had been resolved and that Phase II of the *Air Canada* case would not go ahead.[46] The Commissioner stated that "In light of the passage of time and the significant changes in the industry, we have concluded that it would not be in the public interest to pursue the second part of this case."[47] Prior to this announcement, on September 23, 2004, the Bureau issued a clarification of its enforcement approach in the airline industry:

> In the Bureau's view, the application of the avoidable cost test is only triggered by a significant response by a dominant carrier to competition or new entry.
>
> In general, actions taken by a dominant carrier against competitors which could attract enforcement action include reducing fares to undercut competitors, adding significant capacity, failing to remove capacity in accordance with its seasonal or other usual practices, or substantially increasing the number of tickets offered at fares which match the lowest fares of a competitor.
>
> The Commissioner recognizes the benefits of price competition for consumers. As a general principle, where a dominant carrier's response to competition consists only of reducing fares to levels which match, but do not undercut those of a competitor ("fare matching"), the Bureau will not take enforcement action.
>
> However, if such fare reductions were accompanied by a significant increase in capacity or a significant increase in the number of seats offered at the lowest price, this "safe harbour" would not apply. In such cases, the Bureau would then consider all of the elements of abuse of dominance . . . .
>
> Where a dominant carrier responds to entry or competition by doing something more than fare matching, the Bureau will then consider all of the elements of abuse of dominance, not just the avoidable cost test, in deciding whether to take enforcement action, and in deciding what action to take.[48]

On November 2, 2004, the Government of Canada tabled proposed amendments to the *Competition Act* in the House of Commons. Bill C-19 would, among other things, repeal all of the airline specific amendments to the Act that have been introduced since 2000, including the Airline Regulations. It is too early to tell, at the time of writing, whether Bill C-19 is likely to pass in its original form.

The Competition Tribunal's decision in the *Air Canada* case is the first one in Canada to provide some interpretation of an avoidable cost test in the context of alleged predation. The decision has implications for how an avoidable cost test should be carried out in

---

[46] In August 2003, Konrad von Finckenstein, the Commissioner of Competition under whom the Air Canada case was brought to the Competition Tribunal, was appointed a judge to the Federal Court of Canada. The current Commissioner, Sheridan Scott, joined the Competition Bureau in January 2004.

[47] See "Competition Bureau Settles Case with Air Canada", October 29, 2004, available on the Competition Bureau's website at http://strategis.ic.gc.ca/epic/internet/incb-bc.nsf/en/ct02973e.html.

[48] See "Competition Bureau Clarifies Enforcement Approach in the Airline Industry", September 23, 2004, available on the Competition Bureau's website at http://strategis.ic.gc.ca/epic/internet/incb-bc.nsf/en/ct02952e.html.

future airline predation cases in Canada, as well as how it might be carried out in other jurisdictions.[49] The decision also has more general implications for how an avoidable cost test should be carried out in other possible cases of predation brought under the abuse of dominance provisions. It is therefore of some importance to know both the positions of the two parties with respect to the questions posed by the Tribunal, as well as the conclusion reached on these questions by the Tribunal.

5.2   The Questions and the Issues

The Competition Tribunal accepted the following definition of avoidable costs: all costs that can be avoided by not producing the good or service in question. In general, the avoidable cost of offering a service will consist of the variable costs and the product-specific fixed costs that are not sunk.[50] The Tribunal's decision then reviews the positions of the parties on the questions that it posed prior to providing its analysis.

5.2.1   Units of capacity

The Commissioner's position was that the appropriate unit of capacity for carrying out the avoidable cost test is the schedule flight. Other possible measures of capacity, such as the seat, the route, or the network, are inappropriate since possible predation could go undetected with those units of capacity.[51] A carrier can use schedule flights strategically (e.g., by adding a new schedule flight, increasing aircraft size, or reducing fares on a flight-specific basis) in an attempt to force losses on a rival carrier. By doing so, certain of the alleged predator's flights may also fail to cover their avoidable costs.

Air Canada rejected the schedule flight as the appropriate unit of capacity. It argued that the route is the appropriate unit of capacity, arguing in part that as long as flight operations on a route are profitable, entry by an equally efficient competitor will be possible.[52] The Competition Tribunal accepted the expert evidence that supports the possibility of predatory conduct at the level of the schedule flight, and therefore found that the schedule flight is the appropriate unit of capacity for purposes of the avoidable cost test.

5.2.2   Timing issues

The Tribunal identified the two timing issues as (a) when do avoidable costs become avoidable, and (b) what is the appropriate time period to examine? The Commissioner's position was that substantially all of Air Canada's avoidable costs could be avoided within a period of approximately three months from the time that a decision was made to cancel a flight.[53] In the case where capacity is added to a route in response to entry or to a competitor, all of the costs associated with the new flight should be considered

---

[49] See the Competition Bureau's statements in its press release, *supra* note 47.

[50] See *Commissioner of Competition v. Air Canada, supra* note 45 at paragraph 76.

[51] *Id.* at paragraph 160. For comparison, the DOJ had adopted the incremental capacity to the route as the appropriate unit of analysis in the AMR case.

[52] See *Commissioner of Competition v. Air Canada, supra* note 45 at paragraphs 161–162.

[53] *Id.* at paragraph 170.

avoidable at the outset.[54] In the event of a flight cancellation, some costs could be avoided outright by not incurring or by shedding the cost. Some costs could be avoided by redeployment of resources to other flights. Redeployment of resources would allow the airline to avoid incurring additional costs to support those other flights. A flight cancellation also implies that passengers will redeploy themselves to other flights, and costs are then properly allocated to the flights serving the redeployed passengers.[55]

With respect to the appropriate time period to examine, two questions need to be addressed. First, what is the appropriate time period for which an air carrier can be expected to have reasonably accurate knowledge of its flight performance on a route? Second, what are the appropriate time increments for carrying out the avoidable cost test? The Commissioner submitted that Air Canada's reporting systems produced the relevant information on flight profitability in short time periods,[56] so that Air Canada would know whether a schedule flight was likely to be profitable within a short period of time after the occurrence of the schedule flight. In terms of the appropriate time increments for carrying out the avoidable cost test, the Commissioner proposed that the test be carried out using monthly data. That period of time would be long enough to ensure that observations of poor performance for specific operations of a schedule flight were not random.

Where one is considering whether an established flight's revenues are covering its avoidable costs, the question arises as to whether one tries to determine which costs can be avoided within certain periods of time after the decision is made to cancel a flight. The Commissioner's position was that this is not a reasonable way to proceed. Rather, one should look at whether a cost is avoidable or not at some point in time. All costs that are avoidable at some time should be included as avoidable costs for purposes of the test. This way of carrying out the test is forward looking in the sense that a firm must believe that its revenues cover all of its avoidable costs in order for its conduct to be sustainable in the long run. If revenues do not cover avoidable cost calculated in this way, one would expect an air carrier to make adjustments to its operations (e.g., changing its flight schedule or aircraft size) in order to improve its performance. The lack of such adjustments would be consistent with a predatory response.

Air Canada's position with respect to timing issues was that all costs that are avoidable within a 12-month period of a flight cancellation should be included in the avoidable cost test. Using a 12-month period accounts for seasonality. A cost should only be deemed avoidable if it can be avoided during the relevant time period. The appropriate time period for carrying out the test is the time period during which the alleged predatory behavior was occurring.[57]

On the question of the time period, the Tribunal has stated that the Airline Regulations do not specify a time period for defining what constitutes an anti-competitive act. Therefore, "whenever the dominant carrier operates capacity at fares below the avoidable

---

[54] *Id.* at paragraph 171. In addition, costs should be considered immediately avoidable in the case where an air carrier maintains capacity in the market during a time period when it is usually eliminated (e.g. during low season).

[55] *Id.* at paragraph 88.

[56] *Id.* at paragraph 172.

[57] *Id.* at paragraphs 183–185.

cost of providing the service, it commits an anti-competitive act."[58] Furthermore, it is up
to the Commissioner to decide the relevant time period for determining whether fares
were below avoidable costs. The Tribunal does not accept seasonality as the basis for
selecting a 12-month time period. The Tribunal accepts that the avoidable cost test can
be carried out using monthly data, but that it can be carried out for shorter time periods
as well.

5.2.3   Categories of avoidable costs
According to the Tribunal, the Commissioner's position is that substantially all of Air
Canada's costs, except overhead, are avoidable within three months. Air Canada views
26 cost categories as unavoidable over this time period, and these categories fall into the
broader categories of system labor costs, station labor costs, aircraft labor costs, non-
labor system and sunk costs, and aircraft ownership and insurance costs.[59] The Tribunal
largely accepted the Commissioner's position with respect to which costs are avoidable,
including aircraft costs. The Tribunal was satisfied that the Commissioner had shown
that opportunities for redeployment of aircraft were generally and reasonably available.

5.2.4   Beyond contribution
The beyond contribution of a flight on a particular city-pair route is the difference
between beyond revenue and beyond costs, where the former is the prorated portions of
fares of through and connecting passengers on the route that are allocated to the other
flight segments of the trips of through and connecting passengers. The Commissioner
excluded beyond contribution from the measure of revenue for a given flight, arguing
that in the event of a flight cancellation, Air Canada would retain the beyond contribution
due to passenger redeployment to alternative flights.[60]

Air Canada had a procedure for calculating beyond contribution, and would include the
beyond contribution attributed to a particular flight to the flight's revenue.[61] The Tribunal
found that there was no basis for including beyond contribution as submitted by Air
Canada. The Tribunal further found that when properly estimated, beyond contribution
could be considered as a legitimate business reason for operating a schedule flight with
revenues below avoidable costs, but it is not to be included in the calculation of that test.[62]

5.2.5   Operating below avoidable costs
The Competition Tribunal concluded that Air Canada had operated or increased capacity at fares that did not cover the avoidable costs of providing the service on the
Toronto/Moncton route between April 1, 2000 and March 5, 2001, and on the Hali-
fax/Montreal route between July 1, 2000 and March 5, 2001. While the Tribunal found
that Air Canada had failed the avoidable cost test, it was not yet able to reach a conclusion

---

[58] *Id.* at paragraph 186.
[59] *Id.* at paragraphs 197 and 199.
[60] *Id.* at paragraphs 290 and 295. The DOJ did allow for beyond contribution in its cost based predation test.
[61] *Id.* at paragraph 287.
[62] *Id.* at paragraph 301. The Tribunal stated that it could consider legitimate business justification as part of
Phase II, and as part of the question of whether Air Canada had engaged in a practice of anti-competitive acts
pursuant to section 79 of the Act. See paragraph 55 of the Tribunal's decision.

on whether Air Canada had engaged in an abuse of dominance under section 79 of the Act.[63]

5.3 Commentary

There has been very limited commentary on the Air Canada decision to date. Kay and Kolers (2003–2004), counsel for Air Canada, provide a short summary of the Tribunal's decision. They note, based on a consideration of the *Air Canada* and *AMR* cases, that the price-cost tests used to identify predatory pricing in the airline industry are now different in the U.S. and Canada. They view the Canadian test as over-inclusive of costs that are avoidable, and state that it has the potential to label as anti-competitive behavior that is legitimate.[64]

Musgrove and Edmonstone (2004) provide a more detailed review of the Competition Tribunal's decision, focusing on the legal issues. They disagreed with the Tribunal's conclusion that legitimate business justification for below-cost pricing should be assessed as part of the consideration of whether there was a practice of anti-competitive acts. They argued that the Commissioner should be required to show that there was an anti-competitive purpose before an anti-competitive act can be found. They did not believe that it was appropriate that the Commissioner be allowed to decide the relevant time period for purposes of carrying out the avoidable cost test, or that it made sense that the operation of a single flight could be considered an anti-competitive act given the Tribunal's decision.[65]

Perhaps the most serious criticism that they level with respect to the *Air Canada* case is not at some aspect of the Tribunal's decision, but towards the Airline Regulations themselves. Their concern is that if Air Canada faces a new low cost entrant on a route, it may find itself operating below avoidable costs if it responds to the entrant by lowering fares, or if it maintains its fares and loses customers as a result. While they believe that increasing capacity in the face of entry or undercutting an entrant could be anti-competitive, they view it as problematic that matching the fares of a low cost entrant could be regarded as an anti-competitive act.

McFetridge (2004) has provided both a summary and economic critique of the Tribunal's decision. His main concern (discussed at p. 84) is with the way in which avoidable costs are determined. He states that one view of the avoidable cost test is that it should compare the revenue derived from a product with costs that would be avoided outright (either by shedding or not incurring them) if the product were not offered. The latter costs he calls "inherently avoidable". He interprets the Commissioner's position as being costs that are not inherently avoidable could be treated as if they were. This he

---

[63] *Id.* at paragraph 340.

[64] Houston and Pratt (2004), counsel for the Commissioner of Competition in the *Air Canada* case, also provide a brief summary of the Tribunal's findings, but they do not provide any commentary on the decision. Facey and Ware (2003) touch on the *Air Canada* case, noting that the measure of avoidable cost accepted by the Competition Tribunal was more inclusive than what courts accepted in the *AMR* case. The focus of their paper, however, is to provide a broader comparison of predatory pricing laws and jurisprudence in Canada, the United States, and Europe.

[65] They also note that the Tribunal decided to delay further consideration of the relevant time period until the Phase II issue of whether there was a practice of anti-competitive acts was dealt with.

believes raises the estimated magnitude of Air Canada's avoidable costs significantly. These latter costs are largely the ones identified by the Commissioner as avoidable by passenger recapture, resource redeployment, and asset disposal.[66] His main point seems to be that the opportunity cost of continuing to offer a flight may be higher than the inherently avoidable cost, but that will depend on the extent of passenger recapture.[67] It will also depend on resource redeployment opportunities. McFetridge believes that evidence on the extent of passenger recapture and resource redeployment opportunities should therefore be produced in a predation case involving an avoidable cost test. It should be noted that the Tribunal was satisfied that there was sufficient evidence on the possibilities for passenger recapture and resource redeployment.

6 THE QANTAS CASE

On May 7, 2002, the Australian Competition and Consumer Commission instituted legal proceedings against Qantas Airways Limited. It was alleged that Qantas had misused its market power on the Brisbane-Adelaide route after Virgin Blue Airlines Pty Ltd.'s entry in December 2000.[68] It was alleged that Qantas had misused its market power by increasing the number of seats available on the route and matching or undercutting Virgin Blue's airfares. "The ACCC alleges that Qantas engaged in 'capacity dumping', to eliminate or substantially damage Virgin Blue, or to deter or prevent Virgin Blue from engaging in competitive conduct in the market including the expansion of its network, thereby seeking to lessen competition."[69]

Virgin Blue began serving Australian airline markets as a low-cost carrier on August 31, 2000, with the initiation of service between Brisbane and Sydney. In September 2000, Virgin announced that it would offer two daily schedule flights on the Adelaide/Brisbane route beginning February 1, 2000. In fact, it began service on the Adelaide/Brisbane route with one schedule flight on December 7, 2000, and a second schedule flight one week later. At the time of its entry, Qantas was offering two schedule flights on the route, while Ansett offered one. Qantas began its third schedule flight on the route in February 2001. Ansett discontinued all flight operations in September 2001, leaving the Adelaide/Brisbane route to be served by Qantas and Virgin Blue.[70]

As a result of the increase in capacity on the route and the reduction of fares at the time of Virgin Blue's entry, it was alleged that Qantas, Virgin and Ansett operated at a

---

[66] McFetridge (2004, p. 84) states that, according to Air Canada's Phase I closing argument, the inherently avoidable costs account for 38 percent of Air Canada's fully allocated costs on the two routes involved in the test, whereas costs designated as avoidable by the Tribunal accounted for 90 percent of Air Canada's fully allocated costs to the routes. (Overhead costs and certain common costs were judged unavoidable in the event of a flight cancellation.)

[67] McFetridge (2004, p. 85) interprets the Commissioner as arguing implicitly that the possibilities for passenger recapture, redeployment and disposal of resources are such that the opportunity cost of a flight is just equal to the costs per flight that the Tribunal deemed to be avoidable.

[68] See "ACCC Alleges Qantas Misused Its Market Power in Anti-competitive Manner", available on the ACCC web site at http://www.accc.gov.au/content/index.phtml/itemId/88059 (accessed on October 7, 2004).

[69] *Id.* at p. 1.

[70] See paragraphs 61 to 72 of the Second Amended Statement of Claim in the case of *ACCC v. Qantas Airways Limited.*

loss on the route until the time of Ansett's exit in September 2001.[71] Qantas' ability to engage in the alleged conduct was ascribed to its market power. Its capacity expansion and fare cutting were evidence of taking advantage of market power, for the purpose of eliminating Virgin as a competitor from the Adelaide/Brisbane or Australian market, and/or preventing its entry into other Australian airline markets, and/or deterring Virgin from engaging in competitive conduct in the Australian airline market.[72] In the result, Qantas was alleged to have breached section 46 of the *Trade Practices Act 1974*.

The wording of section 46 is considerably different from the American and Canadian provisions under which a predation case can be taken. According to section 46,

(1) A corporation that has a substantial degree of power in a market shall not take advantage of that power for the purpose of:
    (a) eliminating or substantially damaging a competitor of the corporation or of a body corporate that is related to the corporation in that or any other market;
    (b) preventing the entry of a person into that or any other market; or
    (c) deterring or preventing a person from engaging in competitive conduct in that or any other market.
(2) In determining for the purpose of this section the degree of power that a body corporate or bodies corporate has or have in a market, the Court shall have regard to the extent to which the conduct of the body corporate or of any of those bodies corporate in that market is constrained by the conduct of:
    (a) competitors, or potential competitors, of the body corporate or any of those bodies corporate in that market; or
    (b) persons to whom or from whom the body corporate or any of those bodies corporate supplies or acquires goods or services in that market.

To make out a case under section 46, it must be shown that a firm has a substantial degree of market power in a market, and that it has taken advantage of that power for the purpose of eliminating a competitor, preventing entry, or inhibiting competitive conduct. The terms "predation", "pricing below cost" or "abuse of dominance" are not used in section 46. It must therefore be argued that engaging in predation is a way for a firm to take advantage of its market power.[73]

As expected, Qantas rejected the ACCC's allegations against it. Qantas stated that "The ACCC action relates to a legitimate, commercially justified, competitive response by Qantas to Virgin Blue commencing operations on the Brisbane-Adelaide route in early 2001."[74] The ACCC's economic expert report was filed with the Court on May 30, 2003.

---

[71] *Id.* at paragraph 81.

[72] *Id.* at paragraphs 83–85.

[73] Mr. John Martin, a Commissioner with the ACCC, has written that "Where a company has achieved a position of monopoly or market power (by whatever means), section 46 of the Trade Practices Act restrains the misuse of such power. It prevents a business from using its market power to eliminate, harm or deter competitors. A typical example of this would be predatory pricing, where a company with substantial market power cuts its prices below cost, so as to drive a competitor with less financial resources out of business." See Martin (2002, pp. 4–5).

[74] See Qantas Airways Limited, ABN 16 009 661 901, "Preliminary Monthly Traffic and Capacity Statistics March 2002", available on the Qantas Airways website.

Qantas was then given until November 13 to file economic expert reports in response. The trial was scheduled to commence on November 24, but on November 21 the ACCC announced that it was discontinuing its action against Qantas. The ACCC stated that "Like all section 46 (misuse of market power) cases, final resolution in the courts of this matter would have been extremely difficult, lengthy and expensive. Experience in overseas jurisdictions where similar cases have been instituted shows the uncertainty and delays such litigation faces." It was also noted by the ACCC that the airlines market had changed since the action commenced, and competition had been enhanced. Virgin Blue continued to compete on the Adelaide/Brisbane route.[75]

While we will never know whether the ACCC would have been successful in proving its allegations, we do know something about the economic approach that the ACCC took in this case.[76] Unlike Phase I of the *Air Canada* case, which was focused on the interpretation of the avoidable cost test in an airline predation case, the *Qantas* case required proving a violation of section 46. This required a consideration of market power, market definition, market shares, entry barriers, the predation test, and competitive effects of Qantas' conduct.

With respect to the predation test, the ACCC's proposed price/cost test was a revenue/avoidable cost test that was essentially the same as the one proposed by the Commissioner in the *Air Canada* case. As in the *Air Canada* case, the schedule flight was regarded as the appropriate unit of analysis for purposes of the test. A month was selected as the appropriate time increment for carrying out the avoidable cost test, and four to six weeks after the end of a month was regarded as sufficient time for an air carrier to have accurate flight performance information.

In the case where an incumbent carrier either adds capacity or fails to remove capacity normally removed from a route at a particular time of year, all of the costs associated with that increase in capacity were regarded as avoidable from the outset. With respect to the cancellation of an existing schedule flight, some costs were regarded as avoidable immediately, while others would take more time to avoid through shedding or redeployment. However, for purposes of the avoidable cost test, all costs that can ultimately be avoided by canceling a flight were included in the cost/revenue comparison. Certain allocated costs associated with corporate overhead were excluded from avoidable costs. Aircraft costs were regarded as avoidable through redeployment. As in the *Air Canada* case, avoidable costs were calculated using the cost categories that the airline uses to assess route profitability.

With respect to revenues, all flight specific revenues (including cargo revenue) were included in the revenue/cost comparison, although frequent flyer revenue was excluded.

The *Qantas* case is similar to the *American Airlines* and *Air Canada* cases in terms of the alleged conduct. Once again, the case was terminated before the evidence could be presented and evaluated at a trial. It continues to be unclear what conduct on the part of a dominant air carrier in a relevant market will be sufficient to not only generate an antitrust case, but also to be deemed a violation of the antitrust laws.

---

[75] See ACCC, "Qantas Airlines Matter Discontinued", available on the ACCC's website.
[76] No information is publicly available regarding the positions or arguments contained in the expert reports of economists retained by Qantas.

7   CONCLUSION

The possibility of predatory behavior by an incumbent network carrier directed at entering or expanding LCCs has been a concern of competition authorities in North America, Europe, and Australia. In a number of instances, the incumbent's response to LCCs has been regarded as crossing the line separating aggressive competition from anti-competitive behavior, resulting in antitrust cases. The four cases discussed in this article are based on similar events: an incumbent airline responds to the entry and expansion of one or more low cost carriers by lowering fares, and possibly expanding capacity through additional flights or larger aircraft. Despite the similarity in the cases, however, the approaches of the different antitrust authorities and the findings of the different adjudicating bodies have varied with respect to certain elements that need to be proved.

First, there has been some disagreement among antitrust authorities regarding the unit of analysis for price-cost comparisons. In the *Air Canada* case, it was the Commissioner's position that the schedule flight was the appropriate unit of capacity.[77] An avoidable cost test was then applied to both new schedule flights as well as to schedule flights that had been operating before the alleged anticompetitive behavior. In contrast, the DOJ in the *AMR* case focused specifically on the incremental capacity on a route, challenging the increases to capacity through new flights and larger aircraft.[78] In *Lufthansa*, the Federal Cartel Office accepted the route as the relevant market, but appears to have compared specific low fares to a route level average cost per customer.

The differences in the decisons of the adjudicating bodies was even more dramatic. While the Competition Tribunal accepted the Commissioner's position that the schedule flight was the relevant unit of analysis, the District Court in the *AMR* case held that the appropriate price-cost comparison must encompass the entire route (the Court of Appeals, however, disagreed with this position).

Further disagreements can be found with respect to the costs that should be included in price-cost tests of predation. Both the DOJ and the Commissioner presented avoidable cost measures that included aircraft costs. However, while the Competition Tribunal accepted the inclusion of aircraft costs, the District Court in the *AMR* case rejected the inclusion of such costs, viewing them as being fixed and not avoidable. In addition, the Court of Appeals in the *AMR* case held that certain costs that were accepted by the Competition Tribunal as avoidable were arbitrarily allocated and not avoidable or incremental. There does not seem to be a consensus regarding which costs should be considered avoidable in an airline predation case.

Additional disagreement remains over aspects of an airline predation case other than the measurement of costs. One important issue is whether an allegation of predatory conduct by a carrier can be rejected if the carrier's fares simply matched those of a rival carrier. Both the German Federal Cartel Office and the U.S. DOJ held that price matching by a network carrier to the lower fares of an LCC would constitute effective undercutting if the services and product characteristics offered by the network carrier

---

[77] This position was also taken by the ACCC.

[78] Notably, however, the other two tests regarded route level comparisons of long run costs and revenues.

were superior to those of the LCC.[79] While the German Appellate Court upheld the Federal Cartel Office's decision regarding price matching, the District Court in the *AMR* case granted summary judgment in part based on the finding that AMR merely matched the lower fares charged by rival LCCs.

A second important issue is whether recoupment of predatory losses can include recoupment through the creation of a reputation for predation. This type of recoupment was proposed by the German Federal Cartel Office and the DOJ, although the Federal Cartel Office presented no evidence to substantiate the claim. The German Appellate Court did not reject this claim, but the AMR District Court held that a predatory reputation cannot be distinguished from a reputation earned from legal aggressive conduct, that allowing such arguments could chill competition, and that the government had not proved its claim.

Based on the four predation cases reviewed in this paper, it is clear that there is no international consensus regarding the elements that need to be proved in an airline predation case and on what constitutes proof of the elements. Part of the problem may be that the *AMR*, *Air Canada*, and *Qantas* cases were not completed, so there was no opportunity to have arguments over all of the relevant elements of a predation case. Another part of the problem may be attributed to the lack of guidance offered in the economics literature on how practically to carry out predation tests using real market data. In part, this lack of guidance comes from the level of abstraction of the economic theories of predation. The literature suggests for example that predation for reputation may be possible but provides little discussion of the circumstances under which it is most likely to occur.[80] What is needed is further research into the empirical issues associated with testing for predation and recoupment. If economists can achieve some consensus on how to resolve the empirical issues, then perhaps we might see a greater degree of consensus in actual predation cases and policy.

REFERENCES

Alderighi, M., A. Cento, P. Nijkamp and P. Rietveld (2004) "The Entry of Low-Cost Airlines," Tinbergen Institute Discussion Paper TI 2004-074/3.
Areeda, P. and D. Turner (1975) "Predatory Pricing and Related Practices under Section 2 of the Sherman Act," *Harvard Law Review,* 88: 697–733.

---

[79] While Phase I of the *Air Canada* case was focused on the avoidable cost test, there was some indication that had the case proceeded to Stage 2, price matching as a defense for operating with revenues below avoidable cost would have been an issue. The Competition Bureau states on page 12 of its draft "Enforcement Guidelines on: The Abuse of Dominance in the Airline Industry", February 2001 (available at http://cb-bc. gc.ca/epic/internet/incb-bc.nsf/en/ct02118e.html) that "The Bureau does not consider that matching the dollar price of a competitor for travel on a specific flight is the same as charging the same real price for the same quality and quantity." In contrast, paragraph 31 of Air Canada's Response to the Commissioner's Notice of Application to the Competition Tribunal argues that "Matching a competitor's price cannot constitute anti-competitive or predatory conduct, nor does it "deprive" a competitor of its ability to compete."

[80] Some authors have identified certain conditions that should be met to argue predation for reputation, but it is unclear whether these conditions are sufficiently strict to be of use in practical settings. See Bolton et al. (2000).

Bamberger, G. and D. Carlton (2006) "An Empirical Assessment of Predation in the Airline Industry," in Advances in Airline Economics, Volume 1: Competition Policy and Antitrust, Darin Lee, Editor. Amsterdam, Elsevier.

Baumol, W.J. (1979) "Quasi-Permanence of Price Reductions: A Policy for Prevention of Predatory Pricing," Yale Law Journal, 89: 1–26.

Baumol, W.J. (1996) "Predation and the Logic of the Average Variable Cost Test," Journal of Law and Economics, 39: 49–72.

Bolton, P., J. Brodley and M. Riordan (2000) "Predatory Pricing: Strategic Theory and Legal Policy," The Georgetown Law Journal, 88: 2239–2330.

Clouatre, M. (1995) "The Legacy of Continental Airlines v. American Airlines: A Re-evaluation of Predatory Pricing Theory in the Airline Industry," Journal of Air Law and Commerce, 60: 869–915.

Dresner, M., J.C. Lin and R. Windle (1996) "The Impact of Low-Cost Carriers on Airport and Route Competition," Journal of Transport Economics and Policy, 30: 309–328.

Eckert, A. and D.S. West (2002) "Predation in the Airline Industry: The Canadian Antitrust Approach," Antitrust Bulletin, 47: 217–242.

Edlin, A. (2002) "Stopping Above-Cost Predatory Pricing," Yale Law Journal, 111: 941–991.

Edlin, A. and J. Farrell (2004) "The American Airlines Case: A Chance to Clarify Predation Policy," in J. Kwoka and L. White (eds.), The Antitrust Revolution: Economics, Competition, and Policy, 4th edition, New York: Oxford University Press, 502–527.

Facey, B.A. and R. Ware (2003) "Predatory Pricing in Canada, the United States and Europe: Crouching Tiger or Hidden Dragon," World Competition, 26: 625–650.

Fones, R. (1997) "Predation in the Airline Industry," Remarks Before the American Bar Association Forum on Air and Space Law, Seattle, Washington (June 12, 1997).

Houston, D.B. and J.L. Pratt (2004) "Canadian Predation Laws and Their Application to the Airline Industry," American Bar Association Section of Antitrust Law, Annual Spring Meeting, Washington, D.C., March 2004.

Hüschelrath, K. (2003) "How to Prey on Predators? – The Lufthansa-Germania Case," WHU Graduate School of Management, Institute for Industrial Organization working paper.

Ito, H. and D. Lee (2004) "Incumbent Responses to Lower Cost Entry: Evidence from the U.S. Airline Industry", working paper.

Joskow, P. and A. Klevorick (1979) "A Framework for Analyzing Predatory Pricing Policy," Yale Law Journal, 89: 213–270.

Kay, K.L. and E.N. Kolers (2003–2004) "Canadian Competition Tribunal Rules on "Avoidable Cost" Test for Predatory Pricing in the Airline Industry: Dramatic Divergence from U.S. Approach," International Antitrust Bulletin, ABA Section of Antitrust Law, 15–18.

Kreps, D. and R. Wilson (1982) "Reputation and Imperfect Information," Journal of Economic Theory, 27: 253–279.

Martin, J. (2002) "Role of ACCC in Promoting Competition in Aviation Industry," Regional Aviation Association of Australia Convention, Maroochydore, 24–25 October 2002.

McFetridge, D. (2004) "The Commissioner of Competition v. Air Canada: Phase I," Canadian Competition Record, 21: 81–98.

Milgrom, P. and J. Roberts (1982) "Predation, Reputation, and Entry Deterrence," Journal of Economic Theory, 27: 280–312.

Morrison, S.A. (2001) "Actual, Adjacent, and Potential Competition: Estimating the Full Effects of Southwest Airlines," Journal of Transport Economics and Policy, 35: 239–256.

Morrison, W.G. (2004) "Dimensions of Predatory Pricing in Air Travel Markets," Journal of Air Transport Management, 10: 87–95.

Musgrove, J. and D. Edmonstone (2004) "Stalled on Take-off: Commissioner of Competition v. Air Canada – A Comment," Canadian Competition Record, 21: 64–80.

Niels, G. and A. Ten Kate (2000) "Predatory Pricing Standards, Is There a Growing International Consensus?" *Antitrust Bulletin*, 45: 787–809.

Ordover, J. and G. Saloner (1989) "Predation, Monopolization, and Antitrust," in R. Schmalensee and R. Willig (eds.), *Handbook of Industrial Organization*, Amsterdam: North Holland, 537–596.

Oster, C.V. and J.S. Strong (2001) "Predatory Practices in the U.S. Airline Industry,"U.S. Department of Transportation working paper.

Transportation Research Board (1999) "Entry and Competition in the U.S. Airline Industry: Issues and Opportunities," National Research Council, Special Report 255, Washington, D.C.

U.S. Department of Transporation (2001) "Enforcement Policy Regarding Unfair Exclusionary Conduct in the Air Transporation Industry: Findings and Conclusions on the Economic, Policy, and Legal Issues," Docket OST-98-3713.

Werden, G. (2003) "The *American Airlines* Decision: Not with a Bang but a Whimper," *Antitrust*, 18: 32–35.

Williamson, O.E. (1977) "Predatory Pricing: A Strategic and Welfare Analysis," *Yale Law Journal*, 87: 284–340.

Advances in Airline Economics, Vol 1
Darin Lee (Editor)
© 2006 Published by Elsevier B.V.

3

The Price Effects of International Airline Alliances*

Jan K. Brueckner[†] and W. Tom Whalen
University of Illinois at Urbana-Champaign
Reprinted with Permission From *Journal of Law & Economics*,
vol. XLIII (October 2000), pp. 503–545.
©2000 by The University of Chicago

ABSTRACT

This paper provides evidence on the effect of international airline alliances on fares. The main finding is that alliance partners charge interline fares that are approximately 25 percent below those charged by nonallied carriers. According to our theoretical model, the main source of this fare reduction is internalization of a negative externality that arises from uncoordinated choice of interline "subfares" in the absence of an alliance. The paper also looks for evidence of an anticompetitive alliance effect in the gateway-to-gateway markets. While the point estimates show that an alliance between two previously competitive carriers would raise fares by about 5 percent, this effect is not statistically significant.

1 INTRODUCTION

Deregulation of U.S. airlines spurred the adoption of a number of major innovations by the industry. In the 1980's, the airlines reorganized their route structures into hub-and-spoke networks, while instituting frequent flier programs and building computerized reservations systems. A new innovation has swept the industry in the 1990's: formation of international airline alliances.

---

*We thank Dan Bernhardt, Dennis Carlton, George Deltas, David Figlio, and a referee for helpful comments and discussion. Any errors or shortcomings in the paper, however, are our responsibility.
[†]Corresponding author. Department of Economics, University of California, Irvine, 3151 Social Science Plaza, Irvine, CA 92697. E-mail: jkbrueck@uci.edu.

The oldest of the major alliances is operated by Northwest and KLM, and it is currently expanding to include Alitalia. The newer Star Alliance was initiated by United and Lufthansa, and its additional partners include SAS, Air Canada, Thai, Varig, Air New Zealand, and Ansett Australia. The oneworld alliance, anchored by American and British Airways, also includes Canadian, Qantas, Cathay Pacific, Finnair, Iberia, and Lan Chile. Delta and Air France recently formed a new alliance, which has just added Aeromexico as the first of a number of new anticipated partners. Observers of the industry envision an ongoing competitive battle for international traffic among these four alliances.

Through international alliances, U.S. carriers are able to extend their networks overseas without operating additional flights. The carriers can thus overcome restrictions on international service codified in various bilateral agreements, which still govern much overseas traffic despite a number of new "open skies" agreements. While circumventing such limitations, alliances also allow U.S. carriers to extend their global reach without investing new resources.

Since U.S. airlines, in conjunction with foreign carriers, could always provide "interline" service to any overseas destination, the need for alliances may not be obvious. Their appeal to the airlines arises from several sources. First, by coordinating flight schedules and ensuring gate proximity at connecting airports, the alliance partners can offer greater convenience to the passenger. Alliance travel thus resembles online (single-airline) service, avoiding many of the inconveniences of a traditional interline trip. This effect, which attracts passengers away from nonallied carriers, is reinforced by unification of the partners' frequent flier programs. In addition, the online nature of alliance travel is often formalized in a codesharing agreement, where the component flights are ticketed as if they occurred entirely on one partner airline.

The second advantage of an alliance lies in the realm of pricing. Since the major alliances enjoy antitrust immunity, the alliance partners can engage in cooperative pricing of interline trips. By contrast, pricing of traditional interline travel is best viewed as the result of noncooperative behavior, as argued in the theory developed below. Because of this difference, the theory predicts that the interline fares charged by alliance partners are lower than those of nonallied carriers. Thus, the theory says that, in addition to offering greater passenger convenience than a traditional interline trip, alliance travel is more attractively priced.

In some cases, alliances may generate anticompetitive effects that tend to offset the above benefits. These effects are illustrated by the controversy surrounding the request for antitrust immunity by American (AA) and British Airways (BA), which would have allowed these oneworld alliance partners to engage in cooperative pricing. The problem is that AA and BA currently compete on a number of nonstop routes between U.S. "gateway" cities, such as New York and Chicago, and the major U.K. gateway at London-Heathrow, controlling the majority of U.S.-U.K. traffic. If AA and BA were granted antitrust immunity, government regulators feared that the carriers would collude in setting prices in these "gateway-to-gateway" markets, with the outcome being higher fares. Concern about the resulting detrimental effects on U.S.-U.K. passengers recently led the Department of Transportation to disapprove the carriers' request for antitrust immunity.

It is important to recognize that these anticipated losses for gateway-to-gateway passengers are separate from the benefits accruing to an alliance's interline passengers, who pass through the gateway airports without stopping. These passengers do not suffer a loss of competition from the alliance, but instead enjoy the benefits of cooperation in pricing and scheduling, as noted above. The existence of these two separate effects suggests that alliances may involve a welfare trade-off between two distinct groups of passengers.

The purpose of the present paper is to investigate these issues by presenting empirical evidence on the price effects of international airline alliances. Using fare data from the U.S. Department of Transporation, we document the impact of alliances on interline fares, testing the above hypothesis of a negative effect. In addition, we explore the fare impact of overlapping service by alliance partners in gateway-to-gateway markets, looking for evidence of the fare escalation that has preoccupied regulators. These exercises are carried out in Sections 3 and 4 of the paper. Using the estimates, we present a simulation analysis of the welfare effects of cooperative pricing by AA and BA in subsection 4.5.

To motivate the empirical work, Section 2 presents a theoretical model, built on the previous work by Jan Brueckner and by Brueckner and Pablo Spiller,[1] that illustrates the favorable effect of alliances on interline fares. The model focuses on the impact of cooperative pricing, abstracting from any convenience gains due to alliances, which may affect demand. The key assumption of the model, which follows Brueckner, is that nonallied carriers set interline fares through noncooperative choice of "subfares." The subfare gives the amount earned by a carrier for its portion of an interline trip, with the sum of the subfares giving the interline fare. Such unrestricted fare-setting behavior is consistent with the discussion of Doganis,[2] who indicates that previous formula-based methods of fare determination are now little used. The key implication of the model is that the carriers' non-cooperative subfare choices generate negative externalities. Alliances internalize these externalities through a revenue-sharing arrangement, and the result is a lower fare.

Another key feature of the model is the operation of hub-and-spoke networks by the carriers, with the goal of exploiting economies of traffic density. These economies, whose existence is documented by Douglas Caves, Laurits Christensen and Michael Tretheway and by Brueckner and Spiller,[3] arise because high traffic densities allow carriers to operate larger, more efficient aircraft and to disperse fixed costs over more passengers. In the presence of economies of density, international traffic gains from cooperative pricing of interline trips lead to a lower marginal cost of carrying an additional passenger within the networks of the alliance partners. This cost reduction allows the partners to charge lower fares for purely domestic travel.

In addition to the analysis of Brueckner, the only previous theoretical work on alliances is presented by Jong-Hun Park.[4] Empirical work on alliances is also sparse. Tae Oum, Jong-Hun Park and Anming Zhang present an empirical study of trans-Pacific routes that shows how a codesharing agreement between two small carriers affects the market

[1] Jan K. Brueckner, The Economics of International Codesharing: An Analysis of Airline Alliances (unpublished paper, University of Illinois at Urbana-Champaign 1997); Jan K. Brueckner & Pablo T. Spiller, Competition and Mergers in Airline Networks, 9 Int'l. J. Indus. Org. 323–342 (1991). For another recent theoretical paper on hub-and-spoke networks, see Kenneth Hendricks, Michele Piccione & Guo-Fu Tan, The Economics of Hubs: The Case of Monopoly, 62 Rev. Econ. Studies 83–99 (1995).
[2] Rigas Doganis, Flying Off Course (1985).
[3] Douglas W. Caves, Laurits R. Christensen & Michael W. Tretheway, Economies of Density versus Economies of Scale: Why Trunk and Local Service Costs Differ, 15 RAND J. Econ. 471–489 (1984); Jan K. Brueckner & Pablo T. Spiller, Economies of Traffic Density in the Deregulated Airline Industry, 37 J. Law Econ. 379–415 (1994).
[4] Jong-Hun Park, The Effect of Airline Alliances on Markets and Economic Welfare, 33 Transp. Research-E 181–195 (1997).

leader.[5] Jong-Hun Park and Anming Zhang investigate whether alliances boost traffic
on the partner's gateway-to-gateway routes,[6] while Park and Zhang analyze the fare
impacts of alliances on North Atlantic routes, using published fare data rather than actual
transaction data of the type used below.[7] Finally, Walleed Youssef and Mark Hansen
present a case study of the discontinued SAS/Swissair alliance, showing its effects on
service coordination and market concentration.[8] This small recent literature on alliances
extends a huge previous literature on the airline industry, which is surveyed by Steven
Morrison and Clifford Winston.[9]

2   A MODEL OF AIRLINE ALLIANCES

2.1   An Earlier Model

Before developing the model, it is helpful to discuss the previous analysis of international
alliances presented by Brueckner. In his model, two airlines operate the route structure
shown in Figure 1. Airline 1 operates the routes shown as dotted lines, using city H as its
hub, while airline 2 operates the routes represented by solid lines, using city K as its hub.
Both airlines serve the (transatlantic) city-pair market HK, which connects the hub (or
gateway) cities. In addition to serving this gateway-to-gateway market, airline 1 serves
three domestic city-pair markets, AH, BH, and AB, with service in the latter provided
by connecting flights through the hub H (airline 2 provides parallel domestic service).
Together, airlines 1 and 2 also provide interline service in the international markets AD,

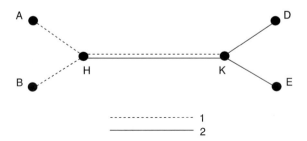

Figure 1   Network Structure from Earlier Model.

[5] Tae H. Oum, Jong-Hun Park & Anming Zhang, The Effects of Airline Codesharing Agreements on Firm
Conduct and International Air Fares, 30 J. Transp. Econ. and Policy 187–202 (1996).
[6] Jong-Hun Park & Anming Zhang, Airline Alliances and Partner Firms' Output, 34 Transp. Research-E
245–255 (1998).
[7] Jong-Hun Park & Anming Zhang, An Empirical Analysis of Global Airline Alliances: Cases in the North
Atlantic Markets, Rev. Indus. Org. forthcoming (1999).
[8] Walleed Youssef & Mark Hansen, Consequences of Strategic Alliances between International Airlines: The
Case of Swissair and SAS, 28 Transp. Research-A 415–431 (1994).
[9] Steven A. Morrison & Clifford Winston, The Evolution of the Airline Industry (1995). See U.S. General
Accounting Office, Airline Alliances Produce Benefits, But Effect on Competition Is Uncertain (1995) and
Gellman Research Associates, A Study of International Codesharing (1994) for excellent discussions of the
mechanics of alliances and codesharing.

AE, BD, and BE, where passengers travel across the networks of both airlines in making their trip. These city-pair markets are denoted "behind-the-gateway" markets, reflecting the nonhub status of their endpoints.[10]

In the absence of an alliance, airlines 1 and 2 compete in the gateway-to-gateway market, HK. They also determine the interline fare in the behind-the-gateway markets, again in noncooperative fashion. The carriers noncooperatively choose "subfares" for their portion of each interline trip, with the sum of the subfares determining the overall fare in the market. When the carriers operate instead as alliance partners, they collude rather than compete in the gateway-to-gateway market, which tends to raise the fare in that market. Collusion also occurs in behind-the-gateway markets, but instead of being anticompetitive, this behavior generates benefits. Since they split the revenue from such markets, the carriers cooperatively choose an overall fare instead of setting individual subfares. This cooperation internalizes the negative externalities from subfare choices, and the result is downward pressure on interline fares. Thus, the expectation is that an alliance leads to higher fares in the gateway-to-gateway market and lower interline fares.[11]

2.2 Setup of the Current Model

Although the above model is suggestive, it is not ideal for motivating an empirical study of airline alliances. The problem is that an international passenger making an interline trip can usually choose between several carrier pairs, either allied or nonallied. The model, however, assumes the absence of interline competition, with service provided only by a single carrier pair. To provide analysis that is empirically more relevant, the present model has four airlines rather than two. Two competing carriers then operate in each set of domestic markets, and the international markets are served by competing carrier pairs, either allied or nonallied.

To prevent this added complexity from making the analysis unmanageable, the model's route structure, shown in Figure 2, is simplified by assuming that all carriers operate

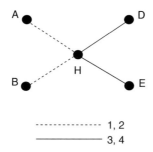

Figure 2 Current Network Structure.

---

out of the same hub, H. This setup, which eliminates the gateway-to-gateway market, is literally impossible in an international context, but the resulting simplification allows empirical predictions regarding interline fares to be derived in a straightforward fashion. As can be seen in Figure 2, carriers 1 and 2 compete in the domestic city-pair markets AH, BH and AB, with carriers 3 and 4 competing in their domestic markets. The international markets AD, AE, BD, and BE again require an interline trip, and for simplicity, we assume that carriers 1 and 3 always form an interline pair, with 2 and 4 forming the other interline pair. The airlines within each of these competing pairs can operate as alliance partners or as nonallied carriers.[12]

In contrast to the analysis of Brueckner and many other models in the literature, we assume that passengers exhibit brand loyalty to particular carriers, implying that airlines sell differentiated products. Because of brand loyalty, a carrier (or carrier pair) can raise its fare above that charged by its competitor without losing all of its traffic. Formally, we assume that when carriers i and k both serve a city-pair market, charging fares of p^i and p^k, carrier i's traffic is given by $q^i = D(p^i, p^k)$, with k's traffic given by $q^k = D(p^k, p^i)$. $D(\cdot)$ is the symmetric demand function, which is decreasing in its first argument and increasing in the second. For example, $q^1_{AH} = D(p^1_{AH}, p^2_{AH})$ gives carrier 1's traffic in market AH when its fare is p^1_{AH} and carrier 2's fare is p^2_{AH}, with $p^1_{AH}D(p^1_{AH}, p^2_{AH})$ giving revenue. Note that the variable q^1_{AH} measures traffic in both directions in market AH, being equal to the number of passengers travelling from A to H and back, *plus* the number of passengers travelling from H to A and back, all on carrier 1. Finally, since we assume symmetry across city-pair markets in the demand for travel, the function $D(\cdot)$ applies to all domestic and international markets.

In the absence of alliances, the interline fares are generated via the noncooperative choice of subfares, as in Brueckner. In city-pair market AD, for example; airline 1's subfare is denoted s^1_{AD}, while the subfare of its interline partner, carrier 3, is denoted s^3_{AD}. The fare in the market is then $s^1_{AD} + s^3_{AD}$, and carrier 1's AD traffic is $q^{13}_{AD} = D(s^1_{AD} + s^3_{AD}, s^2_{AD} + s^4_{AD})$, where the notation q^{13}_{AD} indicates that this also represents carrier 3's traffic. Note that this traffic level depends on the subfares charged by the competing airline pair, which consists of carriers 2 and 4. Carrier 1's revenue in the market is $s^1_{AD}D(s^1_{AD} + s^3_{AD}, s^2_{AD} + s^4_{AD})$, while carrier 3's revenue equals D multiplied by s^3_{AD} instead of s^1_{AD}.

To write carrier 1's total revenue, the symmetry of city pairs can be exploited. Given symmetry, carrier 1's fares and traffic levels will be the same in markets AH and BH, allowing these variables to be written as p^1_{XH} and q^1_{XH}, where X refers to either A or B. Similarly, airline 1's subfares and traffic levels will be same in each of the international markets AD, AE, BD, BE, allowing these variables to be written as s^1_{XX} and q^{13}_{XX}, with the latter traffic level applying also to carrier 3 (note that the first X subscript denotes A or B, while the second denotes D or E). Analogous notation applies to the other carriers. With these conventions, airline 1's revenue is $2p^1_{XH}q^1_{XH} + p^1_{AB}q^1_{AB} + 4s^1_{XX}q^{13}_{XX}$, or

$$2p^1_{XH}D(p^1_{XH}, p^2_{XH}) + p^1_{AB}D(p^1_{AB}, p^2_{AB}) + 4s^1_{XX}D(s^1_{XX} + s^3_{XX}, s^2_{XX} + s^4_{XX}), \qquad (1)$$

where the multiplicative factors 2 and 4 serve to sum revenues across identical markets.

---

[12] Although interline service is feasible in market AB, we assume that consumers use a single carrier, making an online trip.

Now consider the case where each carrier pair (1 and 3, 2 and 4) operates as an alliance. The alliance partners set a total fare in each international market and split the market revenue. Fares are symmetric across international markets, and are denoted p_{XX}^{13} and p_{XX}^{24} for the two alliances. Carrier 1's revenue is now given by $2p_{XH}^1 q_{XH}^1 + p_{AB}^1 q_{AB}^1 + 2p_{XX}^{13} q_{XX}^{13}$, or

$$2p_{XH}^1 D(p_{XH}^1, p_{XH}^2) + p_{AB}^1 D(p_{AB}^1, p_{AB}^2) + 2p_{XX}^{13} D(p_{XX}^{13}, p_{XX}^{24}). \tag{2}$$

The last term in (2) comes from dividing the total international revenue earned by the alliance of carriers 1 and 3, equal to $4p_{XX}^{13} q_{XX}^{13}$, between the two partners.

Carrier 1's costs are equal to the cost of operating the two spokes of its network. The cost of operating a single spoke is $c(Q)$, where Q is the traffic density (i.e., total traffic) on the spoke. With economies of density, this cost function satisfies $c' > 0$ and $c'' < 0$, implying that cost per passenger is decreasing in traffic density. Since density is the same on both of carrier 1's spokes, being given by $Q = q_{XH}^1 + q_{AB}^1 + 2q_{XX}^{13}$, the cost of operating its network equals

$$2c(q_{XH}^1 + q_{AB}^1 + 2q_{XX}^{13}). \tag{3}$$

2.3   Symmetric Alliance and Nonalliance Equilibria

Airline 1's goal is to maximize profit, which equals the difference between revenue, given by (1) or (2), and the cost expression (3). In the nonalliance case, where revenue is given by (1), airline 1 makes decisions independently of all the other carriers. It chooses values for p_{XH}^1, p_{AB}^1, and s_{XX}^1 in Cournot fashion, taking the values of the other airlines' decision variables as given. When carrier 1 is allied with carrier 3, they confer in the choice of the interline fare p_{XX}^{13}. Since the carriers solve symmetric choice problems, they agree on the level of the fare, and as a result, only carrier 1's problem need be considered. The goal of the discussion in this section is to analyze symmetric equilibria, where carriers 2 and 4 mimic carriers 1 and 3, either forming an alliance or not. The asymmetric case, where one pair of carriers are allied and the other nonallied, is considered below.

As usual, the first-order conditions for the alliance and nonalliance cases require that marginal revenue and marginal cost, both appropriate defined, be equated in each market. In developing these conditions, it is useful to focus on the international markets, where the behavioral difference lies. To generate the first-order conditions, (1) minus (3) is differentiated with respect to s_{XX}^1, and (2) minus (3) is differentiated with respect to p_{XX}^{13}. The first expression is simplified using the fact that the equilibrium fare in the nonalliance case equals $p_{XX}^{13} = 2s_{XX}^1$. Then, setting both derivatives equal to zero and dividing by the negative term $\partial q_{XX}^{13}/\partial p_{XX}^{13}$, the first-order conditions for the nonalliance and alliance cases are respectively

$$2q_{XX}^{13} \left(\frac{\partial q_{XX}^{13}}{\partial p_{XX}^{13}} \right)^{-1} + p_{XX}^{13} - 2c' = 0 \quad \text{(nonalliance)} \tag{4}$$

and

$$q_{XX}^{13} \left(\frac{\partial q_{XX}^{13}}{\partial p_{XX}^{13}} \right)^{-1} + p_{XX}^{13} - 2c' = 0. \quad \text{(alliance)} \tag{5}$$

To interpret these equations, note first that $2c'$ gives the marginal cost of serving a passenger in an international market, which equals the sum of marginal costs on the two network spokes used for the trip. Then observe that, while the first two terms in the alliance condition (5) correspond to a standard expression giving marginal revenue as a function of quantity, the corresponding portion of (4) is smaller because the first term, which is negative, is multiplied by two. Because marginal revenue is thus larger in the alliance case, we would expect the first-order condition to be satisfied at a larger value of q_{XX}^{13}, and thus a smaller value of p_{XX}^{13}, than in the nonalliance case. In other words, we would expect airlines 1 and 3 to charge a lower fare as alliance partners than as nonallied carriers, with the same conclusion applying to carriers 2 and 4.

To see the intuitive reason for this outcome, observe that in the absence of an alliance, an increase in carrier 1's subfare depresses carrier 3's profit by reducing traffic in the given market. While carrier 1 has no incentive to take this negative externality into account, revenue sharing under an alliance causes the externality to be internalized, moderating carrier 1's pursuit of a higher fare.

The negative effect of alliances on interline fares can be established analytically in the symmetric case when economies of traffic density are absent (i.e., when c' is a constant). Otherwise, however, the effect is analytically ambiguous. The reason is that, with economies of density, pricing is interdependent across markets, which introduces additional complexity. To generate unambiguous results when economies of density are present, it is helpful to explore a particular example based specific functional forms for cost and demand. Following Brueckner and Spiller,[13] the first assumption imposes linearity on the marginal cost function, which is given by $c'(Q) = 1 - \theta Q$, where $\theta > 0$ (the cost function itself is then quadratic). The second assumption is that brand loyalty to carriers (or carrier pairs) takes a particular form. In a representative market where carriers i and k compete, we assume that a given passenger will fly on carrier i if the fares satisfy $p^i < p^k + a$, or $a > p^i - p^k$, where a gives the individual's dollar-denominated preference for carrier i. If a is uniformly distributed over the interval $[-\alpha/2, \alpha/2]$, then airline 1's traffic is equal to

$$q^i = \int_{p^i - p^k}^{\alpha/2} \frac{1}{\alpha} da = \frac{1}{2} - \frac{p^i - p^k}{\alpha}. \tag{6}$$

Carrier k's traffic is then $q^k = \frac{1}{2} + (p^i - p^k)/\alpha$. A restrictive feature of this formulation is that total demand is insensitive to the level of fares, always being equal to one, with fare differences serving only to divide this fixed total between carriers.

The system of first-order conditions for the symmetric nonalliance and alliance cases consist of (4) or (5) along with conditions for the other markets (these are the same in both cases). As shown in the appendix, the solutions to these conditions are easily derived under the above functional forms. The equilibrium fares in the domestic markets XH and AB, which are the same in the alliance and nonalliance cases, are given by

$$\tilde{p}_{XH} = \frac{\alpha}{2} + 1 - 2\theta \tag{7}$$

---

[13] Brueckner and Spiller, *supra* note 1.

and

$$\tilde{p}_{AB} = \frac{\alpha}{2} + 2 - 4\theta. \tag{8}$$

(These solutions also give the fares charged by carriers 3 and 4 in the the XK and DE markets). Observe that the AB fare is higher than the XH fare, reflecting the higher marginal cost of a connecting trip.[14] Interline fares in the alliance and nonalliance cases are given by

$$\tilde{p}_{XX}^{ally} = \frac{\alpha}{2} + 2 - 4\theta, \quad \tilde{p}_{XX}^{non-ally} = \alpha + 2 - 4\theta. \tag{9}$$

As expected, (9) shows that the interline fare is lower in the alliance case. Also, observe that the alliance fare is the same as the AB fare in (8), reflecting the equivalence of the pricing problems in the two types of markets in the alliance case.[15]

2.4 The Asymmetric Equilibrium

The above analysis focuses on symmetric equilibria, where alliances are totally absent or where each carrier pair constitutes an alliance. However, the case that is perhaps most relevant to the empirical work is asymmetric. In this case, carriers 1 and 3 form an alliance, while carriers 2 and 4 provide interline service without forming an alliance. The interline fare charged by 1 and 3 is thus set jointly, while fare charged by 2 and 4 is the result of noncooperative choice of subfares. As explained in the appendix, the equilibrium in this asymmetric case can be determined using the above functional forms. Letting the asymmetric solutions be denoted by hats, following conclusions emerge:

$$\widehat{p}_{XH}^{1} < \tilde{p}_{XH} < \widehat{p}_{XH}^{2} \tag{10}$$

$$\widehat{p}_{AB}^{1} < \tilde{p}_{AB} < \widehat{p}_{AB}^{2} \tag{11}$$

$$\widehat{p}_{XX}^{13} < \widehat{p}_{XX}^{24} < \tilde{p}_{XX}^{ally} < \tilde{p}_{XX}^{non-ally} \tag{12}$$

From (10) and (11), carrier 1 (the alliance partner) charges lower domestic fares than does carrier 2, the nonallied airline. Moreover, carrier 1's domestic fares lie below those charged in the symmetric cases considered above, while carrier 2's lie above the symmetric fares. With suitable relabeling, (10) and (11) apply to the domestic fares charged by carriers 3 and 4. The major implication of the asymmetric solution, however, is that the alliance partners charge *a lower interline fare* than the nonallied carriers. In contrast to the domestic fares, however, both interline fares are cheaper than those charged in the symmetric cases.[16]

---

[14] Note that the AB fare is less than twice the XH fare. This rules out fare arbitrage, where an AB passenger could reduce his outlay by purchasing separate AH and BH tickets.

[15] Observe that the interline fare in the alliance case is exactly twice the XH domestic fare. This means that an international passenger is indifferent between purchasing an international ticket and two domestic tickets to make his trip.

[16] It can be shown that, as discussed in previous footnotes, there are no possibilities for fare arbitrage in the asymmetric case.

The impact of economies of traffic density helps to explain the pattern of fares in the asymmetric case. As before, internalization of the subfare externality tends to reduce the alliance's interline fare, pushing it below that charged by the nonallied carriers. The resulting gain in international traffic then leads, via economies of density, to lower marginal costs, which puts further downward pressure on the alliance fare. Conversely, the traffic loss for nonallied carriers raises marginal cost, leading to upward pressure on the nonallied fare. These marginal-cost changes in turn affect domestic pricing, allowing the alliance partners to cut fares while forcing nonallied carriers to raise their domestic fares. The resulting gains and losses in domestic traffic further reinforce the marginal-cost advantage of the alliance partners. Confirming the role of economies of density, it may be shown the nonallied/allied fare difference is an increasing function of θ in each market. Thus, stronger economies of density lead to a greater fare advantage for the alliance partners.

3 THE EFFECT OF ALLIANCES ON INTERLINE FARES

3.1 Overview

The first hypothesis we test, which follows directly from the theoretical results above, is that alliance partners charge lower interline fares than nonallied carriers. This hypothesis is tested by estimating the following reduced-form regression:

fare = F(distance; demand; competition; airline-specific effects; alliance dummy). (13)

Under the maintained hypothesis, the alliance dummy variable has a negative coefficient.

To understand this regression, an explanation of the nature of the data is helpful. The data are drawn from the U.S. Department of Transportation's Origin and Destination Survey, Databank 1A (DB1A), for the third quarter of 1997. The DB1A is based on a 10 percent quarterly sample of all airline tickets where one or more route segments is flown on a U.S. carrier. Each record in the DB1A shows the itinerary (route and carriers used), the fare, the distance travelled, and number of passengers observed on the given itinerary at the given fare. The data may contain multiple records for a given itinerary, each showing a different observed fare. These records can be collapsed into a single observation by computing a passenger-weighted average of the multiple fares, which is then assigned to the given itinerary.

Each carrier/route itinerary then generates a single record, and these records constitute the observations for the fare regression in (13). The observation indicates the fare, distance of the trip, and the carriers used, as required in (13). Variables measuring the level of demand and the extent of competition in the itinerary's city-pair market are computed, as discussed below. Then, supplementary information, also discussed below, is used to construct an alliance dummy variable, which assumes the value one if the carriers on the itinerary are allied. While the interline fare depends on the identities of the individual carriers used for trip, this variable captures an additional impact, analogous to an interaction effect, which emerges if the carriers are allied. Assessing the direction of this impact is the goal of the empirical work.

It should be noted that the theoretical model implies that the interline fare should be affected by traffic densities on the various route segments used for the trip, with higher densities leading to a lower fare. Although Brueckner and Spiller[17] included densities in their empirical model of domestic fare determination, this approach is unworkable in an international context. The reason is that traffic-density data for foreign carriers are not readily available.

3.2 Construction of Data Sets

The raw data set contains 2.7 million observations, and it is restricted in various ways to make the empirical work tractable. First, itineraries involving domestic U.S. travel are eliminated, as are itineraries with surface segments. Second, itineraries with fares below $100 are dropped, since these may represent trips purchased with frequent flier miles or made by airline employees at significantly reduced fares. Third, the itinerary must represent round-trip travel, with the same starting and ending airports, and it can have only one trip break. Finally, itineraries involving first class travel are removed. The data set resulting from these conditions is denoted the "restricted" data set.[18]

In order to study the effects of alliances on interline fares, further limitations are imposed on the restricted data set. First, because two-segment itineraries, which are non-stop in both directions, do not involve standard interline trips, such itineraries are eliminated.[19] In addition, to reduce the complexity of the trips considered, itineraries using more than 2 carriers are dropped. For the same reason, highly unusual and circuitous trips are eliminated by restricting attention to itineraries with 3 or fewer segments in each direction (for a maximum of 6 segments over the whole trip). 82 percent of the records in the restricted data set met these conditions. The final step is to compute passenger-weighted fares for each itinerary, as discussed above. The data set resulting from these additional restrictions is denoted the "interline" data set, and it contains 46,620 observations, representing 16,765 distinct city-pair markets.

Because the DB1A is restricted to tickets with at least one segment flown on an American carrier, the interline data set provides an incomplete picture of foreign carrier service. Foreign carriers offering online service in a market, or foreign carrier pairs offering interline service, are unobserved. This can understate the extent of competition in a market, whose measurement is discussed in detail below.

To see whether this problem affects our results, we explore the effect of an additional restriction on the interline data set. This restriction relies on the following observation: any itinerary whose origin or destination is a U.S. airport that has no foreign carrier enplanements must contain at least one route segment flown on a U.S. carrier, making it observable in the data. Endpoints that fit this criterion are simply U.S. behind-the-gateway cities. Thus, if we focus on a data set restricted to itineraries which have a U.S. behind-the-gateway city as origin or destination, the problem of unobserved foreign competition is mitigated. The "behind-the-gateway" (or BTG) data set is constructed

---

[17] Brueckner and Spiller, *supra* note 3.

[18] In most cases, small domestic feeder airlines share the code of the major carrier with whom they operate (for example, American Eagle is listed as American Airlines). Occasionally, however, the feeder carriers are listed under their own airline code. In such cases, the feeder code is changed to the parent carrier's code, although leaving the original code has no significant effect on the results.

[19] Use of different carriers on the inbound and outbound segments would represent interline travel, but this type of itinerary is not our focus.

using information from the Official Airline Guide (OAG), which allows identification of U.S. airports without foreign carrier service.[20] The BTG data set contains 11,694 observations, representing 6,917 city-pair markets.

3.3   Constructing the Alliance Dummy and Demand Variables

To determine which carriers operate alliances, we use the list of codesharing agreements in existence during the sample period, as compiled by the U.S. Department of Transportation, U.S. Air Carrier Licensing Division. The list is shown in Table 1. Since codesharing agreements in some cases may fall short of a true alliance, equating the two may involve an element of inaccuracy. However, to supplement the alliance variable based on codesharing, we also construct an additional variable that indicates whether a carrier pair enjoys antitrust immunity. This variable is discussed further below.

Table 1   Passenger-Weighted Alliance Frequency

Partners	Passengers in Sample	Percent
American-British Midland	323	1.0
American-China Air	217	0.7
American-Canadian Air	4,971	14.9
American-Gulf Air	212	0.6
American-Aero California	43	0.1
American-Kuwait Air	57	0.2
American-LOT (Polish Air)	188	0.6
American-Qantas Air	521	1.6
American-South African Air	423	1.3
American-Singapore Air	195	0.6
American-TACA International	140	0.4
Continental-Air Canada	753	2.3
Continental-Alitalia	953	2.9
Continental-China Air	28	0.1
Continental-Business Air	5	0.0
Continental-Czech Air	176	0.5
Delta-Aeromexico	1,141	3.4
Delta-Finnair	222	0.7
Delta-Aer Lingus	418	1.3
Delta-Korean Air	274	0.8
Delta-Malev (Hungarian Air)	406	1.2
Delta-Austrian Air	412	1.2
Delta-Sabena	859	2.6
Delta-Swiss Air	1,297	3.9
Delta-Aeroflot (Russian Air)	7	0.0
Delta-TAP Air Portugal	44	0.1
Delta-Virgin Atlantic Air	178	0.5

---

[20] An alternative approach is to use a slightly-outdated Federal Aviation Administration (FAA) list of airports that had foreign carrier enplanements (the year is 1996). The regression results under the two approaches are very similar.

Table 1 Passenger-Weighted Alliance Frequency—Cont'd.

Partners	Passengers in Sample	Percent
America West-British Airways	9	0.0
Carnival Air-SEATA	24	0.1
Northwest-Eurowings Luftverkehrs	14	0.0
Northwest-KLM	7,675	23.0
Northwest-Asiana Air	161	0.5
Pan American World-Aeroperu	3	0.0
Pan American World-Royal Jordanian	2	0.0
Trans World-Royal Jordanian	92	0.3
United-Air Canada	3,123	9.4
United-Air India	32	0.1
United-Aeromexico	87	0.3
United-Ansett Australia	634	1.9
United-British Midland	836	2.5
United-Emirates Air	128	0.4
United-Cayman Air	22	0.1
United-Lufthansa	4,176	12.5
United-ALM (Antillean Air)	49	0.1
United-Mexicana	410	1.2
United-Air New Zealand	271	0.8
United-Qantas Air	141	0.4
United-Varig	225	0.7
United-SAS	502	1.5
United-Thai Air	298	0.9

Under the codesharing definition, 50 alliance pairs are observed in the restricted data set, although four pairs dominate. Northwest-KLM carried 23.0 percent of the sampled alliance passengers, American-Canadian Airlines 14.9 percent, United-Lufthansa 12.5 percent and United-Air Canada 9.4 percent. Each of these alliance pairs enjoyed antitrust immunity.

The principal variable used to capture demand effects in a city-pair market is city population. U.S. city populations come from Census data, while foreign city populations are drawn from several sources.[21] Whenever possible, city populations represent the entire metropolitan area. This information yields populations for the itinerary's origin and destination cities, which are denoted POP-ORI and POP-DES, respectively. Following Brueckner and Spiller,[22] we assume the demand for air travel in a city-pair market depends on the market's "population potential," as measured by the geometric mean (in millions) of POP-ORI and POP-DES. This variable is denoted POP-POT.

---

[21] U.S. city populations are estimates as of July 1997. Since these estimates are not available for towns with populations under 10,000, 1990 census data are used instead and adjusted for the state's population growth from 1990–1996. The sources for foreign city populations are the *Rand McNally World Atlas, Cities of the World* encyclopedias, and the U.S. State Department Web Site.

[22] Brueckner and Spiller, *supra* note 3.

Another key determinant of (directional) travel demand in a city-pair market is the level of income at the origin city. However, since a measure of per capita income is not easily available for non-U.S. cities, such a variable can only be used in regressions that restrict attention to U.S. origins. While income performed well in such regressions, these results are not reported below, with attention focusing instead on regressions that mix both U.S. and non-U.S. origins, where use of the income variable is ruled out. For this reason, POP-POT represents the only demand variable used in the present regressions.

3.4   Measuring Competition

The most significant source of competition in a city-pair market is online service, which occurs when an itinerary is flown on a single carrier. In addition, competition can also come from interline flights, operated either by alliances or nonallied carriers. For reasons that are explained below, nonallied interline competition is measured separately from online and alliance competition. Online and alliance competition are measured in one variable, but we construct that variable in several different ways to account for various potential problems.

To construct competition measures, the first step is to determine which airlines offer service in a market, either online or interline. One possibility would be to consult the schedules provided by the Official Airline Guide. However, because the OAG's coverage of connecting flights is incomplete, and because the number of city-pairs in the data is huge, use of this source is ruled out. Instead, our approach is to measure competition using the itineraries observed in the restricted data set.

By decomposing the information in each observed itinerary, we can generate the city-pair combinations served by each airline. For example, suppose the outbound portion of an itinerary shows travel from Indianapolis (IND) to Detroit (DTW) and then to Amsterdam (AMS), all on Northwest, with a final segment to Paris (CDG) flown on KLM. We could then infer that Northwest provides online service in the IND-AMS and DTW-AMS city-pair markets, while KLM provides online service in the AMS-CDG market. The reasoning is that any subset of an itinerary flown on a single carrier must also represent a legitimate trip on that carrier.

The same methodology is applied to capture interline service (both alliance and nonalliance). In this case, subset itineraries flown on two carriers are counted as interline service. In the above example, Northwest and KLM are counted as providing interline service in the IND-CDG and DTW-CDG markets. By repeating this exercise for each itinerary in the restricted data set, we build a picture of available online and interline service in all city-pair markets.[23]

In measuring the extent of competition from this information, a simple count of the different types of online and interline service (both alliance and nonalliance) available in a market may lead to various kinds of double counting. To see the problem, consider the Houston-Toronto market, and suppose that two carriers, United and Air Canada, offer online service in the market. One might be tempted to call this market a duopoly, but because United and Air Canada are alliance partners, there is no reason to believe that

---

[23] Because the DB1A represents a 10 percent sample, existing service may be overlooked in some markets under this approach. However, no better alternate method exists.

they compete in a market where they both offer service. As a result, this market would be better described as a monopoly. The example becomes more complex if we suppose Continental also offers online service. Continental and Air Canada are also alliance partners but United and Continental are not. Is it more accurate to describe this market as a monopoly or a duopoly?

To handle this problem, we construct three measures of online and alliance competition for a city-pair market. The first, which ignores the problem above, is simply a count of the number of airlines providing online service plus the number of alliances offering interline service. An alliance is not counted if one of its partners also offers online service. We call the resulting variable TOTFIRM.

The other two methods are designed to address the problem illustrated above and represent lower and upper bounds on the number of online and alliance competitors. The lower bound assumes that all markets like the one above behave as monopolies. Generally, this measure counts the number of airlines offering online service in the market but assumes that when two nonallied airlines in a market are both allied with a third carrier also in the market, then all three carriers behave as one competitor. From the example above, United and Continental are not allied but are connected through their alliances with Air Canada. Thus, all three carriers are assumed to behave as one firm. This method generates a "lower bound" because it measures the fewest number of competitors one could reasonably believe operates in the market. The resulting competition measure is denoted COM_LOW.

The upper bound on competition also counts the number of airlines offering online service but assumes that each alliance pair (again where both airlines offer online service) behaves as one firm in the market.[24] In the example above, this method considers the market a duopoly, served by the United-Air Canada alliance and the Continental-Air Canada alliance. This measure is called the "upper bound" because it assumes full competition between carriers that are not allied themselves. We call this variable COM_HIGH.

As with the TOTFIRM variable, we add interline alliance competitors, where neither airline offers online service, to both COM_LOW and COM_HIGH. The following relationship between the three measures always holds: TOTFIRM $\geq$ HIGH_COM $\geq$ LOW_COM. The true amount of competition in each market is likely to lie within these bounds.

As mentioned earlier, a separate variable is created to measure the effect of nonallied interline competition. To compute this variable, we begin by eliminating all interline itineraries in a city-pair market where a component carrier operates either online or alliance service. Then, each remaining carrier is counted as $\frac{1}{2}$ of a competitor. The resulting variable is called COM_INT.

3.5 Regional and Directional Effects

To allow for fare differences across regions, the regression in (13) is augmented to include dummy variables indicating the region of the world containing the non-U.S.

---

[24] This calculation is complicated by the presence of "group alliances," which occur when airlines in a group are allied with every other member of the group. For example, Delta, Sabena and Swissair form a group alliance because each is allied with the other two. When all the airlines in a group alliance offer online service in the same market, they are counted as one firm.

endpoint of the itinerary (e.g., South America, Africa). Europe is the default region. In addition, the regression includes another dummy variable indicating the direction of travel for the itinerary. The dummy indicates observations where the destination for the itinerary's round-trip is the U.S. endpoint. Thus, the default corresponds to itineraries that originate in the U.S. While these variables shift the intercept of the regression, they are also interacted with the alliance dummy in some specifications to allow the alliance fare effect to differ by region and by direction of travel.

3.6   Summary Statistics

Table 2 defines the variables used in the analysis, and Tables 3–4 present summary statistics for the interline and BTG data sets. Each table shows statistics for the entire sample, as well as separate statistics for the alliance and non-alliance categories.

AVGFARE is the average passenger-weighted fare for the itinerary. In the regressions, we use its log transformation, LNFARE. ALLY is a dummy variable indicating whether the two carriers for the itinerary are alliance partners, appearing on the list in Table 1. The summary statistics from both data sets show that between 39 and 43 percent of the interline itineraries are flown on allied carriers. Also, alliance fares are lower on average than their non-alliance counterparts. In the interline data set, alliance fares are 19 percent lower than nonalliance fares, and in the BTG markets, the differential is 15 percent.

TOT_DIST is the total distance flown on the itinerary. Two itineraries with the same origin and destination will have different distances if one involves a more circuitous

Table 2   Variable List

Variable	Description
ally	A dummy indicating whether the two firms have an alliance.
avgfare	The average passenger-weighted fare for the itinerary.
com_high	The upper bound on the number of online/alliance competitors in the market.
com_low	The lower bound on the number of online/alliance competitors in the market.
com_int	The number of non-allied interline competitors in a market.
coup	The number of coupon segments in the itinerary.
immunity	A dummy indicating whether two allied firms have antitrust immunity.
inc	The origin city's per capita income (U.S. cities only).
indist	The log transformation of distance.
infare	The log transformation of avgfare.
loss_hi	The number of competitors lost to alliances using the upper bound on competitors.
loss_lo	The number of competitors lost to alliances using the lower bound on competitors.
pop_ori	The origin city's population.
pop_des	The destination city's population.
pop_pot	Population potential, measured as the geometric mean of the origin and destination cities' populations.
tot_dist	The distance traveled on the itinerary.
totfirm	The total number of airlines operating online service plus the number of alliances in the market.
us dest	A dummy indicating that the itinerary's destination is the US.

Table 3 Summary Statistics–Interline Data Set

	All Itineraries–46,620 obs.				Allied Carriers–20,228 obs.				Non-allied Carriers–26,392 obs.			
	Mean	Std Dev	Min	Max	Mean	Std Dev	Min	Max	Mean	Std Dev	Min	Max
avgfare	1,385.87	1,132.2	100	13,391	1,226.35	1,019.1	100	10,876	1,508.13	1,197.4	100	13,391
Infare	6.988	0.688	4.605	9.502	6.877	0.664	4.605	9.294	7.072	0.695	4.605	9.502
coup	4.775	1.006	3	6	4.853	1.001	3	6	4.715	1.005	3	6
tot_dist	9,702.1	5,030.6	207	30,116	9,852.7	4,697.2	752	26,862	9,586.8	5,269.1	207	30,116
indist	8.998	0.672	5.333	10.313	9.047	0.599	6.623	10.198	8.960	0.721	5.333	10.313
ally	0.434	0.496	0	1	1.000	0.000	1	1	0.000	0.000	0	0
pop_ori	2,276,753	4,367,457	500	27,700,000	1,713,019	2,634,306	500	27,700,000	2,708,824	5,286,389	1,127	27,700,000
pop_des	2,298,099	3,805,610	500	27,700,000	1,823,526	2,753,031	500	27,700,000	2,661,833	4,412,410	500	27,700,000
pop_pot	1,300,017	1,419,111	2,305	14,300,000	1,165,716	1,091,202	5,477	14,300,000	1,402,951	1,618,774	2,305	14,300,000
totfirm	3.555	3.120	0	20	4.130	2.814	1	18	3.114	3.268	0	20
com_low	2.849	2.089	0	13	3.250	1.798	1	13	2.542	2.239	0	13
com_high	3.095	2.525	0	18	3.532	2.185	1	16	2.760	2.710	0	18
com_int	1.225	1.218	0	7	0.840	1.128	0	6.5	1.520	1.202	0	7
Regions												
central amer	0.086	0.281	0	1	0.055	0.227	0	1	0.110	0.313	0	1
carib	0.042	0.201	0	1	0.003	0.054	0	1	0.072	0.259	0	1
so amer	0.060	0.238	0	1	0.008	0.090	0	1	0.100	0.300	0	1
europe	0.407	0.491	0	1	0.529	0.499	0	1	0.313	0.464	0	1
africa	0.028	0.164	0	1	0.040	0.197	0	1	0.018	0.133	0	1
mid east	0.041	0.199	0	1	0.044	0.205	0	1	0.039	0.194	0	1
far east	0.145	0.352	0	1	0.057	0.232	0	1	0.212	0.408	0	1
aust	0.033	0.179	0	1	0.041	0.198	0	1	0.027	0.161	0	1
canada	0.158	0.365	0	1	0.223	0.416	0	1	0.108	0.311	0	1
us dest	0.423	0.494	0	1	0.482	0.500	0	1	0.378	0.485	0	1

Table 4 Summary Statistics–Behind-the-Gateway Data Set

	All Itineraries–11,694 obs.				Allied Carriers–4,579 obs.				Non-allied Carriers–7,115 obs.			
	Mean	Std Dev	Min	Max	Mean	Std Dev	Min	Max	Mean	Std Dev	Min	Max
avgfare	1,243.62	1,007.2	101	10,876	1,123.79	884.9	102	8,316	1,320.73	1,071.6	101	10,876
lnfare	6.894	0.663	4.615	9.294	6.816	0.625	4.625	9.026	6.944	0.681	4.615	9.294
coup	5.121	0.954	3	6	5.231	0.931	3	6	5.051	0.962	3	6
tot_dist	8,304.6	4,695.5	460	24,480	8,622.1	4,311.4	1,008	21,812	8,100.3	4,916.4	460	24,480
lndist	8.816	0.707	6.131	10.106	8.899	0.624	6.916	9.990	8.763	0.751	6.131	10.106
ally	0.392	0.488	0	1	1.000	0.000	1	1	0.000	0.000	0	0
pop_ori	1,657,672	4,050,882	500	27,700,000	1,206,566	2,481,471	500	27,700,000	1,947,991	4,774,306	1,127	27,700,000
pop_des	2,201,386	4,139,859	500	27,700,000	1,648,926	2,947,450	500	27,700,000	2,556,932	4,717,660	500	27,700,000
pop_pot	686,446	619,953	2,305	11,000,000	648,749	484,837	5,477	3,872,131	710,707	692,064	2,305	11,000,000
totfirm	1.867	1.758	0	9	2.487	1.712	1	9	1.468	1.670	0	9
com_low	1.767	1.574	0	8	2.315	1.429	1	8	1.415	1.561	0	8
com_high	1.777	1.597	0	8	2.334	1.471	1	8	1.419	1.572	0	8
com_int	1.013	0.980	0	4.5	0.456	0.803	0	4	1.371	0.914	0	4.5
Regions												
central amer	0.116	0.320	0	1	0.070	0.255	0	1	0.146	0.353	0	1
carib	0.047	0.212	0	1	0.002	0.047	0	1	0.076	0.265	0	1
so amer	0.039	0.194	0	1	0.002	0.039	0	1	0.064	0.244	0	1
europe	0.409	0.492	0	1	0.522	0.500	0	1	0.336	0.472	0	1
africa	0.018	0.134	0	1	0.027	0.162	0	1	0.013	0.112	0	1
mid east	0.027	0.163	0	1	0.033	0.180	0	1	0.023	0.151	0	1
far east	0.105	0.307	0	1	0.042	0.201	0	1	0.146	0.353	0	1
aust	0.019	0.138	0	1	0.018	0.133	0	1	0.020	0.141	0	1
canada	0.219	0.413	0	1	0.284	0.451	0	1	0.177	0.381	0	1
us dest	0.362	0.481	0	1	0.408	0.492	0	1	0.332	0.471	0	1

route. In the regressions, distance is log transformed, following the usual practice in the literature (the resulting variable is LNDIST). Because this variable captures the increased variable costs of operating longer flights, we expect it to have a positive coefficient in the regressions. In the summary statistics, it is worth noting that the distance traveled on alliance itineraries, which have lower average fares, is actually longer on average than for nonalliance itineraries.

A related variable, COUP, equals the number of ticket coupons and thus the number of flight segments in the itinerary.[25] From the cost side, more coupon segments should result in higher costs and fares, but from the demand side, consumers should generally need compensation for flights with more coupon segments. In reduced form, the effect of this variable is uncertain.

As discussed above, the sole demand variable is POP_POT, which measures the population potential of the city-pair market. Tables 3 and 4 show that the mean values for POP_POT are smallest in the BTG data set, indicating that cities in the behind-the-gateway markets are smaller on average than those in the interline data set. Because of stronger demand in larger markets, the regression coefficient for POP_POT is expected to be positive.

Competition in the market is measured by the variables whose creation was discussed above, and their coefficients are expected to be negative. TOTFIRM is the number of carriers operating in the market, and COM_INT is the number of nonallied interline partners. COM_LOW and COM_HIGH are the lower and upper bounds on the number of online and alliance competitors in the market. In the interline data set, the average itinerary's city-pair market has 2.8–3.1 online/alliance competitors and 1.2 nonallied interline competitors. In the BTG data set, the number of alliance/online competitors is substantially lower on average, at 1.8, while nonallied interline competition is only slightly lower, with the average number of competitors equal to 1.0. Thus, smaller markets enjoy less competition than larger markets.

The means for the region dummies show that the region with the largest share of non-U.S. endpoints is Europe, which contains 40 percent of the endpoints, followed by Canada, which has 16–22 percent (the share is higher in the BTG data set). The share of itineraries where the U.S. endpoint is the destination ranges between 35 and 42 percent.

Although omitted from the summary statistics, the regressions also include airline-specific effects. Including such variables allows the alliance effect to be separated from the effect of carrier characteristics such as labor cost, which influence fares. While we could simply include a dummy variable for each of the 227 airlines in the data, a measure more closely related to variable costs is used instead. The measure equals the interaction between the carrier dummies and distance flown. For example, suppose the itinerary involves 3000 miles of travel on United and 500 miles of travel on Lufthansa. Our method sets United's variable equal to ln(3000) and Lufthansa's to ln(500), with all other airline variables set equal to zero (the omitted dummy corresponds to American). Also, because United and Lufthansa are allied, ALLY would equal one for this observation. It should be noted that the alliance effect is assumed to be independent of the identities of the allied carriers.

---

[25] When a passenger continues on the same flight after an intermediate stop, the data do not show a segment break. In these cases, which are relatively rare, COUP understates the number of flight segments.

3.7   Regression Results

The estimated model is of the following form:

$$\text{LNFARE}_{ij} = \beta_0 + \beta_1 \text{ALLY}_{ij} + \beta_2 \text{LNDIST}_{ij} + \beta_3 \text{COUP}_{ij}$$
$$+ \beta_4 \text{Online/Alliance Competition}_j + \beta_5 \text{COM\_INT}_j$$
$$+ \beta_6 \text{POP\_POT}_j + \beta_7 \text{Regions}_j + \beta_8 \text{Airline Effects}_{ij} + (v_j + \varepsilon_{ij}). \quad (14)$$

"Online/Alliance Competition" denotes one of the variables TOTFIRM, COM_HIGH or COM_LOW, "Regions" refers to the region and direction dummies, and "Airline effects" denotes the airline variables. In (14), j refers to the city-pair market, i refers to the itinerary within that market, and ε_{ij} is the error term. Note that while the competition, population potential and region dummy variables are constant across the intineraries within a given market, the remaining variables depend on the itinerary. Note also that this specification allows for a fixed effect, v_j, in each city-pair market, which captures unobservable attributes of the market.

We begin with simple OLS regressions on the interline data set, ignoring the possibility of market fixed effects. First, reflecting the pattern seen in Table 3, a regression with the alliance dummy as the only regressor shows that allied carriers charge fares 19.5 percent lower than those charged by nonallied carriers (the R^2 is only 0.02, however). Table 6 shows results with a fuller set of regressors. The 19.5 percent alliance effect increases (in absolute value) to −24.2 percent, as seen in column (1), when the cost, demand, competition (as measured by COM_HIGH and COM_INT) and carrier variables added to the regression. In column (2), where the region and direction dummies are also included, the coefficient is unchanged, indicating that alliance fares are 24 percent lower than those charged by nonallied carriers.

Column (4) adds region/alliance and direction/alliance interactions to the regression. If the alliance effect varies by region and direction of travel, the inclusion of these variables will give a more accurate measures of its magnitude. The results, which are summarized separately in Table 6, indicate that the alliance effect varies markedly. For passengers originating in the U.S. (shown in the first column of Table 6), alliance fares to Europe, Central America and Africa are 15–18 percent lower than those on nonallied carriers, and passengers traveling to Canada see a 52 percent reduction in fares. However, no statistically significant effect is measured for itineraries to the Caribbean, South America, Middle East and Far East. Passengers travelling to Australia face significantly *higher* alliance fares, which are 8.5 percent above those charged by nonallied carriers. The explanation for this fare premium may lie in the web of interlocking alliance relationships among carriers serving Australia, which may reduce competition.[26]

As seen in column (2) of Table 5, passengers whose destinations are U.S. endpoints pay fares 9.6 percent lower than those originating in the U.S. When the alliance interaction

---

[26] Most of the traffic in Australian markets takes place on five carriers: United, Qantas, Ansett, American and Air New Zealand, whose alliances overlap extensively. United operates alliance flights with Qantas, Ansett and Air New Zealand. American operates an alliance with Qantas, and Ansett and Air New Zealand are also allied.

Table 5 Interline Regression Results

	(1) Coef.	(1) t-stat	(2) Coef.	(2) t-stat	(3) Coef.	(3) t-stat	Europe (1) Coef.	Europe (1) t-stat	Europe (2) Coef.	Europe (2) t-stat
ally	−0.2422	−46.09	−0.2426	−32.20	−0.1841	−15.94	−0.2609	−19.86	−0.1910	−12.68
coup	−0.0358	−12.69	−0.0312	−11.23	−0.0337	−12.23	−0.0563	−11.78	−0.0563	−11.81
indist	0.6503	155.87	0.3697	41.43	0.3924	43.97	0.3245	12.25	0.3265	12.35
com_high	−0.0075	−6.04	−0.0101	−8.00	−0.0099	−7.93	−0.0150	−6.54	−0.0154	−6.75
com_int	−0.0163	−7.50	−0.0133	−6.27	−0.0140	−6.68	−0.0152	−4.53	−0.0155	−4.62
pop_pot	4.23E-08	19.82	2.10E-08	9.48	1.87E-08	8.52	3.68E-08	7.09	3.58E-08	6.92
constant	1.4007	41.20	4.1525	51.85	3.9709	50.78	4.6465	20.06	4.5955	19.88
Regions										
central amer	—	—	−0.2298	−12.19	−0.2246	−11.90	—	—	—	—
carib	—	—	−0.4451	−19.69	−0.4341	−19.23	—	—	—	—
so amer	—	—	0.0725	3.72	0.0495	2.55	—	—	—	—
africa	—	—	0.5080	27.09	0.4773	14.78	—	—	—	—
mid east	—	—	0.3827	24.53	0.2856	11.58	—	—	—	—
far east	—	—	0.4547	30.83	0.3780	23.84	—	—	—	—
aust	—	—	0.3524	10.58	0.2634	7.79	—	—	—	—
canada	—	—	−0.1464	−7.44	−0.0759	−3.78	—	—	—	—
us dest	—	—	−0.0959	−20.27	−0.0403	−6.27	−0.2012	−26.01	−0.1141	−9.47
Region/Ally Interactions										
central amer	—	—	—	—	0.0316	1.33	—	—	—	—
carib	—	—	—	—	0.1950	2.82	—	—	—	—
so amer	—	—	—	—	0.1753	4.18	—	—	—	—
africa	—	—	—	—	0.0317	0.92	—	—	—	—
mid east	—	—	—	—	0.1441	5.06	—	—	—	—
far east	—	—	—	—	0.2062	10.51	—	—	—	—
aust	—	—	—	—	0.2686	8.31	—	—	—	—
canada	—	—	—	—	−0.3307	−18.01	—	—	—	—
us dest	—	—	—	—	−0.1142	−12.23	—	—	−0.1468	−9.40
Airline Effects	Yes		Yes		Yes		Yes		Yes	
adj. r^2	0.4289		0.5077		0.5172		0.1280		0.1320	
obs.	46,620		46,620		46,620		18,966		18,966	

Airline effects coefficients omitted from table.

Table 6 Alliance Effect by Region and Direction of Travel (Percent Change in Fare Relative to Non-Alliance Itineraries)

	Interline		BTG	
	US Origin	US Dest.	US Origin	US Dest.
europe	−18.4*	−29.8*	−17.1*	−29.9*
central amer	−15.9*	−26.7*	−10.6†	−23.4*
carib	1.1	−10.3	−6.2	−19.0
so amer	−0.9	−12.3*	22.0	9.1
africa	−15.2*	−26.6*	−19.1*	−31.9*
mid east	−4.0	−15.4*	−11.4	−24.3*
far east	2.2	−9.2*	−0.9	−13.7*
aust	8.5*	−2.9	5.5	−7.3
canada	−51.5*	−62.9*	−33.5*	−46.3*

These results are based on the estimates from column 3 in table 5.
*indicates significance at 1% confidence level.
†indicates significance at 5% confidence level.

terms in column (3) are included, the U.S.-destination discount shrinks to −4.0 percent for nonalliance itineraries but grows to −15.5 percent for alliance travel.[27]

This asymmetry in pricing, which means that the alliance effect is stronger for itineraries originating at foreign airports, generates a constant 11 percent directional differential for each region, as can be seen by comparing the first and second columns of Table 6. Note that the addition of the directional discount causes the alliance effect to become significantly negative, except for Australian and Caribbean origins.

The coefficients of the other regressors in Table 5 are as expected. Greater distance increases the fare, but the consumer must be compensated for additional coupon segments with a lower fare. Greater market size, as measured by a higher population potential, increases the fare as well. An additional online or alliance competitor, as captured by an increase in COM_HIGH, causes the fare to fall by one percent. While this effect is small in magnitude, it is highly significant. An additional interline competitor lowers the fare by 1.4 percent.

Because Europe contains most of the sample's non-U.S. endpoints, the model is estimated separately for European itineraries, with the results shown in last two columns of Table 5. The regression in the last column allows the alliance effect to vary by direction of travel. The results are similar to those discussed previously, with alliance partners charging fares 26 percent lower than those of nonallied carriers. When a directional difference is allowed, the alliance effect is −19 percent for U.S.-originating passengers and −34 percent for passengers originating in Europe.

To address the problem of potential mismeasurement of competition in the interline data set, we run the same regressions on the BTG data set, where all competition is potentially observable. The results are given in Table 7. As can be seen, the alliance

---

[27] This result comes from adding the coefficients on the U.S. destination dummy and the U.S. destination/ally interaction variable.

Table 7 BTG Regression Results

	(1) Coef.	(1) t-stat	(2) Coef.	(2) t-stat	(3) Coef.	(3) t-stat	Europe (1) Coef.	Europe (1) t-stat	Europe (2) Coef.	Europe (2) t-stat
ally	-0.1992	-17.89	-0.2334	-14.91	-0.1707	-7.22	-0.2455	-8.96	-0.1576	-5.17
coup	0.0000	0.01	-0.0065	-1.09	-0.0081	-1.36	-0.0276	-2.73	-0.0266	-2.64
indist	0.5792	75.66	0.2627	15.54	0.2686	15.86	0.0729	1.14	0.0769	1.21
com_high	-0.0315	-8.34	-0.0277	-7.26	-0.0259	-6.81	-0.0303	-4.79	-0.0311	-4.94
com_int	-0.0314	-5.68	-0.0170	-3.18	-0.0151	-2.83	-0.0115	-1.38	-0.0114	-1.37
pop_pot	1.14E-07	12.63	4.47E-08	4.58	3.98E-08	4.09	5.73E-08	3.14	5.36E-08	2.95
constant	1.8749	29.88	5.0586	34.28	5.0065	33.90	6.8643	12.10	6.7943	12.02
Regions										
central amer	–	–	-0.3107	-10.52	-0.3074	-10.40	–	–	–	–
carib	–	–	-0.5697	-14.84	-0.5667	-14.76	–	–	–	–
so amer	–	–	-0.0281	-0.87	-0.0321	-0.99	–	–	–	–
africa	–	–	0.5726	14.12	0.5811	9.07	–	–	–	–
mid east	–	–	0.3446	10.04	0.3075	5.78	–	–	–	–
far east	–	–	0.4129	14.16	0.3829	12.73	–	–	–	–
aust	–	–	0.2341	3.44	0.2201	3.24	–	–	–	–
canada	–	–	-0.2826	-8.47	-0.2736	-8.14	–	–	–	–
us dest	–	–	-0.0202	-2.17	0.0359	2.92	-0.1313	-8.78	-0.0276	-1.26
Region/Ally Interactions										
central amer	–	–	–	–	0.0654	1.35	–	–	–	–
carib	–	–	–	–	0.1086	0.67	–	–	–	–
so amer	–	–	–	–	0.3902	2.13	–	–	–	–
africa	–	–	–	–	-0.0202	-0.28	–	–	–	–
mid east	–	–	–	–	0.0565	0.89	–	–	–	–
far east	–	–	–	–	0.1622	3.69	–	–	–	–
aust	–	–	–	–	0.2261	2.68	–	–	–	–
canada	–	–	–	–	-0.1642	-4.91	–	–	–	–
us dest	–	–	–	–	-0.1283	-6.92	–	–	-0.1912	-6.46
Airline Effects	Yes		Yes		Yes		Yes		Yes	
adj. r^2	0.4361		0.5176		0.5224		0.0792		0.0871	
obs.	11,694		11,694		11,694		4,783		4,783	

Airline effects coefficients omitted from table.

effect in each of the specifications of Table 7 is close to that in the corresponding column of Table 5. This suggests that potential error in the measurement of competition in the interline data set is not a serious source of bias in estimating the alliance effect.

One noteworthy difference between the interline and BTG results is that an additional online or alliance competitor lowers the fare by 2.6 percent, an impact larger than the one-percent decline found in Table 5. However, it is not clear whether this change is due to measurement error in the competition variable or the different nature of behind-the-gateway markets.

Up to this point, we have ignored market-specific effects. If they are significant, then the OLS coefficients will be biased. The traditional solution to this problem is fixed-effects estimation, but such estimation requires at least two observations for each city-pair market. In the interline data set, approximately 71 percent of the data fit this criterion, but only 46 percent the BTG observations do. An alternative approach, which would preserve the smaller markets that are omitted in a fixed-effects regression, is to repeat the OLS regressions on a data set with only one observation selected at random from each market. This approach eliminates the market-specific effect by construction, but it underweights the denser markets.

Table 8 summarizes the results using fixed effects and one randomly selected observation per market, where the specification in column (2) of Tables 5 and 7 is adopted. Under both these alternate approaches, the alliance effect is similar to that found using OLS. This suggests that any omitted market-specific variables are largely uncorrelated with the alliance dummy.

In the OLS regressions, we arbitrarily chose COM_HIGH to measure the effect of online and alliance competition. Table 9 summarizes the effects of using the other competition measures, TOTFIRM and COM_LOW, in both data sets. As can be seen, the choice of the competition variable has little impact on the estimated alliance effect. In addition, all three competition measures have roughly the same coefficient. As before, an extra competitor lowers the fare by one percent in the interline data set, and by approximately 2.5 percent in the BTG data set.

To investigate the effect of a final modification to the regressions, recall that the alliance dummy variable indicates the presence of a codesharing agreement between

Table 8   Alliance Coefficient Using Different Controls for Market-Specific Effects

	Interline		BTG	
	Coef.	Obs.	Coef.	Obs.
OLS	−0.2426	46,620	−0.2334	11,694
	(−32.20)		(−14.91)	
Fixed Effects	−0.2399	33,189	−0.2770	5,383
	(−22.92)		(−9.64)	
1 obs/route	−0.2174	21,508	−0.2034	8,166
	(−19.34)		(−10.72)	

t-statistics are in parenthesis. Regressions included all the variables used in column (2) of Tables 5 and 7.

Table 9 The Effects of Different Competition Measures

	Interline Data Set (OLS)			BTG Data Set (OLS)		
	(1)	(2)	(3)	(4)	(5)	(6)
ally	−0.2426	−0.2410	−0.2431	−0.2334	−0.2329	−0.2349
	(−32.20)	(−31.94)	(−32.27)	(−14.91)	(−14.87)	(−15.01)
com_high	−0.0101	–	–	−0.0277	–	–
	(−8.00)			(−7.26)		
com_low	–	−0.0137	–	–	−0.0288	–
		(−9.43)			(−7.44)	
tot_firm	–	–	−0.0079	–	–	−0.0234
			(−7.56)			(−6.77)
com_int	−0.0133	−0.0132	−0.0132	−0.0170	−0.0172	−0.0161
	(−6.27)	(−6.27)	(−6.25)	(−3.18)	(−3.21)	(−3.02)

t-statistics are in parenthesis. Regressions included all the variables used in column (2) of Tables 5 and 7.

the intinerary's two carriers. Since a codesharing arrangement may fall short of a true alliance, an additional dummy variable is introduced that indicates whether the two carriers enjoy antitrust immunity. A review of Department of Transportation press releases prior to the sample period indicated that the following carrier pairs had immunity: United/Lufthansa, United/SAS, United/Air Canada, Northwest/KLM, American/Canadian, Delta/Swissair, Delta/Sabena, and Delta/Austrian Air. Itineraries involving these carrier pairs account for 71 percent of the alliance itineraries in the interline data set.

The immunity dummy variable is used in the regression along with ALLY, and the results are shown in Table 10. The estimates for the interline data set show that, while a codesharing agreement without immunity leads to a 10 percent fare reduction, the presence of antitrust immunity reduces fares by a further 30 percent, for a net reduction of 40 percent (in the BTG data set, the net reduction is 32 percent). Using the 71 percent immunity share, the weighted average of these effects is approximately 31 percent for the interline sample, which is larger than any of the estimated alliance effects in the regressions using ALLY alone. One explanation for this outcome is that the immunity dummy identifies a relatively small subset of carriers, which may share common characteristics over and above their enjoyment of antitrust immunity. While

Table 10 The Effect of Antitrust Immunity

	Interline		BTG	
	Coef.	t-stat	Coef.	t-stat
ally	−0.1041	−11.07	−0.1012	−4.56
immunity	−0.3279	−24.37	−0.2289	−8.37

Regressions included all the variables used in column (2) of Tables 5 and 7.

such omitted factors might lead to an upward bias in the estimate of the immunity effect, the large size of the coefficient suggests nevertheless that antitrust immunity by itself leads to substantially lower fares. Given that immunity increases the scope of possible price coordination between the carriers, this outcome is expected.

The consistency of the above results across specifications and estimation techniques is remarkable. The results indicate that for interline itineraries, the fares charged by alliance partners are substantially lower than than those charged by nonallied carriers, with an average differential of approximately 25 percent. However, region and direction of travel matter. Passengers travelling to and from Australia and the Caribbean see little or no price benefits from alliances, while passengers whose destination is a U.S. endpoint enjoy a greater fare reduction than U.S.-originating passengers.

4 THE EFFECT OF ALLIANCES ON GATEWAY-TO-GATEWAY FARES

4.1 Overview

Although the gateway-to-gateway market was suppressed in the model of section 2, the impact of alliances in such markets is an important concern of government regulators, as discussed in the introduction. The concern is that when two carriers both provide service in a given gateway-to-gateway market, an alliance between them will be anticompetitive, leading to higher fares in the market.

Given the importance of gateway-to-gateway markets, this section provides empirical evidence on the effect of alliances in such markets. The empirical strategy is to focus on nonstop service between gateway cities, running a regression that relates fares to distance, demand, airline specific effects, and competition variables. The first competition variable is the previous TOTFIRM measure, which counts the total number of carriers in the market. The second variable measures the loss of competition relative to this total due to the presence of alliances among carriers in the market. The hypothesis is that the reduction in competition associated with alliances leads to higher fares, implying a positive coefficient for the loss measure.

4.2 Gateway-To-Gateway Data Sets

To conduct this analysis, we construct a data set of gateway-to-gateway itineraries from our original restricted data set, keeping only round-trip, two-segment itineraries that are operated by one carrier. This "GTG" data set contains 1,313 observations, representing 663 city-pair markets. Note that since interline travel is not represented, each observation involves a round trip on a U.S. carrier. Like the interline data sets, the GTG data set also suffers from unobserved market-specific effects. However, because the parameters of interest in this analysis are constant within a city-pair market, fixed-effects estimation is not an option. Instead, we create two additional data sets that are distinguished by their treatment of market-specific effects. Construction of the first takes the same approach as in the interline analysis, with one observation selected at random from city-pair markets with multiple observations. The other data set aggregates the data to the city-pair level instead of preserving individual itineraries. A passenger-weighted average fare is computed, but in this case, the average is across the itineraries of all the carriers serving the market (the result is denoted the "city-pair" data set). Since only 25 percent of the observations occur in markets with multiple observations, the reduced data sets are not much smaller than the GTG data set, containing 1,137 observations.

4.3 Variables and Summary Statistics

Because attention is restricted to nonstop service, the OAG can be used to determine which carriers operate in each city-pair market.[28] Thus, the mismeasurement issue that arose in the interline data is not present. As noted above, the variable measuring the total number of airlines operating in a market is TOTFIRM. To measure lost competition from alliances, we define two new variables, LOSS_HI and LOSS_LO, which are simply the difference between TOTFIRM and COM_HIGH and COM_LOW, respectively. The loss measure gives the number of airlines in the market that do not provide competition because of the presence of alliances. For example, suppose a market is served by United, American and Air Canada. TOTFIRM in this market equals three. However, because United and Air Canada are allied, both COM_HIGH and COM_LOW equal two. Thus, the loss measures for this market are both equal to one, meaning one of the airlines providing service in the market is not considered a competitor because of alliances. The loss measures differ from zero for only 10 percent of the observations, implying that it is not common for two alliance partners to operate flights in the same gateway-to-gateway market.

Since itineraries in the gateway data sets are flown on the same route by a single airline, we measure airline specific effects with simple airline dummies (the distance interaction is not needed). Only 22 airlines are observed in the gateway-to-gateway markets, and as before, the American dummy variable is omitted from the regressions. In the city-pair data set, where itineraries are aggregated across airlines, the dummy is split between the operating carriers on a passenger-weighted basis.[29]

The summary statistics for the GTG data set are presented in Table 11, which shows that gateway-to-gateway itineraries have a different character than those in the interline data set. The average fare is around \$826, and the average distance is only 5,700 miles. The average number of carriers operating nonstop flights is 2.14, and the mean values of the loss measures, LOSS_LO and LOSS_HI, are 0.21 and 0.16 respectively.

4.4 Regression Results

The model estimated for the gateway-to-gateway markets is

$$\text{LNFARE}_{ij} = \beta_0 + \beta_1 \text{TOTFIRM}_j + \beta_2 \text{Loss measure}_j + \beta_3 \text{LNDIST}_j$$
$$+ \beta_4 \text{POP\_POT}_j + \beta_5 \text{Regions}_j + \beta_6 \text{Airline Dummies}_{ij} + (v_j + \varepsilon_{ij}). \quad (15)$$

---

[28] We count only those carriers listed in the OAG as providing direct service in the market. In some cases, this includes one-stop service where the continuing flight retains the same flight number. Carriers providing connecting one-stop service are not counted, although including such competitors has little effect on the results.
[29] For example, suppose United and Continental are the only airlines operating in a particular gateway-to-gateway market, with 60 passengers observed using United and 40 using Continental. United's dummy for this city pair market would then be set equal to 0.6 and Continental's to 0.4.

Table 11   Summary Statistics-GTG Data Set (1313 obs.)

	Mean	Std Dev	Min	Max
avgfare	826.235	640.134	110	5,179
tot_dist	5,707	4,161	192	19,706
pop_ori	3,485,507	5,433,838	8,000	27,700,000
pop_des	3,424,281	5,393,377	8,000	27,700,000
pop_pot	2.076	2.284	0.010	14.299
totfirm	2.139	1.374	1	9
com_high	1.978	1.166	1	7
com_low	1.930	1.098	1	6
loss_hi	0.161	0.420	0	2
loss_lo	0.209	0.580	0	3
Regions				
central amer	0.164	0.370	0	1
carib	0.153	0.360	0	1
so amer	0.081	0.274	0	1
europe	0.256	0.437	0	1
africa	0.002	0.039	0	1
mid east	0.008	0.091	0	1
far east	0.149	0.356	0	1
aust	0.028	0.166	0	1
canada	0.158	0.365	0	1
us dest	0.480	0.500	0	1

"Loss measure" refers to either LOSS_HI or LOSS_LO. Observe that, with the exception of the airline dummies, all the variables in (15) are constant across different itineraries i within a given city-pair market j.

Notice that by using TOTFIRM along with the loss measure, we can distinguish the effect of adding a nonallied airline to the market from the effect of adding a carrier that is allied with another airline in the market. The effect of adding a nonallied airline is given by the coefficient of TOTFIRM, while the effect of adding an alliance partner is equal to the sum of the coefficients of TOTFIRM and the loss measure. We expect the coefficients on TOTFIRM and the loss measure to be negative and positive, respectively. In addition, the sum of the coefficients should be close to zero, since adding an alliance partner of an existing carrier should have little effect on the fare in the market.

The gateway-to-gateway regression results are presented in Table 12, with two columns devoted to each of the data sets. In all specifications, we meet only two of our three expectations. In particular, the coefficient on TOTFIRM is negative and significant, with its magnitude indicating that an extra competitor reduces fares by about 4–5 percent. In addition, the sum of the coefficients on TOTFIRM and the loss measure is not significantly different from zero. However, the coefficient on the loss measure itself, while negative and of the proper 4–6 percent magnitude, is not significantly different from zero, even at the 10 percent confidence level. This is true regardless of which measure is used. The other coefficients have the expected signs and magnitudes.

Table 12 Gateway-to-Gateway Regression Results

	All Data 1,313 obs.		Random Obs. 1,137 obs.		City-Pair 1,137 obs.	
	(1)	(2)	(3)	(4)	(5)	(6)
totfirm	−0.0449	−0.0454	−0.0445	−0.0447	−0.0389	−0.0385
	(−4.58)	(−4.56)	(−3.93)	(−3.89)	(−3.42)	(−3.34)
loss_hi	0.0500	–	0.0618	–	0.0541	–
	(1.60)	–	(1.64)	–	(1.44)	–
loss_lo	–	0.0377	–	0.0471	–	0.0386
	–	(1.61)	–	(1.60)	–	(1.31)
lndist	0.3731	0.3731	0.3744	0.3743	0.3768	0.3768
	(20.24)	(20.24)	(19.11)	(19.09)	(19.19)	(19.17)
pop_pot	0.0237	0.0231	0.0228	0.0222	0.0222	0.0218
	(4.28)	(4.14)	(3.57)	(3.45)	(3.47)	(3.37)
constant	3.5944	3.5969	3.5967	3.6003	3.5686	3.5695
	(21.28)	(21.27)	(20.03)	(20.00)	(19.83)	(19.79)
Regions						
central amer	−0.4268	−0.4258	−0.4327	−0.4318	−0.4267	−0.4253
	(−10.82)	(−10.84)	(−10.39)	(−10.38)	(−10.22)	(−10.20)
carib	−0.4419	−0.4435	−0.4487	−0.4506	−0.4441	−0.4454
	(−9.62)	(−9.64)	(−9.26)	(−9.28)	(−9.14)	(−9.15)
so amer	0.0560	0.0524	−0.0037	−0.0071	0.0094	0.0065
	(1.39)	(1.30)	(−0.08)	(−0.16)	(0.21)	(0.15)
africa	−0.0024	0.0009	−0.0127	−0.0094	−0.0101	−0.0081
	(−0.01)	(0.00)	(−0.05)	(−0.04)	(−0.04)	(−0.03)
mid east	0.0960	0.0967	0.1307	0.1313	0.1211	0.1211
	(0.87)	(0.88)	(1.08)	(1.09)	(1.00)	(1.00)
far east	0.2144	0.2147	0.1876	0.1877	0.1983	0.1983
	(6.58)	(6.58)	(5.31)	(5.31)	(5.60)	(5.60)
aust	−0.0501	−0.0564	−0.0643	−0.0712	−0.0577	−0.0626
	(−0.78)	(−0.87)	(−0.99)	(−1.08)	(−0.89)	(−0.95)
canada	−0.3290	−0.3270	−0.3174	−0.3159	−0.3141	−0.3122
	(−7.47)	(−7.46)	(−6.78)	(−6.76)	(−6.69)	(−6.67)
us dest	−0.0414	−0.0411	−0.0362	−0.0362	−0.0420	−0.0421
	(−2.08)	(−2.07)	(−1.71)	(−1.71)	(−1.98)	(−1.98)
Adj. r^2	0.7311	0.7311	0.7310	0.7310	0.7313	0.7312
F-test:	0.85	0.69	0.60	0.92	0.65	1.00
totfirm + loss						

t-statistics are in parenthesis. Airline effects coefficients omitted from table.

One drawback to these regressions is that destinations for many itineraries are resort islands such as Tahiti and the Bahamas, which are not gateways in the usual sense, lacking behind-the-gateway endpoints. Since such markets are not a particular concern of regulators, it is appropriate to delete them and evaluate the effect on the results. Dropping itineraries that start or finish in the Caribbean or on any south Pacific island reduces the data set by 23 percent. However, the resulting estimates show that this restriction of the sample has little effect on the magnitude and statistical significance of the loss coefficients.

Another possibility is that our model misspecifies the effect of competition by assuming that an additional competitor has the same fare impact regardless of the level of competition. However, if we allow the marginal impact of the second, third and additional competitors beyond three to differ, the performance of the loss measure is unaffected.

Since the gateway-to-gateway markets connect hub airports, our results may be affected by the absence of a measure of airport dominance, which has been shown in the literature to affect fares (see, for example, the work of Severin Borenstein).[30]

To include such a measure, we compute the Hirschman-Herfindahl Index (HHI) of concentration for U.S. airports, using the DB1A data set to generate enplanements by carrier at each airport. However, since data for a similar calculation at non-U.S. airports are unavailable, the HHI variable is used in regressions restriced to itineraries with U.S. origins. The results, which are shown in Table 13, indicate that an increase in concentration at the U.S. origin airport (reflected in a higher HHI value) raises fares in the relevant gateway-to-gateway markets. Since the level of competition in the market is held constant, this finding must be interpreted as a demand-side effect. In other words, since passengers value the extensive network of the dominant hub carrier, they are willing to pay higher fares for its service.

However, once the HHI measure is included, the coefficients of TOTFIRM become insignificant in the regressions on the GTG data set, with the same outcome occurring in the city-pair data set. Moreover, the loss-measures, which are marginally significant in Table 12, now have much smaller t-statistics. Thus, inclusion of HHI yields less-precise

Table 13 Gateway Regression Results/US Origins only with HHI

	All Data 683 obs.		Random Obs. 590 obs.		City-Pair 590 obs.	
	(1)	(2)	(3)	(4)	(5)	(6)
totfirm	−0.0254	−0.0219	−0.0351	−0.0319	−0.0232	−0.0192
	(−1.75)	(−1.49)	(−2.15)	(−1.93)	(−1.40)	(−1.14)
loss_hi	0.0045	–	0.0595	–	0.0258	–
	(0.10)	–	(1.15)	–	(0.50)	–
loss_lo	–	−0.0101	–	0.0301	–	0.0017
	–	(−0.31)	–	(0.74)	–	(0.04)
hhi	0.2588	0.2603	0.2419	0.2435	0.2603	0.2625
	(3.33)	(3.34)	(2.99)	(3.00)	(3.18)	(3.21)

t-statistics are in parenthesis. Although the coefficients are omitted, these regressions include all variables from Table 11 except us_dest, which does in vary in a data set restricted to US Origins.

---

[30] Severin Borenstein, Hubs and High Fares: Dominance and Market Power in the U.S. Airline Industry, 20 RAND J. Econ. 344–365 (1989).

measures of the effect of competition in individual markets, failing to overturn the previous conclusion that overlapping alliance competition has no effect on fares.

A further issue concerns the potential endogeneity of TOTFIRM and the loss measures. Such endogeneity could arise for two reasons. First, when an alliance is formed, one partner may discontinue overlapping gateway-to-gateway service, relying on the other partner to provide it. Thus, the presence of a given carrier in a market may lead to the exit of its alliance partner, resulting in lower values for the both the loss measures and TOTFIRM. For this reason, the magnitude of the loss measures may understate the anticompetitive effects of the alliance.

Exit of nonallied carriers from gateway-to-gateway routes may also occur in response to formation of an alliance, contributing to the endogeneity of TOTFIRM. To see how such exit may happen, observe that the alliance partners are likely to capture much of the interline traffic passing through the hub airports on a gateway-to-gateway route, leaving nonallied carriers with only the origin-destination traffic between the gateway cities. In some cases, this traffic may be inadequate to justify service, causing the nonallied carrier to exit.[31]

For both these reasons, the coefficients of the key variables in the gateway-to-gateway regression may suffer from simultaneity bias. While the magnitude of such a bias may be small, the difficulty of finding appropriate instruments makes it hard to judge the seriousness of the endogeneity problem. Thus, the absence of a statistically-significant effect from lost competition due to alliances in the gateway-to-gateway markets must be viewed as a tentative conclusion that could be overturned by further investigation.

4.5   Simulation Analysis of the AA/BA Alliance

The estimated effects of alliances on interline and gateway-to-gateway fares can be used to shed light on a regulatory issue discussed in the introduction: the welfare impact from approval of a full-fledged alliance between American and British Airways, including antitrust immunity. To derive this welfare impact, the first step is to compute gains for interline passengers from an AA/BA alliance, recalling that no alliance existed during the 1997 sample period. These gains can be computed by assuming that, with an alliance, fares would fall by 26 percent in each of the sample markets where the partners provide interline service, as in column (4) of Table 5. Combining this figure with a value for the price elasticity of demand, the increase in consumer surplus can be computed for each AA/BA interline itinerary observed in the interline data set. Next, using a representative loss-measure coefficient from Table 12 but ignoring its lack of statistical significance, we assume that fares will rise by 5 percent in each gateway-to-gateway market served by both AA and BA following an alliance. Then, using the same price elasticity value, the loss in consumer surplus can be computed in these markets. The net change in surplus gives an estimate of the welfare impact of the alliance.

---

[31] In private correspondence, Robert Crandall (then CEO of American) provided an example of this phenomenon. He said that after formation of the Delta-Sabena alliance, these partners captured most interline traffic passing through New York and Brussels, leaving American with only a share of the origin-destination traffic between these cities. Because such traffic was viewed an inadequate to justify service, American exited from the route.

The interline data set contains 605 AA/BA itineraries, with a total of 809 sampled passengers. This corresponds to 8090 actual passengers, given the DB1A's 10 percent sampling rate. Assuming a price elasticity of −1, the 26 percent fare decline raises traffic to 10,193 passengers and generates an aggregate consumer surplus gain of $4,881,000. Using the larger elasticity estimate of −2.5 from Brueckner and Spiller,[32] traffic rises to 13,349 passengers, and the surplus gain is $5,723,000. With the still-larger elasticity of −4, traffic rises to 16,504 passengers, and the surplus gain is $6,565,000. These results are summarized in Table 14.

AA and BA compete in six gateway-to-gateway markets, and AA carries 5,309 sampled passengers in these markets, corresponding to 53,090 actual passengers. We assume that BA traffic, which is not observed in the data, is identical to AA's, and that BA passengers experience the same fare effects. With an elasticity of −1, the 5 percent fare increase caused by the alliance reduces AA's gateway-to-gateway traffic to 50,436 and generates a surplus loss of $2,631,000, for a total loss across both carriers of $5,263,000. When the elasticity equals −2.5, AA's traffic falls to 46,454, and total surplus declines by $5,060,000. With an elasticity of −4, AA's traffic falls to 42,472, and total surplus declines by $4,858,000.

The above values, which are summarized in Table 14, generate net consumer surplus changes −$382,000, $663,000, and $1,707,000 when the price elasticities are −1, −2.5, and −4, respectively. These numbers suggest that the welfare impact of the AA/BA alliance on passengers is, at worst, slightly negative, with benefits emerging if demand is relatively elastic.

Fare effects that are harder to quantify, however, would be felt by other passengers in the event of a full-fledged AA/BA alliance, and these must be considered. The first

Table 14 Welfare Effect of American-British Airways Alliance

	Pre-Alliance Passengers	Post-Alliance Passengers	Change in Surplus
Demand Elasticity −1			
Interline	8,090	10,193	4,881,000
Gateway	53,090	50,436	−5,263,000
Net Welfare Change			−382,000
Demand Elasticity −2.5			
Interline	8,090	13,349	5,723,000
Gateway	53,090	46,454	−5,060,000
Net Welfare Change			663,000
Demand Elasticity −4			
Interline	8,090	16,504	6,565,000
Gateway	53,090	42,472	−4,858,000
Net Welfare Change			1,707,000

The alliance is assumed to lower interline fares by 26%. Fares in markets operated by both AA and BA are assumed to rise by 5%.

---

[32] Brueckner and Spiller, *supra* note 3.

affected group consists of AA passengers who made interline trips in 1997 using carriers other than BA. With an alliance, these passengers would presumably switch to BA for the non-AA portion of their trip, enjoying the fare reduction associated with alliance travel. Although, in principle, the resulting gain could be computed using our data, various complications would arise.[33] Note that with the recent emergence of the oneworld alliance, many of these passengers have presumably now switched to AA/BA, although full alliance benefits may not be realized given the absence of antitrust immunity.

Conversely, the loss of competition in gateway-to-gateway markets will lead to higher fares for non-AA/BA passengers in these markets. An obstacle to the computation of this effect is the absence of foreign-carrier traffic information. For example, since we do not observe Virgin Airways' U.S.-U.K. traffic, we cannot compute the surplus loss for its passengers resulting from lower gateway-to-gateway competition.

It is likely that if these additional effects could be reliably computed, their net impact on consumer surplus would be positive. First, since AA and BA control the majority of U.S.-U.K. traffic, the omitted gateway-to-gateway losses would be relatively small. In addition, the benefits for former AA/non-BA interline passengers would be substantial given the large volume of such traffic. Therefore, it is likely that the figures in Table 14 would be adjusted upward, leading to an unambiguous welfare gain from the AA/BA alliance. This conclusion would be reinforced if passenger benefits from the greater convenience of alliance travel, which have not been measured, could be added to the calculation.

Despite the existence of this probable welfare gain, regulators are properly concerned about the anticompetitive effect of an AA/BA alliance. Approval of the antitrust-immunity element of the alliance was made contingent on the release of London-Heathrow landing slots by BA, which would have allowed entry of new competitors in the gateway-to-gateway markets. Failure to secure such a release led to disapproval by the Department of Transportation of the carriers' request for antitrust immunity. Given the large volume of AA/BA gateway-to-gateway traffic, this was probably a prudent regulatory decision.

The welfare impacts of alliances that were in operation during the sample period can also be evaluated. Since interline traffic was already substantial in these cases, the exercise requires a less-speculative approach, as seen in the analysis of Brueckner and W. Tom Whalen.[34] They measure the passenger welfare losses from *termination* of the existing Northwest/KLM alliance, and in parallel calculations, a different study by Brueckner and Whalen computes the welfare losses from terminating the European portion of the Star Alliance, consisting of United's alliances with Lufthansa and SAS.[35] Unlike AA/BA, each of these alliances already carried a large volume of interline traffic during the sample period, while their gateway-to-gateway markets, being less popular

---

[33] While each AA/non-BA interline itinerary that has a European origin or destination could be converted to an AA/BA itinerary, a precise calculation of the fare impact would require a change in the routing so that the trip passes through BA's London-Heathrow hub, with consequent changes in the distance measure and in the distance-based airline specific effects. Given the need for such speculative assumptions, we chose not to carry out these calculations.

[34] Jan K. Brueckner & W. Tom Whalen, Consumer Welfare Gains from United's Alliances with Lufthansa and SAS (unpublished paper, University of Illinois at Urbana-Champaign 1998).

[35] Jan K. Brueckner & W. Tom Whalen, Passenger Welfare Gains from the Northwest/KLM Alliance (unpublished paper, University of Illinois at Urbana-Champaign 1999).

than the U.S.-U.K. routes, had relatively low passenger volumes. In such cases, termination of an alliance generates substantial fare increases for a large number of interline
passengers and small fare declines for relatively few gateway-to-gateway passengers.
The upshot is large welfare losses from alliance termination. In the Northwest/KLM case,
annual consumer surplus losses for interline passengers were estimated to lie between
$111 and $185 million, assuming a range of possible demand elasticities. In the case
of the Star Alliance (which had lower interline volume over the sample period), annual
interline losses were between $50 and $82 million. In each case, these losses dwarfed
the surplus gains for gateway-to-gateway passengers, leading to a substantial overall
welfare loss from termination of the alliance.[36]

5   CONCLUSION

This paper provides strong evidence on the effect of international airline alliances on
fares. Our main finding is that alliance partners charge interline fares that are approximately 25 percent below those charged by nonallied carriers. According to the theoretical
model, this fare reduction arises from two sources. First, cooperative pricing internalizes the negative externalities from the uncoordinated choice of subfares, leading to
lower overall fares. This fare reduction then stimulates traffic, which in turn lowers
marginal costs via economies of traffic density, leading to further downward pressure
on fares. Our results, which confirm this prediction, are extremely robust to changes in
the specification of the empirical model.

The evidence of an anticompetitive alliance effect in the gateway-to-gateway markets
is not as clear. While our point estimates show that an alliance between two previously-
competitive carriers would raise fares by about 5 percent, this effect is not statistically
significant. However, the coefficients in the gateway-to-gateway regression may be
affected by simultaneity bias, suggesting that the absence of an anticompetitive alliance
effect must be viewed as a tentative conclusion.

Although our results compare the interline fares charged by allied and nonallied
carriers, many observers expect most of the world's airlines ultimately to join some
alliance, so that few nonallied carriers will be left. An important question is how
interline fares in this ultimate equilibrium will compare to fares in the prealliance
period. Theoretically, the answer is given by the symmetric solutions from the model of
section 2, where the fare difference between the nonalliance and alliance cases is equal
to $\tilde{p}_{XX}^{non-ally} - \tilde{p}_{XX}^{ally}$ from (9). Our empirical approach, however, applies to the asymmetric
case, where the movement toward alliances is incomplete. In effect, we have estimated
$\hat{p}_{XX}^{24} - \hat{p}_{XX}^{13}$ from (12). Algebra shows that this fare differential is less than $\tilde{p}_{XX}^{non-ally} - \tilde{p}_{XX}^{ally}$,
which implies that our empirical estimates *understate* the interline fare differential
between a fully allied world and the prealliance situation. Of course, since the model is
highly stylized, this conclusion is merely suggestive. The lesson, however, is that our
estimated fare differential may not accurately predict the ultimate effect of the alliance
revolution, with underprediction of its benefits being one possibility.

---

[36] An overall welfare gain is consistent with the theoretical results of Brueckner, who shows that an alliance
leads to higher consumer surplus over most of the feasible parameter space in his model.

Further work on alliances could focus on estimating a structural model to disentangle supply and demand effects. With closer gates, better-timed connections and merged frequent flier programs, alliances are meant to provide the consumer with a better product than traditional interline travel. Thus, the lower fares we observe are net of any increases due to the effect of stronger demand. In principle, this demand effect could be isolated by a structural model.

APPENDIX

Under the functional form assumptions from Section 2.3, the first-order conditions for the symmetric cases can be written

$$q_{XH}^1 - \frac{1}{\alpha}p_{XH}^1 + \frac{1}{\alpha}[1 - \theta\,(q_{XH}^1 + q_{AB}^1 + 2q_{XX}^{13})] = 0 \tag{A1}$$

$$q_{AB}^1 - \frac{1}{\alpha}p_{AB}^1 + \frac{2}{\alpha}[1 - \theta\,(q_{XH}^1 + q_{AB}^1 + 2q_{XX}^{13})] = 0 \tag{A2}$$

$$\phi q_{XX}^{13} - \frac{1}{\alpha}p_{XX}^{13} + \frac{2}{\alpha}[1 - \theta\,(q_{XH}^1 + q_{AB}^1 + 2q_{XX}^{13})] = 0 \tag{A3}$$

where ϕ equals 1 in the alliance case and 2 in the nonalliance case. Because the equilibria are symmetric, with carriers splitting the traffic in each market, all the traffic variables in (A1)–(A3) are equal to $\frac{1}{2}$. Rearrangement then directly yields (7)–(9).

In the asymmetric case, the first set of equilibrium conditions applies to carrier 1, and it consists of $(a1)$–$(a3)$ with $\phi = 1$. The second set of conditions applies to carrier 2, and it consists of (A1)–(A3) with the carrier superscripts changed from 1 to 2 and from 13 to 24. In addition, ϕ is set equal to 2 to reflect the absence of an alliance. The resulting six-equation system is then augmented with 6 demand relationships based on (6), yielding a 12-equation system that determines 6 fares and 6 traffic levels for carriers 1 and 2. The fare solutions are given by

$$\hat{p}_{XH}^1 = \frac{12\alpha + 6\alpha^2 - 48\theta - 49\alpha\theta + 960\theta^2}{12(\alpha - 4\theta)} \tag{A4}$$

$$\hat{p}_{XH}^2 = \hat{p}_{XH}^1 + \frac{\alpha\theta}{6(\alpha - 4\theta)} \tag{A5}$$

$$\hat{p}_{AB}^1 = \frac{12\alpha + 3\alpha^2 - 48\theta - 37\alpha\theta + 960\theta^2}{6(\alpha - 4\theta)} \tag{A6}$$

$$p_{AB}^2 = \hat{p}_{AB}^1 + \frac{\alpha\theta}{3(\alpha - 4\theta)} \tag{A7}$$

$$\hat{p}_{XX}^{13} = \frac{16\alpha + 5\alpha^2 - 64\theta - 54\alpha\theta + 128\theta^2}{8(\alpha - 4\theta)} \tag{A8}$$

$$\hat{p}_{XX}^{24} = \hat{p}_{XX}^{13} + \frac{\alpha^2 - 2\alpha\theta}{8(\alpha - 4\theta)}. \tag{A9}$$

By symmetry, the domestic fares charged by carriers 3 and 4 are given by (A4)–(A7).

To compare fares in the various markets, the sign of the common denominator expression $\alpha - 4\theta$ in the above solutions must be established. Using the second-order condition for the optimization problems, it can be shown that this expression must be positive.[37] Algebraic manipulation then establishes (10)–(12).

REFERENCES

Borenstein, Severin. "Hubs and High Fares: Dominance and Market Power in the U.S. Airline Industry." *RAND Journal of Economics* 20 (1989): 344–365.

Brueckner, Jan K. "The Economics of International Codesharing: An Analysis of Airline Alliances." Unpublished paper, University of Illinois at Urbana-Champaign, 1997.

Brueckner, Jan K., and Pablo T. Spiller. "Competition and Mergers in Airline Networks." *International Journal of Industrial Organization* 9 (1991): 323–342.

Brueckner, Jan K., and Pablo T. Spiller. "Economies of Traffic Density in the Deregulated Airline Industry." *Journal of Law and Economics* 37 (1994): 379–415.

Brueckner, Jan K., and W. Tom Whalen. "Consumer Welfare Gains from United's Alliances with Lufthansa and SAS." Unpublished paper, University of Illinois at Urbana-Champaign, 1998.

Brueckner, Jan K., and W. Tom Whalen. "Passenger Welfare Gains from the North-west/KLM Alliance," Unpublished paper, University of Illinois at Urbana-Champaign, 1999.

Caves, Douglas W., Laurits R. Christensen, and Michael W. Tretheway. "Economies of Density versus Economies of Scale: Why Trunk and Local Service Costs Differ." *RAND Journal of Economics* 15 (1984): 471–489.

Cities of the World. Chicago: Gale Research Inc., 1993.

Doganis, Rigas. *Flying Off Course: The Economics of International Airlines.* London: George Allen & Unwin, 1985.

Gellman Research Associates. *A Study of International Codesharing.* Washington, D.C.: Office of International Aviation, U.S. Department of Transportion, 1994.

Hendricks, Kenneth, Michele Piccione, and Guo-Fu Tan, "The Economics of Hubs: The Case of Monopoly," *Review of Economic Studies* 28 (1995): 83–99.

Morrison, Steven A., and Clifford Winston. *The Evolution of the Airline Industry.* Washington, D.C.: Brookings Institution, 1995.

Official Airline Guide: Worldwide Addition. Oakbrook, IL: Reed Travel Group, 1997.

Oum, Tae H., Jong-Hun Park, and Anming Zhang. "The Effects of Airline Codesharing Agreements on Firm Conduct and International Air Fares," *Journal of Transport Economics and Policy* 30 (1996): 187–202.

Park, Jong-Hun. "The Effect of Airline Alliances on Markets and Economic Welfare," *Transportation Research-E* 33 (1997): 181–195.

---

[37] The second-order conditions for the allied and nonallied carriers are $\alpha - (7/2)\theta > 0$ and $\alpha - (5/2)\theta > 0$, with the first being more stringent (these are derived from the relevant Hessian matrices). If $\alpha - 4\theta < 0$ holds, then the second-order condition implies $(7/2)\theta < \alpha < 4\theta$. But noting that the q_{AB}^1 solution is given by $(3\alpha - 10\theta)/6(\alpha - 4\theta)$, it follows that $3\alpha - 10\theta < 0$ must then hold for q_{AB}^1 to be positive. However, this implies $\alpha < (10/3)\theta$, which contradicts the previous inequality given $10/3 < 7/2$. With $\alpha - 4\theta$ thus positive, inspection of the other traffic solutions generates a necessary condition ensuring that each is positive. This condition is the stronger inequality $\alpha > (14/3)\theta$. Marginal costs should also be positive, indicating that spoke traffic densities lie on the upward-sloping part of the quadratic cost function. The condition for positive marginal costs is $\alpha > 16\theta(1 - 2\theta)/(4 - 9\theta)$, which also ensures that all fares are positive. It can be shown that this constraint is more restrictive than the previous inequality for large θ's, and less restrictive for small θ's.

Park, Jong-Hun, and Anming Zhang. "Airline Alliances and Partner Firms' Output," *Transportation Research-E* 34 (1998): 245–255.

Park, Jong-Hun, and Anming Zhang. "An Empirical Analysis of Global Airline Alliances: Cases in the North Atlantic Markets," *Review of Industrial Organization*, forthcoming, 1999.

Rand McNally World Atlas Chicago: Rand McNally and Company, 1993.

U.S. General Accounting Office. "Airline Alliances Produce Benefits, But Effect on Competition Is Uncertain." Washington, D.C.: General Accounting Office, 1995.

Youssef, Walleed, and Mark Hansen. "Consequences of Strategic Alliances between International Airlines: The Case of Swissair and SAS," *Transportation Research-A* 28 (1994): 415–431.

Advances in Airline Economics, Vol 1
Darin Lee (Editor)
© 2006 Published by Elsevier B.V.

4

Evidence on Pricing from the Continental Airlines and Northwest Airlines Code-Share Agreement*

Olivier Armantier (Université de Montréal)[†] and
Oliver Richard (U.S. Department of Justice)[‡]

ABSTRACT

Recent code-share agreements among major US airlines represent a significant development in the airline industry, as these agreements allow the partner airlines to sell seats on each other's flights across the US. In this paper, we examine with original data how prices and passenger volumes were affected by the first significant alliance among major US carriers, the 1999 alliance between Continental Airlines and Northwest Airlines. We find evidence of higher passenger volumes and lower prices across markets in which CO-NW code-shared. However, we also find evidence of significantly higher prices across markets with nonstop flights from CO and NW. In these markets, our results suggest that, as CO-NW used their agreement to expand the pool of passengers to whom they can sell seats on their aircraft, they have in turn extracted a higher price, on average. Hence, airlines need not be colluding for prices to rise following code-share agreements. This finding is significant for policy-makers traditionally focus on collusion in their reviews of these agreements.

*We are grateful to Darin Lee and to Russell Pittman for insightful comments. The views expressed in this paper do not reflect the views of the U.S. Department of Justice.

[†]Département de Sciences Economiques, CIRANO, CRT, and CIREQ. Université de Montréal, C.P. 6128, succursale Centre-ville, Montréal QC H3C 3J7. E-mail: olivier.armantier@umontreal.ca.

[‡]Corresponding author: Economic Analysis Group, Antitrust Division, US Department of Justice, 600 E Street N.W., Suite 10000, Washington, DC 20530. E-mail: oliver.richard@usdoj.gov.

1   INTRODUCTION

Recent code-share agreements among major US airlines allow the partner airlines to sell seats on each other's flights across the US.[1] Code-share agreements are common at hub airports and internationally, but the new domestic agreements have distinctive features. Namely, the partner airlines are major rivals in the US and, in contrast to international agreements, they face no constraints on entry and must compete in prices, as they are not granted antitrust exemptions. Airline executives emphasize that the new domestic agreements allow the partner airlines to expand their range of products and introduce significant new competition.[2] Consumer advocates, however, are concerned that they may reduce competition and raise prices. In this paper, we analyze with original panel data how prices and passenger volumes across the US were affected by the first significant code-share agreement among major US carriers, the 1999 alliance between Continental Airlines ("CO") and Northwest Airlines ("NW").

The CO-NW code-share agreement was implemented in 1999, without being challenged by the US Department of Transportation or the US Department of Justice.[3] The agreement presumably remains subject to additional investigation under the antitrust laws, should evidence of significant harm be brought forward. In the present paper, we provide evidence that passenger volumes are higher in markets affected by the CO-NW code-share agreement, and that prices are lower in markets in which CO and NW code-share. These findings are consistent with other evidence on domestic and international code-share agreements.[4] However, in markets where CO and NW have nonstop flights, we find that prices are significantly higher in the post-agreement period. In particular, the code-share agreement allows the partner airlines to expand their flight offerings without addition of aircraft and, thereby, increase the pool of passengers to whom they may sell seats on their aircraft. Our results then suggest that CO and NW have used this expansion to extract a higher price, on average. In other words, our analysis suggests that a code-share arrangement like this one sets up incentives for price increases independent of the question of whether it increases the likelihood of collusion. This finding is significant for policy-makers in their recent reviews of domestic and international alliances have focused on collusion when assessing the potential for price increases.

---

[1] See e.g. Continental Airlines and Northwest Airlines in 1999, US Airways and United Airlines in 2003, and Continental Airlines, Delta Airlines, and Northwest Airlines in 2003.

[2] From Gordon Bethune, chairman and CEO of Continental Airlines: "Our alliance demonstrates how consumers can win when two companies work together to provide our customers a dramatically larger range of services than either of us could offer on our own. We will deliver more choice, more frequencies, and more destinations to the traveling public." Source: Detroit Metro News, 12/1998.

[3] Following the CO-NW proposal, NW also acquired a controlling voting interest in CO equity. In October 1998, the US Department of Justice sued to block NW's acquisition. The matter was settled in November 2000, as NW divested most of its voting interest in CO.

[4] See Ito and Lee (2005a,b) for very insightful discussions of the CO-NW code-share agreement, and Bamberger, Carlton and Neumann (2004) for insights on the regional code-share agreements between CO and America West, as well as NW and Alaska Airlines, which were implemented in 1994–1995. See, e.g., Brueckner and Whalen (2000), Brueckner (2001, 2003), as well as Park and Zhang (2000) for discussions of international alliances. See Bamberger, Carlton and Neumann (2004) for valuable insights on the regional code-share agreements between CO and America West, as well as NW and Alaska Airlines, which were implemented in 1994–1995.

The paper is structured as follows. Section 2 outlines the basics of the CO-NW code-share agreement. Section 3 discusses the empirical methodology, and Section 4 describes the data. In Section 5, we discuss our findings, and we conclude in Section 6.

2   THE CO-NW CODE-SHARE AGREEMENT

A code-share agreement is a form of corporate integration that falls in between a traditional arm's length agreement between competitive airlines (known generally as an interline agreement) and an outright merger. In other words, the term "code-share" can mean as little as one airline allowing another airline to use its designator code to sell seats on its flights in markets in which the second airline does not compete, or as much as a comprehensive integration of marketing and operations that involves joint decisions on price, capacity, schedules, and other competitively sensitive matters. The level of integration ultimately depends on the level of antitrust exemptions they receive. For instance, code-share agreements between foreign airlines in international markets are typically granted partial antitrust immunity on prices, whereas domestic agreements, such as the CO-NW code-share alliance, are not granted any antitrust exemptions.[5]

In January 1998, CO and NW announced their intention to form a code-share agreement across the US.[6] Under the terms of this agreement, each airline is able to market seats on some of its partner's flights. The code-share flights are then listed twice in schedules and computer reservation systems, once by each airline with its own flight number and designator code. Moreover, the partners agree to coordinate flight schedules and operations to provide seamless service on code-share flights (e.g. one-stop check-in, automatic baggage transfers). The carrier operating the code-share flight determines seat availability for the marketing partner, but each airline commits to set prices competitively. All sales revenues go to the operating carrier, and the marketing partner gets only a booking fee to cover handling costs (as travel agents do). Finally, the airlines agree to implement linkages in their frequent-flyer programs.[7]

The principal argument advanced in favor of the code-share agreement was the opportunity for CO and NW to expand both flight offerings and markets served without any addition of aircraft. Executives at CO-NW emphasized that their alliance would not only open new markets to their consumers, but also expand the number of flights in markets in which they already operated. For instance, by pairing two of their existing flights, they would generate new code-share flights in addition to the flights they each already offered. Finally, they claimed that their alliance would promote competition over the US market by creating "a fourth network to compete with the existing 'Big Three' airlines

---

[5] For more details, see Brueckner (2003) and pp.140–142 in Special Report 255, *Entry and Competition in the U.S. Airline Industry*, Transportation Research Board.

[6] See Armantier, Giaume, and Richard (2005b) for an analysis of the airlines' incentives and decisions to code-share in specific markets.

[7] These reciprocal linkages allow a customer to use her frequent flyer miles with one airline to book awards from the other airline, but combining mileage across programs to redeem awards was not allowed in the CO-NW agreement. Hence, a consumer may find it preferable to keep accumulating points in a single program and, thus, book seats on code-share flights through her preferred airline.

in the U.S. .... Over 150 cities, 2,000 city-pairs, and three million passengers will gain a new airline competitor and new on-line connections through the alliance."[8]

These claims were consistent with the evidence on regional and international code-share agreements. For instance, major airlines have long-standing code-share agreements at their hub airports with commuter carriers that serve smaller markets. US airlines, faced with restrictions on entry in foreign markets (cabotage laws), have agreements with foreign carriers that allow them to market flights within their partners' domestic network. CO and America West ("HP"), as well as NW and Alaska Airlines, also formed in 1994–1995 agreements in peripheral US markets in which neither partner had previously competed. Across the literature, these agreements have been associated with lower prices and higher passenger volumes. For instance, Brueckner and Whalen (2000) and Brueckner (2003) find that fares are lower by 8% to 17% in markets in which international airlines code-share, even when these airlines are granted antitrust exemptions on prices. Likewise, Bamberger, Carlton, and Neumann (2004) find that the CO-HP agreement has been pro-competitive, as prices fell and passenger volumes rose by an average of 6% in markets in which these airlines code-shared.

The CO-NW proposal generated much controversy at policy levels, however, prompting numerous hearings on its competitive implications.[9] Indeed, this proposal presented distinctive features. In contrast to regional domestic agreements, it would involve major and rival airlines across the US. In contrast to international agreements, CO and NW would face no restrictions on entry across the US, and they would have to compete in prices. Hence, key concerns were that the implementation of the alliance would lower the incentives of CO and NW i) to enter markets in which only one of the partners already operated, ii) to maintain competing flights in markets in which they jointly operated, and iii) to compete in prices. In October 1998, the US Congress granted the US Department of Transportation (DOT) the authority to delay the implementation of domestic alliances pending a review of their effects. In November 1998, the DOT decided to allow the implementation of the alliance without a formal investigation, after CO and NW consented not to code-share flights in markets between their respective hub airports. The CO-NW code-share agreement then became effective in the US in January 1999. The DOT presumably retained the right, however, to investigate the agreement after data become available, to ensure that the alliance is not anti-competitive.

3   EMPIRICAL ANALYSIS

A market is defined as a pair of airports in a quarter. Markets are non-directional. For example, the airport-pairs Miami-Pittsburgh in quarter t and Pittsburgh-Miami in quarter t are the same market. A product in a market is a round-trip ticket for a seat on a sequence of flights (i.e. itinerary) between the two airports in the market. The product is either i) nonstop if it consists of a single flight each way, or ii) connecting if it requires at least one transfer at an intermediate airport. When the airline marketing the product

---

[8] See p. 6, Statement by Hershel I. Kamen, from CO, to the U.S. Senate, 06/04/98.

[9] See, e.g., Statement from Joel Klein, Department of Justice (DOJ), to the Senate Committee on Commerce, Science, and Transportation, 03/12/99.

is the airline operating the flights in the product, as is common in practice, then the product is said to be online. When the airline marketing the product differs from the airline actually operating one of the flights in the product, then the product is either i) a code-share if the two airlines have a domestic code-share agreement, or ii) an interline if the two airlines have no such agreement.[10]

We say that the partner airlines code-share *in* a market if they have code-share products *in* that market. We say that the partner airlines code-share *through* a market if a partner airline operates nonstop flights in the market and the itinerary of a code-share product includes one of these flights. For example, assume that CO pairs a nonstop flight that it operates in a market A-B together with a nonstop flight that NW operates in a market B-C to form a connecting code-share product in market A-C. In other words, a passenger buying this connecting code-share product takes CO's flight between A and B and NW's flight between B and C.[11] Then we say that CO-NW code-share *through* market A-B because the itinerary of the code-share product in market A-C includes CO's nonstop flight in A-B. Likewise, in this example, CO-NW code-share *through* market B-C. Following the code-share agreement, CO may then use the new connecting code-share product in market A-C to sell seats in its A-B aircraft, and it may carry in its A-B aircraft i) passengers from market A-B who buy CO's nonstop product in A-B, and ii) passengers from market A-C who buy the connecting code-share product in A-C. In that regard, the code-share agreement may set up incentives to increase the demand for seats in an aircraft that an airline operates and, therefore, affect the airline's prices and passenger volume. Indeed, throughout the listing of a flight schedule, airlines use sophisticated *yield management* techniques to allocate seats on aircraft to any of a number of passengers with different valuations or origin and destination airports, as to maximize revenues (see, e.g., Boyd 1998 and Netessine and Shumsky 2004).

In the present paper, we examine how airline prices and passenger volumes varied with the set of products that each airline supplied in an airport-pair following the CO-NW code-share agreement. Specifically, we estimate the following models on panel data that overlap the implementation of the CO-NW code-share agreement:

$$Y_{i,t} = X_{i,t}\beta + Z_t\gamma + \mu_{i,t} + \varepsilon_{i,t}, \tag{1}$$

where i indexes the airline and t indexes the market. The dependent variables $Y_{i,t}$ are either i) $PRICE_{i,t}$, the mean ticket price paid by passengers, or ii) $PASS_{i,t}$, the number of passengers. The μ's are fixed-effects for each of the airline, airport-pair, and quarter,

---

[10] Given the focus is on alliances among major airlines, these definitions only apply to products where the carriers are major airlines. When the operating carrier is a commuter carrier that has a regional code-share agreement with the major airline marketing the product, then the product is solely associated to the major airline.

[11] Travelling between A and C was previously possible by purchasing an A-B ticket from CO and a B-C ticket from NW. Such trip arrangements are extremely rare in practice (see Morrison and Winston 1995), as they entail unfavorable features such as the need for double booking, multiple check-ins, longer distance between connecting gates, lack of responsibilities by carriers in case of missed connection or lost luggage, but mostly, higher prices. In contrast, the code-share A-C product is sold as a virtual online product with seamless service and, under the terms of the agreement, competitive prices.

respectively.[12] The $\varepsilon_{i,t}$ is an i.i.d. error term with zero mean. The $X_{i,t}$ and Z_t vectors consist, respectively, in airline and market attributes, and they are subsequently described in Section 4.2.

4 DATA

4.1 Sample Data

The data are for the period 1998 through 2001, which spans the 1999 implementation of the CO-NW code-share agreement. The data consist of quarterly data on flight schedules and prices obtained, respectively, from the US Department of Transportation ("DOT") and the Official Airline Guide (OAG).[13] The DOT data is the Origin-Destination Survey Databank 1B. This Databank is a 10% random sample of tickets sold by US airlines for travel in a quarter. A key feature of Databank 1B, relative to the routinely used Databank 1A, is that it reports each of the operating and marketing carriers, which makes it possible to identify separately online, code-share, and interline tickets. From the observed round-trip tickets, we obtain the number of passengers and mean price per airline in a market.[14] Following Evans and Kessides (1993), we include an airline in a market if the airline has at least 18 passengers in the DOT data (corresponding to an average of 180 in a quarter) and a 1% share of all passengers in the market. The OAG data list the time and itinerary for flights supplied by commercial US airlines. From this schedule, we construct the product set that each airline may supply in a market, and we identify which of these products include which nonstop flight.[15] When the set of products including a CO or NW nonstop flight contains CO-NW code-share products, then we say that CO-NW code-share *through* the market that includes the nonstop flight.[16] We then take our sample data to include airport-pairs between metropolitan areas in the continental US. Descriptive sample statistics are provided in Table 1. The sample data include 1,893 airport-pairs, 29 airlines, and a total of 46,679 airline-market observations. A market averages 288.6 products, 3.7 airlines, and 1385.3 passengers (corresponding to an average of 13,853 passengers in a quarter).

---

[12] For parsimony in the presentation, the indices for airport-pairs and quarters are represented under a single "market" indice t. There are no fixed-effects for the "market" itself in the model, rather there are separate fixed-effects for each of the airport-pair and quarter.

[13] The data are for the 1st quarters of 1998 through 2001, and the 3rd quarters of 1998 through 2000 (7 quarters in total; see http://www.sceco.umontreal.ca/liste_personnel/armantier/index.htm. for details).

[14] We use Borenstein and Rose (1994)'s guidelines to screen unusually high and low ticket prices.

[15] The flight schedule is constructed based on an airline's presence in a market, irrespective of which ticket itineraries are observed for that airline in that market in the DOT data. Following the General Accounting Office (see p. 42 in 2000 report RCED-99-37), we consider connecting products with a transit time at each intermediate airport of at least 30 minutes and no more than 150 minutes. Following Armantier and Richard (2003), we consider connecting products with at most one stop each way.

[16] We hereby recognize that it is the size and mix of the set of *potential* marketing opportunities for flights, not just *realized* ones, that matter. Indeed, assume that an airline has one available seat. Consider two cases: i) the airline has a single potential customer A; and ii) the airline has two potential customers, A and B. Even if we observe that the airline sold the seat to customer A in both cases, its price to customer A may differ across both cases. Indeed, the opportunity cost of not selling the seat in i) is an empty seat, whereas the opportunity cost in ii) may include selling the seat to customer B.

Table 1 Descriptive Sample Statistics

	Aggregates per Market (12,538 markets)				
Variables	Mean (Standard dev.)	Minimum Maximum	Variables	Mean (Standard dev.)	Minimum Maximum
Number of Passengers*	13, 853.3 (17,905.5)	18 16,358	Number of Airlines	3.74 (1.96)	1 10
Mean Price per Passenger ($)	336.81 (130.82)	66.33 1104.05	Number of Products	288.61 (347.17)	1 4,588

	Level Variables in the Model (46,679 observations)				
Variable	Mean (Standard dev.)	Minimum Maximum	Variable	Mean (Standard dev.)	Minimum Maximum
price ($)	342.88 (129.81)	75.36 1231.79	flights	2.27 (5.13)	0 65
pass	367.83 (780.63)	18 13262	flight_online_in	2.38 (5.24)	0 47.53
online_in	68.17 (113.69)	0 2256	flight_online_thru	16.08 (45.70)	0 523.75
csconw_in	6.64 (54.51)	0 1447	flight_csconw_thru	2.22 (22.47)	0 755.3
cscohp_in	2.07 (22.98)	0 981	flight_cscohp_thru	0.83 (12.11)	0 627.4
interline_in	0.65 (19.01)	0 1578	flight_interline_thru	0.18 (2.01)	0 136.5
traveltime_in	602.13 (213.62)	80 1156.1	share	0.16 (0.13)	0 0.91
			herf	0.44 (0.21)	0.12 1

*Predicted quarterly average from DB1B (i.e. value observed in Databank 1B multiplied by 10).

The CO-NW agreement became effective in the US in January 1999. The fraction of markets in which at least one of CO or NW sold tickets increased by 5% between 1998 and 2001, and the fraction of markets in which both CO and NW were present increased by 8%. The number of airport-pairs with nonstop flights from both CO and NW increased from 4 in 1998 to 9 in 2000, which represented only 3% of all airport-pairs where CO and NW had nonstop flights in 2000.[17] As a group, CO and NW supplied only 0.3% of their markets solely with code-share products; that is, without online products.

---

[17] The 9 airport-pairs with nonstop flights from both CO and NW are the ones that pair their respective hub airports together, which are Detroit, Minneapolis-St Paul, and Memphis for NW and Cleveland, Houston, and Newark for CO.

In that regard, this alliance differs notably from traditional regional and international agreements, in which the partners essentially code-share products in markets where none of them would otherwise operate.

We observe that CO and NW code-shared products *in* 26% of the airport-pairs in which at least one of the two airlines was present in 2000–2001. When CO-NW code-shared *in* an airport-pair, an average of 9% of CO-NW passengers used a code-share ticket. CO-NW also code-shared *through* 81% of the markets where they had nonstop flights in 2000–2001. When CO-NW code-shared *through* a market, then the number of products marketing each nonstop flight increased by 136%, and 48% of these products were CO-NW code-share products, on average. Besides its code-share agreement with NW, CO also had a code-share agreement with America West ("HP") during the period 1998 to 2001.[18] In that period, CO and HP code-shared flights in 6.6% of the markets in which at least one of the two airlines was present and, when CO-HP code-shared *in* a market, an average of 9.8% of their passengers used a code-share ticket.

4.2   Variables in the Model

We include in the vector $X_{i,t}$ in (3.1) variables that describe the set of products for airline *i in* market *t*:

– *online_in$_{i,t}$*, the number of online products for the airline in the market. As more products provide more flight options, we expect demand for travel with the airline to increase with the number of products, resulting in higher prices and quantities.
– *csconw_in$_{i,t}$*, the number of CO-NW code-share products in the market. This variable only applies to CO, NW in markets *in* which they code-share. We expect the demand for travel with the airline to increase with the number of code-share products. Competition between the partner airlines may mitigate any price increases as code-share products may be marketed by both airlines.
– *cscohp_in$_{i,t}$*, the number of CO-HP code-share products in the market. This variable only applies to CO, HP in markets *in* which they code-share.
– *interline_in$_{i,t}$*, the number of interline products for the airline in the market.
– *traveltime_in$_{i,t}$*, the average travel time (including transit times) across the airline's products in the market.

When airline *i* operates nonstop flights in market *t*, we have the following variables to denote the set of products marketing these flights:

– *flights$_{i,t}$*, the number of nonstop flights for the airline; and
– *flight_online_in$_{i,t}$*, the number of online products in market *t* that have their customers use a nonstop flight from airline *i* in market *t*, divided by the number of

---

[18] This agreement was implemented in 1994–1995. Alaska Airlines ("AS") and NW also had a domestic code-share agreement at the time, but its presence was negligible in our sample data. For parsimony, we aggregate AS-NW code-share products together with interline products. This is of no significance for our results.

nonstop flights for airline i in market t.[19] In other words, this variable represents the average number of online products *in* the market that may be used by the airline to sell seats on each of its aircraft in the market (i.e. this variable and the following ones are computed on a per-flight basis). How a change in this variable may affect prices and quantities is not clear, a priori. There is evidence of economies of density in the airline industry, whereby a larger passenger volume may be accommodated by larger planes that have a lower cost per passenger.[20] Hence, an increase in the set of products that may be used to sell seats on an aircraft may afford an airline better opportunities to exploit economies of density and lower costs. On the other hand, following yield management practices, an increase in the pool of passengers to whom a seat may be sold may enable an airline, depending on its (lack of) capacity adjustments, to extract a higher yield per passenger.[21]

- *flight_online_thru*$_{i,t}$, the per-flight number of online connecting products *in* markets other than market t that include as part of their itinerary a nonstop flight from airline i in market t (i.e. passengers buying these products fly on a nonstop flight from airline i *through* market t as part of their itinerary).
- *flight_csconw_thru*$_{i,t}$, the per-flight number of CO-NW code-share products that include as part of their itinerary a nonstop flight from airline i in market t. This variable only applies to CO, NW.
- *flight_cscohp_thru*$_{i,t}$, the per-flight number of CO-HP code-share products that include as part of their itinerary a nonstop flight from airline i in market t. This variable only applies to CO, HP.
- *flight_interline_thru*$_{i,t}$, the per-flight number of interline products that include as part of their itinerary a nonstop flight from airline i in market t.

The code-share *through* variable *flight_csconw_thru* is specific to markets where CO-NW have nonstop flights. To ensure that systematic variations (e.g. in costs) that are specific to CO-NW's operation of nonstop flights are not attributed by default to this variable, we include the following dummy variables:

- *dum_conw*$_{i,t}$, which equals 1 for CO or NW when it has nonstop flights.
- *dum_conw_expost*$_{i,t}$, which equals 1 for CO or NW when it has nonstop flights and the period is 1999 to 2001. This variable captures any change in *dum_conw*$_{i,t}$ in the post-agreement period.
- *dum_csconw*$_{i,t}$, which equals 1 for CO or NW when it has nonstop flights and this is an airport-pair *through* which CO-NW code-share ex-post their agreement. This variable captures any change in *dum_conw*$_{i,t}$ for airport-pairs *through* which CO-NW code-share.

---

[19] These online products include nonstop products in the market as well as connecting products where the outbound (inbound, respectively) itinerary is a single nonstop flight and the inbound (outbound, respectively) itinerary requires a stop at an intermediate airport.

[20] See Caves, Christensen, and Tretheway 1984, Brueckner, Dyer and Spiller 1992, and Brueckner and Spiller 1994

[21] Capacity adjustments may include a change in the number of seats supplied or in the fraction of seats filled by passengers at take-off (i.e. load factor). We have no reliable data on either measures.

- $dum\_csconw\_thru_{i,t}$, which equals 1 for CO or NW when it code-shares *through* the market (i.e. when $flight\_csconw\_thru_{i,t} > 0$). This variable captures any change in $dum\_csconw_{i,t}$ ex-post the agreement, beyond that already captured by $dum\_conw\_expost_{i,t}$.

We also denote the presence of code-sharing with the following dummy variables:[22]

- $dum\_csconw\_in_{i,t}$, which equals 1 for CO, NW when they code-share *in* a market; that is, when $csconw\_in_{i,t} > 0$.
- $dum\_cscohp\_in_{i,t}$, which equals 1 when $cscohp\_in_{i,t} > 0$.
- $dum\_cscohp\_thru_{i,t}$, which equals 1 when $cscohp\_thru_{i,t} > 0$.

Finally, the vectors $X_{i,t}$ and Z_t include measures of airline presence and of competitive interactions:

- $dum\_nonstop_{i,t}$ which equals 1 when $nonstop_{i,t}$ is greater than 0;
- $dum\_connect_{i,t}$, which equals 1 when the airline has connecting products;
- $share_{i,t-1}$ is the airline's average share of passenger enplanements at the endpoint airports in the market, lagged by one quarter. Following Borenstein (1989, 1991), we recognize that a larger airport presence may confer an airline greater visibility and allow it to offer a wide array of services and options.
- $herf_t$ is the Hirschmann-Herfindal Index ("HHI", measured as 0 to 1) for passenger enplanements across airlines in the market. As is common in antitrust work, this variable is used as a proxy for competitive interactions. The variable $herf_t$ is endogenous, and we use the following instruments: i) lagged values $herf_{t-1}$ and $herf_{t-2}$, ii) $comp_t$, the number of airline present in the market, and iii) $hairp_t$, the average of the HHI (measured as 0 to 1) for passenger enplanements at the endpoint airports in the market.[23]
- $strike_{i,t}$ is a dummy variable equal to 1 in the 3rd quarter of 1998 for NW in markets where NW competed in the 1st quarter of 1998. This variable should capture the impact that the NW strike may have had during that period. We also interact the variable $strike_{i,t}$ with each of $online\_in_{i,t}$ and $in\_nonstop_{i,t}$.

5 RESULTS

Estimation results are listed in Table 2.[24] Given the large number of observations, we use a 1% level to test for statistical significance. The models fit the data well, with R-square

---

[22] Similar dummy variables were defined for interline products, but they were not statistically significant at standard levels. For parsimony, they were dropped from the model.

[23] $HAIRP_{j,t} = \sum_i (SHAIRP_{i,t} / \sum_i SHAIRP_{i,t})^2$, where both summations apply to all airlines i present in market t.

[24] We consider a simple version of the model that estimates a single parameter, common to all airlines, for each variable, as well as a full version that allows for the parameters to differ across airlines. The estimation results for the simple version are representative, and allowing for the coefficients on the product variables to differ across airlines does not affect the net effect of the code-share variables. Accordingly, we discuss the estimation results for the simple version. The prediction results, listed in Table 3, are computed from the full version, which includes an additional 168 parameters.

Table 2 Estimation Results

Regression for:	Price	Pass		Price	Pass
Variables	Estimate (Standard error)	Estimate (Standard error)	Variables (continued)	Estimate (Standard error)	Estimate (Standard error)
online_in	0.126 (0.007)*	0.412 (0.028)*	dum_cscohp_thru	−14.521 (3.771)*	51.184 (15.844)*
csconw_in	0.015 (0.008)	0.035 (0.035)	dum_nonstop	2.060 (2.681)	−120.299 (11.266)*
cscohp_in	0.145 (0.024)*	0.095 (0.100)	dum_connect	26.237 (2.541)*	274.064 (10.679)*
interline_in	0.012 (0.017)	0.041 (0.072)	share	190.281 (5.742)*	28.762 (24.127)
dum_csconw_in	−4.689 (2.397)	−7.206 (10.072)	herf	253.403 (14.460)*	−142.404 (60.761)
dum_cscohp_in	6.560 (4.245)	30.067 (17.838)	strike	−18.933 (5.797)*	−20.746 (24.361)
traveltime_in	−0.149 (0.008)*	−0.689 (0.034)*	strike*online_in	0.302 (0.082)*	−0.335 (0.344)
flights	−1.068 (0.207)*	119.917 (0.869)*	strike*flights	3.174 (0.946)*	−30.938 (3.974)*
flight_online_in	−0.707 (0.279)	14.946 (1.171)*	1998 quarter 1	9.443 (1.315)*	−14.445 (5.524)*
flight_online_thru	0.120 (0.015)*	−0.749 (0.064)*	1998 quarter 3	−10.274 (1.251)*	13.604 (5.258)*
flight_csconw_thru	0.150 (0.023)*	−0.579 (0.095)*	1998 quarter 1	2.657 (1.243)	−12.857 (5.222)
flight_cscohp_thru	0.013 (0.042)	−0.390 (0.175)	1998 quarter 3	−14.454 (1.219)*	10.144 (5.122)
flight_interline_thru	0.069 (0.173)	−0.856 (0.726)	2000 quarter 1	8.025 (1.216)*	−4.179 (5.111)
dum_conw	−15.979 (8.817)	−135.865 (37.051)*	2000 quarter 3	−4.026 (1.217)*	15.537 (5.113)*
dum_conw_expost	23.551 (5.484)*	−59.025 (23.043)			
dum_csconw	−0.316 (8.580)	261.401 (36.055)*			
dum_csconw_thru	17.450 (5.497)*	91.194 (23.099)*	R^2	0.73	0.87

*indicates statistical significance at a 1% level.

values of 0.76 for the price regression and 0.90 for the passenger one. Coefficients on product, airline, and market variables have the expected signs, which are consistent with findings in the literature. For example, airport presence (*share*) increases prices but not necessarily passenger volumes, suggesting the exercise of market power.[25] We also find that a larger set of online products in a market (*online_in*) is associated with higher prices and passenger volumes, and that nonstop flights (*flights*) are associated with substantially larger passenger volumes (see, e.g., Morrison and Winston 1995, and Richard 2003).[26] This finding is consistent with the DOT data, where we observe that 94% of an airline's passengers fly nonstop, on average, when the airline has nonstop products in a market.

When CO-NW code-share *in* a market, we find that, all else equal, the CO-NW code-share variables are not associated with statistically significant changes in prices and quantities. Indeed, the number of CO-NW code-share products *in* a market (*csconw_in*), and the related dummy variable (*dum_csconw_in*), are not statistically significant in the price and passenger regressions. In contrast, CO's and HP's mean prices and passenger volume in a market are found to be higher the greater the number of their code-share products (*cscohp_in, dum_cscohp_in*).[27] In the DOT data, we observe that CO-HP ultimately code-shared more nonstop products than CO-NW did, as 8.2% of the itineraries that CO-HP code-shared in the DOT data were nonstop compared to only 0.7% for CO-NW.

To determine the net effect of the CO-NW agreement on prices and passenger volumes, we compute the mean prices and passenger volumes that obtain from the model at the estimated coefficient values and the observed values for the right-hand side variables. Within an airport-pair, these predicted values are compared across a pre-agreement and a post-agreement period, where the pre-agreement (post-agreement, respectively) spans all quarters preceding (following, respectively) the start of the code share agreement in that airport-pair.[28] In airport-pairs where CO-NW do not code-share, predictions for 1998 are compared to those for the period 1999 to 2001. Results are listed in Table 3.

Across airport-pairs *in* which CO-NW code-shared, we predict that CO-NW's mean prices were lower by 3.2%, and CO-NW's passenger volumes were higher by 12.3%, in the post-agreement period. For reference, across airport-pairs where CO-NW *never* code-shared, we predict that CO-NW's mean prices were lower by 1.1% during the period 1999 to 2001 relative to 1998, and CO-NW's passenger volumes also were lower by 6.2%. Hence, the prediction results indicate lower prices and higher passenger

---

[25] See, e.g., Berry 1990, Borenstein 1989, 1991, Evans and Kessides 1993.

[26] Nonstop flights are factored in each of the variables *nonstop* and *online_in*. An additional nonstop flight from A to B in airport-pair A-B increases the number of products proportionately to the number of nonstop and connecting flights from B to A. The negative sign on *nonstop* in the price regression may indicate, in this reduced form analysis, that airlines price lower on their demand curve when they have nonstop flights in a market.

[27] The net effect of the *cscohp_in* and *dum_cscohp_in* is a statistically significant increase in passenger volume, in that should either of these variables be removed then the remaining variable becomes significant. The same is not true for the CO-NW code-share variables.

[28] Mean values are computed net of fixed-effects for the quarters and of the *strike* terms, as to control for exogenous variations over time. In the period following the start of the agreement in a market, we only take into consideration the quarters during which CO-NW code-share. A before/after comparison is informative in this paper as at least one of CO or NW is present in 1998 in 97.5% of the airport-pairs *in* which and *through* which they code-share following their agreement.

Table 3 Prediction Results

	Airport-pairs where CO-NW never code-shared	Airport-pairs *in* which CO-NW code-shared	Airport-pairs *through* which CO-NW code-shared
	Post-agreement change (% of pairs with change > 0)	Post-agreement change (% of pairs with change > 0)	Post-agreement change (% of pairs with change > 0)
CO-NW's mean prices	−1.1% (31.5%)	−3.2% (10.5%)	13.6% (94.0%)
CO-NW's passenger volume	−6.2% (36.5%)	12.3% (68.3%)	6.7% (61.6%)
Mean prices across all airlines in airport-pair	−0.5% (41.9%)	−2.8% (16.6%)	10.7% (89.8%)
Passenger volume across all airlines in airport-pair	5.4% (56.8%)	10.5% (73.0%)	10.3% (65.9%)

*Change = (post-agreement mean value − pre-agreement mean value)/pre-agreement mean value.

volumes for CO-NW when they code-shared *in* a market. These results are consistent with Ito and Lee (2005a,b). Interestingly, this increase in passenger volume across airport-pairs *in* which CO-NW code-shared may mostly be traced, not to the CO-NW code-share products in the market (see the previous paragraph), but to an increase in the number of times CO and NW were both present in a market in the post-agreement period. In particular, the number of times that both CO and NW were present in a market increased by 25% following their agreement across airport-pairs *in* which they code-shared, whereas it was unchanged across airport-pairs where they *never* code-shared. Hence, the total number of online products supplied by CO-NW, as a group, increased by 27% in the post-agreement period across airport-pairs *in* which they code-shared, whereas it increased by 16% across all other airport-pairs where they were present.

In the price regression, the coefficient values on the dummy variables *dum_conw_expost* and *dum_csconw_thru* are statistically significant. This means that, across airport-pairs where CO-NW had nonstop flights, we estimate a fixed, statistically significant increase in prices in the post-agreement period, and this increase was relatively larger across airport-pairs *through* which CO-NW code-shared.[29] The sum of the coefficient values on *dum_csconw_thru* and *dum_conw_expost* in the passenger

---

[29] The estimated increases are on the order of (i) $23.6 across airport-pairs where they never code-shared *through* (see *dum_conw_expost*), and (ii) $41.0 (i.e. $41 = $23.6 + $17.4) across airport-pairs *through* which CO-NW code-shared (see *dum_conw_expost* + *dum_csconw_thru*).

regression is not statistically significant, however (p-value=0.11). This means that we estimate that there was no statistically significant fixed change in passenger volume across the pre-agreement and post-agreement periods in airport-pairs *through* which CO-NW code-shared.

The results also indicate that an airline's prices and quantities in a market where it has nonstop flights vary with the set of products that sell seats on these aircraft. In particular, we find that the coefficient on the variable *flight_online_thru* is statistically significant and positive (negative, respectively) in the price (passenger, respectively) regression. This means that prices and passenger volumes *in* a market are, all else equal, adversely affected by an increase in the average number of online connecting products that may be used to sell seats on an aircraft in the market. In other words, this suggests that passengers who buy nonstop products and passengers who buy connecting products may, at the margin, be substitute passengers for the same seat on an aircraft. Likewise, in markets *through* which CO-NW code-shared, we find that an increase in the average number of CO-NW code-share products that market seats on a CO-NW aircraft (*flight_csconw_thru*) is associated with higher prices and lower passenger volumes for CO and NW *in* the market. These findings therefore indicate that, as the set of products that may be used to sell seats on an aircraft in a market increases, the airline may ask for higher prices from its passengers *in* the market, as we might expect under effective yield management practices.

We estimate that the effects associated with the level of code-sharing *through* a market are non-trivial. Indeed, at sample mean values, we find that, all else equal, the effect of the variable *flight_csconw_thru* represents i) a 4.4% increase in CO-NW's mean prices, and ii) a 6.2% decrease in passenger volume across airport-pairs *through* which CO-NW code-shared. Hence, in the case of the CO-NW agreement, the level of code-sharing *through* a market is associated with significant price increases and, at the margin, passenger decreases in that market.

Turning more generally to price and passenger predictions, we predict that, following the implementation of the code-share agreement, CO-NW's mean prices were higher by 13.6%, which represents a significant increase over predicted changes across other airport-pairs (see Table 3). We also predict that CO-NW's passenger volume was higher by 6.7% following their agreement across airport-pairs *through* which they code-shared. This increase is lower than that across airport-pairs *in* which they code-shared, but greater than that across airport-pairs where they *never* code-shared. Interestingly, we predict that the code-share *through* variables (i.e. *flight_csconw_thru* and *dum_csconw_thru*) are associated, all else equal, with i) a net 10.6% increase in CO-NW's mean prices and ii) a net 0.6% decrease in CO-NW's passenger volume.[30] In particular, the increase in passenger volume across airport-pairs *through* which CO-NW code-shared may mostly

---

[30] Under our interpretation that the changes associated with code-sharing *through* a market result from more effective yield management following the code-share agreement, there is no reason to necessarily expect a net decline in passenger volumes, since net changes in volumes also depend on capacity adjustments. We found evidence of a general increase in products supplied following the agreement and of a decrease, at the margin, in volume associated with the level of code-sharing *through* the market. Such changes are consistent with our interpretation of the findings. Note that in 1999, Continental Chairman and CEO Gordon Bethune stated that the CO-NW alliance had been "hugely beneficial" bringing $80 million revenues in 1999, $20 million more than expected (Source: Aviation Week and Space Technology, 01/24/00).

be traced to an increase in the post-agreement period in the number of nonstop flights supplied by CO-NW across these airport-pairs. Indeed, in the OAG data, we observe that CO-NW increased their number of nonstop flights in the post agreement period by 8.8% across airport-pairs *through* which they code-shared, and by 5.3% only across all other airport-pairs.

Aggregating across all airlines in a market, we predict prices that were higher by 10.7%, on average, in the post-agreement period across airport-pairs *through* which CO-NW code-shared. We also predict a mean increase of 10.3% in the total passenger volume, which is comparable to the increase across airport-pairs *in* which CO-NW code-shared. Hence, as CO-NW raised their prices in airport-pairs *through* which they code-shared, other airlines gained in passenger volumes.

Finally, our results on code-sharing *through* a market are robust to alternative specifications. For instance, consider the following model. The dependent variable is $\ln(price_{i,t})$ for the price regression and $\ln(pass_{i,t})$ for the passenger regression. The right-hand side variables include the previously defined (see Section 4.2) dummy variables $dum\_nonstop_{i,t}$, $dum\_csconw_{i,t}$, $dum\_csconw\_thru_{i,t}$, as well as airport-pair, airline, and quarter fixed effects. We also include a new variable: $csconw\_thru\_share_{i,t}$, which is defined for each of CO and NW as the fraction of all products that market CO-NW's non-stop flights that are CO-NW code-share products.[31] This variable proxies for the level of code-sharing *through* the market. Results are in Table 4. In the log-price (log-passenger,

Table 4 Estimation Results for the Alternative Model

Regression for:	In(price)	In(pass)		In(price)	In(pass)
Variables	Estimate (Standard error)	Estimate (Standard error)	Variables (continued)	Estimate (Standard error)	Estimate (Standard error)
dum_nonstop	0.105 (0.003)*	2.234 (0.011)*	1998 quarter 1	0.015 (0.003)*	−0.064 (0.012)*
csconw_thru_share	0.106 (0.031)*	−0.612 (0.115)*	1998 quarter 3	−0.041 (0.003)*	0.050 (0.012)*
dum_csconw	0.056 (0.009)*	0.653 (0.032)*	2000 quarter 1	0.013 (0.003)*	−0.039 (0.012)*
dum_csconw_thru	0.056 (0.017)*	0.329 (0.065)*	2000 quarter 3	−0.025 (0.003)*	0.069 (0.011)*
1998 quarter 1	0.023 (0.003)*	−0.100 (0.012)*			
1998 quarter 3	−0.028 (0.003)*	0.030 (0.012)*	R^2	0.70	0.76

* indicates statistical significance at a 1% level.

---

[31] $csconw\_thru\_share = flight\_thru\_csconw/(flight\_online\_in + flight\_online\_thru + flight\_csconw\_thru + flight\_cscohp\_thru + flight\_interline\_thru)$.

respectively) regression, the estimated coefficient value on *csconw_thru_share* is positive (negative, respectively) and statistically significant. In other words, we again estimate that the level of code-sharing *through* a market increased, at the margin, CO-NW's mean prices and lowered their passenger volumes. At the sample value for *thru_csconw_share* (i.e. 0.48, when positive), we estimate that the effect of the variable *csconw_thru_share* represents a 5.1% increase in CO-NW's mean prices in airport-pairs *through* which they code-shared, which is comparable to the 4.4% increase estimated from our results in Table 3. Computing predictions from the alternative model, we predict that, across airport-pairs *through* which CO-NW code-shared, mean prices for CO-NW were higher by 11.2% in the post-agreement period, and their passenger volume was also higher by 9.5%. These prediction results are in line with those obtained from our model in Table 3, and they attest to the robustness of our findings.

6 CONCLUSION

When Continental Airlines and Northwest Airlines announced in 1998 that they were forming the most significant code-share alliance in the US, expectations among analysts were that the alliance would lead to lower prices and higher traffic volumes. Such a development would have been consistent with the evidence on other code-share agreements at the time. Using a comprehensive and original panel data set, we provided mixed evidence on this matter. We found that passenger volumes were higher across markets affected by the CO-NW code-share agreement, and that CO-NW's mean prices were lower across markets *in* which they code-shared following their agreement. However, we also found evidence of significant price increases across markets with nonstop flights from CO and NW, with prices rising by an average of 13.6%.

The literature on international alliances highlights as well some evidence of higher prices in markets with nonstop flights from both alliance airlines (see Brueckner and Whalen 2000). The suggestion in that literature is that, as international airlines are granted some partial antitrust exemptions on prices, they may collude more generally. The CO-NW alliance, however, has been granted no antitrust exemptions. In fact, not only do CO and NW both offer nonstop flights in just a handful of the same markets, but also our estimation results put forth evidence of lower prices across markets *in* which they code-share. In this paper, we made no claims of collusion. Instead, we provided evidence that CO and NW used their code-share agreement to increase the demand for seats in their aircraft. In conjunction with this increase, then, and consistent with yield management practices, our results suggested that CO-NW maximized revenues, thereby increasing prices.

These findings therefore suggest that greater emphasis be placed on identifying how changes in product offerings in markets *in* which the alliance airlines code-share may in turn adversely affect prices in markets in which the alliance airlines do not code-share. This suggestion is particularly relevant in that policy reviews of the recent domestic code-share agreements, such as the 1999 CO-NW, the 2003 Delta-CO-NW, and the 2003 United-US Airways agreements, focused on the overlap in markets served by the alliance partners, and on the potential for collusion in prices in markets *in* which the alliance airlines code-share. It remains that the reduced-form analysis in the present paper does not allow us to draw unambiguous conclusions on changes in consumer welfare following the CO-NW code-share agreement. To address adequately welfare issues, we need a structural model of demand that accounts for the multi-dimensional effects of the CO-NW agreement on consumer choices. The model in Armantier and Richard (2005a) may offer a blueprint for such an analysis.

REFERENCES

Armantier, O. and Richard, O., 2003, 'Exchanges of Cost Information in the Airline Industry', *RAND Journal of Economics*, 34, 461–477.

Armantier, O. and Richard, O., 2005a, 'Domestic Airline Alliances and Consumer Welfare', Université de Montréal, mimeo.

Armantier, O., Giaume, S. and Richard, O., 2005b, 'An Empirical Analysis of Code-Share Decisions in the Continental and Northwest Airlines Alliance', Université de Montréal, mimeo.

Bamberger G., Carlton, D. and Neumann, L., 2004, 'An Empirical Investigation of the Competitive Effects of Domestic Airline Alliances', *Journal of Law and Economics*, vol. XLVII, pp. 195–222.

Berry, S., 1990, 'Airport Presence as Product Differentiation', *American Economic Review, Papers and Proceedings*, 80, 394–399.

Borenstein, S., 1989, 'Hubs and High Fares: Dominance and Market Power in the U.S. Airline Industry', *RAND Journal of Economics*, 20, 344–365.

Borenstein, S., 1991, 'The Dominant-Firm Advantage in Multiproduct Industries: Evidence from the U.S. Airline Industry', *Quarterly Journal of Economics*, 106, 1245–1265.

Borenstein, S. and Rose, N., 1994, "Competition and Price Dispersion in the U.S. Airline Industry", *Journal of Political Economy*, 102, 653–683.

Boyd, A., 1998, 'Airline Alliances', *OR/MS Today*, October 1998.

Brueckner, J., 2001, 'The Economics of International Codesharing: An Analysis of Airline Alliances', *International Journal of Industrial Organization*, 19, 1475–1498.

Brueckner, J., 2003, 'International Airfares in the Age of Alliances: The Effects to Codesharing and Antitrust Immunity', *The Review of Economics and Statistics*, 85, 105–118.

Brueckner, J., Dyer, N. and Spiller, P., 1992, 'Fare Determination in Airline Hub-and-Spoke Networks', *Rand Journal of Economics*, 23, 309–333.

Brueckner, J. and Spiller, P., 1994, 'Economies of Traffic Density in the Deregulated Airline Industry', *Journal of Law and Economics*, 37, 379–415.

Brueckner, J. and Whalen, T., 2000, 'The Price Effects of International Airline Alliances', *Journal of Law and Economics*, 43, 503–545.

Caves, D., Christensen, L. and Tretheway, M., 1984, 'Economies of Density versus Economies of Scale: Why Trunk and Local Service Airline Costs Differ', *Rand Journal of Economics*, 15, 471–489.

Evans, W. and Kessides, I., 1993, 'Localized Market Power in the U.S. Airline Industry', *The Review of Economics and Statistics*, 75, 66–75.

Ito, H. and Lee, D., 2005a, 'Domestic Codesharing Practices in the US Airline Industry', *Journal of Air Transport Management*, Vol. 11, No. 2, pp. 89–97.

Ito, H. and Lee, D., 2005b, 'The Impact of Domestic Codesharing Agreements on Market Airfares: Evidence from the US', in *Advances in Airline Economics*, Vol. 1, Darin Lee, ed., Elsevier, pp. 141–161.

Morrison, S. and Winston, C., 1995, *The Evolution of the Airline Industry*, Washington, D.C.: Brookings Institution.

Netessine, S. and Shumsky, R., 2004, 'Revenue Management Games: Horizontal and Vertical Competition', *Management Science*, forthcoming.

Park, J. and Zhang, A., 2000, 'An Empirical Analysis of Global Airline Alliances: Cases in North Atlantic Markets', *Review of Industrial Organization*, 16, 367–384.

Richard, O., 2003, 'Flight Frequency and Mergers in Airline Markets', *International Journal of Industrial Organization*, 21, 907–922.

Advances in Airline Economics, Vol 1
Darin Lee (Editor)
© 2006 Published by Elsevier B.V.

5

International Airline Code Sharing and Entry Deterrence*

Stuart D. Gurrea
Economists Incorporated[†]

ABSTRACT

Since 1987 code sharing has required approval from the Department of Transportation (DOT). Under Section 412 of the Federal Aviation Act, the DOT can approve international code-sharing proposals if they are not contrary to the public interest and do not substantially reduce or eliminate competition. Therefore, from a policy perspective, it is important to understand how these cooperative agreements affect competition. We distinguish two effects on competition: a *direct effect*, which results from a reduction in competition between partners, and an *indirect effect* due to the strategic barriers a code-sharing alliance imposes on rivals' entry decisions. Our empirical analysis focuses on identifying the latter. We propose an equilibrium model of entry in which alliances are characterized in terms of airport presence. For a sample of markets in which open skies agreements were approved, we study the effect of alliances and market presence on entry decisions. Our empirical results show that larger airport presence imposes larger reductions on rivals' profits, which may deter entry. From a policy perspective our results suggest that while in a market with an alliance between an incumbent and a new entrant there is no *direct effect*, approval may still deserve scrutiny to account for the *indirect* effect of alliances on competition.

---

*This paper is a revised version of the third Chapter of my Ph.D. dissertation at Northwestern University. I am very grateful to the members of my committee, John Panzar, Rob Porter, and Shane Greenstein, and to Adhamina Rodriguez for her help in preparing this chapter. Financial support from Northwestern University's Transportation Center is gratefully acknowledged. All remaining errors are mine.

[†]Contact information: Economists Incorporated, Emerystation North, Suite 205, 5980 Horton Street, Emeryville CA 94608. E-mail: gurrea.s@ei.com

1 INTRODUCTION

Today, code sharing is a common form of alliance among airlines. This marketing agreement ranges from the simple use of another airline's code when selling tickets on its flights to broader forms of collaboration. Advocates of this form of cooperation highlight its potential gains, such as new "online" service offerings, improvements of existing service, lower costs and greater efficiency. Policy makers and antitrust enforcement authorities need to separate these beneficial effects from possible negative outcomes that may follow cooperation, such as market allocation, capacity limitations, higher fares, or foreclosure of rivals from markets. In this paper we study the effects of code sharing on competition in international airline markets.

Since 1989 the airline industry has been subject to the same merger and antitrust regulation as other industries. The Department of Justice (DOJ) is responsible for approving airline mergers, and reviewing code-sharing agreements for possible antitrust violations. The Department of Transportation (DOT) may challenge mergers approved by the DOJ and has the final authority to approve or disapprove a code-sharing agreement. Alliances that affect an international segment between two countries have received greater scrutiny since they take place between airlines that were direct competitors before the agreement.

This critical view towards code sharing in these markets is supported by theoretical work showing how potential efficiency gains can be offset by a loss in competition. Recent theoretical contributions by Park (1997), Hassin and Shy (2000), Brueckner (2001) and Heimer and Shy (2006) coincide in viewing code sharing as welfare enhancing if it connects airline networks (*complementary alliances*). They also predict that alliances more likely result in higher fares and lower passenger welfare when alliance partners are operating in the same route (*parallel alliances*). Consistent with these theoretical predictions, Brueckner and Whalen (2000) find that alliance partners charge interline fares 25% lower than non-allied airlines. However, the theoretical prediction that code sharing will have a negative effect on prices in gateway-to-gateway markets is not found to be significant in their empirical analysis. More recently, Brueckner (2003) has analyzed further the effects of cooperation on interline fares, finding that antitrust immunity compared to code sharing results in an even larger reduction in fares. These results are confirmed by Whalen (2005) who finds, in addition to a slightly smaller reduction in fares, a significant increase in output.[1]

Generally, earlier studies provide limited evidence of the predicted effects of parallel alliances on competition. Instead of testing for changes in prices or capacity, in this paper we study how airline alliances affect market structure, and in particular how they affect the profitability and subsequent entry decisions of competing carriers in

---

[1] These results justify DOT's generally favorable view towards code sharing. Nonstop traffic between gateway airports accounts for about one-third of all transatlantic traffic, while the rest takes place through connecting markets. As a result, the net gains have justified this policy despite possible reductions in consumer welfare in point-to-point markets.

gateway-to-gateway international airline routes.[2] Competitive effects take place through changes in market structure, which in turn affect fares. These effects can result from a reduction in the degree of competition between airlines forming an alliance, which we refer to as *direct effect*, or from the strategic barriers the alliance imposes on rival potential entrants, the *indirect effect*. In most cases, a code-sharing alliance is viewed as a relatively strong form of integration, and therefore a *direct effect* can readily be assessed. To measure the *indirect effect*, we need to understand the strategic interaction between airlines' entry decisions.

In this paper we propose an empirical model to identify the effects of code sharing on airline oligopoly market structure. Following previous equilibrium models of entry, the observed market configuration is a result of underlying profitability. An equilibrium model of entry allows us to identify the strategic barriers an alliance may impose on rivals' entry decisions. We extend the existing literature by identifying how code sharing affects the market configuration in gateway-to-gateway routes. It is of particular interest to study gateway-to-gateway markets because these are subject to potential direct reductions in competition when former rivals enter an alliance. In our model we characterize an alliance as an airline with presence at both endpoints of an international market. We define in this way a three-type model consisting of airlines with no hubs, one hub, and two hubs (allied airlines), which allows us to measure the strategic interaction between airlines entry decisions. In our empirical analysis we employ a sample of 305 international markets in which the U.S. had open skies agreements during 1999. Unlike regulated markets, in these markets airlines from both countries can make price, capacity and schedule decisions.

Understanding how code sharing affects airline entry decisions is important for evaluating the potential anticompetitive effects of this form of integration.[3] Typically, an agreement in a specific route is characterized by significant cooperation between the parties and is aimed at offering seamless service. Although in principle code sharing is a form of partial integration that varies with the degree of integration of the parties' operations, the standard applied to code sharing is the Clayton Act, which is used to examine mergers. Antitrust authorities' approval will take into account the likelihood of new entry in response to a reduction of service or an increase in fares by alliance partners.[4] The DOJ's standard requires not only the absence of regulatory barriers to entry, but the "timeliness, likelihood and sufficiency of entry".[5]

---

[2] A recent theoretical study by Chen and Ross (2000) considers airline alliances as an example of how a strategic alliance can be a tool of entry deterrence. Their model presents an incumbent firm that offers an entrant to share its fixed facilities. Although this outcome may increase efficiency beyond the pre-entry level, it also may prevent the entrant from building its own facility, which would result in an even more competitive outcome. Their paper focuses on the anticompetitive effect of the alliance on partner airlines -which we refer to as *direct effect*, but does not consider the competitive effects on other rivals' entry or exit decisions -the *indirect effect*.

[3] For example, approval of the alliance between American Airlines and British Airways was not granted based on the absence of conditions conductive to entry. These conditions include, in addition to eliminating government barriers, competitive gate facilities and terminals. See Nannes (1999).

[4] Section 7 of the Clayton Act prohibits the acquisition of stocks or assets "[. . .] where in any line of commerce or in any activity affecting commerce in any section of the country, the effect of such acquisition may substantially to lessen competition or to tend to create a monopoly".

[5] See, Section 3, DOJ and FTC (1997).

The DOJ's entry standard reflects the view that airline markets in the presence of hub airports are not contestable, and the presence of a hub in an airport imposes structural and strategic barriers to other airlines.[6] Levine (1987) and Borenstein (1989) have argued that airport presence gives an advantage to enter new markets. Berry (1992) finds a large impact of airport presence both ends of a market at on airline profitability. In the context of international airline markets, regulation precludes airlines from developing international networks; entry is limited in most international markets and prohibited in domestic markets. For example, a U.S. carrier can develop a domestic hub as an international gateway airport and obtain traffic feed from domestic routes, but cannot parallel this structure in a foreign country. Alliances have become a response to circumvent foreign ownership and entry limitations, allowing airlines to have large airport presence at both ends of a market. In a similar way to domestic markets, airlines with hubs at both ends of the market may impose strategic barriers to other potential entrants in international markets.

Our findings provide evidence of the importance of market presence on profits in international airline markets, which is consistent with previous results for domestic routes. Through the formation of an alliance, code-sharing airlines gain market presence at both ends of the market. The strategic interaction between firms shows a larger competitive effect of airlines with greater market presence on smaller airlines. This result can be explained by efficiency gains and greater traffic feed that result from building an international network. The baseline model is extended to measure how one-hub airlines' nationality affects rivals' profits. We find that hubs located at different endpoints have weaker competitive effects on each other than when they are located at the same end of the market. This can be explained by greater competition for domestic traffic flow and smaller product differentiation between airlines of the same nationality. When evaluating these results from a policy perspective, we find that alliances with new entrants are less likely to yield an increase in profits conducive to new entry. Although there is no direct reduction in competition, profitability of rival firms is more likely to fall. For agreements between incumbent firms we find that the direct effect can be offset by an increase in the profitability of rival firms. According to our model, granting approval for alliances with new entrants imposes stronger barriers to rival airlines' entry. However, the policy applied by the DOJ to some of the major transatlantic alliances has focused on *direct* effects, granting restricted approval to routes in which both airlines operate and not imposing obstacles to routes with only one of the partners operating. We address the *indirect* effects that may follow an agreement and illustrate our predictions with evidence of exit in some of the major transatlantic routes in which only one partner was an incumbent.

The remainder of the paper is organized as follows. Section 2 presents the empirical model. The data and variable definitions are discussed in Section 3. Estimation results for the baseline model are presented in Section 4. In the Section 5, we extend the model to take into account the location of competing hubs. The policy implications are discussed in Section 6, and Section 7 concludes.

---

[6] "For a merger between major air carriers with substantial overlaps in markets in which are the dominant providers of service, it is unrealistic to expect that the prospect of potential competition can fully address the competitive concerns." (Klein, 2000).

2   A MODEL OF ENTRY WITH CODE SHARING

In this section we present an empirical model of airline entry in international markets. In our model each airline's alliance strategy is exogenously given (there is no choice of type) and airlines determine their optimal entry decision simultaneously given their anticipated payoffs in the competition stage. An important assumption in our model is that alliance members make joint entry decisions, and are perceived by competitors as one single airline. As discussed in more detail in the data section below, not all alliances enjoy antitrust immunity and hence not all can overtly coordinate prices or capacity decisions. However, for the purposes of our analysis, we assume competitors perceive alliance partners' entry decisions as a single entry decision.

Our analysis is based on an empirical model identifying what factors drive entry in international airline markets. We build on Berry's (1992) equilibrium model of the domestic airline industry, which proposes an empirical methodology to explain airline entry decisions as a result of the underlying profitability of the route. This model estimates the importance of airport presence on route profitability, taking into account the strategic interaction between competing airlines. In airline oligopoly markets, firms' entry decisions are made taking into account competitors' possible decisions, and therefore decisions must be estimated simultaneously. Since rivals' decisions within an oligopoly market are not independent, estimation is based on the observed market equilibrium outcome. An important assumption of this methodology is to consider entry decisions as independent across markets.

The empirical framework of multiple-agent qualitative response models, as presented in Bresnahan and Reiss (1990) and reviewed in Reiss (1996), relates data on discrete choices – in our case entry in an international airline market – to a game theoretic model specifying payoffs, actions and strategies. Game theory allows modeling interrelated economic decisions that in many cases result in discrete actions or in qualitative information about actions. This literature develops econometric models of games in which players have discrete choices. In an analogous way to single-person choice models in which the parameters of the utility function can be estimated using threshold models of consumer behavior, firms' profit function parameters are estimated using threshold models of games.

The game's solution concept identifies the agent's most preferred strategies. Each observed outcome is a result of a set of threshold conditions. Defining a stochastic payoff function, together with the game's solution concept, allows us to make probability statements for each observed market outcome and construct a likelihood function for the observed configurations in the data. A key feature of these models is that the equilibrium concept must guarantee uniqueness of the equilibrium, ensuring that the sum of the probabilities of the outcomes adds up to one. The assumption made on the equilibrium concept is particularly important given that different equilibrium concepts will determine different probabilities for each outcome.[7] We apply this methodology incorporating the

---

[7] Earlier work by Bresnahan and Reiss (1991), Berry (1992), and more recent by Mazzeo (2002) apply and develop this methodology to analyzing entry decisions in oligopoly markets. Bresnahan and Reiss (1991) study entry in oligopoly car dealer markets. Outcomes are reduced to monopoly and duopoly structures, with payoff functions that may vary with the market's configuration. To the entry decision, Mazzeo (2002) adds product choice in highway motel oligopolies. Players decide whether to enter or not, and in which category to do so. Mazzeo considers two alternative solution concepts and studies how game theoretical assumptions affect the estimation results.

alliance characteristics of the market as a determinant of entry decisions in international airline markets.

A particular feature of airline markets are code-sharing alliances. This characteristic is an important determinant of the strategic interaction between rival airlines in oligopoly markets, and therefore will be a central element of our model of entry in international markets. Earlier models of entry have introduced firm heterogeneity at some level. Berry (1992) considers firm individual heterogeneity based on market presence, and Mazzeo (2002) defines firms based on an endogenous choice of type. In our model we define three types of airlines: allied airlines; airlines with a hub at one end of the route; and airlines with no hub at either end of the route.[8] These types are exogenously given, and firms fall into one of these three categories.[9] The first category consists of code-sharing airlines, which can obtain domestic traffic feed at both endpoints through cooperation. Hereafter, we will refer to them as two-hub airlines or allied, bearing in mind that the alliance does not necessarily include airlines with a dominant hub at both ends.[10] By characterizing code-sharing alliances in terms of market presence we can identify the effect of code-sharing based on the airline's airport presence without adding another dimension of heterogeneity.[11]

Following the methodology described above, we first define a game theory model in which we relate the observed market configurations to a set of actions, information, payoffs and strategies. For this game we define an equilibrium concept with a unique solution. Then, we define a stochastic specification of the payoff function. The uniqueness of the equilibrium allows us to determine the probabilities of each market outcome and construct the likelihood function, which will be the basis for our estimation.

2.1   Equilibrium Concept

Following the framework presented in Berry (1992), we assume that airlines in international markets play a two-stage game. In the first stage firms make their entry decisions and in the second stage they play the competition game in which profits are determined. As noted above, types are exogenously given, and the strategy space is "entry" and "no entry" into a market m. In an international airline market the total number of potential entrants is the sum of potential entrants of each type: N_m^{2h} allied firms, i.e. airlines with hubs at both ends of the route; N_m^{1h} with one domestic hub; and N_m^{0h} no hub at either point. A strategy vector s is defined as a $(N_m^{2h} + N_m^{1h} + N_m^{0h}) \times 1$ vector of zeros (no

---

[8] Here we define an airport as an international hub for an airline if it serves as a gateway for international routes. In the data section below we explicitly define the criteria to include an airport as an airline's domestic hub.

[9] In the long run, alliances can be dissolved and additional ones formed; also airport presence of each airline can change.

[10] We may have in the category of two-hub or allied, carriers with a hub at one end, but the possibility of domestic traffic feed at both ends.

[11] A more complex approach would distinguish airlines based on their airport presence and on their associative structure. In our framework, an allied airline is defined as an airline with airport presence at each end of the market. Therefore, by characterizing airlines by their airport presence we are implicitly defining its associative structure.

entry) and ones (indicating entry). A Nash equilibrium is defined by a strategy vector s^* such that:

$$s_i^* \pi_{mi}\left(s_i^*, s_{-i}^*\right) \geq 0$$
$$\left(1 - s_i^*\right)\pi_{mi}\left(s_i^*, s_{-i}^*\right) \leq 0, \quad \text{for } i = 1, \ldots, N_m^{2h} + N_m^{1h} + N_m^{0h} \qquad (1)$$

The Nash equilibrium pure strategies of the simultaneous-move entry game are such that entrants are profitable and the rest of the potential entrants expect zero profits from entry, given the rival's strategies. In terms of the equilibrium conditions, a non-entrant $(s_i^* = 0)$ has negative profits if it decides to enter $(s_i = 1)$. This condition must hold for each of the three types of firms.

We can illustrate the existence of an equilibrium by considering a hypothetical payoff matrix as defined in Table 1, in which there are only two types: allied and non allied airlines. This simplified example incorporates the natural assumption that profits fall with the number of rivals. In the example we can see that $(2, 1)$ is an equilibrium configuration. An additional allied airline would change the configuration to $(3, 1)$ and airlines' profits would be negative. A non-allied entrant would also have negative profits. Therefore entrants are profitable, and potential entrants are better off not entering the market, which we assume to yield profits equal to zero.

From Table 1 we can see that $(1, 2)$ is also an equilibrium configuration, and hence there does not exist a unique pure-strategy Nash equilibrium. The nonuniqueness of the equilibrium does not allow defining a probability for each event. One approach proposed by Bresnahan and Reiss (1991) to solve this problem is to consider both configurations as one. This method would characterize the market outcome in terms of the number of competitors. In our example, configurations $(1, 2)$ and $(2, 1)$ would be reduced to a single outcome where three firms are observed in the market.

With this approach we would not characterize market configurations by the alliance structure or market presence of the entering airlines. In particular, in our model we want to identify the effect of code sharing on the number of entrants. In the example, we can

Table 1 Payoff Matrix Example

Configuration	Alliance Payoffs	No-Alliance Payoffs
(1, 0)	20	–
(0, 1)	–	14
(1, 1)	13	10
(2, 0)	11	–
(0, 2)	–	8
(2, 1)	6	4
(1, 2)	5	2
(3, 0)	–1	–
(0, 3)	–	–2
(3, 1)	–3	–4
(1, 3)	–2	–6
(2, 2)	–1	–2

see that despite the number of firms being the same, the associative characteristics of the market participants vary.[12]

We address the nonuniqueness of the equilibrium by introducing additional assumptions to the model. In the context of international airline markets, code sharing involves an agreement between a domestic and a foreign carrier. The presence of a partner in each country yields an advantage in terms of entering a route between the two countries. As a result, we may assume that allied airlines have a first-mover advantage in the decision to enter international routes. Following the same logic it is reasonable to assume that airlines with a hub in a domestic market will have advantage over airlines with smaller presence.

Formally we introduce this idea in the model by assuming that airlines play a sequential game in which code-sharing airlines make their entry decisions first, then one-hub airlines, and finally zero-hub airlines. Ordering entry by type ensures a unique equilibrium. This approach is further discussed by Bresnahan and Reiss (1991) and Berry (1992).[13] In the example discussed above, this solution concept eliminates the equilibrium ambiguity: the first-mover advantage determines the unique equilibrium outcome (2, 1).

Next we prove the existence and uniqueness of the Subgame Perfect Nash Equilibrium (SPNE) of the sequential entry game. We assume that firms with airport presence c competing in market m do not differ in their profits, i.e. the effect of competition is the same for firms of the same type. Profits for an airline of type c in market m are:

$$\Pi_{cm} = M_{cm}(n_m^{2h^*}, n_m^{1h^*}, n_m^{0h^*}) + \phi_{cm} \qquad (2)$$

The first element of the profit function measures the portion of profits that depends on the equilibrium number of firms of each type. The second part is unrelated to competition. This equation maintains the basic distinction between type specific fixed costs $(-\phi_{cm})$ and variable costs as presented in Berry (1992). In this general specification we allow both components of profits to be type specific.

First, we construct an equilibrium and then show it is unique. Within types, ϕ_{cm} is the same for all firms in a market:

$$\phi_{1cm} = \phi_{2cm} \cdots = \phi_{N_m^c cm}$$

The SPNE configuration of the sequential game, $(n_m^{2h^*}, n_m^{1h^*}, n_m^{0h^*})$, is the largest number of code-sharing airlines, hub non-allied airlines, and zero-hub airlines satisfying:

$$
(n_m^{2h^*}, n_m^{1h^*}, n_m^{0h^*})
$$

$$
= \max_{0 \leq n^{2h} \leq N_m^{2h}} n^{2h} : \left\{ \max_{0 \leq n^{1h} \leq N_m^{1h}} n^{1h} : \left\{ \max_{0 \leq n^{0h} \leq N_m^{0h}} n^{0h} : M_{cm}(n_m^{2h}, n_m^{1h}, n_m^{0h}) + \phi_{cm} \geq 0 \right\} \right\}
$$

----

[12] A simple way to guarantee uniqueness is to assume a tie-breaking rule in the simultaneous move game. In the case of more than one possible equilibrium, we can assume that the observed outcome will be the one that corresponds to the airline with the largest market presence. In the example our assumed tie-breaking rule implies that the unique equilibrium is (2, 1).

[13] Mazzeo (2002) also uses refinements of the simultaneous-move game to obtain a unique equilibrium in a product type-entry model.

We can construct an equilibrium by taking a vector s, with $s_{k_c}^* = 1$ for $k_c \leq n_m^{c^*}$ and $s_{k_c}^* = 0$ for $k_c > n_m^{c^*}$. By construction, s satisfies the equilibrium condition.

Next, we prove the uniqueness of the equilibrium by contradiction. Suppose there exists a different equilibrium $(n_m^{2h}, n_m^{1h^*}, n_m^{0h^*})$ with $n_m^{2h} > n_m^{2h^*}$. By definition of equilibrium $M_{cm}(n_m^{2h}, n_m^{1h^*}, n_m^{0h^*}) + \phi_{cm} \geq 0$, which is also true for all other entering firms because all firms of the same type have the same profits in a market. This contradicts the definition of $(n_m^{2h^*}, n_m^{1h^*}, n_m^{0h^*})$. In an analogous way, we can prove the case in which $n_m^{2h} < n_m^{2h^*}$, and the possible deviations from $n_m^{1h^*}$ and $n_m^{0h^*}$.

This solution concept based on an assumption of sequential-move decisions enables us to define a unique relation between the observed market configurations and the equilibrium outcomes of the model. Given this relation, we can define probabilities for each market outcome taking into account its associative structure. We cannot make probability statements on the identities of the airlines but we can on the types entering the market. In addition, this solution approach adds to the game the effect of code-sharing alliances, not only through the payoff function but also through the order of entry.

2.2   Profit Function Specification

After defining the game's solution concept, we specify a stochastic function that is the basis for our estimation. The observed market configuration is a result of a set of threshold conditions that hold for the potential entrants' profits. These profits will depend on market characteristics, firm characteristics, and the endogenous market configuration. We parameterize the profit function for an airline of type c in market m as:

$$\Pi_{cm} = X_m \beta_c + M_c(\theta; \vec{n}) + \varepsilon_{cm} \tag{3}$$

X is a vector of market characteristics, and we allow its effect on profits to vary by type. The size of the market or the distance of the route will determine airline's profits. Consistent with the game defined above, the effect of these market characteristics depends on the firm's type. We also allow the effect of competition on profits to vary per type, $M_c(\theta; \vec{n})$. Finally, we assume that the unobserved component of the payoff function, ε_{cm}, varies for each type in a given market. Berry (1992) shows the importance of airport presence as a determinant of entry in domestic markets. In the case of international markets, we have reduced this firm specific characteristic to three possible types, and we allow the stochastic component of profits to vary for each of these types in a given market.

The effect of competition, $M_c(\theta; \vec{n})$, is assumed as in Mazzeo (2002) to be a linear function with indicator variables for each competitor. The parameterization of $M_c(\theta; \vec{n})$ specifies dummy variables to capture the effect of each competitor for each of the three hub types. We define the parameter θ_{ij} as the effect of a rival of type i on the profits of an airline of type j. The effect of competition is therefore parameterized by three intra-type effects (θ_{22}, θ_{11}, and θ_{00}) and six cross-type effects. This results in the following specification for each type:

(a) For a two-hub carrier: $M_2(\theta; \vec{n}) = \theta_{22}{}^*$ (number of rival alliances)
   $+ \theta_{12}{}^*$ (number of one hub airlines) $+ \theta_{02}{}^*$ (number of zero hub airlines).

(b) For a one-hub carrier: $M_1(\theta; \vec{n}) = \theta_{11}{}^*$ (number of one-hub rival airlines)
   $+ \theta_{21}{}^*$ (number of alliances) $+ \theta_{01}{}^*$ (number of zero hub airlines).

(c) For a zero-hub carrier: $M_0(\theta; \vec{n}) = \theta_{00}{}^*$ (number of zero-hub rival airlines)
   $+ \theta_{10}{}^*$ (number of one hub airlines) $+ \theta_{20}{}^*$ (number of alliances).

This specification relies on two assumptions. First, it assumes that there is no distinction between the effect of foreign and domestic competitors. For example, if we observe American Airlines (AA) and Finnair competing in the New York-Helsinki market, this specification will yield: $M_1(\theta; \vec{n}) = \theta_{11}$. If we observe in this same route competition taking place between TWA and AA, the effect of competition would also be measured by θ_{11}. We will maintain this assumption in our baseline specification. In section 5 we relax this assumption allowing the effects to vary with nationality. Second, the effect of competition is assumed to be linear both across and within types; an additional rival of the same type has the same effect as the previous ones. For example, in the Chicago/Montreal market, the effect of the United-Air Canada and American-Canadian Airlines on other firms' profits is the same.[14]

In this parametrization we do not impose a unique incremental effect of market presence. For example, we allow the competitive effect of firms with two hubs on firms with one hub to be different for airlines of one hub on airlines with zero hubs.[15]

2.3 Estimation

In the preceding subsection we have defined a stochastic specification for the profit function. We have also defined in section 2.1 the sequential equilibrium, which guarantees the existence and uniqueness of the equilibrium: for a realization of $(\varepsilon_2, \varepsilon_1, \varepsilon_0)$ and payoff function parameters, we observe a unique market configuration. In order to estimate the model's parameters, we assume that the stochastic component of the profit function is drawn from a trivariate normal distribution.[16]

Uniqueness of the market outcomes allows us to make probability statements for each of the events. Each outcome is a result of a set of threshold conditions for each of the airline types profit functions. For notation simplicity, denote $X_m \beta_c + M_c(\theta; \vec{n}) + \varepsilon_{cm} = \Pi_c(\vec{n}) + \varepsilon_c$, where we redefine $\vec{n}$ as the number of rival airlines of each type.

To observe a market configuration (n_2, n_1, n_0) in the simultaneous move entry game, the following threshold conditions must hold:

---

[14] A more complex specification would distinguish the effect of the first competitor from the second. We might expect the impact of an additional rival to decrease as the number of rival firms' increases.

[15] Mazzeo (2002) assumes a linear parameterization of competition, measuring intra-type and cross-type competition effects. The latter are reduced to one-type and two-type away effects in the three-type version of the model.

[16] Market presence in the second quarter of 1999 determines the possible outcomes in the last quarter of 1999. We will observe at most the number of potential entrants of each type. In addition, we only observe the outcomes of markets in which there is at least one entrant. Therefore we will take the distribution function conditional on these constraints. A more detailed discussion is left to the Appendix.

(1) $\Pi_2(n_2, n_1, n_0) + \varepsilon_2 < 0$ or $\varepsilon_2 < -\Pi_2(n_2, n_1, n_0)$
(2) $\Pi_2(n_2 - 1, n_1, n_0) + \varepsilon_2 > 0$ or $\varepsilon_2 > -\Pi_2(n_2 - 1, n_1, n_0)$
(3) $\Pi_1(n_2, n_1, n_0) + \varepsilon_1 < 0$ or $\varepsilon_1 < -\Pi_1(n_2, n_1, n_0)$
(4) $\Pi_1(n_2, n_1 - 1, n_0) + \varepsilon_1 > 0$ or $\varepsilon_1 > -\Pi_1(n_2, n_1 - 1, n_0)$
(5) $\Pi_0(n_2, n_1, n_0) + \varepsilon_0 < 0$ or $\varepsilon_0 < -\Pi_0(n_2, n_1, n_0)$
(6) $\Pi_0(n_2, n_1, n_0 - 1) + \varepsilon_0 > 0$ or $\varepsilon_0 > -\Pi_0(n_2, n_1, n_0 - 1)$

These conditions result from the Nash Equilibrium defined in section 2.1, according to which firms make entry decisions that are ultimately profitable. Conditions 1, 3 and 5 imply that additional entrants cannot make positive profits; 2, 4 and 6 refer to entrants making positive profits. These conditions delimit a region of the space $\{\varepsilon_2, \varepsilon_1, \varepsilon_0\}$:

1 and 2 imply: $-\Pi_2(n_2, n_1, n_0) > \varepsilon_2 > -\Pi_2(n_2 - 1, n_1, n_0)$;
3 and 4 imply: $-\Pi_1(n_2, n_1, n_0) > \varepsilon_1 > -\Pi_1(n_2, n_1 - 1, n_0)$;
5 and 6 imply: $-\Pi_0(n_2, n_1, n_0) > \varepsilon_0 > -\Pi_0(n_2, n_1, n_0 - 1)$.

The probability of an outcome $\left(n_m^{2h^*}, n_m^{1h^*}, n_m^{0h^*}\right)$ is the integral of the distribution of $(\varepsilon_2, \varepsilon_1, \varepsilon_0)$ over the region for which this outcome holds. As noted above, the simultaneous move game results in multiple equilibria and therefore incorrect probability statements.

To address the nonuniqueness problem, we assume sequential entry: two-hub firms make their entry decisions simultaneously, then one-hub firms, and finally zero-hub firms, guaranteeing a unique equilibrium. The order of entry implies a first mover advantage and therefore the possibility of preemption. Under this alternative equilibrium concept, the unique SPNE is determined by the following conditions:

$-\Pi_2(n_2, n_1(n_2), n_0(n_1(n_2), n_2)) > \varepsilon_2 > -\Pi_2(n_2 - 1, n_1(n_2 - 1), n_0(n_1(n_2 - 1), n_2 - 1))$
$-\Pi_1(n_2, n_1, n_0(n_1, n_2)) > \varepsilon_1 > -\Pi_1(n_2, n_1 - 1, n_0(n_1 - 1, n_2))$
$-\Pi_0(n_2, n_1, n_0) > \varepsilon_0 > -\Pi_0(n_2, n_1, n_0 - 1)$

Estimation of the model's parameters by maximum likelihood yields the parameter values that maximize the probability of the observed market configurations.[17] The likelihood function is the product of the probabilities of each of the observed M market outcomes, which is defined as:

$$L = \prod_{m=1}^{M} Prob(n_2, n_1, n_0)$$

In this three-type model, the region of integration for airlines' entry decisions is nonrectangular. Higher-dimensional multinomial integrals limit the use of maximum-likelihood estimation since the probability of each event can not be evaluated. In order to estimate the parameters of the model, we implement a simulated maximum likelihood estimator in

---

[17] The regions of integration defining the probabilities are constrained in several forms, in particular by the fact that we only consider markets in which entry takes place. This is discussed in detail in the appendix.

which the probability of each market configuration is simulated.[18] This method follows Mazzeo's (2002) implementation of the frequency simulation approach to approximate the likelihood function of a three product-type model.

With the frequency simulation approach we provide an approximation of the probability of each outcome. Then, we construct the likelihood function based on these probabilities. The probabilities are approximated as follows: for each market m, we take a large number K of random draws from $f(\varepsilon_2, \varepsilon_1, \varepsilon_0)$. Then count the number of times, P out of K, for which the market's observed threshold conditions hold. A more detailed discussion of this methodology is provided in the Appendix.

3 DATA AND VARIABLE DEFINITIONS

The main source of information for this study is the DOT's T-100 segment data, which includes all traffic arriving to and departing from U.S. airports on nonstop commercial international flights. These data are for both U.S. carriers with service to a foreign airport and foreign carriers with nonstop service to any point in the U.S. Since our analysis focuses on gateway-to-gateway markets, we can determine which routes and airlines were active in these routes in a given period. We cannot determine from the data the number of passengers for a market, since part of the traffic continues on a connecting flight to a final destination. In determining a market's configuration, we will not consider a firm as active if the number of passengers carried in a quarter is less than 1080.[19] This mainly eliminates charter flights from the sample.

To study airline entry and exit decisions in international markets we can only consider routes in which access is open to each of the domestic carriers. The Office of International Aviation provides a list of bilateral open-skies agreements between the U.S. and other countries. Under these agreements, airlines from both countries have access to the market and to any destination point. Therefore, we constrain our sample to 305 city-pairs with open skies agreements during the last quarter of 1999. Because these routes might have special characteristics, we may question the generality of our results beyond this type of route. This remains an empirical question. In the present study we limit our analysis to routes in which there is a bilateral open skies agreement. Table 2 presents the list of 45 bilateral agreements signed before March 2000. Although there is no open-skies agreement between the U.S. and Canada, we also include the routes between these two countries. Under the 1995 U.S.-Canada Aviation Agreement, Canadian airlines have the right to serve any city in the U.S. Also, U.S. carriers gained unlimited access to any city in Canada.[20]

Entry is identified between the second and fourth quarter of 1999. As in previous studies, a relatively short time interval calls for an explanation of entry and exit decisions based on the strategic behavior of firms and not one based on changes in cost or demand

[18] Reiss (1996) provides evidence of the performance of simulator estimator in a discrete strategic-choice model employing the probability simulator proposed by Axel Borsch-Supan and Vassilis Hajivassiliou (1993). Other simulated methods have been implemented in models of entry. Berry (1992) uses a method of simulated moments to analyze entry in domestic airline markets.

[19] This is equivalent to carrying 90 passengers per week.

[20] Montreal, Vancouver and Toronto were initially excluded from the agreement. These exceptions expired after February 1998.

Table 2   U.S. Open Skies Agreements*

Country	Date	Country	Date
Senegal	2000/12	Chile	1997/10
Benin	2000/11	Aruba	1997/07
Malta	2000/10	Malaysia	1997/06
Rwanda	2000/10	New Zealand	1997/05
Morocco	2000/10	Nicaragua	1997/05
Nigeria	2000/08	Costa Rica	1997/04
The Gambia	2000/05	Honduras	1997/04
Turkey	2000/03	El Salvador	1997/04
Ghana	2000/02	Guatemala	1997/04
Burkina Faso	2000/02	Panama	1997/03
Namibia	2000/02	Taiwan	1997/03
Slovak Republic	2000/01	Brunei	1997/02
Portugal	1999/12	Singapore	1997/01
Dominican Republic	1999/12	Jordan	1996/11
Tanzania	1999/11	Germany	1996/02
Qatar	1999/10	Czech Republic	1995/12
Argentina	1999/08	Austria	1995/05
Baharain	1999/05	Belgium	1995/05
United Arab Emirates	1999/04	Denmark	1995/05
Pakistan	1999/04	Finland	1995/05
Italy	1998/11	Iceland	1995/05
Peru	1998/05	Luxemburg	1995/05
Korea	1998/04	Norway	1995/05
Uzbekistan	1998/02	Sweden	1995/05
Netherlands Antilles	1997/12	Switzerland	1995/05
Romania	1997/12	Canada**	1995/02
		Netherlands	1992/09

*Agreements as of 01/31/01, Office of International Aviation, USDOT.
**The U.S.-Canada Aviation Agreement allows airlines from both countries to have unlimited access to each other's cities.

Table 3   Open Skies Routes in Data Set per World Region

World Region	Observations	Percentage
Canada	109	35.74%
Central America and The Caribbean	55	18.03%
South America	14	4.59%
Europe	108	35.41%
Asia	18	5.90%
Africa	0	0%
Middle East	1	0.33%
	Total: 305	

fundamentals. The analysis of the determinants of entry is based on the observed market
configurations in the second quarter of 1999. As noted above, over this short period
airport presence remains constant and therefore type is taken as exogenous.

In our model, both the number of firms and the associative structure define the market configuration. To characterize markets in terms of code-sharing alliances, we use the
Official Airline Guides (1990–1999) and the DOT's Air Carrier Licensing Division compilation of code-sharing agreements. Based on this information we determine whether the
operating carrier identified in the segment data is also providing service for another airline,
i.e., whether they are code sharing. In Table 4 we provide a complete list of these agreements.

This information does not identify which alliances enjoy antitrust immunity and hence
which member airlines can make joint schedule, price and capacity decisions.[21] While

Table 4 Code-Sharing Alliances

Partner Airlines	Number of Markets	Percentage
Alaska Airlines-Canadian Airlines	6	4%
American-Canadian Airlines	23	15%
American-Asiana Airlines	5	3%
American-Finnair	1	1%
American-LAN Chile	1	1%
American-TAM Mercosur	4	3%
Continental-Alitalia	2	1%
Continental-Compania Panamena	1	1%
Continental-Czech Airlines	1	1%
Continental-EVA Airways	4	3%
Continental-TACA	1	1%
Delta-Austrian	1	1%
Delta-Comair*	2	1%
Delta-Sabena	6	4%
Delta-Swissair	10	7%
Delta-TAP	1	1%
LACSA-TACA	1	1%
Lufthansa-Lauda Air	1	1%
Northwest-KLM	12	8%
Trans World-Royal Jordanian	1	1%
United Airlines-Air Canada	38	26%
United-Air New Zealand	2	1%
United Ailrines-Austrian Airlines	2	1%
United-Lufthansa	17	11%
United-SAS	6	4%
	Total: 149	

Source: OAG, Desktop Guide.
*Delta owned subsidiary.

[21] For example, the 1996 Alliance Expansion Agreement between United Airlines and Lufthansa states that
"[. . .] the joint applicants will plan and coordinate service over their respective route networks as if there had
been an operational merger between the two airlines."

many of the alliances in our sample do not enjoy antitrust immunity, throughout the analysis we assume that partner carriers make joint entry decisions, and are perceived as one single competitor by rival airlines. Since code sharing is public information, we assume rivals are aware of allied firms' entry decisions and perceive them as a single entry decision.

A key element of our empirical model is the definition of each of the three types of airlines: zero-hub, one-hub and two-hub airlines. As defined above, two-hub airlines correspond to alliance airlines, which can operate in each of the domestic markets beyond the international segments.

The definition of hub tries to identify airlines for which an airport is an international gateway airport. Since we do not have information on all the international operations of the foreign carriers we use different definitions for U.S. and foreign airlines. A U.S. airport is a hub for a carrier when it operates in at least four international markets from that airport during the second quarter of 1999. In the case of foreign carriers, there is typically a major domestic airline which concentrates its operations in an international gateway airport or hub. These definitions of market presence result in the set of potential entrant configurations reported in Table 5.

Table 6 presents the distribution of observed market configurations for the 305 markets in our sample. These correspond to the actual entry decisions for the fourth quarter of 1999. Although the single non-allied carrier market is largest in number of routes, the biggest configuration in terms of number of passengers presents multiple competing airlines. In the empirical analysis we collapse some of these groups by assuming that adding additional competitors of a type beyond 4 has no effect on airline profitability.

In addition to the structure of competition and to an airline's type, payoffs are explained by market characteristics. Market size is proxied by the variables *income* and *population*, defined as the product of the population and income respectively at the segment's end-point cities. Costs are proxied by the distance between the two cities. The units and sources of the variables are summarized in Table 7, and summary statistics are presented in Table 8. The typical international route has close to two airlines and, on average, airlines with one hub are more frequently observed than two or zero hubs.

4 ESTIMATION RESULTS

We first present reduced form results for the determinants of entry in international airline markets. With this approach we do not take into account the strategic behavior of airlines in oligopoly markets, and focus on market characteristics rather than on the interaction between firms. In all four specifications reported in Table 9, the dependent variable is the number of firms observed in a market. This is defined as the total number of firms carrying passengers in an international airline market m during the fourth quarter of 1999.

The right hand side variables include *income* and *population* as measures of demand. The interpretation of *population* as a proxy for demand is straightforward, and we expect the number of carriers to increase with the size of the market. We also include the dummy variable *island* that takes value one if the origin or destination of the market is an island. For these routes, we expect to find a stronger effect of population for two

Table 5 Observed Potential Entrants for 3-Type Model

Alliance	One Hub	Zero Hub*	Frequency	Percentage
0	0	1	1	0.3%
0	0	2	3	1.0%
0	0	3	2	0.7%
0	0	4	6	2.0%
0	1	1	5	1.6%
0	1	2	8	2.6%
0	1	3	7	2.3%
0	1	4	32	10.5%
0	2	0	1	0.3%
0	2	1	3	1.0%
0	2	2	4	1.3%
0	2	3	7	2.3%
0	2	4	25	8.2%
0	3	3	3	1.0%
0	3	4	11	3.6%
0	4	3	2	0.7%
0	4	4	42	13.8%
1	0	1	1	0.3%
1	0	2	1	0.3%
1	0	3	1	0.3%
1	0	4	10	3.3%
1	1	1	2	0.7%
1	1	2	3	1.0%
1	1	3	2	0.7%
1	1	4	14	4.6%
1	2	2	2	0.7%
1	2	3	5	1.6%
1	2	4	20	6.6%
1	3	3	4	1.3%
1	3	4	24	7.9%
1	4	3	3	1.0%
1	4	4	35	11.5%
2	1	4	3	1.0%
2	3	4	8	2.6%
2	4	4	5	1.6%
			Total: 305	

*Assuming competitive effect only relevant up to four airlines.

reasons: first, many of the islands are tourist destinations; and second, the nature of the islands makes air transportation more necessary. The second measure of demand, *income*, has been found to have a positive effect on domestic markets, since demand increases with consumers' purchasing power. In the case of international markets some additional factors may determine the direction in which income affects demand. First, *income* has a positive effect on demand, with a similar interpretation as in domestic markets. Second,

Table 6 Observed Market Configurations for 3-Type Model

Alliance	One Hub	Zero Hub	Frequency	Percentage
0	0	1	56	18.4%
0	0	2	6	2.0%
0	0	3	2	0.7%
0	1	0	86	28.2%
0	1	1	6	2.0%
0	1	2	3	1.0%
0	2	0	5	1.6%
0	2	1	2	0.7%
0	2	3	2	0.7%
0	2	4	1	0.3%
0	3	0	3	1.0%
1	0	0	68	22.3%
1	0	1	7	2.3%
1	0	2	3	1.0%
1	0	3	1	0.3%
1	1	0	26	8.5%
1	1	1	3	1.0%
1	1	2	2	0.7%
1	1	5	1	0.3%
1	2	0	2	0.7%
1	2	1	1	0.3%
1	3	0	2	0.7%
1	3	2	1	0.3%
2	0	0	9	3.0%
2	0	1	2	0.7%
2	1	0	1	0.3%
2	1	1	1	0.3%
2	2	0	1	0.3%
2	2	1	1	0.3%
2	3	0	1	0.3%
			Total: 305	

*Assuming competitive effect only relevant up to four airlines.

Table 7 Variable Definitions

Variable	Definition	Units	Source
Distance	Distance between origin and destination cities	10^5 Km	U.S. DOT O&D
Population	End cities' product of population	10^{14} people	Various Sources*
Island	Dummy variable indicating at least the origin or destination points are an island	Indicator	
Income	End cities' product of income	10^8 $	Various Sources*
Income Difference	End cities' absolute value of income difference	10^8 $	Various Sources*

*U.N. Demographic Year Book, Europa World Year Book, Statistical Abstract of the U.S. and World Almanac.

Table 8 Descriptive Statistics

Variable	Mean	Standard Deviation	Min	Max
Number of Airlines	1.515	0.967	1	7
Population	0.127	0.261	0.0001	2.176
Income	0.357	0.480	0.0004	3.009
Income Difference	0.984	0.863	0.005	3.148
Distance	0.045	0.030	0.002	0.131
Island	0.111	0.315	0	1
Number of 0 hub	0.436	0.741	0	5
Number of 1 hub	0.590	0.693	0	3
Number of 2 hub	0.488	0.597	0	2

Table 9 Determinants of The Number of Entrants in International Markets

Variable	Alternative Specifications				
	(i)	(ii)	(iii)	(iv)	(v)
Constant	0.860***	0.767***	0.844***	0.760***	0.779***
	(0.156)	(0.161)	(0.155)	(0.161)	(0.161)
Population	0.314	0.367*			
	(0.206)	(0.206)			
Income			−0.136	−0.100	
			(0.111)	(0.112)	
Income Difference					−0.102*
					(0.061)
Island		0.353**		0.294*	0.314**
		(0.161)		(0.163)	(0.160)
Distance	−5.010**	−4.673***	−4.519***	−4.184**	−3.820**
	(1.697)	(1.693)	(1.674)	(1.678)	(1.686)
Number Alliances	0.464***	0.496***	0.507***	0.525***	0.052***
	(0.084)	(0.085)	(0.089)	(0.090)	(0.026)
Number 1 hub	0.102**	0.098**	0.120***	0.118***	0.128***
	(0.031)	(0.031)	(0.030)	(0.030)	(0.031)
Number 0 hub	0.064**	0.068*	0.066**	0.070***	0.070***
	(0.084)	(0.026)	(0.026)	(0.026)	(0.086)
Number of Observations:	305	305	305	305	305
R-squared:	0.215	0.240	0.226	0.234	0.224

***, **, *: Statistically significant at the 1, 5 and 10-percent level.

income differentials, which between countries are much larger than between cities in the same country, may determine demand in a different way. Migration from poorer, highly populated countries can determine a high demand when income levels are low. In this same direction, a high-income differential can also determine tourism to poorer regions of the world, increasing demand. In addition to measures of demand, we include the variable *distance* as a proxy of the cost of operating the flight in each market.

Berry (1992) shows the importance of airport presence as a determinant of the number of firms operating in a domestic market. Airport presence is measured by the number of firms operating at one and both endpoints. Our analysis aims to identify how the alliance structure of a market determines the observed market outcomes. In section 2 we have defined the association characteristics of an airline by the number of hubs the airline has in that market. Therefore, in the context of international markets, we also include a measure of market presence, but the definition and the interpretation of the variable is different. The number of firms with no hubs, one hub, or two hubs operating in a market during the first quarter of 1999 is introduced in the analysis to measure both the importance of market presence as well of the associative structure on the number of entrants.

Table 9 presents the OLS coefficient estimates of the determinants of the number of airlines operating in an international market. Specifications *i* and *ii* include *population* as a proxy for market demand, while *iii* and *iv* use *income*. *Population* has a strong effect on the number of entrants with greater markets sustaining a larger number of competitors. This effect is statistically significant when we control for the presence of islands as the origin or destination of a route. The *island* dummy doubles the effect of *population* on number of entrants in these routes, which is consistent with tourism or transportation characteristics of these markets. When measuring demand with *income*, we find a positive but not statistically significant effect on the number of entrants. As noticed above, *income*, which might have a more straightforward interpretation as a measure of demand in domestic markets, does not have a clear effect in the international markets of our sample.[22] We further explore the relation between *income* and number of airlines in specification *v*. We define *income difference* between the origin and destination cities as a measure of demand. In this case we do find a significant negative effect, with smaller expected number of entrants for lower income differences. In all five specifications *distance*, as a measure of costs, has a significant negative effect on the expected number of entrants.

Airport presence is found to have a strong effect on the number of entrants in all specifications. An increase in an airline with no hubs in the market increases the expected number of airlines by 0.07. Greater market presence, with a hub in the domestic city increases the number of entrants by 0.10. As expected the effect is stronger for allied airlines, which increase the expected number of entrants by 0.5.

4.1 Frequency Estimator Results

In this section we present the results for the empirical model of entry presented in Section 2. This approach allows us to study how the interaction between different types of carriers determines the observed market outcome and in particular, how do alliances affect other airlines' entry decisions. In our analysis we assume that $f(\varepsilon_2, \varepsilon_1, \varepsilon_0)$ is a

---

[22] In order to identify the effect of income we considered additional specifications including dummy variables for each of the different world regions presented in Table 3. These results did not reveal continent specific differences in income's effect.

Table 10   Estimates for Three Type Model of Entry in International Airline Markets

Variable	Parameter	Parameter Estimate	Standard Error
Constant of Two Hub	α_2	2.2780	0.1532
Constant of One Hub	α_1	1.5686	0.0355
Constant of Zero Hub	α_0	1.1324	0.0137
Competition:			
Effect on 2 Hub Rival of:			
2 Hub airline	θ_{22}	−0.5201	0.0030
1 Hub airline	θ_{12}	−0.4009	0.1514
0 Hub airline	θ_{02}	−0.2630	0.0243
Effect on 1 Hub Rival of:			
2 Hub airline	θ_{21}	−0.4236	0.0414
1 Hub airline	θ_{11}	−0.6664	0.0067
0 Hub airline	θ_{01}	−0.0922	0.0134
Effect on 0 Hub Rival of:			
2 Hub airline	θ_{20}	−0.5781	0.0178
1 Hub airline	θ_{10}	−0.3812	0.0147
0 Hub airline	θ_{00}	−0.4738	0.0063
Population: 2 Hub airline	$\beta_{2H,1}$	0.4596	0.8903
1 Hub airline	$\beta_{1H,1}$	0.3714	0.0347
0 Hub airline	$\beta_{0H,1}$	2.0205	0.0487
Island: 2 Hub airline	$\beta_{2H,2}$	1.4194	2.9633
1 Hub airline	$\beta_{1H,2}$	0.3385	0.0363
0 Hub airline	$\beta_{0H,2}$	1.0273	0.0277
Distance: 2 Hub airline	$\beta_{2H,3}$	−0.5918	2.2696
1 Hub airline	$\beta_{1H,3}$	−0.4939	0.1971
0 Hub airline	$\beta_{0H,3}$	−0.7225	0.1350
Number of Observations:		305	

trivariate normal distribution with correlation coefficient equal to zero.[23] In what follows we discuss the results for the sequential move entry game.[24]

Table 10 presents the frequency estimator parameter estimates, taking *population* as a proxy for demand. The profit function estimates for each type allow us to compare the profitability of each type given the market and competition characteristics. The first three coefficients reported in Table 10 are the constant terms of the profit function; for similar market and competition characteristics, expected profits are greater for allied airlines, second for airlines operating with one-hub, and third for airlines with no hubs

[23] For a version of the model with weaker assumptions on the distribution we did not obtain converge in the optimization procedure. Recall that the estimation procedure relies on approximating the probabilities based on random draws from the distribution of ε. Weaker assumptions on the distribution difficult convergence.

[24] Results under the alternative simultaneous move game with tie-breaking rule are very similar for the benchmark model. We therefore limit the discussion to the results for the sequential game which corresponds to a more realistic assumption of the entry decisions.

($\alpha_2 = 2.28$, $\alpha_1 = 1.57$, and $\alpha_0 = 1.13$). According to our definition of international hub based on the number of international flights, profitability differences are smaller between zero-hub and one-hub airlines than between one-hub and allied airlines. In the second case, building an international network through an alliance yields greater profits than by increasing presence in one side of the market. These results indicate that allied airlines face much smaller fixed costs in the operation of their flights. This is consistent with the multiple efficiency gains derived from code sharing, such as sharing baggage handling, check in desks, and other ground services and through the rationalization of capacity.

The next set of coefficients measures the effect of rivals on airline profitability. The effect of allied airlines, is stronger on the profits of airlines with no hubs ($\theta_{20} = -0.58$), which appear to be more vulnerable to the large market presence of an alliance. Alliances also have a strong negative effect on other alliances. This strong intra-type effect can be explained by a higher degree of competition between airlines competing at both ends of the market.

If we compare the effect of airlines with one hub to the effect of allied airlines on rivals with no hubs we find a smaller competitive effect ($\theta_{10} = -0.38$ vs. $\theta_{20} = -0.58$). For single hub airlines we also find a very strong intra-type effect ($\theta_{11} = -0.67$). The interpretation for this type is more difficult since we do not make a distinction between foreign and domestic hubs. In this model, this is not always a result of competing hubs at the same end of the market. This relatively strong effect between airlines of the same type is also found for airlines with no hubs.

For the zero-hub type we find a relatively smaller effect on rival airlines' profits, which is consistent with the importance of market presence as a determinant of each type's competitive effects. Indeed, these are smaller than the competitive effect of higher types ($\theta_{01} = -0.09$ vs. $\theta_{10} = -0.38$, and $\theta_{02} = -0.26$ vs. $\theta_{20} = -0.58$).

The coefficients on demand show much larger coefficients for airlines with small airport presence. As we might expect, profits of smaller airlines will depend on the demand at the end points. As airlines build greater networks, there is greater traffic feed from other points of the network. In addition, the rationalization of capacity and schedule coordination achieved through alliances allows operating flights more efficiently. The results on the *island* dummy are also consistent with these relative differences across types and with the expected higher demand in routes including an *island*. We do not find, however, a significant effect on the allied airline's profits. The coefficients on *distance* also have a stronger effect for smaller airlines. Variable costs measured by *distance* is not found to be significant in determining profitability for allied airlines.[25]

5   THE EFFECT OF DOMESTIC AND FOREIGN RIVALS

In the baseline model discussed above we have assumed that the effect of rival airlines does not vary with nationality. In the case of alliance airlines, this distinction is irrelevant since they have large airport presence at both ends of the route. This assumption is more significant for hub airlines, since the location of the rival's hub-same or different

---

[25] Coefficients estimates for the case in which demand is measured by *income* are similar. As with *population*, we find a statistically significant effect of income for airlines with no hubs.

airport – is likely to be a determinant of profits. For example, in the New York-Buenos Aires route we observe competition between American Airlines (AA) and Aerolineas Argentinas (AR). We expect the negative effect of AR's presence on AA's profits to be smaller than if the rival airline were from the U.S. In a similar way we could characterize the effect of small airlines according to their nationality. In this section we extend the model presented in Section 2 by relaxing this assumption, and allowing for a more general specification in which the effect of a hub rival on profits depends on its nationality.[26]

The distinction between domestic and foreign one-hub airlines results in the existence of multiple equilibria in the sequential-type game defined above. Within a type, we can observe more than one type-nationality configuration for which the equilibrium conditions hold. In order to guarantee the uniqueness of the equilibrium we define an alternative equilibrium concept. In this section, we assume that foreign airlines, within a type, move first. The rationale behind this assumption is that U.S. carriers have more alternative foreign destinations, while foreign carriers are likely to be more committed to entry in markets serving the U.S. This equilibrium concept imposes more structure to the sequential entry game defined above, introducing an additional stage in the one-hub decision stage. The uniqueness of the SPNE relies on the assumption that airlines make their alliance decisions sequentially and that, within a type, foreign airlines move first. The proof of the existence and uniqueness of the SPNE are analogous to the game with no nationality differences.

The parameterization of the profit function captures the distinction between the effect of domestic and foreign airlines. The benchmark profit function is extended with the following specification of competition:

(a) For the two-hub carrier it remains unchanged: $M_2(\theta; \vec{n}) = \theta_{22}{}^*$ (number of rival alliances) $+ \theta_{12}{}^*$ (number of one hub airlines) $+ \theta_{02}{}^*$ (number of zero-hub airlines).

(b) For the foreign one-hub carrier: $M_1^f(\theta; \vec{n}) = \theta_{21}{}^*$ (number of alliances) $+ \theta_{1f1f}{}^*$ (number of foreign one-hub rival airlines) $+ \theta 1_{d1f}{}^*$ (number of domestic one-hub rival airlines) $+ \theta_{01}{}^*$ (number of zero-hub rival airlines).

(c) For the domestic one-hub carrier: $M_1^d(\theta; \vec{n}) = \theta_{21}{}^*$ (number of alliances) $+ \theta_{1f1d}{}^*$ (number of foreign one-hub rival airlines) $+ \theta_{1d1d}{}^*$ (number of domestic one-hub rival airlines) $+ \theta_{01}{}^*$ (number of zero-hub rival airlines).

(d) The parameterization of the zero-hub carrier is: $M_0(\theta; \vec{n}) = \theta_{00}{}^*$ (number of zero-hub rival airlines) $+ \theta_{10}{}^*$ (number of one-hub airlines) $+ \theta_{20}{}^*$ (number of alliances).

We maintain the profit function's stochastic specification and, as above, assume that the unobserved component of profits does not vary with nationality. This assumption is quite restrictive since it fixes the differences between airline types' profits within a market. For one-hub airlines of the same nationality differences in profitability are zero; when hubs are located in different countries we have:

$$\prod_m^f - \prod_m^d = \alpha_{1f} - \alpha_{1d} + M_c^d(\theta; \vec{n}) - M_c^f(\theta; \vec{n})$$
$$= \alpha_{1f} - \alpha_{1d} + (\theta_{1d1d} - \theta_{1f1f}) + (\theta_{1f1d} - \theta_{1d1f})$$

---

[26] We could further extend the model by considering the effect of the nationality of zero-hub airlines. We expect the effect on profitability to be much smaller than the dominant carrier.

This specification assumes that $M_2(\theta; \vec{n})$ does not change, because the alliance will always face direct competition from a hub airline regardless of its nationality. We have also assumed that $M_0(\theta; \vec{n})$ remains unchanged, implying that zero-hub airlines are not affected by the nationality of the hub. Similarly, we assume that the competitive effects of zero-hub and two-hub airlines are the same on both types of one-hub airlines (domestic and foreign).

In Table 11 we report coefficient estimates for this model. The constant terms for each type are similar to the baseline model. By making the distinction between foreign and domestic markets, and under the assumption of first-mover advantage for foreign

Table 11 Three Type Model, with Nationality, Foreign First-Mover Advantage

Variable	Parameter	Parameter Estimate	Std. Error
Constant of Two Hub	α_2	2.3253	1.4935
Constant of One Hub-Foreign	α_{1f}	1.4209	0.0201
Constant of One Hub-Domestic	α_{1d}	1.3719	0.0471
Constant of Zero Hub	α_0	1.1314	0.0172
Competition:			
Effect on 2 Hub airline of:			
2 Hub airline	θ_{22}	−0.5188	0.0460
1 Hub airline	θ_{12}	−0.4009	0.7844
0 Hub airline	θ_{02}	−0.2643	0.1716
Effect on 1 Hub airline of:			
2 Hub airline	θ_{21}	−0.4162	0.0852
0 Hub airline	θ_{01}	−0.0924	0.0311
Effect on Domestic 1-Hub of:			
1 Hub Domestic	θ_{1d1d}	−0.4636	0.0246
1 Hub Foreign	θ_{1f1d}	−0.3694	0.0487
Effect on Foreign 1-Hub of:			
1 Hub Foreign	θ_{1f1f}	−0.4989	0.0393
1 Hub Domestic	θ_{1d1f}	−0.3654	0.0378
Effect on 0 Hub Rival of:			
2 Hub airline	θ_{20}	−0.5924	0.0927
1 Hub airline	θ_{10}	−0.3894	0.0184
0 Hub	θ_{00}	−0.4508	0.0351
Population 2 Hub airline	$\beta_{2H,1}$	0.4626	0.0704
1 Hub airline	$\beta_{1H,1}$	0.3740	0.0878
0 Hub airline	$\beta_{0H,1}$	1.9937	0.1144
Island: 2 Hub airline	$\beta_{2H,2}$	1.3760	5.4740
1 Hub airline	$\beta_{1H,2}$	0.3374	0.0733
0 Hub airline	$\beta_{0H,2}$	1.0429	0.0652
Distance: 2 Hub airline	$\beta_{2H,3}$	−0.6255	4.1504
1 Hub airline	$\beta_{1H,3}$	−0.5010	0.3810
0 Hub airline	$\beta_{0H,3}$	−0.7333	0.4818
Number of Observations:		305	

airlines, we find a small difference in profitability between one-hub airlines ($\alpha_{1f} = 1.42$ vs. $\alpha_{1d} = 1.37$) and an increase in the coefficient on two-hub airlines from 2.21 to 2.40.

In this model we can identify the effect of competition between one-hub airlines based on at what endpoint they are located. We expect that a hub airline will experience a smaller reduction in profits if the competing hub is located at the other endpoint of the market. Consistent with this intuition, we find more negative effects when hubs are concentrated at the same end of the market for both domestic ($\theta_{1d1d} = -0.46$ vs. $\theta_{1d1f} = -0.36$) and foreign carriers ($\theta_{1f1f} = -0.50$ vs. $\theta_{1f1d} = -0.37$).

This result can be explained by greater competition for domestic traffic flow. Airlines of the same nationality will have domestic networks at the same end-point of the market, while hubs of different nationalities obtain traffic feed from different domestic networks. In addition, smaller product differentiation leads to greater competition between carriers of the same nationality. Indeed, consumers perceive differently foreign from domestic carriers, which may be driven by convenience, brand loyalty (enhanced through frequent flyer programs), etc.

6 POLICY IMPLICATIONS

The empirical results presented above show how market presence affects the profitability of entry in international airline markets. According to these results, in a model of sequential entry, larger market presence imposes strategic barriers to entry for subsequent entrants.

Unlike domestic markets in which market presence at one or both ends of the market responds to an airline's business decisions, in international markets it is also a policy decision. Before 1985 international code sharing was permitted by the DOT as long as the carriers involved had underlying route authority between cities in the route. This initial policy changed in 1988 after United Airlines/British Airways proposed to code share on the Chicago-Seattle segment of the London-Chicago-Seattle route. Since then, the DOT requires approval based on the agreement being in the "public interest". Therefore from a policy perspective understanding the effects of code sharing is important not to undermine competition.

Section 412 and 414, 49 U.S.C. §41308 and 41309 set the DOT's approval standards for intercarrier agreements. Under Section 412 of the Federal Aviation Act, the DOT can approve agreements with foreign carriers if they are not contrary to the public interest, and do not substantially reduce or eliminate competition. In the case that competition is reduced, the agreement may be approved if there is an important transportation need or if it is the only alternative to secure public benefits. Since 1989 the airline industry is subject to the same merger and antitrust regulation as other industries. The Department of Justice (DOJ) is responsible for approving airline mergers, and reviewing code-sharing agreements for possible antitrust violations. The DOT may challenge mergers approved by the DOJ and has the final authority to approve or disapprove a code-sharing agreement. Therefore, evaluating the effect of code sharing on competition is a requirement for obtaining approval.

In addition to the direct reduction in competition between partner airlines, horizontal concerns arise from the possibility of affecting rivals entry decisions. The question is whether allowing for greater market presence through an alliance has anticompetitive effects. Our model incorporates the assumption that incumbent airlines with a more significant presence have a first-mover advantage. This may lead to preemption as earlier movers take actions that limit options to later movers. According to this model, granting approval to an alliance provides a first-mover advantage to the alliance, which might have significant effect on competition.

In many alliances, members are not direct competitors and hence there are no horizontal concerns. The U.S. Air Carrier Licensing Division defines an agreement as type 1 when the foreign carrier operates the flight from its homeland to the U.S., and a U.S. carrier transports the foreign carrier's passengers within the U.S. Analogously, type 2 are defined as agreements in which code sharing takes place in the foreign leg, i.e., U.S. carrier's passengers are transported on a foreign carrier between foreign points. In these complementary alliances, competition is not directly undermined and new destinations can be offered. In type 3 alliances, however, the agreement affects the international segment between gateway airports and either partner could fly the route between the countries before entering the agreement. These parallel alliances raise stronger antitrust concerns because they involve potential competitors. Our analysis has focused on the assessment of the indirect competitive effects of code sharing on this type of alliance. In these cases in which partners can be rivals, approval requires understanding which will be the competitive response of rival airlines to the agreement.

To evaluate the effects on competition based on our results we compare several possible market configurations. Table 12 and 13 evaluate the changes in profitability for non-allied airlines in the absence of entry. In order to assess whether entry would take place we would need to consider, in addition to the presence of potential entrants, the effect of the alliance on profits.

Table 12 evaluates the changes in profitability based on our estimates of the baseline model, which does not distinguish between nationalities. An important determinant of profitability and entry is whether the alliance takes place between actual competitors or an airline which did not operate in the market. The table shows that if both partners were active, code sharing leads to an increase in profitability for all rival types. If an alliance

Table 12 Competitive Effects of Code Sharing on Rival's Profitability

Pre-alliance Market configuration*	Post-alliance Market configuration	Direct Reduction in Competition	Change in Rival's Profitability
Alliance with an incumbent:			$\Delta \pi_1 = n_2(\theta_{21}) - n_2(2\theta_{11}) = +0.909 \, n_2$
$(0, n_1, n_0)$	$(n_2, n_1 - 2n_2, n_0)$	1	
			$\Delta \pi_0 = n_2(\theta_{20}) - n_2(2\theta_{10}) = +0.184 \, n_2$
Alliance with a new entrant:			$\Delta \pi_1 = n_2(\theta_{21}) - n_2(\theta_{11}) = +0.243 \, n_2$
$(0, n_1, n_0)$	$(n_2, n_1 - n_2, n_0)$	0	
			$\Delta \pi_0 = n_2(\theta_{20}) - n_2(\theta_{10}) = -0.197 \, n_2$

*Configuration is the vector: (alliances, one-hub airlines, zero hub airlines).

Table 13 Competitive Effects of Code Sharing on Rival's Profitability, Controlling for Nationality of Hub Airlines

Pre-alliance Market configuration*	Post-alliance Market configuration	Direct Reduction in Competition	Change in Rival's Profitability
Alliance with an incumbent:			
			$\Delta\pi_{1f} = n_2(\theta_{21}) - n_2(\theta_{1d1f} + \theta_{1f1f})$
			$\quad = +0.448n_2$
$(0, n_{1f}, n_{1d}, n_0)$	$(n_2, n_{1f} - n_2, n_{1d} - n_2, n_0)$	1	$\Delta\pi_{1d} = n_2(\theta_{21}) - n_2(\theta_{1d1d} + \theta_{1f1d})$
			$\quad = +0.417n_2$
			$\Delta\pi_0 = n_2(\theta_{20}) - n_2(2\theta_{10}) = +0.187n_2$
Alliance with a new entrant:			
			$\Delta\pi_{1d} = n_2(\theta_{21}) - n_2(\theta_{1f1d}) = -0.047n_2$
$(0, n_{1f}, n_{1d}, n_0)$	$(n_2, n_{1f} - n_2, n_{1d}, n_0)$	0	$\Delta\pi_{1f} = n_2(\theta_{21}) - n_2(\theta_{1f1f}) = +0.083n_2$
			$\Delta\pi_0 = n_2(\theta_{20}) - n_2(\theta_{10}) = -0.203n_2$
			$\Delta\pi_{1d} = n_2(\theta_{21}) - n_2(\theta_{1d1d}) = +0.047n_2$
$(0, n_{1f}, n_{1d}, n_0)$	$(n_2, n_{1f}, n_{1d} - n_2, n_0)$	0	$\Delta\pi_{1f} = n_2(\theta_{21}) - n_2(\theta_{1d1f}) = -0.051n_2$
			$\Delta\pi_0 = n_2(\theta_{20}) - n_2(\theta_{10}) = -0.203n_2$

*Configuration is vector: (alliances, one-hub domestic, one-hub foreign, zero hub airlines).

takes place with a new entrant, profits decrease by -0.20 for the zero-hub firm, while for one-hub firms we still get greater profits after the alliance, with an increase of 0.24.

The model incorporating nationality allows us to examine further this question. In Table 13, the results for the zero-hub airlines are consistent with the baseline model, finding a decrease in profits when the partner is a new entrant. However, positive effects are not found for both one-hub types; the positive effect is only found for the type the airline entering the alliance belonged to. E.g., when a domestic one-hub airline forms an alliance with a new entrant, profits decrease for all types except for the one-hub domestic airlines.

6.1   An Example: LH-UA

The policy question that motivates our analysis is to understand when an alliance would likely result in a reduction of competition, and when would is it likely to be offset by the timely, likely and sufficient entry. Our results indicate that the necessary increase in profitability for firms to enter will be more likely when code sharing takes place between incumbent firms than with new entrants. When an alliance takes place between incumbent firms, the integration of two rival hubs should increase the profitability of rival firms. Actual entry will depend on whether this increase in profits is sufficient given the market characteristics, and whether there are potential entrants in that particular market. If only one of the members of the alliance is an incumbent, the reduction in profits can drive actual competitors out of the market.

This prediction contradicts the policy applied by the DOJ and DOT which has focused on what we have defined as the *direct effect*: "exclude city pairs in which the proposed alliance partners are two of very few or likely future competitors".[27] This policy is reflected in the final order granting antitrust immunity between Lufthansa and United Airlines. On one hand markets with a *direct effect* were granted limited immunity:

> "Regarding city-pair markets, the applicants undertook to exclude from the scope of their requested immunity capacity, fares, and yield management decisions for particular U.S.-source local passengers in the only two markets where both applicants operate their own flights, the Chicago-Frankfurt and Washington, D.C.-Frankfurt markets consistent with Appendix A."
> (OST-96-1116, p. 8)

On the other hand routes with only one incumbent partner were granted unrestricted immunity:

> "As to the other twelve city-pair markets, we found that there were no barriers to entry and that no party had argued to the contrary.[28] We noted that the recent and planned entry by other U.S. airlines into U.S.-Germany markets confirmed our tentative finding that entry is both possible and likely, notwithstanding the applicants' large market share". (OST-96-1116, p. 8)

Table 14 illustrates the outcome in terms of competition of this alliance. In May of 1998, in four out of the twelve routes there were less competitors than before immunity was

Table 14   An Example: LH-UA*

	1996**	1997	1998	1999
Atlanta-Frankfurt	LH, UA	LH-UA	LH-UA	LH-UA
Boston-Frankfurt	US, LH	US, LH	LH	LH
Chicago-Düsseldorf	UA	UA	UA	UA
Chicago-Munich	LH	LH	LH	LH
Dallas/Ft.Worth-Frankfurt	AA, LH	AA, LH	AA, LH	AA, LH
Houston-Frankfurt			LH	LH
New York-Düsseldorf	LH	LH, LT	LH	
New York-Frankfurt	DL, KU, LH, TW, PK, SQ	DL, KU, LH, PK, SQ	DL, KU, LH, PK, SQ	AA, DL, KU, LH, SQ
Los Angeles-Frankfurt	DL, LH, NZ	DL, LH, NZ	LH, NZ	LH, NZ
Miami-Frankfurt	AA, LH	AA, LH	LH	LH
Newark-Frankfurt	CO, LH	CO, LH	CO, LH	CO, LH
San Francisco-Frankfurt	LH	LH	LH	LH
Washington-Frankfurt***	DL, LH, UA	LH-UA	LH-UA	LH-UA
Chicago-Frankfurt***	AA, LH, UA	AA, LH-UA	AA, LH-UA	AA, LH-UA

*In June of 1996 LH and UA were granted immunity.
**Operating carriers in May of each year. "LH-UA" means they where both operating.
***Routes in which partners where both operating.

---

[27] Klein (1999), p. 7.
[28] These routes are Atlanta-Frankfurt, Boston-Frankfurt, Chicago-Dusseldorf, Chicago-Munich, Dallas/Ft.Worth-Frankfurt, Houston-Frankfurt, New York-Dusseldorf, New York-Frankfurt, Los Angeles-Frankfurt, Miami-Frankfurt, Newark-Frankfurt, and San Francisco-Frankfurt.

granted. This example is consistent with the predictions of our model, which suggest that in order to measure the competitive effect of an alliance we should also account for the *indirect effect* on competition.

7 CONCLUSION

In this paper we investigate the effect of international code sharing on airline profitability. Our empirical analysis proposes an equilibrium model of entry in which we study the effect of competition on airlines' profits. We characterize markets both in terms of their alliance structure and airport presence. Because to have a hub at both ends of the route requires entering an alliance, we can characterize routes in these two dimensions and still have a tractable problem. Our findings indicate that airport presence and therefore the alliance structure is a determinant of profitability.

Unlike domestic routes, large airport presence at both end-points of the route requires authorization. Our results indicate that approval should take into account how an alliance affects the profitability of potential entrants. A competitive response to an increase in prices or a reduction in service will depend on whether in a particular market the presence of an alliance imposes large negative effects on rivals' profits, which ultimately can deter entry. We find that it is more likely that the direct reduction in competition is offset by entry when alliances take place between incumbents. If a partner is a new entrant, while there is no direct reduction in competition, the *indirect effect* is stronger and hence may determine other rivals' decisions to continue in the market.

We extend our analysis to allow for differences in nationality. Our results indicate that it is important to take into account not only total competition and airport presence, but also whether competition is concentrated at the same end of the market or not. The equilibrium relies on an assumption regarding the order of entry.

We can not make a welfare statement based on the identified interactions between rival's profitability. A possible outcome may still be a more concentrated market, operating more efficiently, with higher margins, and lower prices. Our analysis contributes to the evaluation of these agreements based on the potential competitive effects and the likelihood of entry.

APPENDIX

In this appendix we provide a more detailed explanation of the calculation of probabilities and estimation method presented in Section 2 for the simultaneous entry game with tie-breaking rule. There are three types of airlines (two-hub, one-hub and zero-hub airlines), which we label with subscripts 2, 1 and 0 respectively. The number of airlines observed for each type $(n_m^{2h^*}, n_m^{1h^*}, n_m^{0h^*})$, results from of a set of threshold conditions holding for the potential entrants' profits. To simplify notation we denote this vector of entrants as (n_2, n_1, n_0). In any given market, m, there is a vector of potential entrants $p_m = (p_2, p_1, p_0)$, and therefore the possible market outcomes are bounded: $0 \leq n_2 \leq p_2$, $0 \leq n_1 \leq p_1$, and $0 \leq n_0 \leq p_0$.

For notation convenience we rewrite the profit function defined in equation 3, $X_m\beta_c +$ $M_c(\theta; \vec{n}) + \varepsilon_{cm} = \Pi_c(\vec{n}) + \varepsilon_c$. In section 2 we have assumed that the stochastic component of profits has a trivariate normal distribution. To observe a market configuration (n_2, n_1, n_0) entry must be profitable (conditions 2, 4 and 6) and firms not entering can not make positive profits (conditions 1, 3 and 5). This yields the following threshold conditions:

(1) $\Pi_2(n_2, n_1, n_0) + \varepsilon_2 < 0$ or $\varepsilon_2 < -\Pi_2(n_2, n_1, n_0)$
(2) $\Pi_2(n_2 - 1, n_1, n_0) + \varepsilon_2 > 0$ or $\varepsilon_2 > -\Pi_2(n_2 - 1, n_1, n_0)$
(3) $\Pi_1(n_2, n_1, n_0) + \varepsilon_1 < 0$ or $\varepsilon_1 < -\Pi_1(n_2, n_1, n_0)$
(4) $\Pi_1(n_2, n_1 - 1, n_0) + \varepsilon_1 > 0$ or $\varepsilon_1 > -\Pi_1(n_2, n_1 - 1, n_0)$
(5) $\Pi_0(n_2, n_1, n_0) + \varepsilon_0 < 0$ or $\varepsilon_0 < -\Pi_1(n_2, n_1, n_0)$
(6) $\Pi_0(n_2, n_1, n_0 - 1) + \varepsilon_0 > 0$ or $\varepsilon_0 > -\Pi_0(n_2, n_1, n_0 - 1)$

These conditions delimit the following region:

(1) (1) and (2) imply $-\Pi_2(n_2, n_1, n_0) > \varepsilon_2 > -\Pi_2(n_2 - 1, n_1, n_0)$
(2) (3) and (4) imply $-\Pi_1(n_2, n_1, n_0) > \varepsilon_1 > -\Pi_1(n_2, n_1 - 1, n_0)$
(3) (5) and (6) imply $-\Pi_1(n_2, n_1, n_0) > \varepsilon_0 > -\Pi_0(n_2, n_1, n_0 - 1)$

Denoting this region as A, its probability is:

$$Prob(A) = \int_{-\Pi_2(n_2-1,n_1,n_0)}^{-\Pi_2(n_2,n_1,n_0)} \int_{-\Pi_1(n_2,n_1-1,n_0)}^{-\Pi_1(n_2,n_1,n_0)} \int_{-\Pi_0(n_2,n_1,n_0-1)}^{-\Pi_1(n_2,n_1,n_0)} f(\varepsilon_2, \varepsilon_1, \varepsilon_0) d\varepsilon_2 d\varepsilon_1 d\varepsilon_0$$

This probability is defined over regions in which multiple equilibria are possible. The sequential entry guarantees uniqueness by defining the order of entry: type 2 firms make their entry decisions simultaneously, then type 1 firms, and type 0 firms last. Therefore, to calculate the probability of (n_2, n_1, n_0) we must subtract from A the probability over the regions in which other equilibria have a first mover advantage. The intersections, which we label as regions B and C, will depend on the profit functions. In our model we do not impose any assumptions regarding competitive effects being greater intra or inter-types, and therefore we can not order profits based on the number of firms. As a result, the regions of intersection will depend on the realization of the profit function. For example, suppose competition of the same type had a more negative effect on profits. Then, regions B and C have probabilities:

$$Prob(B) = \int_{-\Pi_2(n_2,n_1-1,n_0)}^{-\Pi_2(n_2,n_1,n_0)} \int_{-\Pi_1(n_2,n_1-1,n_0)}^{-\Pi_1(n_2+1,n_1-1,n_0)} \int_{-\Pi_0(n_2,n_1,n_0-1)}^{-\Pi_1(n_2,n_1,n_0)} f(\varepsilon_2, \varepsilon_1, \varepsilon_0) d\varepsilon_2 d\varepsilon_1 d\varepsilon_0$$

$$Prob(C) = \int_{-\Pi_2(n_2-1,n_1,n_0)}^{-\Pi_2(n_2,n_1,n_0)} \int_{-\Pi_1(n_2,n_1,n_0-1)}^{-\Pi_1(n_2,n_1,n_0)} \int_{-\Pi_0(n_2,n_1,n_0-1)}^{-\Pi_1(n_2,n_1+1,n_0-1)} f(\varepsilon_2, \varepsilon_1, \varepsilon_0) d\varepsilon_2 d\varepsilon_1 d\varepsilon_0$$

Therefore, the probability of observing (n_2, n_1, n_0) is given by:

$$Prob(n_2, n_1, n_0) = Prob(A) - Prob(B) - Prob(C)$$

Prob(B) is the region corresponding to an alternative equilibrium with type 2 first mover advantage. Realizations of ε in this region correspond to a $(n_2 + 1, n_1 - 1, n_0)$

configuration. In a similar way, we subtract $Prob(C)$, which corresponds to an alternative equilibrium with type 1 advantage, $(n_2, n_1 + 1, n_0 - 1)$.

The region and distribution defining the probabilities are constrained in several ways. First, in each market we observe no fewer than zero firms of each type, and at most a number of entrants equal to the number of potential entrants. If the number of entrants is equal to the number of potential entrants, the probability is not bounded by the profits of an additional entrant, and the integration limit is plus infinity. Similarly, the region is unbounded below when the number of firms is zero. Second, the distribution of the error term is truncated at zero and we only study markets in which entry takes place, i.e., the distribution is conditional on observing at least one entrant of one type, $min(n_2, n_1, n_0) > 0$.

Since the region of integration for airlines entry decisions is nonrectangular, higher-dimensional multinomial integrals limit the use of maximum-likelihood estimation. In order to estimate the parameters of the model we employ a frequency simulation approach. Lerman and Manski (1981) propose to simulate the probability of each event by an observed frequency. For a large number of random draws this simulator counts the number of times the event is true. This approach has two drawbacks: consistency requires a large number of draws; and second, the discontinuity of the simulator causes discrete changes in the frequency count for small changes in the parameters, impeding numerical optimization.

The literature proposes a number of simulators which overcome the limitations of the "crude" frequency simulator.[29] In the context of entry models, Berry (1992) implemented a simulated method-of-moments estimator, using the moment conditions for the number of firms in the market. Reiss (1996) provides evidence of the performance of simulator estimator in a discrete strategic-choice model employing the probability simulator proposed by Axel Borsch-Supan and Vassilis Hajivassiliou (1993). More recently Mazzeo (2002) uses a frequency simulation method to approximate the likelihood function of a three product-type model. We will apply this approach to our problem.

The likelihood function is the product of the probabilities of each of the observed outcomes, which is defined as:

$$L = \prod_{m=1}^{305} Prob(n_2, n_1, n_0)$$

Given the complexity of the limits of integration we approximate the probability as follows: for each market m, take a large number K of random draws from $f(\varepsilon_2, \varepsilon_1, \varepsilon_0)$. We count the number of times, P out of K, for which the market's observed threshold conditions hold. For example, the $Prob(A)$ is approximated by:

$$Pm(\beta, \theta) = \frac{1}{K} \sum_{K=1}^{K} \left\{ \begin{array}{l} I\left[-\prod_2(n_2, n_1, n_0) > \varepsilon_2 > -\prod_2(n_2 - 1, n_1, n_0)\right] \\ *I\left[-\prod_1(n_2, n_1, n_0) > \varepsilon_1 > -\prod_1(n_2, n_1 - 1, n_0)\right] \\ *I\left[-\prod_0(n_2, n_1, n_0) > \varepsilon_0 > -\prod_0(n_2, n_1, n_0 - 1)\right] \end{array} \right\}$$

---

[29] A detailed discussion of the properties of the alternative methods can be found in Hajivassiliou, McFadden, and Ruud (1996). Stern (1997) reviews the different simulation methods and their empirical applications in the literature.

This is the product of the indicator function for each of the inequalities that must hold to get the observed market configuration. To overcome the discontinuity of the frequency count, the estimated function is smoothed replacing the indicator function by the cumulative normal distribution.

REFERENCES

Airline Business (1994–1999) *Survey of Airline Alliances.*

Bailey, E.E., Graham, D.R., and Kaplan, D.P. (1985) *Deregulation and The Theory of Contestable Markets*, Cambridge, MA: MIT Press.

Berry, S. (1992) "Estimation of a Model of Entry in the Airline Industry," *Econometrica*, vol. 60(4), pp. 841–917.

Bingaman, A.K. (1996) "Consolidation and Code Sharing: Antitrust Enforcement in the Airline Industry," *Address before the American Bar Association, Forum on Air and Space Law*, Washington: US Department of Justice.

Borenstein, S. (1989) "Hubs and High Fares: Dominance and Market Power in the U.S. Airline Industry," *Rand Journal of Economics*, vol. 21, pp. 344–365.

Borenstein, S. (1990) "Airline Mergers, Airport Dominance, and Market Power," *American Economic Review*, vol. 80, pp. 400–404.

Borsch-Supan, Axel and Vassilies A. Hajivassiliou (1993) "Smoothed Unbiased Multivariate Probability Simulators for Maximum Likelihood Estimation of Limited Dependent Variable Models," *Journal of Econometrics*, vol. 58(3), pp. 347–368.

Bresnahan, T. and P.C. Reiss (1990) "Entry in Monopoly Markets," *Review of Economic Studies*, vol. 57, pp. 531–553.

Bresnahan, T. and P.C. Reiss (1991) "Models of Discrete Games," *Journal of Econometrics*, vol. 48(1), pp. 57–81.

Brueckner, J.K. and P.T. Spiller (1991) "Competition and Mergers in Airline Networks," *International Journal of Industrial Organization*, vol. 9, pp. 323–342.

Brueckner, J.K. and W.T. Whalen (2000) "The Price Effects of International Airline Alliances," *The Journal of Law and Economics*, vol. 43(2), pp. 503–545.

Brueckner, J.K. (2001) "The Economics of International Code Sharing: An Analysis of Airline Alliances," *International Journal of Industrial Organization*, vol. 19, pp. 1475–1498.

Brueckner, J.K. (2003) "International Airfares in the Age of Alliances: The Effects of Codesharing and Antitrust Immunity," *The Review of Economics and Statistics*, vol. 85(1), pp. 105–118.

Burton J. and P. Hanlon (1991) "Airline alliances: Cooperating to Compete?" *Journal of Air Transport Management*, vol. 1(4), pp. 209–227.

Chen, Z. and T. Ross (2000) "Strategic Alliances, Shared Facilities, and Entry Deterrence," *Rand Journal of Economics*, vol. 31(2), pp. 326–344.

Cox, D.R. (1972) "Regression Models and Life Tables," *Journal of The Royal Statistical Society B*, vol. 34. pp. 187–202.

Department of Justice and Federal Trade Commission (1997) *Horizontal Merger Guidelines.*

Department of Transportation, Office of the Secretary (1995) "Statement of United States International Air Transportation Policy," Docket No. 49844.

Hajivassiliou, V., D. McFadden, and P. Ruud (1996) "Simulation of Multivariate Normal Rectangle Probabilities and their Derivatives: Theoretical and Computational Results," *Journal of Econometrics*, vol. 72(2), pp. 85–134.

Hassin, O. and O. Shy (2000) "Code-Sharing Agreements, Aircraft Capacity and Interconnections in the Airline Industry," *Department of Economics, University of Haifa.*

Heimer, O. and O. Shy (2006) "Code-Sharing Agreements, Frequency of Flights and Profits under Parallel Operation," in Darin Lee, ed., Advances in Airline Economics, vol. 1, Elsevier, pp. 163–181.

Klein, J.I. (2000) "Antitrust Issues in the Airline Industry," Testimony before the Committee on Commerce, Science and Transportation, United States Senate.

Klein, J.I. (1999) "Competition in the airline industry," Testimony before the Committee on Commerce, Science and Transportation, United States Senate.

Lerman, S. and C. Manski (1981) "On The Use of Simulated Frequencies to Approximate Choice Probabilities," in Structural analysis of discrete data with econometric applications, Eds.: Charles Manski and Daniel McFadden. Cambridge: MIT Press, 1981, pp. 305–319.

Levine, M. (1987) "Airline Competition in Deregulated Markets: Theory, Firm Strategy and Public Policy," Yale Journal of Regulation, vol. 4, pp. 393–494.

Mazzeo, M.J. (2002) "Product Choice and Oligopoly Market Structure: An Empirical Analysis of the Motel Industry," Rand Journal of Economics, vol. 33, pp. 221–242.

Morrison, S.A. and C. Winston (1987) The Implications of Airline Deregulation, Washington DC: The Brookings Institution.

Morrison, S.A. and C. Winston (1987) "Empirical implications and tests of the contestability hypothesis," Journal of Law and Economics, vol. 30, pp. 53–56.

Nannes, J.M. (1999) "The Importance of Entry Conditions in Analyzing Airline Industry Issues," Address before the International Aviation Club, Washington, DC.

Nannes, J.M. (1998) "Consolidation in the Airline Industry," Testimony before the Committee on Commerce, Science and Transportation, United States Senate.

Official Airline Guides (1990–1999) OAG: Worldwide Edition, OAG, Chicago, IL.

Office of International Aviation (2000) Code Share Report. Department of Transportation. http://ostpxweb.dot.gov/aviation/IntAv/coderpt.PDF.

Oum T.H., Park, J. and A. Zhang (1996) "The Effects of Airline Code-sharing Agreements on Firm Conduct and International Air Fares," Journal of Transport Economics and Policy, vol. 30(2), 187–202.

Oum, T.H., C. Yu, and A. Zhang (2001) "Global Airline Alliances: International Regulatory Issues," Journal of Air Transport Management, vol. 7(1), pp. 57–62.

Park, J. (1997) "The Effects of the Airline Alliances and Markets Economic Welfare," Transportation Research, vol. 33E(2), June.

Park, J. and A. Zhang (1998) "Airline Alliances and Partner Firms. Outputs," Transportation Research, vol. 34E(4), December.

Park, J. and A. Zhang (2000) "An Empirical Analysis of Global Airline Alliances: Cases in North Atlantic Markets," Review of Industrial Organization, vol. 16, pp. 367–384.

Reiss, P.C. (1996) "Empirical Models of Discrete Strategic-Choices," American Economic Review, vol. 86(2), pp. 421–426.

Stern, S. (1997) "Simulation-Based Estimation," Journal of Economic Literature, vol. 35(4), pp. 2006–2039.

Stern, S. (1992) "A Method of Smoothing Simulated Moments of Discrete Probabilities in Multinomial Probit Models," Econometrica, vol. 60(4), pp. 943–952.

U.S. Department of Transportation (1994): A study of International Code sharing. Gellman Research Associated, Inc.

Whalen, T. (2005) "A Panel Data Analysis of Code Sharing, Antitrust Immunity and Open Skies Treaties in International Aviation Markets," Mimeo.

Advances in Airline Economics, Vol 1
Darin Lee (Editor)
© 2006 Published by Elsevier B.V.

6

The Impact of Domestic Codesharing Agreements on Market Airfares: Evidence From the U.S.*

Harumi Ito[†] and Darin Lee[‡]

ABSTRACT

Recent codesharing agreements among the many of the largest U.S. carriers (i.e., US Airways/United and Delta/Continental/Northwest) has resulted in nearly two-thirds of all domestic passengers traveling on carriers with domestic codesharing agreements. This paper examines the impact of domestic codeshare agreements on airfares at the market level between 1998 and 2003. Results from our fixed-effects analysis indicate that even when codesharing does not combine the networks of two different carriers (thus internalizing the double-marginalization problem associated with interline tickets), average fares tend to be lower after codesharing is introduced into a market.

1 INTRODUCTION

The impact of international airline alliances and codesharing on airfares and competition has received much attention over the past few years (Brueckner 2003, Brueckner and Whalen 2000, Park and Zhang 2000). And while codesharing between large carriers has primarily been thought of as an international practice, codeshare agreements among major domestic carriers has also become a widespread phenomenon in the U.S. airline

---

*The authors thank W. Tom Whalen and participants of the 2005 American Economic Association annual meetings for helpful comments. The views expressed in this paper are those of the authors and do not necessarily reflect those of LECG, LLC. All errors are ours alone.
[†]NBER.
[‡]Corresponding author. LECG, LLC. 350 Massachusetts Avenue, Suite 300, Cambridge, MA 02139. E-mail: darin_lee@lecg.com. Tel: (617)-761-0108, Fax: (617)-621-8018.

industry.[1] Over the past few years, and as summarized in Table 1, virtually all of the largest U.S. hub and spoke carriers have entered into broad domestic codesharing partnerships, including the United/US Airways alliance that began in January 2003, and even more recently, the three-way alliance between Northwest, Continental and Delta initiated in June 2003.[2] In light of this recent trend towards increased cooperation and the fact that carriers comprising the three largest U.S. alliances at the end of 2003 (Continental/Northwest/Delta, United/US Airways and American/Alaska) accounted for nearly two-thirds of all domestic origin and destination ("O&D") passengers, there are legitimate policy and antitrust concerns regarding the impact of these cooperative marketing agreements on airfares. Indeed, numerous reports (i.e., U.S. General Accounting Office 1998, U.S. General Accounting Office 1999, Transportation Research Board 1999) have raised significant questions regarding the potential negative effects of domestic codeshare agreements.

This paper asks a simple question: has increased domestic codesharing by the large U.S. carriers in recent years led to higher airfares? In order to shed some light onto this important question, we construct a five year panel (1999–2003) of city-pair markets. We then analyze the impact of codesharing on average fares within markets generally, but also on the average fares of the different market participants (i.e., non-codeshare tickets of the codeshare partners as well as other carriers serving the market).

Predicting the impact of domestic codeshare agreements on market fares is a controversial topic. On the one hand, there is much evidence that cooperative marketing agreements in international markets has resulted in lower fares (Brueckner 2003, Brueckner and Whalen 2000, Park and Zhang 2000, Oum, Park, and Zhang 1996). These results, however, rely critically on the fact that international codesharing has served to greatly reduce the double-marginalization problem associated with "interline" fares between two carriers. That is, since no single carrier can viably offer (both due to cost and regulatory factors) a route network that serves all major international markets, absent international alliances, many international passengers would be required to make an interline connection between two carriers. And while international carriers routinely sell such joint tickets, the fare setting procedure for two unaffiliated carriers typically involves both carriers independently setting their segment fare to maximize their own profit. Since most international alliances have antitrust immunity, however, alliance partner carriers can typically set prices on codeshare itineraries as though they were a single carrier, thus substantially reducing—or eliminating all together—the double marginalization problem (Brueckner 2003, Brueckner 2000).

While international air travel often necessitates combining the network resources of two or more carriers, there is already substantial overlap between the domestic networks of the large U.S. carriers. For example, among the 1,000 largest city-pair markets— which collectively account for over three quarters of all domestic passengers—the mean and median number of the six largest hub-and-spoke carriers (American, United, Delta,

---

[1] It is important to note that codesharing between mainline and regional carriers (i.e., American/American Eagle, Northwest/Mesaba, Delta/Comair, etc.) has been an integral part of the U.S. airline industry for several decades.

[2] Even more recently (January 2005), two of the nation's largest low cost carriers—Southwest and ATA— announced that they would also begin codesharing.

Northwest, Continental and US Airways) offering service using their own aircraft is 5.0 and 6 respectively.[3] Thus, as demonstrated by Ito and Lee (2004), most domestic codesharing within the U.S. does not involve connecting service on two different carriers (a practice they refer to as "traditional" codesharing). Rather, Ito and Lee (2004) find that the vast majority of domestic codeshare tickets are "virtual" in nature, whereby the codeshare carrier sells tickets for flights operated entirely by another carrier.[4]

Consequently, it should come as no surprise that domestic codesharing alliances have typically been met with much greater regulatory skepticism than their international counterparts. For example, in its 1998 assessment of domestic alliances, the U.S. General Accounting Office noted that "Unlike international alliances, which largely extend domestic airlines' route networks into areas that they could not enter by themselves, the networks of the domestic airlines generally overlap to a much greater extent, and therefore the proposed alliances pose a greater threat to competition" (U.S. General Accounting Office 1998, p. 8). Commonly cited potential anti-competitive consequences of domestic codesharing agreements that could lead to higher prices include CRS "crowding-out" (i.e., the fact that codeshare flights are listed numerous times in computer reservations systems, potentially travel agents away from non-alliance carriers), reduced incentives by carriers that are part of an alliance to enter new markets already served by its codeshare partners and less competition (or tacitly collusive behavior) among alliance carriers bidding for corporate travel contracts (Whalen 1999, Transportation Research Board 1999).

In sum, the impact of domestic codeshare agreements on overall market fares is not at all obvious, at least at first glance. Not only is there substantial overlap between many alliance partners, the majority of codesharing that currently takes place under these agreements does not result in additional competitors serving markets using their own network resources, a fact that has raised numerous anti-competitive concerns. And while Ito and Lee (2004) also find—somewhat surprisingly—that virtual codeshare itineraries are priced lower than comparable itineraries offered by a single carrier, the number of codeshare tickets sold as a proportion of all tickets is still quite small (i.e., less than one half of one percent.[5] Therefore, it is not clear if or how the availability of less expensive virtual tickets could exert competitive downward pressure on overall fares within a market. One potential channel by which less expensive codeshare fares could exert competitive pressure on non-codeshare fares is via in the Internet. If—as argued by numerous airline executives—the proliferation of Internet-based search and booking tools has led to unprecedented price transparency for airfares, carriers would be forced to respond to lower priced codeshared itineraries, even if few passengers actually purchased such tickets.[6]

---

[3] Among the largest 2,500 city pairs—which account for 89% of domestic passengers—the mean is 4.6 and the median is 5.

[4] For example, a typical codeshare ticket in the U.S. might involve a passenger purchasing a ticket marketed by US Airways consisting of flights operated entirely by United.

[5] Ito and Lee (2004) argue that carriers use virtual codesharing as another form of product differentiation, selling their "branded" product to passengers willing to pay for all the benefits of their premium product (i.e., upgradeability and full elite-qualifying frequent flyer miles) while positioning their virtual tickets as a "generic", less expensive, and slightly inferior brand.

[6] See, for example, *Remarks of David N. Siegel, President and Chief Executive Officer, US Airways, Potomac Officers Club, February 25, 2004.*

Despite the recent proliferation of large domestic codeshare agreements, they have thus far received only limited attention in the economics literature. The paper most related to ours is Bamberger, Carlton, and Neumann (2004), which studies the change in average market fares before and after the introduction of codesharing by Northwest/Alaska and Continental/America West.[7] While our empirical findings support those of Bamberger, Carlton, and Neumann (2004), our analysis extends their findings in three important respects. First, since our panel of data covers the period 1999–2003, our analysis captures the dramatic expansion of domestic codesharing that began in 1999, including the recent United/US Airways agreement and the Northwest/Continental agreement.[8] For example, while less than 45,000 passengers travelled on domestic codeshare tickets during the third quarter of 1998, this number had grown over thirteen-fold to more than 586,000 by the third quarter of 2003. Second, while Bamberger, Carlton, and Neumann (2004) focus solely on those markets where an alliance converts a potential interline itinerary into a traditional codeshare itinerary (i.e., those which combine the networks of the two alliance partners), our analysis also takes into account the more recent—and much more widespread—phenomena of virtual codesharing whereby one carrier markets flights operated entirely by another carrier.[9] Finally, by also estimating itinerary-level (in addition to market-level) models, we are able to decompose the effect of codesharing on alliance members and their competitors.

In general, we find that the introduction of domestic codesharing has not led to higher average fares. To the contrary, we find that introducing codesharing into a market slightly reduces averages fares. When we decompose codesharing into its traditional and virtual types, we also find—not surprisingly—that traditional codesharing exerts greater downward pressure on average fares within a market than virtual codesharing. Thus, our analysis reinforces earlier findings by Bamberger, Carlton, and Neumann (2004) and suggests that increased cooperation between carriers in the sales and marketing of airline tickets has not led—in any systematic way—to higher average fares.

The remainder of this paper is organized as follows. Section 2 defines some notation and terminology that will be used throughout the paper. Section 3 presents an overview of our data and empirical model. In Section 4, we analyze the impact of codesharing on average fares at the market (i.e., city-pair) level. In Section 5, we assess whether or not codesharing has different effects on various market participants by estimating itinerary-level models. Brief concluding remarks are presented in Section 6.

---

[7] The latter of these two agreements was terminated in 2002. Two other papers (Whalen 1999, Armantier and Richard 2003) estimate the welfare effects arising from domestic alliances (some of which were proposed but never implemented), and find that they are likely to reduce consumer welfare.

[8] Bamberger, Carlton, and Neumann (2004) study the Northwest/Alaska agreement during the period 1994–96 and the Continental/America West agreement during the 1994–95 period. While Delta joined the Northwest/Continental agreement in June 2003, codeshare itineraries involving Delta were not yet present in the third quarter data from 2003.

[9] For example, while fewer than 10% of codeshare itineraries during the third quarter 1998 were virtual, the proportion had grown to more than 75% by the third quarter of 2003. During the period of analysis in Bamberger, Carlton, and Neumann (2004), virtual codesharing had not yet been introduced.

2   CODESHARING IN THE U.S. AIRLINE INDUSTRY

We begin by briefly discussing some important concepts of airline cooperation and marketing: codesharing, interlining and alliances. A flight is said to be "codeshared" when the operating and marketing carrier for that flight can differ. For example, Alaska Airlines operates non-stop flights between Seattle and Los Angeles. However, the Seattle–Angeles flights operated by Alaska are listed in computer reservation systems ("CRSs") and flight schedules of both Alaska Airlines and American Airlines. Next, an airline itinerary or ticket is said to be "online" when the operating carrier for each flight coupon of the itinerary remains the same.[10] In contrast, an itinerary is said to be "interline" when there are two or more operating carriers. Finally, carriers can form cooperative marketing "alliances" that may cover a wide array of joint activities, up to–but not necessarily including–codesharing. Generally speaking, a typical domestic alliance may include costs reduction initiatives (i.e., sharing or consolidating airport facilities such as gates, lounges, etc.), schedule and gate coordination to provide more convenient connections between flights of alliance partners, and frequently flyer program and/or airport lounge reciprocity. Unlike many international alliances, no domestic alliance currently has antitrust immunity that would allow them to jointly determine pricing on interline or codeshare flights. Table 1 summarizes the main domestic codesharing alliances in effect in the U.S.

   From an institutional standpoint, all domestic codesharing agreements in the U.S. use the "free-sale" model. Under a free-sale agreement, the operating carrier maintains and controls the seat inventory, but allows its codeshare partner(s) to market and sell seats on designated codeshare flights under their own marketing code. Hence, both the operating and codeshare carriers sell seats out of the same general inventory, and the operating carrier receives all of the ticket revenue, regardless of which carrier actually sells the seat. In practice, there may be technological differences between the seat inventories available to the operating and codeshare carriers. For example, while the operating carrier will have "real time" access to its seat inventory, the codeshare partner's inventory may be delayed if the particular agreement calls for its inventory to be updated only periodically throughout the day. In return for selling a seat on a codeshare flight, the operating carrier usually pays the marketing carrier a nominal commission to cover costs (for example, the "cost" to the marketing carrier of issuing its frequent flyer miles). Since virtually all of the revenue from a codeshare flight accrues to the operating carrier, codeshare agreements are carefully negotiated so that they are "balanced" in the sense that partners exchange their operating/marketing roles across different routes so as to roughly equalize the benefits from the agreement.

   A less common type of institutional agreement (and one that is not currently used among any of the large domestic codeshare alliances in the U.S.) is the so-called block-space agreement. Under this form of codeshare arrangement, the operating carrier sells a block of its seats on a given flight to another carrier (the codeshare partner) which then assumes the sole responsibility for marketing and selling the inventory of seats it has purchased, which it does under its own marketing code. Since the codeshare carrier

---

[10] We assume throughout our analysis–as is standard in the industry–that connections between mainline and affiliated regional carriers are also online.

Table 1 U.S. Domestic Alliances/Codeshare Agreements (2003)

Carriers	Combined Domestic Share (%)	Notes
Continental/Delta/Northwest	30.4	Three-way codesharing began in June 2003. Excludes local hub markets. Northwest and Continental entered into a bilateral codeshare agreement in December 1999.
United/US Airways	17.6	Commenced January 2003.
American/Alaska	16.2	Commenced 1999. Codeshare on select flights to/from Los Angeles/Portland/San Francisco/Seattle.
American/Hawaiian	13.9	Commenced March 1998. American codeshares on Hawaiian Airlines services within Hawaii. Hawaiian codeshares on American Eagle services at Los Angeles.
Northwest/Alaska	11.4	Commenced August 1999. Systemwide codeshare except select flights to/from Mexico and transcontinental flights.
Continental/Alaska	10.5	Commenced March 1999.
Northwest/Hawaiian	9.2	Commenced 1995. Codeshare on intra-Hawaii flights and Trans-Pacific flights.
Continental/Hawaiian	8.3	Commenced August 1999. Codeshare on inter-island flights.
American West/Hawaiian	5.2	Commenced October 2002.
Alaska/Hawaiian	5.0	Commenced October 2001.

Notes and Sources: Share is of domestic O&D passengers for the third quarter of 2003 based on U.S. DOT OD1B Database. Effective dates from "Airline alliance survey 2003", *Airline Business*, July 2003.

purchases the inventory from the operating carrier, it keeps all of the revenue associated with the codeshare seats it sells.

3 NOTATION AND DEFINITIONS

We begin by defining some terminology and notation. We define a market to be a directional city pair.[11] An itinerary or ticket consists of one or more flight coupons, each coupon representing travel on a particular flight segment between two airports. While

---

[11] For the purposes of our analysis, we group airports in the following metropolitan area: Washington, D.C. (BWI, DCA, IAD), San Francisco Bay Area (SFO, SJC, OAK), Los Angeles (LAX, BUR, LGB, SNA, ONT), Houston (IAH, HOU), Dallas (DAL, DFW), Chicago (ORD, MDW), New York City (LGA, JFK, EWR, HPN) and Miami (MIA, FLL).

every flight segment has, by definition, a single operating carrier (the airline whose plane is used to operate the flight) it can have one or more marketing carriers (airlines that have the ability to list the flight as part of their flight schedule, set its fares, and in turn, market seats on the flight to travelers).

When referring to a flight segment, we use the convention operating carrier code/marketing carrier code and we denote a connection between two flight segments with the symbol "→". For example, AA/AA → AA/AA denotes a connecting itinerary between two flights in which both the operating and marketing carrier is American Airlines. Likewise, NW/NW → CO/CO denotes a connecting itinerary where the first segment is operated and marketed by Northwest, while the second segment is operated and marketed by Continental.

An itinerary is said to be *online* when the operating carrier for each flight coupon of the itinerary remains the same (i.e., AA/AA → AA/AA). In contrast, an itinerary is said to be *interline* if the operating carrier changes at some point throughout the journey (i.e., DL/DL → AA/AA).

A particular flight is said to be *codeshared* when the operating and marketing carrier for that flight can differ. We denote codeshare flight segments with an asterisk (*). Thus, NW/CO* → CO/CO denotes a connecting itinerary where the first segment is operated by Northwest, but is marketed by Continental as a codeshare flight, and the second segment is both operated and marketed by Continental. This leads us to our first definition:

Definition 1 *An itinerary is said to be* **traditional codeshare** *if it is interline and has at least one codeshare segment. Examples: (i.e., AA/AA → AS/AA*, UA/UA → UA/UA → US/UA*).*

While the existing codeshare literature (i.e. Brueckner and Whalen 2000, Brueckner 2003, Bamberger, Carlton, and Neumann 2004) has implicitly assumed that codesharing entails a connection between two (or more) different operating carriers, Ito and Lee (2004) recently demonstrated that domestic codesharing practices within the U.S. do not conform to the "traditional" concept of codesharing. Rather, the authors showed—somewhat surprisingly—that the majority of domestic codeshare tickets involve a single operating carrier, practice they refer to as "virtual" codesharing. That is, a typical domestic codeshare ticket might involve US Airways marketing and selling tickets on flights operated solely by its codeshare partner United Airlines (i.e., UA/US* → UA/US*).[12] This leads us to our next definition:

Definition 2 *An itinerary is said to be a* **virtual codeshare** *itinerary when it is online and has at least one codeshare segment. Examples: UA/US* → UA/US*, AA/AS*.*

In addition to the two codeshare itinerary types define above, we also define two non-cooperative types of itineraries.

---

[12] Ito and Lee (2004) further differentiate between "fully" and "semi" virtual codesharing based on whether or not all—or only some—of the ticket's segments are codeshared. As the main purpose of the current analysis is to study the impact of codesharing more generally on market fares, we do not distinguish between these sub-cases.

Definition 3 *An itinerary is said to be* **pure online** *if it is online and has no code-share segments. Examples: (i.e.,* $DL/DL \rightarrow DL/DL, WN/WN, UA/UA \rightarrow UA/UA \rightarrow UA/UA$).

Definition 4 *An itinerary is said to be* **standard interline** *if it is interline and has no codeshare segments. Examples: (i.e.,* $DL/DL \rightarrow HP/HP, UA/UA \rightarrow AA/AA$).

Pure online and standard interline itineraries are the two extreme cases on the spectrum of integration/cooperation. While pure online itineraries are fully integrated and presumably the most desirable from the point of view of the traveler, standard interline itineraries are the least integrated, potentially most inconvenient and the most costly type of itinerary to provide. Likewise, while pure online itineraries constitute the overwhelming majority of domestic tickets sold in the U.S., standard interline tickets are extremely rare, accounting for less than one half of one percent of all tickets sold in 2003.

Table 2 summarizes the number of domestic passengers travelling on each of the four itinerary types described above during the third quarter of each year between 1999 and 2003. Of particular interest to our analysis is the fact that virtual—rather than traditional—has become the predominant form of codesharing. In 2003, for example, more than three quarters of all the codeshare itineraries were virtual, a trend that appears to be growing. While traditional codesharing can be expected to introduce downward price pressure on fares within a market since it typically creates "new" integrated service—a result confirmed by Bamberger, Carlton, and Neumann (2004)—it is not altogether obvious why the introduction of virtual codesharing, which is effectively a re-branding of existing online service, would have the same effect.

4   THE DATA & MODEL

Data for our analysis was drawn from the U.S. Department of Transportation's (DOT) domestic origin and destination Databank 1B, a 10% sample of passengers traveling on U.S. certified carriers. The period of time covered in our study is 1999–2003 and we use data from the third quarter of each year. Each observation in the raw DOT data consists of a unique airline itinerary, including the starting and ending airports of each flight coupon, the operating and marketing carrier for each flight coupon, the price paid, class of service, and (among other things) the number of passengers traveling on that particular itinerary. In order to focus our analysis on common types of trips, we place the following restrictions on the raw data. First, we restrict our analysis to passengers purchasing round-trip, coach class (both restricted and unrestricted) tickets in which the passenger started and ended at the same airport (i.e., we exclude "open jaw" tickets). Second, we limited our analysis to tickets with three or fewer coupons per directional trip leg. Third, we excluded tickets with reported one-way fares less than $25 or greater than $1,500, since these might represent incorrectly coded non-revenue tickets (i.e., employee travel or frequent flyer tickets) or first/business class tickets. Fourth, we excluded itineraries where the marketing carrier of either segment was a non-U.S.

Table 2 Classification of Dataset Itineraries

	Example	Passengers (000s)					
		1998	1999	2000	2001	2002	2003
Pure Online	AA/AA → AA/AA	38,001,795	39,797,867	41,610,384	38,914,735	38,587,888	38,735,542
Interline	NW/NW → UA/UA	268,440	227,980	230,250	202,720	190,040	179,120
Traditional Codeshare	NW/NW → CO/NW*	39,620	78,310	88,770	87,010	81,660	142,710
Virtual Codeshare	UA/US* → UA/US*	3,590	52,150	88,090	122,250	160,250	443,660
Total		38,313,445	40,156,307	42,017,494	39,326,806	39,019,837	39,501,032

Notes and Sources: Data is from the third quarter of each year. Source: U.S. DOT OD1A domestic database. Includes roundtrip, coach class tickets with less than three coupons per directional trip leg. Examples represent connecting itineraries between operating carrier/marketing carrier flight segments with codeshare segments denoted by*.

carrier. Finally, we limited our analysis to directional city-pair markets generating, on average, at least one passenger per day.[13]

We define a market as a directional city pair. That is, we (a) consider passengers traveling from Los Angeles to Chicago to be in different markets than passengers traveling between Chicago to Los Angeles, and (b) group itineraries with originating and terminating airports in the same metropolitan area. Likewise, since there are often numerous routings with different prices that are otherwise identical, we collapsed the data by market and connecting status (either non-stop or connecting), retaining the passenger weighted average fare and total number of passengers for each final observation. Since the low-level DOT data is inclusive off all taxes and fees, we net out the federal excise, segment and security tax from each ticket.[14]

Previous studies (Ito and Lee 2004) have shown that virtual codeshare itineraries are priced lower than the itineraries of single carriers (i.e., pure online itineraries) by 5–6%. That analysis, however, focussed on a cross sectional analysis of market equilibria, comparing itineraries with codesharing to otherwise similar itineraries without codesharing. Like Bamberger, Carlton, and Neumann (2004), our current analysis focusses on the before and after change in market equilibria in order to assess the fare impact of codesharing.

We take advantage of the panel nature of our dataset by including both market and time fixed effects, and control for the time-variant market characteristics using a number of independent variables. Our period of analysis was undeniably one of the most turbulent times in U.S. airline history. The industry experienced an unprecedented boom—fueled in large part by the "dot-com" boom—and a subsequent bust that was punctuated further by the September 11th terrorist attacks. While all of large hub-and-spoke network carriers have been struggling to stay afloat—United and US Airways are both in Chapter 11 reorganization while Delta and American narrowly averted filing for bankruptcy—low-cost carriers such as Southwest, jetBlue and AirTran have continued to rapidly expand and have remained profitable. Since the practice of domestic codesharing grew throughout our sample period, we separate its effects from the ongoing industry dynamics using time fixed effects.

Table 3 summarizes the number of markets in which each codeshare alliance carried passengers purchasing codeshare tickets, by year. While our data set includes observations from eleven different codeshare agreement, the majority of codeshare observations are from the two largest alliances—as of 2003—Continental/Northwest and United US Airways.[15] During the period of our analysis, one significant codesharing agreement—

---

[13] Since the purpose of our analysis is to study the fare implications of codesharing between large carriers, care must be taken to ensure that itineraries involving the regional "codesharing" partners of the larger hub-and-spoke carriers are appropriately accounted for. Since the marketing carrier code for a flight segment operated by a regional affiliate (i.e., American Eagle ("MQ")) will be that of its mainline partner (i.e., American ("AA")), we recoded the operating carrier code for each coupon operated by a codesharing regional carrier with the code of its mainline partner.

[14] The federal excise tax was 7.5% for our quarters in 2000–2003, was 8.0% for 1999 and was 9.0% for 1998. The segment tax was $3.00 for 2002 and 2003, $2.75 for 2001, $2.50 for 2000, $2.00 for 1999 and $1.00 for 1998. The security tax of $2.50 per coupon (with a maximum of $5.00 per one way ticket) took effect in February 2002, but was waived between June 1 and Sept 30, 2003.

[15] Since Delta joined the Continental/Northwest alliance during the summer of 2003, our data does not include any codesharing observations involving Delta and either Continental or Northwest.

Table 3   Active Codeshare Markets in Dataset

Alliance	Number of Markets with Codesharing in Dataset					
	1998	1999	2000	2001	2002	2003
Alaska/Hawaiian	0	1	1	1	13	21
America West/Hawaiian	0	2	0	1	3	39
American/Hawaiian	128	106	132	128	113	149
American/Alaska	0	1	91	109	219	221
Continental/Alaska	0	76	69	100	72	140
Continental/America West	607	1,037	604	397	19	3
Continental/Hawaiian	1	11	32	61	59	89
Continental/Northwest	3	2,750	3,955	5,035	6,240	5,823
Northwest/Alaska	185	183	182	203	219	270
Northwest/Hawaiian	95	95	135	100	94	90
United/US Airways	0	0	0	0	0	5,901
Total	1,026	4,262	5,201	6,135	7,051	12,746

Notes and Sources: Data is from the third quarter of each year, U.S. DOT OD1A domestic database. Includes roundtrip, coach class tickets with three or fewer coupons per directional trip leg.

between Continental and America West—was discontinued. Continental/America West represented the largest codesharing alliance in our sample in 1998 and was one of the two alliances studied by Bamberger, Carlton, and Neumann (2004). The termination of the this alliance, however, coincides with America West dramatically shifting its business model from one that largely resembled that of a traditional legacy network carrier to one that today more closely resembles that of a low cost carrier.[16] Likewise, we suspect that the effects of introducing and terminating codesharing in a market may not be symmetric. Since it is unclear, *a priori* how these factors might influence our results, we run each of our models with and without the Continental/American West alliance.[17]

We examine the effect of codesharing both at the market and itinerary level. In our market level analysis presented in Section 4, we ask the following simple question: what has been the impact of introducing codesharing on average market fares? In addition to our market-level analysis, we also estimate three itinerary-level models in Section 5. We are interested in an itinerary-level analysis to determine whether or not the introduction of codesharing affects the non-codeshare fares of various market participants in different ways.[18] Consequently, we introduce carrier-year interaction effects and consider the impact of codesharing on: (1) the average pure online (i.e., non-codeshare) fares of the codeshare partners in market where they introduce codesharing, and (2) the average pure online fares of other competitors in the same market. By estimating these itinerary-level

---

[16] In particular, American West radically simplified its pricing structure, eliminating many walk-up fares. See, for example, "America West Introduces Flexible Everyday Fare Structure", Company Press Release, March 25, 2002.

[17] In the model excluding this alliance, we code the observations as if there were no alliance between the two carriers.

[18] Likewise, we would like to make sure that the deteriorating financial conditions of some codeshare partners do not influence our key estimates.

models, we hope to shed some additional light onto the question of whether or not increased concentration at the marketing and distribution-level of tickets has provided alliances members with market power that translates into higher fares.

5   MARKET-LEVEL ANALYSIS

Let j denote a "market" and t denote a year.[19] In our market-level analysis, our dependent variable is $\ln(fare)_{jt}$, the passenger-weighted market average fare (in natural log) in market j at time t. Since codeshare itineraries have been shown to have lower prices than non-codeshare itineraries (Ito and Lee 2004), we estimate our market-level models both with and without the codeshare itineraries. Our baseline market model (Model 1) assumes the following relationship between the logged average market fare and our independent variables:

Model 1

$$\ln(fare)_{jt} = \alpha_j + \alpha_t + Z_{jt}\alpha_Z + \alpha_{CS}D(CS)_{jt} + \varepsilon_{jt},$$

where α_j is a market fixed effect, α_t is a time fixed effect and Z_{jt} is a vector of time-variant market characteristics. The key independent variable is $D(CS)_{jt}$ a dummy variable that takes value 1 if there is at least one codeshare itinerary in market j at time t and 0 otherwise. In Model 1, the coefficient on this variable measures the overall market impact of introducing codesharing on the average market fare. To determine whether or not there is any difference between traditional and virtual codesharing, we also consider the following alternative model.

Model 2

$$\ln(fare)_{jt} = \alpha_j + \alpha_t + Z_{jt}\alpha_Z + \alpha_{TCS}D(traditionalCS)_{jt} + \alpha_{VCS}D(virtualCS)_{jt} + \varepsilon_{jt}$$

Model 2 decomposes $D(CS)_{jt}$ into two separate dummy variables, $D(traditionalCS)_{jt}$ and $D(virtualCS)_{jt}$, which represent the presence of any traditional or virtual codesharing itineraries in each market.

It is natural to wonder if the alliance carriers introduced codesharing into markets with certain characteristics. However, the presence of market fixed effects should absorb any time-invariant market characteristics, including common regressors such as distance or market density. Therefore, after controlling for these two fixed effects, we only need to control for the time-varying market characteristics.

To control for any potential pricing power afforded by high market share at the originating city (Evans and Kessides 1993, Lee and Luengo Prado 2005), we include

---

[19] Formally, our "market" definition for estimation purposes is a non-directional city-pair by connecting or non-stop status. While the appropriate definition of a relevant market for the purposes of antitrust analysis is no doubt much larger, we believe that we can obtain more precise estimates using a narrower definition for the current analysis.

$max(orgshare)_{jt}$, the maximum share of domestic O&D passengers among all carriers serving the origin. Likewise, we control for the growth of low-cost carriers (LCCs) within the market by including $lccshare_{jt}$, the combined market share of low-cost carriers in market j and year t.[20] Naturally, increased LCC market share should lead to lower average market fares (Dresner, Lin, and Windle 1996, Morrison 2001). Finally, we include two other measures of market competition and structure, $mktHHI_{jt}$, the market-level Herfindahl-Hirschman index of O&D passengers and $\#(carriers)_{jt}$, the number of carriers offering pure online service in the respective market. Summary statistics for our market variables are presented in Table 4.

5.1   Market-Level Estimation Results

Tables 5 and 6 present the estimation results for our market level regressions, with and without codeshare itineraries respectively. While Continental and America West represented the largest codeshare agreement in the early part of our sample, it was quickly dissolved after Continental and Northwest formed their alliance in 1999. We

Table 4   Summary Statistics—Market-Level Variables

	Mean/(Standard Error)					
	1998	1999	2000	2001	2002	2003
ln(fare)	5.147	5.144	5.157	5.042	5.025	5.123
	(0.499)	(0.488)	(0.500)	(0.497)	(0.472)	(0.447)
max(orgshare)	0.275	0.266	0.258	0.248	0.257	0.256
	(0.212)	(0.204)	(0.201)	(0.194)	(0.198)	(0.199)
lccshare	0.064	0.069	0.073	0.082	0.087	0.095
	(0.173)	(0.179)	(0.180)	(0.189)	(0.193)	(0.203)
mktHHI	0.554	0.541	0.525	0.518	0.517	0.520
	(0.234)	(0.233)	(0.229)	(0.219)	(0.224)	(0.226)
#(carriers)	3.942	4.084	4.208	4.065	4.041	4.074
	(2.168)	(2.248)	(2.303)	(2.131)	(2.128)	(2.110)
D(CS)	0.062	0.216	0.261	0.306	0.330	0.463
	(0.241)	(0.412)	(0.439)	(0.461)	(0.470)	(0.499)
D(traditional CS)	0.053	0.122	0.126	0.140	0.129	0.223
	(0.224)	(0.327)	(0.332)	(0.347)	(0.335)	(0.416)
D(virtual CS)	0.016	0.139	0.188	0.226	0.262	0.376
	(0.126)	(0.346)	(0.391)	(0.418)	(0.440)	(0.484)
	27,411	27,085	27,238	27,212	27,473	27,325

Notes: Includes Continental/America West codeshare itineraries.

---

[20] The LCCs we include are: Southwest, AirTran, Frontier, ATA, jetBlue, Spirit, Sun Country, Allegiance, Vanguard, National, ProAir and Reno Air.

Table 5   Market-Level Regression (All Itineraries)

	With CO/HP Alliance		Without CO/HP Alliance	
	Model 1	Model 2	Model 1	Model 2
	ln(*fare*)	ln(*fare*)	ln(*fare*)	ln(*fare*)
max(orgshare)	0.635†	0.637†	0.635†	0.640†
	(0.043)	(0.042)	(0.043)	(0.042)
lccshare	−0.256†	−0.253†	−0.253†	−0.249†
	(0.025)	(0.025)	(0.025)	(0.025)
mktHHI	0.069*	0.066*	0.068*	0.064*
	(0.030)	(0.030)	(0.030)	(0.030)
#(*carriers*)	−0.011†	−0.012†	−0.011†	−0.011*
	(0.003)	(0.003)	(0.003)	(0.003)
D(CS)	−0.006		−0.018†	
	(0.006)		(0.007)	
D(virtual CS)		−0.008		−0.015*
		(0.007)		(0.007)
D(traditional CS)		−0.024†		−0.037†
		(0.005)		(0.006)
yr1999	0.003	0.006	0.006	0.010
	(0.006)	(0.006)	(0.006)	(0.006)
yr2000	0.044†	0.048†	0.049†	0.054†
	(0.007)	(0.007)	(0.007)	(0.007)
yr2001	−0.085†	−0.081†	−0.079†	−0.074†
	(0.008)	(0.008)	(0.008)	(0.008)
yr2002	−0.102†	−0.098†	−0.095†	−0.089†
	(0.007)	(0.007)	(0.007)	(0.007)
yr2003	−0.011	−0.003	−0.002	0.011
	(0.007)	(0.007)	(0.007)	(0.007)
constant	5.021†	5.027†	5.021†	5.019†
	(0.023)	(0.023)	(0.023)	(0.023)
Adj. R^2	0.7767	0.7771	0.7769	0.7775
N	163,560	163,560	163,560	163,560

Notes: *Significant at 5%; †Significant at 1%. Robust standard errors in parentheses. All models control for market and time fixed effects. For estimation purposes, markets are analytically weighted by passengers.

found our results to be slightly sensitive to the inclusion of this codeshare agreement.[21] Consequently, Tables 5 and 6 present results with and without the Continental/America

---

[21] As discussed earlier, there are at least two factors that could be driving this result. First, it is not clear that the effects of introducing and terminating codesharing in a market are symmetric. Second, the termination of the CO/HP agreement coincides with America West's transformation into a low cost carrier.

Table 6   Market-Level Regressions Excluding Codeshare Itineraries

	With CO/HP Alliance		Without CO/HP Alliance	
	Model 1	Model 2	Model 1	Model 2
	ln(*fare*)	ln(*fare*)	ln(*fare*)	ln(*fare*)
max(*orgshare*)	$0.628^\dagger$	$0.629^\dagger$	$0.630^\dagger$	$0.633^\dagger$
	(0.043)	(0.042)	(0.043)	(0.042)
lccshare	$-0.256^\dagger$	$-0.253^\dagger$	$-0.252^\dagger$	$-0.248^\dagger$
	(0.025)	(0.025)	(0.025)	(0.025)
mktHHI	$0.070^\dagger$	$0.067^\dagger$	0.068*	0.064*
	(0.030)	(0.030)	(0.030)	(0.030)
#(*carriers*)	$-0.011^\dagger$	$-0.011^\dagger$	$-0.011^\dagger$	$-0.011^\dagger$
	(0.003)	(0.003)	(0.003)	(0.003)
D(CS)	-0.003		$-0.016^\dagger$	
	(0.006)		(0.007)	
D(virtual CS)		-0.008		-0.015*
		(0.007)		(0.007)
D(traditional CS)		$-0.019^\dagger$		$-0.033^\dagger$
		(0.005)		(0.006)
yr1999	0.003	0.006	0.006	0.010
	(0.006)	(0.006)	(0.006)	(0.006)
yr2000	$0.044^\dagger$	$0.048^\dagger$	$0.049^\dagger$	$0.054^\dagger$
	(0.007)	(0.007)	(0.007)	(0.007)
yr2001	$-0.085^\dagger$	$-0.080^\dagger$	$-0.079^\dagger$	$-0.073^\dagger$
	(0.008)	(0.008)	(0.008)	(0.008)
yr2002	$-0.103^\dagger$	$-0.098^\dagger$	$-0.095^\dagger$	$-0.089^\dagger$
	(0.007)	(0.007)	(0.007)	(0.007)
yr2003	-0.011	-0.002	-0.002	0.011
	(0.007)	(0.007)	(0.007)	(0.007)
Constant	$5.021^\dagger$	$5.027^\dagger$	$5.020^\dagger$	$5.019^\dagger$
	(0.023)	(0.023)	(0.023)	(0.023)
Adj. R^2	0.7769	0.7771	0.7769	0.7774
N	162,676	162,676	162,758	162,758

Notes: *Significant at 5%; †Significant at 1%. Robust standard errors in parentheses. All models control for market and time fixed effects. For estimation purposes, markets are analytically weighted by passengers.

West ("CO/HP") agreement. Since codeshare itineraries comprise only a small fraction (i.e., 2% in 2003) of all tickets, the estimations results are extremely similar in the two tables, and therefore, we will focus the discussion of our results on Table 6 (excluding codeshare tickets).

Model 1 shows that introducing codesharing into a market does not raise average fares. To the contrary, in the model where we exclude the CO/HP agreement, new codesharing in a market reduces average fares by roughly 1.6% (when we include the CO/HP agreement, there is no statistically significant effect). In Model 2, we find—not surprisingly—that traditional codesharing has a much larger effect that virtual codesharing on average fares. While introducing traditional codesharing lowers average fares by roughly 3.3% (or 1.9% when we include the CO/HP agreement), new virtual competition lowers average fares by less than half as much, or 1.5% (.8% when we include the CO/HP agreement). The fact that traditional codesharing has a larger impact than virtual codesharing makes sense because in many markets, traditional codesharing often adds an entirely new competitor, potentially internalizing the double marginalization problem associated with interline tickets. In contrast, virtual codesharing—by definition—is effectively a re-branding of an existing service, which, in many cases does not result in new service *per se*.

The estimated coefficients on all other variables are reasonable both in sign and magnitude. For example, a 1% increase in the share of the largest carrier at the origin increases average fares by 0.635%. Similarly, as the share of low-cost carriers increase by 1%, average market fares decrease by 0.25%. Likewise, higher market concentration, measured by the market HHI, leads to the higher average market fares and the coefficients on year dummies captures the rapid cycle of boom and bust during the sample period. Finally, adding pure online service from an additional carrier lowers average market fares by 1.1%.

Comparing the outcome of our market analysis with the previous literature, Bamberger, Carlton, and Neumann (2004) find that average market fares dropped by 6–8% in codeshare markets where the alliance members had previously offered only interline service. While our findings are largely similar to theirs—in particular, we find that codesharing has not led to higher fares—we do find somewhat smaller price effects. We offer several reasons to explain the difference. First, the effect measured by Bamberger, Carlton, and Neumann (2004) only reflects traditional codesharing, while our generic codesharing definition includes both traditional and the now much more common virtual type. Indeed, traditional codesharing in our analysis is found to have a much larger price effect that virtual codesharing. Second, our dataset contains more recent and larger codeshare alliances (e.g., Northwest/Continental, United/US Airways) which have far greater network overlap than the alliances studied by Bamberger, Carlton, and Neumann (2004). Third, since our sample period is more recent, our estimates likely reflect the fact that the industry has become more price-competitive, both due to increased low cost carrier penetration as well as increased price transparency due to Internet travel agencies such as Orbitz or Expedia.[22] In such an environment, the competitive effect of introducing new codesharing into a market may be much smaller than before. Nevertheless, despite the difference in the measured magnitude between our results and those of Bamberger, Carlton, and Neumann (2004), our findings provide further evidence that widespread domestic codesharing has not led—in any systematic fashion—to higher fares.

---

[22] For example, while only 5% of all airline revenue was booked online in 1999, the proportion had grown to 27% by 2003. Source: *The Online Travel Marketplace 2001–2003: Forecasts, Business Models and Best Practices for Profitability*, PhoCusWright, 2001.

6 ITINERARY-LEVEL ANALYSIS

We now turn our attention to decomposing the effect of codesharing on the pure online fares of different market participants. In particular, we are interested in determining the effect of codesharing on: (1) the pure online (i.e., non-codeshare) fares of the alliance partners and (2) the pure online fares of other non-alliance carriers.[23]

Let i denote an itinerary and t a calendar year. An itinerary is defined as a unique combination of market and operating/marketing carriers (for example, CO/CO → NW/NW between Memphis and El Paso). k_i (k for brevity) denotes the carrier(s) of itinerary i and j_i (j for brevity) denotes the market of itinerary i. Our dependent variable, $\ln(fare)_{it}$ is the natural log of the passenger-weighted average fare for itinerary i in year t.

The advantage of estimating itinerary-level models is that we can include carrier-year interaction effects, in addition to itinerary and time fixed effects. In particular, the year-carrier interaction effects should absorb any carrier-specific events such as bankruptcy that may impact a carriers' system-wide fares. We re-estimate Models 1 and 2 from Section 5 using itinerary-level data in order to test the robustness of our estimates to such factors. We also estimate a third model (Model 3) that compares the effects of codesharing on alliance members and their competitors. By doing so, we should be able to determine if alliances generate an unfair marketing advantage over their competitors that translates into higher fares for alliance members, a concern commonly expressed by policy makers (U.S. General Accounting Office 1999, Transportation Research Board 1999). In particular, we estimate the following model:

Model 3

$$\ln(fare)_{it} = \alpha_i + \alpha_{kt} + X_{it}\alpha_X + Z_{jt}\alpha_Z$$
$$+ \alpha_{CSOWN}D(CS)_{jt} \cdot D(OWN)_{it} + \alpha_{CSCOMP}D(CS)_{jt} \cdot D(COMP)_{it} + \varepsilon_{it}$$

Like Model 1, $D(CS)_{jt}$ is a dummy variable that takes the value 1 if there is a codeshare itinerary in market j in year t, and 0 otherwise. We interact $D(CS)_{jt}$ with another dummy that indicates the type of itinerary. $D(OWN)_{it}$ is a dummy variable that takes the value 1 if itinerary i in year t is one of the codeshare partners' own pure online itinerary in the same market.[24] Thus, the coefficient α_{CSOWN} measures how the partners' own pure online (i.e., non-codeshare) fares in the same market were impacted by introducing codeshare service. If the introduction of codeshare enabled the alliance partners to exercise market power, we would expect this coefficient to be positive.

Similarly, $D(COMP)_{it}$ is a dummy variable that takes the value 1 if itinerary i in year t is a pure online itinerary of a competing carrier.[25] Thus, α_{CSCOMP} measures the impact

---

[23] We focus only on pure online itineraries because these fares reflect the pricing decisions of a single carrier.

[24] For example, if Continental and Northwest offered codesharing in the Seattle to New Orleans market in 2001, $D(OWN)_{it}$ takes the value 1 for all Seattle to Boston itineraries in 2001 that represent pure online service on either Continental or Northwest.

[25] For example, if Continental and Northwest offered codesharing in the Seattle to New Orleans market in 2001, $D(COMP)_{it}$ takes the value 1 for all Seattle to New Orleans itineraries in 2001 that represent pure online service on carriers not offering codesharing in this market in 2001.

of introducing codesharing on competitors' fares. If the introduction of codesharing results in competitors pricing more aggressively, we would expect this coefficient to be negative.

In all three models, we include itinerary-specific effects, α_i, to control for the time-variant itinerary/market characteristics. Likewise, since industry dynamics affected carriers somewhat differently during the sample period (i.e., some carriers filed for bankruptcy, while others did not) we include α_{kt}, the interaction between the year and carrier-specific fixed effects.[26]

Each of the time-variant market characteristic variables used in the market-level analysis from Section 5 are included in the vector Z_{jit}, with the exception of $orgshare_{k_it}$, which is replaced with the market share of O&D passengers in the originating city of carrier k_i. Likewise, since the itinerary fixed effects are controlled for, the coefficients on the CS interaction dummies can be interpreted as the change in the fare before and after the introduction of codesharing in the market. Summary statistics of our itinerary-level variables are presented in Table 7.

6.1   Itinerary-Level Estimation Results

Itinerary-level results are presented in Table 8. As we did in Section 4.1, we present results with and without the CO/HP alliance.

Table 7   Summary Statistics—Itinerary Level Variables

	Mean/(Standard Error)					
	1998	1999	2000	2001	2002	2003
orgshare	0.198	0.190	0.184	0.182	0.187	0.186
	(0.201)	(0.195)	(0.190)	(0.185)	(0.189)	(0.187)
lccshare	0.072	0.076	0.082	0.093	0.098	0.106
	(0.165)	(0.166)	(0.168)	(0.177)	(0.180)	(0.189)
mktHHI	0.471	0.458	0.442	0.443	0.440	0.440
	(0.208)	(0.205)	(0.201)	(0.192)	(0.196)	(0.197)
#*(carriers)*	5.008	5.172	5.345	5.050	5.024	5.086
	(2.401)	(2.481)	(2.569)	(2.440)	(2.405)	(2.365)
D(CS)	0.115	0.333	0.392	0.439	0.472	0.627
	(0.319)	(0.471)	(0.488)	(0.496)	(0.499)	(0.484)
D(traditional CS)	0.097	0.199	0.203	0.216	0.197	0.334
	(0.297)	(0.399)	(0.402)	(0.411)	(0.397)	(0.472)
D(virtual CS)	0.039	0.231	0.299	0.339	0.388	0.539
	(0.193)	(0.422)	(0.458)	(0.473)	(0.487)	(0.498)
N	81,397	84,778	89,571	86,827	87,786	93,045

Notes: Pure online itineraries only. Includes Continental/America West codeshare itineraries.

---

[26] For a codeshare itinerary, we turn on carrier-year effects for the operating carrier. Due to the limited degrees of freedom, all the low cost carriers are grouped together in the year-carrier interaction effects.

Table 8 Itinerary-Level Regressions

	With CO/HP Alliance			Without CO/HP Alliance		
	Model 1	Model 2	Model 3	Model 1	Model 2	Model 3
orgshare	−0.188[†]	−0.185[†]	−0.188[†]	−0.187[†]	−0.183[†]	−0.187[†]
	(0.029)	(0.029)	(0.029)	(0.029)	(0.029)	(0.029)
lccshare	−0.206[†]	−0.200[†]	−0.205[†]	−0.203[†]	−0.197[†]	−0.202[†]
	(0.017)	(0.017)	(0.017)	(0.017)	(0.017)	(0.017)
mktHHI	0.000	−0.001	−0.000	−0.001	−0.002	−0.001
	(0.019)	(0.019)	(0.019)	(0.019)	(0.019)	(0.019)
#(*carriers*)	−0.018[†]	−0.018[†]	−0.018[†]	−0.018[†]	−0.018[†]	−0.018[†]
	(0.002)	(0.002)	(0.002)	(0.002)	(0.002)	(0.002)
D(CS)	−0.007*			−0.015[†]		
	(0.003)			(0.003)		
D(CS COMP)			−0.004			−0.012[†]
			(0.003)			(0.003)
D(CS OWN)			−0.018[†]			−0.026[†]
			(0.006)			(0.006)
D(traditional CS)		−0.037[†]			−0.036[†]	
		(0.004)			(0.004)	
D(virtual CS)		−0.006*			−0.014[†]	
		(0.003)			(0.003)	
yr1999	0.023*	0.030[†]	0.023*	0.027[†]	0.032[†]	0.025[†]
	(0.009)	(0.009)	(0.009)	(0.009)	(0.009)	(0.009)
yr2000	0.100[†]	0.107[†]	0.099[†]	0.103[†]	0.109[†]	0.102[†]
	(0.010)	(0.010)	(0.010)	(0.010)	(0.010)	(0.010)
yr2001	−0.122[†]	−0.114[†]	−0.122[†]	−0.117[†]	−0.110[†]	−0.118[†]
	(0.008)	(0.008)	(0.008)	(0.008)	(0.008)	(0.008)
yr2002	−0.171[†]	−0.162[†]	−0.171[†]	−0.166[†]	−0.158[†]	−0.167[†]
	(0.010)	(0.009)	(0.010)	(0.010)	(0.009)	(0.010)
yr2003	−0.079[†]	−0.062[†]	−0.079[†]	−0.072[†]	−0.057[†]	−0.073[†]
	(0.010)	(0.010)	(0.010)	(0.010)	(0.010)	(0.010)
Constant	5.069[†]	5.067[†]	5.070[†]	5.068[†]	5.066[†]	5.069[†]
	(0.016)	(0.016)	(0.016)	(0.016)	(0.015)	(0.016)
N	424,843	424,843	424,843	424,843	424,843	424,843
Adj. R^2	0.894	0.895	0.894	0.894	0.895	0.894

Notes: *Significant at 5%; [†]Significant at 1%. Pure online itineraries only. Robust standard errors in parentheses. All models control for market and time fixed effects. For estimation purposes, itineraries are analytically weighted by passengers.

The estimation results of Models 1 and 2 confirm the robustness of our market-level estimates. The introduction of codesharing does not lead to higher average fares. Rather, Model 1 confirms that codesharing—defined generically—results in a small (1.5%) drop in the overall fares (0.4% when CO/HP alliance is excluded). Likewise, results from Model 2 indicate, once again, that traditional codesharing leads to a larger decline in fares (3.6%–3.7%) relative to virtual codesharing (0.6%–1.4%).[27]

Turning to Model 3, we find that the pure online fares of the alliance members dropped by 2.6% when they introduced codesharing into a market. Somewhat surprisingly, the fares of the alliance's competitors only fall by 1.2%. Thus, it does not appear that alliance members are exercising greater market power at the expense of their competitors. To the contrary, it appears as though codesharing leads to competitive pressures both on alliance members and their competitors.

Finally, we find that the estimated coefficients on other variables are reasonable. As was the case in our market-level analysis, we find that a 1 percent increase in *lccshare* leads to 0.2% drop in fares. Likewise, an additional pure online carrier leads to 1.8% decrease in fares. Interestingly, the estimated coefficient on *orgshare* becomes negative and significant in all three itinerary-level models. On the surface, this is somewhat surprising because high market share at the origination airport is often suspected as a source of market power. However, during our sample period, most network carriers faced dramatically increased low cost carrier penetration at their hubs. We suspect that this variable is picking up such changes in the competitive landscape faced by the large hub-and-spoke carriers.[28]

7 CONCLUSIONS

Although increased cooperation and codesharing between large carriers was a dominant theme in international aviation during the 1990s, widespread codesharing among large carriers in domestic markets is a much more recent phenomenon, and consequently, it is much less well-understood. This paper investigates the impact of domestic codesharing on airfares and expands upon work by Bamberger, Carlton, and Neumann (2004) by: (a) utilizing a more recent panel of data that covers the recent proliferation of domestic codesharing agreements, (b) extending the definition of codesharing to include its more prevalent "virtual" implementation, and (c) decomposing the price effects of codesharing on alliance members and their competitors.

Like Bamberger, Carlton, and Neumann (2004), we find no evidence that increased domestic codesharing has led to higher airfares. To the contrary, we find that codesharing has led to slightly lower average fares. Not surprisingly, the fare impact tends to be larger when traditional codesharing is introduced into a market, relative to virtual codesharing.

---

[27] Although we do not present the carrier-year interaction effect estimates in our table for brevity, they reflect turbulence experienced by the large network carriers (e.g. a bankruptcy and subsequent financial crisis) and we find the time path is uniquely different from one carrier to another. It is comforting to find our key estimates remain robust to such factors.

[28] See, for example, *Memorandum in Support of the Debtors' Motion to Reject Their Collective Bargaining Agreements Pursuant to 11 U.S.C. §1113(c)*. In re: UAL Corporation, et. al., United States Bankruptcy Court For the Northern District of Illinois, Eastern Division.

Moreover, we also find that the introduction of codesharing leads to slightly larger fare declines for alliance members than their competitors. Thus, contrary to some initial concerns of the increased concentration resulting from these alliances (U.S. General Accounting Office 1998, U.S. General Accounting Office 1999, Transportation Research Board 1999) we find no evidence that codesharing provides alliance members with an umbrella of pricing power at the expense of their non-alliance competitors.

REFERENCES

Armantier, O., and O. Richard (2003): "Domestic Airline Alliances and Consumer Welfare," Unpublished Manuscript.

Bamberger, G., D. Carlton, and L. Neumann (2004): "An Empirical Investigation of the Competitive Effects of Domestic Airline Alliances," *Journal of Law and Economics*, XLVII, 195–222.

Brueckner, J. (2000): "The Economics of International Codesharing: An Analysis of Airline Alliances," *International Jouranl of Industrial Organization*, 19, 1475–1498.

—— (2003): "International Airfares in the Age of Alliances: The Effects to Codesharing and Antitrust Immunity," *Review of Economic Statistics*, 85, 105–118.

Brueckner, J., and T. Whalen (2000): "The Price Effects of International Airline Alliances," *Jounal of Law and Economics*, 43, 503–545.

Dresner, M., J.-S. C. Lin, and R. Windle (1996): "The Impact of Low-Cost Carriers on Airport and Route Competition," *Journal of Transport Economics and Policy*, 30, 309–328.

Evans, W., and I. Kessides (1993): "Localized Market Power in the U.S. Airline Industry," *Review of Economics and Statistics*, 75, 66–75.

Ito, H., and D. Lee (2004): "Alliances and Prices: The Case of Codesharing in the U.S. Airline Industry," Unpublished Manuscript.

Lee, D., and M. Luengo Prado (2005): "The Impact of Passenger Mix on Reported Hub Premiums in the U.S. Airline Industry," *Southern Economic Journal*, Vol. 72, No. 2, pp. 372–394.

Morrison, S. A. (2001): "Actual, Adjacent and Potential Competition: Estimating the Full Effect of Southwest Airlines," *Journal of Transport Economics and Policy*, 35, 239–256.

Oum, T., J. H. Park, and A. Zhang (1996): "The Effects of Airline Codesharing Agreements on Firm Conduct and International Airfares," *Journal of Transport Economics and Policy*, 30, 187–202.

Park, J. H., and A. Zhang (2000): "An Empirical Analysis of Global Airline Alliances: Cases in the North Atlantic Markets," *Review of Industrial Organization*, 16, 367–384.

Transportation Research Board (1999): "Entry and Competition in the U.S. Airline Industry: Issues and Opportunities," National Research Council, Special Report 255, Washington, D.C.

U.S. General Accounting Office (1998): "Airline Competition: Proposed Domestic Airline Alliances Raise Serious Issues," June 1998, GAO/RCED 98-215, Washington, D.C.

—— (1999): "Airline Competition: Effects on Consumers From Domestic Alliances Vary," January 1999, GAO/RCED 99-37, Washington, D.C.

Whalen, W. T. (1999): "The Welfare Effects of Domestic Airline Alliances," Unpublished Manuscript, Department of Economics, University of Illinois, Urbana-Champaign.

Advances in Airline Economics, Vol 1
Darin Lee (Editor)
© 2006 Published by Elsevier B.V.

7

Code–Sharing Agreements, Frequency of Flights, and Profits Under Parallel Operation[*]

Orit Heimer
ZIM Integrated Shipping Services LTD

Oz Shy[†]
University of Haifa and WZ-Berlin

ABSTRACT

We investigate the market consequences of code-sharing agreements among airline firms competing on the same route. Our approach relies on defining frequency of flights as the output of airline firms, hence code-sharing agreements affect passengers in two opposing ways. First, the agreements increase the frequency of flights available to passengers. Second, they reduce competition because of the semi-collusive agreements on compensatory fees each airline must pay for selling tickets for flights to be operated by the other airline. We find that code-sharing agreements increase airfares and profits, reduce passengers' welfare, but improve social welfare.

1 INTRODUCTION

Following the 1978 deregulation of the airline industry in the U.S., the industry has been going through major structural changes. Such changes include: (i) a complete redesign of the route structures, most notably, the movement from nonstop flights to

[*]We thank Yossi Berechman, Volodymyr Bilotkach, Darin Lee, and Moshe Kim for most valuable comments on earlier drafts. The views expressed are those of the authors and do not necessarily correspond to the views of ZIM or other institutions.
[†]*Corresponding Author*: WZB – Social Science Research Center, Reichpietschufer 50, D–10785 Berlin, Germany. E-mail: ozshyMail@gmail.com

hub-and-spoke networks during the 1980s; (ii) Transition to computerized reservation systems (CRS), enabling a sophisticated pricing system based on a multidimensional price discrimination; (iii) Establishment of frequent-flyer programs which enable airline companies to lock-in their passengers and prevent switching to competing carriers; (iv) During the 1990s, a large number of airline companies found it profitable to engage in international alliances constituting two or more airline companies (Berechman and de Wit, 1999). The main characteristic of these alliances was the enactment of *code-sharing* agreements.

Our paper analyzes the market consequences of code-sharing agreements. A code-sharing agreement affects the reservation system of each airline, as it allows each participating airline company to sell tickets on flights operated by other carriers under its own code. Thus, a passenger buying a flight ticket from one airline company may end up flying on an aircraft operated by another airline. The passenger is unlikely to observe it before he actually boards the aircraft since flights operated under code-sharing agreements bear all the individual airline-specific codes.[1] Every commercial flight is marked with a code composed of two parts. The first part is a unique airline code which is allocated by the International Civil Aviation Organization (ICAO). This two-letter code identifies the airline on every computer reservation system. The second part of the code is the flight number which is determined by the airline itself for the purpose of identifying the places of origin and destination of the flight.

For example, a code-sharing agreement between United Air Lines and Lufthansa enables the companies to list the flights from Chicago to Frankfurt as UA940 and LH6431, respectively, despite the fact that the flight is operated on a single plane which is generally operated by United. Those passengers who purchase the ticket from Lufthansa are unlikely to notice the name of the operator before they actually board the plane, unless as a few airlines do, the name of the operator is also marked on the ticket. As we discuss below, the major advantage to passengers from these agreements is the increase in the number of available flights. Some other advantages include an improved service at the origin and destination cities since clearly United has better facilities at Chicago whereas Lufthansa has better facilities in Frankfurt. These services become even more important when flights get cancelled or delayed as passengers are more likely to get a hotel when the domestic airline assumes responsibility.

Code-sharing agreements worry antitrust authorities as they fear that code sharing may result in reduced competition. The present research attempts to investigate this issue by investigating the effects of code-sharing agreements on airfares, profits, passengers' welfare, and aggregate social welfare. Our model is based on the assumption that passengers have preferences according to which they can rank the different airline firms. Since our paper deals mainly with international carriers, this assumption can be justified on the basis that *some* passengers do not speak any foreign language and therefore prefer to fly with their own national airline. Others, may prefer the foreign airline, say because they expect a better service at destination. Another interpretation for different preference rankings over airline companies is the prevalence of switching costs resulting

---

[1] Although codeshare operations must be disclosed to passengers, a large number of passengers are actually not aware in advance of the change in carriers.

from frequent-flyer programs. For example, if, for historical reasons in each country, half of the passengers have flown their national-flag carrier, whereas the other half have flown the foreign carrier, generous frequent-flyer programs can maintain this passenger distribution in the future.

The above discussion is linked to the (now historical) case of the proposed partnership between American Airlines and British Airways. In the early 2000s the carriers had trouble approving their proposed code-sharing agreement. The regulators specifically frowned of the fact that the partnership between the two carriers would obtain dispro-portionately large share of the London – New York and London – Chicago markets.

An important feature of this paper, which makes it different from the literature is the way we define units of output for airline companies. Following Berechman, Poddar, and Shy (1998), and Shy (1996, Ch.17), instead of relying on the conventional definitions of output, such as passenger/unit of distance or occupancy level, we view the *flight frequency* as the output level. One advantage of this approach is the separation of the costs associated with the operation of the aircraft from the costs associated with handling the passengers. A second advantage of using flight frequency as output, is that flight frequencies play a major role in code-sharing agreements since such agreements significantly enhance passengers' utility by multiplying the number of flights accessible to passengers. Thus, in this paper we emphasize that the major potentially-improving welfare aspect of code sharing is the *increase in the number of flights* available to passengers.

We can classify the effects of code sharing into two types. The first type, analyzed in the present paper, is called *parallel operation* in which two airlines competing on the same route sign a code-sharing agreement thereby increasing the frequency of flights as viewed by passengers. The second type is called *complementary operation* which involves facilitating interconnections.

In the theoretical literature, Park (1997) examined the consequences of two types of strategic alliances (parallel and complementary) on output levels, profits, and social welfare. The market is modeled as a Cournot competition, where it is assumed that in a state of alliance the carriers equally share the profit from the joint operation. His results show that parallel alliances reduce social welfare whereas complementary alliances raise social welfare. The present paper, which deals only with parallel alliances, obtains a different result as we show that the utility gain from an increase in flight frequencies dominates the welfare loss associated with reduced competition.

Brueckner (2001) extends Park's analysis by adding routes that require the service of two carriers. He demonstrates a reduction in the combined airfare for the routes in which the service of two airlines is needed, but an increase in airfare for routes connecting hub cities, where alliances completely remove any competition. Using simulations, he concludes that alliances increase social welfare. Brueckner and Whalen (2000) predict that the overall airfare on the combined route will decline and demonstrate empirically how airfares fell by 25% compared to the sum of airfares collected by each airline for its part of the route. Other empirical investigations on codesharing alliances include Whalen (1999), Bamberger, Carlton, and Neumann (2004), Brueckner (2003), Ito and Lee (2005), Armantier and Richard (2005). Hassin and Shy (2004) combines parallel with complementary routes to investigate code sharing of international flights.

On the empirical side, Gellman Research Associates (1994) examined using an econometric model the effects of code-sharing agreements between British Airways and USAir, and between KLM and Northwest. They found that the market shares of the contracted carriers have increased as well as passengers' welfare. This research focused on the quality of service (frequency, scheduling, etc.) but did not address the effects on airfares. Oum *et al.* (1996) examined the effect of code sharing on small carriers and the market share of the leading airline in the market. Park and Zhang (1998) examine the effects of regional alliances on output by looking at changes in the number of passengers on the relevant routes and compare it to routes that were excluded from the alliance. Looking at four major North-Atlantic alliances during 1992–94, they found a significant increase in the number of passengers traveling on the contracted routes. Park and Zhang (2000) examine airfares, number of passengers, and passengers' surplus by looking at international oligopolies. The compare the periods before and after alliances are formed, thereby taking into account structural changes that may have occurred as a result of the alliances. They concluded that parallel alliances tend to decrease output and passengers' surplus, but complementary alliances tend to increase output as well as passengers' surplus.

The remainder of this chapter is organized as follows. Section 2 sets up the environment, passengers' preferences for travel, and airline technologies. Section 3 solves for the equilibrium in the airline industry in the absence of code-sharing agreements. Section 4 solves for an airline industry equilibrium when the carriers sign a code-sharing agreement. Section 5 analyzes the welfare effects of code-sharing agreements. Section 6 concludes.

2 THE MODEL

Consider two countries labeled A and B with two national airlines labeled α and β, respectively. Both airline companies provide international service to and from their countries. There are n passengers who wish to fly between countries A and B. The direction of their travel is irrelevant as each airline firm provides flights in both directions.

2.1 Airfares and Passengers

The n passengers are heterogeneous with respect to their preference for the two airline companies. Let f_α $(f_\alpha \geq 1)$ denote the frequency of flights (number of flights at a given time period) provided by airline α. Similarly, let f_β $(f_\beta \geq 1)$ be the frequency of flights offered by airline β. Also, let p_i denote the airfare charged by airline $i, i = \alpha, \beta$. Passengers are uniformly distributed on the interval $[0, 1]$ with density n. Formally, these passengers are indexed by x on the unit interval $[0, 1]$ according to an increase preference for flying with airline β. Thus, the utility of a passenger x $(0 \leq x \leq 1)$ is given by

$$U(x) \stackrel{\text{def}}{=} \begin{cases} f_\alpha - \tau x - p_\alpha & \text{flies with carrier } \alpha \\ f_\beta - \tau(1-x) - p_\beta & \text{flies with carrier } \beta, \\ 0 & \text{does not travel by plane,} \end{cases} \tag{1}$$

where $\tau > 0$ measures the degree of differentiation between the two airline companies. The utility function (1) reveals the following behavior. First, the utility of each passenger is enhanced with an increase in the frequency of flights offered by the airline in which the passengers holds a ticket. This is because a higher frequency of flights allows greater flexibility to each passenger, especially to business passengers whose schedule could be less predictable. Second, passengers indexed by a low x, whom we call airline α-oriented passengers, would choose to fly carrier α over carrier β if both airline offer similar airfares and flight frequency. In contrast, passengers indexed by a high x, whom we call airline β-oriented passengers, would choose β over α if both offer similar airfares and flight frequency. Third, when airfares are high, passengers may refrain from traveling by air. Clearly, the passengers most likely to opt out of this service are those who are indexed around $x = 1/2$, and the passengers that are least likely to opt out are those with the strongest preference for their national airline, $x = 0$ and $x = 1$.

Suppose now that all the market is served (that is, all passengers choose to travel by air). From (1) we define the passengers who are indifferent between flying α and β by

$$\hat{x} = \frac{f_\alpha - f_\beta - p_\alpha + p_\beta + \tau}{2\tau}. \tag{2}$$

Thus, all passengers indexed by $[0, \hat{x}]$ will fly α. The passengers indexed on $(\hat{x}, 1]$ will fly airline β.

Suppose now that airfares are relatively high, so that some passengers prefer not to travel by air. From (1) we define the passengers who are indifferent between flying carrier α and not flying at all by

$$\hat{x}_\alpha = \frac{f_\alpha - p_\alpha}{\tau}. \tag{3}$$

Similarly, we define the passengers who are indifferent between flying carrier β and not traveling by air by

$$\hat{x}_\beta = \frac{\tau - f_\beta + p_\beta}{\tau}. \tag{4}$$

Clearly, if $\hat{x}_\alpha \geq \hat{x}_\beta$, then the entire market is served so (2) is the valid market division rule. In this case, we will say that the market is *fully served*. Otherwise, (3) and (4) are the market division rules, in which case all passengers indexed on the interval $(\hat{x}_\alpha, \hat{x}_\beta)$ are not served. In this case, we will say that the market is only *partially served*.

2.2 Airline Firms

Airline companies are subjected to two types of costs:

(a) The costs associated with aircraft operation. We simplify the analysis by assuming that all aircraft operating costs can be accounted for each flight separately. Such costs consist of fuel for the duration of the flight, airport maintenance, renting the gate to board and disembark the passengers, landing and air-traffic control fees. The cost function of each airline increases quadratically with the frequency of flights, so we assume that the aircraft operation costs of carrier i ($i = \alpha, \beta$) are given by $\delta(f_i)^2$, where $\delta > 0$. The reason why cost per departure is increasing with frequency is that airport gate slots are scarce, therefore an increase in congestion results in higher landing fees during peak hours.[2]

(b) The costs associated with serving the passengers. Let q_i denote the number of passengers flying carrier i, $i = \alpha, \beta$, and let ϕ denote the cost per passenger, which involves the labor hours needed to serve the passenger on the ground and in the air, as well as the cost of service. Thus, the aggregate passenger cost of airline i is $\phi \cdot q_i$.

Altogether, the total cost of airline i, when operating a frequency of f_i of flights and carrying q_i passengers is

$$TC(f_i) \stackrel{\text{def}}{=} \delta(f_i)^2 + \phi q_i \quad i = \alpha, \beta. \tag{5}$$

Thus, if the market is fully served, the profit levels of airline α and airline β are given by

$$\pi_\alpha = n\hat{x}(p_\alpha - \phi) - \delta(f_\alpha)^2, \quad \text{and} \quad \pi_\beta = n(1 - \hat{x})(p_\beta - \phi) - \delta(f_\beta)^2. \tag{6}$$

However, if the market is only partially served, the profit levels are given by[3]

$$\pi_\alpha = n\hat{x}_\alpha(p_\alpha - \phi) - \delta(f_\alpha)^2, \quad \text{and} \quad \pi_\beta = n(1 - \hat{x}_\beta)(p_\beta - \phi) - \delta(f_\beta)^2, \tag{7}$$

where $\hat{x}_\alpha$ and $\hat{x}_\beta$ are given in (3) and (4), respectively.

Finally, we make the following assumptions.

ASSUMPTION 1 *(a) Passengers view the two national carriers as sufficiently differentiated. Formally, $\tau > n/(18\delta)$.*
(b) The passenger population size is sufficiently large relative to the cost per departure. Formally, $n > \max\{6\delta, 12\delta\phi\}$.

Assumption 1(a), which is commonly utilized in 'location' models, ensures the existence of airfare and frequency competition between the carriers. Assuming otherwise would intensify the airfare competition between the carriers in which case each carrier attempts to undercut the airfare of the competing carrier in order to gain control over the entire market. Assumption 1(b) makes it profitable for carriers to provide flight frequencies exceeding one flight per time period. In addition, this assumption assures that in equilibrium in the absence of code sharing, all passengers gain a strictly positive utility from flying with one of the carriers under a certain restriction on the differentiation parameter τ.

---

[2] However, since multiple frequencies allows the carrier to spread out certain costs across flights (such as, gate rental, check-in facilities, etc.) it may be that these cancel out some of the congestion costs associated with higher frequency.
[3] Clearly, the airline companies have some control of whether the market is fully served or only partially served. For example, when the market is fully served and airfares are sufficiently high, if one of the carriers raises its airfare it may transform the market into a partially-served market. We will get back to this issue once we solve the carriers' profit-maximization problems.

3 EQUILIBRIUM WITHOUT CODE SHARING

Consider the following two-stage game.

Stage I: Each airline firm sets its yearly schedule by specifying its frequency on this route.

That is, airline α sets f_α knowing f_β, and airline β sets f_β knowing f_α.

Stage II: Airline firms compete in airfares, p_α and p_β.

We are looking for a subgame perfect equilibrium for this two-stage game. We need to solve the model for two cases: One case in which the market is fully served, and the second case in which the market is only partially served. However, Appendix A demonstrates that with the absence of code-sharing agreements, a partially-served market equilibrium does not exist. We can therefore assume that the market is fully served.

3.1 Solving for the second stage equilibrium

Let f_α and f_β be given. Substituting (2) into (6) and then maximizing π_α with respect to p_α, and then maximizing π_β with respect to p_β yield the following best-response functions.

$$p_\alpha(p_\beta) = \frac{f_\alpha - f_\beta + \tau + \phi + p_\beta}{2}, \quad \text{and} \quad p_\beta(p_\alpha) = \frac{f_\beta - f_\alpha + \tau + \phi + p_\alpha}{2}. \tag{8}$$

Second-order conditions are given by $\partial^2 \pi_i / \partial(p_i)^2 = -n/\tau < 0, i = \alpha, \beta$. Solving (8) yields the equilibrium airfares as functions of the flight frequencies offered by both carriers. Thus,

$$p_\alpha = \frac{f_\alpha - f_\beta + 3\tau + 3\phi}{3}, \quad \text{and} \quad p_\beta = \frac{f_\beta - f_\alpha + 3\tau + 3\phi}{3}. \tag{9}$$

Hence, $p_\alpha \geq p_\beta$ if and only if $f_\alpha \geq f_\beta$, meaning that the carrier providing a higher frequency of flights charges a higher airfare.

Substituting (9) into (2) yields

$$\hat{x} = \frac{1}{2} + \frac{f_\alpha - f_\beta}{6\tau}. \tag{10}$$

Thus, the airline which provides a higher frequency of flights maintains a higher market share, and if both carriers provide the same frequency of flights ($f_\alpha = f_\beta$), the market is equally divided between the two carriers.

3.2 Solving for the first stage equilibrium

Substituting (9) and (10) into (6) yields the equilibrium profit levels of the two airline companies. Therefore,

$$\pi_\alpha = \frac{n(f_\alpha - f_\beta + 3\tau)^2}{18\tau} - \delta(f_\alpha)^2, \quad \text{and} \quad \pi_\beta = \frac{n(f_\beta - f_\alpha + 3\tau)^2}{18\tau} - \delta(f_\beta)^2. \tag{11}$$

Maximizing each profit function yield the airline firms' frequency best-response functions. Thus,

$$f_\alpha(f_\beta) = \max\left\{1, \frac{n(3\tau - f_\beta)}{18\delta\tau - n}\right\}, \quad \text{and} \quad f_\beta(f_\alpha) = \max\left\{1, \frac{n(3\tau - f_\alpha)}{18\delta\tau - n}\right\}. \quad (12)$$

The second-order conditions for maxima are $\partial^2 \pi_i / \partial(f_i)^2 = 2n/18\tau - 2\delta < 0$ by Assumption 1. Hence, the equilibrium frequency levels are

$$\bar{f} \stackrel{\text{def}}{=} f_\alpha = f_\beta = \frac{n}{6\delta}, \quad (13)$$

which are greater than 1 by Assumption 1. Therefore, as expected, with no code sharing, flight frequencies increase with an increase in the number of passengers, and decrease with the cost per departure. Substituting (13) into (10), and into (9) yields the equilibrium market shares and airfares. Thus,

$$\hat{x} = \frac{1}{2}, \quad \text{and} \quad p_\alpha = p_\beta = \tau + \phi. \quad (14)$$

Substituting into (6) yields

$$\pi_\alpha = \pi_\beta = \frac{n\tau}{2} - \frac{n^2}{36\delta}, \quad (15)$$

which is nonnegative by Assumption 1. Finally, in order for the fully-served market equilibrium to exist, it must be that all passengers gain a strictly-positive utility level. Clearly, if the passenger indexed by $x = 1/2$ gains a strictly positive utility, then all others do. Thus, for a fully-served market equilibrium to exist, we must have for $i = \alpha, \beta$ that

$$U(0.5) = f_i - \frac{\tau}{2} - p_i = \frac{n}{6\delta} - \frac{\tau}{2} - (\tau + \phi) \geq 0, \quad \text{or} \quad \tau \leq \frac{n - 6\delta\phi}{9\delta}. \quad (16)$$

Notice that for such a range to be nonempty, more precisely for τ to satisfy both Assumption 1(a) and (16), we need to impose the restriction that $n \geq 12\delta\phi$, which constitutes the last part of Assumption 1(b).

We now state the main proposition of this section. The proof is given in Appendix B.

Proposition 1 *Suppose that there is no code-sharing agreement between the two airline companies. Then,*
(a) A unique subgame-perfect fully-served market equilibrium exists and is given by (13) and (14) if and only if $\tau \leq (n - 6\delta\phi)/(9\delta)$.
(b) A subgame-perfect partially-served equilibrium does not exist.

Finally, Doganis (1993) reports about the rapid growth in U.S. passenger population. Therefore, it is instructive to check the effect of an increase in passenger population on profits. The following proposition is proved in Appendix C.

Proposition 2 *(a) An increase in number of passengers n on the route (i) reduces the profits of both national carriers, (ii) increases the frequency of flights, and hence (iii) increases passengers' welfare.*
(b) An increase in the flight frequency cost parameter δ would decrease equilibrium fight frequency, increase carriers' profits, but would leave airfare unchanged.
(c) An increase in the passenger cost parameter φ would be rolled over the passengers in the form of higher airfares, thereby leaving profits unchanged.

Proposition 2 highlights the (network) externality nature of air-transport services, which is clearly manifested in (13) which shows that flight frequencies increase with the number of passengers. This explains why passengers' utility is enhanced. However, Proposition 2(a)(i) reveals that airlines lose from an increase in passenger population because it intensifies competition so that the cost of supplying a higher frequency of flights dominates the increase in revenue collected from a larger number of passengers. Furthermore, (14) shows that in the absence of code sharing, equilibrium airfares are invariant with respect to the number passengers. All this means is that in the absence of code sharing airline firms tend to compete in frequencies rather than in airfares.

Proposition 2(b) and (c) demonstrates how the total costs are allocated between carriers and passengers. As it turns out, carriers bear the entire cost associated with flight frequency, whereas passengers bear their own service cost.

4 EQUILIBRIUM UNDER CODE SHARING AGREEMENTS

4.1 The Nature of the Code-Sharing Agreement

A code-sharing agreement allows each national airline to issue a ticket for flights operated by any contracting airline. Passengers choose from which airline to purchase the ticket according to their preference for the two carriers, and then, with the same ticket they can board any flight operated by either carrier, if this flight happens to fit their schedule better. However, our assumption here is that even if a passenger boards a flight operated by a carrier other than the carrier which issued the ticket, she still considers it as a flight operated by the carrier which issued the ticket.

Thus, the frequency of flights facing each passenger is now $f_\alpha + f_\beta$. Under code sharing, the utility of a passenger indexed by x is given by[4]

$$U(x) \overset{\text{def}}{=} \begin{cases} f_\alpha + f_\beta - \tau x - p_\alpha & \text{flies } \alpha \\ f_\alpha + f_\beta - \tau(1-x) - p_\beta & \text{flies } \beta \\ 0 & \text{does not travel by air.} \end{cases} \quad (17)$$

From the above, if the market is fully served we can define

$$\hat{x} = \frac{p_\beta - p_\alpha + \tau}{2\tau}. \quad (18)$$

---

[4] This utility function implies that the two carriers remain differentiated from passengers' point of view. This assumption is somewhat too strong considering the fact code-sharing agreements allow passengers to gain full mileage on their frequent-flyer programs regardless of which carrier operates the specific flight.

However, if the market is only partially served, we define

$$\hat{x}_\alpha \stackrel{\text{def}}{=} \frac{f_\alpha + f_\beta - p_\alpha}{\tau}, \quad \text{and} \quad \hat{x}_\beta \stackrel{\text{def}}{=} \frac{\tau - f_\alpha - f_\beta + p_\beta}{\tau}. \tag{19}$$

A code-sharing agreement must specify a compensation mechanism under which airline firms must be compensated for carrying passengers who purchased a ticket from the other airline. Let t_α denotes the compensation carrier α pays to carrier β for each passenger who boards a flight operated by β using a flight ticket issued by carrier α. Similarly, let t_β denotes the compensation carrier β pays to carrier α for each passenger who boards a flight operated by α using a flight ticket issued by carrier β. We now make the following assumption.

ASSUMPTION 2 *Each passenger boards an aircraft operated by carrier α with probability $f_\alpha/(f_\alpha + f_\beta)$, and an aircraft operated by carrier β with probability $f_\beta/(f_\alpha + f_\beta)$. These probabilities are invariant with respect to from which airline the passengers purchase their tickets.*

Assumption 2 implies that if $f_\alpha > f_\beta$ the passenger, holding a ticket issued by either carrier, is more likely to board an aircraft operated by carrier α than carrier β, simply because carrier α operates a higher frequency of flights.

The profit of carrier α is given by

$$\pi_\alpha = n\tilde{x}_\alpha p_\alpha - n(\tilde{x}_\alpha + 1 - \tilde{x}_\beta)\frac{f_\alpha}{f_\alpha + f_\beta}\phi + n(1 - \tilde{x}_\beta)\frac{f_\alpha}{f_\alpha + f_\beta}t_\beta - n\tilde{x}_\alpha\frac{f_\beta}{f_\alpha + f_\beta}t_\alpha - \delta(f_\alpha)^2, \tag{20}$$

where $\tilde{x}_\alpha = \tilde{x}_\beta = \hat{x}$ is defined in (18) if the market is fully served; whereas $\tilde{x}_\alpha = \hat{x}_\alpha$ and $\tilde{x}_\beta = \hat{x}_\beta$, both are defined in (19) if the market is only partially served. The first term in (20) is carrier's α revenue from selling tickets. The second term measures the total passenger-handling costs which equals to the number of passengers actually carried by the airline times the per-passenger cost, ϕ. The third term measures the total revenue generated from compensatory fees collected from carrier β for flying passengers holding a ticket issued by β. The fourth term measures the compensation carrier α pays carrier β for flying passengers holding α's tickets. The last term measures α aggregate aircraft departure cost. Similarly, the profit function of carrier β is given by

$$\pi_\beta = n\tilde{x}_\beta p_\beta - n(\tilde{x}_\alpha + 1 - \tilde{x}_\beta)\frac{f_\beta}{f_\alpha + f_\beta}\phi - n(1 - \tilde{x}_\beta)\frac{f_\alpha}{f_\alpha + f_\beta}t_\beta + n\tilde{x}_\alpha\frac{f_\beta}{f_\alpha + f_\beta}t_\alpha - \delta(f_\beta)^2. \tag{21}$$

We now specify the details of the code-sharing agreement between the two national carriers.

Definition 1 *A code-sharing agreement (contract) is $\langle t_\alpha, t_\beta, f_\alpha, f_\beta \rangle$ specifying the compensatory fee each airline pays the other for carrying their passengers, and the frequency of flights each airline must maintain.*

We now place further restrictions on the specific formulation of this agreement.

ASSUMPTION 3 *(a) Both carriers agree to maintain the same flight frequencies they maintained prior to signing the code-sharing agreement. Formally, $f_\alpha = f_\beta = \bar{f}$, where $\bar{f}$ is given in (13).*
(b) Both carriers set a common compensatory fee, $t_\alpha = t_\beta = \bar{t}$, where $\bar{t}$ is set to maximize joint profits (first stage).
(c) After setting up the contract, airline carriers engage in noncooperative airfare competition, and set p_α and p_β accordingly (second stage).

The logic behind the code-sharing agreement specified in Assumption 3 is that such an agreement must be approved by the antitrust authorities regulating this agreement. Antitrust authorities, of course, will not tolerate any price fixing, so for this reason the carriers must convince the authorities that airfare competition is maintained. Next, antitrust authorities will also not tolerate a significant cut in flight frequencies associated with this agreement, since any cut in flight frequencies constitutes a clear manifestation of a monopoly power which results in an immediate reduction in passengers' welfare. For this reason, we assume that the carrier agrees to maintain the same flight frequencies as they provide without the code-sharing agreement. Finally, by 'negotiating' the compensatory fees, t_α and t_β, the two carriers engage in quasi-collusion as they implicitly set these fees to maximize joint profits.

4.2 Fully-Served Market Equilibrium Under Code Sharing

Substituting (13) and (18) into (20), in the second stage, carrier α chooses p_α that solves

$$\pi_\alpha = \frac{n[p_\alpha(p_\beta + \bar{t} + \tau) - (p_\alpha)^2 - p_\beta \bar{t} - \phi\tau]}{2\tau} - \delta\bar{f}^2, \tag{22}$$

yielding, assuming $p_\alpha = p_\beta$,

$$p_\alpha = p_\beta = \bar{t} + \tau. \tag{23}$$

The second-order condition is $\partial^2 \pi_\alpha / \partial(p_\alpha)^2 = -n/\bar{t} < 0$. Substituting (23) into (22) yields the profit of carrier α as a function of the negotiated compensatory fee, $\bar{t}$. Hence,

$$\pi_\alpha = \frac{n(\bar{t} + \tau - \phi)}{2} - \delta\bar{f}^2, \tag{24}$$

which is strictly increasing with $\bar{t}$. Therefore, (24) does not have a maximum for the first-stage maximization problem. However, (23) shows that the compensatory fee is rolled over to the passengers. Hence, for large values of $\bar{t}$, some passengers will choose not to fly with any airline. More precisely, the maximum value of $\bar{t}$ which is consistent with having the entire market being served is found by equating the utility of a passenger indexed by $x = 1/2$ to zero. Thus,

$$0 = U(0.5) = 2\bar{f} - \frac{\tau}{2} - (t^{\max} + \tau), \quad \text{or} \quad t^{\max} = \frac{4\bar{f} - 3\tau}{2} = \frac{2n - 9\delta\tau}{6\delta}, \tag{25}$$

where the last equality is obtained by substituting (13) for $\bar{f}$. Substituting t^{max} into (24) we obtain the maximum obtainable profit each airline can earn under the constraint that the entire market has to be served. Therefore,

$$\pi_\alpha^{\mathrm{max}} = \frac{n[5n - 9\delta(2\phi + \tau)]}{36\delta} \geq 0 \quad \text{if} \quad \tau \leq \frac{5n - 18\delta\phi}{9\delta}. \tag{26}$$

Our results of code-sharing under a fully-served market are given in the following proposition, which is proved in Appendix D.

Proposition 3 *Under code sharing, the profits of airline firms increase with an increase in the number of passengers, n, and decrease with an increase in the differentiation parameter, τ.*

The first part of Proposition 3 predicts exactly the opposite of the prediction made in Proposition 2. We explain this difference in Section 6.1 in the concluding section. The second part follows from (25) since an increase in τ reduces passengers' utility, hence it places a lower upper bound on the maximal compensatory fees.

4.3 Partially-Served Market Equilibrium Under Code Sharing

We now solve for the equilibrium under code sharing when the market is only partially served. Substituting (19), and then $f_\alpha = f_\beta = \bar{f}$ and $t_\alpha = t_\beta = \bar{t}$ into (20), in the second stage, airline α chooses p_α to solve

$$\max_{p_\alpha} \pi_\alpha = \frac{n\left[4\bar{f}(p_\alpha - \phi) - 2(p_\alpha)^2 + p_\alpha(\phi + \bar{t}) + p_\beta(\phi - \bar{t})\right]}{2\tau} - \delta\bar{f}^2. \tag{27}$$

The second-order condition yields $\partial^2 \pi_\alpha / \partial(p_\alpha)^2 = -2n/\tau < 0$. This maximization problem yields

$$p_\alpha = \frac{4\bar{f} + \phi + \bar{t}}{4}, \quad \text{hence} \quad \hat{x}_\alpha = \frac{4\bar{f} - \phi - \bar{t}}{4\tau}. \tag{28}$$

Substituting (13) into (28) yields

$$\hat{x}_\alpha = \frac{2n - 3\delta(\phi + \bar{t})}{12\delta\tau} \leq \frac{1}{2} \quad \text{if} \quad \bar{t} \geq \frac{2n - 3\delta(\phi + 2\tau)}{3\delta}, \tag{29}$$

a condition which is needed to maintain a partially-served market equilibrium.

Substituting (28) into (27) yields the profit of carrier α under code sharing. By symmetry, the profit earned by carrier α equals the profit earned by carrier β. Hence,

$$\pi_\alpha = \pi_\beta = \frac{n\left[16\bar{f}^2 - 16\bar{f}\phi + (\phi + \bar{t})(3\phi - \bar{t})\right]}{16\tau} - \delta\bar{f}^2. \tag{30}$$

In the first stage both carriers choose a common compensatory fee, $\bar{t}$, to maximize joint profits $\pi_\alpha + \pi_\beta$, which, by (30) is strictly concave. Therefore,

$$\bar{t} = \phi > \frac{2n - 3\delta(\phi + 2\tau)}{3\delta} \iff \tau > \frac{n - 3\delta\phi}{3\delta}. \tag{31}$$

The last condition in (31) is needed for a partially-served market equilibrium to exist. Under this condition, the equilibrium $\bar{\iota}$ exceeds the minimum fee needed for ensuring that the market is not fully served given in (29). Equation (31) implies that the joint-profit maximizing compensatory fee equals the cost of handling each passenger, ϕ, which is rather intuitive since it equals the marginal cost of carrying an additional passenger. Finally, substituting (13) for $\bar{f}$, and (31) for $\bar{\iota}$ into the profit of carrier α yields

$$\pi_\alpha = \frac{n\left[9\phi^2\delta^2 - \delta n(6\phi + \tau) + n^2\right]}{36\delta^2\tau}. \tag{32}$$

5   A WELFARE ANALYSIS OF CODE SHARING AGREEMENTS

We now approach the main purpose of our analysis which is the investigation of the effects of code sharing agreements. The questions to be answered below are: (i) Can airline firms increase their profits by engaging in a code-sharing agreement? (ii) How does the signing of a code-sharing agreement affect passengers' welfare? (iii) What is the effect on social welfare?

In order to be able to compare the market equilibria before and after the code-sharing agreement is signed, we must restrict the parameter range so that an equilibrium in the absence of code sharing will exist. Thus, Proposition 1(a) implies that we must make the following assumption.

ASSUMPTION 4 *The differentiation parameter τ is sufficiently low so that there exists an equilibrium in the absence of a code sharing agreement. Formally, $\tau \leq (n - 6\delta\phi)/(9\delta)$.*

However, under Assumption 4 the condition in (31) does not hold, which means that, under code sharing, a partially-served market equilibrium does not exist whenever an equilibrium exists in the absence of code sharing. All this means is that, in a welfare analysis, we need only compare the market equilibrium in absence of code sharing to the market equilibrium under code sharing when the market is fully served, i.e., Section 4.2.

We begin by comparing the profit levels before and after a code-sharing agreement is signed. The proof of the following proposition is given in Appendix E.

Proposition 4 *The code-sharing agreement enhances the profit of both airline companies compared to the profit they earn in the absence of this agreement.*

The intuition behind Proposition 4 is as follows. First, the code-sharing agreement increases the potential surplus that can be extracted from passengers since passengers increase their willingness to pay for flight tickets because the agreement exposes passengers to twice the frequency of flights compared to the frequency of flights provided by each airline prior to the agreement.

Second, the agreement allows the carriers to collude on the compensatory fees they must compensate each other for carrying passengers holding a ticket purchased by the competing airline. As can be observed in (20) and (21), these fees cancel out, however, they artificially increase the marginal passenger handling costs thereby enabling the carriers to raise airfares. To see this, (14) and (23) imply

$$\tau + \bar{t} > \tau + \phi \Longleftrightarrow \tau < \frac{2n - 6\delta\phi}{9\delta},$$

which is clearly satisfied if Assumption 4 is satisfied.

Therefore, we can say that the compensation mechanism imbedded into the code-sharing agreement relaxes airfare competition. Such an effect is not unique to the airline industry. For example, Laffont, Rey, and Tirole, (1998) and their references have demonstrated a similar result in the telephony industry where mutual negotiation on access pricing raises the marginal cost of transmitting a call via a competitor results in an increase in the equilibrium price of phone calls. Altogether, the code-sharing agreement increase airfares while leaving the carriers with the same market shares and total costs. This implies that profits must increase.

We now turn to analyzing the effects of the code-sharing agreement on passengers' welfare. The following proposition is proved in Appendix F.

Proposition 5 *All passengers are worse off when airline companies enter into a code-sharing agreement.*

Proposition 5 is not surprising. Despite the increase in frequency, the code-sharing agreement enables airline companies to extract a higher surplus since the agreement facilitates airfare competition.

Finally, we define the social welfare function as the sum of the utilities of the n passengers plus the sum of profits made by the national airlines. Analyzing world's welfare rather than the welfare of an individual country allows us not to specify whether the carriers are domestically owned, or whether foreign ownership is allowed. Social welfare in the absence of code sharing (NCS) is given by

$$W^{\text{NCS}} = nU^{\text{NCS}}(0.25) + \pi_\alpha^{\text{NCS}} + \pi_\beta^{\text{NCS}} = n\left[\frac{4n - 9\delta\tau - 36\delta\phi}{36\delta}\right], \tag{33}$$

where the first term is the utility of the 'average' passenger (indexed by $x = 0.25$) multiplied by the world passenger population, n. The second and third terms are from (15). Social welfare under code sharing is given by

$$W^{\text{CS}} = nU^{\text{CS}}(0.25) + \pi_\alpha^{\text{CS}} + \pi_\beta^{\text{CS}} = n\left[\frac{10n - 9\delta\tau - 36\delta\phi}{36\delta}\right]. \tag{34}$$

Subtracting (34) from (33) yields

$$\Delta W \overset{\text{def}}{=} W^{\text{CS}} - W^{\text{NCS}} = \frac{n^2}{6\delta} = n\bar{f} > 0. \tag{35}$$

This proves our last proposition.

Proposition 6 *Code sharing improves social welfare.*

The intuition behind Proposition 6 can be clearly seen from (35) which shows the net gain to this economy equals to the sum of utility gains from the increase in frequency, resulting from the code sharing agreement. The utility loss to passengers from the increase in airfares is obviously a transfer to the airline firms which does not affect aggregate welfare.

6   DISCUSSION

6.1   Implications of Code-Sharing Agreements

Section 5 has already summarized the welfare effects of code sharing. Here, we would like to point out further implications of these agreements. Comparing Propositions 2 and 3 reveals that code sharing *changes the nature of competition* between airline firms. In the absence of code sharing airline firms utilize flight frequencies as their major strategic instrument, whereas under code sharing airlines utilize airfares as their strategic instrument. As demonstrated in Propositions 2 and 3, these differences in the form of competition contribute to the results that profits decline with the number of passengers in the absence of codes sharing, and increase under code sharing. Also, in the absence of code sharing profit increase with the differentiation parameter τ, as expected; however, it declines with τ under code sharing.

Finally, the present paper is perhaps the only theoretical study so far suggesting that parallel code sharing may improve social welfare. However, the reader should bear in mind that Proposition 6 relies on Assumption 3(a) stating that the carriers are not allowed to reduce flight frequency after a code sharing agreement is signed. If this assumption is relaxed, carriers will find it profitable to reduce flight frequency in which case the reduction in consumer welfare may overweigh the increase in profit.

6.2   Extensions

Our investigation of the market consequences of code-sharing agreements focused on the direct effect on the degree of competition *between the contracting airline companies*. This makes our analysis incomplete as it neglects to take into account how a code-sharing agreement between two airline companies creates an advantage for the contracting carriers over other airline companies operating on the same routes. This advantage is created partly because flights under code sharing happen to be listed at the top of the screen on some reservation systems thereby gaining a significant marketing advantage over flights listed only under a single airline, see Oum *et al.* (1996). To model this effect one has to construct a model with more than two operators, and to check the effects of asymmetric advantage gained by contracting airlines whose flight frequencies are enhanced relative to noncontracting airlines. This asymmetry will enable the contracting carriers to charge higher airfares relative to noncontracting carriers.

Another aspect of code sharing which is not analyzed in the present paper is how it affects *interconnections*. Interconnections are used mainly in international travel where passengers from one country would like to arrive at a non-hub city (or a small city) in their destination country. Since national airlines generally do not provide internal flights in foreign countries, interconnection means that passengers must switch carriers upon their arrival to the foreign country. Brueckner (2003) provides empirical evidence showing the effect of airline cooperation on the interline fares paid by international passengers. A code sharing agreement can facilitate the transition from one aircraft to another simply by having both carriers sharing the same terminal and ground crews so that no extra check-in procedures are needed. Although such services can be maintained without code-sharing, it turns out that such a commitment is most likely to be maintained when carriers sign a code-sharing agreement, see Gellman Research Associates (1994).

APPENDIX A. NONEXISTENCE OF A PARTIALLY-SERVED MARKET EQUILIBRIUM IN THE ABSENCE OF CODE SHARING

Since the market is segmented, i.e., $\hat{x}_A < \hat{x}_B$, it is sufficient to focus our analysis on carrier α only. By symmetry, all the restrictions that apply to carrier α need also apply to carrier β. Substituting (3) into (7), in the second stage carrier α chooses its airfare, p_α, to solve

$$\max_{p_\alpha} \pi_\alpha = n \frac{(f_\alpha - p_\alpha)(p_\alpha - \phi)}{\tau} - \delta(f_\alpha)^2. \tag{36}$$

The second-order condition for a maximum is $-2n/\tau < 0$. Hence, the first-order condition implies that

$$p_\alpha = \frac{f_\alpha + \phi}{2}. \tag{37}$$

Substituting into (3) yields

$$\hat{x}_\alpha = \frac{f_\alpha - \phi}{2\tau}. \tag{38}$$

Substituting (37) into (36), in the first stage, carrier α chooses its flight frequency, f_α, to solve

$$\max_{f_\alpha} \pi_\alpha = \frac{n(f_\alpha - \phi)^2}{4\tau} - \delta(f_\alpha)^2, \quad \text{s.t.} \quad f_\alpha \geq 1. \tag{39}$$

For an interior maximum to exist, the second order condition must hold, i.e.,

$$\frac{\partial^2 \pi_\alpha}{\partial (f_\alpha)^2} = \frac{n - 4\delta\tau}{2\tau} < 0, \quad \text{or} \quad \tau > \frac{n}{4\delta}. \tag{40}$$

However, the first-order condition implies that

$$f_\alpha = \frac{n\phi}{n - 4\delta\tau}, \tag{41}$$

which, together with the second-order condition, implies that $f_\alpha < 0$; a contradiction to our assumption that (39) has an interior maximum. Therefore, when (40) holds, $f_\alpha = 1$ is a unique maximum, meaning that the carrier provides the lowest possible flight frequency equals to a single flight per unit of time. Substituting $f_\alpha = 1$ into (38) and then, also, into (39), yield

$$\hat{x}_\alpha = \frac{1-\phi}{2\tau}, \quad \text{and} \quad \pi_\alpha = \frac{n(1-\phi)^2}{4\tau} - \delta. \tag{42}$$

Hence, $x_\alpha > 0$ implies that $\phi < 1$, and $\pi_\alpha \geq 0$ implies that

$$\tau \leq \frac{n(1-\phi)^2}{4\delta}, \tag{43}$$

which contradicts (40).

Suppose now that the second-order condition (40) does not hold. Therefore, $\tau \leq n/4\delta$ which means that (39) is a convex profit function where (41) constitutes a unique minimum. There are two cases to analyze: $f_\alpha < 1$, and $f_\alpha > 1$, where f_α is given in (41).

If $f_\alpha \leq 1$ in (41), then $\partial\pi_\alpha/\partial f_\alpha > 0$ for all $f_\alpha \geq 1$. This means the carrier will increase its flight frequency until $\hat{x}_\alpha = 1$, where $\hat{x}_\alpha$ is given in (38). This means that the market is fully served, a contradiction.

If $f_\alpha > 1$ in (41), then either the entire market is served (since the carrier will profitably increase f_α until $\hat{x}_\alpha = 1$), or it will maximize profit by setting $f_\alpha = 1$. Then, (41) implies

$$\tau > \frac{n(1-\phi)}{4\delta},$$

which contradicts (43).

APPENDIX B. PROOF OF PROPOSITION 1

(a) The condition is taken from (16) which is necessary to ensure that all consumers are served. (b) See Appendix A.

APPENDIX C. PROOF OF PROPOSITION 2

(a) (i) Differentiating (15) with respect to n reveals

$$\frac{\partial\pi_\alpha}{\partial n} = \frac{\tau}{2} - \frac{n}{18\delta} < 0 \Longleftrightarrow \tau < \frac{n}{9\delta},$$

which holds by Proposition 1(a). (ii) Immediate from (13). (iii) Follows directly from (16) also for all consumers indexed by $0 \leq x \leq 1/5$.

(b) The statements follow immediately by inspecting (13), (15), and (14), respectively.

(c) (14) implies that equilibrium airfares are composed of ϕ, meaning that the cost of handling passengers are fully borne by the passengers themselves. The equilibrium profits levels (15) are independent of ϕ.

APPENDIX D. PROOF OF PROPOSITION 3

The two statements follow directly from (26), which clearly shows that profit increases with n and declines with τ.

APPENDIX E. PROOF OF PROPOSITION 4

The profit earned by each carrier under a code-sharing agreement (26) exceeds the profit of an airline in the absence of a code-sharing agreement (15) if $\tau < (2n - 6\delta\phi)/(9\delta)$, which is clearly satisfied if Assumption 4 is satisfied.

APPENDIX F. PROOF OF PROPOSITION 5

The equilibrium airfare under code sharing is found by substituting (25) into (23). Then, comparing with the equilibrium airfare in the absence of code sharing given in (14) reveals that airfares are higher under the code-sharing agreement. More precisely, subtracting (14) from (23) reveals that when the carriers enter into the code sharing agreement, airfare rises by

$$\Delta p = \frac{2n - 9\delta\tau - 6\delta\phi}{6\delta}.$$

However, passengers gain some utility from the doubling of the frequency of flights from $\bar{f} = n/(6\delta)$ to $2\bar{f} = 2n/(6\delta)$. Now, consumer welfare declines if the negative price effect dominates the positive increase in utility generated by higher frequency. This is indeed the case since $\bar{f} < \Delta p$ if $\tau < (n - 6\delta\phi)/9\delta$ which holds by Assumption 4.

REFERENCES

Armantier, O., and O. Richard. 2005. "Domestic Airline Alliances and Consumer Welfare." Working Paper, University of Montreal.

Berechman, J., and J. de Wit. 1999. "On the Future Role of Alliance." In: Gaudry, M., Mayes, R. (eds.), *Taking Stock of Air Liberalization.* Boston: Kluwer Academic Publishers.

Bamberger, G., D. Carlton, and L. Neumann. 2004. "An Empirical Investigation of the Competitive Effects of Domestic Airline Alliances." *Journal of Law and Economics.* 47: 195–222.

Berechman, J., S. Poddar, and O. Shy. 1998. "Network Structure and Entry in the Deregulated Airline Industry." *Keio Economic Studies.* 35: 71–82.

Brueckner, J. 2001. "The Economics of International Codesharing: An Analysis of Airline Alliances." *International Journal of Industrial Organization.* 19: 1475–1498.

Brueckner, J. 2003. "International Airfares in the Age of Alliances: The Effects of Codesharing and Antitrust Immunity." *The Review of Economics and Statistics.* 85: 105–118.

Brueckner, J., and T. Whalen. 2000. "The Price Effects of International Airline Alliances." *Journal of Law and Economics.* 43: 503–545.

Doganis, R. 1993. *Flying off Course: The Economics of International Airlines.* New York: Routledge. (2nd Edition).

Gellman Research Associates. 1994. "A Study of International Airline Code Sharing." Office of Aviation and International Economics, U.S. Department of Transportation, Washington, D.C.

Hassin, O., and O. Shy. 2004. "Code-Sharing Agreements and Interconnections in Markets for International Flights," *Review of International Economics*, 12: 337–352.

Ito, H., and D. Lee. 2005. "Domestic Codesharing Practices in the US Airline Industry." *Journal of Air Transport Management*. 11: 89–97.

Laffont, J-J., P. Rey, and J. Tirole. 1998. "Network Competition: I. Overview and Nondiscriminatory Pricing." *Rand Journal of Economics* 29: 1–37.

Oum, T., J. Park, and A. Zhang. 1996. "The Effect of Airline Codesharing Agreements on Firm conduct and International Air Fares." *Journal of Transport Economics and Policy*. 30: 187–202.

Park, J. 1997. "The effect of Airline Alliances on Markets and Economic Welfare." *Transportation Research* 33: 181–195.

Park, J., and A. Zhang. 1998. "Airline alliances and partner firms' output," *Transportation Research* 34: 245–255.

Park, J., and A. Zhang. 2000. "An Empirical Analysis of Global Airline Alliances: Cases in the North Atlantic markets." *Review of Industrial Organization* 16: 367–383.

Shy, O. 1996. *Industrial Organization: Theory and Applications*. Cambridge MA: The MIT Press.

Whalen, T. 1999. "The Welfare Effects of Domestic Airline Alliances." University of Illinois Working Paper.

Advances in Airline Economics, Vol 1
Darin Lee (Editor)
© 2006 Published by Elsevier B.V.

8

Airline Hubs: Costs, Markups and the Implications of Customer Heterogeneity[1]

Steven Berry, Michael Carnall, and Pablo T. Spiller[2]

1 INTRODUCTION

There is by now a large empirical literature on the post-deregulation airline industry. This literature has focused on a number of issues regarding the provision and pricing of airline services.[3] One of the most debated aspects of the industry restructuring is the almost complete shift in network organization, from "point-to-point" to "hub-and-spoke." Hub and spoke networks, in which passengers change planes at a hub airport on the way to their eventual destinations, have been criticized as increasing entry barriers and driving up prices for hub-originating passengers (e.g., Borenstein, 1989, 1991).[4] Others, including some airline executives, have suggested that hub-and-spoke networks reduce costs (e.g. Caves, Christensen and Trethway, 1984; Brueckner, Dyer and Spiller, 1992,

---

[1] The authors would like to acknowledge the useful comments of Severin Borenstein, Shane Greenstein, Ariel Pakes and participants at various seminars and conferences. The computing for this research project was supported by grants from the National Center for Supercomputer Applications at the University of Illinois, Urbana-Champaign, and from the Pittsburgh Supercomputing Center through the National Science Foundation (NSF).
[2] The authors are, respectively, James Burrows Moffatt Professor of Economics, Yale University, <steven.berry@yale.edu>; Senior Managing Economist, LECG LLC, <mcarnall@lecg.com>; and Jeffrey A. Jacobs Distinguished Professorship in Business and Technology Chair, Haas Business and Public Policy Group, Haas School of Business, University of California, Berkeley, <spiller@haas.berkeley.edu>.
[3] Deregulation removed restrictions on entry and exit and gave carriers the freedom to set fares. For discussion of the impact of the new regulatory environment on airline operations, see Bailey and Williams (1988), Bailey, Graham and Kaplan (1985), Brueckner and Spiller (1994), Levine (1988), Moore (1986), and Morrison and Winston (1986).
[4] Critics also mention several other negative features of hub-and-spoke networks, like increased number of connections, and the increase in hub airport congestion (as planes land and depart in bunch).

hereafter, BDS; Brueckner and Spiller, 1994).[5] The claim of the cost-efficiency of hubs has been challenged by the success of non-hub carriers, like Southwest.[6]

These two effects, increasing markups and reducing costs, though, are not mutually exclusive (Berry 1990). Airline hubs could raise prices for some consumers by substantially increasing markups over marginal cost, while at the same time reducing costs. In this paper, we use a differentiated products supply-and-demand model to disentangle the separate effects of hubs on costs and markups. We think of hubs as shifting out the product specific demand curve for flights of the hubbing airline out of its hub city. Flights originating at hubs and provided by the hub-airline may appeal especially to relatively price inelastic consumers. This shift in the level and elasticity of demand can lead to both higher output levels and prices for the hubbing airline, consistent with previous empirical results. On the cost side, we allow for economies of "spoke density:" more densely traveled spokes may have lower marginal costs. Economies of spoke density will lead to economies of scope across itineraries that share a common spoke.[7] These economies of scope in turn imply network economies, so that itineraries that include a hub airport, by increasing spoke density, may have lower costs (see BDS).

In this paper we provide the first estimates of a model of airline competition which capture the two major features of the industry: product differentiation and economies of density. On the demand side, we attempt to capture the fact that airline customers are heterogenous by allowing customers' preferences over various product specifications to be drawn from a binary distribution. On the cost side, we estimate a very flexible spoke marginal cost function, so as to allow economies of density to vary across different ranges.

Our estimates not only provide support to some of the traditional common wisdom in the industry, but are also useful to understand major puzzles concerning the evolution of the industry and of its operational, marketing and pricing practices. First, we provide estimates of the differential willingness to pay for different air travel features by what can be called tourist and business travelers. Indeed, our results show the existence of two very distinct types of passengers, one with the standard attributes of a tourist traveler (i.e., high price sensitivity, low willingness to pay for frequent flyer features, low willingness to pay for frequency, low disutility from connecting flights, etc) and another with a strong business-traveler flavor (i.e., low price sensitivity, high willingness to pay for frequent-flyer features, high willingness to pay for frequency, high disutility from connecting flights, etc). These estimates are the key to uncovering the ability of hub-airlines to increase their markups in hub-originating flights. In this regard, we provide evidence that hubs provide two major competitive advantages to companies: they reduce costs and allow for higher markups on hub originating passengers.

---

[5] For an industry defense of the hub-and-spoke system, see Michael Levine's editorial page article in Northwest Airlines's February issue of its in-flight magazine.

[6] Southwest has been the only consistently profitable carrier since deregulation. See, US Department of Transportation, Air Carriers Financial Statistics Quarterly, various issues.

[7] For example, the itinerary New York-Chicago-San Diego shares a spoke with New York-Chicago-Seattle. Thus, an increase in demand for the airline's New York-San Diego service, increases traffic in its New York-Chicago leg, and if economies of density are present, it reduces the marginal cost of providing service in the New York-Seattle market. See Brueckner and Spiller (1991, 1994).

Second, our estimates show that a hubbing airline's ability to raise prices at its hub is not universal, but rather is focused on tickets that appeal to relatively price-inelastic consumers, (i.e., business travelers). Indeed, we find that hub airlines do not find it profitable to raise prices much to non-business travelers. Thus, business travelers' higher willingness to pay for flying a hub-airline coupled with their price inelastic demands, provides hub airlines with the ability to offer higher priced products to which business travelers will self-select.

Third, our estimates suggest that in spite of the higher markups of the hubbing airlines, the price inelastic consumers (i.e., business travelers) drastically move their flying patterns towards the origin hub airline, even though they have to pay an average premium of 20% or so over the prices charged by the non-hub competitors.

Fourth, our estimates show that the existence of a hub airline does not provide a "monopoly umbrella" to the other non-hub airlines serving the hub airport. Indeed, non-hub airlines competing with a hub-airline face the workings of a particularly strong competitive scissor: a reduction in the proportion of their travelers who are price insensitive, and a reduction in market share. Both are the result of the shift of the price insensitive passengers (business travelers) towards the hub airline. The increased price sensitivity of their average passenger, however, reduces the non-hub airlines' average yield and, as a consequence, the profitability of serving all routes connected to that airport. Thus, competing airlines will reduce service out of an airport where a competitor starts operating a hub. Our results, then, provide a possible explanation for the increase in airport concentration that has taken place following airline deregulation (Brueckner and Spiller, 1994). Such increase in airport concentration, however, is not necessarily the result of increased entry-barriers, but rather of the price insensitivity of business travelers' demands and of their valuation of flying the hub-originating airline.

Finally, on the cost side, we find strong evidence of economies of density. Indeed, airlines operating large hubs are found to have, on average, significantly lower marginal costs, out of the hub, than their competitors in the same routes. We show, however, that economies of density may depend on the nature of the route. In particular, we do not find economies of density at distances less than 500 miles or so. This may help to explain the "Southwest effect," which relates to the apparent profitability of Southwest Airlines, a non-hubbing airline offering frequent flights on short routes. According to our estimates, the "Southwest effect" may not be exclusively the result of lower labor costs, but rather may be the result of Southwest's having found a particularly effective "cost" niche.[8]

2   COSTS AND DEMAND: PRELIMINARIES

Costs. The cost efficiencies of hubs may arise from the use of large, cost-effective aircraft on the densely trafficked spokes of a hub-and-spoke system. This idea relies in part on an engineering argument that larger planes are cheaper to fly per seat mile, at least on longer routes. For a given flight frequency, more "dense" spokes can efficiently

---

[8] This result puts in question Southwest's recent strategy of moving "national." Such move implies moving into a range where economies of density, and hence, hub-and-spoke networks, may be more efficient.

use larger aircraft. Economies of scale at the level of airline spokes in turn imply network economies, for hubbing airlines can combine passengers who have different final destinations on a single large plane that flies to a hub city. At that hub the passengers switch to different planes, which in turn combine passengers from various initial origins.

There is some empirical evidence in favor of hubs reducing costs. Caves, Christensen and Tretheway (1984), for example, estimate economies of density by analyzing the relationship between airline total costs, route structure, and total passenger traffic. They find that, holding the airline's route structure (e.g., the number of points served) constant, total cost increases only 80% as rapidly as total traffic, indicating significant economies of traffic density. While this is an important finding, the underlying methodology ignores details of a carrier's route structure that critically affect density levels, an omission that may bias the estimate of economies of density.[9] In order to capture such detail, a more disaggregated approach is needed that makes use of density information at the individual route level. Use of such detailed output information, however, is impossible within the traditional cost-function framework because the required cost accounting data are not available at the route level. Therefore, estimation of economies of density using disaggregated data must proceed in a way that does not require direct cost information.[10]

Brueckner and Spiller (1994) provide an alternative method to estimate economies of density that is not based on traditional cost function approaches, but rather directly model the role of spoke densities. In their model, the marginal cost of adding a passenger to a given spoke changes with an airline's total traffic, or density, on that spoke. The marginal cost of a multisegment passenger is then found as the sum of the marginal costs of each segment. This marginal cost in turn affects price. Thus, the high spoke densities that are a feature of hub-and-spoke networks are allowed to affect costs and prices in a natural way. Brueckner and Spiller (1994) focus on flights that pass through hub airports, rather than originating at hubs. (This is an attempt to control for the higher markups that may be found on flights out of hub airports.) They find evidence that by funneling passengers through a hub airport, the switch to hub-and-spoke operations raised traffic densities and allowed carriers to reduce their costs.

For the cost side of our model, we take an approach similar to Brueckner and Spiller (1994). We model the effect of density on the marginal costs of each spoke in the network, which we infer from the markup equation, and make inferences from the effect of density on prices, holding markups constant via techniques discussed below. The marginal cost of flying a given itinerary is then the sum of the marginal costs of the spokes defining that itinerary.

There are several issues to be faced in using such a model. First, depending on demand conditions, airlines may respond to increased density by increasing flight frequency rather than by increasing plane size. Therefore, in the empirical work we try to control for flight frequencies. Second, high traffic, and thus low cost, on some spokes may be a consequence of high demand for associated itineraries, resulting in low prices as well as

---

[9] For example, holding the number of endpoints fixed, densities will fall as the number of hubs operated by the airline increases.

[10] We are not the first to estimate an oligopoly model, including a marginal cost function, without *direct* cost information. For prior attempts, see, for example Porter (1983) and, more generally, Bresnahan's (1989) survey of structural estimation of oligopoly models. We use, though, cost shifters in estimating both the demand and the marginal cost functions.

high markups. This suggests that densities are endogenously determined, together with price. Our estimation procedure tries to account for this endogeneity. Third, density may affect fixed as well as marginal costs, an effect that we will simply not capture. Finally, marginal cost may vary with factors that we do not observe, such as capacity levels that vary across time of day. We do not observe these factors and so cannot account for them.

Demand. Many authors have suggested reasons why flights on hubbing airlines originating out of hub airports may be associated with higher markups (e.g. Borenstein, 1989, Levine, 1987). It has been suggested that various marketing programs, such as frequent flier plans and non-linear travel agent commission programs, both build brand loyalty and may exploit various principal-agent problems. Hubbing airlines may also offer superior service via their control over airport resources: for example more convenient gates and better departure times.

Evidence for this markup effect has been provided in various regressions of price on characteristics of routes and markets, including whether the flight originates from a hub. Borenstein (1989), for example, finds that flights on airlines with a hub at one or both endpoints command higher prices. This effect seems to be particularly large at the high end of the price distribution. Borenstein (1989) does not provide a model of costs or demand, but attempts to control for market-level unobservables by, for example, introducing city-pair level fixed effects. In Borenstein (1991), he introduces *directional* city-pair effects, looking at the difference between routes into and out of the hub city. He finds higher prices on flights out of the hub which might, for example, be consistent with the effect of marketing efforts such as frequent flyer programs.

Reduced form regressions, however, do not allow us to make statements about how prices relate to costs, or what are the determinants of markups over cost. Our approach is to introduce hubs as one characteristic in a differentiated products model of demand for airline flights. When combined with the cost model and a notion of market equilibrium, we will obtain estimates of markups for various products. In such a model, high markups can result both from a lack of competition and from high levels of product-specific demand.

To obtain an empirically implementable model of product differentiation, we adapt recent advances in empirical models of such markets (Berry, 1994, Berry, Levinsohn and Pakes - henceforth BLP-, 1995). In these models, consumers differ in their valuations of the characteristics of different products. In particular, we model two types of potential consumers ("business" and "tourist", perhaps) who differ in their "taste" for direct flights, low fares, and other features of airlines' products. A ticket on a direct flight with few restrictions, for example, can be sold to business travelers at a high price, while other tickets may be sold primarily to tourists at low prices. Our model of markups allows for the possibility that flights out of hub airports are offered at higher prices, even if costs are low.

We believe that the restrictions placed on tickets, such as advance purchase requirements and Saturday stayover rules, are an important explanation for the wide variety of fares offered within given routes. Unfortunately, our data do not contain information on ticket restrictions. Previous authors have generally used this same data set and have not been able to control for such restrictions. We introduce an explicit unobserved product characteristic, which is correlated with prices, to help control for these unobserved restrictions.

Equilibrium. Following Berry (1990) equilibrium model of airline prices, we assume that prices are set according to a static Nash equilibrium in prices. It is this equilibrium

Second, we recognize that the publicly available data do not tell us what restrictions are placed on a ticket. To account for this, we follow Berry (1994) and introduce an unobserved (to us) product characteristic, ξ_j. The term ξ_j, which is perfectly observed by firms and consumers, will also capture other unmeasured characteristics of the product, such as the quality of the food and the service. This characteristic enters utility in much the same way as the observed x's. Since there is one unobserved characteristic for each product, we cannot consistently estimate the ξ_j from product level data. Therefore, as the estimation section will make clear, to estimate the model we must place some restrictions on their distribution. We could assume some parametric distribution for the unobserved product characteristics, but instead we will use the weaker assumption that the ξ_j are uncorrelated with some vector of instruments.

We do not want to assume that the unobserved product characteristics are uncorrelated with price, because we believe that tickets with different restrictions have systematically different prices. We will assume that the ξ_j are uncorrelated with other observed demand variables, such as the distance between the two cities and a dummy variable for whether the flight is direct. Whether these exogeneity restrictions are reasonable depends on the economic process that generates restrictions on tickets. To give one extreme case, if the same restrictions are offered on each airline/itinerary, then the exogeneity restrictions are correct. For example, an airline might always offer an unrestricted fare, an advanced-purchase Saturday night stayover fare and an advanced purchase fare with no stayover restriction. In this case, there will be no correlation between the (un)restrictiveness of the ticket and x. On the other hand, it is not hard to think of stories which would violate our exogeneity restriction. In any case, our assumptions strictly generalize previous work.

As a third extension, we generalize the distribution of tastes across consumers (see Hausman and Wise, 1978 and BLP, 1995.) In particular, we consider a random coefficients framework in which the taste for product characteristics and prices, (β_i, α_i), varies across consumers. For example, we might assume that utility is given by

$$u_{ij} = x_j \beta_i - \alpha_i p_j + \xi_j + \varepsilon_{ij}.$$

where (β_i, α_i) is assumed to have some distribution across consumers. Unlike the logit model, this allows markups to systematically vary with observed characteristics. In the random coefficients model the tastes of consumers who purchase a product vary systematically with x and p. Thus, a change in price will have systematically different effects on products with different characteristics and prices. For example, a high priced product will be purchased, on average, by consumers who do not care much about price. Thus, a price increase may not have a large effect on the demand for this product. In contrast, in the logit model price effects (measured by the slope of demand) are always equal for products with equal market shares, regardless of the values of x and p. Indeed, this last feature is true of any discrete choice model in which consumer tastes enter only as an additive i.i.d. term.

There is an important question of how to model the distribution of the random coefficients. One traditional model would assume that (β_i, α_i) are distributed i.i.d. normal across consumers. The correlation of tastes across characteristics is often assumed to be zero for simplicity (as in BLP). However, we believe that the distribution of consumer tastes may be bi-modal. This is because there is a group of business travelers for whom the price of a ticket is not an important consideration in their decision to fly. There is another, probably much larger, group of potential travelers for whom the price of a ticket is, however, an important factor.[11] Furthermore, business travelers may have systematically different tastes for observed x's, such as flight frequency and whether the flight is direct. This last point suggests that tastes are correlated across characteristics.

We adopt the simplest distribution that is bi-modal and features correlation in tastes across characteristics.[12] This is a two point distribution. We estimate two different taste parameters, (β_1, α_1) and (β_2, α_2), together with the probability, γ, that a potential consumer is of "Type 1". Note that this distribution has $2K + 1$ parameters if there are K characteristics with random coefficients. In contrast, the simplest normal distribution would have $2K$ parameters – a mean and a variance of tastes for each characteristic. Our discrete distribution also has the advantage that it will provide a simple closed form expression for market shares. In contrast, the normality assumption requires numeric integration to obtain market shares.

There are obvious extensions of our two point discrete distribution. For example, one could model tastes as being drawn from two different normal distributions. This would allow for within type variance in tastes, as seems reasonable, but would also return us to the problem of numeric integration. Alternatively, we could allow for more than two discrete types of consumers. Although this specification would lose any neat interpretation as "business" and "tourist" travelers, it might more accurately reflect the data. Each of these extensions, however, would require a significant increase in the number of parameters to be estimated.

Random coefficients introduce a correlation in utility between products with "similar" characteristics. We believe that the outside good is not at all similar to the inside goods, so we also want to introduce correlation among the utilities of the "inside" goods. To do this in a simple way, we use a nested logit framework, where the only "nesting" groups products into an inside group and an outside good; the latter group, of course, has only one element. Note that the nested logit assumption could be extended to include other nests – on airports within cities, firms within markets, etc. – but we have not yet estimated such a model.

The Final Form for Utility and Market Shares. With all of these extensions, the utility function becomes:

$$u_{ij} = x_j\beta_i - \alpha_i p_j + \xi_j + \nu_i(\lambda) + \lambda\epsilon_{ij}.$$

[11] This difference in price sensitivity may arise from several factors including the urgency or need of the trip, tax considerations (travel is a deductible expense for business but not for tourists), and even the extent by which business travelers fully internalize the costs of their tickets.

[12] There is some evidence that the distribution of fares may be a mixture of distributions. Looking at the distribution of fare per mile (available from the authors upon request) we observe that such distribution has a fat upper tail, which is inconsistent with a normal distribution. Fitting fare per mile to a mixture of normal distributions we find that it provides a much better fit than a simple normal distribution (adj R^2 of .999 against 0.972). The linear combination is given by Fare $= 0.5987^*N(0.2375, 0.0781)$ $+ (1 - 0.5987)^*N(0.5946, 0.2752)$. It is interesting to note that the fare/mile means from the full estimation match these distributions fairly well. As will be presented in more detail below, our full estimation provides a Type 1 mean fare/mile of 0.237 the same mean as estimated through this method. The Type 2 mean fare/mile from the full estimation is 0.414, against 0.589 using this method. The proportions are a bit different, 0.73 are from the "Type 1" distribution in the full estimation and only 0.598 using this simple estimate.

To summarize, the characteristics of the product are x_j, p_j, and ξ_j. The fare is denoted by p_j and the vector x_j contains the other observed product characteristics and market-level demand factors. The term ξ_j captures unobserved (to us) characteristics of the product, such as advance purchase restrictions. The "taste" vectors β_i and α_i vary across the two types of consumers.

The additive error, represented by the sum $\nu_i + \lambda\varepsilon_{ij}$ is chosen to yield the familiar nested logit market share function (see McFadden, 1978 and Cardell, 1992). The distribution of this sum is parameterized by λ, which is to be estimated. As in the logit, ε captures idiosyncratic tastes for a particular product; for example, consumer I may prefer a particular departure time. In contrast, ν_i does not vary across products and represents the random taste for air travel, relative to the outside good. Cardell (1992) gives the distributional assumption that implies the nested logit market share function, conditional on values of β_i and α_i. Under this assumption, as λ goes to 1 the within market correlation goes to zero while as λ goes to zero, the correlation of choices within the market goes to one.

Conditional on β_i and α_i, the nested logit market share function is given by the product of the within group market shares (the share of this product out of the total number of tickets sold) times the group share (the number of tickets sold in the market divided by the number of potential consumers). For consumer Type 1, the within market share is:

$$s^1_{j/g} = \frac{e^{(x_j\beta_1 - \alpha_1 p_j + \xi_j)/\lambda}}{\sum_j e^{(x_j\beta_1 - \alpha_1 p_j + \xi_j)/\lambda}}$$

whereas total share of the market, the group share, is

$$\bar{s}_1 = \frac{D_1^\lambda}{1 + D_1^\lambda}$$

where the term D_1 is just the denominator of $s^1_{j/g}$.[13] The market share of product j is then given by the appropriate weighted average across the two types of consumers:

$$s_j = \gamma s^1_j(p, x, \xi) + (1 - \gamma)s^2_j(p, x, \xi),$$

where γ is the proportion of Type 1 consumers in the population and s^1_j is the share of Type 1 consumers who purchase product j.

Costs. In our model, the total and marginal cost, respectively, of operating a given spoke, s, are given by $C(Q_s, w_s)$ and $c(Q_s, w_s)$, where Q_s is spoke density and w_s is a vector of exogenous variables. These exogenous variables include distance between the endpoint cities and characteristics of the origin and destination airports. In addition to modeling spoke costs, we assume that there is a random, idiosyncratic component to product cost. In particular, we will assume that the product specific component of total cost for product j in market m is given by $\omega_{jm}q_{jm}$. The only reason for this particular specification is so that marginal cost of product j will have a linear random error term, ω_{jm}. This makes for a convenient empirical specification.

---

[13] The "1" in the denominator reflects the assumption that $u_{i0} = 0$.

Total variable cost for the firm is the sum of the total costs of each spoke flown by the firm plus the product-specific costs. Let S_f be the complete set of spokes flown by firm f, $S_f(j, m)$ be the set of spokes in the itinerary of firm f for product j in market m, and $J(f, m)$ be the set of products offered by firm f in market m. Then total firm cost is given by:

$$C_f = \sum_{s \in S_f} C(Q_{sf}, w_{sf}) + \sum_m \sum_{j \in J(f,m)} \omega_{jm} q_{jm} + FC_f$$

Note that fixed costs, FC_f could be affected in some way by hubbing, but our empirical work will make use only of estimates of marginal cost and so will not capture any such effect.

In this specification, there are common costs across products because the same spoke can enter into the production of many demand-side products. Thus, is it not possible to speak of a well-defined total cost for any given product. However, product marginal cost is well-defined and is given by sum of spoke marginal cost across the spokes in the itinerary, plus the product-specific component.

$$mc_{jmf} = \left[\sum_{s \in S_f(j,m)} c(Q_s, w_s) \right] + \omega_{jm}.$$

To derive an estimator, we will assume that ω is uncorrelated with the exogenous variables of the model. We treat price and spoke density as endogenous, and other observed variables as exogenous.

Our prior belief is that there may be a complicated relationship between distance, density, and flight frequency. At shorter distances, air travel competes heavily with auto travel (and, in a few places, with trains). There may be pressure in these markets to use any potential cost savings that stem from density to increase flight frequency, so as to the better compete with auto travel that allows travelers to choose a fairly precise departure and arrival time. We think of the East and West Coast air shuttles, as well as Southwest airlines, as potential examples of this.[14] Also, in shorter markets it may not be cost effective to fly larger planes, because a large fraction of cost involves take-offs and landings. In short markets, this fixed-cost with respect to distance is not offset by large savings once in the air. We do not have a model of flight frequency, but we do have data on the number of flights flown per quarter on each spoke. Ideally, we would like to treat flight frequency as an endogenous variable, but in this paper we merely include it in some specifications as an exogenous cost shifter.

To avoid imposing much structure on spoke costs, we want to use a fairly flexible functional form in distance, density and flight frequency. In the empirical work reported below, we use polynomials of these variables. Consider, for example, a case where spoke costs are quadratic in distance and density and d_s is the distance of spoke s. Then, for a multi-spoke ticket, product marginal cost is given by a linear combination of $\Sigma_s d_s$, $\Sigma_s Q_s$, $\Sigma_s d_s^2$, $\Sigma_s Q_s^2$ and $\Sigma_s d_s Q_s$, plus the error term ω.

Note that we provide no role in costs for capacity constraints or for firms' uncertainty about future costs and demand. This is in large part because we have no information at

---

[14] Southwest Airlines is not in our data set, as it reports all its sales as being composed of one way tickets. As a consequence, it does not fit our product definitions. See Data section below.

the level of individual flights at a particular day and time. The data are aggregated to the level of the airline/route/fare on a quarterly basis. Therefore we cannot identify which flights might be subject to capacity constraints. Nor can we tell how uncertainty about the number of passengers on a flight is resolved as the time of departure approaches.

Capacity constraints, together with demand uncertainty, have been proposed as possible explanations for some features of airline pricing, such as the apparent price discrimination in favor of tickets purchased in advance. Other features of pricing, such as Saturday stayover rules appear to be harder to explain as purely cost-based phenomena. In any case, there is always the possibility that some of what we label as a markup in fact represents a shadow price of capacity.

As another caveat, our estimation techniques can at best identify only the parameters of marginal cost. One of the cost reducing effects of hubs may be to reduce fixed cost, but we will not capture any such effect.

Markups and the Pricing Equation. To close the model, we assume price-setting behavior by the multi-product firms in each origin and destination market. In the pricing equation that we derive, each firm takes into account the effect of a change in price on the demand and cost of its own products in this market, and (through the spoke densities) on the cost of its products in other markets.

Our assumption of a static Nash equilibrium in prices is obviously a simplification. Airline "yield management" techniques attempt to allocate seats across different fare classes in a complicated fashion that depends on the sales history of a particular flight. Therefore, the true equilibrium involves more choices than just prices and it has some dynamic component. This dynamic component would be even more complicated if, as some allege, airlines engage in some form of tacit collusion. Unfortunately, these interesting extensions to our equilibrium model are very difficult to implement and are left for future research.

In our model, profits of firm f, which in each market m produces the products in the set $J(f, m)$ are given by the sum over the revenue generated by each product minus total cost:

$$\pi_f = \sum_m \sum_{j \in J(f,m)} q_{jm}(p) p_{jm} - \sum_{s \in S_f} C(Q_s, w_s) - \sum_m \sum_{j \in J(f,m)} \omega_{jm} q_{jm}(p) - FC_f$$

Differentiating with respect to the price of product j in market m gives a first order condition of

$$\frac{\partial \pi_f}{\partial p_{jm}} = q_{jm} + \sum_m \sum_{k \in J(f,m)} \frac{\partial q_k}{\partial p_{jm}} \left[p_{km} - \omega_{jm} - \sum_{s \in S(k,m)} c(Q_{sf}, w_{sf}) \right] = 0.$$

But since the marginal cost of product k in market m is

$$mc_k = \left[\sum_{s \in S(k,m)} c(Q_s, w_s) \right] + \omega_k,$$

we can rewrite the first order condition in the more familiar form of

$$\frac{\partial \pi_f}{\partial p_{jm}} = q_{jm} + \sum_{k \in F_m} \frac{\partial q_k}{\partial p_{jm}} (p_k - mc_k) = 0.$$

Then, following BLP, define the matrix Δ which has elements (j, k) equal to $\partial s_k / \partial p_j$, if j and k are produced by the same firm, and equal to zero otherwise. In vector notation, the pricing equation is then:

$$p = \Delta^{-1} s + mc$$

where the first term on the right-hand side is the markup.

To derive the matrix Δ, note first that it is possible to get analytic forms for the derivatives of shares conditional on each type, $\partial s_k^1 / \partial p_j$ and $\partial s_k^2 / \partial p_j$. Let Δ_1 be the matrix of derivatives of market share with respect to mean utility for consumers of Type 1, (with j, k elements not produced by the same firm again set to zero). Then, using the analogous definition for Δ_2, the derivative matrix is:

$$\Delta = \gamma \alpha_1 \Delta_1 + (1 - \gamma) \alpha_2 \Delta_2$$

which is enough to give us the markup term. The markup depends only on the derivatives of market shares with respect prices and therefore does not depend on any cost-side parameters.

Remember that we should not confuse markups with profits. Airlines may not be profitable even if markups over marginal cost are large, because fixed costs are potentially large and because marginal may be declining in output over a substantial range.

4   ESTIMATION

The estimation techniques are taken from Berry (1994) and Berry, Levinsohn and Pakes (1995). These depend on an assumption that the two "errors" in the model, ξ and ω, are mean independent of some vector of observed instruments. (This is analogous to the OLS assumption that the error is mean independent of x.) We want to allow for the endogeneity of price and density, so we do not include these in the instrument vector. However, we do treat the other product characteristics (and indeed the network structure of each firm) as exogenous. While our econometric assumptions are still restrictive, they are in many ways less restrictive than the assumptions found in previous work.[15]

Estimation of the parameters of the model is undertaken by the method of moments, which exploits the mean independence assumption on the errors of the model. In particular, at the true parameter vectors, the errors of the model should be orthogonal to the vector of instruments. Thus, we choose the vector of parameters which sets the covariance of the errors and the instruments "as close as possible" to zero.

Because the basic procedure is described in much detail in BLP (1995), we will not belabor it here. The method of moments framework requires us to solve for unique values of the unobservables as a function of the data. On the demand side, unique values of ξ are guaranteed by a result in Berry (1994). We calculate them using a slight variation of a

---

[15] Entry into airline networks was modeled in previous work undertaken separately by two of the current authors. These attempts, though, involved much less detailed models of product markets and, in any case, did not endogenize the entire network structure. See, Berry (1990) and Reiss and Spiller (1989).

contraction mapping technique used in BLP. This calculation requires us to compute the market share function itself. Unlike the BLP specification, our assumptions on demand give us analytic market share and so, unlike BLP, we do not require any Monte Carlo integration techniques. Given the size of our data set, this is fortunate. On the cost side, we note that marginal cost can be computed simply as price minus the markup, where the markup is a function of demand side parameters and of ξ. The cost side unobservable is then just a linear term in marginal cost.

Thus, for any values of the parameters, θ, we can compute two vectors of unobservables, $\xi(\theta)$ and $\omega(\theta)$. At the true value of θ, these unobservables have mean zero, conditional on our assumed vector of instruments. This is the restriction that drives the estimation procedure.

To calculate standard errors of the estimates, we have to make some assumptions on the correlation structure of the errors. Across markets, the errors are assumed to be independent. Within markets, we assume a factor structure for the demand and cost errors. Both errors have a market-specific component and these components are correlated across demand and cost. Thus, demand and cost errors are assumed to be correlated within markets. The factor structure is used in calculating the variance matrix of the moment conditions, which is one component of the formula for the variance of the estimates.

Berry (1994) makes a simplifying assumption that the econometrician observed the expected market share. In actual data, we observe this only with sampling error. In BLP (1995), this sampling error in observed market shares was not large, because the shares were calculated as a fraction of the population of U.S. households, which on the order of 100 million. In this paper, we also have a large sample size, of more than one million. Unfortunately, this sample is divided into more than 120,000 products across more than 14,000 markets. Thus, the average number of sampled passengers choosing a given product is less than 10. While in other contexts a sample size of one million might lead one to ignore sampling error, in our case it is not so obvious. However, we must leave the topic of how to correct our standard errors for this source of variation for future research. Our current standard errors correct for the very large variation across products and markets.

Instruments. Our estimation procedure requires us to specify a vector of exogenous instruments. As noted, we treat product price, product market shares and spoke densities as endogenous, but treat all other product and market characteristics as exogenous shifters of cost and/or demand. Instruments for spoke densities include population and network characteristics at the endpoint cities. Additional instruments for price and markups include the characteristics of other products in the market. To create our instrument vector, we experimented with various combinations of the exogenous data on simple versions of our model on a 10% sample of our data. We then held this vector fixed as we moved onto estimating our full model on the entire data set.

5 DATA

The spoke density data used in the empirical work are drawn from the Department of Transportation's Service Segment Databank DB27R, which shows a carrier's total monthly traffic on each nonstop route segment that it serves (traffic is aggregated across individual flights). Data on fares and traffic levels in individual city-pair markets also used below, are drawn from Databank 1A (DB1A) of the Department of Transportation's *Origin and Destination Survey* (O&D). This databank shows fare and route information for a quarterly 10% sample of all airline tickets sold in the U.S. Each record of the databank contains an airline itinerary (a route flown on a given carrier, with the direction of travel indicated), a dollar fare, the distance of the trip, and a number of passengers flown on the itinerary at the given fare during the quarter.

We follow the earlier studies of spoke density, BDS and Brueckner and Spiller (1994), by using data from the fourth quarter of 1985. However, these two studies focused on 4-segment round-trip flights that do not originate out of hub cities. This restriction is intended to avoid demand-side effects of hubs. In the present work, we allow for markups which vary with hubs and so we do not restrict ourselves to non-hub origins, nor to 4-segment fares. We do use only round-trip itineraries. We eliminate itineraries that are chosen by only one passenger, as these may represent coding errors. For similar reasons, we eliminate very low and very high prices from the data.

Our data set contains 122,871 unique Origin-Destination-Carrier-Fare products in 14,122 unique Origin-Destination directional markets. These products comprise 4,963 unique Carrier-Legs flown by 32 carriers from 262 Origins representing the itineraries of 1,107,894 passengers. Approximately 30% of the markets have only one product and another 30% have between one and five products. About 1% of the markets have more than one hundred products, the maximum number being 874 products in the New York City to Miami market. In approximately 50% of the markets with more than one product, fares vary less than 20% from the mean fare but in 10% of the markets fares vary more than 50% from the mean.

As noted, the "population potential," or market size, M_m, of each market is measured as the geometric mean of the population of the endpoint cities, measured in millions (in the tables, this variable is MPOP). Sampled output of each product is the number of passengers (NPASS) in the O&D sample. Price (or FARE) is the observed fare in the O&D.

The x variables that determine consumer utility relative to the outside good include a constant, distance between the origin and destination cities (MDIST), distance squared and a dummy variable (DIRECT) equal to one if the flight is direct. To capture the possibility that consumers may avoid congested airports we include a variable (CONGEST-D) equal to the number of the origin or destination airports (0, 1 or 2) that are slot controlled.[16] We have experimented with a number of measures of hub size, including a dummy variable for hubs and the number of points served by an airline out of an airport. However, neither of these measures accounts for the relative importance of the city-pair. Therefore, if an airport is a hub for a given carrier, our HUBSIZE variable is equal to the sum of the population potential for all city-pairs connected by that airline-through that hub. If the airport does not serve as a hub for a carrier, then the hubsize measure is zero. Our measure of appeal to tourists is the (signed) January temperature difference (TEMPDIFF) between the origin and destination. Since TEMPDIFF is the same for all products in a given market, it has no power to explain the choice between products, but

---

[16] The FAA has established slot allocation mechanisms at Chicago O'Hare, Kennedy and La Guardia in New York City and Washington National in Washington D.C.

it helps explaining the choice between flying and the outside good. Furthermore, it may help separate customer types. There is no direct measure of flight frequency in the data. However, from the Service Segment Databank, one observes the number of trips (per quarter) between the two cities comprising the route. As a demand-side flight frequency variable (TRIPS-D) we include the minimum number of such trips across the one or two segments of the flight. We allow the coefficients on the direct, hub size, tourist and flight frequency variables, together with the coefficient on price, to vary across consumer types.

On the cost side, segment marginal cost depends on a the number of spoke end-points (0, 1 or 2) that are congested (CONGEST-C), segment distance (DIST) and spoke density (DENS). CONGEST-C is equal to the number of take offs and landings, (0, 1, 2, 3 or 4), on the route which occur at "slot controlled" airports. We also include a second cost-side measure of congestion, (DOT-CONGEST), equal to the number of takeoffs and landings which occur at one of the twenty-four airports which operate under FAA "flow control."[17] Finally, a cost-side flight frequency variable (TRIPS-C) is included in some specifications. This is just the segment number of trips per quarter from the Service Segment Databank.

Remember that product marginal cost is the sum of spoke marginal costs, so that a linear specification for marginal cost would include the sum of distance and density across segments. We include a constant (equal to one) in the specification of segment marginal cost and so the number of segments (NSEG), which is just the sum of this constant across segments, enters product marginal cost. The mean of any product-specific marginal costs that are unrelated to segment costs (*i.e.* the mean of ω) is then captured by including a additional constant in the specification for product marginal cost.

Since we expect that any cost-reducing effect of density would be greater at longer distances, we experiment with different functional forms for the interaction between distance, density and frequency. In particular, we use second and third order polynomials as approximations to more general functional forms. A quadratic specification adds the sum across spokes of squared distance, the sum of distance times density and so forth.

Table 1 presents some descriptive statistics on the data, including means, maximums, standard deviations, etc, as measured across products in the sample. (The spoke 2 densities are set to zero on direct flights.) The variables in Table 1 are scaled so as to give easy-to-present coefficients in the later tables. Table 2 presents some simple correlations between exogenous variables, taking products as the unit of observation. (The two densities are for up to two outbound segments.) Note that in the raw sample, densities are positively correlated with price, which is consistent with the idea that it is necessary to correct for the effects of markups and distance if we are to find any evidence of economies of density.[18]

Table 3 presents some simple regressions of price on other variables. These regressions are for descriptive purposes only, as the estimated coefficients bear little necessary relationship to the parameters of the model. There are two price regressions. The first involves only the "cost" variables of distance and density. Density has the expected sign,

---

[17] This list of 24 airports also includes Orange County and Long Beach, California, each of which is under strict local limits on takeoffs and landings.

[18] When we look only at a subsample of small 4-segment markets, consistent with the Brueckner-Spiller sampling framework, we do find a negative raw correlation between price and density.

Table 1 Descriptive Statistics   122,871 Unique Origin-Destination-Fare-Carrier Observations

	Mean	Std dev	Min	Max
FARE ($100)	2.764	1.488	0.110	18.33
NPASS (Passengers)	9.017	31.299	1.000	2798.0
DIRECT (Fraction)	0.466	0.498	0.000	1.000
HUBSIZE	0.017	0.045	0.000	0.210
TEMPDIFF (10°F)	0.286	2.077	−6.520	6.520
TRIPS-D (MIN 1,000/QTR)	0.293	0.179	0.001	1.595
CONGEST-D(# of airports)	0.202	0.413	0.000	2.000
MDIST (1,000 MI)	1.009	0.608	0.030	2.776
DIST (1ST Outbound Leg) 1,000 MI	0.710	0.503	0.021	2.704
DIST (2ND Outbound Leg) 1,000 MI	0.351	0.479	0.000	2.611
DENS (1ST Outbound Leg) 100,000 PASS/QTR	0.593	0.475	0.00003	4.553
DENS (2ND Outbound Leg) 100,000 PASS/QTR	0.361	0.493	0.000	4.553
TRIPS-C (1ST Leg) 1,000 DEP/QTR	0.349	0.214	0.001	1.595
TRIPS-C (2ND Leg) 1,000 DEP/QTR	0.212	0.249	0.000	1.594

Table 2 Correlation of Endogenous Variables

	Price	Quantity	Dens(1)	Dens(2)
PRICE	1.000	−0.063	0.084	0.122
NPASS		1.000	0.068	−0.120
DENS(1)			1.000	0.164
DENS(2)				1.000

Table 3 Regression of Price on Cost and Demand Variables

	Cost only		Cost and Demand		Mean
	Parm	S.E.	Parm	S.E.	
CONSTANT	1.704	0.013	1.545	0.022	1.000
NSEGS	−.113	0.013	−0.011	0.017	1.533
CONGEST-S	0.084	0.007	0.082	0.008	0.315
CONGEST-C	0.012	0.005	0.012	0.005	1.766
DIST	1.004	0.008	1.004	0.008	1.062
DENS	−.088	0.012	−0.094	0.012	0.954
TRIPS-C	0.362	0.029	0.310	0.037	0.561
CONGEST-D			0.009	0.013	0.202
HUBSIZE			2.097	0.094	0.017
TEMPDIFF			−0.011	0.002	0.286
TRIPS-D			0.019	0.040	0.294
R^2		0.173		0.177	

but a small magnitude, about a $9 decrease in price for a 100,000 passenger increase in spoke density. As measured by the R^2, distance and density do not "explain" much of the variance in price. When some demand variables are added, the magnitude of the coefficient on density decreases further. Both direct and the hubsize variable are positive and significantly different than zero. The positive coefficient on hubsize is consistent with early descriptive regressions that have been used to support the "Borenstein" effect of hubs on markups. The magnitude of the coefficient on direct is fairly large, about $75.

These results suggest room for improvement, and we turn next to results from our model.

6   RESULTS

We begin by briefly characterizing the demand and cost parameters and then move on to the more interesting implications of those parameters.

The Estimated Parameters. Table 4 summarizes the results for the demand side for various versions of the model. Table 5 provides the estimated parameters and standard errors for both demand and cost for the various estimated models. In each case marginal cost includes a cubic in distance and density. In addition, the marginal-cost specification includes the number of segments in the itinerary and the two variables measuring airport congestion. In both tables the first column provides estimates for a special case with only one type of consumer. The second column lets the coefficient on price vary across two types of consumers, while the third column lets a number of the demand parameters vary. The fourth column differs from the third in adding flight frequency ("trips") to the cost function.

Table 4   Summary of Demand Results

	I Single Type of Consumer	II 2 Types of Consumers Differ only in Price		III 2 Types of Consumers No Trips in MC		IV 2 Types of Consumers Leg Trips in MC	
VARIABLE		Type 1	Type 2	Type 1	Type 2	Type 1	Type 2
FARE	0.455	0.696	0.068	0.829	0.077	0.986	0.111
DIRECT	0.656	0.542	–	0.414	1.014	0.293	0.876
HUBSIZE	0.437	0.213	–	0.285	0.761	0.616	0.368
TEMPDIFF	0.050	0.049	–	0.052	0.049	0.049	0.050
TRIPS	0.551	0.393	–	0.329	0.954	0.388	0.493
PERCENTAGE OF PASSENGERS	100%	70.99%	29.01%	73.19%	26.81%	60.13%	39.87%
PERCENTAGE OF POPULATION	100%	92.35%	7.65%	97.48%	2.52%	95.21%	4.79%
AVERAGE FARE	–	$205	$338	$204	$351	$191	$323
AVERAGE ξ	–	0.97	1.19	0.86	1.30	0.87	1.22
AVERAGE TRIPS	–	0.39	0.36	0.37	0.39	0.39	0.36

Table 5 Results of Estimation

	I Single Type of Consumer		II 2 Types of Consumers Differ only in Price		III 2 Types of Consumers No Trips in MC		IV 2 Types of Consumers Leg Trips in MC	
	Parm	S.E.	Parm	S.E.	Parm	S.E.	Parm	S.E.
LAMBDA	0.605	0.020	0.638	0.020	0.599	0.027	0.617	0.026
MU	4.766	0.464	8.652	2.079	8.651	2.471	9.532	1.625
PROB TYPE 1	1.000	Fixed	0.924	0.018	0.975	0.013	0.952	0.019
DEMAND								
FARE 1	0.455	0.039	0.696	0.054	0.829	0.075	0.986	0.084
FARE 2	–	–	0.068	0.014	0.077	0.017	0.111	0.024
DIRECT 1	0.656	0.023	0.542	0.022	0.414	0.060	0.293	0.063
DIRECT 2	–	–	–	–	1.014	0.070	0.876	0.070
HUBSIZE 1	0.437	0.026	0.213	0.013	0.285	0.047	0.615	0.075
HUBSIZE 2	–	–	–	–	0.761	0.423	0.368	0.127
TEMPDIFF 1	0.050	0.003	0.049	0.003	0.052	0.005	0.049	0.007
TEMPDIFF 2	–	–	–	–	0.049	0.017	0.050	0.016
TRIPS-D 1	0.551	0.058	0.393	0.041	0.329	0.055	0.388	0.061
TRIPS-D 2	–	–	–	–	0.954	0.395	0.493	0.231
CONSTANT	−10.305	0.034	−10.621	0.033	−10.207	0.034	−10.172	0.034
CONGEST-D	−0.158	0.030	−0.215	0.030	−0.186	0.031	−0.203	0.030
MDIST	0.528	0.070	0.562	0.069	0.772	0.071	0.752	0.070
MDIST^2	−0.126	0.029	−0.176	0.028	−0.206	0.029	−0.209	0.029
COST								
NSEGS	−1.453	0.157	−0.922	0.088	−0.656	0.095	0.081	0.234
CONGEST-S	0.125	0.030	0.046	0.017	0.060	0.019	−0.033	0.015
CONGEST-C	0.041	0.012	0.073	0.007	0.071	0.008	0.072	0.010
DIST	4.510	0.395	2.965	0.223	3.181	0.241	0.155	0.631
DIST^2	−2.117	0.241	−1.297	0.136	−1.420	0.147	1.117	0.446
DIST^3	0.402	0.044	0.168	0.247	0.178	0.027	−0.410	0.096
DIST*DENS	−5.229	0.794	−3.540	0.448	−3.891	0.486	−6.651	1.287
DIST^2*DENS	1.419	0.254	1.045	0.143	1.270	0.155	2.986	0.454
DENSITY	2.060	0.506	1.818	0.282	1.584	0.307	4.827	1.259
DENSITY^2	0.376	0.384	−0.252	0.213	0.164	0.232	1.537	0.522
DENSITY^3	−0.379	0.081	−0.102	0.046	−0.238	0.050	−1.012	0.341
DENS^2*DIST	1.140	0.277	0.564	0.156	0.524	0.169	0.392	0.361
TRIPS	–	–	–	–	–	–	−4.544	2.536
TRIPS^2	–	–	–	–	–	–	13.540	4.826
TRIPS^3	–	–	–	–	–	–	−13.612	2.524
TRIPS*DIST	–	–	–	–	–	–	6.989	3.868
TRIPS*DIST^2	–	–	–	–	–	–	−5.075	1.374
TRIPS^2*DIST	–	–	–	–	–	–	4.913	2.360
TRIPS*DENS	–	–	–	–	–	–	−14.381	3.247
TRIPS^2*DENS	–	–	–	–	–	–	9.237	2.114
TRIPS*DENS^2	–	–	–	–	–	–	2.008	1.605

There are so many parameters to be estimated that Table 5 is broken into three panels. The first two panels present the demand parameters, while the third panel presents the cost estimates.

Columns one of Tables 4 and 5 give results from a nested logit with only one type of consumer. We can reject the pure (non-nested) logit model, as the coefficient λ is less than one, indicating the expected result that the values of within market choices are correlated. The other demand-side coefficients are of the expected sign. The coefficient on FARE applies to the negative of price; the positive coefficient indicates that consumers do not like price increases. They prefer direct flights out of uncongested airports on the hubbing airline. The signs of DIST and DIST^2 have the expected inverse U shape: as distance increases, air travel becomes more attractive relative to auto travel, but total demand for travel may fall. At short distances we expect the first effect to dominate, but the second to dominate at longer distances.

In columns two, we allow the coefficient on FARE to differ across two groups of consumers. The coefficients on the other variables continue to have sensible signs. Looking at the coefficient on FARE, we find evidence in favor of the existence of different types of consumers with differing disutility from price increases. The Type 1 consumers place a much greater negative weight on price increases, as the coefficient on price is nearly ten times as large for group one as opposed to the group two. The price sensitive consumers make up about 92.4% of the potential travelers. However, such price sensitive potential consumers are much less likely to actually buy a ticket; we shall see in the last panel of the table that they make up a much lower percentage of the actual travelers.

Column three allows the coefficients on FARE, DIRECT, HUBSIZE, TEMPDIFF and TRIPS to vary across customer type. This additional differentiation reduces the population of Type 2 customers from almost eight percent of the population to less than three percent of the population. The price insensitive Type 2 consumers exhibit tastes, relative to Type 1, that we might expect from business travelers. They care more about direct flights, more about the size of hub at the origin and more about flight frequency. Their valuation of the tourist variable, TEMPDIFF, is a little less than that of Type 1 customers, but is less precisely estimated. Thus, even though we have no customers' characteristics in our data set, the data and the model together can identify two types of consumers that can sensibly be labeled "tourist" and "business."

In column four, the demand side specification does not vary but the cost side specification does: the trips variable is added to the cubic portion of segment marginal cost. Here the only puzzling result is that the Type 1 HUBSIZE coefficient is larger than the Type 2 coefficient. This puzzle can be resolved by considering the marginal willingness to pay for HUBSIZE. Our linear utility specification implies linear indifference curves in HUBSIZE/FARE space, with a slope given by the ratio of the coefficient on HUBSIZE to the coefficient on FARE. It is easy to see that the marginal willingness to pay for increases in hub size is much greater for the Type 2 business traveler.

The third panel of Table 5 gives the estimated parameters of segment marginal cost. Given the flexible functional form on our cost side, it is hard to interpret the these parameters. In all specifications but the last, congestion appears to raise segment marginal cost. The negative sign on NSEGS indicates a negative intercept in the segment marginal cost function, which may indicate problems with the cost specification for distances and densities near zero. The estimated coefficient on the linear term in DIST is positive, which seems reasonable. The coefficient on the linear term in DENSITY is also positive, which by itself does not support economies of density. However, the other terms do lend support to the presence of economies of density at many distances and densities, as we will see below.

We turn next to the economic implications of these parameters. The demand parameters have important implications for pricing behavior and markups, while the cost side parameters determine the extent of economies of density.

Implications of the demand parameters. In this section we focus on implications of the demand side results in column III of Table 4. The last panel of that table summarizes the demand side results. First note that both types of consumers are important in the market. While Type 2 consumers make up less than three percent of the potential travelers, the column III estimates imply that they make up more than a quarter of actual passengers (and this percentage increases to almost 40% in column IV). These proportions are consistent with the results of a recent Gallup survey which reports that in 1993, 8 percent of air travelers accounted for 44 percent of all trips.[19]

Based on results shown in column III, the mean price paid by Type 1 consumers is $204 while the mean price paid by the "business" travelers is almost $150 higher. However, the business traveler is getting something for these extra dollars. In particular, consider the demand unobservable, ξ, which captures, for example, the unrestrictiveness of the ticket. Across all products, ξ is mean zero (i.e. its mean is captured by the constant in the utility function). Passengers have a preference for high "quality" flights and so the mean across all tickets sold is estimated to be about 0.98. The level of ξ is 30% higher for Type 2 customers and about 12% less for the Type 1s.

Table 6 considers the implication of the parameters for the relationship between prices, markups and hubs. Specifically we examine in some detail the effect of a carrier's usage of an airport as a hub on the demand and fare paid for products in markets originating at those airports given our estimates, for each product in each market we can estimate the proportion of each type of consumer buying the product. We can then discuss the average product characteristics bought by different types of consumers flying different airlines in different markets.

Table 6 presents a summary of product characteristics across categories of markets, consumers and airlines using the results of Table 5 Column III. Within a market, we take weighted averages of product characteristics, where the weights are the predicted number of passengers of each type. The weighted product characteristics are separately averaged (within market) across hubbing and non-hubbing airlines. These market averages are then averaged across market (weighting by the number of passengers in each market) to produce summary statistics. The point of taking averages of within market averages is to control for across market variation in distance, populations size and other market characteristics. However, such variation in market-level variables makes it dangerous to compare levels the different market categories (i.e. across the vertical panels

---

[19] See, Air Travel Association, *Air Travel Survey 1993*, Washington, DC, 1993.

Table 6 Comparison of Shares and Fares   Based on Column III, Table 5

Market Type	Non-Hub 31% of Pass. 82% of Mkts Av Dist 800 mi		Small-Hub 32% of Passengers 9% of Markets Avg Dist 954 mi Avg Pop 3.8 Million				Large-Hub 37% of Passengers 9% of Markets Avg Dist 842 mi Avg Pop 3.0 Million			
Customer Type Pct of Mkt	Typ 1 75.8%	Typ 2 24.2%	Type 1 73.2%		Type 2 26.8%		Type 1 70.4%		Type 2 29.6%	
Carrier Type	N/Hub	N/Hub	Hub	N/Hub	Hub	N/Hub	Hub	N/Hub	Hub	N/Hub
Pct of Car Tot	100%	100%	73.6%	73.0%	26.4%	27.0%	67.0%	76.8%	33.0%	23.2%
Pct of Typ	100%	100%	40.0%	60.0%	39.3%	60.7%	62.3%	37.7%	72.9%	27.1%
Avg Fare $	224	296	206	206	306	295	215	205	319	268
Avg MC $	93	111	96	95	111	106	91	109	98	133
Avg Markup	58.6%	62.4%	53.4%	53.8%	63.7%	63.9%	57.8%	46.7%	69.2%	50.4%
Ave Fare $/mi	0.387	0.488	0.301	0.302	0.398	0.398	0.336	0.313	0.474	0.403
Avg ξ	0.601	1.005	0.650	0.771	0.942	1.074	0.875	0.566	1.321	0.836
Avg Direct	0.522	0.542	0.792	0.778	0.809	0.819	0.922	0.622	0.927	0.665
Avg Trips	336	340	399	404	410	430	469	362	484	371
Hub Premium										
Fare			0.1%		3.7%		5.0%		19.0%	
Marginal Cost			−1.1%		−4.5%		16.8%		26.1%	
Markup			−0.8%		3.3%		29.9%		63.4%	

Notes:

Markets There is a total of 14,122 Origin-Destination markets in the data. Of that number, 778 are markets, representing 5.2% of total passengers, in which only Hub carriers participate. These markets are not used in the compilation of these tables.

Market Type The distinction among market types is based on the maximum HUBSIZE of all carriers participating in the market. The specific division used is:

Non-Hub – HUBSIZE = 0.0 (93.5% of all unique Origin-Carrier combinations).

Small-Hub – 0 < HUBSIZE < 0.01

Large-Hub – HUBSIZE >= 0.01 (Approximately 34% of all unique Origin-Carrier combinations with non-zero HUBSIZE)

See Description of Variables for a complete description of HUBSIZE. See Appendix 1 for a list of all Origin-Carrier combination with non-zero HUBSIZE.

Averages are calculated as follows: first the passenger weighted average is calculate for each of the O&D markets within each market type. The average, weighted by the total number of passengers in the O&D market, of these averages is then calculated to produce the final values. This method was chosen to best represent the average relationship among the various components of each market.

Markup is calculated as (Avg Fare − Avg MC)/Avg Fare.

Hub Premiums are calculated as follows:

Fare: [Fare(Hub) − Fare(N/Hub)]/Fare(N/Hub).

MC: [MC(N/Hub) − MC(Hub)]/MC(N/Hub).

Markup: [Fare(Hub) − MC(Hub) − Fare(N/Hub) − MC(N/Hub) − MC(N/Hub)]/[Fare(N/Hub) − MC(N/Hub)].

of the table). Therefore we will focus on the hub/non-hub differences within market categories.

The first (horizontal) panel of Table 6 divides the products into three categories of markets. The first category, non-hub markets, includes all markets in which no carrier uses the origin as a hub airport. The other two categories are comprised of all hub markets, those in which at least one carrier uses the origin as a hub. The hub markets are distinguished by the size of their connected network, as measured by HUBSIZE. Large hub markets include all those in which at least one of the hub carriers has a HUBSIZE of 0.01, approximately the largest third of all hubs. Small hubs then include all other hub markets. The second panel of the table divides the customers into the two estimated types (with average percentage of each type given in the third panel.) The fourth panel then further separates the products into the products of non-hubbing and (where appropriate) hubbing airlines. The next panel then gives the averaged product characteristics.

Note that although 82% of the markets are non-hub markets, these markets include only 31% of the total passengers flown. The remaining markets and passengers are distributed almost evenly between the large and small hub markets. The makeup of the passengers in each type of market is also notable, with non-hub markets having the highest percentage of Type 1, "tourist", passengers, and the large hub markets having the highest percentage of Type 2, "business", passengers.

Even more interesting is the distribution, within hub markets, of customer types between the hub and non-hub carriers participating in each market. In small hub markets the distribution of customer types, "Pct of Car Tot", is almost identical for each carrier type. In the large hub markets, however, the hub carrier, or carriers, serve a substantially higher percentage of Type 2 customers, 33.0% versus 23.2% for non-hub carriers. In all markets the fare paid by Type 2 customers is higher than that paid by Type 1 customers. In the small hub markets these fares are almost identical for hub and non-hub carriers. In the large hub markets, however, the average fare realized by the hub carriers is almost 19% higher than that of the non-hub carriers for Type 2 customers and only 5% higher for Type 1 customers. This advantage is labeled the "Hub Premium" and is shown not only for fare but also for estimated Marginal Cost and markup.

Also shown in Table 6 are the average values of DIRECT, TRIPS and then unobserved characteristic, ξ, for each customer type in each market. Note that in small hub markets, where the non-hub carriers carry 60 percent of the passengers, average TRIPS is higher for non-hub carriers than for hub carriers. In all markets, however, Type 1 customers fly, on average, less frequent products than do Type 2 customers. Similar comments can be made about DIRECT. Hub carriers generally provide a higher percentage of direct flights and Type 2 customers consume more direct flights than Type 1 customers from both carrier types. In the small hub markets, the products of non-hub carrier's products have 14 to 18 percent higher values for the unobserved characteristic. In large hub markets, however, their products have values 35 percent smaller than those of the hub carriers.

The last panel of Table 6 then decomposes the fare premium obtained by hubbing airlines. In large hubs, Type 2 passengers are paying 19% more ($305 vs. $255) originating from a large hub on the hubbing airline. However, the average cost of the hubbing flights is 20% *less* ($94 vs. $118). An interesting part of the "hub premium" is then that markups are 53% higher ($211 vs. $137). Another way to present the results is to take all the differences as a percentage of non-hub average fare. In this case, the 19% hub premium is found by subtracting an approximately 10% marginal cost advantage from a 29% markup premium.

Figure 1 provides these results in a visual way.[20] We see that for small hub markets, hub carriers are able to charge Type 2 customers 4% above non-hub carriers. Hub carriers also have 4% lower marginal costs for these traveler types. On the other hand, the average Type 1 customer pays the same to a hub or a non-hub carrier. Furthermore, carriers have similar marginal cost of providing Type 1 service. Because the hub premia for Type 2 customers is so small, Type 1 and Type 2 customers divide themselves evenly between hub and non-hub carriers.

In large hub markets, however, we observe the working of the hub premium. First, Type 2 customers are not just willing to pay the 20% premia that hub airlines charge, but that price differential does not deter them from flying more often with a hub than a non-hub carrier. Hub carriers are even able to extract a small premium over Type 1 customers (5%).

Figure 1 shows, then, the origins and the workings of the origin hub premium. The hub premium originates in Type 2 (business) customers. They value flying an airline with a larger network much more than Type 1 customers do. In large hubs, then, hub-airlines are able to charge Type 2 customers a substantial premium over non-hub airlines. That premium, however, is very small for Type 1 (tourist) travelers.

The ability to charge a large premium and still capture a larger share of the business travel, implies that non-hub airlines in hub markets have a strong competitive disadvantage. Not only does the hub airline not create a "monopoly umbrella" (the price non-hub carriers are able to charge Type 1 or Type 2 customers is indeed found to be smaller than in non-hub markets), but the hub airline takes a larger share of the Type 2 customers. Thus, the average yield of a non-hub airline is smaller in hub markets than in non-hub markets, reducing the profitability of serving hub-markets.

This result may suggest a dynamic explanation (untested here) to the increase in airport concentration that has taken place since deregulation. Once an airline decides to develop a major hub in a given airport, their competitors find business customers moving away, reducing their average yield. Marginal airlines, then, will find it profitable to drastically cut service to that city. On the other hand, hubs do provide substantial price and cost benefits to airlines, facilitating entry out of hubs into new city-pair markets, thus potentially explaining the decrease in market level concentration that has taken place since deregulation (for a start on empirical models of airline entry, see Reiss and Spiller (1989) and Berry (1992)).

Implications of the Cost Parameters. We have just seen that flights by hubbing airlines out of hubs are associated with lower costs. Our proposed explanation for this is economies of density. Figure 2 and Figure 3 present plots of estimated marginal cost, corresponding to the estimates in columns II and III, in distance and density space. Information similar to that depicted in the figures is also found in Table 7. Although there are some differences between the two figures, the basic shape is the same. The surface of

---

[20] Some readers have found this representation useful and some have not; in any case all the relevant numbers are in Table 6.

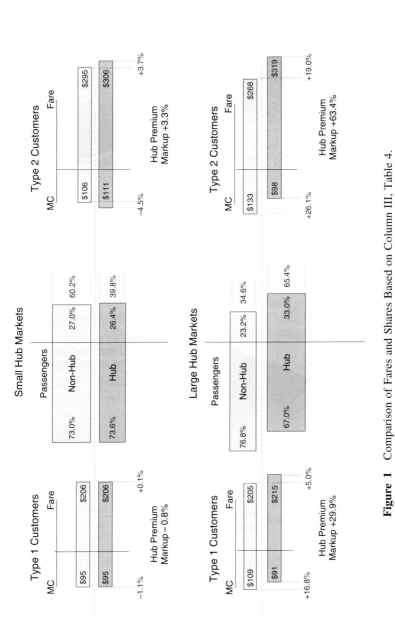

Figure 1 Comparison of Fares and Shares Based on Column III, Table 4.

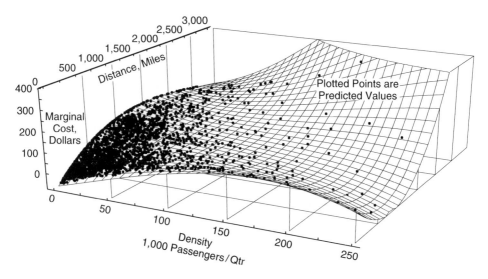

Figure 4 Marginal Cost vs. Distance and Density (Column III, Table 4) Predicted MC Plotted for 4,963 Legs.

We have not addressed all the issues of potential importance in the airline industry. There may be important dynamic aspects in the pricing and production decisions. On the pricing side, there may be some sort of tacit or explicit collusion. On the production side, some of what we call markups or marginal cost may reflect capacity constraints on some flights at some times of day. Also, network structure may affect entry and exit decisions in important ways. Finally, we have not modeled any agency problems related to frequent flier programs or travel agent commissions. These marketing devices might exploit differences in incentives between decision-makers and the ultimate consumers of the product.

This paper, though, provides a first attempt to analyze the role of hub-and-spoke operations in a product differentiation framework. Our results confirm that hubs are an important production and marketing tool for the airlines. First, the existence of economies of density implies that hubs provide important cost savings. Second, hubs provide the airlines with an ability to charge a hub-premium. Their ability to raise prices, however, is much greater for price-insensitive business-type travelers. When flying out of large hubs, these travelers pay a premium of approximately 20%, while the hub-premium for non-business travelers is estimated to be only 5% or less. The welfare consequences of this hub premium need not be negative. Business travelers are seen to receive a higher quality good, in terms of observed and unobserved (by us) characteristics and, indeed, business travelers represent a higher percentage of total passengers for hub-carriers than for non-hub carriers. Add to this the low demand elasticities of business travelers and, aside from the unmodeled issues mentioned in the last section, the negative welfare consequences of hubs appear to be rather small.

APPENDIX

Description of Variables
Descriptions are for Product j, in Market i, Carrier k

DEMAND VARIABLES	
MPOP	Population Potential[1] for market I.
FARE	Fare paid for product j. UNITS – $100.00
DIRECT*	1 if product j is a direct flight, 0 otherwise
HUBSIZE*	If the origin is a hub airport for carrier k then HUBSIZE is the Population Potential for all city pairs connected through the origin city. If the airport does not serve as a hub for carrier k then HUBSIZE is zero.
TEMPDIFF*	Difference between origin and destination mean January temperatures. UNITS – 10 Degrees Fahrenheit
TRIPS*	Minimum of the number of trips flown by carrier k on each leg of the route. UNITS – 1000 Departures/Quarter
CONSTANT*	1.0
CONGEST-D*	Sum, over the origin and destination, of a dummy variable indicating that an airport is "slot controlled"[2]
MDIST*	Great circle distance between origin and destination airports. UNITS – 1000 Miles
MDIST^2*	MDIST squared.

COST VARIABLES	
NSEGS	Number of segments in the route of product j. (1 or 2)
CONGEST-C*	Number of takeoffs and landings at "slot controlled" airports in the route of product j.
DOT-CONG*	Number of takeoffs and landings at airports which operate under FAA "flow control"[3]
DISTANCE	Sum of actual leg distances over the one or two legs of the route. UNITS – 1000 Miles
DENSITY	Sum of the number of passengers per month flown by carrier k on each leg[4] of the route. UNITS – 100,000 Passengers/Quarter
TRIPS	Sum over both legs of the number of trips flown per quarter by carrier k. UNITS – 1000 Departures/Quarter.

[1] SQRT(origin population * destination population).

[2] The FAA has established slot allocation mechanisms at Chicago O'Hare, Kennedy and La Guardia in New York City and Washington National.

[3] This list of 24 airports also includes Orange County and Long Beach, California, each of which is under strict local limits on takeoffs and landings.

[4] Because trips are round trips, we measure densities as the sum of the two directions.

Descriptive Statistics Demand/Cost Variables

Variable	Mean	Std Dev	Minimum	Maximum
MPOP	227387.12	192268.08	1130.40	1191781.00
FARE	2.7638407	1.4880484	0.1100000	18.3300000
DIRECT	0.4666602	0.4988892	0	1.0000000
TEMPDIFF	0.2864697	2.0774947	−6.5200000	6.5200000
TRIPS	0.2934735	0.1795864	0.0010000	1.5950000
HUBSIZE	0.0170110	0.0448443	0	0.2106280
CONGEST	0.2022039	0.4130535	0	2.0000000
MDIST	1.0090688	0.6084302	0.0300000	2.7760000
MDIST^2	1.3884041	1.5944844	0.000900	7.7061760
NSEGS	1.5333398	0.4988892	1.0000000	2.0000000
CONGEST	0.3149401	0.6041807	0	3.0000000
DOT-CONG	1.7655997	0.9916804	0	4.0000000
DISTANCE	1.0621377	0.6249192	0.0300000	5.0610000
DIST^2	1.1119420	1.2418665	0.000900	12.8130210
DIST^3	1.5190454	2.6297537	0.0000270	32.4545279
DIST*DEN	0.6679041	0.7026942	0.00001674	5.2785213
DIS^2*DEN	0.7055024	1.1366410	4.67046E-6	13.0132275
DENSITY	0.9544737	0.7384137	0.0000300	7.9023200
DENSITY^2	0.9511442	1.3970802	9E-10	31.9492227
DENSITY^3	1.3074138	3.5029454	2.7E-14	131.9727217
DENS^2*DIST	0.6751575	1.1904563	5.256E-10	11.4191792
TRIPS	0.5610866	0.3638758	0.0010000	3.0850000
TRIPS^2	0.2753029	0.3046792	1E-6	4.7639170
TRIPS^3	0.1679641	0.3080066	1E-9	7.3647064
TRIPS* DIST	0.3382569	0.2554679	0.00012900	2.2982620
TRIPS*DIST^2	0.3175201	0.3843447	9.8E-6	3.3692860
TRIPS^2*DIST	0.1479861	0.1695250	1.29E-7	2.8692971
TRIPS*DENS	0.4777567	0.5866136	3E-8	12.1272763
TRIPS^2*DNS	0.2948855	0.5751647	3E-11	18.6315668

REFERENCES

Bailey, E., D. Graham and D. Kaplan, (1985) *Deregulating the Airlines*, Cambridge, MA: MIT Press.

Bailey, E. and J. Williams (1988) "Sources of Economic Rent in the Deregulated Airline Industry," *Journal of Law and Economics*, 31, 173–203.

Berry, S. (1990) "Airport Presence as Product Differentiation," *American Economic Review*, 80, 394–399.

Berry, S. (1994) "Empirical Models of Product Differentiation," *RAND Journal of Economics*, 25, 242–262.

Berry, S. (1992) "Estimation of a Model of Entry in the Airline Industry," *Econometrica*, 60, 889–917.

Berry, S., J. Levinsohn and A. Pakes (1995) "Automobile Prices in Market Equilibrium," *Econometrica*, 63, 841–890.

Borenstein, S. (1989) "Hubs and High Fares: Airport Dominance and Market Power in the U.S. Airline Industry," 20, 44–65.

Borenstein, S. (1991) "The Dominant Firm Advantage in Multiproduct Industries: Evidence from U.S. Airlines," *Quarterly Journal of Economics*, 106, 1237–1266.

Borenstein, S. and N. Rose (1994), "Economies of Traffic Density in the Deregulated Airline Industry," *Journal of Political Economy*, 102, 65–95.

Bresnahan, T.F. (1989), "Empirical Studies of Industries with Market Power," in R. Schmalensee and R.D. Willig, *Handbook of Industrial Organization*, Vol 2, North-Holland.

Brueckner, J., N. Dyer and P.T. Spiller (1992); "Fare Determination in Airline Hub and Spoke Networks," *RAND Journal of Economics*, 23, 309–333.

Brueckner, J. and P.T. Spiller (1991) "Competition and Mergers in Network Airlines," *International Journal of Industrial Organization*, 9, 323–342.

Brueckner, J. and P.T. Spiller (1994) "Economies of Traffic Density in the Deregulated Airline Industry," *Journal of Law and Economics*, 37, 379–415.

Caves, D., L. Christensen and M. Tretheway (1984) "Economies of Density versus Economies of Scale: Why Trunk and Local Airline Costs Differ," *RAND Journal of Economics*, 15, 471–489.

Cardell, N. (1992) "Variance Component Structures for the Extreme Value and Logistic Distributions," mimeo, Washington State University.

Hausman and Wise (1978) "A Conditional Probit Model for Qualitative Choice: Discrete Decisions Recognizing Interdependence and Heterogeneous Preferences," *Econometrica*, 46, 403–426.

Levine, M. (1987) "Airline Competition in Deregulated Markets: Theory, Firm Strategy and Public Policy," *Yale Journal on Regulation*, 4, 393–494.

McFadden, D. (1978) "Modeling the Choice of Residential Location," in A. Karlgvist, *et al.*, ed. *Spatial Interaction Theory and Planning Models*, Amsterdam: North-Holland.

Morrison, S. and C. Winston (1986) *The Economic Effects of Airline Deregulation*, Washington, DC: Brookings Institution.

Porter, R.H. (1983) "A Study of Cartel Stability: The Joint Executive Committee, 1880–1886," *Bell Journal of Economics*, 14, 301–314.

Reiss, P. and P.T. Spiller (1989) "Competition and Entry in Small Airline Markets," *Journal of Law and Economics*, 32, 179–202.

Advances in Airline Economics, Vol 1
Darin Lee (Editor)
© 2006 Published by Elsevier B.V.

9

The Home Carrier Advantage
in Civil Aviation

Mark G. Lijesen,
Netherlands Bureau for Economic Policy Analysis (CPB),
The Hague and Free University, Amsterdam[1]

Peter Nijkamp, Eric Pels, and Piet Rietveld
Free University, Amsterdam

ABSTRACT

This paper analyzes the relative market power position of home carriers in hub-and-spoke systems. Hub-and-spoke systems may lower costs on densely traveled routes and enable economically viable operations on less densely traveled routes. The reverse side is probably that carriers enjoy significant market power at their home base, often labeled the "home carrier" advantage. The paper offers a concise overview of the literature in this field, and empirically addresses this issue for European home carriers. We find that at least some European carriers charge premiums for flights originating from their hubs. The hub premiums of Lufthansa, Swissair and Air France are significantly higher than those of the other companies in our sample.

1 INTRODUCTION

Air transportation is a transport mode that is already more than one century old. It started off as an adventurous activity of a few pioneers, but soon turned into a commercial activity oriented toward the physical transport of both people and goods. Its strategic-military value was also soon recognized, in particular during World War I. Land and airspace became national territories with a strong involvement of governments. The Chicago Convention was a clear sign of the complexity of treating airspace both as a closed area for national competence and as an open area for transborder transport.

---

[1] Corresponding Author. CPB, PO Box 80510 2508 GM The Hague, The Netherlands, m.g.lijesen@cpb.nl

The national perspective on airspace also favored the emergence of national airlines, as they were enabled to start up in the protected and non-competitive area of individual nations. Airlines became the symbol of national feelings and pride, comparable to the national flag or hymn. Efficiency motives were overruled by national interests. In the period after World War II, the protected aviation market led to a patchwork of rather disconnected network segments dominated by home carriers (national flag carriers) representing national interests and feelings. Its development was hampered by an overwhelming amount of institutional barriers which made air transport a relatively expensive and inefficiently operated mode of transportation.

A real breakthrough—with rapidly increasing geographical mobility—took place as a result of the deregulation movement which started in North America, but which also reached other regions where national interests historically played a prominent role (e.g., Europe) in less than a decade (see Berechman and Shy 1998).

The deregulation movement has exerted an unprecedented impact on the operation, logistics and market organization of airlines, as unnecessary restrictions on airfares, freedom of entry and exit, route structures, airport development and flight frequencies were abolished. Consequently, competition became a driving force in the dynamics of the airline industry, where network constellations (route structures, hub-and-spoke systems) acted as critical parameters for economizing on airfares in the competitive multi-actor transport market (see Brueckner and Zhang 2001, Pels *et al.* 1997). Another critical parameter for competitive pricing turned out to be service-quality competition (see Morrison and Winston 1995). Those issues will be addressed in this paper from the perspective of domestic (home) carriers.

We have outlined above that the importance of civil aviation to modern society is quite significant. This sector is not only a large and rapidly growing industry by itself, it also fuels several other important industries directly (e.g. tourism) or indirectly, through increased travel possibilities.

We start with a concise sketch of recent developments in Europe. The airline industry has seen rapid growth over the past three decades. The number of passenger kilometers in EU-15 countries rose from 33 billion in 1970 to 281 billion in 2000, an average annual growth of 7.4 percent. Over the same period, major institutional and regulatory changes have occurred. Civil aviation has for long been a heavily regulated sector, mainly because of the strategic importance of air transport. The era of regulation ended in 1978, when US Congress adopted the Airline Deregulation Act. In the same year, the US and the Netherlands signed a very liberal bilateral agreement ("open skies") inducing an increase in competition in Trans-Atlantic markets.

Europe's airline industry was by then still heavily regulated, often with domestic monop- olies for the national flag carrier and duopolies of two flag carriers on international routes. Passengers had the choice between the home carrier of the country of origin and the home carrier of the country of destination. In 1984, The UK and The Netherlands signed a new bilateral agreement that effectively deregulated the air services between these countries. It was the first serious step towards the deregulation of the European airspace, which neared completion in 1992, in time to serve the now integrated European market.

Like in the US in 1978, the 1992 deregulation fuelled the emergence of hub-and-spoke systems in Europe. Together with the entry of former charter airlines and the new low cost carriers into the deregulated market, the hub-and-spoke system increased competitive pressure. Besides the home carrier of the country of origin and the home carrier of the country of destination, passengers could now choose from several other carriers serving the route through their hub.

This paper focuses on the relative competitive position of the home carriers in hub-and-spoke systems. We will, however, not deal with the subject in isolation, but rather give a somewhat broader review of important themes in civil aviation. To an economist, civil aviation offers a rich variety of research subjects, such as market failure, externalities, the network structure of the industry and its successive deregulation (in both the US and Europe). The next section will briefly touch upon some prominent research subjects present in the current stream of economic literature on civil aviation.[2] Section 3 will explore in more detail the hub-and-spoke system, which acts as a central theme in aviation economics. We will introduce the phenomenon of the home carrier advantage in section 4 followed by an empirical analysis on the subject in Section 5. Section 6 offers concluding remarks and discusses policy implications.

2   IMPORTANT ISSUES IN MODERN AVIATION ECONOMICS

In this section we will briefly address three major economic issues in the airline industry: externalities, regulatory systems and the network ramification of modern airlines.

2.1   External Costs

External costs of a good or service are the costs that an agent imposes on others by consuming the good or service. Schipper *et al.* (2003) mention emissions of pollutants, aircraft noise and accidents as external costs of air transport. Wit *et al.* (2003) provide a somewhat more extensive list. They distinguish between several types of emissions by their effects (climate change, ozone layer depletion, local air quality effects and odor nuisance). They also mention aircraft noise (nuisance and health impacts, as well as indirect land use impacts) and accidents (direct risks and indirect land use impacts), Furthermore, Wit *et al.* (2003) mention water and soil pollution, congestion of runways and air space, land use impacts of airports and impacts on nature conservation (e.g. loss of tranquillity). Whether congestion of runways and air space are considered external is merely a matter of aggregation. It depends on whether one looks at the level of the individual traveler or the entire industry.

Borenstein and Zimmerman (1988) analyze the effect of airplane accidents on a carrier's demand. They find a negative effect, as was to be expected. However, they also conclude that most of the effect is gone after two months. Rose (1992) explains this short period by the relatively small serial correlation of accidents with the same carrier, implying that an airline's safety record hardly informs travelers on accident probability.

From a welfare-theoretic and policy perspective, the presence of externalities is important due to its implications for taxation schemes for airlines, for airport development

---

[2] For an extensive overview of recent literature, see Nijkamp and Button (2003).

plans and for regulatory frameworks for the airline sector. Inclusion of externalities in airline cost schemes and regulations should avoid privileges for home carriers in a certain country or at a given airport.

2.2   Deregulation

As mentioned earlier, the airline industry is historically regarded as a strategically important sector for any nation. The ensuing regulation of this sector has caused large economic inefficiencies. The deregulation of civil aviation in the United States in 1978 and the early nineties in Europe induced great changes in the airline industry (see Doganis, 1991) for an overview). Following these changes, a vast volume of literature emerged. Winston (1993) provides an extensive overview of the literature on deregulation in the US, Marín (1995) is an example of the relatively small amount of European studies. Specific topics related to deregulation are contestability (Baker and Pratt, 1989 and Button, 1996), yield management strategies and airline productivity.

Since the implementation of deregulation, airlines have engaged in dynamic price discrimination to maximize total revenues once flight schedules are set. This phenomenon is known as yield management. Reece and Sobel (2000) link yield management to price discrimination under capacity constraints. One of the issues here is how to distinguish between passengers based on their willingness to pay for a flight. The main mechanism for this distinction is to differentiate fares by the amount of time they are booked ahead of departure. The subject has attracted the attention from economists, both from an operations research viewpoint (e.g. Dana, 1999; see McGill and Van Ryzin (1999) for an extensive review) and from a perspective of economic efficiency (Botimer, 1996).

Efficiency is also the main concern of another stream of recent literature, albeit from a different viewpoint. Productive efficiency is the main theme of a stream of literature devoted to productivity analysis. Oum and Yu (1998) perform a broad and comprehensive assessment of carrier productivity. Marín (1998) focuses on productivity differences between European carriers, whereas Ahn et al. (1999) compare Asian and North-American carriers.

The issue of deregulation has prompted economists to study the airline sector also from the perspective of industrial organization, and this has in the past led to interesting and novel analytical frameworks for investigating regulatory systems' impact on the aviation sector.

2.3   Aviation as a Network Industry

Aviation is commonly known as a network industry. The lines in the network are neither visible nor physical, but create nevertheless a connectivity infrastructure. Aviation is a nodal network, the nodes in the network being the airports. Network economics has become a new angle for studying the airline industry.

Economic literature on airports traditionally focussed on financing and investment decisions. Contemporary airport economics cover a much wider range of subjects, such as privatization and liberalization, pricing strategies and performance measurement (Doganis, 1996). Furthermore, the concept of airport choice and valuation of airport attributes has gained increasing interest, both from the point of view of the traveler (e.g. Pels *et al.*, 2002) and the point of view of the airline (Berechman and De Wit, 1996).

Aviation networks require an efficient operation and management because of their capacity limits. The increase in air traffic has created the problem of airport congestion. Economists almost instinctively propose to battle congestion by prices, explaining why congestion pricing is such a well-covered topic in economic literature. Recent advances in airport congestion pricing may be found in Daniel and Pahwa (2000), Brueckner (2002) and Pels and Verhoef (2004). The latter contribution shows that airport congestion pricing need not be optimal when airlines have significant market power.

Network structure also impacts the cost structure of the industry. Networks are often characterized by economies of density, implying that higher densities, e.g. more passengers per flight leg, bring down unit costs. Economies of density are a special case of scale economies. The main difference is that economies of density relate to an increase of output at a given geographical scale, whereas economies of scale relate to an increase of output in general (Oum and Waters, 1996).

Economies of density have two important implications for the airline industry, each of them representing a way to utilize economies of density. The first implication is the formation of hub-and-spoke networks, which will be discussed more extensively in the next section. The second implication regards code-sharing and alliances between airlines.

Park (1997) distinguishes between two types of alliances. The first type is the complementary alliance, in which the networks of the two carriers complement each other. The second type is the parallel alliance, where two competitors join their networks. Park shows that complementary networks increase welfare, whereas parallel networks decrease welfare. Bissessur and Alamdari (1998) also mention network complementarity as an important factor affecting the operational success of alliances. Brueckner and Pels (2004) show that the consolidation of the (largely parallel) Northwest-KLM and Sky Team alliances, following the merger between KLM and Air France, has anti-competitive effects, decreasing overall welfare.

It is thus clear that network constellation and usage, as well as network policies (on the side of both airlines and airports) have wide-ranging implications for the development of this sector, including issues like point-to-point flight schedules, the size of new generations of aircraft and the role of the public sector.

3   THE HUB-AND-SPOKE SYSTEM

The abolishment of regulation and the entry of new competitors forced existing airlines to rethink their operations and urged them to exploit economies of density. The hub-and-spoke system enabled carriers to concentrate passengers on flight legs, thus inducing lower costs per passenger through the exploitation of density economies. The hub-and-spoke system rapidly developed in the US as a consequence of the 1978 liberalization. Somewhat similar systems had been in use in Europe. Although similar in appearance, the 'old' European hub-and-spoke systems were different from those in the US and from those presently evolving in Europe. Europe's tradition of national carriers, each concentrating its operations at one or more national airports, created a system of star-shaped networks without emphasis on connecting flights. The latter is a central feature in the present hub-and-spoke system, as we will see further on.

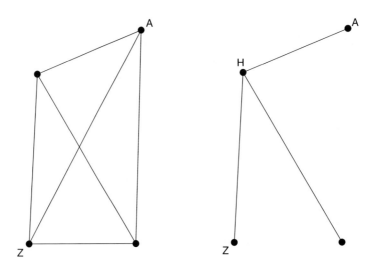

Figure 1   A Fully-Connected Network Versus a Hub-and-Spoke Network.

The advantage of a hub-and-spoke system may be best described by sketching a simple airline network with four nodes. Figure 1 depicts two ways of connecting all nodes together. The figure on the left hand side represents a fully connected network in which all nodes are connected through point-to-point relations. The figure on the right hand side is a hub-and-spoke network. Airport H is the hub airport through which all other airports are connected.[3]

It is clear from the figure that it takes only three routes to connect all the nodes in the hub-and-spoke network, whereas it takes six routes in the fully connected network. Based on this simple example, one can easily imagine why the hub-and-spoke system can be a much more efficient way to connect all the nodes. Whether a hub-and-spoke network is more efficient depends on the number of nodes in the network and the density of travel demand on each nodal pair. Both effects may be illustrated using Figure 1. Suppose we added an extra node to both networks. This would require four extra routes in the fully-connected network, and only one in the hub-and-spoke network, increasing the relative efficiency of the hub-and-spoke network. The effect of the density of travel demand may be illustrated by assuming that nodal pair A-Z has very high travel demand. In this case it would not be efficient to connect A and Z through hub H, as the economies of density are already exhausted and the extra connection imposes costs on the airline as well as its travelers.

If an airline centers its operations at a hub airport, the airline is likely to be an important airline at that airport. Table 1 lists the market shares of home carriers on their hubs. For the European hubs, we distinguish between US Department of Transport-data and European data. The former reflect market shares on combined routes from the listed European airports to destinations in the US (e.g., British Airways and its code-sharing partners carry 45 percent of all passengers from London Heathrow to US destinations).

---

[3] For a more extensive discussion on hub-and-spoke operations, see Chapter 5 in Hanlon (1999).

Table 1 Market Shares (% of Departing Passengers) of Home Carrier on Main Hubs in the US and Europe, January 2003

Hub airport	Home carrier	Market share	
		European data	US-DOT data
US			
Atlanta	Delta		70%
Chicago O'Hare	United		42%
	American		28%
Dallas Fort Worth	American		61%
Denver	United		53%
Miami	American		54%
Houston Intercontinental	Continental		70%
Minneapolis St Paul	Northwest		70%
Detroit	Northwest		66%
Newark	Continental		51%
San Francisco	United		48%
Europe			
London Heathrow	British Airways	45%	45%
	British Midlands	14%	NA
Paris CDG	Air France	57%	74%
Frankfurt	Lufthansa	60%	73%
Amsterdam	KLM	48%	81%
Milan Malpensa	Alitalia	NA	66%

Sources: DOT, T100 market database, European airlines and airports websites.

European data relate to the market share of all flights leaving from the hub, but come from different sources, which may cause some inconsistencies. For instance, in the cases of KLM and Air France airline data relate to calendar year 2003, whereas airport data relate to the fiscal year 2003/2004. The impact of these inconsistencies on the general image is probably minor. The difference between US data and European data is especially large for KLM.

An airport is always almost used as a hub by a single airline, the only exceptions being Chicago O'Hare, acting as a hub for both American Airlines and United Air Lines, and London Heathrow, serving as a hub for British Airways and British Midland. We refer to the hub-based airline as the *home carrier*, expressing that the carrier is at home at its hub airport. In a city pair-market, *we define the home carrier as the carrier whose hub is either the origin airport or the destination airport.* The special position of the home carrier makes one wonder whether it has an advantage competing for passengers, following from the nature of its hub-and-spoke operations, and how to interpret this advantage.

To understand the aspects of the possible advantage of the home carrier, we need to place the position of the home carrier in a wider perspective. First, we need to acknowledge that carriers compete for travelers on city pair markets. As far as a traveler is concerned, the product he buys is getting from his origin to his destination. The traveler makes a combined choice of carrier and itinerary, depending on the availability

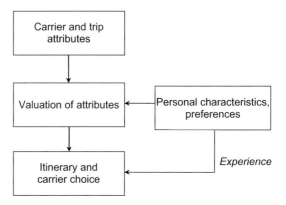

Figure 2   The Process of Itinerary and Carrier Choice.

of combinations. If a traveler were to fly from Amsterdam to Florence, for instance, he may choose between a direct KLM flight and an Air France flight via Paris. As Air France does not offer direct flights from Amsterdam to Florence, carrier choice and itinerary choice are connected.

Each trip alternative that takes the passenger from his origin to his destination is judged on its trip characteristics as well as on the characteristics of the carrier operating the flights. Figure 2 depicts a stylized version of the process of itinerary and carrier choice.

Each traveler takes into account the attributes (e.g., frequency, in-flight time, transfer time, access time) of all possible combinations of carriers and itineraries on the city pair he plans to travel. The traveler values each of the attributes before making his choice. The traveler's valuation depends on his personal characteristics, such as age, gender, trip purpose, income and experience. After making the choice, the traveler completes the trip, thus gaining new experience, which may alter his valuation of some of the attributes.

Present debates relate to the question whether the hub-and-spoke system will remain the dominant organization principle in the airline industry. Airfares and inconvenience for the traveler have to be traded-off against each other. Especially in the emerging open European skies it is questionable whether a few dominant hubs will arise, given the national interests of individual nations and the relatively small distances in Europe. National flag carriers have lost their dominant position, but the system of home carriers is a very prominent feature of European aviation.

4   ADVANTAGES OF HOME CARRIERS

In the previous section we argued that the home carrier may have an advantage over its competitors because of favorable flight characteristics. Apart from flight characteristics, other factors may play a role as well, like grandfathering rights in airport slot allocation, familiarity with the local situation and good relations with the home airport. (see e.g. Levine, 1987 and Borenstein, 1989 for an extensive discussion) In the remainder of this section, we will focus on flight-related advantages however. To assess the relative position of the home carrier it is important to know which trip and carrier characteristics differ between the home carrier and the other carriers. We distinguish between five main characteristics:

- route
- frequency
- fare
- frequent flier programs
- other attributes

We will now briefly discuss each of these five items.

4.1 Route

The obvious advantage of a home carrier over its competitors is that it generally offers direct flights, whereas its competitors (other than the destination's home carrier) offer indirect flights. Direct flights have two advantages over indirect flights. First, travel time is shorter. In-vehicle time is shorter because the overall distance on a direct flight is shorter. Fridström and Thune-Larsen (1989) and Bhat (1995, 1997) find that in-vehicle travel time influences travel choices. Furthermore, total travel time will be shorter, as the transfer itself takes time as well.

The second advantage is that the transfer may be experienced as a negative characteristic, because of the discomfort of having to find your way at an unknown airport and risks like losing luggage and missing connecting flights. Kanafani and Ghobrial (1985) find a strong route choice effect for non-direct flights. Ghobrial (1993) also finds a negative effect of intermediate stops. Harvey (1987) finds that connecting flights are poor alternatives for direct flights, but finds no difference between non-stop and multi-stop flights without a transfer. This suggests that the change of plane aspect of non-direct flights weighs heavier than the extra travel time involved and the possible discomfort of an extra landing and take off. Clearly, route advantages are a key element in home carrier policy.

4.2 Frequency

A carrier is more likely to offer a high frequency from its home airport than carriers operating a hub elsewhere. Chances of departing or arriving at a desired time are positively related to flight frequencies. Therefore, frequency is often used as a proxy for schedule convenience (Ghobrial, 1993, Kanafani and Ghobrial, 1985, Bhat, 1995, Proussaloglou and Koppelman, 1995, Suzuki 2000). Frequency is one of the quality aspects of modern airlines and therefore plays an important role in consumer choices.

4.3 Cost Advantages

The hub-and-spoke system is based on economies of density. It allows carriers to collect passengers at all nodes and concentrate them in the hub. This enables the carrier to use larger planes and reach a higher load factor on them, thus decreasing the costs per passenger. Lower fares for longer flights are actually observed in practice. On the other hand, costs are also raised somewhat by the hub-and-spoke system, because indirect flights span longer distances and require extra landings and take-offs. Berry, Carnall and Spiller (2005) find empirical evidence for the cost-reducing effect of the hub-and-spoke system. Brueckner, Dyer and Spiller (1992) as well as Brueckner and Spiller (1994) focus on economies of density as an explanation for differences in fares.

Being the home carrier also gives a carrier some market power, allowing it to raise fares above cost levels. Brueckner, Dyer and Spiller (1992) find that hub-originating and hub-terminating passengers pay higher fares, but cost advantages due to economies of density are passed on to passengers, thus reducing fares overall. The issue of fares in hub airports will be discussed in more detail below.

4.4   Frequent Flyer Programs

Frequent flyer programs (FFPs) are a well-known marketing device in civil aviation worldwide and may be viewed as a carrier characteristic. Customers acquire credit points from a specific carrier in relation to distance traveled. These points can then be used for gifts, free travel or for upgrades (i.e., to have an economy class ticket upgraded to a business class ticket).

FFP's favor the home carrier because of their non-linearity: the awards grow as points accumulate. This feature causes increasing marginal returns, thus rewarding loyalty, especially so for the home carrier. After all, the home carrier is the carrier that flies most routes from the traveler's home town, thereby offering the largest opportunities to both collect and use points. The latter is confirmed by Toh and Hu (1988), who name frequent flier programs as a factor affecting carrier choice. They state that small airlines with limited networks have a disadvantage in this respect. FFP's may essentially be seen as a fringe benefit of the airline sector for frequent travelers.

4.5   Other Attributes

Other trip and carrier characteristics are generally not related to the home airport of the carrier, although some aspects may play a role. Language may influence carrier choice, especially in countries where citizens have little education in other languages than their mother tongue. (Swait and Bernardino, 2000). For some consumers, flying with a carrier from their own nationality may be a favorable characteristic as well, either in the form of national pride or feeling at home.[4]

Furthermore, if cultural taste variations (for instance, with respect to food or leg space) are large, the home carrier will find it easier to adjust to local preferences. Swait and Bernardino (2000) find that, on three routes from different origins, there are some taste differences regarding food, in-flight entertainment and the design of the frequent flyer program.

A final point to be mentioned is that a home carrier may encounter economies of density in marketing in its home region, as a general marketing campaign can be expected to have an effect on all routes offered from the home airport.

---

[4] Recent KLM-advertisements relate to the latter by mentioning a place abroad, then stating 'home at last' over a picture of a traveler being welcomed aboard a KLM plane.

4.6   Consequences of Home Carrier Advantages for Fares

Existing studies analyzing features of the hub-and-spoke system mainly focus on the situation in the US, e.g. Borenstein (1989) and Evans and Kessides (1993). The focus of our analysis is on European cihvil aviation, more specific on Europe's large traditional carriers. Relatively new carriers like Ryanair and easyJet, however successful some of them may be, are not taken into account in our analysis, as they do not adopt the hub-and-spoke system. The European focus is an important contribution to earlier work. Almost all studies relating to the home carrier advantage have a US background. Europe's airline industry has a different structure than that in the US, as it evolved from a history of national carriers. The networks that these carriers operate sometimes still bear the signs of Europe's history, especially with regard to connecting former colonies to their homeland.

The saying that time flies is very true for civil aviation. Developments in Europe's civil aviation market place are following each other rapidly. Some of the carriers mentioned in the text of this study no longer exist, with their successors operating under different names, and with a different scope and scale of operations. CrossAir and SN Brussels Airways, successors of SwissAir and Sabena respectively, can hardly be labeled as large carriers operating a hub-and-spoke network anymore. The recent merger of Air France and KLM may change the landscape of European civil aviation again, once they start coordinating their networks and flight schedules.

The literature has devoted some attention to the home carrier advantage under the label of 'airport dominance' or hub premium. The first to tackle the problem of airport dominance empirically was Severin Borenstein in his 1989 paper. The variable reflecting hub dominance in Borenstein's paper is the average of a carrier's share of daily passengers originating at the two endpoints of the route, weighted by the proportion of passengers on the route who originate at each endpoint. Borenstein finds the effect of this variable on fare differences to be significantly positive, indicating that carriers with dominant positions at their hubs are able to charge higher prices. In his 1991 paper, Borenstein finds significant positive results, indicating that carriers exercise some market power over their hubs.

Berry (1990) estimates a structural model using airport presence as an explanatory variable in both cost and demand equations. Airport presence is defined as the number of top 50 cities served by an airline out of a given city. Berry finds that airport presence has a positive effect on demand and at the same time lowers costs. Though Berry interprets airport presence as product differentiation, which is different from Borenstein's market power approach of hub dominance, their results point into the same direction.

Evans and Kessides (1993) test whether airport and route market shares have a significant effect on fares. They find that airport dominance confers substantial pricing power upon the carrier, and that the isolated impact of route dominance on fares is insignificant. Evans and Kessides explain this difference by stating that, contrary to airports, routes are contestable since planes can easily be switched between routes, whereas airport facilities and FFPs can not.

Berry, Carnall and Spiller (2005) extend Berry's earlier work on the influence of airport presence on costs and demand. They find that airport presence has a positive effect on demand and a negative effect on costs. The cost-reducing effect of airport presence can be interpreted as the returns stemming from the economic rationale of the hub-and-spoke system. The effects are labeled 'hub premium', leaving aside whether it stems from product differentiation, market power or both.

The cost aspect is also present in Brueckner, Dyer and Spiller (1992) and in Brueckner and Spiller (1994), who focus on economies of density as an explanation for fares. Brueckner, Dyer and Spiller (1992) find that hub-originating and hub-terminating passengers pay higher fares, but cost advantages due to economies of density are passed on to passengers, thus reducing fares.

Goetz and Sutton (1997, p. 258) also find some indications of market power on concentrated hub markets. They find that '. . . passengers flying from small-city airports to major airports paid 34 percent more if the major airport was concentrated and 42 percent more if both the small-city and the major airport were concentrated.' Lee and Luengo-Prado (2005) find that hub premiums may be partly explained by differences in passenger mix. Their empirical analysis suggests that controlling for passenger mix lowers the hub premium from 19 to 12% at primary hubs and from 16 to 13% at secondary hubs. They also find that hub premiums tend to be larger for passengers traveling on unrestricted tickets, which is consistent with Ramsey pricing. Carbonneau (2003) finds that fares are higher in markets with a higher proportion of business passengers traveling from an airline's hub, but lower in markets with a higher proportion of business passengers traveling *to* an airline's hub. He explains this phenomenon by stating that entry in the spoke-hub market is easier than in the hub-spoke market.

Marín (1995) was the first to address the issue in a European context, by estimating both a market share and a price equation, in a regulated and a deregulated segment.[5] Marín finds that the effect of airport presence is not significant in a regulated environment and significantly negative in a deregulated environment. This implies that, contrary to the U.S. situation, European carriers in a deregulated environment tend to exploit the cost reducing effect of airport presence in order to compete in prices. Marín explains the difference between his European results and earlier U.S. estimates by signaling significant differences in the causes of market power. In Europe at that time, computer reservation systems were owned by multiple European carriers and FFPs hardly existed in Europe. Furthermore, Marín uses intra-European city pairs in his analyses. For these types of routes the hub and spoke system had not yet gained as much ground yet as it had in the U.S. aviation industry. Because of these differences, several causes of hub dominance had less impact than in the U.S., which may explain the absence of hub dominance in Marín's results.

5 EMPIRICAL INDICATIONS FOR HOME CARRIER ADVANTAGES

5.1 Theoretical Framework

We use a simple hub-and-spoke network, as depicted in the right hand side of Figure 1. Airport A is an origin close to hub H and Z is defined as distant destination. This combination represents the common practice of Europe originating flights to other continents.

---

[5] Marín uses a similar interpretation of airport presence as Berry (1990). His definition is also much alike, though fit to the European situation.

We base our analysis on the assumption that fares depend on distance traveled, because costs are likely to be distance related—though not exclusively—and fares are at least partly related to costs. Hansen (1990) and Windle and Dresner (1999) are examples of empirical studies on the relationship between fare and distance. Brander and Zhang (1993) find that costs per passenger are increasing but concave in distance. We capture this by using a logarithmic relationship between distance and fares. We define the fare from hub H to destination Z as:

$$\log fare_{HZ} = \alpha_{HZ} + \beta_{HZ} \log dist_{HZ} + \chi C + \varphi_H H + \varphi_Z Z + hdp \tag{1}$$

where $dist_{HZ}$ is the distance from airport H to airport Z, C is a vector of unobservable company-specific factors, H and Z are airport dummies[6] and $\alpha_{HZ}, \beta_{HZ}, \phi_H, \phi_Z$ and χ are corresponding parameters. The variable hdp represents the hub departure premium, an *extra* markup that the home carrier is confident enough to place on hub originating fares. This premium may be caused by market power, as Borenstein (1989) suggests, or may be a form of product differentiation or both. The latter explanation, suggested by Berry (1990), implies that the carrier anticipates a higher willingness to pay for direct flights.

We should keep in mind that the premium as it is defined above, is a *relative* measure. Consider a situation where we, as we will do later in the paper, analyze fares of eight different companies. If we use the maximum number of seven company specific hdp's in our specification, the choice of the 'numéraire' would determine the sign of the hdp's. The 'numéraire' company is the one with the weakest airport dominance, which doesn't necessarily mean it has no dominance at all. This implies that the hub premiums estimated from the model measure the hub premium of a carrier on top of the lowest premium in the sample. Similar to equation (1), we define the fare of a flight from origin A via hub H to destination Z as:

$$\log fare_{AHZ} = \alpha_{AHZ} + \beta_{AHZ} \log dist_{AHZ} + \chi C + \varphi_A A + 2\varphi_H H + \varphi_Z Z \tag{2}$$

Note that we entered the dummy for the hub airport twice, since a return flight lands and takes off at the hub twice. Next, we use the distinction between close and distant spokes for scaling purposes, by defining relative fare, *Rfare* as $\frac{fare_{AHZ}}{fare_{HZ}}$. We may now write the equation for log *Rfare* as:

$$\log Rfare = \alpha + \beta_{AHZ} \log Rdist + \varphi_A A + \varphi_H H + (\beta_{AHZ} - \beta_{HZ}) \log dist_{HZ} - hdp \tag{3}$$

where $\alpha = \alpha_{AHZ} - \alpha_{HZ}$, $Rdist = dist_{AHZ}/dist_{HZ}$ and parameter β represents the fare elasticity of a small increase in distance, which should be comparable to the cost elasticity of a small increase in distance.

In aviation, costs are positively related to distance, but less than proportionally, so we expect β to be between 0 and 1. Brueckner and Spiller (1994) point out that hub and spoke operations induce economies of density, which would imply that the sign of $\beta_{AHZ} - \beta_{HZ}$ should be negative.

---

[6] We have also tried to model airport specific factors by entering the country's income per capita. This implicitly denotes price discrimination, but it did not yield statistically significant results.

Route competition, measured by the Herfindahl-Hirschman index (HHI) may also influence fares.[7] Consistency in scaling would require the use of HHIs for both routes A-H-Z and H-Z. No major carriers share hubs in Europe however, so that any route A-H-Z is almost certainly only operated by H's home carrier. This problem may be mitigated by considering competition on city pair level rather than the level of individual itineraries.[8] On city pair A-Z, itinerary A-H-Z is considered a close substitute to the direct flight. We use this notion to compute the HHI for city pairs A-Z as well as for city pair H-Z. Next we add the HHI's to equation (3):

$$\log Rfare = \alpha + \beta_{AHZ} \log Rdist + \varphi_A A + \varphi_H H + (\beta_{AHZ} - \beta_{HZ}) \log dist_{HZ}$$
$$- hdp + \phi_{HZ} HHI_{HZ} + \phi_{AZ} HHI_{AZ} \qquad (4)$$

5.2   Data and Empirical Results

We retrieved fare and frequency data from the internet.[9] We collected fare data for unrestricted economy class, which more or less means that we focus on the lower part of the market for business travelers.[10] Our data on fares, travel times and distance relate to February 2000, and are retrieved from the internet page of Travelocity, using a strict set of rules to ensure comparability of fares.

We built our database around the five largest European carriers and their intercontinental hubs: London Heathrow, Paris Charles de Gaule, Frankfurt, Amsterdam and Milan Malpensa. We selected ten European origins, among which these five main airports. The other European origins have different characteristics. Three of them (Zürich, Brussels and Athens) are also intercontinental hubs, be it hubs of medium sized international carriers. Another origin (Prague) is the hub of a carrier that operates mainly on European routes. The final origin to be mentioned here (Venice) is an airport that is not used as a hub by any carrier, but it is served by the main European carriers.

For the purpose of our analysis, we need five important non-European airports with a substantial amount of destination traffic. Worldwide, important destination airports are almost always some carrier's hub however. For these reasons, picking destinations is always slightly arbitrary. Trying to obtain a more or less global image, we picked New York (North America, East Coast), Los Angeles (North America, West Coast), Tokyo (far East), Cairo (Africa/Middle East) and Singapore (Southeast Asia).

We summarize our data in Table 2. Note that the minimum of *Rfare* is quite a bit below unity, indicating the existence of lower fares for connecting flights. In our sample, *Rfare* is below unity for 47 observations, be it that 33 of them are less then four percent below unity. Nevertheless, this indicates the presence of a hub departure premium.

Table 3 presents the results from the estimation. Apart from the coefficients of the Herfindahl index and the constants, all parameters are statistically significant. Only one

---

[7] Comparing direct and one-stop flights creates the need to correct for the inconvenience of the latter. We use the result found by Lijesen *et al.* (2004), giving a higher (1.63) weight to direct flights than to indirect ones.
[8] Note that competition at the city-pair level also implies that a flight from London Heathrow to New York JFK competes with a flight from London Gatwick to Newark.
[9] Many of the studies from the US use publicly available data on sold tickets and actual travel behaviour. Such data are not available in Europe.
[10] This is consistent with the findings of Berry, Carnal and Spiller (1996).

Table 2   Descriptive Statistics

	Mean	Stand. Dev.	Minimum	Maximum
Fare (US$)	3094.08	1092.67	1073.60	5367.90
Distance (Miles)	5388.22	1658.92	1609	8242
Rfare	1.141	0.278	0.479	3.023
Rdist	1.106	0.180	1.015	3.153

Table 3   Regression Results for Log *Rfare* (t-values between Brackets)

		Equation (4)
Constant	α	0.68
		(2.2)
log *Rdist*	β	0.48
		(3.6)
cost difference between legs	$\beta_{AHZ} - \beta_{HZ}$	−0.08
		(−2.5)
hub dominance premium for Air France	hdp_{AF}	0.14
		(4.4)
hub dominance premium for Lufthansa	hdp_{LH}	0.15
		(4.4)
hub dominance premium for Swissair	hdp_{SR}	0.13
		(3.5)
Brussels originating dummy		−0.58
		(−7.8)
log of HHI of city pair	ϕ_{AZ}	−0.06
		(−1.2)
log of HHI of main leg	ϕ_{HZ}	−0.03
		(−0.5)
Log likelihood		83.3
adjusted R^2		0.44
Number of observations		213

of the airport dummies (Brussels originating flights) yielded a significant parameter, the other ones were omitted from the analysis. We found positive and significant hub premiums for Swissair, Air France and Lufthansa.[11] The parameter for the Herfindahl indices are not significantly different from zero. The hypothesis that economies of density arise from the hub-and-spoke operations is confirmed by the negative sign of $\beta_{AHZ} - \beta_{HZ}$.

For Swissair, the hub premium is about 13 percent, for Air France it is slightly higher at 14 percent. Lufthansa (15 percent) has the highest premium in this sample. Similar results

---

[11] As stated before, the company with the lowest hdp should be the 'numéraire'. In the specification used here, Sabena is the 'numéraire', with Alitalia, Olympic, KLM and British Airways not differing significantly. These dummies were therefore omitted from the analysis.

are found by Berry, Carnal and Spiller (2005), who compute a hub premium of 19% for type 2 passengers on large hubs, roughly the US equivalent of the fares studied here.

Comparing these results with the market shares of Europe's main hubs in Table 1 gives some room for the hypothesis that hub premiums are related to market power at airports, since Air France and Lufthansa (for which we found relatively high hub premiums here) have higher airport market shares than the other carriers.[12] This result is consistent with Dresner and Windle (1992), who find that premium yields are positively related to airport market shares, and it suggests that favorable product characteristics are not the only reasons why fares from hub-originating flights are higher.

6 CONCLUSION AND DISCUSSION

This paper addresses the issue of relative position of the home carriers in hub-and-spoke systems. Hub-and-spoke systems are used by airlines to concentrate large numbers of passengers at their hub, thus giving rise to the exploitation of economies of density. Economies of density may lower costs on densely traveled routes and enable economically viable operations on less densely traveled routes. The reverse side is probably that carriers enjoy market power at their home base, labeled the home carrier advantage.

The home carrier advantage follows from carriers' favorable positions at their home base. Exploiting economies of density, they offer a higher number of direct flights from their hub at a higher frequency. This results in a higher product quality, as travelers are known to prefer direct flights, shorter travel times and higher frequencies. Other possible advantages for the home carrier follow from nonlinearities in Frequent Flyer Programs, language advantages, national pride and economies of density in advertisement in the home country.

We have developed a framework to establish empirically whether European carriers have a home carrier advantage or not. We use a cost-base approach of pricing flight tickets, taking a hub premium into account. We correct for unknown carrier specific characteristics by scaling all parameters of the indirect flights to their counterparts of the main leg of that same flight. Assuming a loglinear relationship between costs and distance, we establish an empirical relationship between fares, distance, route competition and hub premiums.

Borenstein (1989, 1991), Berry (1990), Evans and Kessides (1993) and Berry, Carnall and Spiller (2005) found positive hub premiums in the U.S. We established empirically that at least some European carriers charge premiums for flights originating from their hubs as well. We would like to stress that our results are *relative* results. This implies that the hub premiums of Lufthansa, Swissair and Air France are significantly higher than those of Sabena, British Airways, KLM, Olympic and Alitalia. These other companies do not necessarily refrain from charging hub premiums: they may also charge premiums, but lower than the ones that Lufthansa, Swissair and Air France charge. Also note that hub premiums may be used to cross-subsidize feeder flights in order to make optimal use of economies of density. This implies that hub premiums do not per se raise average fares.

---

[12] Unfortunately, lack of data of sufficient quality did not allow us to include variables of this type in the empirical analysis.

One may wonder whether 'hub premiums' follow from market power or from product differentiation. Both are probably true. The approach in Berry (1990) clearly follows the latter interpretation, whereas Borenstein (1989, 1991) looks at the phenomenon from the point of view of market power. The approach adopted in this paper follows the approach adopted by Borenestein, but does not explicitly exclude the product differentiation aspect.

An analysis slightly different from the one in this paper (Lijesen *et al.*, 2002a) shows that product differentiation affects relative fares, and it does so in two ways. First, travelers are willing to pay more for higher quality (i.e., direct flights). Second, product differentiation limits competition because imperfect substitutes do not compete perfectly. The latter finding is a standard result from product differentiation in oligopoly models. So, fare differences stem partly from differences in product characteristics and partly from rents following from those differences. Furthermore, our findings in this paper that relative fares deviate from relative costs and that these deviations differ significantly between carriers suggest the presence of market power.

The relevance for competition policy is clear. Competition between full-service airlines using hub-and-spoke systems is imperfect in the sense that travelers will have to choose between imperfect substitutes. The hub carrier advantage involves rents which are likely to be sought by airlines. If we include routes also served by low cost carriers the hub carrier advantage decreases, since its main elements, direct flights and high frequencies, are generally also offered by the low cost carrier. This implies that the presence of a low cost carrier may seriously limit the home carrier in extracting rents from its home carrier advantage. It is therefore interesting to figure out how the entry of a low cost carrier on a route would influence the hub-based carrier's pricing decisions on that route, as well as on itineraries involving that route (see for example Alderighi *et al.*, 2004). In the summer of 2003 British Airways was chosen as the best low-cost carrier during the Guardian/Observer travel awards, indicating that conventional airlines have responded to the emergence of low-cost carriers by lowering fares. On the other hand Pels and Rietveld (2004) find that in terms of yield management strategies, network carriers (British Airways, Air France) hardly react to price changes of low-cost carriers (easyJet, Buzz) in the London-Paris market. We may thus conclude that low-cost carriers have the potential to limit a hub-and-spoke airline's opportunity the charge hub-premiums. But further research is needed in this field to better comprehend the effects of market entry of low cost carriers on hub and spoke operations and on fare structures.

The home carrier advantage provides a rent-seeking opportunity for hub-and-spoke airlines. Passengers flying directly to their destination pay a relatively high fare due to a lack of direct competition from similar carriers (unless they fly with a low-cost carrier operating in a different market segment). Competition may be low because the market is too 'thin' to support multiple carriers, or simply because the necessary airport capacity is lacking. The passenger flow in markets with a relatively high hub premium will be relatively low; the airline extracts all rents, while revenues for the airport are relatively low. However, the airline can support this system because of the indirect passengers it transports, which cause the average costs per passenger to be relatively low. The airport thus also benefits from this system. For the surrounding economy, however, the origin-destination passengers (both business travelers and tourists) will be more interesting. While the business travelers may have a relatively high willingness-to-pay, leisure travelers (tourists) are price-sensitive. When the hub-premium is too high, tourists will find another destination, unless the market is also served by other, possibly low-cost carriers. Low-cost carriers will enter a market when the number of (potential) passengers is high enough to guarantee reasonable returns, and when slots are available at relatively low cost.

The obvious policy implication is that problems associated with the home carrier advantage may thus be mitigated by ensuring the possibility of entry. Apart from that, the hub carrier advantage calls for caution when measuring concentration, e.g. when assessing the competitive effects of a merger.[13]

REFERENCES

Ahn, S.C., D.H. Good, R.C. Sickles, 1999, The relative efficiency and rate of technology adoption of asian and north american airline firms, in T.-T. Fu, C.J. Huang, C.A.K. Lovell (eds) *Economic Efficiency and Productivity Growth in the Asia-Pacific Region*, Cheltenham, Edward Elgar, pp. 67–91.

Alderighi, M.A. Cento, P. Nijkamp and P. Rietveld, 2004, The entry of low cost airlines: price competition in the European airline market, Tinbergen Institute, Amsterdam.

Baker, S.H. and J.B. Pratt, 1989, Experience as a barrier to contestability in airline markets, *The Review of Economics and Statistics*, 71(2), pp. 352–6.

Berechman, J. and O. Shy, 1989, The structure of airline equilibrium networks, *Recent Advances in Spatial Equilibrium Modelling* (J.C.J.M. van den Bergh, P. Nijkamp and P. Rietveld, eds), Springer-Verlag, Berlin 1998, pp. 138–56.

Berechman, J. and J. de Wit, 1996. An analysis of the effects of European aviation deregulation on an airline's network structure and choice of a primary west European hub airport, *Journal of Transport Economics and Policy*, 29, pp. 251–74.

Berry, S., 1990, Airport presence as product differentiation, *American Economic Review, papers and proceedings*, 80, pp. 394–99.

Berry, S., M. Carnall and P.T. Spiller, 2005, Airline hubs: costs, markups and the implications of customer heterogeneity, in Lee, D. (ed) *Advances in Airline Economics, volume I: Competition Policy and Antitrust*, Elsevier, North Holland.

Bhat, C.R., 1995, A heteroscedastic extreme value model of intercity travel mode choice, *Transportation Research, Part B*, 29(6), pp. 471–83.

Bhat, C.R., 1997, An endogenous segmentation mode choice model with and application to intercity travel, *Transportation Science*, 31(1), pp. 34–48.

Bissessur, A. and F. Alamdari, 1998, Factors affecting the operational success of strategic airline alliances, *Transportation*, 25, pp. 331–55.

Borenstein, S., 1989, Hubs and high fares: dominance and market power in the US airline industry, *Rand Journal of Economics*, 20, pp. 344–65.

Borenstein, S., 1991, The dominant firm advantage in multi-product industries: evidence from the U.S. airlines, *Quarterly Journal of Economics*, 106, pp. 1237–66.

Borenstein, S. and M.B. Zimmerman, 1988, Market incentives for safe commercial airline operation, *American Economic Review*, 78(5), pp. 913–35.

Botimer, T.C., 1996, Efficiency considerations in airline pricing and yield management, *Transportation Research Part A*, 30, pp. 307–17.

Brander, J.A. and Zhang, A., 1990, Market conduct in the airline industry: an empirical investigation. *RAND Journal of Economics* 21, pp. 567–83.

---

[13] See Lijesen *et al.* (2002b, 2004).

Brander, J.A. and Zhang, A., 1993, Dynamic oligopoly behaviour in the airline industry, *International Journal of Industrial Organization* 11, pp. 407–35.

Brueckner, J.K., 2002, Airport congestion when carriers have market power, *American Economic Review*, 92(5), pp. 1357–75.

Brueckner, J.K., N.J. Dyer and P.T. Spiller, 1992, Fare determination in airline hub-and-spoke networks, *The RAND Journal of Economics*, 23(3), pp. 309–33.

Brueckner, J.K. and E. Pels, 2004, European airline mergers, alliance consolidation, and consumer welfare, CESifo Working paper no. 1154.

Brueckner, J.K. and P.T. Spiller, 1994, Economies of traffic density in the deregulated airline industry, *Journal of Law and Economics*, 37, pp. 379–415.

Brueckner, J. and Y. Zhang, 2001, A Model of scheduling in airline networks, *Journal of Transport Economics and Policy*, 35, pp. 195–222.

Button, K., 1996, Liberalising European Aviation, is there an empty core problem? *Journal of Transport Economics and Policy*, 29, pp. 275–91.

Carbonneau, S.E., 2003, Measuring the Hub Carriers' Market Power in Directional Hub-Spoke Markets, unpublished manuscript, University of Texas, http://www.eco.utexas.edu/graduate/ Carbonneau/ Carbonneau_Paper1.pdf.

Dana, J.D., 1999, Using yield management to shift demand when the peak time is unknown, *RAND Journal of Economics*, 30(3), pp. 456–74.

Daniel J.I. and M. Pahwa, 2000, Comparison of three empirical models of airport congestion pricing, *Journal of Urban Economics*, 50(2), pp. 230–58.

Doganis, R., 1991, *Flying off course, the economics of international airlines*, 2nd edition, London, Routledge.

Doganis, R., 1996, *The Airport Business*, 2nd edition, London, Routledge.

Doganis, R., 2001, *The Airline Business in the 21st Century*, London, Brunner-Routledge.

Dresner, M. and R. Windle, 1992, Airport dominance and yields in the U.S. airline industry, *Logistics and Transportation Review*, 28(4), pp. 319–39.

Evans, W.N. and I.N. Kessides, 1993, Localized market power in the U.S. airline industry, *Review of Economics and Statistics*, 70(1), pp. 66–75.

Fridström, L. and H. Thune-Larsen, 1989, An econometric air travel demand model for the entire conventional domestic network: the case of Norway, *Transportation Research Part B*, 23(3), pp. 213–23.

Ghobrial, A., 1993, A model to estimate the demand between US and foreign gateways, *International Journal of Transport Economics*, 20(3), pp. 271–83.

Goetz, A.R. and C.J. Sutton, 1997, The geography of deregulation in the U.S. airline industry, *Annals of the Association of American Geographers*, 87(2), pp. 238–63.

Hanlon, P., 1999, *Global Airlines*, Oxford, Butterworth Heinemann, 2nd edition.

Hansen, M., 1990, Airline competition in a hub-dominated environment: an application of noncooperative game theory, *Transportation Research Part B*, 24, pp. 27–43.

Harvey, G., 1987, Airport choice in a multiple airport region, *Transportation Research Part A*, 21, pp. 439–49.

Kanafani, A. and A. Ghobrial, 1985, Airline hubbing – some implications for airport economics, *Transportation Research Part A*, 19, pp. 15–27.

Lee, D. and M.J. Luengo-Prado, 2005, The impact of passenger mix on reported "hub premiums" in the U.S. airline industry, *Southern Economic Journal,* 72(2), pp. 372–394.

Levine, M.E., 1987, Airline competition in deregulated markets: theory, firm strategy and public policy, *Yale Journal on Regulation*, 4(2), pp. 393–494.

Lijesen, M.G., P. Rietveld and P. Nijkamp, 2002a, How do carriers price connecting flights? Evidence from intercontinental flights from Europe, *Transportation Research Part E*, 38, pp. 239–52.

Lijesen, M.G., P. Rietveld and P. Nijkamp, 2002b, Measuring competition in civil aviation, *Journal of Air Transport Management*, 8, pp. 189–97.

Lijesen, M.G., P. Rietveld and P. Nijkamp, 2004, Adjusting the Herfindahl index for close substitues, an application to pricing in civil aviation, *Transportation Research Part E*, 40(2), pp. 123–34.

Marín, P.L., 1995, Competition in European aviation: pricing policy and market structure, *The Journal of Industrial Economics*, 18(2), pp. 141–59.

Marín, P.L., 1998, Productivity differences in the airline industry: partial deregulation versus short run protection, *International Journal of Industrial Organization*, 16, pp. 395–414.

McGill, J.I. and G.J. van Ryzin, 1999, revenue management: research overview and prospects, *Transportation Science*, 33(2), pp. 233–56.

Morrison, S.A. and C. Winston, 1995, *The Economic Effects of Airline Deregulation*, Brookings Institution, Washington D.C.

Nijkamp, P. and K. Button, 2003, Recent advances in air transport economics, in Cederlund, K. and U. Silbersky (eds), *New Trends in the European Air Traffic*, Rapporter och Notiser 164, Lund University.

Oum, T.H. and W.G. Waters II, 1996, A survey of recent developments in transportation cost function research, *Logistics and transportation review*, 32(4), pp. 423–63.

Oum, T.H. and C. Yu, 1998, *Winning Airlines, Productivity and Cost Competitiveness of the World's Major Airlines*, Norwell MA, Kluwer.

Park, J.-H., 1997, The effects of airline alliances on markets and economic welfare, *Transportation Research, part E*, 33(3), pp. 181–95.

Pels, E., P. Nijkamp and P. Rietveld, 1997, substitution and complementarity in aviation, *Transportation Research E*, 33, pp. 275–286.

Pels, E., P. Nijkamp and P. Rietveld, 2002, Airport and airline competition for passengers departing from a large metropolitan area, *Journal of Urban Economics*, 48, pp. 29–45.

Pels, E. and E.T. Verhoef, 2004, The economics of airport congestion pricing, *Journal of Urban Economics*, 55, pp. 257–277.

Proussaloglou, K. and F. Koppelman, 1995, Air carrier demand, an analysis of market share determinants, *Transportation*, 22, pp. 371–88.

Reece, W.S. and R.S. Sobel, 2000, Targeting teaching: diagrammatic approach to capacity-constrained price discrimination, *Southern Economic Journal*, 66(4), pp. 1001–08.

Rose, N.L., 1992, Fear of flying? Economic analyses of airline safety, *Journal of economic perspectives*, 6(2), pp. 75–94.

Schipper, Y., P. Rietveld and P. Nijkamp, 2003, Airline deregulation and external costs: a welfare analysis, *Transportation Research B*, 37(8), pp. 699–718.

Suzuki, Y., 2000, The relationship between on-time performance and airline market share: a new approach, *Transportation Research, Part E*, 36, pp. 139–54.

Swait, J. and A. Bernardino, 2000, Distinguishing taste variation from error structure in discrete choice data, *Transportation Research Part B*, 34, pp. 1–15.

Toh, R.S. and M.Y. Hu, 1988, Frequent-flier programs: passenger attributes and attitudes, *Transportation Journal*, 28(2), pp. 11–22.

Windle, R. and M. Dresner, 1999, Competitive responses to low cost carrier entry, *Transportation Research Part E*, 35, pp. 59–75.

Winston, C., 1993, Economic deregulation: days of reckoning for microeconomists, *Journal of Economic Literature*, 31(3), pp. 1263–89.

Wit, R.C.N., M.D. Davidson and J.M.W. Dings, 2003, *Meeting External Costs in the Aviation Industry*, CE Delft.

Advances in Airline Economics, Vol 1
Darin Lee (Editor)
© 2006 Published by Elsevier B.V.

10

Actual, Adjacent, and Potential Competition Estimating the Full Effect of Southwest Airlines

Steven A. Morrison
Reprinted with Permission, *Journal of Transport Economics and Policy*, Volume 35, Part 2, pp. 239–256, May 2001

Address for correspondence: Department of Economics, Northeastern University, Boston, MA 02115 (saml@neu.edu). This paper is based on research undertaken on behalf of Southwest Airlines. The views expressed are the author's own and are not necessarily those of Southwest Airlines. The author would like to thank Tae Oum, Cliff Winston, and an anonymous referee for helpful comments.

ABSTRACT

Southwest Airlines is frequently credited with having an important influence on the success of airline deregulation in the United States. This paper uses an original set of competition variables to estimate the extent of that influence in 1998. The estimated savings – due to actual, adjacent, and potential competition from Southwest – were $12.9 billion. Southwest's low fares were directly responsible for $3.4 billion of these savings to passengers. The remaining $9.5 billion represents the effect that actual, adjacent, and potential competition from Southwest had on other carriers' fares. These savings amount to 20 per cent of the airline industry's 1998 domestic scheduled passenger revenue and slightly more than half the fare reductions attributed to airline deregulation. From a policy perspective, these results are both troubling and encouraging. On the one hand, it is troubling to find that a large part of the fare reductions from airline deregulation is due to one carrier. On the other hand, if entry by a carrier with the appropriate characteristics can make such a difference, policies that encourage entry – for example, relaxing the restriction on entry by foreign-owned carriers – may have a large impact on passenger welfare.

1   INTRODUCTION

"Probably the most significant development in the U.S. airline industry during the past decade has been the continued expansion of Southwest Airlines and the resurgence of low fare entry generally."

Transportation Research Board (1999)

Southwest Airlines has a unique position in the US domestic aviation industry. It was one of two carriers (along with Pacific Southwest Airlines) whose low fares as intrastate carriers not regulated by the federal government led to airline deregulation in 1978[1]. Indeed, its combination of low fares, high frequency, and point-to-point service has become a model for other carriers both in the United States and abroad. As exemplified by the quote above, Southwest Airlines is often cited as a major reason for the success of airline deregulation in the United States. This paper uses an original set of competition variables to quantify the impact that Southwest Airlines has on airfares through actual, adjacent, and potential competition.

2   PREVIOUS RESEARCH

Previous research has estimated Southwest's aggregate impact on fares on the routes that it serves[2]. Dresner *et al.* (1996) hypothesized that the effect of Southwest (and other low-fare carriers) may be greater than previously estimated because of possible spillover effects that Southwest's service on one route has on adjacent competitive routes that involve nearby airports. They found a significant effect of service on adjacent competitive routes but did not aggregate the results to estimate the aggregate impact of Southwest. This paper's contribution is to specify the effect that Southwest may have on a route's fares in an original disaggregate way, which includes the effect of various forms of actual, adjacent, and potential competition from Southwest. The results are then aggregated to obtain an estimate of the effect that Southwest has had on airfares. This estimate is compared with estimates of the fare reductions attributed to airline deregulation to gauge Southwest's role in this policy's success.

3   METHODOLOGY

Airfares on a route can be influenced by an airline in three ways. First, the airline can serve the route in question. Second, the airline can serve an adjacent route that consumers view as a reasonable substitute for the route in question. Third, although the airline may not serve the route in question or an adjacent route, it may still affect fares on the route

---

[1] See Breyer (1982). Southwest Airlines started service in 1971 as a Texas intrastate carrier serving three Texas cities. It began interstate service shortly after airlines were deregulated in 1978. In 1999, it served 57 airports (in 29 of the 48 contiguous states) and had operating revenue of $4.7 billion, which placed it seventh among US passenger airlines.

[2] See, for example, Bennett and Craun (1993) and US Department of Transportation (1996).

if airlines lower their fares to make entry by potential competitors less attractive[3]. This could happen if the airline has a presence at the airports in question or at nearby airports.

Figure 1 illustrates the various ways that an airline may affect fares on a particular route. In the figure, the route of interest is from airport A to airport B. The dashed circles around airports A and B form the boundaries of zones of influence any carrier serving

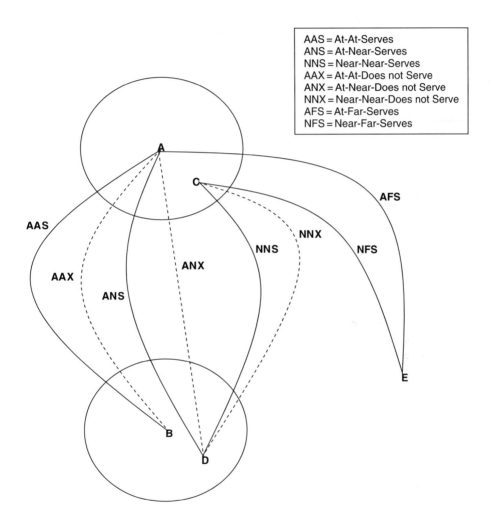

AAS = At-At-Serves
ANS = At-Near-Serves
NNS = Near-Near-Serves
AAX = At-At-Does not Serve
ANX = At-Near-Does not Serve
NNX = Near-Near-Does not Serve
AFS = At-Far-Serves
NFS = Near-Far-Serves

A solid line means the airline serves both airports and the route.
A dashed line means the airline serves both airports but not the route.

Figure 1 Ways in Which a Carrier May Affect Fares on Route A-B.

[3] The role of potential competition was formalized by Baumol *et al.* (1982). In their model, the threat of entry by potential competitors disciplines those firms serving the market to price at a level that maximizes consumer welfare.

an airport within those zones may exert a competitive influence on the carriers serving the airports in question. In the diagram, airports C and D fall within the zones of A and B, respectively, and airport E is outside both zones.

The possible ways in which a carrier may affect fares on a given route A-B are:

- It may serve the route A-B (denoted by AAS, for At the origin airport, At the destination airport, and Serves the route).
- It may serve a route A-D, where airport D is "near" airport B (denoted by ANS, for At, Near, Serves).

It may serve a route C-D, where C is near airport A and D is near airport B (denoted by NNS, for Near, Near, Serves).

- It may serve both airports A and B but not serve the route (denoted by AAX, for At, At, does not serve the route).
- It may serve airport A and airport D, which is near airport B, but not serve the route (denoted by ANX, for At, Near, does not serve the route).
- It may serve airports C and D but not serve the route (denoted by NNX, for Near, Near, does not serve the route).
- It may serve a route A-E, where E is not near B (denoted by AFS, for At, Far, Serves).
- It may serve a route C-E, where C is near A, but E is not near B (denoted by NFS, for Near, Far, Serves).

In the first of these cases, the airline serves the route in question. In the next two cases, the airline provides service on adjacent routes. In the remaining five cases, a carrier provides various degrees of potential competition (the extent of which will be estimated) by serving one or both of the airports A and B or airports nearby, but not serving routes connecting them[4].

4   THE DATA AND THE MODEL

The primary dataset for this study was the US Department of Transportation's Ticket Origin and Destination Survey (Data Bank 1A) for the calendar year 1998, a 10 per cent sample of airline tickets, which carriers report quarterly to the Department[5]. Although the effect of Southwest Airlines will be empirically estimated below, the

---

[4] The last two cases are considered as potential competition even though the carrier offers service on A-E or C-E because airport E is outside the zone of influence for the A-B route.

[5] In order to be reasonably assured that the tickets for a particular trip reflect travel from one origin to one destination, only tickets with one (directional) destination were used. Round trips had to return to the initial point of departure (with no ground segments, i.e., "open jaw" tickets). Only one-way tickets with two or fewer coupons (i.e., flight segments) and round-trip tickets with two or fewer coupons on the outbound and return legs were used. Further, only tickets involving airports in the 48 contiguous states were used. Finally, tickets that were coded with the generic codes for Chicago, Detroit, New York City, and Washington, DC were omitted because it was not possible to identify the airport actually used.

Table 1 Competitive Profile of Southwest Airlines in 1998

Category	Variable		Percentage of Domestic Passenger Miles
Actual Competition			44.8%
	At-At-Serves	21.0%	
	At-Near-Serves	18.0%	
	Near-Near-Serves	5.7%	
Potential Competition			49.4%
	At-At-Does not Serve	6.5%	
	At-Near-Does not Serve	2.7%	
	Near-Near-Does not Serve	0.1%	
	At-Far-Serves	30.7%	
	Near-Far-Serves	9.4%	
Total			94.2%

Source: Author's calculations. See text for a detailed explanation of the variables. Calculations are based on a zone of influence with a 75-mile radius. Totals may not add due to rounding.

extent of its possible influence is shown in Table 1, which shows the percentage of domestic passenger miles flown on routes in each of the categories above. To avoid double counting, Southwest's (potential) influence on each route was classified into the highest category for which it qualified. During 1998, Southwest was in a position to (potentially) influence fares on the routes it served and on adjacent routes amounting to 44.8 per cent of domestic passenger miles flown. In addition, in its role as a potential competitor, it was in a position to (potentially) influence fares on routes accounting for an additional 49.4 per cent of domestic passenger miles. Thus, Southwest was in a position to potentially influence fares on routes comprising 94 per cent of domestic passenger miles[6].

The standard approach to assessing the effect of competition – both actual and potential – on airfares is to estimate a fare equation[7]. In a fare equation, the average fare on a route is regressed on measures of actual and potential competition and other control variables that are believed to influence the cost and demand characteristics of the route. Here, quarterly data from the 1,000 most heavily traveled routes in 1998 were used to estimate a fare equation to assess the effect of Southwest Airlines on fares[8].

---

[6] What characterizes those routes that are beyond any (potential) impact of Southwest? The 20 most heavily traveled routes (based on passenger miles) that Southwest did not (potentially) influence in 1998 (amounting to 24 per cent of the passenger miles of that unaffected group) involved routes between the following 13 airports: Atlanta, Buffalo, Charlotte, Denver, Hartford, LaGuardia, Memphis, Minneapolis-St. Paul, Newark, Raleigh-Durham, Richmond, Philadelphia, and Pittsburgh. Eight of these airports are hubs for major airlines. Eleven are in the eastern US. One is slot constrained. (In 1999, Southwest entered Hartford and Raleigh-Durham.)
[7] This fare equation may be regarded as a reduced form equation derived from a structural model. See, for example, Bailey and Panzar (1981), or Morrison and Winston (1995).
[8] The 1,000 routes account for 70 per cent of passengers and 67 per cent of passenger miles in the full dataset containing more than 29,000 routes.

4.1   The Dependent Variable

For each ticket in the sample, the price each passenger paid was reduced by the amount of ticket taxes and passenger facility charges (PFCs)[9]. Average one-way fare (logarithm) was then calculated for each route in the sample[10].

4.2   The Competition Variables

As above, Southwest's (potential) influence on each route was classified into the highest category for which it qualified. In addition, competition variables giving the number of carriers from each group serving the route were included for three other groups of carriers:[11] Low-Fare carriers (other than Southwest), Major carriers (other than Southwest), and Other carriers[12]. A zone of influence with a radius of 75 miles was used because it provided the best fit compared with zones of 25, 50, 100, and 125 miles.[13]

4.3   Control Variables

Although we are primarily interested in the effect that Southwest Airlines has on fares, it is important to control for other influences in order that we are reasonably certain that the competition variables capture just that, rather than some other effect.

4.3.1   Distance

Other things being equal, we expect fares to be higher the longer the trip because costs are higher. The logarithm of the (great circle) distance from the origin to the destination was used.

---

[9] During the first three quarters of 1998, the federal domestic ticket tax was 9 per cent of the ticket price plus $1 per flight segment. During the fourth quarter of 1998, the tax was 8 per cent plus $2 per segment. 290 airports assessed PFCs during 1998; all but one airport charged the statutory maximum of $3 per enplanement; one airport charged $2.

[10] Because of possible coding errors in the data carriers submit to the Department of Transportation, the US General Accounting Office's (1990) fare screen was used to screen out fares that seemed too high. In order to keep frequent flier tickets, a low-fare screen was not used. The effect on the results of omitting frequent flier tickets is discussed below in the section on sensitivity.

[11] A carrier was considered as serving a route if it had at least a 10 per cent share of the route's passengers. Attempts to estimate an equation with a complete set of competition variables to capture the effect of adjacent and potential competition for major, low fare, and other carriers resulted in implausible estimates for all competition variables.

[12] The Low-Fare carriers identified by the US Department of Transportation that were operating during 1998 (other than Southwest) were AirTran, American Trans Air, Frontier, Kiwi, ProAir, Reno, Spirit, Tower Air, Vanguard, and Western Pacific. The US Department of Transportation defines a Major carrier as one with annual revenue over $1 billion. In 1998, the Major (passenger) carriers (in addition to Southwest) were Alaska, American, America West, Continental, Delta, Northwest, Trans World, United, and US Airways. The Other carriers used in this analysis were Casino Express, Eastwind, Hawaiian, Midway, and Midwest Express. Carriers with fewer than 1,000 sampled passengers during 1998 were not assigned a competition variable, nor were trips involving changing airlines, i.e., interline connections.

[13] Dresner et al. (1996) used a 50-mile radius to define adjacent competitive routes. Sensitivity results for zones of 25, 50, 100, and 125 miles are reported below.

4.3.2   Density

Because of fixed station costs and economies of aircraft size, airline service is character-ized by economies of density[14]. An airport is classified into one of four "hub" categories (Large, Medium, Small, and Non) based on its share of enplanements nationwide[15]. Since there are four hub classifications, a given route is in one of ten possible origin-hub-destination-hub classifications (for example, Large-Small). To control for density, nine dummy variables were used representing all but one of the possible combinations of service between the four airport hub classifications. (A Non-Hub-Non-Hub variable was not used because there were no routes in the top 1,000 in that category.) Because dummy variables were included for all hub categories in the sample, a separate constant term was not included.

4.3.3   Slots

Four airports in the United States have limits on the number of takeoffs and landings that may take place during any given hour. To account for the effect on fares of the demand restrictions at these so-called "slot-controlled" airports, four dummy variables were included for the four airports: Chicago O'Hare; New York Kennedy and LaGuardia; and Washington Reagan National. The variable equaled one if the airport was on the route in question, and zero otherwise.

4.3.4   Percentage Business

Airlines use yield management to charge business travelers higher fares than pleasure travelers. Thus, other things being equal, trip purpose is expected to affect airfares. Data used were the percentage of air travelers traveling between the states where the origin and destination airports were located, whose trip purpose was business.[16]

4.3.5   Concentrated Hubs

Previous research (see, for example, Borenstein, 1989) has shown that other things being equal, fares at concentrated hub airports are higher than at other airports. This analysis uses the US General Accounting Office's (1990) definition, in which an airport was considered concentrated if it was among the top 75 in the country in terms of passenger enplanements and one carrier accounted for 60 per cent or more of enplaned passengers at the airport, or two carriers accounted for 85 per cent or more of enplaned

---

[14] See, for example, Caves et al. (1984).

[15] Those airports that accounted for 1 per cent or more of passenger enplanements were classified as Large Hubs; those enplaning 0.25 per cent or more but less than 1 per cent were classified as Medium Hubs; airports enplaning 0.05 per cent or more but less than 0.25 per cent were classified as Small Hubs; airports enplaning less than 0.05 per cent were classified as Non Hubs. These classifications were determined based on the US Department of Transportation's Airport Activity Statistics data (Form 41, Schedule T-3, Data Bank 22) for 1998. This definition differs from the US Federal Aviation Administration's definition of hub class in that here airport level enplanements were used, whereas the FAA aggregates airport level data into metropolitan area data.

[16] This was calculated from data in the US Department of Transportation's (Bureau of Transportation Statistics), 1995 American Travel Survey. Given that state-level data were used and that the data come from an earlier year, this variable is likely to be exogenous.

5.3   Comparison with Other Studies

Table 5 compares the results of this study with the results of three previous studies of the aggregate impact of Southwest Airlines on airfares. These previous studies assessed Southwest's effect on the routes that it served, but did not capture the additional effects of competition on adjacent routes or from potential competition.

Based on a fare model and entry and exit models, and using data from 1988–1992 for the 1,000 most heavily traveled routes, Morrison and Winston (1995) estimated that if Southwest Airlines exited the airline industry, fares nationwide would increase by 8.5 per cent after five years, even after taking into account the subsequent entry that would probably occur. Bennett and Craun (1993) found that if fares on Southwest's routes in 1992 were raised to the level of fares on non-Southwest routes, industry revenue would rise by $2.5–$3.0 billion (holding traffic constant), which amounts to 5.6–6.7 per cent of 1992's domestic scheduled passenger revenue. The US Department of Transportation (1996) estimated that low-fare carriers saved passengers $6.3 billion during the four quarters ending in 1995:3. If we conservatively assume that Southwest's and other low-fare carriers' effect on fares is the same, because Southwest accounted for 71 per cent of low-fare carriers' revenue passenger miles during the four quarters studied, Southwest's effect would be $4.5 billion, amounting to 8.4 per cent of domestic scheduled passenger revenue. If, on the other hand, we assume that Southwest's presence on a route exerts a stronger influence on fares as indicated by the estimates in this paper, Southwest's effect rises to $5.4 billion, amounting to 10.1 per cent of domestic scheduled passenger revenue.[28]

The Table also shows Southwest's relative size during the time periods covered by these studies. Given that Southwest accounted for a larger share of the industry in 1998,

Table 5   Comparison with Other Studies

Study	Year of Data	Amount that Southwest Lowers Fares as a Percentage of Industry Domestic Passenger Revenue	Southwest's Share of Domestic Scheduled Revenue Passenger Miles
Morrison and Winston (1995)	1988–92	8.5% on routes served	2.9% (1990)
Bennett and Craun (1993)	1992	5.6–6.7% on routes served	4.0% (1992)
U.S. DOT	1995	8.4–10.1% on routes served	5.9% (1995)
Morrison	1998	10.2% on routes served 4.7% on adjacent routes 5.2% from potential competition	6.9% (1998)

Source: Listed above and Air Transport Association (various issues) and Southwest Airlines (www.southwest.com).

---

[28] Here, we assume that the effect of a Southwest passenger mile is 2.25 times more powerful than other low-fare carriers' passenger miles; 2.25 is the ratio of the effect of Southwest $(1 - \exp(-0.62))$ to the effect of other low-fare carriers $(1 - \exp(-0.23))$.

and that this study includes both the effect of competition on adjacent routes and the effect of potential competition from Southwest, which the other aggregate studies did not, the results seem reasonable, although dramatic.[29]

6   SUMMARY AND CONCLUSION

This paper reports estimates of the savings that Southwest Airlines has brought to air travelers in the United States during 1998 using an original set of actual, adjacent, and potential competition variables. The estimated savings due to competition from low fares were directly responsible for $3.4 billion of these savings to passengers. The remaining $9.5 billion represents the effect that actual, adjacent, and potential competition from Southwest had on other carriers' fares. These savings amount to 20 per cent of the airline industry's 1998 domestic scheduled passenger revenue and slightly more than half of the fare reductions attributed to airline deregulation – a sizable impact from a carrier that accounts for about 7 per cent of the industry's domestic scheduled passenger miles. From a policy perspective, these results are both troubling and encouraging. On the one hand, it is troubling to find that a large part of the fare reductions from airline deregulation is due to one carrier – albeit one, along with Pacific Southwest Airlines, whose performance as an intrastate carrier not regulated by the Civil Aeronautics Board provided a natural experiment that contributed to the passage of the Airline Deregulation Act. On the other hand, if entry by the "right" carrier can make such a difference, policies that encourage entry – for example relaxing the restrictions on entry by foreign-owned carriers may have a large impact on passenger welfare.

APPENDIX

Ordinary Least Squares Regression Results
Dependent Variable: Logarithm of Average Fare
White Heteroskedasticity-Consistent Standard Errors

Variable	Coefficient	Standard Error	t-Statistic	Probability
Quarter 1 Dummy	0.052490	0.010539	4.980753	0.0%
Quarter 2 Dummy	0.015028	0.009772	1.537867	12.4%
Quarter 3 Dummy	0.000123	0.009831	0.012493	99.0%
Large Hub-Large Hub Dummy	2.377770	0.059735	39.805390	0.0%
Large Hub-Medium Hub Dummy	2.364472	0.058763	40.237720	0.0%

(Continued)

---

[29] The US Department of Transportation (1996) notes that the impact of low-fare carriers has been growing at an increasing rate.

Ordinary Least Squares Regression Results—Cont'd

Variable	Coefficient	Standard Error	t-Statistic	Probability
Large Hub-Small Hub Dummy	2.268900	0.056298	40.301470	0.0%
Large Hub-Non Hub Dummy	2.053422	0.065934	31.143380	0.0%
Medium Hub-Medium Hub Dummy	2.305377	0.059215	38.932040	0.0%
Medium Hub-Small Hub Dummy	2.247348	0.061191	36.726570	0.0%
Medium Hub-Non Hub Dummy	2.217791	0.068890	32.193100	0.0%
Small Hub-Small Hub Dummy	1.956237	0.054875	35.648990	0.0%
Small Hub-Non Hub Dummy	2.177449	0.089147	24.425440	0.0%
Washington Reagan National Dummy	−0.022675	0.021961	−1.032517	30.2%
New York Kennedy Dummy	−0.159651	0.026972	−5.919129	0.0%
New York LaGuardia Dummy	0.029887	0.015915	1.877973	0.0%
Chicago O'Hare Dummy	0.068581	0.018123	3.784230	0.0%
Percent Business Travel	0.494438	0.024715	20.005290	0.0%
Distance (logarithm)	0.408168	0.007605	53.674420	0.0%
Number of Airport in Sunbelt	−0.057146	0.006638	−8.608938	0.0%
Concentrated Hub Dummy	0.055875	0.009511	5.875008	0.0%
Southwest: At-At-Serves	−0.619880	0.022826	−27.156370	0.0%
Southwest: At-Near-Serves	−0.306484	0.023236	−13.190140	0.0%
Southwest: Near-Near-Serves	−0.167483	0.028573	−5.861661	0.0%
Southwest: At-At-Does Not Serve	−0.401170	0.027317	−14.685750	0.0%
Southwest: At-Near-Does Not Serve	−0.140334	0.033032	−4.248364	0.0%
Southwest: Near-Near-Does not Serve	0.188314	0.032628	5.771554	0.0%
Southwest: At-Far-Serves	−0.124500	0.020706	−6.012689	0.0%
Southwest: Near-Far-Serves	−0.066610	0.023775	−2.801657	0.5%
Number of Low Fare Carriers on Route	−0.233511	0.010366	−22.525530	0.0%

Ordinary Least Squares Regression Results—Cont'd

Variable	Coefficient	Standard Error	t-Statistic	Probability
Number of Major Carriers on Route	−0.029259	0.004696	−6.230184	0.0%
Number of Other Carriers on Route	−0.117270	0.020069	−5.843354	0.0%
Number of Observations = 4,000				
$R^2 = 0.739$				

Source: Author's calculation. See text for a detailed explanation of the variables.

REFERENCES

Air Transport Association (various years): *Annual Report.* Washington, DC: Air Transport Association.

Bailey, Elizabeth E., David R. Graham, and Daniel P. Kaplan (1985): *Deregulating the Airlines.* Cambridge, MA: The MIT Press.

Bailey, Elizabeth E. and John C. Panzar (1981): "The Contestability of Airline Markets during the Transition to Deregulation." *Law and Contemporary Problems*, 44, 125–45.

Baumol, William J., John C. Panzar, and Robert D. Willig (1982): *Contestable Markets and the Theory of Industrial Structure.* New York: Harcourt Brace Jovanovich.

Bennett, Randall D. and James M. Craun (1993): "The Airline Deregulation Evolution Continues: The Southwest Effect." Office of Aviation Analysis, Office of the Secretary, US Department of Transportation.

Borenstein, Severin (1989): "Hubs and High Fares: Dominance and Market Power in the US Airline Industry." *Rand Journal of Economics*, 20, 344–65.

Breyer, Stephen (1982): *Regulation and its Reform.* Cambridge: Harvard University Press. Caves, Douglas W., Laurits R. Christensen, and Michael W. Tretheway (1984): "Economies of Density versus Economies of Scale: Why Trunk and Local Service Airlines Costs Differ." *Rand Journal of Economics*, 15, 471–89.

Dresner, Martin, Jiun-Sheng Chris Lin, and Robert Windle (1996): "The Impact of LowCost Carriers on Airport and Route Competition." *Journal of Transport Economics and Policy*, 30, 309–28.

Morrison, Steven A. and Clifford Winston (1987): "Empirical Implications and Tests of the Contestability Hypothesis." *Journal of Law and Economics*, 30, 53–66.

Morrison, Steven A. and Clifford Winston (1995): *The Evolution of the Airline Industry.* Washington, DC: The Brookings Institution.

Strassmann, Diana L. (1990): "Potential Competition in the Deregulated Airlines." *The Review of Economics and Statistics*, 72, 696–702.

Transportation Research Board, National Research Council (1999): *Entry and Competition in the US Airline Industry: Issues and Opportunities.* Washington, DC: National Academy Press.

US General Accounting Office (1990): *Airline Competition: Higher Fares and Reduced Competition at Concentrated Airports.* GAO/RCED-90–102, Washington, DC.

US Department of Transportation (1996): "The Low Cost Airline Service Revolution." Windle, Robert and Martin Dresner (1995): "The Short and Long Run Effects of Entry on US Domestic Air Routes."

Advances in Airline Economics, Vol 1
Darin Lee (Editor)
© 2006 Published by Elsevier B.V.

11

Does Competition Influence Airline On-Time Performance?*

Nicholas G. Rupp[†], Douglas H. Owens[‡], and L. Wayne Plumly[§]

ABSTRACT

We investigate how route competition influences airline on-time performance. Examining the link between service quality and competition is especially relevant given recent bankruptcy filings (US Airways and United Airlines) and scheduling cutbacks since September 11th, 2001. Unlike Mayer and Sinai (2002), which use excess travel time to measure flight delays, this paper's delay calculation compares actual versus scheduled arrival times. Using a sample of over 27,000 monthly route observations between 1997 to 2000 involving more than 5.8 million flights, we find some evidence of lower service quality (both more frequent and longer flight delays) on less competitive routes.

1 INTRODUCTION

Airline on-time performance has attracted congressional attention ever since a January 1999 incident at a Detroit airport that left hundreds of passengers stuck in planes on snow-covered runways for nearly eight hours. The Senate and House held hearings in 1999 to discuss passenger treatment and a passenger bill of rights. On 17 June 1999

---

*We thank Bernie Stankus and Robert Nazreth of the Bureau of Transportation Statistics for providing the data. We thank Keith Brown, Jeff DeSimone, Mark Holmes, and Dong Li for their helpful comments and suggestions. Jim Goodman, Joe Bunting, and Michael Hopkins provided excellent research assistance.

[†]Corresponding author. Department of Economics, East Carolina University, Greenville, NC 27858-4353. E-mail: ruppn@mail.ecu.edu or (252)-328-6821.

[‡]Welch Consulting, Silver Spring, Maryland 20910.

[§]Department of Marketing and Economics, Valdosta State University, Valdosta, GA 31685-0075.

performance averages for 48 months along 150 routes of various sizes, which results in about 27,000 monthly observations involving over 5.8 million flights. In addition to data differences, the papers also use different explanatory variables. For example, Mazzeo includes some aircraft specific variables such as manufacturer, age of aircraft, and seating capacity, while this paper includes each carrier's route yield (defined as passenger revenue divided by revenue passenger miles) and the number of scheduled flights on the route. Other differences include Mazzeo uses six measures of severe weather while this study uses only two, and this paper considers four measures of route competition: the number of carriers, effective competitors, market share and a monopoly route indicator, while Mazzeo uses the monopoly route indicator.

3 ON-TIME PERFORMANCE DATA

3.1 The Sample

Airlines that account for at least 1 percent of domestic scheduled passenger revenues are required to submit monthly reports to the BTS.[3] These BTS data cover all nonstop scheduled-service domestic flights by the ten largest U.S. carriers, which account for more than 85 percent of domestic revenues in 2000 (Air Travel Consumer Report, January 2001). There are 29 U.S. airports in which these ten carriers are required to report flight operations. All of these airlines, however, have chosen to report all domestic operations voluntarily to the BTS. The result is the best source of on-time performance data for the airline industry.

Our sample includes the 100 largest domestic airport-pair routes[4] (i.e., most passengers flown in 1999), and 50 randomly selected small and mid-size routes between January 1997 and December 2000.[5] Following Borenstein (1990) and Berry (1990), travel from city A to city B is treated as a different market than travel from city B to city A. To be included as an observation, the carrier must offer a minimum of sixteen scheduled flights on a route per month. The result is a sample of 27,379 monthly observations involving 5,804,542 flights along 150 routes. Unless otherwise indicated, all variables come from or are constructed from BTS data. Descriptive statistics appear in Table 1. Flights in the sample are grouped into one of three categories: on-time (74 percent), late (23 percent), and cancelled (3 percent).[6] Flights that arrive at the gate within fifteen minutes of the scheduled time are considered "on-time". Hence *percent on-time* is the percentage of on-time arrivals on route i for carrier j at month t. Likewise, late flights arrive at the gate more than fifteen minutes after the scheduled time.

Minutes late is the average number of minutes that flights for carrier j on route i arrived after the scheduled gate arrival time in month t. This variable is constructed

[3] We thank Bernie Stankus and Robert Nazreth of the Bureau of Transportation Statistics for providing the data.
[4] We exclude international flights and intra-Hawaii island flights.
[5] Specifically, we randomly select small and medium-size routes as follows: ten routes which averaged between 1,100 and 1,500 daily passengers; ten routes with 700 to 1,100 average daily passengers; ten routes with 300 to 700 daily passengers; ten routes with 200 to 300 daily passengers; and ten routes with less than 200 daily passengers.
[6] There is also a fourth category, diverted flights, which constitute just 0.03 percent of the sample.

Table 1 Descriptive Statistics

Variable	Mean	Std. Dev.
Percentage of On-time Arrivals (Within 15 Minutes of Scheduled Time)	74.05	12.62
Minutes Late (Time Between Scheduled and Actual Gate Arrival)	12.12	8.06
Number of Carriers on Route	2.37	1.05
Effective Competitors on Route	1.97	0.75
Carrier's Market Share on Route	0.52	0.31
Monopoly Route	0.20	0.40
Carrier's Scheduled Flights on Route (Monthly)	212.0	161.6
Airport Operations at Origination (Monthly)	10,758	6,691
Airport Operations at Destination (Monthly)	10,753	6,693
Airport Hub at Origination	0.68	0.46
Airport Hub at Destination	0.68	0.46
Airline Hub at Origination	0.43	0.50
Airline Hub at Destination	0.43	0.50
Another Airline's Hub Origination	0.25	0.44
Another Airline's Hub Destination	0.25	0.43
Slot Controlled Airport at Origination	0.14	0.35
Slot Controlled Airport at Destination	0.14	0.35
Distance (miles)	936.5	723.8
Yield (dollars per mile)	0.115	0.078
Total Monthly Snowfall at Origination (inches)	0.94	3.52
Total Monthly Snowfall at Destination (inches)	0.95	3.53
Days with 0.5+ inches of precipitation at Origination	1.62	1.81
Days with 0.5+ inches of precipitation at Destination	1.61	1.81

Note: The sample includes monthly observations for all flights by major carriers on the Top 100 passenger routes between January, 1997 – December, 2000 and fifty randomly selected small and mid-size routes (monthly observations = 27,379 involving 5,804,542 flights).

from BTS data as follows: average minutes of arrival delay for late flights multiplied by the probability of being late (e.g., if late flights are delayed an average of 60 minutes and one-fourth of a carrier's flights on the route are late, then average *minutes late* equals 15 minutes). In this construct, *minutes late* treats all on-time flights as having zero minutes of arrival delay.[7] During this four-year period, flights arrived an average of 12 minutes after their scheduled time.

Various measures of route competition are considered. These include *carriers*, which is the total number of carriers on route *i*. There were an average of slightly more than two *carriers* on a route. *Market share* is a route-level measure of the percentage of flights scheduled by carrier *j* on route *i*. *Market share* provides an alternative measure of

---

[7] The BTS provided data only include the total number of arrival delay minutes for flights at least 15 minutes behind schedule, not the actual minutes delayed for all flights. We manually pulled actual minutes delayed data from the BTS web site for one-third of our sample and found the correlation between the constructed *minutes late* and actual minutes delayed to be 0.90. Similar empirical results were obtained when using actual minutes delayed instead of *minutes late*. Hence we believe that the constructed average *minutes late* variable is a reasonable proxy for delay length.

where y_{ijt} is a vector of the monthly average *percent on-time* on the ith routing[16] $(i = 1, \ldots, 300)$ of the jth carrier $(j = 1, \ldots, 10)$ for the tth month $(t = 1, \ldots, 48)$, x is a vector of route, airline, and airport characteristics, and ε is an error term. Since the dependent variable *percent on-time* is a monthly average of the on-time arrival rate for each carrier, we would like to assign more weight to observations involving more flights. More formally, we use the weighted least squares (WLS) estimation of airline on-time performance with the weight being the number of *scheduled flights* per month on the ith routing for the jth carrier at month t.

Various route level characteristics considered in the estimations include: the number of *carriers* serving the route, *effective competitors*, each carrier's route *market share*, *monopoly* routes, and *distance* between airport-pairs. Airline characteristics include the number of *scheduled flights* each month, flights originating or destined for an airline's hub airport, and *yield* for the airline on the route. Airport characteristics include the number of *airport operations* at both origination and destination airports, whether the airport serves as an *airline hub*, and *snowfall* and *rain* at origination and destination airports. Hence the typical model is specified as follows:

$$
\begin{aligned}
On-time = {} & \alpha + \beta_1 Carriers + \beta_2 Scheduled\ Flights + \beta_3 Airport\ Operations\ Orig \\
& + \beta_4 Airport\ Operations\ Dest + \beta_5 Airline\ Hub\ Orig \\
& + \beta_6 Airline\ Hub\ Dest + \beta_7 Distance + \beta_8 Yield \\
& + \beta_9 Snowfall\ Origination + \beta_{10} Snowfall\ Destination \\
& + \beta_{11} Rain\ Origination + \beta_{12} Rain\ Destination + \varepsilon_{ijt} \qquad (2)
\end{aligned}
$$

All estimations include carrier dummy variables to control for carrier specific differences such as quality of service, propensity to pad flight schedules, and fleet age. In addition, monthly dummies are included to control for seasonality in airline travel. Most estimations also use origination and destination airport dummies to control for airport congestion, among other things. Finally, we examine the length of flight delays by using a different dependent variable *minutes late* in equation (2) with the same set of explanatory variables.

5 RESULTS

5.1 The Occurrence of Flight Delays: Which Flights are Late?

Table 2a presents WLS regressions of on-time arrivals. The dependent variable in these estimations is *percent on-time*, which is the percentage of monthly flights that arrive at the gate within 15 minutes of their scheduled time. The first estimated equation shows that more competitive routes have worse on-time arrival rates with an additional *carrier* reducing on-time arrival rates by 0.85 percentage points. Additional factors which contribute to more late flights include bad weather (more *snow* and *rain*) at origination

---

[16] Routing refers to a directional route (i.e., LGA to BOS) whereas routes have no directional notation.

Table 2a WLS Regressions of On-time Flight Arrivals

Dependent Variable: Monthly Percentage of Flights Arriving Within 15 Minutes of Scheduled Time

	Entire Sample (1)			Entire Sample (2)			Top 100 Routes (3)		
	Coeff	Std. Error	t-Stat	Coeff	Std. Error	t-Stat	Coeff	Std. Error	t-Stat
Carriers	-0.8467	0.0863	-9.81	0.2080	0.1170	1.78	0.3074	0.1236	2.49
Scheduled Flights	-0.0090	0.0006	-15.56	-0.0034	0.0007	-4.57	-0.0032	0.0008	-4.14
Airport Operations Origination	-0.0002	0.0000	-16.60	-0.0037	0.0002	-21.40	-0.0037	0.0002	-19.53
Airport Operations Destination	-0.0002	0.0000	-16.03	-0.0035	0.0002	-19.78	-0.0036	0.0002	-19.01
Airline Hub Origination	-0.9895	0.2016	-4.91	-3.2007	0.2488	-12.86	-3.3429	0.2689	-12.43
Airline Hub Destination	2.1048	0.1992	10.56	-0.1588	0.2468	-0.64	-0.4737	0.2662	-1.78
Distance	-0.0007	0.0002	-4.70	0.0014	0.0002	6.55	0.0019	0.0003	7.22
Yield	13.4787	0.5598	12.04	15.3268	1.6032	9.56	21.1995	2.5223	8.40
Snowfall Origination	-0.3990	0.0216	-18.50	-0.3708	0.0221	-16.79	-0.3703	0.0251	-14.75
Snowfall Destination	-0.2571	0.0219	-11.75	-0.2841	0.0220	-12.91	-0.3012	0.0248	-12.15
Rain Origination	-0.8573	0.0433	-19.79	-0.9500	0.0429	-22.16	-0.9768	0.0478	-20.43
Rain Destination	-0.9509	0.0436	-21.81	-1.0693	0.0427	-25.05	-1.0950	0.0478	-22.91
Constant	77.8253	0.5228	148.87	97.3325	2.5815	37.70	251.9019	4.7474	53.06
Airport Fixed Effects	No			Yes			Yes		
R-squared	0.26			0.39			0.38		
Monthly Observations	27,379			27,379			20,743		
Number of Flights	5,804,542			5,804,542			4,930,070		

Note: Robust standard errors are reported. Regressions also include month and carrier dummies. The number of monthly scheduled flights for each airline on each route between 1997 and 2000 is the "weight" in the Weighted Least Squares estimations.

and destination airports, carriers with more monthly *scheduled flights* on a route, flights to and from airports with more operations, and flights that originate from an *airline hub*. The estimates suggest significantly better on-time arrival rates occur for *airline hub destination* flights (2.1 percentage points higher), long *distance* and high *yield* routes.

One limitation of the previous estimations, however, is that airport specific effects (e.g., congested airport facilities), are not controlled for. The inclusion of airport fixed effects wipes out any time invariant airport parameter such as airport capacity and more generally any factors impacting supply and demand that don't change much over the sample period (e.g., local population). The cross-sectional variation over routes and time-series variation during these four years are used to identify the airport hubbing and route competition effects.

Model 2 uses the same explanatory variables as the first model and it includes airport fixed effects. We find four notable changes using airport fixed effects. First, the positive and marginally significant *carriers* coefficient indicates that more competitive routes have slightly better on-time performance (0.21 percentage point increase in the on-time arrival rate for an additional carrier). Second, *airline hub destination* flights are neither more likely nor less likely to be on-time. By contrast Mayer and Sinai (2003) report slightly longer excess travel times (2 to 3 minutes) for flights destined for larger airline hubs. While we do not distinguish between hub size, our results indicate that hub destination flights are not significantly delayed on the basis of scheduled arrival times. This is an important finding, because if hub destination flights were systematically late, then such actions would jeopardize passenger connections. Third, the *airline hub origination* coefficient increases three-fold indicating that hub carriers have difficulty in satisfying on-time arrival schedules. We find that *airline hub origination* flights have 3.2 percentage points lower on-time arrival rates. Mayer and Sinai (2003) report a similar finding as hub carriers have longer excess travel times (between 3 and 6 minutes) primarily due to the banking of hub flights around peak travel times. Certainly, it is more costly for flights destined for a carrier's hub to arrive late (due to missed connections) than flights departing a carrier's hub. And fourth, long *distance* flights are now associated with better on-time arrival rates.

To check the robustness of these results, we re-estimate the model using only the Top 100 largest passenger routes (hence excluding the 50 small and medium size routes). The results (model 3) change little from the previous entire sample estimation (model 2) with the only modest change being more *carriers* along the Top 100 routes have significantly better on-time arrival rates, whereas *carriers* is only marginally significant in the entire sample. Given that so few changes occur, the remainder of the paper (unless otherwise specified) uses the entire sample representing over 5.8 million flights.

To further explore the relationship between route competition and on-time arrival rates Table 2b includes various competitive measures: *effective competitors* (the inverse of the route's Herfindahl index), route *market share*, and *monopoly* routes. Regardless of how route competition is defined, we find a consistent result: more competitive routes have better on-time performance. Since counting the number of route carriers makes no distinction between those large and small, model 4 uses *effective competitors* instead of *carriers*. The results indicate that routes with more *effective competitors* have significantly higher on-time flight arrival rates. Specifically, an additional *effective competitor* increases the on-time arrival average by 0.37 percentage points, a larger effect

Table 2b WLS Regressions of On-time Flight Arrivals – The Effect of Route Competition

Dependent Variable: Monthly Percentage of Flights Arriving Within 15 Minutes of Scheduled Time

	Entire Sample (4)			Entire Sample (5)			Entire Sample (6)		
	Coeff	Std. Error	t-Stat	Coeff	Std. Error	t-Stat	Coeff	Std. Error	t-Stat
Effective Competitors	0.3723	0.1574	2.37	—	—	—	—	—	—
Market Share	—	—	—	−2.5956	0.4546	−5.71	—	—	—
Monopoly	—	—	—	—	—	—	−0.4216	0.2480	−1.70
Scheduled Flights	−0.0030	0.0007	−4.11	−0.0013	0.0009	−1.50	−0.0033	0.0007	−4.53
Airport Operations Origination	−0.0037	0.0002	−21.51	−0.0037	0.0002	−21.76	−0.0037	0.0002	−21.44
Airport Operations Destination	−0.0035	0.0002	−19.85	−0.0035	0.0002	−20.06	−0.0035	0.0002	−19.76
Airline Hub Origination	−3.1983	0.2477	−12.91	−3.0422	0.2461	−12.36	−3.2539	0.2440	−13.33
Airline Hub Destination	−0.1532	0.2464	−0.62	0.0079	0.2451	0.03	−0.2096	0.2435	−0.86
Distance	0.0014	0.0002	6.76	0.0018	0.0002	8.34	0.0014	0.0002	6.42
Yield	15.5323	1.6108	9.64	16.7835	1.5977	10.50	15.6534	1.6064	9.74
Snowfall Origination	−0.3707	0.0221	−16.80	−0.3701	0.0220	−16.80	−0.3708	0.0221	−16.79
Snowfall Destination	−0.2840	0.0220	−12.91	−0.2835	0.0220	−12.90	−0.2842	0.0220	−12.91
Rain Origination	−0.9502	0.0429	−22.17	−0.9495	0.0429	−22.16	−0.9502	0.0428	−22.18
Rain Destination	−1.0696	0.0427	−25.08	−1.0691	0.0426	−25.08	−1.0695	0.0427	−25.07
Constant	97.3941	2.5824	37.72	100.6732	2.6323	38.25	98.0656	2.6007	37.71
Airport Fixed Effects	Yes			Yes			Yes		
R-squared	0.39			0.39			0.39		
Monthly Observations	27,379			27,379			27,379		
Number of Flights	5,804,542			5,804,542			5,804,542		

Note: Robust standard errors are reported. Regressions also include month and carrier dummies. The number of monthly scheduled flights for each airline on each route between 1997 and 2000 is the "weight" in the Weighted Least Squares estimations.

than found for an additional *carrier* of 0.21 percentage points (from model 2). Moreover, *carriers* is only marginally significance in model 2. Finally, we find similar results for all other explanatory variables in model 4 (i.e., same signs and statistical significance as previously reported in model 2).

Model 5 includes route *market share* to analyze the effect of route competition. Carriers with a larger route *market share* have significantly lower on-time flight arrival averages. For examples, a one standard deviation (or 31 percentage points) increase in route *market share* reduces on-time arrival rates by 0.80 percentage points. The magnitude of a carrier's presence on a route is also captured by the number of monthly *scheduled flights* on a route. The negative coefficient for *scheduled flights* suggests a consistent story with *market share*, a route with more *scheduled flights* has lower on-time performance. Yet, in model 5 *scheduled flights* is not statistically significant. This is likely due to the inclusion of both *market share* and *scheduled flights* in the same equation, since carriers that have more *scheduled flights* typically have a larger route *market share*. Hence *market share* may capture most, if not all, of the *scheduled flights* effect. In every other estimation (models 1 through 9) *scheduled flights* achieves statistical significance and tells a consistent story: carriers with more *scheduled flights* on a route have worse on-time performance. The magnitude of *scheduled flights* remains small, yet significant: an additional daily *scheduled flight* on a route reduces the average on-time arrival rate by 0.09 percentage points (i.e., from model 4: $0.003*30 = 0.09$).

The on-time performance of *monopoly* carriers is presented in model 6 of Table 2b. The results indicate that monopolist carriers have marginally worse on-time flight arrival averages. Specifically, a *monopoly* route has an on-time arrival rate that is 0.42 percentage points lower than routes served by two or more carriers. While caution should be exerted in inferring too much from a marginally significant variable, the pattern remains clear. Using various measures of route competition, i.e., the number of *carriers*, *effective competitors*, *market share*, and *monopoly* routes, we find statistically worse on-time performance, in terms of arriving within 15 minutes of the scheduled time, on less competitive routes. The magnitude of these route competition effects, however, is small, since an additional route *carrier*, an additional *effective competitor*, a one-standard deviation in a carrier's route *market share* or a *monopolist* route change the average on-time arrival rate by less than one percentage point.

Next, we explore how hub airports affect on-time flight arrivals. The magnitude of the hub airport effect is considerably larger (three to five times larger) than the effect of route competition. In models 2–6 from Tables 2a and 2b, we find two consistent hub results: first, *airline hub origination* flights have significantly lower on-time arrival rates (between 3.0 and 3.3 percentage points); second, on-time performance for flights that are destined for an airline's hub are neither more likely nor less likely to be on-time. The importance of the origination airport is not surprising given that the FAA reports that 75% of all flight delays in 2000 occurred before the flight leaves the ground (U.S. DOT Report AV-2001-020).

Table 2c further investigates the effect of *airport hubs* and *airline hubs*. Recall that *airport hub* represents an airport which serves as a hub for at least one carrier (i.e., Atlanta Hartsfield), whereas *airline hub* indicates that a particular airline has a hub at that airport (i.e., US Airways at Charlotte Douglas). We begin by first considering the *airport hub* effect in model 7. We find a surprising result: *airport hub origination*

Table 2c WLS Regressions of On-time Flight Arrivals – The Effect of Hub Airports

Dependent Variable: Monthly Percentage of Flights Arriving Within 15 Minutes of Scheduled Time

	Entire Sample (7)			Entire Sample (8)			Entire Sample Except Slot Controlled Airports (9)		
	Coeff	Std. Error	t-Stat	Coeff	Std. Error	t-Stat	Coeff	Std. Error	t-Stat
Carriers	0.3351	0.1137	2.95	0.0714	0.1175	0.61	0.1796	0.1307	1.37
Scheduled Flights	−0.0060	0.0006	−9.44	−0.0032	0.0007	−4.34	−0.0019	0.0008	−2.24
Airport Operations Origination	−0.0037	0.0002	−21.64	−0.0037	0.0002	−21.51	−0.0031	0.0002	−16.65
Airport Operations Destination	−0.0034	0.0002	−19.67	−0.0035	0.0002	−19.85	−0.0030	0.0002	−15.96
Airport Hub Origination	2.3104	0.8551	2.70	–	–	–	–	–	–
Airport Hub Destination	5.9813	0.7601	7.87	–	–	–	–	–	–
Airline Hub Origination	–	–	–	0.8190	0.8796	0.93	1.5872	1.0817	1.47
Airline Hub Destination	–	–	–	4.8164	0.7811	6.17	4.6824	0.9934	4.71
Another Airline's Hub Origination	–	–	–	4.2582	0.8656	4.92	5.4174	1.0479	5.17
Another Airline's Hub Destination	–	–	–	5.2288	0.7680	6.81	5.7246	0.9636	5.94
Distance	0.0012	0.0002	5.65	0.0016	0.0002	7.70	0.0019	0.0002	7.69
Yield	14.846	1.6097	9.22	15.496	1.5987	9.69	5.8294	1.7044	3.42
Snowfall Origination	−0.3712	0.0221	−16.78	−0.3706	0.0221	−16.76	−0.3263	0.0300	−10.86
Snowfall Destination	−0.2842	0.0222	−12.82	−0.2837	0.0220	−12.87	−0.1917	0.0284	−6.74
Rain Origination	−0.9493	0.0431	−22.04	−0.9492	0.0428	−22.18	−0.9582	0.0475	−20.17
Rain Destination	−1.0694	0.0427	−25.06	−1.0692	0.0426	−25.12	−1.0820	0.0468	−23.10
Constant	97.933	2.6478	36.99	98.374	2.6529	37.08	93.906	2.8226	33.27
Airport Fixed Effects	Yes			Yes			Yes		
R-squared	0.39			0.39			0.41		
Monthly Observations	27,379			27,379			19,797		
Number of Flights	5,804,348			5,804,348			4,150,570		

Note: Robust standard errors are reported. Regressions also include month and carrier dummies. The number of monthly scheduled flights for each airline on each route between 1997 and 2000 is the "weight" in the Weighted Least Squares estimations.

flights have significantly better on-time performance (2.3 percentage points higher) than flights that originate from non-hub airports. More than two-thirds of the flights in the sample originate from hub airports. The *airport hub destination* effect is even larger in magnitude as these flights had approximately 6.0 percentage points higher on-time flight arrival rates than flights not destined for hub airports. Since at a typical hub, a majority of the passengers make connections (Morrison and Winston, 1995, p. 44), an airline can minimize customer inconvenience (i.e., reissuing tickets for missed connections), by providing better service to flights destined for hubs. This also becomes a profit maximizing issue for evening flights, since airlines are responsible for providing overnight food and lodging for passengers missing connections due to a factor within the airline's control. The sign and significance of the remaining explanatory variables closely resemble previously reported findings with one minor exception: more route *carriers* significantly improve on-time flight arrival rates (model 7) instead of being only marginally significant (model 2).

Given the counter-intuitive result of better on-time performance from hub airports, we decompose the *airport hub* effect into performance by hub airlines and non-hub airlines at a hub airport. Model 8 shows that the primary factor contributing to better performance from hub airports is the significantly better on-time rates of the non-hub carriers at the hub airport. Specifically, flights which originate from *another airline's hub* have 4.3 percentage points higher on-time arrival rates. Whereas flights from an airline's own hub airport show no noticeable improvement in on-time performance. A test that the *airline hub origination* and *another airline's hub origination* coefficients are equivalent is easily rejected (p-value $= 0.000$). The results are consistent with the Mayer and Sinai (2003) finding that hub carriers bank flight departures around peak travel times to minimize passenger connection times. Without the connection concerns, non-hub airlines at hub airports more evenly disperse flights throughout the day, hence avoiding peak airport congestion periods and resulting in significantly better on-time performance. Or alternatively, non-hub airlines may provide better service due to diseconomies of scale since one gate crew is responsible for only one gate (e.g., America West has just one gate at DFW and United has just three DFW gates).

Model 8 also indicates that on-time performance rates for hub airport destinations involving hub and non-hub airlines are significantly better: 4.8 and 5.2 percentage points higher, respectively. We are unable to reject the equivalence of *airline hub destination* and *another airline's hub destination* coefficients at standard significance levels (p-value $= 0.095$). In sum, these on-time arrival results indicate significant service quality differences exist for flights originating from hub airports for hub and non-hub airlines, with the non-hub airline providing better service. For flights destined for hub airports we do not find a gap in service quality for hub and non-hub airlines.

Finally, we exclude observations from the four slot-controlled airports and re-estimate the previous model 8 equation. The results appear as model 9 in Table 2c. Notice that all variables maintain their previous sign and level of significance. While some of the coefficient magnitudes may have changed slightly, all qualitative implications remain unchanged.

While this paper has emphasized the effects of route competition and airport hubs, there are other delay factors such as weather, *distance*, and *yield* which are also important. In models 1–9, we find more *snowfall* at both origination and destination airports is associated with significantly worse on-time performance. The estimations indicate that an additional inch of *snowfall* during a month at the origination and destination airports reduces on-time performance by 0.37 and 0.28 percentage points, respectively. Service quality also suffers on wet-weather days. Specifically, an additional day in which precipitation exceeds one-half an inch reduces *percent on-time* by about 0.95 and 1.07 percentage points at the origination and destination airports, respectively.

In all of the models that include airport fixed effects (models 2–9) we find that long *distance* flights have significantly better on-time arrival rates. For example, these estimations indicate that increasing the flight distance by 100 miles raises *percent on-time* by between 0.14 and 0.19 percentage points. These results suggest that pilots may "make-up" time while airborne, hence the better on-time performance of longer flights. Alternatively, these longer flights might be considered more important and the airline may give them priority over shorter flights.

Finally, a novelty of this paper is the inclusion of a carrier's *yield* in the on-time performance estimation. Previous airline service quality studies (Foreman and Shea 1999; Mazzeo 2003; Mayer and Sinai 2003) have not directly controlled for revenue or revenue per mile.[17] We find that higher *yield* (dollars per mile) flights have significantly better on-time performance in models (1–9). Given that Suzuki (2000) finds passengers are more likely to switch carriers after experiencing flight delays, carriers may provide better service quality on high yield routes in order to retain these passengers. In the next section, we examine the length of the flight delay.

5.2   The Magnitude of Flight Delays: How Late was the Flight?

Tables 3(a-c) investigate average *minutes late*, which is the difference between scheduled and actual gate arrival. Again, we construct average *minutes late* by multiplying the average number of minutes delayed if the flight is late times the probability of being late. The first estimation of average delay length is model 10, which appears in Table 3a. We initially find longer delays on routes with more *carriers* and more monthly *scheduled flights*. In addition, it is not surprising to see that busier airports (both origination and destination) also have longer delays. Flights originating from an *airline hub* have little effect on *minutes late* while flights destined for an *airline hub* had significantly shorter delays. *Minutes late* decreases for long *distance* and high *yield* flights. Longer delays occur at airports that experience more *snowfall* and *rain*. Since the above estimations do not control for important airport specific effects such as airport capacity, we down-play the importance of the model 10 results. Hence all remaining estimated models (11–18) include airport fixed effects and should provide a more accurate depiction of the relevant delay factors.

After including airport specific effects in the estimation, we find four notable changes. First, more competitive routes, measured by the number of *carriers*, now have significantly shorter average delays. Specifically, model 11 indicates that an additional *carrier* on a route reduces *minutes late* by 0.26 minutes. This finding is also consistent with the results discussed in the previous section (more *carriers* have better on-time arrival rates).

---

[17] Prior studies have included distance, which is a rough proxy for revenue.

Table 3a WLS Regressions of Average Delay Length

Dependent Variable: Monthly Average Minutes Late (Time Between Scheduled and Actual Gate Arrival)

	Entire Sample (10)			Entire Sample (11)			Top 100 Routes (12)		
	Coeff	Std. Error	t-Stat	Coeff	Std. Error	t-Stat	Coeff	Std. Error	t-Stat
Carriers	0.5886	0.0563	10.45	-0.2611	0.0763	-3.42	-0.2845	0.0814	-3.50
Scheduled Flights	0.0024	0.0004	5.99	-0.0010	0.0005	-1.97	-0.0010	0.0006	-1.83
Airport Operations Origination	0.0001	0.0000	12.58	0.0023	0.0001	20.65	0.0023	0.0001	18.67
Airport Operations Destination	0.0001	0.0000	10.81	0.0021	0.0001	18.00	0.0021	0.0001	16.77
Airline Hub Origination	0.1755	0.1276	1.38	1.3241	0.1595	8.30	1.3936	0.1725	8.08
Airline Hub Destination	-1.0300	0.1255	-8.21	0.1148	0.1587	0.72	0.2572	0.1718	1.50
Distance	-0.0005	0.0001	-5.53	-0.0021	0.0001	-14.98	-0.0024	0.0002	-13.59
	—			—			—		
Yield	14.3407	0.7400	19.38	14.1165	1.0149	-13.91	17.2469	1.6650	-10.36
Snowfall Origination	0.2232	0.0160	13.93	0.2010	0.0162	12.39	0.1976	0.0187	10.59
Snowfall Destination	0.1089	0.0147	7.43	0.1280	0.0146	8.78	0.1399	0.0164	8.51
Rain Origination	0.6326	0.0294	21.50	0.6511	0.0295	22.04	0.6784	0.0334	20.33
Rain Destination	0.5885	0.0299	19.71	0.6623	0.0293	22.59	0.6948	0.0331	21.02
Constant	7.8815	0.3261	24.17	-3.9936	1.4146	-2.82	92.0404	3.0834	-29.85
Airport Fixed Effects	No			Yes			Yes		
R-squared	0.24			0.39			0.39		
Monthly Observations	27,379			27,379			20,743		
Number of Flights	5,804,542			5,804,542			4,930,070		

Note: Robust standard errors are reported. Regressions also include month and carrier dummies. The number of monthly scheduled flights for each airline on each route between 1997 and 2000 is the "weight" in the Weighted Least Squares estimations.

Table 3b WLS Regressions of Average Delay Length – The Effect of Route Competition

Dependent Variable: Monthly Average Minutes Late (Time Between Scheduled and Actual Gate Arrival)

	Entire Sample (13)			Entire Sample (14)			Entire Sample (15)		
	Coeff	Std. Error	t-Stat	Coeff	Std. Error	t-Stat	Coeff	Std. Error	t-Stat
Effective Competitors	−0.2933	0.1000	−2.93	—	—	—	—	—	—
Market Share	—	—	—	2.4770	0.2864	8.65	—	—	—
Monopoly	—	—	—	—	—	—	0.6140	0.1561	3.93
Scheduled Flights	−0.0013	0.0005	−2.43	−0.0030	0.0006	−4.94	−0.0010	0.0005	−1.99
Airport Operations Origination	0.0023	0.0001	20.77	0.0024	0.0001	21.09	0.0023	0.0001	20.68
Airport Operations Destination	0.0021	0.0001	18.05	0.0021	0.0001	18.39	0.0021	0.0001	17.98
Airline Hub Origination	1.3792	0.1604	8.60	1.2096	0.1579	7.66	1.3771	0.1573	8.76
Airline Hub Destination	0.1675	0.1597	1.05	−0.0075	0.1581	−0.05	0.1643	0.1575	1.04
Distance	−0.0020	0.0001	15.20	−0.0024	0.0001	17.25	−0.0020	0.0001	−15.00
Yield	14.1923	1.0187	13.93	15.4512	1.0076	15.33	14.6290	1.0111	−14.47
Snowfall Origination	0.2010	0.0162	12.39	0.2005	0.0162	12.38	0.2011	0.0162	12.39
Snowfall Destination	0.1279	0.0146	8.78	0.1274	0.0145	8.77	0.1280	0.0146	8.79
Rain Origination	0.6515	0.0295	22.10	0.6507	0.0295	22.06	0.6512	0.0295	22.09
Rain Destination	0.6627	0.0293	22.65	0.6623	0.0293	22.62	0.6626	0.0293	22.64
Constant	−4.1592	1.4159	−2.94	−4.9133	1.4551	−3.38	−5.0110	1.4302	−3.50
Airport Fixed Effects	Yes			Yes			Yes		
R-squared	0.39			0.39			0.39		
Monthly Observations	27,379			27,379			27,379		
Number of Flights	5,804,542			5,804,542			5,804,542		

Note: Robust standard errors are reported. Regressions also include month and carrier dummies. The number of monthly scheduled flights for each airline on each route between 1997 and 2000 is the "weight" in the Weighted Least Squares estimations.

Table 3c WLS Regressions of Average Delay Length – The Effect of Hub Airport
Dependent Variable: Monthly Average Minutes Late (Time Between Scheduled and Actual Gate Arrival)

	Entire Sample (16)			Entire Sample (17)			Entire Sample Except Slot Controlled Airports (18)		
	Coeff	Std. Error	t-Stat	Coeff	Std. Error	t-Stat	Coeff	Std. Error	t-Stat
Carriers	-0.2952	0.0751	-3.93	-0.1758	0.0773	-2.27	-0.2732	0.0846	-3.23
Scheduled Flights	0.0001	0.0005	0.31	-0.0011	0.0005	-2.17	-0.0014	0.0006	-2.28
Airport Operations Origination	0.0024	0.0001	20.83	0.0023	0.0001	20.74	0.0020	0.0001	16.26
Airport Operations Destination	0.0021	0.0001	17.96	0.0021	0.0001	18.06	0.0017	0.0001	13.92
Airport Hub Origination	-1.7808	0.4143	-4.30	–	–	–	–	–	–
Airport Hub Destination	-3.6163	0.4730	-7.65	–	–	–	–	–	–
Airline Hub Origination	–	–	–	-1.1129	0.4305	-2.58	-2.1320	0.4873	-4.37
Airline Hub Destination	–	–	–	-3.0764	0.4855	-6.34	-3.8670	0.5922	-6.53
Another Airline's Hub Origination	–	–	–	-2.5833	0.4223	-6.12	-3.6505	0.4666	-7.82
Another Airline's Hub Destination	–	–	–	-3.3524	0.4775	-7.02	-4.2063	0.5760	-7.30
Distance	-0.0020	0.0001	-14.84	-0.0022	0.0001	-16.04	-0.0026	0.0002	-15.73
Yield	-13.9272	1.0160	-13.71	-14.2223	1.0110	-14.07	-8.2800	1.1298	-7.33
Snowfall Origination	0.2012	0.0162	12.41	0.2010	0.0162	12.37	0.1735	0.0207	8.37
Snowfall Destination	0.1279	0.0146	8.74	0.1277	0.0146	8.76	0.0835	0.0181	4.62
Rain Origination	0.6506	0.0295	22.02	0.6506	0.0295	22.07	0.6480	0.0330	19.63
Rain Destination	0.6624	0.0292	22.68	0.6623	0.0292	22.66	0.6447	0.0325	19.85
Constant	-4.5245	1.4387	-3.14	-4.7207	1.4414	-3.27	1.2591	1.4594	0.86
Airport Fixed Effects	Yes			Yes			Yes		
R-squared	0.39			0.39			0.41		
Monthly Observations	27,379			27,379			19,797		
Number of Flights	5,804,542			5,804,542			4,150,570		

Note: Robust standard errors are reported. Regressions also include month and carrier dummies. The number of monthly scheduled flights for each airline on each route between 1997 and 2000 is the "weight" in the Weighted Least Squares estimations.

Second, routes with more *scheduled flights* on a route now have slightly shorter flight delays. Specifically, an additional daily *scheduled flight* (or 30 more *scheduled flights* per month) shortens average *minutes late* by 0.03 minutes (or less than two seconds). Third, flights that originate from an airline's hub have significantly longer flight delays. Whereas previously *airline hub* did not achieve standard statistical significance levels, we find that flights from an *airline hub* arrive an average of 1.32 minutes later than flights by a non-hub airline. Finally, flights destined for an *airline hub* are no longer associated with significantly shorter delays. Instead, we find that *airline hub destination* has minimal effect on average *minutes late* after controlling for airport specific effects. The results for the remaining variables were similar to those previously reported in model 10.

More take-offs and landings at both origination and destination airports contribute to longer flight delays.[18] Weather remains an important factor in determining on-time performance as more *snow* and *rain* lengthen airport delays. For example, another day of *rain* at the origination airport increases the monthly average *minutes late* by 0.65 minutes. Likewise, *rain* at the destination airport causes delays of similar length. Long *distance* and high *yield* flights have shorter average delays. This result is more evidence that carriers provide better service quality on higher *yield* routes. It is also interesting to note that according to the model 11 estimations, each of the following events would increase the average monthly *minutes late* by a similar magnitude (between 0.20 and 0.23 minutes): an additional 100 monthly flights (take-offs or landings) at the origination airport, one more inch of snow at the origination airport, and a 100 mile reduction in flight distance.

To verify the robustness of these delay results we re-estimate the model using only the Top 100 largest passenger routes (as of 1999). Few changes are found. The explanatory power of *scheduled flights* is slightly diminished as it is only marginally significant in the Top 100. Statistically, this is a minor change, since the coefficient is identical and the *t*-statistic changes by less than two-tenths of a point. The effect of *scheduled flights*, however, remains minimal, since an additional daily *scheduled flight* still only changes average *delay length* by less than two seconds. Since the results appear to be robust to the alternative sample of only the largest passenger routes, the remaining estimations use the entire sample (unless otherwise specified).

Table 3b examines the effect of route competition on average *minutes late*. Consistent with our previous finding that more competitive routes have higher on-time arrival rates (see Table 2b), we now show in Table 3b that more competitive routes also have shorter flight delays. We again use three different measures of route competition: *effective competitors*, *market share*, and *monopoly routes*. Model 13 shows that routes with an additional *effective competitor* reduces average *minutes late* by 0.29 minutes. Likewise, a one-standard deviation (or 31 percentage points) increase in a carrier's route *market share* lengthens average *minutes late* by 0.77 minutes (see model 14). Finally, *monopoly* routes in model 15 have 0.61 minutes longer average *minutes late*. Similar results are found for the remaining explanatory variables.

Table 3c considers the effect of hub airports on average flight delay. Once again, the magnitude of the airport hub effect is considerably larger than the route competition

---

[18] For a theoretical model relating on-time performance and airport concentration see Brueckner (2003).

effect. Model 16 shows that *airport hubs* have significantly shorter delays of 1.78 and 3.61 minutes at origination and destination airports, respectively. This result is consistent with the previously documented higher on-time flight arrival rate at both hub origination and destination airports (see model 7). We decompose the *airport hub* effect by separating carriers that serve hub airports into two types: hub airlines and non-hub airlines in model 17. We find that at the origination airport *airline hub* and *another airline's hub* have significantly shorter *minutes late* of 1.11 and 2.58 minutes, respectively. Once again, non-hub airlines perform relatively better than their hub airline counterparts, since we can easily reject the equivalence of *airline hub* and *another airline's hub origination* coefficients (p-value = 0.000). Nonetheless, the finding that hub airlines have shorter flight delays is surprising given the banking of flights at peak travel times. Flights destined for an *airline hub* or *another airline's hub* also experience shorter flight delays of similar magnitude: 3.08 and 3.35 minutes early, respectively. We cannot reject the equivalence of these coefficients at standard significance levels (p-value = 0.083). Again, it is important that flights destined for an airline's hub arrive on-time and have shorter delays to enable passengers to make connecting flights.

Finally model 18 excludes the nation's four slot-controlled airports. Results are little changed except that the magnitude of the airline hub and another airline's hub coefficients are larger in absolute value. This suggests that excluding the slot-controlled airports, both hub and non-hub airlines have even shorter delays at hub airports.

6 CONCLUSION

Since September 11th, airline scheduled service has been drastically reduced, two major carriers (US Airways and United Airlines) have declared bankruptcy while Delta Airlines and American Airlines have experienced tremendous financial pressure. US Airways and United have recently announced a code-share agreements as have Continental, Northwest, and Delta. Southwest Airlines has taken an equity stake in financially troubled low cost carrier ATA. US Airways and America West have recently proposed a merger. Further consolidation in the airline industry appears inevitable. This paper establishes a link between airline service quality and route competition. Using various measures of route competition (number of carriers, effective competitors, route market share, or monopoly route indicator) the result is the same: competitive routes have slightly higher on-time arrival rates (between 0.2 and 0.8 percentage points) and shorter average flight delays (between 0.3 and 0.7 minutes). Should further consolidation occur in the airline industry, consumers may expect slightly worse service quality.

The paper finds that hub airports have a larger influence on airline service quality than the effect of route competition. We find significantly worse service quality for flights that originate from an airline's hub as these flights have between 3.0 and 3.3 percentage points lower average on-time arrival rates and these flights have between 1.2 to 1.4 minutes of additional flight delay. Lower service quality of hub airlines does not necessarily indicate that social welfare suffers; we have not accounted for the network benefits from hubbing such as short connection times, possibly lower operating costs, and access to a larger set of destinations.[19] In fact, we find that flights to and from hub airports are also more likely to arrive on schedule and have shorter average delays than non-hub airports. The primary reason for better performance from hub airports is the significantly higher on-time arrival rates of the non-hub carriers at the hub airport. Non-hub airlines also have relatively shorter average flight delays than their hub airline counterparts. We suspect that the better performance of non-hub airlines is related to fewer peak-time departures. For flights destined for hub airports we find no difference in service quality of hub and non-hub airlines.

REFERENCES

Adelman, M.A. 1969. 'Comment on the 'H' Concentration Measure as a Numbers-Equivalent', *Review of Economics and Statistics*, 51, pp. 99–101.

Berry, Steven T. 1990. 'Airport Presence as Product Differentiation', *American Economic Review Papers and Proceedings*, 80:2, pp. 394–99.

Borenstein, Severin. 1989. 'Hubs and High Fares: Dominance and Market Power in the US Airline Industry', *Rand Journal of Economics*, 20, pp. 344–68.

——. 1990. 'Airline Mergers, Airport Dominance, and Market Power', *American Economic Review Papers and Proceedings*, 80:2, pp. 400–04.

Borenstein, Severin and Janet Netz. 1999. 'Why Do All the Flights Leave at 8 am?: Competition and Departure-time Differentiation in Airline Markets', *International Journal of Industrial Organization*, 17, pp. 611–40.

Foreman, Stephen Earl and Dennis G. Shea. 1999. 'Publication of Information and Market Response: The Case of Airline on Time Performance Reports', *Review of Industrial Organization*, 14, pp. 147–62.

Kim, E. Han and Vijay Singal. 1993. 'Mergers and Market Power: Evidence from the Airline Industry', *American Economic Review*, 83:3, pp. 549–69.

Kocher, Daniel. 2001. 'Airline Competition, Flight Delays Continue to Worry Congress', *Nation's Cities Weekly*, 24:13, p. 12.

Mann, Paul. 2001. 'Congress Bearish on Big Carriers', *Aviation Week & Space Technology*, 154:11, pp. 66–67.

Mayer, Christopher and Todd Sinai. 2003. 'Network Effects, Congestion Externalities, and Air Traffic Delays: Or Why All Delays Are Not Evil', *American Economic Review*, 93:4, pp. 1194–215.

Mazzeo, Michael. 2003. 'Competition and Service Quality in the U.S. Airline Industry", *Review of Industrial Organization*, 22:4, pp. 275–96.

Morrison, Steven and Clifford Winston. 1989. 'Enhancing the Performance of the Deregulated Air Transportation System', *Brookings Papers on Economic Activity: Microeconomics*, 1, pp. 61–112.

——. 1990. 'The Dynamics of Airline Pricing and Competition', *American Economic Review Papers and Proceedings*, 80:2, pp. 389–93.

——. 1995. *The Evolution of the Airline Industry*. Washington, D.C.: The Brookings Institution.

Rupp, Nicholas G., George M. Holmes, and Jeff DeSimone. 2005. 'Airline Schedule Recovery after Airport Closures: Empirical Evidence since September 11th', *Southern Economic Journal*, 71:4, pp. 800–20.

---

[19] See Mayer and Sinai (2002) for a discussion of the benefits provided by a hub network.

Rupp, Nicholas G. and George M. Holmes. 2006. 'An Investigation Into the Determinants of Flight Cancellations', forthcoming *Economica*.

Rupp, Nicholas G. 2005. 'Flight Delays and Cancellations', working paper East Carolina University Department of Economics.

Suzuki, Yoshinori. 2000. 'The Relationship between On time Performance and Airline Market Share', *Transportation Research: Part E: Logistics and Transportation Review*, 36:2, pp. 139–54.

U.S. Department of Transportation. 2001. Office of Aviation Enforcement and Proceedings, *Air Travel Consumer Report* (January 2001 and February 2001), Washington, D.C.: US Government Printing Office.

U.S. Department of Transportation. 2001. Office of Inspector General, *Final Report on the Airline Customer Service Commitment*, Report AV-2001-020, Washington, D.C., US Government Printing Office.

Wall Street Journal. 1999. 'Airlines Promise Measures to Boost Customer Service', 18 June, p. A6.

——. 2001. 'Airline Workers Decry Use of Clause Excluding Them from Bailout Plan', 26 September.

Advances in Airline Economics, Vol 1
Darin Lee (Editor)
© 2006 Published by Elsevier B.V.

12

Concentration, Market Share Inequality and Prices: An Examination of European Airline Markets[*]

Stephanie GIAUME
University of Nice-Sophia Antipolis, CNRS[†]

Sarah GUILLOU
University of Nice-Sophia Antipolis, CNRS

ABSTRACT

This paper investigates the link between market structure and ticket prices on intra-European airline routes. Our database contains ticket prices offered by all the carriers serving Nice Airport (France) flying to European destinations. Our analysis has two aims: first, to examine how concentration and other route- and ticket-specific factors affect offered prices; second, to test the hypothesis that higher market concentration reduces price discrimination. The market structure is examined using three measures of concentration: the Herfindahl-Hirschman Index (HHI), the decomposed HHI, and the Gini coefficient. We find that concentration has a negative effect on the prices offered for a particular route. We also show that concentration, measured by the inequality of market shares, reduces the price discrimination practices of European carriers. In other words, our results show that the discounts offered are smaller on the least competitive routes, and consequently, price dispersion is smaller on these routes.

[*]We would like to thank J. Stavins, N. Rupp, M. Rainelli, V. Bilotkach, P. Barla, D. Lee and M. Lijesen for their helpful comments.
[†]Lavoisier post-doctoral fellowship at the Centre for Research on Transportation (CRT) at the University of Montreal. Corresponding Author. E-mail addresses: giaume@idefi.cnrs.fr or giaume@crt.umontreal.ca (S. Giaume), guillou@idefi.cnrs.fr (S. Guillou).

This measure is not adequate because it does not differentiate firm size inequality and number of firms. Moreover, the analysis of firm size inequality appears to be important to the extent that European routes are nearly always served by the same number of carriers. So, based on Adelman (1969), we split the HHI into two parts in order to show the respective contributions of the number of firms and market share inequality to the HHI. The decomposed HHI is given by:

$$HHI = cv^2/N + 1/N$$

In this form, we can easily discern the separate contributions of the two terms. The first term represents the market share inequality of firms (cv^2/N) where cv is the coefficient of variation of market shares on a route, and the second term corresponds to the value of HHI when the firms have equal market shares ($1/N$)[16]. To control for market share inequality, we also use the Gini coefficient. Unlike the HHI, the Gini coefficient can be very sensitive to data on small firms[17]. The Gini of market shares may be written as (see Barla, 2000):

$$Gini = \frac{(N + 1 - 2\sum_j jS_{ij})}{(N - 1)}$$

where N represents the number of carriers on each route and S_{ij} reflects the market share of carrier j on route i. Carriers are ordered by decreasing size, $j = 1$ being the largest, $j = 2$ the next largest, and so on. Moreover, to avoid having the value range of Gini dependent on N, as Barla did, we replaced the denominator N with $(N - 1)$.

2.4   Airline Price Discrimination

Price discrimination is present when the same commodity is sold at different prices to different consumers, and when the price difference cannot be fully explained by differences in cost. This practice is profitable for firms because some consumers are willing to pay more than others. In the airline industry, carriers discriminate by offering consumers a variety of discount fares with restrictions attached to the tickets. We retained three kinds of restriction. Based on Pigou's (1920) classification, these restrictions correspond to two degrees of discrimination.

Requirements such as advance purchase or Saturday night stay-over are considered second-degree price discrimination. These restrictions reduce the flexibility of the ticket and introduce a quality differentiation (Salop, 1977; Mussa and Rosen, 1978; Chiang and Spatt, 1982). They allow carriers to associate a "time cost" to a ticket leading travellers to report their private information about their value of time. The extraction

---

[16] Clearly, if all firms are of the same size $cv^2 = 0$ then the HHI becomes the inverse of the number of firms. In case of a monopoly, the HHI-value is 1, and HHI diminishes as the number of firms increases. Similarly, for a given number of firms, HHI increases with the inequality of firms' market shares, i.e., as cv^2 increases.

[17] For instance, the disappearance of five small firms leaving only five large ones each with 20 per cent of the market, would rapidly reduce the value of the Gini to zero because inequality of size has disappeared, although such a situation would probably have very little effect on market behaviour and, in any event, would intuitively be considered as an increase in concentration.

of the consumer surplus by carriers becomes easier. This type of discrimination leads to self-selection because consumers reveal their reservation price through their actual purchases. Gale and Holmes (1992; 1993) demonstrate that using the advance purchase condition to screen travellers for peak time travel is an optimal profit maximization mechanism. This second-degree discrimination spreads prices and allows carriers to sort consumers in order to address the specific constraints of the airline[18].

Restrictions based on exogenous criteria (such as age) are consistent with third-degree price discrimination. Exogenous segmentation allows carriers to differentiate between customers with respect to demand price elasticity. They can successfully discriminate between different consumer groups only if the difference in demand elasticities is significant. This leads to "exogenous market segmentation" and carriers can charge a different price to the members of different groups. In practice, carriers apply the same discounts to consumers within a group. For example, students and the elderly benefit from discount prices with respect to their high price elasticity of demand.

The empirical analysis allows us to specify the relationship between pricing behaviour and market structure by introducing ticket restrictions and different measures of concentration.

3 EMPIRICAL STUDY

We propose two empirical regressions which are reduced-form regressions of airfares. In the first regression, we study how concentration, restrictions and other specific factors affect the prices offered. We assume that price discrimination does not vary with market concentration. In the second regression, we relax this assumption and assume that price discrimination depends on market concentration. For each regression, three specifications are estimated depending on the index of concentration: HHI, decomposed HHI, and Gini Coefficient. All regressions are estimated in log-linear form[19].

3.1 Concentration and Inequality of Market Share: The Impact on Prices

The first regression is estimated through the following three specifications. Each specification includes a specific index of concentration, IC. The IC is i) the HHI in the first specification; ii) in the second specification H1 and H2 replace HHI, where H1 reflects the carrier market share inequality cv^2/N and H2 captures the value of HHI when all the carriers are equal to $1/N$; and iii) Gini replaces H1 in the third specification, which controls for the distribution of market share between carriers on each route[20]:

$$\log P_{ijk} = \beta_0 + \beta_1 R_{hijk} + \beta_{2IC} IC_i + \beta_3 DAY + \beta_4 DIST_i + \beta_5 DIST_i^2$$
$$+ \beta_6 AVGPO_i + \beta_7 ONEWAY_{ijk} + \beta_8 BUSS_{ijk} + \beta_9 CSHARE_{ij}$$
$$+ \beta_{10} HUB_i + \beta_{11} LCOST_i + \beta_{12} CAR_{ij} + \varepsilon_{ijk} \qquad (1.1)$$

---

[18] These constraints are mainly: capacity constraint, a non-storable service, and uncertain demand.

[19] We also used linear-linear form and log-log form and obtained similar results.

[20] We decided not to introduce market share as this causes endogeneity problems with prices and collinearity problems with indices of concentration.

P_{ijk} is the price of round trip tickets for the route i from company j at fare k. So, i denotes the European city destination from Nice, the subscript j represents the airline company and subscript k is a particular ticket on that route. The explicative variables vary with i and/or j and/or k.

Ticket restrictions are used as proxies for price discrimination. We retained three ticket restrictions (R_{hijk}, $h = 1, 3$). First, R_1, the advance purchase time needed (number of days) to obtain that price; second, R_2, whether or not a Saturday-night stay-over is required; and third, R_3, the exogenous segmentation (family, age, student, events)[21]. R_1 and R_2 represent second-degree price discrimination. R_3 represents third degree price discrimination. To avoid multicollinearity, one restriction at a time was introduced into each specification[22].

DAY is a variable giving the number of days before the departure day when the particular ticket prices were available. This variable implicitly represents the rationing device applied to each date for which we have selected fares. Other explicative variables included are: DIST and DIST^2 which are the distance between Nice and the destination, and this distance squared; and AVGPO, the average population of the two cities. In order to take account of major influential qualitative variables, we added six dummies: (i) ONEWAY takes the value 1 when tickets are one-way; (ii) BUSS takes the value 1 when tickets are business-class tickets[23]; (iii) HUB takes the value 1 when the destination airport is a hub airport[24]; (iv) CSHARE takes the value 1 when carriers have concluded code share agreements on the route[25]; (v) LCOST takes the value 1 when a low cost carrier serves the route. We did not include the low cost carriers in our sample because their fares are not available from the Amadeus GDS. However, we introduce a dummy variable to indicate the presence of these carriers which become effective competitors[26] in the European market. Lastly, a dummy variable, CAR, for each carrier is introduced allowing us to keep costs and other carrier-specific characteristics influencing ticket prices separate. These carrier dummies stand for the fixed-effects, which control for all the unobserved factors on carriers such as carrier reputation, fleet structure, availability of gates, etc.

In the first regression, we evaluate the effect of the restrictions on prices along with the effect of all variables, which should explain the level of the airfare. We expect that restrictions reduce the price of the ticket: travelers benefit from a cut in the fare in exchange for a loss of flexibility due to restrictions. We assume that concentration positively affects prices. Standard results establish a positive correlation between prices and concentration. The coefficient DAY should be negative because fares increase as the departure date gets closer. Since the cost of flying largely depends on the distance, DIST should have a significantly positive effect on the fare. However, considering the fixed costs of landing and take off, the coefficient of squared DIST should be negative. We also expect the coefficient of AVGPO to have a positive sign as a demand effect

---

[21] Everyone belonging to each of these categories receives the same discount.

[22] The Farrar and Glauber (1967) test confirms the presence of multicollinearity.

[23] On the intra-European route, carriers have abolished first class, and only business class fares are available.

[24] This dummy should capture the effect associated with spoke-hub routes.

[25] These agreements refer to collaboration between two carriers operating on the same direct route.

[26] The traffic growth of these "no-frills" carriers has been outstanding in the European market. In 2002, low cost carriers represented 18% of the traffic at Nice Airport (DTA, 2003).

could exist[27]. Except for the coefficient LCOST, denoting competition from a low cost carrier which should reduce the level of fares, the remaining dummy variables should have positive coefficients as they all positively affect the prices offered.

3.2 Concentration and Inequality of Market Share: The Impact on Price Discrimination

In the second regression we estimate three other specifications with the same explicative variables, but with a possible relationship between price discrimination and concentration of routes. We test the hypothesis that higher market concentration and higher market share inequality reduces price discrimination in the European airline market. As in the previous section, we applied the three indices of concentration successively.

Price discrimination is measured by the effect of ticket restrictions on fares, in other words, price discrimination is revealed through discounts. Hence, changes in price discrimination involve changes in the discounts being offered to more price elastic consumers. In this case, if higher competition reduces the fares charged to price-elastic travelers, it involves an increase in price discrimination. Also, the discount associated with any given ticket restriction may increase making prices more dispersed.

We estimated the following specifications:

$$\log P_{ijk} = \alpha_0 + R_{hijk}(\gamma_h + \gamma_{1HHI}HHI_i) + \alpha_{1HHI}HHI_i + \alpha_2 DAY + \alpha_3 DIST_i$$
$$+ \alpha_4 DIST_i^2 + \alpha_5 AVGPO_i + \alpha_6 ONEWAY_{ijk} + \alpha_7 BUSS_{ijk}$$
$$+ \alpha_8 CSHARE_{ij} + \alpha_9 HUB_i + \alpha_{10} LCOST_i + \alpha_{11} CAR_{ij} + \varepsilon_{ijk} \qquad (2.1)$$

$$\log P_{ijk} = \alpha_0 + R_{hijk}(\gamma_h + \gamma_{hH1}Gini_i + \gamma_{hH2}H2_i) + \alpha_{1H1}H1_i + \alpha_{1H2}H2_i + \alpha_2 DAY$$
$$+ \alpha_3 DIST_i + \alpha_4 DIST_i^2 + \alpha_5 AVGPO_i + \alpha_6 ONEWAY_{ijk} + \alpha_7 BUSS_{ijk}$$
$$+ \alpha_8 CSHARE_{ij} + \alpha_9 HUB_i + \alpha_{10} LCOST_i + \alpha_{11} CAR_{ij} + \varepsilon_{ijk} \qquad (2.2)$$

$$\log P_{ijk} = \alpha_0 + R_{hijk}(\gamma_h + \gamma_{hGini}Gini_i + \gamma_{hH2}H2_i) + \alpha_{1Gini}Gini_i + \alpha_{1H2}H2_i + \alpha_2 DAY$$
$$+ \alpha_3 DIST_i + \alpha_4 DIST_i^2 + \alpha_5 AVGPO_i + \alpha_6 ONEWAY_{ijk} + \alpha_7 BUSS_{ijk}$$
$$+ \alpha_8 CSHARE_{ij} + \alpha_9 HUB_i + \alpha_{10} LCOST_i + \alpha_{11} CAR_{ij} + \varepsilon_{ijk} \qquad (2.3)$$

The relationship between the sensitivity of price to restrictions and concentration is given by following equations where which measure the effects of market concentration and more specifically of market share inequality on price discrimination are measured:

$$\partial P / \partial R_h = (\gamma_h + \gamma_{hHHI}HHI_i)P \qquad \text{with } h = 1, 2, 3 \qquad (2.4)$$

$$\partial P / \partial R_h = (\gamma_h + \gamma_{hH1}H1_i + \gamma_{hH2}H2)P \qquad \text{with } h = 1, 2, 3 \qquad (2.5)$$

$$\partial P / \partial R_h = (\gamma_h + \gamma_{hGini}Gini_i + \gamma_{hH2}H2_i)P \qquad \text{with } h = 1, 2, 3 \qquad (2.6)$$

---

[27] We ignore the possibility of economies of density due to larger populations as there are no really huge cities in Europe, its biggest cities being all of roughly the same size.

4 RESULTS

The tables in this section show the estimations of two regressions using Ordinary Least Square (OLS). We apply heteroskedasticity-robust standard error and covariance procedures using the White method in order to correct for standard errors.

4.1 Results on Prices

Tables 2 to 4 present the results of each of the three specifications with the three different restrictions. Whatever the specification, restrictions always have a negative impact on

Table 2 Results of HHI on Prices

	R_1	R_2	R_3
R_h	−0.032***	−0.132***	−0.327***
	(0.002)	(0.023)	(0.021)
HHI	−0.491***	−0.516***	−0.473***
	(0.144)	(0.148)	(0.138)
DAY	−0.001	−0.001	−0.001
	(0.001)	(0.001)	(0.001)
DIST	0.001**	0.001**	0.001**
	(0.0004)	(0.0004)	(0.0004)
$DIST^2$	$-6.15e^{-7}*$	$-6.77e^{-7}*$	$-6.40e^{-7}*$
	$(3.31e^{-7})$	$(3.34e^{-7})$	$(3.30e^{-7})$
AVGPO	$1.76e^{-7}***$	$1.84e^{-7}***$	$1.45e^{-7}***$
	$(4.65e^{-8})$	$(4.82e^{-8})$	$(4.75e^{-8})$
ONEWAY	0.188***	0.179***	0.186***
	(0.031)	(0.031)	(0.028)
BUSS	0.793***	0.77***	0.748***
	(0.028)	(0.032)	(0.029)
HUB	0.08*	0.08*	0.08*
	(0.041)	(0.042)	(0.041)
LCOST	−0.671***	−0.683***	−0.618***
	(0.072)	(0.075)	(0.071)
CSHARE	0.227***	0.211***	0.153***
	(0.055)	(0.056)	(0.054)
intercept	5.224***	5.172***	5.162***
	(0.246)	(0.183)	(0.18)
Sample	2016	2016	2016
Adj R^2	0.554	0.537	0.57
SCR	388.92	402.72	373.93
LogL-Ratio	−1201.45	−1236.51	−1161.939
F-statistic	87.01***	81.69***	93.23***

*** significant at 1%; ** significant at 5% and * significant at 10%. Fixed-effects not reported.

Table 3 Results of H1 and H2 on Prices

		R_1	R_2	R_3
R_h		−0.032***	−0.137***	−0.327***
		(0.002)	(0.023)	(0.021)
HHI	H1	−1.188***	−1.248***	−1.160***
		(0.205)	(0.211)	(0.198)
	H2	−0.096	−0.104	−0.086
		(0.171)	(0.175)	(0.167)
DAY		−0.001	−0.001	−0.001
		(0.001)	(0.001)	(0.001)
DIST		0.001***	0.001**	0.001**
		(0.0004)	(0.0004)	(0.0004)
DIST^2		−6.37e^{-7}*	−5.98e^{-7}*	−7.60e^{-7}*
		(3.29e^{-7})	(3.31e^{-7})	(3.27e^{-7})
AVGPO		1.24e^{-7}***	1.30e^{-7}***	9.44e^{-8}**
		(4.77e^{-8})	(4.93e^{-8})	(4.90e^{-8})
ONEWAY		0.187***	0.177***	0.185***
		(0.031)	(0.03)	(0.027)
BUSS		0.795***	0.769***	0.75***
		(0.028)	(0.031)	(0.028)
HUB		0.071*	0.069*	0.079*
		(0.04)	(0.04)	(0.04)
LCOST		−0.508***	−0.513***	−0.457***
		(0.081)	(0.084)	(0.082)
CSHARE		0.277***	0.264***	0.202***
		(0.057)	(0.057)	(0.055)
INTERCEPT		5.114***	5.062***	5.053***
		(0.257)	(0.187)	(0.174)
Sample		2016	2016	2016
Adj R^2		0.557	0.541	0.574
SCR		385.62	399.11	370.7
LogL-Ratio		−1192.87	−1227.44	−1153
F-statistic		85.35***	80.23***	91.43***

*** significant at 1%; ** significant at 5% and * significant at 10%. Fixed-effects not reported.

the level of prices. In the first specification, increasing the advance-purchase requirement (R_1) by a day results in a 3.2% decrease in the ticket price. Evaluated at the median price, the tickets sold 7 and 14 days before departure date have a discount of 72 euros and 144 euros respectively. As would be expected, the more restrictions that apply, the bigger the discount on the ticket, and therefore the lower will be, the price. A ticket that includes the restriction (R_2), i.e., Saturday-night stay-over requirement, is less expensive, by 13–14% than an unrestricted ticket. For instance, passengers who buy a ticket that

Table 4   Results of Gini and H2 on Prices

	R_1	R_2	R_3
R_h	−0.032***	−0.140***	−0.327***
	(0.002)	(0.023)	(0.021)
Gini	−0.489***	−0.515***	−0.469***
	(0.073)	(0.075)	(0.071)
H2	−0.229	−0.243	−0.210
	(0.174)	(0.178)	(0.170)
DAY	−0.001	−0.001	−0.001
	(0.001)	(0.001)	(0.001)
DIST	0.001***	0.001***	0.001***
	(0.0004)	(0.0004)	(0.0004)
$DIST^2$	$-7.86e^{-7}$**	$-6.52e^{-7}$**	$-9.05e^{-7}$***
	$(3.25e^{-7})$	$(3.28e^{-7})$	$(3.23e^{-7})$
AVGPO	$1.17e^{-7}$**	$1.22e^{-7}$**	$8.82e^{-8}$*
	$(4.77e^{-8})$	$(4.93e^{-8})$	$(4.90e^{-8})$
ONEWAY	0.185***	0.174***	0.183***
	(0.029)	(0.03)	(0.027)
BUSS	0.795***	0.768***	0.75***
	(0.027)	(0.031)	(0.028)
HUB	0.075*	0.076*	0.068*
	(0.04)	(0.041)	(0.039)
LCOST	−0.455***	−0.458***	−0.409***
	(0.083)	(0.086)	(0.083)
CSHARE	0.236***	0.221***	0.165***
	(0.058)	(0.058)	(0.056)
INTERCEPT	5.164***	5.116***	5.096***
	(0.264)	(0.191)	(0.174)
Sample	2016	2016	2016
Adj R^2	0.559	0.543	0.575
SCR	384.13	397.45	369.54
LogL-Ratio	−1188.99	−1223.26	−1150.05
F-statistic	85.93***	80.84***	91.93***

*** significant at 1%; ** significant at 5% and * significant at 10%. Fixed-effects not reported.

includes this restriction get a discount of 45 euros. The exogenous segmentation (R_3) is the most influential on the price reduction. For example, a student would pay 32% less for a ticket than a passenger not included in the segmentation group (Appendix B).

The explicative variables have the expected sign:

- The distance (DIST) and the population (AVGPO) are positive and significant, and the distance squared is negative and significant at 10%. We can see that the coefficient of these variables approximates to zero. These results seem consistent with our sample of routes and thus with all intra-European routes. The distances between cities are short and quasi-identical.

- Single tickets (ONEWAY) affect prices significantly. Buying two one-way tickets is more expensive than purchasing a one round-trip ticket. Generally, one-way tickets are always more expensive than round trip tickets: additional cost is generated by demand uncertainty.

- Business class (BUSS) induces significantly higher fares than economy class tickets. Business class tickets buy higher quality and do not have any restrictions. Business class tickets are thus more expensive.

- The presence of a hub airport at the destination (HUB) slightly influences prices; the variable is positive and significant at 10% level[28]. This result is consistent with the European airline market where intense use of hub-and-spoke networks is reduced making hub airports of little consequence on intra-European routes. Burghouwt and Hakfoort (2001) have shown that there is no clear trend towards concentration of intra-European traffic on hubs. Hubs have increased their market share in relation to intercontinental flights, which suggests that smaller airports have become more important for intra-European traffic.

- Code sharing agreements permit carriers to increase market share on the route, so CSHARE is positive and significant. This result contradicts the recent literature on domestic code sharing in the US airline industry (see Bamberger et al., 2004; Ito and Lee, 2005; Armantier and Richard, 2005). However, it seems consistent with the structure of the European airline industry where carriers have code share agreements on direct flights. Also, Armantier and Richard (2005) found evidence of significantly higher prices in the US market on routes with direct flights on Continental and Northwest airlines.

- The presence of a low-cost carrier (LCOST) reduces the prices being offered. The coefficient of the dummy LCOST is positively significant meaning that the "Southwest effect"[29] is also present on intra-European routes.

- The coefficient of the DAY variable is always negative, but is not significant.

In the first specification, the variable of concentration HHI is significant at the 1% level. However, the HHI coefficient is negative. This result is not in accordance with the standard relationship between the concentration and price[30]. Increases in the HHI generally indicate a gain in pricing power and a loss in competition, whereas decreases imply the reverse. To better explain this result, we decomposed the HHI in a second specification. This specification shows that only H1 is significant and negatively alters

---

[28] We also defined and estimated HUB dummy as airline specific, but in this case the coefficient was insignificant. This result may be explained by the fact that hub airports are only at the destination. Much of the literature shows that carriers charge higher prices for flights originating from their hubs. Thereby, it seems that prices are more affected by the route effect than the specific carrier effect.

[29] When the *Southwest* carrier started to compete on a route, this produced a particular phenomenon: the average fare for the route decreased, and the number of passengers increased. This phenomenon was called the "Southwest effect" by DOT officials in a 1993 study. Moreover, recent research found that the entry of a low cost carrier leads to lower prices on routes it has entered (Whinston and Collins, 1992; Bennett and Craun, 1993; Morrison and Winston, 1995; Windle and Dresner, 1995; Windle et al., 1996; Windle and Dresner, 1999).

[30] It should be remembered that unlike the existing empirical literature on airline market, our study uses actual prices and not the average fares for each route.

Results of specification (2.2)

$$\partial P/\partial R_1 = (-0.043 + 0.007H1 + 0.022H2)\,P \tag{2.10}$$

$$\partial P/\partial R_2 = (-0.428 + 1.032H1^{***} + 0.081H2)\,P \tag{2.11}$$

$$\partial P/\partial R_3 = (-0.253 + 0.60H1^{**} + 0.014H2)\,P \tag{2.12}$$

Results of specification (2.3)

$$\partial P/\partial R_1 = (-0.043 + 0.002Gini + 0.023H2) \tag{2.13}$$

$$\partial P/\partial R_2 = (-0.48 + 0.298Gini^{***} + 0.046H2) \tag{2.14}$$

$$\partial P/\partial R_3 = (-0.272 + 0.196Gini^{**} + 0.06H2) \tag{2.15}$$

The sensitivity of price discrimination to concentration depends on the type of restriction. Price discrimination is not significantly affected by concentration when R_1 type restrictions i.e., advance-purchase restrictions are involved. One explanation for this lack of sensitivity to advance purchase requirements can be found in the nature of the R_1 restriction. This device is more the application of a policy of allocation than pricing. The advance purchase restriction provides an efficient mean of allocating the limited capacity on peak flights. Carriers are confronted with the problem of limited capacity allocation as an airline service is not storable and demand is uncertain. Thus, the sensitivity of price to this restriction is not directly linked to price competition. This probably explains why concentration on price discrimination has little effect in the presence of R_1.

When R_2 and R_3 restrictions are involved, and concentration is measured by the inequality of market shares on a route, price discrimination is negatively affected by concentration. That is, the higher the market concentration on a route, the lower is the effect of the restrictions on airfares. In this case, the discounts related to restrictions R_2 and R_3 decrease. For example, equation (2.11) shows the estimated price discounts at the 25th, 50th, and 75th percentiles of H1 are 137 €, 132 € and 102 € respectively (Appendix D). Indeed, since the relationship between price and restrictions is negative, the positive influence of concentration leads to less price discrimination. This means that more competitive routes are associated with greater price discrimination. On competitive routes, carriers mainly compete over passengers with a low willingness to pay. These passengers have a higher price-elasticity, but a lower value for time. Carriers attract them by increasing the discounts offered in exchange for restrictions. The passengers who suffer "time costs" prefer to pay the full price for an unrestricted ticket. Airlines try to attract and retain this type of passenger (usually business travelers) by improving the quality of service through frequent-flyer schemes. These practices, therefore, allow price discrimination to increase with competition.

5 CONCLUSION

In this study, we empirically investigated the link between concentration and price in the European airline market. We used offered ticket prices for all flights from Nice Airport (France) to European destinations on one departure day. Because our dataset covers a large number of intra-European flights and is representative of the European route market structure, our results contribute to the understanding of the European airlines market with regard to pricing policy.

We first showed that the relationship between concentration and price is negative, meaning that the less competitive the route, the higher the level of offered prices. This result was established along with the result that only the indicator of market share inequality (market share coefficient of variation or Gini coefficient) explains the influence of the concentration on price behaviour. We conclude that this negative relationship is a characteristic of the European market where inequality of market shares is a distinctive feature of airlines routes. In routes with high market share inequality, the behaviour of the small carrier may deviate first, leading to competitive price behaviour.

Second, our empirical analysis showed that concentration significantly and positively affects the sensitivity of airline prices to purchase restrictions. Consequently, we conclude that price discrimination decreases with market concentration. This latter result is consistent with (i) the fact that price dispersion is lower on routes with more concentration; (ii) the theoretical literature on price discrimination, which shows that price discrimination persists and may increase as a market moves from monopoly to imperfect competition (Borenstein, 1985; Holmes, 1989; Stole, 1995; Valletti, 2000); (iii) Stavins' (2001) results for the US airline market.

Our results provide strong evidence of the relationship between prices and market structure on the intra-European routes and show that the pricing policies of airlines are of great importance in evaluating the degree of competition among European airlines. Given that market structures are subject to modification in the European airlines market, pricing policies are likely to reflect these changes. This calls for further and continuous economic analyses regarding the relationship between price discrimination and market structure.

We plan to extend this empirical analysis by extending the sample to include other main European airports in order to control for the presence of a selection bias due to unobserved specificities in the international airport of Nice, and by including a longitudinal dimension in the analysis in order to use information on the cross-sectional and time dimensions. This would enhance the analysis of the dynamic relationship between pricing policies and market structure.

Appendix A Summary Statistics (Prices Expressed in Euros)

ROUTES	Carriers	Mean Day-22	Mean Day-1	CV (Day − 22)	CV (Day − 1)
Amsterdam	KL	581	656	0,53	0,46
	HV	232,5	304	0,85	0.71
Barcelona	FU	390,4	452	0,54	0,45
	AF	435	485,5	0,48	0,44
	IB	431,5	523	0,59	0,48
Bordeaux	FU	252	264	0,56	0,56
	AF	306	323	0,44	0,41

(*Continued*)

Appendix A   Summary Statistics (Prices Expressed in Euros)—Cont'd

ROUTES	Carriers	Mean Day-22	Mean Day-1	CV (Day − 22)	CV (Day − 1)
Brussels	TV	220,5	240	0,46	0,4
	SN	487	487	0,71	0,71
Dusseldorf	LH	520	618	0,59	0,55
	EW	616	711	0,55	0,48
Frankfurt	LH	501	593,5	0,55	0,5
Geneva	LX	301,6	358	0,57	0,54
Lille	FU	308	298	0,47	0,44
	AF	293	319	0,37	0,32
Lisbon	NI	508	508	0,59	0,59
	TP	618	737	0,62	0,53
London	BA	533,5	687	0,7	0,5
	AF	584	680	0,57	0,43
	BD	1480	1735	1,31	1,17
Lyon	AF	200	211	0,49	0,48
Madrid	FU	503	526	0,62	0,6
	AF	550	626	0,57	0,51
	IB	541	668	0,62	0,48
Milan	AZ	359	379	0,31	0,28
	AF	497	548	0,54	0,52
Munich	FU	522	506	0,51	0,58
	LH	445,5	513,5	0,6	0,58
Nantes	FU	285	290	0,47	0,4
	AF	270	284	0,39	0,42
Paris	IW	181	226	0,78	0,6
	AF	268,5	273	0,69	0,68
Rennes	AF	345	358	0,3	0,29
Rome	AZ	450,5	519	0,48	0,4
	AF	619	786	0,62	0,46
	FU	390	445	0,56	0,45
	AP	376	445	0,57	0,45
Strasbourg	FU	255	250	0,43	0,42
	AF	253	260	0,44	0,43
Toulouse	FU	254	259	0,48	0,42
	AF	237	248	0,41	0,39

Appendix B Descriptive Statistics

Variables	Mean	Median	Standard Deviation
PRICE	436,02	321	483,48
R_1	1,07	0	3,26
R_2	0,36	0	0,49
R_3	0,298	0	0,45
HHI	0,54	0,52	0,19
H2	0,492	0,50	0,18
H1	0,053	0,01	0,06
Gini	0,24	0,13	0,22
DIST	707,09	686,83	272,17
AVGPO	896711	483780	901901,53
ONEWAY	0,08	0	0,26
BUSS	0,16	0	0,37
DAY	11,67	14	7,77
HUB	0,40	0	0,49
LCOST	0,17	0	0,37
CSHARE	0,38	0	0,48

Appendix C Concentration and Inequality of Market Share in European Airline Markets

DEST	Carriers	HHI	H1	Gini
Amsterdam	2	0,52	0,02	0,2
Barcelona	3	0,3446	0,0146	0,13
Bordeaux	2	0,545	0,045	0,3
Brussels	2	0,5008	0,0008	0,04
Düsseldorf	2	0,5	0	0
Frankfurt	1	1	0	0
Geneva	1	1	0	0
Lille	2	0,6058	0,1058	0,46
Lisbon	2	0,5	0	0
London	3	0,3974	0,0674	0,35
Lyon	1	1	0	0
Madrid	3	0,3414	0,0114	0,11
Milan	2	0,5	0	0
Munich	2	0,50125	0,00125	0,05
Nantes	2	0,6682	0,1682	0,58
Paris	2	0,58	0,08	0,4
Rennes	1	1	0	0
Rome	4	0,2536	0,0036	0,0792
Strasbourg	2	0,6058	0,1058	0,46
Toulouse	2	0,7145	0,2145	0,68
	Mean	0,6039175	0,0419175	0,39196
	Standard deviation	0,2305693	0,06294245	0,37000852
	CV	0,38178941	1,50157917	0,94399561

Appendix D   Percentiles of HHI, Decomposed HHI, and Gini Coefficient

| | Indexes of Concentration | | | |
	HHI	H1	H2	Gini
25th percentiles	0.3974	0.001025	0.33	0.045
50th percentiles	0.52	0.0146	0.5	0.13
75th percentiles	0.6058	0.1058	0.5	0.46

REFERENCES

Adelman, M. A. (1969) "Comment on the "H" Concentration Measure as a Numbers-Equivalent", *Review of Economics and Statistics*, 51, 99–101.

Armantier, O. and O. Richard (2005) "Evidence on Pricing from the Continental Airlines and Northwest Airlines Code-Share Agreement", *Université de Montréal*, mimeo.

Bamberger, G. E., D. W. Carlton and L. R. Neumann (2004) "An Empirical Investigation of the Competition Effects of Domestic Airline Alliances", *Journal of Law and Economics*, Vol. XLVII, (April 2004), pp. 195–222.

Barla, P. (2000) "Firm Size Inequality and Market Power", *International Journal of Industrial Organization*, 18, 693–722.

Bennett, R. D. and J. M. Craun (1993) "The Airline Deregulation Evolution Continues: The Southwest Effect", *US Department of Transportation*, Washington, DC.

Borenstein, S. (1985) "Price Discrimination in Free-Entry Market", *Rand Journal of Economics*, 16, 380–397.

Borenstein, S. (1989) "Hubs and High Fares: Dominance and Market Power in the U.S. Airline Industry", *Rand Journal of Economics*, 20, 344–365.

Borenstein, S. and N. L. Rose (1994) "Competitive and Price Dispersion in the U.S. Airline Industry", *Journal of Political Economy*, 102, 654–683.

Burghouwt, G. and J. Hakfoort (2001) "The Evolution of European Aviation Network, 1990–1998", *Journal of Air Transport Management*, 7, 311–318.

CAA (1998) The Single European Aviation Market: The First Five Years: Westward Digital, London.

Chiang, R. and C. Spatt (1982) "Imperfect Price Discrimination and Welfare", *Review of Economic Studies*, XLIX, 153–181.

DTA (2003) L'envolée des Compagnies à bas-coûts en France: n°11: Paris.

Evans, W. N. and I. N. Kessides (1993) "Structure, Conduct, and Performance in the Deregulated Airline Industry", *Southern Economic Journal*, 59, 450–467.

Farrar, D. E. and R. R. Glauber (1967) "Multicolinearity in Regression Analysis", *Review of Economics and Statistics*, 49, 92–107.

Gale, I. and T. J. Holmes (1992) "The Efficiency of Advance-Purchase Discounts in the Presence of Aggregate Demande Uncertainty", *International Journal of Industrial Organization*, 413–437.

Gale, I. and T. J. Holmes (1993) "Advance-Purchase Discounts and Monopoly Allocation of Capacity", *American Economic Review*, 83, 135–145.

Graham, D. R., D. P. Kaplan and D. S. Sibley (1983) "Efficiency and Competition in the Airline Industry", *The Bell Journal of Economics*, 14, 118–138.

Holmes, T. J. (1989) "The Effects of Third-Degree Price Discrimination in Oligopoly", *American Economic Review*, 79, 244–250.

Ito, H. and D. Lee (2005) "Domestic Codesharing Practices in the Us Airline Industry", *Journal of Air Transport Management*, 11, 89–97.

Morrison, S. and C. Winston (1987) "Empirical Implications of the Contestability Hypothesis", *Journal of Law and Economics*, 30, 53–66.

Morrison, S. and C. Winston (1995) *The Evolution of the Airline Industry*. Brookings Institutions. Washington D.C.

Mussa, M. and S. Rosen (1978) "Monopoly and Product Quality", *Journal of Economic Theory*, 78, 301–317.

Pigou, A. C. (1920) *The Economy of Welfare*. 4th Ed. London, Macmillan.

Reiss, P. C. and P. T. Spiller (1989) "Competition and Entry in Small Airline Markets", *Journal of Law and Economics*, S179–S202.

Salop, S. (1977) "The Noisy Monopolist: Imperfect Information, Price Dispersion and Price Discrimination", *Review of Economic Studies*, 44, 393–406.

Stavins, J. (2001) "Price Discrimination in the Airline Market: The Effect of Market Concentration", *The Review of Economics and Statistics*, 83, 200–202.

Stole, L. A. (1995) "Nonlinear Pricing and Oligopoly", *Journal of Economics and Management*, 4, 529–562.

Valletti, T. M. (2000) "Price Discrimination and Price Dispersion in a Duopoly", *Research in Economics*, 54, 351–374.

Whinston, M. D. and S. C. Collins (1992) "Entry and Competitive Structure in Deregulated Airline Markets: An Event Study Analysis of People Express", *Rand Journal of Economics*, 23, 445–462.

Windle, R. and M. Dresner (1995) "The Short and Long Run Effects of Entry on U.S. Domestic Air Routes", *Transportation Journal*, 35, 14–25.

Windle, R. and M. Dresner (1999) "Competitive Responses to Low Cost Carrier Entry", *Transport Research Part E*, 35, 59–75.

Windle, R., J. Lin and M. Dresner (1996) "The Impact of Low-Cost Carriers on Airport and Route Competition", *Journal of Transport Economics and Policy*, 30, 309–328.

Advances in Airline Economics, Vol 1
Darin Lee (Editor)
© 2006 Published by Elsevier B.V.

13

Patterns of Low Cost Carrier Entry: Evidence from Brazil

Alessandro Vinícius Marques de Oliveira, PhD
Center for Studies of Airline Competition and Regulation
(NECTAR)* Instituto Tecnológico de Aeronáutica, Brazil
June 2005

ABSTRACT

Competition between low cost carriers in rapid expansion and full-service network carriers has recently become one of the most relevant issues of the airline industry. The present paper addresses this matter by analyzing the entry of the low cost Gol Intelligent Airlines, in the Brazilian domestic market, in 2001. A route-choice model is estimated by making use of a flexible post-entry equilibrium profits equation and accounting for endogeneity of the main variables. Results indicate the relevance of market size and rival's route presence as underlying determinants of profitability. Furthermore, it is also performed an analysis of the consistency of Gol's entry patterns with the route choice behavior classically established by the pre-eminent US low cost carrier Southwest Airlines – that is, a focus on short-haul and high-density markets. Evidence is found that although Gol initiated operations by reproducing the behavior of Southwest, it quickly diversified its portfolio of routes and, at the margin, became more in accordance with the pattern of entry of JetBlue Airways (another successful US low cost carrier), that is, incorporating many longer-haul markets, albeit with some relevant country-specific idiosyncrasies.

* Homepage: http://www.ita.br/~nectar. Email address: nectar@ita.br. The author would like to thank Michael Waterson, Margaret Slade, Adalberto Febeliano, Jorge Silveira, Robson Ramos, Allemander Pereira Filho, Cristiano Miranda, Cristian Huse, Dante Aldrighi Mendes, the participants of a seminar at IBMEC (São Paulo, 2004), the participants of the annual conference of ESRC Econometric Study Group (Bristol, 2004), CAPES and FAPESP. Special thanks to Rachel Oliveira. All errors are the author's.

1 INTRODUCTION

Competition between rapidly expanding low-cost carriers (LCC's) and traditional network full-service carriers (FSC's) has recently become one of the most significant issues regarding the airline industry. Although basically a phenomenon of fully or partially liberalized markets – and thus dating back to the US deregulation process of the 1970s – it was only recently, however, that the LCC segment won recognition as a relevant and distinct business strategy as well as a profitable market niche. Following the successful paradigm of the pioneer Southwest Airlines in the United States, airlines such as Ryanair and EasyJet, in Europe, flourished in the market, and soon the concept has spread worldwide. Moreover, this segment is expected to expand considerably within the next few years, and this has undoubtedly been forcing legacy carriers to respond progressively – a movement that is shaping the frontiers of competition in the industry.

The present paper addresses this matter by examining the entry of low-cost carrier Gol Intelligent Airlines in the Brazilian domestic market in 2001. By making use of this case study, one is able to make inferences on the strategy of a successful and fast-growing newcomer LCC in an airline industry with recent liberalization. The ultimate objective here is therefore to inspect Gol's route choice decisions in order to identify entry patterns which could be associated with notable benchmarks of the LCC niche.

Gol Airlines was not only the first scheduled LCC of Brazil, but also of Latin America. Initially with operations confined to domestic flights[1], Gol soon represented the most effective threat to the so-called "Big Four" legacy majors, Varig, Vasp, Tam and Transbrasil, since the establishment of liberalization in 1992. By offering basic air transport service (without frills), and prices that were lower than the average in the market, and above all with lower costs and careful choice of routes, Gol started a successful path of growth and penetration in the domestic market. The consequence was that, according to Department of Civil Aviation, after only two years of operations the carrier was already Brazil's only profitable airline among major players, with 5.8% of operating margin and 12% share in the domestic segment – that is, 3.2 billion pax-km in a market with 26.8 billion pax-km in 2002[2].

The literature on LCC was, until recently, rather scarce and the few existing studies were usually related with the investigation of the FSC's pricing behavior in response to entry. Dresner, Lin and Windle (1996) examined and found significant spillover impacts of LCC entry onto other competitive routes, as on other routes at the same airport and on routes at airports in close proximity to where entry occurred. Their analysis was performed by inspecting, among others, the entry of Southwest Airlines into Baltimore-Washington International Airport, in 1993. Windle and Dresner (1999) investigated the impact of entry by ValuJet into Delta Air Line's hub, Atlanta, and refuted the US DOT's claim that the latter increased fares on non-competitive routes to compensate for lost revenues on competitive routes. More recently, Morrison (2001) assessed the total extent of Southwest Airlines' influence on competition by investigating the impacts of its actual, adjacent and potential route presence, on other carriers' fares in 1998, and

---

[1] Actually, Gol has started entering international routes only recently, by serving Guarulhos Airport (São Paulo) – Ezeiza Airport (Buenos Aires).
[2] Source: Statistical Yearbook of Department of Civil Aviation, 2002.

reached the conclusion that the presence of the LCC permitted savings to consumers that amounted to 20% of US airline industry's domestic schedule passenger revenue for that year.

In contrast, Ito and Lee (2003b) and Bogulaski, Ito and Lee (2004) focused on route entry decisions and entry patterns by LCC's. Whereas the former was aimed at studying the implications for further growth of the LCC's in the US market, by considering their propensity to enter high-density routes, the objective of the latter was to determine and quantify "*the market characteristics which have influenced Southwest's entry decisions*". The authors' main conclusions were that LCC's are no longer a niche segment restricted to particular geographic regions or leisure travelers and that legacy airlines' degree of exposure to LCC competition is very likely to increase from "*roughly 30% today to just under 50% in the future*" (Ito and Lee, 2003b). The authors also found that markets with high traffic density are becoming increasingly contestable, with relevant implications to market structure and performance. Other examples of empirical airline literature on entry are Berry (1992), Whinston and Collins (1992) and Joskow, Werden and Johnson (1994).

In order to study Gol's entry decisions in the Brazilian domestic market, an empirical model of route choice was designed in the same fashion of Boguslaski, Ito and Lee (2004). By considering a fairly flexible post-entry equilibrium profits equation, the model was estimated by making use of Newey (1987)'s methodology, and therefore Amemiya's Generalized Least Squares (AGLS) was employed. This approach results in consistent and asymptotically efficient estimation of the parameters of a limited-dependent variable – such as the newcomer's entry decisions – for the case of the presence of some endogenous regressors.

Results indicated the relevance of market size and rival's route presence as underlying determinants of profitability. Unobservables at the airport/city levels, such as sunk costs and economies of scope, were also found to be significant. Furthermore, the consistency of Gol's entry patterns with the route-choice behavior classically established by Southwest Airlines for the LCC segment – short-haul and high-density markets – was investigated; evidence was found that although Gol initiated operations by reproducing standards of Southwest, the carrier quickly diversified its portfolio of routes and became more in accordance with JetBlue Airways' entry pattern, that is, incorporating longer-haul markets, albeit with some relevant country-specific idiosyncrasies.

This paper has the following structure: Section 2 portrays the background of the entry of Gol Airlines in the Brazilian airline industry, with a description of the main paradigms related to LCC entry patterns along with some facts about the deregulation process in Brazil and Gol Airlines. Section 3 presents the empirical model and the econometric issues. Section 4 reports the results and includes an analysis of Gol's entry patterns consistency. Section 5 presents concluding remarks.

2 BACKGROUND: LCC NICHE AND ENTRY OF GOL AIRLINES IN BRAZIL

2.1 The LCC Market Niche and its Paradigms

The entry of low-cost carriers providing basic air transportation service with no frills and lower fares has considerably transformed competition in the airline industry.

Notwithstanding a phenomenon of partially or fully liberalized airline markets dating back to the US deregulation process of the seventies, it was only recently that this "*low-cost revolution*" (Doganis, 2001) has resulted in the formation of a well recognized and distinct business strategy and a sustainable market niche.

The LCC niche is usually associated with the *Southwest Airlines Paradigm* (hereafter **SWP**), mainly because the US carrier pioneered this sort of operations with standards that are now deliberately reproduced around the world[3]. The most widely known characteristics of this paradigm are (Doganis, 2001): single fleet type; simplification or elimination of in-flight service; use of less congested secondary airports; direct sales to consumers; e-ticketing; short-haul, point-to-point flights in dense markets with no inter-lining or transfers, which means a simple network structure, with absent or weak feed to long-range flights; single-class cabin lay-out; simple or no frequent-flyer program; high level of fleet utilization; and highly motivated employees[4]. Moreover, LCC's are typically associated with a very aggressive pricing strategy, with the use of a simplified fare structure with few or no restrictions, and low one-way fares[5].

The cost advantage permitted by the SWP is not merely an issue of paying lower salaries or operating at cheaper airports, and, contrary to common sense, not even due only to the lack of frills; instead it is rather a function of fundamental differences in the business model associated with it, emerging mainly from a very careful choice of markets, targeting dense, short-haul routes in order to exploit economies due to higher seating density and higher aircraft utilization, especially with non-stop service. According Boguslaski, Ito and Lee (2004), Southwest has resulted in unit costs that are 28 to 51 per cent lower than the US major airlines, considering 2001 US DOT unit cost figures.[6]

Since the early nineties, and in particular very recently, a plethora of *de novo*, LCC entry, has been observed around the world. Inspired by the more than three decades of success of Southwest Airlines, and stimulated by market liberalization, airlines such as Ryanair and EasyJet in Europe, Air Asia and Virgin Blue in the South Pacific, 1 Time and Kulula in Africa, and Gol and U Air in South America, flourished in the market, meaning that the LCC concept has rapidly achieved global recognition.

In parallel to the worldwide spread of the low-cost operations based on the SWP, alternative standards for the segment have been successfully implemented. The *AirTran-Frontier Paradigm* (**AFP**), with a clear focus on the low-fare business market by making use of multi-service operations, usually with mini-hubs to provide convenient connections and more possibilities in terms of origin-and-destination markets, and with a more

---

[3] As the Chief Executive of Ryanair (UK) once said: "*We went to look at Southwest. It was like the road to Damascus. This was the way to make Ryanair work*" (Doganis, 2001).

[4] This description refers to what can be considered "classic" Southwest paradigm. One has to bear in mind, as we will see below, that Southwest's actual patterns of operations has had some changes recently: "*its strategy evolved during the latter half of the decade to include a much more heterogeneous mix of markets, including a number of markets which were both long-haul and surprisingly thin*" (Boguslaski, Ito and Lee, 2004).

[5] Tretheway (2004) points out that the introduction of low one way fares ultimately served to undermine the ability of the FSC's to price discriminate, and not only resulted in a considerable increase in competition but also in an exposure of the problems associated with the FSC business model.

[6] Moreover, Southwest Airlines' average stay length is shorter than most other carriers, understating its unit cost advantage.

complex fare structure and even business class[7]; secondly, the *JetBlue Airways Paradigm* (**JBP**), which is associated with the focus on long-haul routes (usually more than 1,500 kilometers), resulting in the highest average stage length of the LCC segments[8].

And finally, one has the Ryanair Paradigm (RYP). Ryanair, the most successful LCC in the world in terms of profitability, is extremely focused in selecting only destinations with underutilized secondary and tertiary airports. Contrary to all other major LCC's like EasyJet or even Southwest Airlines, the Irish carrier has always resisted entering either primary or congested airports; this permitted it to always be in a position to negotiate airport fees (cost control) and to focus almost completely on the leisure travelers segment, which makes this paradigm completely distinct from, for example, the AFP.

It is important to emphasize two caveats on the above-mentioned paradigms. First, while newer standards of operation have clearly emerged in the segment, the essence of the SWP remains dominant for most of LCC's, namely the absence or weak presence of frills and the lower costs, typically resulting in low prices. From this point of view, the SWP is still the major benchmark for LCC's. In addition to that, it is clear that, due to the ever-changing state of the competition in deregulated airline markets, it is rather unlikely to observe the above-mentioned paradigms in a strict basis, but rather as a **mixture** of them. Indeed, the volatile frontier of competition along with the need of market expansion have forced LCC's to also enter atypical markets, with relevant examples being the recent entry of Southwest in the coast-to-coast markets of the United States (US Department of Transportation, 2001 and 2002), and even more recently, into major carriers' hubs. This trend has resulted in LCC's serving a variety of short/medium/long haul, business/tourism, direct/indirect routes, which has ultimately increased the exposure not only to FSC competition but also among LCC's.

Nevertheless, even with carriers having a more diversified range of routes nowadays, it is clear that, by making use of the notion of paradigms as benchmarks one has useful reference in order to analyze and pinpoint patterns of entry behavior by LCC's. Nevertheless, despite those caveats, my argument here is that the idea of paradigms is still useful for a better identification of actual LCC behavior, especially because the industry all over the world is observing a wave of small entrants, most of them claiming to be LCC's. Actually it is not always straightforward to identify if a given airline is really operating as a LCC and this causes much confusion among industry analysts. Therefore, in order to better understand and pinpoint patterns of entry behavior by entrants that are truly consistent with LCC operations, some form of representation, such as the paradigms, is needed.

For example, one can study a carrier's marginal propensity to enter a market with respect to flight haul in order to make inferences on its conformity with either the SWP or the JBP. The analysis of preference with respect to flight haul, in this specific case, is crucial to distinguish between both paradigms; in addition, a thorough investigation

---

[7] AirTran Airways operates in the eastern United States with Atlanta as its hub, being the second-largest carrier at Hartsfield International Airport, and providing service to 45 cities within the country. Frontier Airlines operates routes linking its Denver hub to 38 cities in 22 states and Mexico.

[8] With operations started in 2000, JetBlue Airways focuses on non-stop transcontinental routes in the US. The airline serves point-to-point routes between 22 destinations in 11 states, Puerto Rico and the Dominican Republic. It is important to emphasize that both JBP and AFP are usually considered in a different category from Southwest when it comes to passenger amenities and in-flight entertainment (IFE).

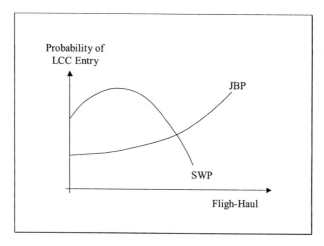

Figure 1   SWP versus JBP: Effects of Flight-Haul on LCC Entry Probability.

of the commercial and operational practices of the newcomer (with respect to strategic choices regarding frills, network, airports, labor, advertising, etc.), can be very effective in permitting its correct classification.

Figure 1 presents a diagram showing the flight-haul analysis of paradigms. As Figure 1 shows, the probability of entry of a SWP-like LCC is increasing in flight haul but with diminishing returns, in such a way that the highest probability is associated with relatively shorter-haul markets. On the other hand, a JBP-like LCC has typically an ever-increasing entry probability with respect to flight distance, with highest levels associated with long-haul domestic flights.

Therefore, by performing a simple inspection of the marginal effects of distance on the probability to enter a market by an alleged LCC, it is possible to have a straightforward analysis of consistency with either SWP or JBP. Similarly, it would be possible to make inferences on the conformity of a given carrier with AFP by inspecting, for example, its degree of hubbing and propensity to enter business-related cities[9].

2.2   LCC Entry in Brazil

The removal of regulatory barriers in the Brazilian airline industry since the early nineties was undoubtedly a major determinant of Gol Airlines' entry in 2001, and of the unprecedented increase in competition in the market. Started at the beginning of the nineties within a broader governmental program for deregulation of country's economy, regulatory reform was then performed gradually, in three main rounds, by the Department of Civil Aviation, DAC (Oliveira, 2005).

---

[9] In this case, however, an analysis of a carrier's overall service attributes is probably more useful to infer the conformity with AFP than a focus on route entry decisions. None of them are accomplished in this paper, however.

Gol Intelligent Airlines was not only the first scheduled LCC of Brazil, but also of Latin America, with operations commencing in January 2001[10]. It is owned by Grupo Áurea – a conglomerate that owns 38 companies and a major operator of urban and long-distance coach services across Brazil.

By offering a simple fare structure, and thus with an average yield that at the beginning was 31% below those of FSC competitors[11], Gol started a successful path of growth and penetration in the domestic market. After only two years of operations, it was already Brazil's only profitable airline with operating profits of BRL 39 million[12] and an operating margin of 5.8% of total revenues. Table 1 presents some characteristics of Gol, compared with the major legacy airlines within the country in 2002; Gol's figures of 2001 are also presented to demonstrate the airline's rapid growth. One can see that Gol's unit costs and yields were roughly a third lower than its competitors and its average stage length was approximately 20% lower; also, it is possible to visualize the pace of expansion of the LCC, which, from the start-up year, 2001, to 2002, increased RPK's by 156% and RPK market share by 151%.

Some additional characteristics of the newcomer are: absence of complete food service (only snacks and cereal bars); standardized fleet (Boeing 737-700s and 800s, the largest operator of Next-Generation 737 aircraft in Latin America); availability of full e-ticketing service and heavy distribution via the internet (65% of sales, according to Silva and

Table 1 Comparison of Gol and Incumbent FSC's (2002) – Domestic Market[13]

Variable	Unit	FSC			LCC		
		Tam 2002	Varig 2002	Vasp 2002	Gol 2002	Gol 2001	Growth 2001–02
Revenue Passenger Kilometers (RPK)	pax * km (billion)	9.34	10.48	3.39	3.22	1.26	156%
Market Share RPK	fraction	0.35	0.39	0.13	0.12	0.05	151%
Traffic per Employee	pax * km (million)	1.23	0.75	0.70	1.56	1.08	44%
Load Factor	fraction	0.53	0.59	0.55	0.63	0.60	5%
Unit Cost	BRL/(pax * km)	0.33	0.33	0.31	0.20	0.18	10%
Yield	BRL/(pax * km)	0.29	0.31	0.27	0.21	0.18	14%
Operating Margin	fraction	−0.12	−0.05	−0.16	0.06	0.02	153%
Average Stage Length	km	868	1,017	1,016	792	772	3%

Notes:
 (i) BRL means Brazilian currency (Real, current values);
 (ii) pax means number of passengers traveled;
(iii) market share is equal to a firm's RPK over industry's RPK;
(iv) Operating margin is equal to operating profits or losses over total revenues.

---

[10] Gol Airlines and U Air (Uruguay) are the only scheduled LCC's currently based in Latin America. Some North-American LCC's provide service to Mexico and the Caribbean, such as JetsGo, Frontier and JetBlue, but do not have operational basis at the region (Source: website lowcostairlines.org).
[11] Statistical Yearbook of Department of Civil Aviation, volume II, 2001.
[12] Approximately 13 million dollars.
[13] Source: DAC's Statistical Yearbook, vols. I and II.

Espírito Santo Jr., 2003); reservation system software acquired from JetBlue ("Open Skies"); around half of the original staff coming from outside the industry and half recruited from other airlines – especially flight crew and technical staff –, although not more than 15% from any particular carrier[14].

At the beginning, Gol's marketing efforts were clearly oriented to become "the people's airline", concentrating more on potential travelers with lower income than on current traveling-public (Zalamea, 2001, mentions "*small business officials, blue collar workers, students, farmers and others who have never flown before*" as targeted segments of consumers). For example, Tarcisio Gargioni, Gol's Vice President for Marketing and Services, once revealed: "*Our business plan identified that in 2000, out of the 170 million Brazilian population only 6 million flew commercial aviation. Out of the remaining 164 million, some 25 million could also become potential fliers provided fares were reduced 30%*" (Lima, 2002).

Nevertheless, demand stimulation from non-traveling, lower-income consumers was eventually not enough to guarantee the expansion rate targeted by the airline; in fact Gol's rapid growth was achieved primarily at the expense of existing legacy carriers, and also enhanced by Transbrasil Airlines' exit in 2001: "*We did a market survey in September [2001] and found only 4% of our passengers had never flown before*" (Gargioni, as in Lima, 2002).

Undoubtedly, Brazil's macroeconomic instability, lower *per capita* income and high wealth concentration can be regarded as major sources of Gol's lack of success in attracting the non-traveling public. Also, the country's high interest rates, which increase the risk of enterprise, probably forced Gol not to venture providing service to new domestic destinations where new demand could be created, but to focus only on already existing routes. Another relevant restriction is the lack of infrastructure for typical LCC operations in other cities than the major conurbations in Brazil (suitable secondary airports, for example).

This does not mean, however, that Gol's entry was totally ineffective in stimulating new demand on **existing** routes. On the contrary, if one considers the top-500 densest routes in Brazil, and by comparing traffic density of 2002 with 2000 (previous to entry), it is possible to arrive at the conclusion that routes entered by Gol observed a 13.1% average increase in traffic density (pax), against a 7.0% increase on all 500 routes. In fact, routes not entered by Gol had an 11.5 decrease in traffic density within the same period[15].

A major issue is whether the above-mentioned difficulty in attracting new travelers and therefore not generating the amount of additional traffic expected of a LCC[16], has ultimately forced the airline to substantially alter its initial route entry strategy in order not to affect growth. Indeed, this may be particularly true with respect to the effect on route choice of flight haul – as seen before, a crucial variable with respect to analysis of conformity with LCC paradigms. For example, it was observed that, since 2002,

---

[14] According to Lima (2002), hiring personnel from other carriers was made easier due to the downsizing process taken place at Vasp and especially at the bankrupt Transbrasil (Lima, 2002). According to Silva and Espírito Santo Jr. (2003), Gol had the following internal slogan: "*the youngest and most experienced airline in Brazil*".

[15] Calculations based on figures of DAC's Statistical Yearbook (Volume I). Results are consistent with findings of Dresner, Lin and Windle (1996), for the US market, and the so-called "Southwest Airlines Effect".

[16] Although some increase in traffic density was actually observed after Gol's entry (see Section 4).

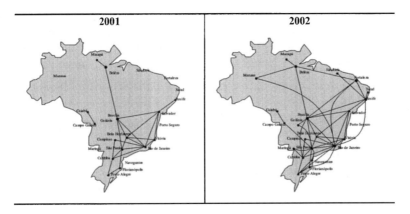

Figure 2 Evolution of Gol's Network within Brazil

Source: DAC's HOTRAN reports.

medium-to-long haul routes were increasingly added to Gol's network, as one can see from the maps of Figure 2.

At the beginning of 2001, Gol had only six 737-700's, providing service between São Paulo, Rio de Janeiro, Belo Horizonte, Florianópolis, Brasília, Porto Alegre and Salvador (i.e. the maximum haul below 1,500 kilometers). This straightforward link with the SWP is not surprising since, during the start-up of operations, Gol admitted it was reproducing the model of Southwest Airlines in the same way Ryanair did in the United Kingdom (Guimarães, 2002). In fact, this recipe permitted the newcomer to rapidly achieve levels of efficiency that were notably higher-than-average, with aircrafts having 10 to 12 flights a day and very fast ground turn-around times, within fifteen to thirty minutes. In fact, by December 2001 there was only one city-pair in the entire network which could be classified as direct long-haul route: Brasília-Belém, with 1,610 km.

By the end of 2002, on the other hand, the situation was clearly very different. Gol had 22 aircraft in operation, serving a much wider network with many routes with longer-than-average distance and certainly an additional target of feeding long-range flights. For example, routes like Rio de Janeiro – Manaus (2,860 km), Rio de Janeiro – Recife (1,863 km) and Brasília – Fortaleza (1,690 km) were added to the network structure, indicating a higher propensity to enter direct, long-haul routes and rapidly increasing the possibilities of connections between extreme regions like the South and the North/Northeast.

Table 2 gives some details on the route profile of the airline with respect to flight haul, by considering entry on the top-500 densest routes. As one can observe in Table 2, Gol increased by 21 the number of direct routes served from 2001 to 2002 (54-33). Out of these 21 new routes, two-thirds (14) were medium-to-long-haul routes (that is, with flight haul above the median, 716 kilometers). Indeed, as Gol doubled its presence on longer-haul routes in 2002 (28 routes above the median, against 14 in 2001), it consolidated a very different portfolio of routes, notably atypical for a SWP-like LCC; in fact, the portfolio changed from a set in which there was a minority of long-haul routes in 2001 (14 out of 33), to a slight majority in 2002 (28 out of 54).

Table 2 Direct Routes Served by Gol – Flight Haul Distribution

Flight-Haul Intervals – kilometres	#500 Top Routes	Direct Routes Served 2001		Direct Routes Served 2002	
		#	%	#	%
$Q_0 - Q_1$ *Less than 390*	125	8	6.4%	11	8.8%
$Q_1 - Q_2$ *390 to 716*	125	11	8.8%	15	12.0%
$Q_2 - Q_3$ *716 to 1,466*	125	9	7.2%	18	14.4%
$Q_3 - Q_4$ *more than 1,466*	125	5	4.0%	10	8.0%
Total	500	33	6.6%	54	10.8%

Notes:
(i) Q_1, Q_2, Q_3 and Q_4 mean the quartiles considering a sample with the 500 densest routes;
(ii) # means number of routes and % means percentage out of the top routes.

All these facts raise questions about the actual standard of operations undertaken by Gol in the Brazilian airline industry, especially with respect to the paradigm with which it might be consistent. One might doubt whether Gol, although claiming itself as initially inspired by Southwest Airlines (Guimarães, 2002), could resist entering a wider range of markets in order to expand or even to exploit unobservable (to the analyst) economies of scope throughout Brazil, increasing the number of actual origin-and-destination markets served. In fact, by a simple inspection on Gol's website, one can quickly arrive at the conclusion that flights with more than two stops and/or connections are much more frequently available than non-stop flights, which clearly represents a departure from the typical SWP.

The start of operations of "red-eye" flights in 2003 in order to attract more travelers from coach and to persist in expanding serves as an additional argument to the claim that the LCC's standards are probably not consistent with the SWP, but could be potentially associated with a variant of the JBP; as seen before, Jet Blue Airways is well-known for its red-eye, transcontinental flights in the US market. In fact, it is known that, just before starting-up operations in Brazil, Gol's executives made visits to both Southwest Airlines and JetBlue Airways in order to conceive the newcomer's strategic planning.

By analyzing Gol's entry patterns, it is possible to collect further evidence on the change of directions by the LCC from 2002 and beyond and to make inferences about the determinants of entry decisions by a LCC in a recently liberalized airline market, which is the focus of Section 3.

3 EMPIRICAL MODELING

In this section I present an empirical modeling for the route-entry decisions of Gol Intelligent Airlines. Firstly, the LCC's route entry problem is analyzed under a discrete-choice model framework; secondly, issues like sample selection, functional form and chosen empirical specification are discussed. And finally, the issue of endogeneity is examined along with a discussion of the instrumental variables and the estimator employed. Empirical results are presented in Section 4.

3.1   Discrete-Choice Framework

The main objective here is to develop a framework of discrete choice with random utility[17] for the analysis of the patterns of entry decisions of the newcomer Gol Airlines. It is straightforward that here we have Gol as the decision maker, and the set of decisions "to enter a route" and "not to enter a route" as the alternatives in this "route-choice problem". Consider the binary variable representative of choice, $PRES_{kt}$, which accounts for the presence of Gol on the k-th route at time t. The probability of entry can then be regarded in the following way:

$$\Pr[PRES_{kt} = 1] = \Pr[\delta \pi_{kt}^* - SC_k > 0] \tag{1}$$

Where the multiplicative term $\delta \pi_{kt}^*$ is the present value of the stream of equilibrium profits of the newcomer (δ is the discount factor) in case of entry. SC_k is the amount of sunk costs on the k-th route. One can develop (1) in the following way:

$$\Pr[\delta \pi_{kt}^* - SC_k > 0] = \Pr\left[\frac{\delta \pi_{kt}^*}{SC_k} > 1\right] = \Pr[\ln \pi_{kt}^* + \ln \delta - \ln SC_k > 0] \tag{2}$$

By introducing ε_{kt}, the disturbances associated with the choice mechanism within a random utility framework, in (2), we have the following random variable representative of equilibrium net present value profits at the route level (Π_{kt}^*):

$$\Pi_{kt}^* = \ln \pi_{kt}^* + \ln \delta - \ln SC_k + \varepsilon_{kt} \tag{3}$$

where ε_{kt} is assumed to be iid $\sim N(0,1)$[18].

As in a typical discrete-choice model (ex. Amemiya, 1978), we have only $PRES_{kt}$ as an observable, whereas the other terms δ, π_{kt}^* and SC_k are latent. Actually, only the sign of Π_{kt}^* is observed:

$$PRES_{kt} = \tau\left(\Pi_{kt}^*\right) = \begin{cases} 1 & if \ \Pi_{kt}^* > 0 \\ 0 & if \ \Pi_{kt}^* \leq 0 \end{cases} \tag{4}$$

Therefore we have $PRES_{kt}$ assigned with one in case of entry (expectation of positive route profitability) and zero in case of no entry (no expectation of route profitability).

---

[17] In the random utility approach, "*the observed inconsistencies in choice behavior are taken to be a result of observational deficiencies on the part of the analyst*" (Ben-Akiva and Lerman, 1985); therefore, contrary to the constant utility approach, which assume a probabilistic behavior for the decision maker, by assuming random utility I assume that the individual always select the alternative with the highest utility (profits). By doing this, here we have the standard interpretation of the error term as representing factors that are observable to the firm but not to the econometrician.

[18] This is a convenient assumption, as the literature on binary probit estimation within a simultaneous equations framework is vast (examples being Amemiya, 1978, Smith and Blundell, 1986, Rivers and Vuong, 1988 and Lee, 1991), in opposition to the binary logit with endogenous variables.

on route k. Finally the DC's ($l = 1, 2, \ldots, L$) are city-specific dummies. The translog representation of (5) would then be:

$$\Pr\left[PRES_{kt} = 1\right] = \Pr\left[\Pi_{kt}^* > 0\right] =$$

$$\Pr\left[\begin{array}{c} v_0 + v_1 \ln den_{kt} + v_2 \ln km_k + v_3 \ln sdr_{kt} + v_4 \ln den_{kt}^2 + \\ v_5 \ln km_k^2 + v_6 \ln sdr_{kt}^2 + v_7 \ln den_{kt} \ln km_k + v_8 \ln den_{kt} \ln sdr_{kt} + \\ v_9 \ln km_k \ln sdr_{kt} + \sum_l u_l DC_l + v_1 cpres_{kt-1} + v_2 tbapres_{kt-1} + \varepsilon_{kt} > 0 \end{array}\right] \quad (6)$$

where the v's, u's and v's are parameters. Let us now present details of each of the variables present in (5) and (6):

$PRES_{kt}$, is a binary variable that accounts for route presence of Gol Airlines, being assigned with one if entry has occurred in any year lower or equal than t, and with zero otherwise. $PRES_{kt}$ then means the presence of the LCC on route k in year t.

"Route" is defined as discussed before (see 3.2); therefore one has to precisely define "entry". Here I define entry as Gol's presence in any of the possible origin-to-destination (O–D) markets, within the period under consideration (2001–2002); for more details, see the discussion of $cpres_{kt-1}$ below. The information of the presence of Gol in the O–D markets was collected from Panrotas's Domestic and International Schedules and Fares Guide and from Airwise's website[24].

The definition of $PRES_{kt}$ including all O–D traffic is certainly in contrast with Boguslaski, Ito and Lee (2004), which considers only non-stop markets and thus disregards routings with flight connections and stops within a given route. That procedure is certainly more reasonable for their case of Southwest Airlines, which is usually associated with non-stop and short-haul flights (the SWP, as discussed in 2.1). In the present case, however, one may be unconvinced whether Gol has typical SWP standards, but, on the contrary, would believe that it has some propensity to enter a more diversified range of markets, especially longer-haul routes with stops and connections (see 2.2). Therefore, it would not be a reasonable procedure to include only either non-stop or direct flights in the definition of "route", as it would not be representative of Gol's operations; also, it would be impossible to investigate the conformity of Gol with either SWP or JBP (see Figure 1). Therefore, broader definitions of both route and entry were considered in this study.

Another issue regarding the definition of entry is related to the minimum level of operations (MLO) within a year for Gol's presence to be accounted for. Previous literature usually had either absolute or relative definitions of MLO. For instance, whereas Oum, Zhang and Zhang (1993) and Berry (1992) used MLOs of, respectively, 100 and 90 passengers per quarter in the ten per cent sample collected by the US DOT[25], Evans and Kessides (1993) used a fractional definition, considering effective presence as more than 1% of total traffic on the route. The latter is certainly a more flexible filtering criterion which could be adapted for the Brazilian conditions; however, as here traffic disaggregated by airline is not observed, a proxy used was to adapt Evans and Kessides

---

[24] Panrotas is a database that is similar to OAG's of flight schedules guide, the world's most comprehensive schedules database; Airwise's website: http//www.airwise.com.
[25] U.S. Department of Transportation (DOT) Origin and Destination Survey.

(1993)'s approach, and therefore use the minimum percentage of seats available at the endpoint cities[26], considering then "entry" when actual figures are higher than 1%.

den_{kt} is route density of traffic (in million passengers) and was collected from the Statistical Yearbook of the Department of Civil Aviation (volume II) for the years 2001–2002. Consisting of origin-and-destination traffic figures, this variable represents total (non-airline-specific) domestic number of trips, aggregating all direct and indirect, single-trip and round-trip, traffic (that is, revenue passengers).

km_k represents route distance, that is, the one-way distance between origin and destination airports. This information was provided by Department of Civil Aviation's Laboratory of Simulation and was calculated by using the polar coordinates method. One important issue about km_{kt} is related to its calculation in case of an observation with more than one airport in one or both endpoint cities of the given route. In both cases the latitude and longitude of the airports closest to the city centre was employed and considered representative of the distance between cities[27].

Another aspect of km_k it that it represents the *minimum* distance between two given airports, and therefore does not take into account neither actual airway distance nor the effect of flight connections and/or stops. In principle, one would object using this proxy for flight distance, especially for medium-to-long-haul routes because their higher availability of seats in flights with stops represents a higher actual distance flown than can be assessed by km_k.

Besides that, the lower the participation of non-stop flights on one given route the more one would underestimated the effect of actual flight distance on profits, specially because the higher distance would permit lower unit costs – a phenomenon known as "cost taper" in the transport literature, see Brander and Zhang, 1990. One has to be cautious with that argument, however, as more stops are also known for increasing costs – for instance, by additional landing/departure fees and higher fuel consumption; besides that, on the demand side, stops usually increase passengers' flight disutility, generating competitive disadvantage and also reducing profitability – a product differentiation effect. In spite of these arguments, we can therefore interpret km_{kt} as capturing the broad effect – the balance of the two effects mentioned above – of flight distance on the probability of entry by the LCC[28].

sdr_{kt} is the number of total seats available per passenger on direct flights of FSC's on route k and time t. A relative measure, that is seats *per* passenger, was considered better than the absolute figure of seats available, as it avoids strong colinearity with den_{kt}. Figures of total number of flights disaggregated by airline is available in Department of Civil Aviation's HOTRAN, "Horário de Transporte", a data system that generates reports containing operational information of all scheduled flights within the country (non-published data). This information was extracted from their system in every month for the period 2001–2002, and was subsequently aggregated by year. Sdr_{kt} is then both a measure of product differentiation – that is, more seats available meaning more

---

[26] Source: Department of Civil Aviation's HOTRAN's (various).
[27] As mentioned before, there were only three cities in this situation found in the data sample: Rio de Janeiro, Sao Paulo and Belo Horizonte. In all cases the largest city airport (in terms of figures of number of passengers and movement of aircrafts) is located closer to the city centre. Source: INFRAERO's website (February, 2004).
[28] Some colinearity with sdr_{kt} is expected *ex-ante*, however.

convenient flights and service levels generated by the FSC's –, and of the degree of how well or underserved a given route actually is.

cpres$_{kt-1}$ is a binary variable that controls for entry at any of the endpoint cities of a route in the previous year. It is assigned with one for each route in 2002 that had one of the endpoint cities entered by Gol in 2001, and zero otherwise. This variable is crucial in the present framework as it is designed to control for the effects of sunk costs at the city level, that is, once one given airport/city was entered, it is then easier for the newcomer to provide services to other routes out of it, as it had already incurred in most of the sunk costs, such as start-up costs, advertising, sales and operational structure at the airport, etc. Therefore, it is useful to control for the fact that the probability that Gol enters a given route B–C is related to the probability that Gol has entered route A–B, for example.

Finally, cpres$_{kt-1}$ also controls for the effects of routes already entered in the year before and thus making a distinction between "new" or "true" entry and "previous" entry; in this sense, this variable makes this study in line with Toivanen and Waterson (2001)[29].

tbapres$_{kt-1}$ is a binary variable representative of the presence of the bankrupt (and no-longer existing) Transbrasil Airlines on route k and time $t-1$. On the one hand, one would think of this exit as an opportunity to any newcomer; this would be certainly the case in city-pairs with endpoint airports subject to slots; on the other hand, however, one would think of the exit of Transbrasil as a clear signal for Gol that those routes were not profitable.

DC$_l$$(1 = 1, \ldots, L)$, which are *city-specific dummies*: assigned with 1 if the city is one of the endpoint cities of the city-pair, and 0 if not. The city dummies provide an economical way to capture and control for a large number of truly significant variables, which can be regarded as being actually city-specific, instead of route-specific; also, most of them are in fact either unobservables or potentially measured with noise by the researcher.

Below is a list of some of the potential effects that may be controlled by the city dummies:

(a) **Characteristics of travelers from/to a city:** consumers' purchasing behavior and attributes, like the percentage of the travelers which frequently makes use of the internet when searching and buying; consumers' attributes: income, niche preferences, propensity to make either tourism-related or business-related trips, etc.; city's gross domestic product and wealth in general, as a factor of business-trips generation; percentage of migrants established in one city (ex: large participation of migrants from Northeast in São Paulo, a fact that is potentially trip-generation enhancing); geographic idiosyncrasies;

(b) **Characteristics of the airports of a city:** sunk costs; airport accessibility and costs of the access to the airport (price of taxi, distance from the zones-of-trip-generation,

---

[29] The authors criticize the common procedure found in the entry literature, of treating "entry" of existing firms, meaning the continuation of operations, in a similar way to entry of new firms; this would be equivalent to *"making the assumption that firms can in every period, without a change in costs, review their entry decision"*. They state: *"Given sunk costs, we believe that particular assumption to be unwarranted and we do no utilize it"* (Toivanen and Waterson, 2001, p. 3).

etc.), the size of the zone of influence of the city's airport(s) in terms of trip generation (nearby cities); operational costs and expenses related to a particular city (airport fees, cost of hiring personnel, cost of contracts in general, etc.); presence of airports with constrained capacity (slots) or with spare capacity; subsides and incentives given by authorities to operations in one given city; presence of airports owned by the public enterprise Infraero; vacant slots or frequencies left by the bankrupt Transbrasil; airport/airway infrastructure: size of the runway, air traffic control capacity;

(c) **Characteristics of network out of a city:** size of the airlines' network (unobservable degree of product differentiation, economies of scope, etc. at the airport level); presence of hub or mini-hub in a city; frequent flyer effect: number of possible destinations out of a city;

(d) **Characteristics of the competition in a city:** quality/availability of motorways out of a city; tolls; presence of charter; number of travel agents; commission fees to travel agents of a city; airport dominance by particular airlines; number of airlines operating out of a city and concentration levels; levels of advertising and forms of effective media in one city; number of flights and excess capacity out of a city.

Most of these effects are expected to generate persistent heterogeneity in the error-term structure **across cities** (but not routes), which can be controlled via the city-specific dummies, DC's.

Another relevant feature of the dummies-specific city is that one is able to identify only the effects of actually entered cities. This is a common problem of any discrete-choice model, in which one cannot use as a regressor a dummy variable if for any of the values it takes, there is no variation in the dependent variable (see, for example, Toivanen and Waterson, 2001). This is precisely the case of non-entered cities, all of them with no variation in $PRES_{ikt}$, that is, in which $PRES_{ikt} = 0$ for all routes[30]. On the other hand, it is not a good procedure to create one dummy for each actually entered city, as this would be certainly inducing somewhat artificially designed correlation with the dependent variable, due to the obvious fact that only routes from and to actually chosen airports will be entered. The extreme alternative, namely the drop of all city dummies, would probably be inappropriate as it would induce omitted variables bias.

Thus, in order to balance between the gains of controlling for effects which are city-specific and to avoid the aforementioned sort of artificial correlation, I then focused on the *network decisions of any potential newcomer* in the Brazilian domestic market. In fact, given that "*there are no secondary airports near major Brazilian cities able to handle midsize jet operations (737s, A320/319, etc.)*" (Silva and Espírito Santo Jr., 2003), any major player considering entering the market would not be able to avoid having operations at the airports of some of the most important cities within the country. Indeed, this is a sort of network decision that is expected *ex-ante*, irrespective of the type of operations and specific niche of the potential competitor. This evidence can be regarded as a justification for the inclusion of dummies for the major cities present in

---

[30] The other extreme would be the case of the sample containing cities with all routes actually entered (that is, $PRES_{ikt} = 1$ for all routes), and thus generating the same problem of lack of variation in $PRES_{ikt}$ – a case not present in the current data sample.

predicted endogenous variables and the residuals as regressors; then, in the final stage, a generalized least square estimator is performed in order to obtain efficient estimates of the structural parameters. This estimator requires consistent standard errors correction to account for the first-stage estimation, which is performed here by making use of Newey (1987)'s approach[37].

The basic procedure for identification here was to employ lagged variables as instruments and to test for their validity. The list of instrumental variables was den_{kt-1}, sdr_{kt-1}, stt_{kt-1} (total direct seats available), swe_{kt-1} (total direct seats available during weekends) and asz_{kt-1} (average size of aircraft); it also comprised the respective second-order terms: $(\ln den_{kt-1})^2$, $(\ln sdr_{kt-1})^2$, $\ln den_{kt-1}*\ln km_k$, $\ln den_{kt-1}*\ln sdr_{kt-1}$, $\ln km_k*\ln sdr_{kt-1}$. The validity of instruments is supported by the following diagnostics described below.

Firstly, in terms of **relevance** of the instruments, by having a look at the matrix of correlations between endogenous and instrumental variables one can have an idea of the reasonably high correlation among them (Appendix 1, Table 12).

Also in terms of relevance of the instruments, by inspecting the partial R-squared and the F-test of joint significance of the excluded instruments in the first-stage regressions; the minimum R-squared was 0.55 and the minimum F-statistic was 105.20 (P-value of 0.00), which further indicated they are fairly correlated with the endogenous variables (Appendix 1, Table 13).

Since the number of instruments exceeds the number of endogenous regressors I made use of over-identification restrictions tests to check for the **validity** of the instruments proposed (tests of orthogonallity, as in Davidson and MacKinnon, 1993; see Baum, Schaffer and Stillman, 2003, for a survey); by regressing a linear probability model in two-stages least squares (LPM/2SLS) one could confirm the validity of instruments. The tests used were the Sargan N*R-squared test and the Basmann test, and both failed in rejecting the null hypothesis that the excluded variables are valid instruments (Appendix 1, Table 13).

With the intention of emphasizing the relevance of controlling for endogeneity, I perform comparison between the standard (single stage) probit with the AGLS in the results presentation of Section 4; this is specially useful to have an idea of the magnitude (and sign) of the underlying simultaneous equations bias.

4   ESTIMATION RESULTS

Table 4 presents the results obtained from models with and without simultaneous equations bias correction – respectively, AGLS in column (1) and ordinary Probit in column (2).

By analyzing the results presented in column (1), one can see that, in spite of the expected multicolinearity among the terms of the translog profits equation, most variables related to density (den_{kt}), distance (km_k) and rivals' presence (sdr_{kt}) are at least significant at 10% level. $cpres_{kt-1}$ is very significant and with a positive sign, and thus some evidence is found on the existence of sunk costs at the city level; $tbapres_{kt-1}$ is also

---

[37] Stata's routine "ivprob" was used to perform all estimations and standard error corrections in Newey (1987)'s fashion (Harkness, 2001).

Table 4 Estimation Results

Dependent Variable	PR [ENTRY = 1]	
	(1) AGLS	(2) PROBIT
ln den$_{kt}$	0.078*	0.057
	(0.039)	(0.032)
(ln den$_{kt}$)^2	0.003	0.006‡
	(0.003)	(0.002)
ln km$_k$	0.464†	0.562†
	(0.211)	(0.205)
(ln km$_k$)^2	−0.033†	−0.038†
	(0.015)	(0.015)
ln sdr$_{kt}$	−0.183*	−0.105*
	(0.072)	(0.054)
(ln sdr$_{kt}$)^2	0.012*	0.006†
	(0.006)	(0.003)
ln den$_{kt}$ * ln km$_k$	−0.012*	−0.007
	(0.006)	(0.005)
ln den$_{kt}$ * ln sdr$_{kt}$	0.014*	0.005*
	(0.006)	(0.003)
ln km$_k$ * ln sdr$_{kt}$	0.015	0.011
	(0.009)	(0.007)
cpres$_{kt-1}$	0.049‡	0.061‡
	(0.023)	(0.021)
tbapres$_{kt-1}$	−0.035†	−0.042†
	(0.016)	(0.014)
Control for Endogeneity	YES	NO
Second-Order Terms	YES	YES
LR χ^2 Statistic	462.00‡	460.25‡
# Predicted = 0/# Actual = 0	673/719	683/719
# Predicted = 1/# Actual = 1	118/177	109/177
Lave-Efron Pseudo-R2	0.493	0.514
McKelvey-Zavoina Pseudo-R2	0.803	0.750
N. Observations	896	896

Notes:
(i) marginal-effects reported;
(ii) standard errors in parentheses;
(iii) *means significant at 10%, † at 5% and ‡ at 1% level;
(iv) city-specific dummies not reported.

significant and with a negative sign, meaning that routes exited by a bankrupt (Trans-brasil) were probably not perceived as profitable by the newcomer – and thus one can reject the hypothesis that Transbrasil's exit served as a market opportunity for Gol.

In order to investigate the *full effects* of variables den_{kt}, km_k and sdr_{kt}, one needs a measure that takes into account the coefficients of all related terms, and thus including the quadratic and interactions terms of equation (6). Therefore, *arc elasticities* were extracted, calculated by computing the full effect on the estimated probability of an arbitrary percentage change in each variable; the elasticity was considered a better measure than the marginal effects as it is invariant to the unit of measure. Figures were calculated by making use of the formula $(Pr_1 - Pr_0)/0.10$, where Pr_1 is the predicted probability with the explanatory variables at the sample mean, except for the one under analysis, which is increased by ten percent (represented by 0.10), and Pr_0 is the predicted probability holding all variables at the sample mean[38]. It is important to emphasize that, as here we have a translog specification, which engenders interactions between terms, the elasticity of any variable always depends on the values of the other variables in the model. Table 5 presents the estimated elasticities.

Figures in Table 5 are interpreted in the following way: if, for instance, den_{kt} is increased by 10%, the probability of entry (at the sample mean) is increased by 1.5%. By examining the differences (in percentage) between estimated elasticities between estimators, one can see that a significant bias is generated when endogeneity is not controlled. As expected, there seems to be a positive bias related to density (the difference between estimators is +88%), indicating that this variable is positively correlated with the error term, and, as discussed before, this is likely due to new demand generation caused by LCC entry[39]. Likewise, the positive simultaneity bias caused by not controlling for the endogeneity of sdr_{kt} (associated with +7% difference between elasticities) provides some evidence that LCC entry causes FSC presence to adjust upwards, and therefore providing basis for the rejection of the hypothesis of "crowding-out"; this is consistent with Winston and Collins (1992)'s results of an increase in 25% of incumbents' seats offered in response to low cost airline entry[40].

Table 5 Estimated Elasticities

Variable	(1) AGLS	(2) PROBIT	(2)–(1) %
den_{kt}	0.151	0.283	88%
km_k	0.061	0.194	220%
sdr_{kt}	0.166	0.179	7%

Notes:
(i) figures calculated at the sample mean;
(ii) calculated as a 10% increase in each variable at the mean.

---

[38] In terms of the binary explanatory variables, $cpres_{kt-1}$ and $tbapres_{kt-1}$ were set equal to zero and the DC's were considered by extracting the average effect times two (as each route has two endpoint cities).
[39] As mentioned in Section 1, routes entered by Gol had 13.1% increase in traffic density against a 7.0% increase on all 500 top-routes, when comparing figures of 2002 (after entry) with 2000 (previous to entry).
[40] For an analysis of FSC's price responses to Gol's entry, see Oliveira and Huse (2006).

Finally, one has that the coefficient of km_k presents a large positive difference between estimators (+220%); although flight distance is not *per se* an endogenous variable, its full effect measured by the elasticity in Table 5 is formed by endogenous variables, namely, the second-order terms $\ln den_{kt}{}^* \ln km_k$ and $\ln km_k{}^* \ln sdr_{kt}$. On account of these interactions, one would expect that, the estimated sensitivity of an additional kilometer to be higher because the estimated effects of both variables are higher – that is, because of the simultaneity bias of, respectively, den_{kt} and sdr_{kt}[41].

We now turn to the analysis of the signs and magnitudes of the estimated elasticities (the AGLS column). From Table 5 one can see that the elasticities of the original, not log-transformed, variables den_{kt}, km_k, and sdr_{kt} were, respectively 0.151, 0.061 and 0.166, all measured at the sample mean. Apart from the results of den_{kt}, which can be naturally thought of having positive overall effects – that is, the more is a given route's density of traffic the more it is attractive for LCC entry – special attention is required with respect to the analysis of the effects of km_k, and sdr_{kt}.

Firstly, we have an overall positive elasticity of sdr_{kt}, considering everything else held constant at the sample mean. The immediate conclusion implied by this result is that the higher is the presence of the FSC competitors in terms of seats available on direct flights (*per* route passenger) the higher is the propensity to enter of Gol; in other words, the more is the market underserved by direct FSC supply the less is the entry probability. On the one hand, one could interpret this finding as an indication that Gol does not follow the typical LCC practice of avoiding market contact with the legacy carriers but, quite the opposite, prefers behaving like a follower, learning from the others' past entry decisions in order to make its own route choices. The "learning" argument is in line with the results of Toivanen and Waterson (2001): "*Structural form estimations show that the positive effect of rival presence on the probability of entry is due to firm learning: rival presence increases the estimate of the size of the market*". Also, this would be clearly suggestive that route presence is quite an indication of underlying profitability, in opposition to Evans and Kessides (1993), which found evidence only of airport presence effects in the US market.

On the other hand, however, one could have the "market niche" argument of the LCC's: by positioning itself close to well-served direct markets, Gol is able to detect market opportunities once not perceived by the FSC's; this is especially true if one observes that, contrary to both SWP and JBP, and as discussed before, Gol provides a wider range of origin-and-destination products with stops and flight connections, and therefore placing in the market as the low fare alternative for less time-sensitive passengers.

Table 6 below presents a disaggregation of the elasticity of sdr_{kt} with respect to own values of that variable, with both den_{kt} and km_k held constant; one can observe decreasing but always positive elasticity figures, which means that a point of probability maximization is reached at higher levels of sdr_{kt}. This pattern confirms that Gol has a lower preference for creating new markets or entering underserved routes, contrary to the SWP.

---

[41] One has to be cautious with those arguments, however, as here we have only the difference between the estimated effects, and not the real simultaneity bias. The difference between the results of the estimator is indicative of the problems engendered by not controlling for the endogeneity of the regressors, however.

Table 6 Sdr$_{kt}$ Disaggregated Elasticities (1)

sdr$_{kt}$	0.70	1.00	1.50	3.00	6.00	10.00
Elasticity	0.82	0.66	0.45	0.14	0.02	0.00

Notes:
 (i) figures calculated holding km$_k$ and den$_{kt}$ at the sample mean;
 (ii) calculated as a 10% increase in each variable at the mean;
 (iii) values of sdr$_{kt}$ are representative of the following percentiles: 0.35, 0.50, 0.65, 0.80, 0.90 and 0.95.

Table 7 Sdr$_{ikt}$ Disaggregated Elasticities (2)

km$_k$ \ den$_{kt}$	350	500	750	1,150	1,850	2,250	2,600
1,000	2.32	2.31	2.26	2.21	2.20	2.22	2.24
3,000	2.55	2.36	2.15	1.98	1.89	1.88	1.90
6,000	2.40	2.11	1.83	1.62	1.51	1.50	1.51
15,000	1.85	1.50	1.20	0.99	0.89	0.88	0.90
50,000	0.80	0.53	0.35	0.25	0.21	0.22	0.23
150,000	0.12	0.06	0.03	0.02	0.01	0.02	0.02
300,000	0.01	0.00	0.00	0.00	0.00	0.00	0.00

Notes:
 (i) figures calculated holding sdr$_{kt}$ at the sample mean;
 (ii) calculated as a 10% increase in each variable at the mean;
 (iii) values are representative of the following percentiles: 0.20, 0.35, 0.50, 0.65, 0.80, 0.90 and 0.95.

Table 7 presents another disaggregation of the elasticity of sdr$_{kt}$, with respect to kilometers and density, this time holding sdr$_{kt}$ constant at the mean.

Table 7 is quite useful in showing a detailed analysis of Gol's route choice preferences regarding opponents' presence. Indeed, it is possible to observe two regimes: one, for the great majority of the routes, of ever positive elasticities – for routes with density below 150,000 pax/year –, and one with elasticities that are almost null – associated with very high density routes (for Brazilian standards), above 150,000 pax/year. This likely means that opponent's presence is a good indicator of underlying profitability for low-to-medium sized markets (in terms of density of traffic) but it is irrelevant for high-sized ones. In other words: actual market size is much more observable for the newcomer the higher is traffic density, and for routes in which traffic is rather thin, opponents' presence becomes a better signal for entry.

To sum up on the effects of sdr$_{kt}$, one has, contrary to traditional Industrial Organization literature, that rival's market presence does not inhibit entry but, on the contrary, is used as a warning sign for underlying profitability (mainly in markets with lower size). This is consistent with the results of Toivanen and Waterson (2001) which unveiled learning processes regarding entry[42]. There are three explanations for these results: first, as Brazil's very high interest rates are well-known for increasing the risk of enterprise, firms usually prefer not taking additional risk of venturing to create new markets; second, the airline market all over the world has been highly volatile and uncertain in the past few years; and third, as regulators were stimulating entry and forcing entry barrier to vanish, it was relatively easy for Gol to enter the same markets of its opponents and without much competitive disadvantage in terms of slots, access to airport facilities, etc.

The other result that needs to be carefully addressed is related to the marginal effects of km_k. A more detailed analysis of this variable is not only essential for proper understanding of the model's most relevant outcomes but also for performing an analysis of Gol's consistency with either SWP or JBP, detailed in Section 1. The positive elasticity of flight haul, presented in Table 5, does not reveal much as it is a rather aggregate figure, measured at the sample mean; once again, one useful alternative is to extract the same measure for a broader set of combinations of density and flight-haul values.

As one can see in Table 8, Gol's propensity to enter a route is marked by diminishing returns of flight-haul, and also with steadily decreasing effects of density. Again, one can observe two regimes: first, for routes with traffic density values up to approximately 50,000 pax/year, where distance has an ever increase effect on entry (although with diminishing returns), probably meaning that Gol is willing to substitute density by kilometers since it is able to force passengers to have stops or connect; this seems to be in line with a modified version of the JBP. And second, for routes with very thick density (higher than 50,000 pax/year), flight haul has no influence on entry; this is the outcome of the same factors affecting the elasticities of sdr_{kt} on the same set of routes, as seen above.

Table 8 Disaggregated Elasticities of km_k

km_k / den_{kt}	350	500	750	1,150	1,850	2,250	2,600
1,000	15.59	10.05	6.16	3.62	1.83	1.28	0.92
3,000	9.22	5.90	3.54	1.99	0.90	0.56	0.33
6,000	6.28	3.95	2.30	1.24	0.49	0.26	0.10
15,000	3.39	2.02	1.09	0.53	0.16	0.04	−0.04
50,000	1.00	0.50	0.22	0.08	0.01	−0.02	−0.04
150,000	0.12	0.04	0.01	0.00	0.00	0.00	−0.01
300,000	0.01	0.00	0.00	0.00	0.00	0.00	0.00

Notes:
  (i) figures calculated holding sdr_{kt} at the sample mean;
  (ii) calculated as a 10% increase in each variable at the mean;
(iii) values are representative of the following percentiles: 0.20, 0.35, 0.50, 0.65, 0.80, 0.90 and 0.95.

---

[42] In the present case, one could think of Gol learning from the FSC's previous entry decisions, that is, from the number of direct seats available, in order to infer the amount of business traffic on a given route, which is usually associated more with direct flights.

One would claim, however, that Gol changed operational standards from 2002 on, as discussed in 2, and probably started to enter a broader range of markets, especially with respect to long-haul routes and flight connections. This might be due to the opportunities emerged after some events of 2001, such as the exit of Transbrasil Airlines, the barriers to expansion at São Paulo city, the DAC's authorization to operate Rio de Janeiro's city-centre airport, and the fiercer incumbents' reactions on short-haul routes (Oliveira and Huse, 2004).

If the above argument is correct, however, the aggregated 2001-2002 regressions of Table 4 would present a rather "average" entry behavior, and disaggregation with respect to time would then be required. In order to perform that, variables $\ln km_k$, $(\ln km_k)^2$, $\ln den_{kt}* \ln km_k$ and $\ln km_k* \ln sdr_{kt}$ were multiplied by a dummy representative of year 2002, in order to test for possible structural change from that year on; thus the following variables were generated: $\ln km_k* d02$, $(\ln km_k)^{2*} d02$, $\ln den_{kt}* \ln km_k* d02$ and $\ln km_k* \ln sdr_{kt}* d02$. Table 9 reports the results for the same AGLS estimates but with those variables included.

By making use of the results of Table 9, it is possible to compare the elasticities of km_k across flight distance and route density *disaggregated by year*, in order to inspect how Gol's sensitivity to kilometers changed from 2001 to 2002. Tables 10 and 11 report the results.

Using Table 10 one can assess Gol's entry strategy in its start-up year. In this case a parabolic curve is clearly observed, meaning that the highest probability of entry is located within 1,150 and 1,850 kilometers for most cases; this could be associated with the SWP; in comparison, the average stage length of Southwest Airlines in 2003 was approximately 1160 kilometers[43]. On the other hand, in Table 11, the estimates for 2002 resulted in ever-positive flight-haul elasticities for any route density lower than 150,000 pax/year, and this is certainly more in line with JBP. Therefore we have that a pattern of entry that was in accordance with the SWP, observed in 2001, seems to be replaced by a propensity to enter a more diversified set of routes, and thus also considering higher flight sectors in 2002 (JBP). In both cases, however, a set of almost null elasticities for thick-density routes was observed.

The aforesaid findings noticeably reject the notion that Gol follows a pure standard of operations like the SWP or the JBP, but, consistently with a recent trend in the LCC segment, preferred to develop a more diversified portfolio of markets. Some evidence is found, however, that, for a great deal of medium-sized markets, Gol behaved more consistently with the SWP, but this was limited to its first year of operations; in contrast, there is evidence that she accomplished a deviation towards a more JBP-like standard of operations, implemented since 2002.

Two caveats must be considered with respect to the above mentioned results on flight distance: firstly, as discussed before, country idiosyncrasies (for example, unobserved economies of scope) probably influenced Gol in the strategic decision of not to focus only on non-stop short flight markets, but to put into practice a modified version of JBP – that is, also considering long-haul markets but with many stops and connections. Also, it is important to emphasize that, from 2002 on, Gol's pace of expansion ultimately made it the third biggest domestic airline; it is no surprise, therefore, that its entry behavior

---

[43] Source: Southwest Airlines Annual Reports (2003).

Table 9   Estimation Results Disaggregated by Year

Dependent Variable	PR [ENTRY = 1]
	AGLS
$\ln \text{den}_{kt}$	0.067
	(0.038)
$(\ln \text{den}_{kt})^2$	0.004
	(0.004)
$\ln \text{km}_k$	0.525‡
	(0.222)
$(\ln \text{km}_k)^2$	−0.039‡
	(0.016)
$\ln \text{sdr}_{kt}$	−0.157*
	(0.073)
$(\ln \text{sdr}_{kt})^2$	0.011
	(0.005)
$\ln \text{den}_{kt} * \ln \text{km}_{kt}$	−0.011*
	(0.006)
$\ln \text{km}_k * \ln \text{sdr}_{kt}$	0.012
	(0.009)
$\ln \text{den}_{kt} * \ln \text{sdr}_{kt}$	0.013
	(0.006)
$\ln \text{km}_k * \text{d}02$	−0.050†
	(0.031)
$(\ln \text{km}_k)^2 * \text{d}02$	0.007†
	(0.004)
$\ln \text{den}_{kt} * \ln \text{km}_k * \text{d}02$	0.001
	(0.001)
$\ln \text{km}_k * \ln \text{sdr}_{kt} * \text{d}02$	0.000
	(0.001)
apres_{kt-1}	0.008
	(0.034)
tbapres_{kt-1}	−0.033†
	(0.016)
LR χ^2 Statistic	468.36‡
Predicted = 0/Actual = 0	670/719
Predicted = 1/Actual = 1	119/177
Lave-Efron Pseudo-R2	0.504
McKelvey-Zavoina Pseudo-R2	0.810
N. Observations	896

Notes:
 (i) marginal-effects reported;
 (ii) standard errors in parentheses;
 (iii) *means significant at 10%, † at 5% and ‡ at 1% level;
 (iv) city-specific dummies not reported.

Table 10   Disaggregated Elasticities of km_k – 2001

km_k \ den_{kt}	350	500	750	1,150	1,850	2,250	2,600
1,000	11.09	6.81	3.83	1.85	0.32	−0.21	−0.58
3,000	6.65	4.02	2.17	0.92	−0.09	−0.47	−0.75
6,000	4.52	2.67	1.37	0.51	−0.21	−0.51	−0.73
15,000	2.37	1.31	0.61	0.16	−0.24	−0.43	−0.58
50,000	0.61	0.28	0.10	0.00	−0.11	−0.18	−0.25
150,000	0.05	0.02	0.00	0.00	−0.01	−0.02	−0.04
300,000	0.00	0.00	0.00	0.00	0.00	0.00	−0.01

Table 11   Disaggregated Elasticities of km_k – 2002

km_k \ den_{kt}	350	500	750	1,150	1,850	2,250	2,600
1,000	23.02	14.55	8.83	5.26	2.87	2.17	1.73
3,000	13.98	8.84	5.31	3.08	1.59	1.16	0.89
6,000	9.76	6.10	3.58	2.01	0.98	0.69	0.50
15,000	5.54	3.32	1.82	0.94	0.41	0.26	0.17
50,000	1.90	0.96	0.42	0.17	0.05	0.03	0.01
150,000	0.29	0.10	0.03	0.01	0.00	0.00	0.00
300,000	0.03	0.01	0.00	0.00	0.00	0.00	0.00

Notes:
  (i) figures calculated holding sdr_{kt} at the sample mean;
  (ii) calculated as a 10% increase in each variable at the mean;
 (iii) values are representative of the following percentiles: 0.20, 0.35, 0.50, 0.65, 0.80, 0.90 and 0.95.

has became more similar to the incumbent majors as Gol began to enter every single dense route across the country, irrespective of other market attributes, such as flight haul or rival's presence[44]. Once the decision of rapid expansion was taken it actually made the airline path-dependent, which can potentially undermine its LCC attributes and cost advantage.

5   CONCLUSIONS

This paper aimed at developing an empirical model for the analysis of entry decisions of Gol Airlines, the first low cost carrier in Latin America. By making use of Amemiya's Generalized Least Squares (AGLS) it was possible to estimate a route-choice model

---

[44] The increase in market contact among LCC's and FSC's is also reported by Boguslaski, Ito and Lee (2004).

associated with a flexible post-entry equilibrium profits equation, and in which some of the regressors were treated as endogenous.

Results revealed market size and rivals' route presence to be relevant indicators of underlying determinants of profitability; the relevance of rivals' presence is probably in accordance with a learning process (Toivanen and Waterson, 2001). The consistency of Gol's decision making with the pattern of entry classically established by Southwest Airlines – with stronger preference for dense and short-haul routes – was investigated and was not rejected for the start-up year (2001). Unambiguous evidence was found, however, that Gol deviated from this paradigm towards a standard of operations more in accordance with the JetBlue Airways' paradigm (higher average stage length), in 2002, when compared to 2001. This tendency engendered diversification of portfolio of routes, instead of specialization in one single business approach.

The main reason for that deviation is associated with country idiosyncrasies like unobserved economies of scope, which probably influenced Gol in the strategic decision of not to focus only on non-stop short flight sector markets, but to put into practice a modified version of JBP – that is, considering long-haul markets but with many stops and connections.

APPENDIX 1 – ADDITIONAL STATISTICS

Table 12 Matrix of Correlations of Variables

Variable	$\ln den_{kt}$	$\ln sdr_{kt}$	$(\ln den_{kt})^2$	$(\ln sdr_{kt})^2$	$\ln den_{kt}$ $* \ln km_k$	$\ln den_{kt}$ $* \ln sdr_{kt}$	$\ln km_k$ $* \ln sdr_{kt}$
$\ln den_{kt}$	1.000						
$\ln sdr_{kt}$	0.422	1.000					
$(\ln den_{kt})^2$	0.374	−0.177	1.000				
$(\ln sdr_{kt})^2$	0.206	0.943	−0.287	1.000			
$\ln den_{kt} * \ln km_k$	0.992	0.420	0.375	0.208	1.000		
$\ln den_{kt} * \ln sdr_{kt}$	0.847	0.310	0.630	0.083	0.844	1.000	
$\ln km_k * \ln sdr_{kt}$	0.412	0.973	−0.168	0.933	0.427	0.321	1.000
$\ln km_k$	0.074	−0.003	−0.059	0.061	0.131	0.058	0.194
$(\ln km_k)^2$	0.067	−0.002	−0.064	0.066	0.124	0.052	0.194
$\ln den_{kt-1}$	0.795	0.282	0.497	0.104	0.787	0.763	0.270
$(\ln den_{kt-1})^2$	0.568	−0.018	0.862	−0.154	0.566	0.700	−0.019
$\ln sdr_{kt-1}$	0.246	0.734	−0.079	0.695	0.246	0.275	0.729
$(\ln sdr_{kt-1})^2$	0.083	0.658	−0.189	0.698	0.085	0.102	0.673
$\ln den_{kt-1} * \ln km_k$	0.788	0.277	0.497	0.103	0.795	0.762	0.285
$\ln den_{kt-1} * \ln sdr_{kt-1}$	0.762	0.347	0.602	0.156	0.762	0.865	0.340
$\ln km_k * \ln sdr_{kt-1}$	0.244	0.717	−0.079	0.694	0.259	0.280	0.763
$\ln seats_{kt-1}$	0.125	−0.425	0.383	−0.371	0.131	0.184	−0.379
$\ln swe_{kt-1}$	0.667	0.596	0.427	0.460	0.667	0.762	0.604
$\ln asz_{kt-1}$	0.289	0.017	0.315	0.073	0.309	0.396	0.118

Table 13 Hypothesis Tests – AGLS Model

Test	Description	H_0	Statistic	P-Value
Endogeneity	*Smith-Blundell Test (1986)*	*All explanatory variables are exogenous*	15.49	*0.03*
Heteroskedasticity	*Likelihood-ratio/Maximum-likelihood heteroskedastic Probit*	*Homoskedasticity*	1.23	*0.75*
Relevance of Instruments (test of correlation with included endogenous variable)	*Partial R-squared of excluded instruments (min)*		0.55	
	F Test of excluded instruments – joint significance (min)	*Instruments are not relevant*	105.20	*0.00*
Validity of Instruments (overi-dentification/ort hogonality test of all instruments)	*Sargan Test*	*Instruments are valid*	1.87	*0.60*
	Bassman Test	*Instruments are valid*	1.82	*0.61*

REFERENCES

Amemiya, T. (1978) The Estimation of a Simultaneous Equation Generalized Probit Model. *Econometrica* 46, 1193–1205.

Baum, C., Schaffer, M. and Stillman, S. (2003) Instrumental Variable and GMM: Estimation and Testing. *Department of Economics Working Paper – Boston College* 545.

Ben-Akiva, M. and Lerman, S. (1985) *Discrete Choice Analysis: Theory and Application to Predict Travel Demand*, Cambridge, Massachusetts: The MIT Press.

Berry, S. (1992) Estimation of a Model of Entry in the Airline Industry. *Econometrica* 60, 889–917.

Berry, S., Carnall, M. and Spiller, P. (1996) Airline Hubs: Costs, Markups and the Implications of Customer Heterogeneity. *NBER Working Paper Series* 5561, 41 (Forthcoming in this volume).

Blundell, R. and Smith, R. (1989) Estimation in a Class of Simultaneous Equation Limited Dependent Variable Models. *Review of Economic Studies* 56, 37–57.

Boguslaski, R., Ito, H. and Lee, D. (2004) Entry Patterns in the Southwest Airlines Route System. Review of Industrial Organization, vol. 25(3), 317–350.

Borenstein, S. (1989) Hubs and High Fares: Dominance and Market Power in the U.S. Airline Industry. *Rand Journal of Economics* 20, 344–365.

Brander, J. and Zhang, A. (1990) Market Conduct in the Airline Industry: An Empirical Investigation. *Rand Journal of Economics*. 21(4):567–583.

Davidson, R. and MacKinnon, J. (1993) *Estimation and Inference in Econometrics*, 2nd edn. New York: Oxford University Press.

Doganis, R. (2001) *The Airline Industry in the 21st Century*, London: Routledge.

Dresner, M., Lin, J. and Windle, R. (1996) The Impact of Low-Cost Carriers on Airport and Route Competition. *Journal of Transport Economics and Policy* 30, 309–328.

Evans, W. and Kessides, I. (1993) Localized Market Power in the U.S. Airline Industry. *Review of Economics and Statistics* 75, 66–75.

Fox, J. (1997) *Applied Regression Analysis, Linear Models, and Related Methods.* Sage Publications, London.

Guimarães, C. (2002) Feita Para Voar. *Revista Exame*, vol. 01–04.

Harkness, J. (2001) IVPROB-IVTOBIT: Stata Modules to Estimate Instrumental Variables Probit and Tobit. *Statistical Software Components from Boston College Department of Economics.*

Ito, H. and Lee, D. (2003a) Low Cost Carrier Growth in the U.S. Airline Industry: Past, Present, and Future. *Department of Economics Working Papers – Brown University.*

Ito, H. and Lee, D. (2003b) Market Density and Low Cost Carrier Entries in the US Airline Industry: Implications for Future Growth. Forthcoming in *"Low Cost Carriers: A Global Experience"*, IBS Press, 2006.

Joskow, A., Werden, G. and Johnson, R. (1994) Entry, Exit, and Performance in Airline Markets. *International Journal of Industrial Organization* 12, 457–471.

Lee, L. (1991) Amemiya's Generalized Least Squares and Tests of Overidentification in Simultaneous Equation Models with Qualitative or Limited Dependent Variables. *Discussion Paper Series – Center for Economic Research – Department of Economics – University of Minnesota*, Minneapolis, Minnesota; n. 262:12p.

Lima, E. (2002) Brazil's Daring Wings. *Air Transport World*, May. Cleveland.

Morrison, S. (2001) Actual, Adjacent, and Potential Competition: Estimating the Full Effect of Southwest Airlines. *Journal of Transport Economics and Policy* 35, 239–256.

Mullineaux, D. (1978) Economies of Scale and Organizational Efficiency in Banking: A Profit-Function Approach. *Journal of Finance* 33, 259–280.

Newey, W. (1987) Efficient Estimation of Limited Dependent Variable Models with Endogenous Explanatory Variables. *Journal of Econometrics* 36, 231–250.

O'Connor, W. (1995) *An Introduction to Airline Economics*, 5th Edition edn. Westport, Connecticut: Praeger.

Oliveira, A. V. M. (2005) The Impacts of Liberalization on competition on an Air Shuttle Market. Working Paper N. 006 – Center for Studies of Airline Competition and Regulation (NECTAR) Working Paper Series. São José dos Campos, SP. Available at http://www2.ita.br/~nectar/dt006-05.pdf.

Oliveira, A. V. M. and Huse, C. (2006) Localized Competitive Advantage and Price Reactions to Low Cost Carrier Entry in the Brazilian Airline Industry. Center for Studies of Airline Competition and Regulation (NECTAR) Working Paper Series. São José dos Campos, SP. Available at http://www2.ita.br/~nectar/dt009-05.pdf.

Oum, T. H., Zhang, A. and Zhang, Y. (1993) Inter-Film Rivalry and Firm-Specific Price Elasticity in Airline Markets. *Journal of Transport Economics and Policy* 27(May), 171–192. Reprinted in Oum, T. H. et al. (eds.) (1995). *Transport Economics: Selected Readings*. Harwood Academic Publishers, pp. 313–342.

Oum, T., Zhang, A. and Zhang, Y. (1997) Inter-Firm Rivalry and Firm-Specific Price Elasticities in Deregulated Airline Markets. Oum, T. et al, editor. *Transport Economics – Selected Readings*. Amsterdam: Harwood Academic Publishers, p. 691.

Richard, O., Flight Frequency and Mergers in Airline Markets. *International Journal of Industrial Organization* 21(6):907–922.

Rivers, D. and Vuong, Q. (1984) Limited Information Estimators and Exogeneity Tests for Simultaneous Probit Models. *Social Science Working Paper – California Institute of Technology, Pasadena, CA* 539.

Rivers, D. & Vuong, Q. (1988) Limited Information Estimators and Exogeneity Tests for Simultaneous Probit Models. *Journal of Econometrics* 39, 347–366.

Silva, E. and Espírito Santo Jr. (2003) Introducing the Low Cost-Low Fare Concept in Brazil: Gol Airlines. *7th Annual World Conference of the Air Transport Research Society* (proceedings).

Slade, M. (1986) Taxation of Non-Renewable Resources at Various Stages of Production. *Canadian Journal of Economics* 19, 281–297.

Smith, R. and Blundell, R. (1986) An Exogeneity Test for a Simultaneous Equation Tobit Model with an Application to Labor Supply. *Econometrica* 54, 679–686.

Toivanen, O. and Waterson, M. (2001) Market Structure and Entry: Where's the Beef? Warwick Economic Research Papers, n. 593 (Forthcoming in Rand Journal of Economics).

Tretheway, M. (2004) Distortions of Airline Revenues: Why the Network Airline Business Model is Broken. *Journal of Air Transport Management* 10, 3–14.

US Department of Transportation (2001) Special Feature: The Low-Fare Evolution II. *Domestic Airline Fares Consumer Report*, Q3.

US Department of Transportation (2002) Special Feature: The Low-Fare Evolution. *Domestic Airline Fares Consumer Report*, Q3.

Whinston, M. and Collins, S. (1992) Entry and Competitive Structure in Deregulated Airline Markets: An Event Study Analysis of People Express. *Rand Journal of Economics* 23, 445–462.

Windle, R. and Dresner, M. (1999) Competitive Responses to Low Cost Carrier Entry. *Transportation Research – Part E* 35, 59–75.

Zalamea, L. (2001) Brazil's Gol Airlines Aims for Low-Cost, No-Frills Niche. *Aviation Week & Space Technology*, March. New York.

Advances in Airline Economics, Vol 1
Darin Lee (Editor)
© 2006 Published by Elsevier B.V.

14

Understanding Price Dispersion in the Airline Industry: Capacity Constraints and Consumer Heterogeneity[1]

Volodymyr Bilotkach[2]
Department of Economics, University of California, Irvine

ABSTRACT

This paper analyzes across-airline differences in economy class fares, aimed at consumers of different types. We use the sample of fares offered on the London–New York City market. Different booking scenarios are employed to obtain offered fares to resemble those aimed at customers of different types. We determine that fares aimed at business customers are different across airlines, while leisure fares are not. Such conduct appears to be consistent with airlines applying yield management techniques to manage uncertain demand under short-term fixed capacity. Yet, empirical support of this contention in our sample is weak. We hope that this finding sheds lights on the role of uncertain demand and constrained capacity in price dispersion in the airline and similar industries.

---

[1] This paper has benefited from comments by Stan Reynolds, Greg Crawford, Ron Oaxaca, Price Fishback, Alessandro Oliveira and Darin Lee. Any remaining errors are my responsibility. Part of this paper was completed during my appointment at the Economics Education Research Consortium (EERC) in Kiev, Ukraine. I thank EERC for support. The views presented here are mine and do not reflect those of the EERC or any of the Consortium's members.
[2] Address: University of California, Irvine, Department of Economics, 3151 Social Science Plaza, Irvine, CA, 92697, USA. E-mail: vbilotka@uci.edu.

1 INTRODUCTION

Research on price dispersion in the airline industry has thus far yielded two stylized facts. First, business travelers pay higher fares than do leisure travelers. Second, the degree of fare dispersion depends positively on competition (Dana 1999a, Hayes and Ross, 1998, Stavins, 2001, Borenstein and Rose, 1991, Giaume and Guillou, 2005). Constrained capacity with uncertain demand (Dana, 1999a) and price discrimination (Borenstein, 1985) have been suspected as the main sources of such price dispersion. Yet, the relative contribution of these factors remains open question. It is important to stress that constrained capacity and price discrimination need not be entirely conflicting explanations. Rather, as Dana (1999a) points out, apparent price discrimination might be a carrier's response to fixed capacity with uncertain demand. So, the issue is not whether the cause is price discrimination or constrained capacity, but rather whether capacity constraints with uncertain demand cause price discriminating behavior of airlines.

This paper looks at the issue of price dispersion from a somewhat different angle to provide a first approach to the question described above. We look at dispersion of fares aimed at consumers of different types, using a new sample of fares offered on the London–New York City market. Our aim is to compare across-airlines dispersion of fares, aimed at consumers of various types, to suggest a testable hypothesis for further exploration of the price dispersion puzzle.

The London–New York City route was chosen due to the large number of airlines (seven) providing non-stop service on this market, a significant number of competitors as compared to many other markets. The data for this study was collected from the Sabre computer reservation system through its Travelocity.com web site. A sample of offered round-trip economy class fares was obtained over an eight week period during the Spring of 2002. This method of data collection (together with certain empirical regularities of the airline markets) allows us to adequately control for the group at which a specific fare is targeted, which is generally not possible with the datasets usually employed in empirical research on airline industry.[3] Even though airlines do not specifically indicate what types of customers they are targeting with specific economy class fares, different screening devices (restrictions and/or penalties for changing the departure date and/or cancellation) are successfully used to make sure that business customers do not take advantage of the low fares aimed at leisure travelers. Further, airlines tend to offer lower fares with more restrictions, the further away the departure date, on the premise that leisure travelers tend to plan ahead more than business travelers.

Our analysis shows that on the London–New York City market, the fares aimed at business travelers are heterogeneous across airlines, while leisure fares do not vary much across carriers. We also suggest that capacity constraints are an important determinant of fare dispersion. Even though results are only marginally significant due to little within-carrier capacity variation over the period of data collection, the signs do point in the expected direction. It is hoped that the pattern of fare dispersion we observed can serve as the basis for future research to answer the question of the cause of fare dispersion in the airline and similar industries.

---

[3] For example, the U.S. Department of Transportation's Origin and Destination survey, the most widely used dataset in the literature, has no information indicating when tickets were purchased.

The remainder of the paper is organized as follows. Section 2 describes the London–New York City market and the dataset used. Section 3 presents estimation results and discusses possible econometric issues. Section 4 concludes the paper.

2 DESCRIPTION OF MARKET AND DATA

The market for passenger air transportation between London and New York City is the second largest international market worldwide in terms of number of passengers[4] (Williams, 2002), and the busiest transatlantic route. It should also be noted that both endpoints are served by several airports. The International Air Transport Association (IATA) code LON refers to all airports in the London area, which includes Heathrow (LHR), Gatwick (LGW), Stansted (STN), Luton (LTN) and City (LCY) airports. Of those, transatlantic services in the spring and summer of 2002 were only offered from LHR and LGW. On the other side of the ocean, the code NYC refers to all airports in the New York City area, including the John F. Kennedy (JFK), LaGuardia (LGA), Newark (EWR) and Islip Long Island (ISP) airports. However, non-stop transatlantic services are performed only from JFK and EWR. Thus, we have four distinct airport-pair markets (APM), of which only three were operational (there were no non-stop services between JFK and LGW).

As on every international route, travel between London and New York City is subject to some regulatory constraints. More specifically, it is governed by the Bermuda agreement, which is a bilateral air services agreement between the United States and the United Kingdom. The Bermuda agreement is considered more liberal than other similar bilaterals, since it does not govern everything in travel between the two countries[5]. Yet, it is also less liberal than a typical "open-skies" agreement, as it only provides for at most two UK and two US carriers on any given route between the two countries[6]. Important restrictions not directly included into the Bermuda agreement relate to access to London's Heathrow airport, the busiest and one of the most congested gateways in Europe. More specifically, access to LHR with direct non-stop services to/from the US is limited to British Airways (BA), Virgin Atlantic (VS), American Airlines (AA), and United Airlines (UA) (the so-called incumbent carriers). While other carriers performing services between London and the United States using their "fifth-freedom rights"[7] also can access LHR, these are not important players in the market, and fare setting for these carriers is subject to more stringent regulation. Otherwise, US and UK incumbent carriers are rather free to select frequency of service and fares charged.

---

[4] The largest one is the Taipei–Hong Kong market (classified as international by Williams (2002).

[5] There is a considerable literature describing the details of regulation of international air transportation (Doganis, 1991, 2001, de Murias, 1989, Sohor, 1991, Williams, 1993, 2002), and the reader wishing to learn about further details is directed to these sources.

[6] In their most liberal form, the only restriction in the "open-skies" agreements is that airlines performing direct services between the two countries be owned and controlled by nationals of either of the two states.

[7] Carrying passengers between London and the United States in conjunction with their services from other countries to the US through London.

For the purposes of our data analysis, a sample of roundtrip economy class fares, offered through the Sabre computer reservation system was collected[8]. The data were collected through the Travelocity.com website from March 5 until April 23, 2002. This means that we collected fares during a low travel season. The reason for using Sabre and Travelocity.com for the purpose of data collection is as follows. Travelocity is directly connected to Sabre, which means that the fares found on that web site are actual fares offered by airlines, not consolidator or some other special fares often offered by some travel agencies[9]. And, due to mandatory disclosure requirements, in effect as of spring of 2002, carriers were under obligation to participate in all major computer reservation systems, which means that the choice of CRS for data collection is not critical. Consequently, we chose Sabre/Travelocity, which offered us the friendliest interface and was also one of the industry's leaders in airline ticket distribution.

Fares were collected weekly, on Tuesdays (at approximately 7 a.m. Eastern standard time, which corresponds to noon in London) in the following way. We attempted to book roundtrip tickets for non-stop travel between London to New York City, for each airport-pair market and airline offering non-stop services on this APM. We played three different 'roles' when attempting to purchase tickets, so as to collect offered fares aimed at different types of consumers. First, we requested fares for trips which would require departure on Thursday of the current week and return on Saturday of the same week (this way one should obtain rather high fares, since most 'leisure' fares require a Saturday night stay). This would correspond to a typical business traveler embarking on a short business trip. We will refer to this as Booking Scenario 1. This booking scenario mostly yielded unrestricted economy class fares. The second booking scenario (Booking Scenario 2) involved departure within the next 48 hours and return 10 days after departure. This could correspond to either a longer-term business trip or a last minute vacation, so a typical pattern of fares is less certain than under the first scenario, and will probably depend on whether the airline already decided to offer discounted 'last minute' fares. Booking Scenario 3 involved departure a month from the date of booking and return 10 days after departure. This corresponds to pre-planned leisure travel, and should therefore result in the lowest fare of the three. For each of the three above-described scenarios we collected offered fares for travel originating in London and in New York City. Thus, for each airline and APM we could obtain up to six offered fares each week. Over the eight weeks of data collection, a total of 499 offered fares were obtained. Note that each of the fare types were not available every week, especially for airlines with low frequency service. If the first attempt to obtain a fare quote for a given airline under a given scenario was unsuccessful, no further attempts were made.

---

[8] Due to mandatory disclosure requirements, in effect as of spring of 2002, carriers are under obligation to participate in all major computer reservation systems, which means that the choice of CRS for data collection is not critical.

[9] A series of checks was performed in the process of data collection to ensure that the same fares as found on Travelocity.com could be obtained directly from airlines' web sites. Fares on Travelocity were usually only several dollars higher, a difference that could be attributed to fees charged by the travel agent. Collecting fares through a single web site is a much less time consuming process than doing it through several different web sites, especially since the actual difference in fares was negligible. Plus, many customers still tend to book travel through travel agencies and thus end up paying the fees.

Over the time period considered, seven different airlines offered non-stop service on the LON–NYC market. However, only five of those offered direct non-stop flights. Two airlines (Air India – AI and Kuwait Airways – KU) offered service between LHR and JFK in conjunction with their flights from New Delhi and Kuwait City, respectively. So, these flights were non-stop, but not direct. As both AI and KU have the respective "fifth freedom rights", they are able to sell tickets for the London to New York portion of their flights. The other five airlines are BA, AA, VS, UA (the above-mentioned incumbent airlines, present at LHR and offering service between LHR and both JFK and EWR), and Continental Airlines (CO), the only carrier offering non-stop service between EWR and LGW.

Over the course of data collection, no entry took place. However, BA, AA and AI increased frequencies on LHR–JFK route. Overall, the frequency of service on all airport-pair markets increased from 158 to 171 flights per week (excluding British Airways Concorde Supersonic service, the frequency of which also increased from six to seven flights a week; this service is not considered in our analysis).

Table 1 includes summary statistics of fares.

Numbers in the table show that variability of fares is more than substantial, both for the entire sample, and within each booking scenario. Fares under the first scenario are higher than those under the second scenario. Moreover, fares under the third scenario are generally the lowest ones (the extraordinarily high ones were offered by Air India and Kuwait Airways – in fact, the highest fare under the third booking scenario, quoted by one of the five US/UK carriers was equal to $1,350.1, the second highest being equal to $605.5). Note that search results always reflected the lowest fares offered by a given airline for given departure and return dates[10]. This pattern is as expected. Another

Table 1 Descriptive Statistics of Fares

	Average	Standard Deviation	Maximum	Minimum
Whole Sample	**1483.40**	**1619.55**	**9457.4**	**305.6**
Booking Scenario 1	2160.55	1792.70	9457.4	315.5
Booking Scenario 2	1665.06	1701.58	9457.0	319.8
Booking Scenario 3	578.83	634.16	5029.7	305.6
Heathrow – JFK Market	1686.60	1892.18	9457.4	305.6
Heathrow – Newark Market	1268.67	1253.89	7391.75	305.6
Gatwick – Newark Market/ Continental Airlines	1177.31	940.56	5168.05	311.9
British Airways	1020.03	800.04	6536.75	315.6
American Airlines	1019.38	563.23	2549.41	311.6
United Airlines	1646.71	1650.71	7391.75	324.6
Virgin Atlantic	1052.56	941.16	4762.5	305.6
Air India	3856.33	2984.66	9457.4	668.4
Kuwait Airways	2087.81	1960.05	8764.1	315.5

All numbers are in US Dollars and represent offered roundtrip fares, including applicable taxes.

---

[10] In some cases, higher fares were also available for different flights on the same dates. Yet, such occurrences were infrequent and not systematic.

interesting yet expected fact is the difference between fares offered by British and US carriers on one hand and the Asian airlines on the other hand. Asian carriers offer significantly higher fares, which is the result of the different institutional environment under which they operate. We will return to this issue in the next section.

3   DATA ANALYSIS AND DISCUSSION OF RESULTS

The purpose of the data analysis is to compare dispersion of fares under different booking scenarios. We begin by defining and describing variables to be used and hypotheses to be tested. This is followed by presentation of the simple pooled OLS estimation results. Afterwards, we discuss some alternative estimation techniques and interpret the results.

3.1   Description of Variables and Pooled OLS Estimation Results

The dependent variable in our estimation will be *LNFARE*, or the natural logarithm of the offered fare. Our analysis will be restricted to reduced-form price regressions. The independent variables can be divided into two broad groups. The time-invariant variables include AMP – specific and airline – specific dummies, (note that LGW–EWR dummy coincides with CO dummy variable), as well as the *UKUS* dummy, which takes the value of 1 if the itinerary originates in London and zero if it originates in New York[11]. Time-varying variables include *FREQUENCY* (weekly frequency of airline's service on a given APM – also used in logarithmic form in some specifications), and *TOTCOMP*, the weekly frequency of all competing airlines' services across all airport-pair markets (this variable serves as the measure of competition a given airline faces on the market). For reader's convenience, variables are listed and described in Appendix A.

The main focus of this paper is on the differences in fares across airlines for different booking scenarios. In particular, we will be interested in looking at Booking Scenario 3 (fares aimed at leisure travelers) versus the other two scenarios.

Let us now turn to estimation. The purpose of this study suggests estimating separate regressions for different booking scenarios. The relevant estimation issues are as follows. First, the discussion above suggests that Air India and Kuwait Airways should be excluded from the data analysis; so, we would like to see whether such exclusion is justifiable. Also, since airline fares are known to exhibit seasonal, weekly, daily and other types of temporal variation, some way of controlling for time effects will be needed.

We begin by presenting results of a simple pooled OLS model, using time dummy variables to control for inter-temporal variation, and excluding fares offered by Air India and Kuwait Airways. Justification for reporting these particular results can be found in the next sub-section of the paper. We run separate regressions for each booking scenario and correct for heteroscedasticity using White robust variance-covariance matrix.

We also attempted excluding frequency measures as potentially endogenous, as well as controlling for frequency with the number of seats offered using number of seats offered as an instrument for frequency. Yet, no significant effect on results was observed.

---

[11] The reason for including this variable is evidence that fares on the transatlantic market depend on which side of the ocean the trip originates. Brueckner (2003) finds higher fares for US-originating trips.

As can be seen from the tables below, substantial differences in fares across airlines are observed for the first two booking scenarios. This suggests that business travelers view airlines' services as rather differentiated (or at least such is the airlines' perception – remember that we are looking at offered fares, and not at purchased trips). On the other hand, advance purchase fares apparently aimed at leisure travelers are much less dispersed across airlines. Our task is indeed to approach the question of reasons behind this observation. Many factors can influence the inter-airline differences in offered fares. We actually can attempt considering impact of one of such factors, which is airline's short-term capacity constraints. This factor seems relevant, since estimation results suggest negative correlation between offered fares (under Scenarios 1 and 2) and the carriers' market shares.

Intuitively, we can offer the following link between constrained capacity and the observed pattern of fare dispersion. We can suspect that last minute fares offered by an airline which has larger market share could be lower than those of the smaller players in the low travel season due to the fact that the former may run a greater risk of letting higher proportion of its seats go empty. This could explain lower last minute fares offered by British Airways and American Airlines in comparison with other carriers. For advance purchase fares, we should not expect substantial differences in prices across airlines, as they all should have about the same unutilized capacity at that time (due to more unfilled seats). This intuition is consistent with airlines using the yield management technique to manage their realized demand (see Dana (1999b) for a detailed theoretical model).

To explore this issue further, we included airline – number of seats interaction variables into regressions. One problem with this variable is little variation, which in part explains only marginal significance of the coefficients below. In fact, variation in the number of seats has been observed for AA and BA (as they changed frequency of service) and for UA, as it varied aircraft type without changing frequency of service. The expectation is that for a potentially seat-constrained (low market share) airline this variable should exhibit negative and significant impact on fares for the first and the second booking scenarios. For the carriers with substantial market share and therefore potentially many unfilled seats this variable should not be statistically significant for Scenarios 1 and 2. For the third booking scenario, we should not observe any differences. Effectively, if number of seats is an indication of constrained capacity, the coefficients on airline – number of seats variables should represent some kind of 'shadow price' of increasing the capacity.

Estimation results are presented in Table 5. Only coefficients on airline – number of seats interaction variables are reported to save space. Coefficients on other variables are quantitatively and statistically similar to the ones found in Tables 2, 3 and 4.

Results from Table 5 could be interpreted as the evidence that constrained capacity (perhaps through realization of yield management) contributes to across-airline fare differences under the first and the second booking scenarios. Note that United Airlines can be considered the most capacity-constrained carrier of the three, and the coefficient on UA* Number of Seats variable is the only one exhibiting marginal statistical significance. Further, all the coefficients have the expected negative sign.

Yet, if we are correct in stating that more constrained capacity is behind higher fares under Scenarios 1 and 2, we should observe lower load factors for airlines offering larger capacity on the market. This is, actually, not true, as Table 6 demonstrates. In fact,

Table 2 Booking Scenario 1 (Short Business Trip)

Independent Variables	Specification 1	Specification 2	Specification 3
LHRJFK	−0.1656 (0.1019)	−0.1259 (0.2630)	−0.1285 (0.2517)
CO	0.4472** (0.0350)	0.4885** (0.0221)	0.4673** (0.0347)
BA	−1.1924** (0.0048)	−1.1946** (0.0048)	−1.3243** (0.0101)
AA	−0.5377** (0.0115)	−0.5354** (0.0113)	−0.5559** (0.0226)
UA	0.4674** (0.0001)	0.4715** (0.0001)	0.4700** (0.0001)
UKUS	−0.1316** (0.0048)	−0.1311** (0.0051)	−0.1311** (0.0053)
FREQUENCY	0.0038 (0.3881)	—	—
LNFREQUENCY	—	0.0193 (0.8358)	0.0233 (0.8016)
TOTCOMP	−0.0377** (0.0091)	−0.0393** (0.0063)	—
LNTOTCOMP	—	—	−5.4633** (0.0149)
	N = 141 d.f. = 125 Adj. R-squared = 0.51	N = 141 d.f. = 124 Adj. R-squared = 0.51	N = 141 d.f. = 125 Adj. R-squared = 0.50

Notes:
(1) Dependent variable is LNFARE
(2) Time dummy variables are used in each specification, but not reported
(3) Constant term is included into each regression but not reported
(4) Numbers in parentheses are p-values
(5) Results corrected for heteroscedasticity using White robust variance-covariance matrix
(6) ** – significant at 5% level
(7) * – significant at 10% level.

United Airlines' load factor is not that different from that of most other carriers. In fact, the only carrier whose load factor clearly stands out is Virgin Atlantic. This carrier's average load factor over the time period considered was about 15% higher than that of its main competitors.

Thus, even though there is an indication that the lower number of seats offered by an airline is associated with higher prices aimed at business travelers, we cannot claim with certainty that constrained capacity is the source of this phenomenon. Available data does not permit a deeper analysis of this issue. Yet, we can hypothesize that, in addition to the number of seats offered, other airline or maybe even route-specific factors can explain the phenomenon we report here. For example, UA may offer higher fares under Scenarios 1 and 2 as it tries to single out price-insensitive passengers exhibiting high

Table 3 Booking Scenario 2 (Extended Business Trip or Last Minute Vacation)

Independent Variables	Specification 1	Specification 2	Specification 3
LHRJFK	−0.1534 (0.3634)	−0.0723 (0.7131)	−0.0755 (0.7013)
CO	1.0093** (0.0052)	1.0834** (0.0053)	1.0962** (0.0042)
BA	−1.8928** (0.0064)	−1.8840** (0.0065)	−2.2634** (0.0074)
AA	−0.7467** (0.0284)	−0.7461** (0.0276)	−0.8421** (0.0301)
UA	0.9081** (0.0000)	0.9027** (0.0000)	0.9212** (0.0000)
UKUS	−0.6243** (0.0000)	−0.6240** (0.0000)	−0.6220** (0.0000)
FREQUENCY	0.0036 (0.6282)	—	—
LNFREQUENCY	—	−0.0313 (0.8520)	−0.0259 (0.8773)
TOTCOMP	−0.0712** (0.0030)	−0.0734** (0.0020)	—
LNTOTCOMP	—	—	−10.8304** (0.0036)
	N = 141 d.f. = 125 Adj. R-squared = 0.58	N = 141 d.f. = 125 Adj. R-squared = 0.58	N = 141 d.f. = 125 Adj. R-squared = 0.57

Notes:
(1) Dependent variable is LNFARE
(2) Time dummy variables are used in each specification, but not reported
(3) Constant term is included into each regression but not reported
(4) Numbers in parentheses are p-values
(5) Results corrected for heteroscedasticity using White robust variance-covariance matrix
(6) ** – significant at 5% level
(7) * – significant at 10% level.

degree of brand loyalty. It could also be the case that airlines on this market practice yield management in different ways. On one hand, this explanation may seem strange, as competition should punish the airline for inefficient yield management practices. On the other hand, one should keep in mind that for some carriers the London–New York market is one of the routes in their hub-and-spoke network (this is so for British Airways, Virgin Atlantic and Continental Airlines), while for others this market is almost like a stand-alone route (especially so for United Airlines[12]). In either case, while we detect

---

[12] In fact, Bilotkach (2004) finds that United Airlines (in 1999) channeled almost no transatlantic traffic through New York. American Airlines, however, did channel some passengers to Europe through JFK.

The usual problem of testing for pooled OLS versus the fixed effects model is in our case complicated by the fact that some explanatory variables do not vary over time. Time invariant variables are captured by the fixed effects, and fixed effects model does not allow us to obtain estimates of coefficients on those variables. This is not a problem when time invariant variables are used as controls. However, time invariant airline dummy variables are the most important ones in our study, so we cannot simply let them be swept away by fixed effects, in case fixed effects model happens to be the model of choice. A technique for estimating the coefficients on time invariant variables in fixed effects models has been developed by Polacheck and Kim (1994) and improved by Oaxaca and Geisler (2003).

Suppose we can divide our explanatory variables into two groups. The first group will consist of k_1 time varying variables X, while the second group will include k_2 time invariant variables Z. In this case the original pooled OLS model can be written as:

$$Y_{it} = \alpha + Z_i\gamma + X_{it}\beta + \varepsilon_{it} \qquad i = 1, \ldots, n \quad t = 1, \ldots, T_i$$

The idea of Polacheck and Kim (1994) is to estimate the model

$$Y_{it} = \alpha_i + X_{it}\beta + \varepsilon_{it} \qquad i = 1, \ldots, n \qquad t = 1, \ldots, T_i$$

by fixed effect and use the fixed effects coefficient on time varying variables to estimate, as the second stage, the following model:

$$Y_{i\bullet} - X_{i\bullet}\beta_{FE} = \alpha + Z_i\gamma + \varepsilon_{it} \quad i = 1, \ldots, n \qquad t = 1, \ldots, T_i$$

where $Y_{i\bullet}$ and $X_{i\bullet}$ are respective group means. The estimation technique is FGLS to correct for heteroscedasticity. The appropriate statistic to test for existence of fixed effects in this case is:

$$\frac{\left(\varepsilon'_{OLS}\varepsilon_{OLS} - \varepsilon'_{FE}\varepsilon_{FE}\right)/(n - 1 - k_2)}{\varepsilon'_{FE}\varepsilon_{FE}/(n\overline{T} - n - k_1)} \sim F_{n-1-k_2, n\overline{T}-n-k_1}$$

Where $\overline{T} = \sum T_i/n$. The null hypothesis is no fixed effect. Test results for various specifications (along with values for adjusted R-squared and Akaike information criterion) are given in Appendix B.

The first thing to note from Appendix B is that we were not able to reject pooled OLS in 26 out of 36 cases, and where AI/KU variables were omitted from the analysis, there was not a single case where pooled OLS could be rejected. Thus, the issues of model selection and inclusion of AI and KU into the analysis are indeed inter-related. The specification selection decision we have to make here is different from the 'classical' model selection problem, since new variables here also bring in new observations. We use Akaike information criterion (AIC) to address this issue. We observe that in all specifications the value of AIC with AI and KU dummies included is higher than without them. Thus, AIC favors the specifications without AI and KU fares to those with them.

We conclude the following. First, models with time dummy variables outperform those with the time trend. Second, observations corresponding to AI and KU appear to add more to noise than to explaining the phenomena studied. Third, pooled OLS is preferred to the fixed effects estimation technique. We do not report results of the tests of OLS versus random effects model here: it sufficed to say that where positive variance of the error term was obtainable by standard techniques (which was rare), relative efficiency of pooled OLS over random effects model was not rejected.

3.3   Discussion of Results

To conclude this section, analysis of dispersion of fares, aimed at different types of travelers, revealed that economy class fares, targeted at business travelers, differ substantially across airlines, whereas leisure fares are largely homogeneous. Obviously, we do not observe actual purchases made by travelers. Yet, a customer attempting to book a ticket at roughly the time of our data collection would have faced the same fares as those included into our sample and could only have a choice between purchasing at the quoted fare or attempting to purchase from a different carrier. Second, in their fare setting decisions airlines should have a specific customer in mind; moreover, current technology allows carriers to observe and track competitors' fares, which means that it is very likely that fares we observe in the sample have been set taking into account fares offered by competing airlines at roughly the same time.

We also suggest that short-term capacity constraints appear to contribute to the dispersion of last-minute fares we have observed here. Yet, evidence to this end is not conclusive, as relevant coefficients exhibit only marginal significance and there is no correlation between the numbers of seats offered by an airline and realized load factors. The most plausible explanation for this result is use of yield-management techniques by airlines, even though other airline or route-specific factors cannot be ruled out at this stage. As noted in Dana (1999a), at any given moment an airline faces the choice between selling a ticket for sure at a lower price, or waiting for a high valuation consumer to show up. Then an airline having more empty seats left as the flight's departure date nears would be in pressure to lower prices. And we do observe that airlines with larger market share (and potentially more unfilled seats before departure date) charge lower last-minute fares than do carriers with smaller market share.

4   CONCLUSIONS

This paper analyzes the issue of across-airline dispersion of economy class fares, aimed at consumers of different types (namely, business versus leisure travelers). We use a sample of economy class roundtrip fares, offered by various carriers for travel between London and New York. The data was collected weekly over eight weeks in the spring of 2002 from Sabre computer reservation system through the Travelocity.com website. Three booking scenarios were used, one of which clearly corresponds to the business travel, one profiles a leisure traveler, and the third one can be construed as either a prolonged business trip or a last-minute vacation (so, it is located in between the two extremes).

Data analysis shows that across-airline dispersion of fares, aimed at business travelers, appears to be more than substantial, with some airlines offering fares several times higher than others. For leisure travelers, however, no substantial variation in fares across airlines is observed. Further analysis suggests that short-term capacity faced by airline companies appears to contribute to the pattern of price dispersion we observe. This appears consistent with the use of yield management to cope with uncertain demand when capacity is fixed. Thus, we can suggest that capacity constraints do contribute to dispersion of fares. Yet, further analysis is needed for this suggestion to turn into a solid conclusion.

We should caution that our results cannot be claimed to state that capacity constraints (coupled with uncertain demand and consumer heterogeneity) is *the* source of price dispersion in the airline industry, as we have not explicitly rejected the hypothesis that price discrimination contributes to price dispersion. Rather, one should view our conclusion as suggesting a direction for further research. Our hope is that the result we observe (heterogeneous prices for business travelers with more capacity constrained airline offering higher fares, and uniform fares for leisure travelers) will point us towards a test for determining the primary reason for price dispersion in the airline and similar industries.

APPENDIX A – DESCRIPTION OF VARIABLES

Variable	Description
LHRJFK	Dummy variable taking the value of 1 for trips between London Heathrow and John F. Kennedy airports
CO	Dummy variable taking the value of 1 for trips on Continental Airlines
BA	Dummy variable taking the value of 1 for trips on British Airways
AA	Dummy variable taking the value of 1 for trips on American Airlines
UA	Dummy variable taking the value of 1 for trips on United Airlines
AI	Dummy variable taking the value of 1 for trips on Air India
KU	Dummy variable taking the value of 1 for trips on Kuwait Airways
UKUS	Dummy variable taking the value of 1 for trips originating in London
FREQUENCY	Number of weekly services by an airline on a given airport-pair market
LNFREQUENCY	Natural logarithm of FREQUENCY
TOTCOMP	Number of weekly services by other airlines on the market (includes all airport-pair markets)
LNTOTCOMP	Natural logarithm of TOTCOMP

APPENDIX B TESTING FOR POOLED OLS VERSUS FIXED EFFECTS MODEL

Note: The null hypothesis in the test, which uses the test statistic is that pooled OLS is more efficient than fixed effects model.

Table B.1 Booking Scenario 1 (Short Business Trip)

Dependent Variables Used	Time Dummy Variables						Time Trend					
	AI/KU Excluded			AI/KU Included			AI/KU Excluded			AI/KU Included		
	Test Result	Adjusted R-squared	Akaike	Test Result	Adjusted R-squared	Akaike	Test Result	Adjusted R-squared	Akaike	Test Result	Adjusted R-squared	Akaike
FREQUENCY, TOTCOMP	Accept	0.51	0.441	Accept	0.43	1.352	Accept	0.23	0.868	Accept	0.32	1.508
LNFREQ, TOTCOMP	Accept	0.51	0.446	Reject	0.49	1.315	Accept	0.23	0.867	Reject	0.37	1.503
LNFREQ, LNTOTCOMP	Accept	0.49	0.458	Reject	0.48	1.318	Accept	0.20	0.907	Reject	0.37	1.505

Note: "Accept" means that we failed to reject the null hypothesis at 5% significance level; "Reject" indicates that the null hypothesis was rejected at 5% significance level.

Table B.2 Booking Scenario 2 (Extended Business Trip or Last Minute Vacation)

Dependent Variables Used	Time Dummy Variables						Time Trend					
	AI/KU Excluded			AI/KU Included			AI/KU Excluded			AI/KU Included		
	Test Result	Adjusted R-squared	Akaike	Test Result	Adjusted R-squared	Akaike	Test Result	Adjusted R-squared	Akaike	Test Result	Adjusted R-squared	Akaike
FREQUENCY, TOTCOMP	Accept	0.57	1.418	Accept	0.53	1.780	Accept	0.42	1.707	Accept	0.45	1.902
LNFREQ, TOTCOMP	Accept	0.57	1.419	Accept	0.53	1.781	Accept	0.42	1.701	Accept	0.45	1.906
LNFREQ, LNTOTCOMP	Accept	0.57	1.431	Accept	0.53	1.770	Accept	0.38	1.769	Accept	0.44	1.925

Note: "Accept" means that we failed to reject the null hypothesis at 5% significance level; "Reject" indicates that the null hypothesis was rejected at 5% significance level.

Table B.3 Booking Scenario 3 (Pre-Planned 10-Day Vacation)

Dependent Variables Used	Time Dummy Variables						Time Trend					
	AI/KU Excluded			AI/KU Included			AI/KU Excluded			AI/KU Included		
	Test Result	Adjusted R-squared	Akaike	Test Result	Adjusted R-squared	Akaike	Test Result	Adjusted R-squared	Akaike	Test Result	Adjusted R-squared	Akaike
FREQUENCY, TOTCOMP	Accept	0.61	−1.184	Reject	0.61	0.348	Accept	0.46	−0.893	Reject	0.59	0.363
LNFREQ, TOTCOMP	Accept	0.61	−1.190	Reject	0.61	0.348	Accept	0.46	−0.898	Reject	0.59	0.365
LNFREQ, LNTOTCOMP	Accept	0.61	−1.195	Reject	0.60	0.352	Accept	0.47	−0.904	Reject	0.59	0.365

Note: "Accept" means that we failed to reject the null hypothesis at 5% significance level; "Reject" indicates that the null hypothesis was rejected at 5% significance level.

WORKS CITED

Bilotkach, Volodymyr (2004) *Asymmetric Regulation and Airport Dominance in International Aviation: Evidence from London – New York Market*, University of Arizona Department of Economics Working Paper 04-07.

Borenstein, Severin (1985) *Price Discrimination in Free-Entry Markets* RAND Journal of Economics, Vol. 16, No. 3, Autumn 1985, 380–397.

Borenstein, Severin and Nancy L. Rose (1994) *Competition and Price Dispersion in the U.S. Airline Industry* The Journal of Political Economy, Vol. 102, Issue 4, August 1994.

Brueckner, Jan K. (2003) *International Airfares in the Age of Alliances: The Effects of Codesharing and Antitrust Immunity* Review of Economics and Statistics, February 2003, 105–118.

Dana, James (1999a) *Equilibrium Price Dispersion under Demand Uncertainty: The Roles of Costly Capacity and Market Structure* RAND Journal of Economics, Winter 1999.

Dana, James (1999b) *Using Yield Management to Shift Demand when the Peak Time is Unknown* RAND Journal of Economics, Fall 1999.

de Murias, Ramon (1989) *The Economic Regulation of International Air Transport* McFarland and Company.

Doganis, Rigas (1991) *Flying Off Course: The Economics of International Airlines* 2nd ed. Harper Collins Academic.

_____ (2001) *The Airline Business in the 21st Century* Routledge.

Giaume, Stephanie and Sarah Suillou (2005) *Concentration, Market Share Inequality and Prices: An Examination of European Airline Markets*, in Darin Lee, ed., Advances in Airline Economics, Vol. 1, Elsevier.

Hayes, Kathy J. and Leola B. Ross (1998) *Is Airline Price Dispersion the Result of Careful Planning or Competitive Forces?* Review of Industrial Organization, Vol. 13, No. 5.

Oaxaca, Ronald L. and Geisler, Iris (2003) *Fixed Effects Models with Time Invariant Variables: A Theoretical Note*, Economics Letters, Vol. 80, No. 3, September 2003.

Polachek, S.W. and Kim, M. (1994) *Panel Estimates of the Gender Earnings Gap: Individual-Specific Intercept and Individual-Specific Slope Models*, Journal of Econometrics, Vol. 61, pp. 23–42.

Sohor, Eugene (1991) *The Politics of International Aviation* Macmillan.

Stavins, Joanna (2001) *Price Discrimination in the Airline Market: The Effect of Market Concentration* Review of Economics and Statistics, Vol. 83, No. 1. (February 2001).

Williams, George (1993) *The Airline Industry and the Impact of Deregulation* Ashgate.

_____ (2002) *Airline Competition: Deregulation's Mixed Legacy* Ashgate.

Advances in Airline Economics, Vol 1
Darin Lee (Editor)
© 2006 Published by Elsevier B.V.

15

Airport Competition: Regulatory Issues and Policy Implications[1]

Peter Forsyth

Department of Economics, Monash University[2]

1 INTRODUCTION: THE EMERGENCE OF AIRPORT COMPETITION

Airport competition is an issue which has been attracting more attention of late, especially now that many airports in Europe, the Asia Pacific, and Canada have been either privatised or commercialised. Under public ownership, airports were regarded as regional natural monopolies, not competing with airports in other cities or regions. They were supposed to produce efficiently and keep charges low (whether they achieved this is another matter). Under privatisation or commercialisation, it was recognised that airports would possess market power, and that they would use it to increase prices. To constrain this, when most airports were privatised they were subjected to price regulation – in a few cases, such as in New Zealand, they were subjected to a less prescriptive form of control, such as the threat of explicit regulation. Regulation, however, is well recognised as having its limitations, particularly in regard to incentives for productive efficiency. Thus the question arises of whether competition can be an effective substitute for regulation.

Over the same period, more airports have been entering the market. Former military airports, especially in Europe, have been sold off to local communities, and these are looking for traffic to use the airports. Airports which previously only served local

---

[1] This paper was first presented at the HWWA Workshop "Congestion and Competition-Major Problems of the Airport Industry" Hamburg, February 2004. I am grateful for comments received at this Workshop. All errors are mine.
[2] Address: Department of Economics, Clayton Campus, Monash University, Vic, 3800, Australia. Email: peter.forsyth@buseco.monash.edu.au.

have fixed capacities, with limited ability to expand capacity in the short term. Under oligopoly, competition will be imperfect in several ways. Depending on the competitive strategies adopted, prices may not be bid down to costs. Tacit collusion may exist. This is a particular concern with fixed capacity industries, like electricity generators and airports – given that the ability to handle additional output is strictly limited, there is no incentive for the firms to enter price competition. In the longer term, excess capacity can result from capacity wars. Airports can use excess capacity as a strategic weapon, to deter entry. Thus it has been suggested that BAA has been willing to create excess capacity at Stansted to deter competition from other airports in the region such as nearby Luton (Starkie, 2004).

Scale economies and entry barriers. It is not easy for a new airport to enter and compete with an existing airport. One of the main reasons for this is legal – entry may be prohibited for environmental reasons. While it is difficult for existing airports to expand, it is usually even more difficult for new airports to establish in urban areas. There have been few new airports established in recent decades in Europe, North America an Australia (though additional competition has come from existing secondary airports outside urban areas).

Even when a new airport is permitted, it will have problems in achieving sufficient scale to compete effectively with the incumbent. Scale is important partly for costs; minimum per unit costs cannot be achieved with small airports, though costs may level out with airports of medium rather than large size. However, medium sized airports cannot achieve the network economies that large incumbent ones can; they will not be as attractive as hubs because they will not have services to as many destinations, and they will not be as attractive to origin destination traffic because they will not have as good frequencies. These, combined with the almost inevitable poorer location, on the urban fringe, makes it difficult for the new airport to compete with the incumbent – second airports usually take decades to build up sufficient networks and frequencies to challenge the incumbent airport – examples such as Montreal Mirabel airport and Milan Malpensa airport come to mind.

Excess demand and congestion. Often it is the case that the major airport in a city is subject to excess demand – this excess demand may be rationed by congestion, administrative methods such as slots, or both (as is the case with London's Heathrow and Gatwick airports, and New York's La Guardia and Kennedy airports). Congestion creates a competitive disadvantage, which the newer airports in the city/region can take advantage of, and slot controls mean that the major airport faces excess demand which the other airports can satisfy. However, in this capacity and congestion constrained situation, the airports are not really competing. The major airport has no incentive to lower prices to win demand from the other airports because it does not have the capacity to serve it. The other airports may have an incentive to win demand from the major airport, but their ability to do so is limited by the fact that they are inferior substitutes – travellers and airlines prefer to use the major airport. Competition from the fringe airports is not likely to be a strong restraint on the pricing of the major airport. Indeed, in these circumstances, efficiency is compromised by prices of the major airport being too low (probably because they are regulated) than by being too high.

Sunk costs and inflexibility. Airports represent substantial sunk costs, in runways and terminals. The demand for their services varies considerably over time, however. Sunk costs and capacity inflexibility do not prevent competition, but they do make it work less smoothly. Other industries, such as motor vehicles, hotels and telecommunications infrastructure face considerable sunk costs and manage to compete. However, responses are not always quick, and profitability can vary sharply over the cycle. Thus a secondary airport may offer basic terminal facilities to appeal to a LCC; the major airport, which may have just completed an expensive terminal upgrade, may have excess terminal capacity, but it may have difficulties in offering the LCC a low price to use the terminal, especially if it is currently trying to recoup the costs from its existing customers. If an airport has excess runway capacity, it may be many years before prices set at efficient levels will cover costs.

Regulation of competitors. Most major airports in urban areas are either government or locally owned, or if they are privately owned, directly regulated. In Australia and New Zealand, privately owned airports are not directly regulated, though they are subject to price monitoring or the threat of regulation (Forsyth, 2004; McKenzie-Williams, 2004). The working of regulation impacts on the working of competition. Cost plus regulated airports do not have a strong incentive to maximise profits, so that their responses to competition need not be those of a typical private firm. A competitor may reduce prices and win customers from the regulated major airport, but it may not respond – it may increase prices to remaining customers to cover its cost. Regulation typically allows airports to cover their costs on a year to year basis (which is strictly arbitrary). The result is that sometimes their prices are well above marginal costs (when there is excess capacity), and at other times, prices are well below the opportunity cost of the capacity (when there is excess demand, but prices are kept low and cannot be used to ration demand). High prices during periods of excess capacity may mean that airlines are encouraged to use less convenient secondary airports even when they can be served very cheaply at major airports. It is not easy to generalise about the response of a regulated airport to competition – the response depends critically on the nature of the regulation and how it works. What is certain is that it is inaccurate to assume that the response is the same as that of a profit maximising private firm. How competition works in the presence of regulation has to be analysed on a case by case basis.

Subsidies. Airports are often subsidised. Much attention has been given recently to the subsidies which local regions have been granting to secondary airports, especially in Europe. Some major airports are permitted to operate without generating a commercial return, and some have been provided with assets at less than market prices. Competition works best when none of the competitors is in receipt of a subsidy – when subsidies are present, the airports in receipt of a subsidy gain an advantage, and there is a loss of efficiency due to a distortion in the allocation of traffic to airports. Sometimes subsidies might be justified in terms of correcting externalities. A region may believe that it gain economic benefits if more traffic flows through its airport (and then travels directly to the large city which is the primary destination) – if so, an airport subsidy could correct the externality. If the major airport is congested, there could be a case for subsidising the substitute airport (though it would be better to eliminate the congestion by pricing the major airport properly). This is similar to the argument for subsidising public transport based on the congestion externalities created by private road transport. Whether subsidies are justified or not, they will impact on the way competition works, and this needs to be factored into any assessment of airport competition.

2.2   Airport Prices and Price Discrimination

Airports typically impose price structures which embody considerable price discrimination. They charge different prices to different users for the use of the same facility at the same time. There are good reasons for this; such a price structure is likely to be a reasonably efficient way of achieving cost recovery when the airport has large sunk costs, low marginal costs and excess capacity. The ability to price discriminate is put under pressure by competition, and at the very least, the airport may be forced to adjust its price structure when competition emerges.

This is evident when a major central city airport begins to face competition from a urban fringe or regional airport for LCC traffic. Whether as a result of lower cost or subsidies, the secondary airport may seek to attract LCCs by offering lower charges than the central city airport. If the airport is a cost plus regulated airport, it may not respond. However, if the city airport wished to retain the traffic, it will have to adjust its price structure. It may do this by rearranging prices so that it matches charges at the secondary airport in the pricing category in which the LCC falls – all airlines will face the same charges if their flights fall into this category. Other charges will be increased to recoup the revenue lost. The implications of competition for price structures is considered in detail later.

2.3   Competition and Efficiency in Airports

One of the primary reasons why competition is promoted is that it can be the most effective device for ensuring efficiency. With airports there are several aspects of efficiency which are relevant.

Allocative efficiency at airports embraces some distinct aspects. Firstly, it is desirable that price levels be set at an efficient level – in the airports case, prices should reflect the opportunity cost of use of the facility. By this criterion, efficiency is often not achieved, since prices are set above marginal costs in airports with ample capacity, and well above opportunity cost in busy, capacity constrained, airports. Competition encourages firms to keep prices down, close to marginal cost, under certain circumstances. Secondly, it is desirable that the price structure be efficient. As noted above, when there are cost recovery constraints, it may not be feasible to have prices equal to marginal cost, but price structures may be efficient or inefficient. Airports frequently have weight based or passenger based charges – these may be an imperfect approximation to Ramsey prices, and the deadweight losses, as compared to an ideal structure, may be low (see Morrison, 1982). Competition influences price structures – additional competition for a category of user will induce the airport to lower prices for that category, if necessary increasing other prices to achieve that revenue constraint. More competition does not necessarily induce a more efficient price structure (e.g. see Braeutigam, 1979).

Another aspect of efficiency which is relevant to airports arises with the allocation of flights to airports. When there are several airports competing, it is efficient that flights are allocated to their most preferred airport to the extent possible. If capacity is constrained, this would mean that the flights which have the greatest willingness to pay use the preferred airport, but when capacity is not constrained, it is efficient that flights use their most preferred airport as long as they are prepared to pay the marginal costs of doing so. Competition between airports influences the allocation of flights between them – sometimes this process may not work efficiently however.

Productive efficiency is another important aspect of efficiency – it is desirable that services be produced at minimum cost. Competition puts pressure on firms to achieve efficiency because it puts pressure on the prices they can charge; lower prices force firms to be productively efficient. Productive efficiency issues are becoming increasingly an issue with airports, and benchmarking studies (e.g. ATRS, 2003) suggest a wide range of productivity levels – see Oum, Zhang and Zhang (2003) for a recent investigation.

While efficiency is often taken as being the objective which policy makers are, or at least should, be pursuing, it may be the case that policy makers are also seeking to keep profits of firms with strong market power at modest levels. It can be argued (see Forsyth, 2002) that much price regulation, particularly as it applies to airports, seeks to constrain monopoly profits per se, rather than necessarily promote efficiency. Governments may be worried not so much about monopoly welfare losses as about monopoly firms earning high profits. The clearest example of this arises with airports which are subjected to substantial excess demand, such as London Heathrow, yet prices for which are regulated to be well below market clearing levels (see Andrew and Hendriks, 2004). Regulation of this nature does not promote efficiency – in fact it probably lessens it (depending on whether other allocative devices such as slots markets work). It does however keep profits down, and prices close to (arbitrarily measured) costs.

To this extent, regulation may be implemented which imposes greater costs in terms of productive inefficiency than savings it achieves through lessening of deadweight losses from monopoly pricing. Increased competition should lessen profitability. However, an airport system which embodies some competition between firms could be quite efficient in overall terms, yet it might still earn "unacceptably" high returns.

3   ASSESSING AIRPORT COMPETITION

As is often the case with assessing the strength of competition in a market, it is not feasible to draw on a set of reliably estimated demand cross elasticities for the products of the different suppliers. Rather it is necessary to draw on information about a range of factors which could influence the extent that the products of one seller are substitutes for those of another. There will be various imperfect indicators, which, when considered together, will provide some evidence on competition. Indicators for airports are summed up in Table 1.

3.1   Airline Demand Elasticities

Demand elasticities for airports are derived demand elasticities, and they depend in part on the elasticity of demand for the final product, airline travel. It is normally taken that the elasticity of demand for airline travel is moderately high – typically above 1.0

3.2   Share of Airline Costs

Airport charges normally only account for a small proportion – often less than 5% – of total airline costs. Other things equal, this would suggest a very low demand elasticity for airports.

Table 1 Indicators of Competition

Indicator	Comment
Air Transport Demand Elasticity	Higher demand elasticity implies higher airport demand elasticity
Share of Airline Costs	Low share implies low airport demand elasticity
Destination Competitiveness	Greater competitiveness of alternative destinations Implies higher airport demand elasticity
Proximity of Other Airports	More airports imply more intense competition
Price Discrimination	Presence indicates competition is not strong
Responses to new Competition	Strong response consistent with effective competition in market segment
Responses to Pricing Freedom	Price increases indicate lack of strong competition
Different Prices	Different prices indicate lack of strong competition

3.3   Destination Competitiveness

To the extent that an airport serves a city which is a destination, the competitiveness of destinations will affect demand elasticities. Different leisure destinations may be substitutes, and this will mean that, to an extent, the airports are substitutes are substitutes. Destination competitiveness is likely to be limited for business or visiting friends and relatives travel.

3.4   Proximity of Other Airports

Competition for an airport is likely to be stronger if there are other airports in the vicinity which can handle origin traffic from the city and destination to the city. If there were several comparable airports in a city region, competition between them could be quite strong.

3.5   Existence of Price Discrimination

Price discriminatory charges schedules are difficult to support if competition is strong. When competition is imperfect, price discrimination can survive, as airline fares have indicated (though strong competition from low cost carriers is breaking down the overt discriminatory mechanisms, such as Saturday night stays). Typical central city airports have long operated with weight or passenger based charging structures, which embody a distinct discriminatory element (since costs of runway use are little related to weight or passenger loads). The ability of airports to maintain these structures is evidence that they have faced limited competition.

3.6   Responses to New Competition

When smaller, urban fringe or regional airports enter the market and attract low cost carriers, how does the city centre airport respond? If it does not respond, this could be evidence that the new airport is not a serious competitor (or that the airport does not want to attract low cost carrier traffic). On the other hand, if it responds by offering discounts to attract such traffic, this is evidence that competition is effective, at least in this market segment. In fact, many such airports have responded in this way. At these airports, discriminatory price structures are not eliminated, but rather changed. Competition is strong enough to affect prices, but not to make discrimination completely non viable.

3.7   Responses to Pricing Freedom

In a number of cases, airports have been permitted to change their prices, sometimes to increase them substantially. For example, before privatisation, Sydney airport was permitted to almost double its aeronautical charges–in the next year, passenger numbers increased (ACCC, 2005). After direct airport regulation was removed in late 2001, Canberra airport increased its aeronautical revenue per passenger by 108%. The volume of passengers did fall, but this was more due to the collapse of one of the two major airlines (Ansett, which had about 40% of the traffic) – by 2003–04, passenger numbers were above what they had been in 2000–01 (ACCC, 2005). These responses suggest very low demand elasticities, and the absence of strong competition.

3.8   Different Prices

If prices charged by different airports for essentially the same services are different, this suggests that they are not strong competitors for one another in the same market. Within individual countries, in North America, Europe and Australasia, there are wide differences in per passenger or per movement revenues between city airports (some are more than 80% higher than the lowest) (TRL, 2002). This suggests that these airports are not strong competitors for one another.

In summary, these indicators suggest that the competitive picture is a mixed one. They suggest that some airports are not likely to be too constrained by competition, but that competition may be quite effective for some traffic types, and between some close airports, moderately strong.

3.9   Factors Influencing Substitutability

The strength of competition between airports depends on how substitutable they are for each other. There are several factors which will influence this.

Perhaps the most obvious and important factor is proximity. Close airports can compete intensively, whereas airports separated by large distances are not likely to be able to do so. Distance influences both access time and cost. If there is substantial overlap between the catchment areas of airports, access times and costs for them can be similar, and they may be potentially close competitors. If one airport has a distinct advantage over the other, for example access to and from the central city airport is quicker and cheaper, then competition from other airports will be weak.

Proximity of airports also depends, in turn on population densities. In low population density countries such as Canada and Australia, cities and their airports will be widely

likely to be the most willing to switch between airports on price. Price sensitive business travellers may be the next most willing to switch. Home leisure travellers seeking log haul flights will be prepared to travel to more distant airports, especially if parking charges are low. Visiting foreign leisure travellers on long haul flights are likely be less familiar with the region, and may still prefer to use a central city airport to arrive at. Hub passengers may have some sensitivity to airport prices, though it is difficult to be definitive on this. The typical passengers on regional and short haul full service carriers are likely to have a strong preference for the central city airport, as will business and foreign leisure travellers on international long haul flights.

Depending on the traffic they serve, the strength of competition between various types of airports will be as outlined in Table 4.

Central city airports are likely to be separated from each other by moderate to large distances. They may compete with each other for low cost traffic, especially if population densities are high, as in Germany and the UK. The may also compete to a limited extent as hubs. In addition, a less central airport (e.g. Hamburg in Germany) will compete with the more central airport for direct services rather than services through the hub (e.g Frankfurt).

Urban fringe or regional airports may be quite strong competitors for central city airports for low cost traffic. They are likely to be located much closer to the central city airport than airports in other cities, and may be quite attractive to leisure travellers. In Europe, secondary airports targeting low cost carriers have been successful in attracting them, lessening the traffic which might otherwise go to the central city airports.

Finally, especially in countries with high population densities, and with a number of airports within moderately close proximity, there can be moderately strong competition between these airports.

This pattern of competition will have distinct implications for policy – these are considered in the next section.

Table 4   Competition between Airport Types

Airport Types	Types of Competition
Central City with Central City	Some competition in leisure/low cost markets if sufficiently close Possibility of some hub competition Limited competition in long haul point to point
Central City with Urban Fringe/Regional Airports	Possible strong competition in leisure/low cost markets Limited competition in niche higher fare markets No hub competition No competition in long haul point to point
Fringe/Regional Airports with other Fringe/Regional Airports	Strong competition in leisure/low cost markets if moderately close Little involvement with other types of traffic

4   AIRPORT COMPETITION POLICY PROBLEMS

With competition between airports becoming a reality, several policy problems emerge. They involve various different aspects, and include:

- Whether competition can be used as a substitute for price regulation;
- Impacts of competition from secondary airports on city airport price structures and allocation of flights to airports;
- Subsidies and Competition Merger (and horizontal separation) policy;
- Subsidies and Competition; and
- Asset sales and privatisation processes.

These are considered in turn.

4.1   Competition as a Substitute for Regulation

Price regulation is often instituted when competition is not strong enough to discipline the price behaviour of firms with market power. Regulation can be effective in keeping overall prices down, but it usually involves a cost. This cost is in terms of weakened incentives to minimise costs – regulated firms do not keep costs at a minimum because they do not enjoy the full benefit of their cost reduction efforts. Incentive regulation, such as price caps, attempts to strengthen the incentives for cost reduction, but even good regulation, in practice, weakens incentives for efficiency. Thus, in practice, regulation has a cost which is manifest in cost levels being higher than they need to be (on regulation in general, see Armstrong, Cowan and Vickers, 1994, and as applied to airports, see Productivity Commission, 2002, Chs 4, 8).

In spite of this, many firms with strong market power are subjected to regulation. When airports have been privatised, they have almost always been subjected to price regulation. In some cases, price monitoring has been substituted for explicit regulation in the hope that it will have less of an adverse impact on incentives. In most situations where airports have been privatised, it has been assumed that competition would not be strong enough to discipline price behaviour. In its review of price regulation, the Australian Productivity Commission (Productivity Commission, 2002) did examine whether competition would be strong enough – it concluded that, in most cases, it would not be, but it recommended monitoring as a substituted for regulation. Starkie (2002) has also examined the issue. However, Australian airports are widely separated geographically, and it is possible that competition may be an effective regulator of prices in countries with higher population densities, such as Germany and the UK.

If competition can work as an effective substitute for regulation, it would be a preferable option, since it does not entail the efficiency costs which are associated with regulation. From an efficiency perspective, competition may not work perfectly – it may be strong enough to keep prices fairly close to costs, but it may not be strong enough to reduce them to optimal levels. If so, it could be preferable to regulation, since the efficiency costs (specifically monopoly deadweight losses from prices being too high) are likely to be less than the costs from lower productivity under regulation. In short, from an efficiency perspective, competition between airports may not be very strong, yet moderate competition may be preferable to regulation.

This presupposes that the objective of regulation is efficiency – regulation is necessary to curb deadweight losses from excessively high prices. As noted earlier, the underlying objective of price regulation may not be the reduction of deadweight losses – rather it may be to keep prices close to costs, and profit levels moderate. If this is the objective, competition is less attractive as the constraint. Competition may result in a more efficient outcome than regulation, yet under it, prices may still be moderately high and profits very high. Competition may have to be quite strong to achieve a situation under which prices are very close to costs. Thus competition which is sufficiently strong to achieve a tolerable level of efficiency may not be strong enough to achieve the political objective of low prices and profits. For much of the discussion which follows, it will be taken that efficiency is the objective, though it should be borne in mind that in reality, regulators may be paying attention to profit levels as well.

The effectiveness of competition as a regulator of prices can be considered for a number of distinct cases.

4.1.1   Competition between Regional Airports

There are situations when across-the-board product range competition may take place between airports. Urban fringe and regional airports may concentrate on charter and low cost carrier traffic. Several such airports may be in direct competition with one another to handle such traffic, and to be the base for these airlines' operations. Airlines do have some bargaining power since they can credibly threaten to take their business elsewhere. In such a situation, competition may be an effective discipline on the airports pricing, and it may force them to minimise their costs.

In fact, smaller airports are often not regulated. This partly reflects ownership – many are owned by local or regional governments, which seek to attract business rather than maximise airport profits through charging high prices. There are, however, several airports which are now privately owned or operated. Bristol airport in the UK is privately owned, and London Luton airport, a major airport for charter and low cost carrier flights, is privately operated. Luebeck airport in Germany, which serves the low cost carrier market, is being privatised. These airports are not directly regulated, reflecting the view that there is a reasonable chance that competition between secondary airports would be strong enough to discipline their price behaviour and promote efficiency. Competition may be a more cost effective discipline on such airports than explicit regulation.

4.1.2   Competition between Distant City Airports

Many cities have one major airport, and often these cities are separated by moderate to large distances from other cities with comparable airports. These airports serve traffic which is less sensitive to access time (e.g. leisure travellers on low cost carriers) and traffic which is highly sensitive to access time. Granted the distances between such airports, and the significant proportions of time sensitive traffic, it is unlikely that they will be effective competitors for one another. These airports may face competition from urban fringe or regional airports, but this will cover only some of their product range (for more discussion of this issue, see below). For city airports, competition will not be an effective price regulator.

4.1.3   Potential for Competition in Multiple Airport Cities

There are several large cities around the world which have two, three or occasionally more airports capable of handling a broad range of traffic – London, New York and Paris are examples. Evidence suggests that they are sufficiently close together for them to be effective substitutes when passengers are evaluating their options (see Pels, 2000, Chs 6, 7). Could competition between these airports, if owned separately, be strong enough to make regulation redundant?

This seems unlikely. Leaving aside the chance that the airports in such cities would recognise their strategic interdependence and tacitly maintain high prices, there are doubts whether they compete strongly against one another even if they wanted to. For a start, many of the major airport are subject to excess demand, and are either slot constrained, congested or both. They have little incentive to compete to gain traffic which they cannot handle.

Secondly, city airports tend to be very unequal. One airport usually has a much preferred location, and the advantage of a wider choice of destinations and greater frequencies. Second airports are often built to relieve congestion at major airports, yet in spite of this, they struggle to become viable. Several cities have "white elephant" second airports on the urban fringe which fail to compete with congested central airports. While the second or third airport may have a locational advantage for some parts of a large city (Stansted may be preferred to London Heathrow by residents of the North East suburbs of London), overall they will be at a strong disadvantage. It would take a lot of encouragement for most airlines which use Heathrow to switch to Stansted. Second airports are normally further out and more expensive to travel to than the central airports. If the second airport costs only US \$5 more to travel to, the central airport can charge US \$5 more per passenger and still be competitive. Given the level of most airport charges (generally around US\$5–US\$15 per passenger for major airports – TRL, 2002), this would be a substantial price increase, which would lead to very high profits.

Whether this is consistent with efficiency depends on the nature of the premium that the preferred airport can charge. If the preferred airport is capacity constrained, the premium which it charges over less preferred airports earns it a locational rent. This rent is consistent with efficiency, especially in the sense of allocation of flights to airports. The higher price rations the use of the preferred airport, and it promotes efficiency. Thus a higher price for Heathrow over Stansted is efficient – indeed, efficient rationing prices for Heathrow would be much higher than current charges.

However, not all rents which arise from higher prices at preferred airports are efficient locational rents. For a rent to be a genuine locational rent, consistent with efficient allocation, it is necessary that the higher price be allocating scarce capacity. Consider a city airport, with a preferred location, competing against one or more secondary airports on or beyond the urban fringe. It can, if it wishes, charge higher prices than its competitors. But suppose that it has ample capacity, and that the marginal costs of use are low. If it does charge higher prices, it will discourage use of its facilities, and it will create a deadweight loss. Higher prices are not necessary to ration scarce capacity, and the rent created is a monopoly rent, which is inefficient, and not a locational rent, which is consistent with efficiency.

When capacity is constrained, as it is with Heathrow, the inability of competition to keep prices down, because competitors are less well located, does not have efficiency

implications. At the same time, actual regulation which *does* keep prices down is inefficient, unless there is some efficient allocation mechanism, such as a well functioning slot
market, to take the place of prices. When capacity is not constrained, the fact that competitors are unequally well located means that competition is less effective in lessening
the efficiency cost of using market power.

In the short run, it is unlikely that there will be the conditions for competition between
established airports in major cities to discipline pricing. In the long run, new competitors
could enter if existing airports are earning high profits. Entry into the urban airport
market is difficult, however. To start with, environmental factors make it difficult to
obtain permission to develop new airports in urban areas. New airports are likely to be
fringe airports with unattractive locations. It will take a long time to develop airports
which can compete across the product range, and new airports are likely to have inferior
ranges of destinations and lower frequencies than established airports.

Major airports may also be in competition with each other for airlines to use them as
hubs. Thus in this sense, Heathrow may be in competition with Amsterdam Schiphol,
Paris and Frankfurt. However, this competition, to the extent that it exists, must be
regarded as limited and very long term. At the moment, and for the foreseeable future,
these airports are tightly slot constrained and it would be extremely difficult for large
airlines to switch hubs. They would have to sell their (extremely valuable) slots at the
airport they are leaving at bargain prices and buy many slots at their new hub-essentially
they would lose much of the rents they currently enjoy from their grandfathered slots (for
some airlines, their most valuable asset). Airlines have substantial physical investments
at their hubs. Airlines which switch would lose the strong advantages of combining hub
with origin destination traffic. For the large city airports which function as hubs, hub
competition is unlikely to be a strong discipline on pricing.

In summary, for airports which are currently regulated or monitored, or which would
be regulated if they were privatised, the possibility of airport competition does not
change the regulatory equation by very much. Major city airports are not likely to subject
to strong competition for much of their product range. If there is only one airport in
the city, it is likely that the nearest other city airports will be too distant to provide
effective competition except in niche markets. Where large cities have several airports,
it is usually the case that such airports are congested or capacity constrained, which
severely limits their ability and incentive to compete. Secondary urban fringe or regional
airports typically have inferior locations than major city airports, and they can effectively
challenge them for only a small proportion of their traffic. Competition between airports
to act as hubs is limited and very long term.

By contrast, competition between regional airports, especially in high population
density countries, may be sufficiently strong to do away with direct regulation. These
airports tend to target the same low cost markets, and there may be several airports in
the same catchment area. Travellers will tend to have low values of time, and this leads
to low access costs, and similar access costs for the airports in the catchment. The ability
of these airports to charge high prices is effectively constrained by competition.

4.2   Competition from Secondary Airports

In a number of locations, especially in Europe but also elsewhere, competition is opening
up between established city airports and airports on the urban fringe or regional airports.

The urban fringe or regional airports are typically focussed mainly on low cost traffic. These airports are often able to offer lower charges than the city airports, possibly because they operate at lower cost, possibly because they offer a reduced range of services, and possibly because they may be subsidised. The emergence of this competition poses several efficiency questions, associated with price structures and the allocation of traffic between airports (see Forsyth, 2003).

Many city airports have adequate capacity, and they cover their costs by imposing a quasi Ramsey price structure, in which prices are based on aircraft weight, passengers, or both (these in turn are inversely related to elasticity of demand). When a monopoly which is implementing Ramsey pricing is opened up to competition, this price structure becomes unsustainable, and at the very least, will need to be revised.

When the new airport enters with lower charges for a particular market segment, namely flights of low cost carriers, the city airport can choose not to respond. For example, Hamburg airport in Germany did not seek to match the charges offered by nearby Luebeck airport when it started attracting low cost carriers. If an airport does not respond, it will lose low cost carrier traffic, and it must recover its costs from a lower base. It can do this by restructuring its charges, and the efficiency cost is not likely to be high granted that demand elasticities are low. However there will be an efficiency cost when flights switch to the urban fringe or regional airport, because they could be handled at zero or low marginal cost at the more convenient city airport, but they are induced to use the less convenient urban fringe or regional airport by its lower charges. This misallocation comes about as a result of prices being set above marginal costs at the city airport to achieve cost recovery.

Alternatively, suppose that the city airport does respond to the lower charges being offered by the urban fringe or regional airport. The airport will seek to adjust its charges so as to attract the low cost traffic while not reducing its charges across its whole product range. Airports may price discriminate overtly, and offer the low cost carriers lower charges, or they may offer lower charges on a general basis but for categories which target the low cost carriers. Thus they will offer discounts for new flights by an airline, or flights to new destinations. While established carriers can take advantage of some of these discounts, they are primarily of benefit to the low cost carriers which are flexible in their choice of airport. Again, to achieve cost recovery, the airport will need to revise its price structure, possibly increasing charges for categories of flights not likely to switch airports. In the recent years of rapid growth of low cost carriers, discounts for new flights have been an effective means of implementing price discrimination – over time, as these flight cease to be new, it remains to be seen how effectively these airports can continue to implement discriminatory price structures.

This response has the effect of encouraging the low cost carriers to use the more preferred airport when capacity is available at low marginal cost. However, it can have an efficiency cost through its impact on airline competition. Two airlines offering services on the same route will be paying different airport charges – the established full service carrier will be paying more for using the airport than the low cost carrier which can access discounts on its new routes. This will lead to a less efficient allocation of traffic between the two airlines.

Over the longer term there is also the issue of whether there will be excessive investment in airport capacity. If the city airport has adequate capacity, incurring the fixed costs of developing urban fringe or regional airports to enable them to handle airline traffic would be inefficient. However, local communities may make these investments in order to attract economic activity and tourism to their region. If the city airport signals in advance that it is prepared to match prices, it is less likely that excessive investment in airport capacity will take place.

In summary, competition need not always be efficiency enhancing, especially when it is imposed on a situation in which there are already significant distortions. When existing prices are well above marginal cost, there is a danger that additional competition will lead to inefficient duplication of facilities.

4.3   Subsidies and Competition

When some, but not all, of a group of competitors are subsidised, patterns of competition are distorted. Subsidised competitors will gain at the expense of unsubsidised ones, even though their cost of provision is not lower – as a result there will be an inefficient allocation of business to competitors. There are several examples of subsidy in airports. Secondary airports are often explicitly subsidised by local regions, and some airports may be have obtained implicit subsidies by purchasing assets at lower prices than their competitors. Some secondary airports have been winning traffic away from major airports by offering lower charges – to the extent that these are underpinned by subsidies, an inefficient allocation of flights to airports may have resulted. Further, LCCs which use secondary airports may be gaining an artificial advantage over the full service competitors, and airline competition could be being distorted.

Airport subsidies are now a big issue in Europe. The issue is not a simple one, as there are several possible justifications of these subsidies. A subsidy to a small secondary airport with ample capacity may enable it to set a price close to marginal cost, which could be very low. If it had to cover costs on a small traffic base, charges might have to be very high and traffic would be lost. When major airports are subject to congestion, there is an external cost to their use; if secondary airports are subsidised and draw traffic away from them, a more efficient allocation of traffic may result (this is like the argument for subsidising urban public transport). If local communities believe that there are external economic benefits to be obtained if they can attract air traffic and tourism, should they not be permitted to offer subsidies to correct the externality which they perceive? If urban areas are congested and facilities are underpriced, shifting business and tourism to surrounding areas could be efficient.

While airport subsidies can be justified in some circumstances, they do have efficiency costs and need not be justified in all circumstances. Guidelines developed by competition authorities may be a means of addressing the problem.

4.4   Merger Policy and Horizontal Separation

While the actuality or possibility of competition between airports may not have a large impact on regulatory policy, it can have major implications for merger and industry structure policy. Airports may seek to merge or and some are currently talking about strategic alliances. When airports are privatised, decisions must be made as to privatise them as a bloc, or to sell them separately. When the UK privatised BAA, it sold it as a going concern and did not separate the London airports, Heathrow, Gatwick and

Stansted. By contrast, when Australia privatised its airports, it insisted that major airports be sold to separate owners, even though most of them were at least 800 km apart. There is also a question as to whether competition regulators should actively intervene to alter industry structure – for example to separate Stansted from the other London airports.

As a general rule, if competition between firms is not very strong, then there is not going to be much of a competitive detriment if they are allowed to merge. There is unlikely to be much loss of benefits from competition between widely separated airports such as Sydney and Brisbane, or Hamburg and Duesseldorf if they were permitted to merge. However, even though competition between some airports may not span the product range, some competition does exist and it could be welfare enhancing. Secondary airports compete to an extent with major airports, and to some extent, with each other.

As always, merger or structural separation policy relies on determining the balance of benefits from a merger compared to the losses of efficiency entailed by the reduction in competition. There is not much literature on what the benefits of having two locationally separated airports under a single owner. Some economies may depend on proximity – there may be some economies of operation if the airports are close by each other. Airports which are serving overlapping markets may be able to coordinate services and allocate capacity better if they are under one owner – within firm coordination could work better than the price mechanism especially if price flexibility is constrained by regulation. When firms are subject to a cost recovery constraint which results in prices above marginal cost, there are gains in spreading cost recovery over a wider base; these gains, though real, are not likely to be large however. In some cases there will be substantial economies at the plant level (e.g. when traffic is concentrated at one airport), but most merger issues arise with separate airports. There are likely to be some benefits from horizontal integration, though it is not obvious that they are very large.

There are a some situations where the balance between benefits of integration need to be considered against the costs of reduced competition. These include competition between secondary airports, competition between regional airports and major city air-ports, and competition between hub airports.

The situation of common ownership of major and secondary airports, such as that with Frankfurt and Hahn, is more complex. While the two airports may be competing for some traffic, notably LCC traffic, competition may not be impacting very strongly on the major airport. In addition, as noted above, competition need not always deliver an efficient allocation of traffic between separately owned airports. As against this, it is not clear that the major airport will gain much from owning the secondary airport. It may be able to coordinate and allocate traffic, but would the result be any better than if the airports were competing?

A more potent objection to common ownership might lie in the scope for this to distort competition between secondary airports. Many major airports are very unlikely to be profit maximisers – rather they are almost certain to be regulated private firms or public firms. They have the ability, and often the incentive, to cross subsidise one airport from another. A secondary airport owned by a major airport need not compete on equal terms with other secondary airports. It may indulge in provision of excess capacity, to forestall competition. It could indulge in predatory pricing (though determining what is and is not predatory when airports have substantial excess, fixed, capacity is no easy task).

It has been claimed, by competitor airports, that BAA's London Stansted has behaved in a predatory manner – while competition regulators did not act, they accepted that

REFERENCES

Air Transport Research Society (2003) *2003 Airport Benchmarking Report: Global Standards for Airport Excellence,* ATRS, University of British Columbia, Vancouver (www.atrsworld.org).

Andrew, D and N Hendriks (2004) "Airport Regulation in the UK", in P Forsyth, D Gillen, A Knorr, O Mayer, H-M Niemeier, and D Starkie (eds) *The Economic Regulation of Airports: Recent Developments in Australasia, North America and Europe,* Aldershot, Ashgate.

Armstrong, M, S Cowan and J Vickers (1994) *Regulatory Reform: Economic Analysis and British Experience,* Cambridge Mass, MIT Press.

Australian Competition and Consumer Commission (ACCC) (2005) *Airports Price Monitoring and Financial Reporting 2003–04,* Canberra and Melbourne, ACCC, February (www.accc.gov.au).

Barrett, S (2000) "Airport competition in the deregulated European Aviation Market", *Journal of Air Transport Management,* pp 13–27.

Braeutigam, R (1979) "Optimal Pricing with Intermodal Competition", *American Economic Review,* March, 69, 1, pp. 38–49.

Davy European Transport & Leisure (2004) *Late Arrival: A Competition Policy for Europe's Airports,* Dublin, Davy Research Department.

Forsyth, P (2002) "Airport Price Regulation: Rationales, Issues and Directions for Reform", Department of Economics, Monash University, *Discussion Paper 19/02.*

Forsyth, P (2003) "Airport Competition and the Efficiency of Price Structures at Major Airports", Paper presented at German Aviation Research Society, Research Seminar, Leipzig November.

Forsyth, P (2004) "Replacing Regulation: Airport Price Monitoring in Australia", in P Forsyth, D Gillen, A Knorr, O Mayer, H-M Niemeier, and D Starkie (eds) *The Economic Regulation of Airports: Recent Developments in Australasia, North America and Europe,* Aldershot, Ashgate.

Graham, A (2003) *Managing Airports An International Perspective,* (2nd Edn) Elsevier Butterworth Heinemann, Oxford.

McKenzie-Williams, P (2004) "A Shift towards Regulation? The Case of New Zealand" in P Forsyth, D Gillen, A Knorr, O Mayer, H-M Niemeier, and D Starkie (eds) *The Economic Regulation of Airports: Recent Developments in Australasia, North America and Europe,* Aldershot, Ashgate.

Morrison, S (1982) "The Structure of Landing Fees at Uncongested Airports", *Journal of Transport Economics and Policy,* 16, pp 151–159.

Oum, T, A Zhang and Y Zhang (2003) "Concession Profit and its Efficiency Implications on Alternative Forms of Economic Regulation of Airports", Paper presented at Air Transport Research Society Conference, Toulouse, July.

Pels, E (2000) *Airport Economics and Policy: Efficiency, Competition and Interactions with Airlines,* Vrije Universiteit Amsterdam, Tinbergen Institute Research Series No 222.

Productivity Commission (2002) *Price Regulation of Airport Services, Report No 19,* AusInfo Canberra January.

Starkie, D (2002) "Airport regulation and competition", *Journal of Air Transport Management,* 8, pp 63–72.

Starkie, D (2004) "Testing the Regulatory Model: The Expansion of Stansted Airport", *Fiscal Studies* 25 (4) pp 389–413.

Starkie, D and D Thompson (1985) "Privatising London's Airports: Options for Competition", *IFS Report Series 16,* Institute for Fiscal Studies, London.

Transport Research Laboratory (TRL) (2002) *Airport Performance Indicators 2002,* Crowthorne, Berkshire, UK, TRL, August.

Advances in Airline Economics, Vol 1
Darin Lee (Editor)
© 2006 Published by Elsevier B.V.

16

Access to Airport Facilities: Its Impact on Market Competition

Monica E. Hartmann
University of St. Thomas*

ABSTRACT

Airlines must have sufficient access to airport facilities in order to be a viable competitor. The literature has established that landing slots and long-term gate leasing arrangements reduce airport entry and raise ticket prices. The role contracts play in governing access to *all* facilities – baggage handling, ticket counters, airfield facilities – has yet to be determined. This paper empirically examines how changes in contractual arrangements between airports and airlines over airport usage affect a carrier's decision to operate a route. Results indicate that the recent trend toward using hybrid agreements will increase the number of flight options at airports that switch from residual contracts, but reduce them at airports that switch from compensatory contracts.

1 INTRODUCTION

Access to an airport's facilities is essential for an airline to be a viable competitor at an airport. Abramowitz and Brown (1993) and Dresner et al. (2002) find that slot and gate controls deter entry and raise ticket prices. In 2000, Congress raised airline passenger fees to help our nation's airports finance construction of gates and other facilities to ease congestion and promote competition. These congestion problems, however, are only expected to get worse. Air travel is near its pre-9-11 levels and carriers have switched to smaller regional aircrafts to transport passengers. But, focusing *solely* on expanding facilities is not the answer to our congestion problems. The literature has shown that the price system can help alleviate congestion [Brueckner (2002, 2005) and Yuen and Zhang (2005)]. While efficient utilization of resources can be addressed with tolls, it

---
*Department of Economics, University of St. Thomas, 2215 Summit Avenue, St. Paul, MN 55105, U.S.A. Tel: 1-651-962-5681, Fax: 1-651-962-5682, Email: mehartmann@stthomas.edu

is as much a function of the contracts airport operators use to specify terms to use their facilities. If contractual agreements limit entrant's access to an airport's facilities, then the highest value user may not gain access to them and market competition is not enhanced.

Forty-one percent of airport operators at large hub airports use residual agreements to specify the terms in which carriers use and pay for airport facilities. These contracts tend to grant signatory airlines long-term terminal leases, reduced landing fees, and majority-in-interest approval rights over airport capital improvements in exchange for taking on the risk of a shortfall in airport revenue to cover operation costs. The increased power potentially gives signatory airlines the ability to block entry or expansion of rivals' operations at the airport. These contracts have been used by some localities to push the financial burden from airport expansions onto airlines. Tax payers' money may have been saved from financing terminal expansions, but at what cost? Higher ticket prices? Reduction in route service?

In recent years, some airline operators have switched to contracts that allow for more mobility of airport resources among airlines. For example, the operator of the Dallas-Fort Worth (DFW) Airport intends to allocate more access to airport facilities through short-term and preferential leases when its current Airport Use Agreement expires on December 31, 2009 (*DFW International Airport*, 2000). This movement toward hybrid agreements is not only expected to increase access to facilities, but enhance price competition. This raises interesting questions about how changes in airport contractual agreements shape price competition in the airline industry.

Existing literature documents the importance of slot and gate controls on market competition. But, the role contracts play in governing access to all facilities – baggage handling, ticket counters, airfield facilities – has yet to be established. This paper empirically examines how changes in contractual arrangements between airports and airlines over terms in which carriers gain access to airport facilities affect a carrier's decision to operate a flight between two airports. Pricing and enplanement data are gathered on approximately 1470 nonstop flights between cities serviced by large and medium sized airports. Results indicate that the recent trend toward using hybrid agreements will increase the number of flight options at airports that switched from residual contracts. In contrast, those airports switching from a compensatory agreement will observe a decrease in flight options or at least a slow down in growth in flight options. This probably reflects that hybrid agreements contain elements of both contract types; it is more restrictive than compensatory but less restrictive than residual. The results also suggest that ticket prices will rise (although by a small amount) despite the increased number of flight options as airports switch to these hybrid contracts.

2   HISTORY OF AIRPORT FACILITY ALLOCATION

Although excess demand for airport facilities is increasingly becoming a problem across the United States, it is not a new problem. In 1969, capacity at four major airports – JFK, LaGuardia, O'Hare, and Reagan National – was deemed insufficient and take-off and landing slots were rationed. Observing capacity problems across the nation, Congress passed the Aviation Safety and Capacity Enhancement Act of 1990 to help alleviate it. The Act authorized airports to collect Passenger Facility Charges (PFC) to finance expansions of airport runways and facilities. Congress recognized that expanding capacity would not foster market competition if smaller airlines or entrants could not gain access to these newly created resources. In order to ensure mobility, PFCs could not finance facilities later leased on a long-term basis or through exclusive arrangements. While this provision was essential, capacity limits and gate leasing arrangements are not the only factors that dictate how accessible facilities are. This also depends on the contractual agreements that define conditions to use *all* airport facilities. If these agreements limit admission to these newly created facilities, then increasing capacity may not lead to price competition as hoped.

There are three types of contracts airport operators use to specify the terms and conditions for using and leasing airfield and terminal facilities. Under a *compensatory agreement*, airlines are charged only for facilities actually used. Airports assume the financial risk of a revenue shortfall if airline demand drops. Under a *residual agreement*, signatory airlines[1] bear the risk. They are financially responsible for airport operating expenses not covered by nonairline revenue or other fees paid by airport users. The final contractual agreement is a *hybrid agreement* that contains elements of the previous two agreements. Both the carriers and the airport operator bear the financial risk.

The degree to which and how long carriers control airport resources and limit competition depends on which party – the airport and/or the airlines – bears the financial risk. Under residual agreements, contracts last on average twenty-eight years (FAA/OST, 1999).[2] Signatory carriers are given long-term contracts in exchange for assuming the revenue shortfall risk. Eighty-four percent of these contracts also include a majority-in-interest (MII) clause; a clause stipulating that signatory airlines have the right to review and approve airport development projects. Signatory airlines then potentially may vote against projects that grant entrants and smaller carriers greater access to airport facilities that would increase airport competition.[3] Conversely, airline carriers are given short-term contracts under compensatory agreements. This is not surprising given that airlines do not need to be compensated for bearing some risk. On average, these agreements are for seventeen years and only twenty percent of them include a MII clause. Finally, under the hybrid agreement where both the airlines and the airport operator bear the risk, the average contract length – twenty years – and the percentage of contracts containing the MII provision – seventy four percent – are between the averages for the other two contractual types.

3   LITERATURE SURVEY

Ever since Borenstein (1989) demonstrated that an airline's airport presence determines the degree in which a carrier can mark-up over costs, economists have investigated the source of the market power. Airlines have been found to enjoy a competitive advantage

---

[1] As of December 2000, DFW Airport has twenty-nine signatory airlines (DFW, 2000).
[2] Contract figures are based upon a 1998 survey conducted by the Airport Council International–North America (ACI-NA).
[3] There are exceptions to what the signatory airlines can veto. For example, they must approve construction of passenger terminal facilities if it is shown to be in the interest of public safety.

derived from a larger network of flights [Berry (1990), Borenstein (1991), Evans and Kessides (1993), and Henricks et al. (1997)], a greater frequency of flights [Pels et al. (2000, 2001, and 2003)], and economies of density – increase traffic volume decreases costs per passenger [Berry et al. (1997), Brueckner and Spiller (1994), and Brueckner et al. (1992).] Airport presence also has been shown to play a role in city-pair entry decisions [Berry (1992), Brueckner et al. (1992), and Reiss and Spiller (1989)].

Several other studies examine how access to airport facilities, potentially correlated with airport presence, shapes market competition. Marin (1995) concludes that price competition was enhanced with passage of bilateral agreements that allowed entry on several European routes. Ticket prices are found to rise with slot controls [Abramowitz and Brown (1993), Morrison and Winston (1990), and Dresner et al. (2002)], exclusive use of gates [Dresner et al. (2002)], and inclusion of majority-in-interest clauses in contracts between airport operators and airlines [Abramowitz and Brown (1993)]. But, facilities that airlines need access to, in order to be viable competitors, extend beyond gate and landing slots. The contracts airport operators use to govern admission to *all* facilities, terminal and airfield, also shape market competition. In recent years, there has been a shift toward using hybrid agreements to allow smaller carriers and entrants greater access to airport facilities. This study will substantiate and quantify the effect on market competition from switching to hybrid agreements.[4]

4 MODEL

This paper presents an empirical model to estimate carriers' routing decisions. In each period, domestic airline carriers simultaneously choose which routes to fly. A route is defined by the airports in which the flight originates and concludes and not by the city-pair. Also a flight between Airport A and Airport B is considered to be a different route than a flight between Airport B and Airport A [Borenstein (1989)]. All other carrier decisions – pricing, maintenance, and other flight characteristics – are assumed to be exogenously determined. Finally, product differentiation allows carriers to price above marginal cost and to earn positive profits.

A carrier's expected profits influence its decision to operate a flight between two airports. A route's profitability depends on 1) the carrier's market power on a given route, 2) the carrier's market power at a given airport, and 3) the carrier's ability to gain sufficient access to an airport's facilities to exhaust economies of scale and be a viable competitor. In addition to profitability considerations, the carrier's routing decision depends on an airport's capacity, especially when alternative airport destinations with no capacity constraints exist.

A carrier's decision to offer airline service between two airports is determined by a latent unobserved variable reflecting the expected profitability of operating that route, Π_{jrt}, where j is the carrier, r is the flight route, and t is the time period. Assume that

---

[4] This study also differs from Dresner et al. (2002) because the sample period, two years, is twice as long. The increased sample length allows for more variation in the data to extract information on how gate controls and contractual arrangements shape market competition. Furthermore, the sample period – 1992 and 1998 – covers a seven year span and thus captures market competition that existed pre and post entry by discount carriers.

the carrier's decision to operate flights on a given route indicates that the carrier expects profits to be positive on that route. Unobservable route profitability is defined to depend on the market size, route demand and cost conditions, and a random component of profit.

More specifically, the functional form for the unobserved expected profitability for route r on carrier j in time t is

$$\pi_{jrt} = V_{jrt}S_{jt} - F_{jrt} + \varepsilon_{jrt}. \tag{1}$$

V_{jrt} is a measurement of the per flier markup for carrier j in period t on route r. S_{rt} represents the market size and expectations about future growth for that market. F_{rt} denotes the fixed costs associated with the rth route in period t. It contains variables that reflect differences in fixed costs and entry barriers across routes. Finally, ε_{jrt} is the error in measuring carrier j's profitability on route r in period t. This error is distributed i.i.d. $N(0, \sigma^2)$. These differences in expected profitability are due to unobserved demand and costs conditions. This model allows one to predict, given demand and cost conditions, the routes carriers operate. With this understanding, one can anticipate how changes in access to airport facilities affect routing decisions.

5   DATA

5.1   Airline and Airport Data

Quarterly price and quantity data to construct average fares for each route is obtained from the Department of Transportation's *Origin and Destination (O&D) Survey of Air Passenger Traffic*. This microlevel data set consists of a random sample of 10 percent of all airline tickets issued by U.S. airlines for each quarter in 1992 and 1998. Segment distance, number of departures, and number of enplanements for nonstop flights are drawn from the Department of Transportation's *Service Segment Databank DB27R*. This route information is observed by carrier and quarter. Finally, a survey conducted by the Airports Council International-North America (ACI-NA) collects information on each airport's leasing arrangements, use of majority-in-interest clauses, gate usage practices, peak hour gate usage, and length of contractual agreements. The survey results are reported in the FAA's 1999 publication titled "Airport Business Practices and Their Impact on Airline Competition."

5.2   Market Size Data

Demand for air travel on a given route depends on the amount of business, the amount of tourism, and the population base between the originating and concluding metropolitan statistical areas (MSAs). The number of travelers on a given route is obtained from travel figures in the *O&D Survey*. The *1992 and 1997 Economic Census* report the number of employees in the service sector in 1000s for each MSA. Finally, the *Statistical Abstract of the United States* lists annual population figures for each MSA in 1000s as well.

5.3 Cost Variables

The profitability of operating flights out of a given airport depends highly on labor costs, a key input. The Bureau of Labor Statistics' *Metropolitan Area Occupational Employment and Wage Estimates* reports the median hourly wage for Aircraft Mechanics (OES Code Number 85323) by MSA. These wage figures are taken from the Occupational Employment Statistics (OES) Survey.

5.4 Sample

The model described in the previous section assumes that a carrier's decision to operate on a given route is independent of decisions made on other routes. If one maps a carrier's network of flights, one knows this assumption is violated constantly. This is particularly true for carriers that utilize a hub-and-spoke network of flights. Because there is a large number of routes from which a carrier can choose, estimating the model with a multinomial probit – each choice representing a different combination of routes flown – is not feasible. Alternatively, one can estimate the model if one limits the sample to passengers who fly nonstop to their destination. This allows one to ignore the correlation in routing decisions among alternative flight paths between two airports. The correlation in routing decisions across airports within the same city-pair is captured in a gravity type variable to be discussed in the next section.

Table 1 Airports in Sample By Classification

Medium-Sized Airport	Large-Sized Airport
	Atlanta
Austin	Baltimore
Colorado Springs	Boston
Dulles (Washington)	Chicago O'Hare
Fort Lauderdale	Cincinnati
Fort Myers	Dallas-Fort Worth
Jacksonville	Detroit
Kansas City	Houston
Memphis	JFK (New York)
Milwaukee	LaGuardia (New York)
Nashville	Las Vegas
New Orleans	Los Angeles
Oakland	Miami
Omaha	Newark
Ontario, CA	Orlando
Orange County	Phoenix
Portland, OR	Pittsburgh
San Antonio	Reagan National
San Jose	Salt Lake City
Spokane	San Diego
Tucson	San Francisco
Tulsa	Seattle
West Palm Beach	St. Louis
	Tampa

The sample is further reduced to nonstop flights between large and medium size hub airports in the years 1992 and 1998. See Table 1 for list of airports included in sample. Based on this criterion, there are 1470 routes from which carriers can choose to operate. The sample was limited to these routes because information on peak hour gate usage, airport-leasing arrangements, and gate usage practices are only available for these sized airports in these years. Finally, for each carrier, only those routes where it already operates flights at both endpoints are considered as potential routes to fly. This is because the true economic model of firm's routing decisions consists of two decisions. In the first stage, the carrier chooses whether or not to offer flights out of Airport A. If it chooses to operate, then in stage two the carrier decides which flights to offer at that airport. This final sample criterion is necessary because the first decision is ignored in this analysis. It allows for isolation of the impact contractual agreements have on routing decision from the decision to operate at a given airport. Table 2 provides the descriptive statistics for each variable used in this study, including means, maximums, minimums and standard deviations.[5]

Table 2 Descriptive Statistics

Variable Name	Mean	Std Dev	Min	Max
Carrier Discount	0.153	0.360	0	1
Carrier Hub (Origin)	0.416	0.493	0	1
Compensatory Agreement (Origin)	0.292	0.455	0	1
Discount Carrier on Route	0.208	0.406	0	1
Contract Length (Origin)	26.616	11.595	1	45
Ln (# of Passengers on Route)	7.009	1.258	2.303	9.980
Ln (Average Route Fare)	5.278	0.493	3.741	7.707
Ln (Flight Distance)	6.661	0.750	2.398	7.910
*Ln (# of Employees in Service Sector)	16.748	0.951	13.934	19.292
*Ln (# of Departures)	10.179	0.440	8.835	11.433
*Ln (Population)	8.223	0.641	6.311	9.887
*Ln (Hourly Aircraft Mechanic Salary)	2.936	0.082	2.641	3.102
Market Size Gravity Variable	6.975	1.451	−0.312	11.401
MII Clause (Origin)	0.784	0.412	0	1
Peak Usage of Gates (%) (Origin)	0.117	0.127	0	0.47
Gates For Exclusive Use (%) (Origin)	0.475	0.412	0	1
Quarter	2.502	1.117	1	4
Residual Agreement (Origin)	0.467	0.499	0	1
**Route Concentration Dummy Variable	0.784	0.411	0	1
Route HHI	7641	2427	1799	10000
Slot Constrained Airport on Route	0.285	0.451	0	1
Year	1.479	0.500	1	2

No. of observations = 5,235

* The natural logarithm of the geometric mean of each variable at the route's endpoints is calculated.

** The route concentration dummy variable equals 1 for routes where one carrier services at least 60% of the passengers.

---

[5] When constructing the sample for the probit estimation of the carrier-route decision, a carrier is considered operating a route only if it has at least 12 departures on that route in that quarter. This translates to at least one flight per week.

6 ESTIMATION

This section describes in more detail each component of expected route profitability in Equation (1). The first term, V_{jrt}, quantifies carrier j's variable profit per flier in period t on route r. It reflects the variation in demand and cost conditions across routes. It can be rewritten as

$$V_{jrt} = \alpha X_{rt} + \delta Z_{jrt}. \tag{2}$$

The vector of X_{rt} captures factors that influence per capita profits on a given route that do not vary across carriers. It includes 1) a dummy variable that equals one if a low cost carrier operates on that route,[6] 2) the average ticket price on route excluding taxes, 3) a dummy variable that indicates if either airport on the route is slot constrained – JFK, LaGuardia, O'Hare, and Reagan National – during the sample period, and 4) the median-hourly wage for aircraft mechanics by MSA. Employees' salaries proxies the difference in operating costs across cities. A geometric mean of the endpoints' hourly wages is used. It measures the central tendency, similar to a median, and thus a better measure of operating costs at the endpoints instead of the standard mean value.

The vector of Z_{jrt} captures factors that influence per capita profits on a given route that varies by carriers. Route specific variables comprise of 1) a dummy variable that equals one if the originating airport is a hub for the carrier – measuring airport presence, and 2) a dummy variable that equals one if the carrier is a low-cost carrier.

The dummy variable for low-cost carriers captures the variation in how airlines decide when to offer service on a route. Major carriers fly between two cities only if there is sufficient number of business travelers to cover expenses, while the low cost carriers are more concerned with the total number of fliers on the route (Boydston, 1999). Furthermore, this dummy variable will capture the differences in cost structure and price sensitivity of fliers across carrier type.

The second term in Equation (1), expected route profitability, is the market size. S_{rt} reflects expectations about route demand that is the same across carriers. It depends on the average fare, route population base, and amount of economic activity at the endpoints. Market demand is expressed as[7]

$$S_{rt} = \ln(Passengers_{rt}) = B_0 + B_1 \ln(Population_{rt}) + B_2 \ln(Departures_{rt})$$
$$+ B_3 \ln(Employment_{rt}) + B_4 \ln(Distance_r) + B_5 \ln(Avg\_fare_{rt}) + v_{rt}. \tag{3}$$

Specifically, the geometric mean of the population of the originating and concluding MSAs quantifies the size of the potential flier base. The geometric mean of the number of departures at airport endpoints is correlated with the amount of business activity that generates travel demand. This also reflects demand elasticity, the intensity of preferences for traveling. The geometric mean of the number of employees in the service sector proxies the amount of tourism that takes place in these cities. Note that market demand is estimated at the city-pair level and not at the route level. This is done to capture the

---

[6] Whether or not a low cost carrier operates on an alternative route is not explored. Goolsbee and Syverson (2005) show that incumbents do not cut fares on alternative routes, only on threatened routes where Southwest Airlines already operates at both endpoints.
[7] The natural logarithm is used to get rid of outliers and correct for heteroscedasticity.

correlation in flight demand across airports servicing the same city, New York City for instance.[8] This gravity type variable also allows for correlation in profitability across flights to similar destinations in different city-pairs, such as tourist destinations like Miami and Orlando both with large service sectors. Essentially, S_{rt} is constructed to capture why fliers gravitate to certain itineraries over others even if the flight distance and airfare are equivalent. For example, more people fly between Chicago and Las Vegas than between Chicago and Boise, Idaho because of the greater business and tourist travel that takes places between the two cities.

The final term in Equation (1) captures the role fixed costs, F_{rt}, play in the operation of airline carriers. Thus, a model of route profitability must reflect those costs operating at an airport that do not vary with the number of routes offered, but influence a carrier's operation decisions. Factors that affect operating costs include: 1) a measurement of airport congestion – percent of gate capacity used during peak periods,[9] 2) a dummy variable that equals one if the agreement the airport uses contains MII clauses, 3) a dummy variable that indicates the type of airport leasing arrangement used – compensatory, residual or hybrid, and 4) the percentage of gates granted for exclusive use. These final variables capture how access to airport facilities at originating airports dictates routing decisions.

7 RESULTS

The first set of results to report is the estimated coefficients for the gravity term, i.e., city-pair demand, as specified in Equation (3). See Table 3. To control for the endogeneity of

Table 3 Gravity Equation – Market Demand

Instrumental Variables Estimation Method
Instruments for Ln (Average Route Fare): *Slot Dummy Variable, HHI*

Parameter	Coefficient	Std. Error
Constant	−5.3933	0.3139*
Ln (Distance)	0.6779	0.0560*
Ln (Average Route Fare)	−2.9207	0.1722*
Ln (Geometric Mean of Departures)	1.7843	0.0437*
Ln (Geometric Mean of # of Employees in Service Sector)	0.2799	0.0221*
Ln (Geometric Mean of Population)	0.0510	0.0328
Quarter 1 Dummy Variable	0.2680	0.0364*
Quarter 3 Dummy Variable	−0.2513	0.0317*
Quarter 4 Dummy Variable	−0.0129	0.0301
Adjusted R^2	0.0215	
F(8,14174)	539.24	
Number of Observations	14183.00	

*Significant at the 5% level.

---

[8] BWI, Reagan National, and Dulles Airports also are considered servicing the same set of potential fliers.
[9] Phoenix's Sky Harbor airport is an example of an airport that is not slot constrained but due to its physical limitations cannot accommodate new airlines. The airport already is currently operating at 99% of gate capacity during peak periods.

price, the slot dummy variable and route Herfindahl-Hirschman Index (HHI) were used as instruments for price. As expected, consumers are more likely to fly on routes where the city-pair has a large population base and a strong tourist industry as proxied by the service sector. A positive relationship also is found between the number of fliers and economic activity as captured by the number of departures at the end points. Finally, city-pair demand rises with longer flights – reflecting fewer viable substitutes – and drops with higher ticket prices as expected. These findings are consistent with Marin's (1995) estimates of route demand.

Table 4 presents the results from a 2SLS estimate of average ticket prices by route. These give some insight on how fares are affected by the type of contract that specify

Table 4   Average Route Fare

Two Stage Least Square Estimation Method		
Parameter	I	II
Contract Variables:		
Compensatory Agreement		−0.0570*
		0.0173
Residual Agreement		−0.0353*
		0.0106
MII Clause	0.0754*	0.0422*
	0.0092	0.0157
Length of Contractual Agreement	0.0004	0.0010
	0.0004	0.0004
Facility Constraint Variables:		
Peak Usage of Gates (%)	−0.3483*	−0.3516*
	0.0344	0.0347
Gates for Exclusive Use (%)	0.0811*	0.1046*
	0.0092	0.0111
Slot Constrained Airport on Route	0.0394*	0.0397*
	0.0086	0.0088
Carrier-Route Characteristics:		
Route Concentration Dummy Variable	−0.0940*	−0.0951*
	0.0080	0.0080
Discount Airline Operates on Route	−0.1507**	−0.1480**
	0.0103	0.0104
Discount Airline	−0.0197*	−0.0269*
	0.0112	0.0111
Flight Distance	0.0003*	0.0003*
	0.0000	0.0000
Gravity Variable	−0.2549*	−0.2548*
	0.0024	0.0024
Aircraft Mechanic Salary	0.9929*	1.0248*
	0.0440	0.0461

Notes: Top entry in each cell indicates parameter estimates while bottom entry lists corresponding standard error.

The route concentration dummy variable equals 1 when one carrier services at least 60% of the market and zero otherwise.

Table 4 Average Route Fare—Cont'd

Parameter	I	II
Miscellaneous:		
Constant	3.8417*	3.7814*
	0.1301	0.1328
Quarter 1	0.0794*	0.0792*
	0.0087	0.0087
Quarter 3	−0.0697*	−0.0695*
	0.0087	0.0087
Quarter 4	0.0007	0.0008
	0.0087	0.0087
Year	0.0056	0.0055
	0.0064	0.0064
Adjusted R^2	0.795	0.7954
F Statistic	1354.04	1198.26
Number of Observations	5235	5235

*Significant at the 5% level
**Significant at the 10% level
Note: Top entry in each cell indicates parameter estimates while bottom entry lists corresponding standard error.

terms to use airport facilities. To control for the endogeneity of market demand, the gravity variable is first estimated and then the predicted value is used as a regressor. Column one shows the regression results when one only includes the typical variables that determine average fare. In column two, dummy variables for the type of contracts used at the originating airport are added as regressors. Signs and magnitude of the coefficients are similar across the two specifications. The type of contract used to grant access to facilities is found to have a statistically significant effect on average fares.

As expected, average fares rise with flight distance; there are fewer transportation alternatives to keep prices low. The presence of a discount carrier on a route lowers fares as well. Routes that fly into or out of a slot-constrained airport are more expensive as previously found. Also consistent with the literature, ticket prices rise with the use of contracts containing MII clauses and the percentage of gates granted for exclusive use. Both of these factors increase signatory airlines' ability to block entry or expansion of rivals' airport operations, thereby reducing price competition.

The negative coefficient on the gravity term suggests that average ticket prices are lower for routes with greater market demand. This probably reflects the cost savings passed onto consumers from economies of density on a route. Dresner et al. (2002) observe the opposite, but price falling with traffic volume is consistent with Abramowitz and Brown (1993) who also control for MII clauses in their study.

Interestingly, routes where the originating airport operator uses compensatory agreements are less expensive than routes where the operator uses hybrid agreements. This is as expected and is consistent with intuition. Airport facilities are more mobile under compensatory agreements, allowing more access to these facilities and promoting market competition. Unexpectedly, flights are more expensive at airports that use hybrid agreements than ones that use residual agreements. One may have hypothesized that these flights would be less expensive because the decreased mobility of airport facilities under residual agreements would inhibit price competition. But, the lower average fare for flights flown out of airports with residual agreements is observed even after controlling for contract length, slotting, gate exclusivity, and gate peak usage. Possibly, the fact that the signatory airlines are financially responsible for any shortfall in airport revenue may induce them to use airport facilities more cost effectively and pass savings onto their customers.

Table 5 reports the probit estimation results that allow for carrier random effects. A carrier's decision to operate a given route depends on route-specific profitability, carrier-specific route profitability, and potential entry barriers. Airlines are more likely to operate on routes where the originating airport allocates a lower percentage of gates for exclusive use and have a greater percentage of unused gates during peak periods. The slot

Table 5 Carrier-Route Operation Decision

Random Effects Probit Estimation Method

Parameter	Coefficient	Std. Error
Contract Variables:		
Compensatory Agreement	0.6479	0.192*
Residual Agreement	−0.0252	0.003**
MII Clause	0.0664	0.165
Length of Contractual Agreement	0.0113	0.005*
Facility Constraint Variables:		
Peak Usage of Gates (%)	−1.0106	0.390*
Gates for Exclusive Use (%)	−0.4098	0.149*
Slot Constrained Airport on Route	0.1443	0.099
Carrier-Route Characteristics:		
Carrier Hub	−0.5628	0.094*
Discount Airline Operates on Route	−0.5741	0.079*
Discount Airline	1.6384	0.135*
Flight Distance	−0.0005	0.000*
Gravity Variable	−0.1569	0.047*
Ln (Average Fare on Route)	−0.1229	0.146
Aircraft Mechanic Salary	−2.2528	0.579*
Miscellaneous:		
Constant	8.9903	1.728*
Quarter 1 Dummy Variable	0.0113	0.091
Quarter 3 Dummy Variable	−0.0606	0.092
Quarter 4 Dummy Variable	0.0074	0.091
Year	−0.1532	0.108
Sigma	0.7096	0.048
Rho	0.3349	0.030

*Significant at the 5% level   Log Likelihood = −6733.94
**Significant at the 10% level   # of observations = 27415
Likelihood ratio test of rho = 0: chi2(1) = 16037.13   Prob > chi2 = 0.0000

dummy variable, another proxy of airport congestion, has the reverse effect on routing decisions. One may hypothesize that carriers are more likely to operate flights on these routes because of the bigger market. But this slot effect is observed even after controlling for city-pair demand, i.e., the gravity variable. The slot coefficient then must be capturing the higher expected profitability for flights out of slot-constrained airports than flights out of alternative airports in the same city-pair, reflecting a superior flight option to fliers. The carrier-route characteristics also reveal some interesting insights about routing decisions. The likelihood of offering service falls with ticket price, mechanic salaries (i.e., labor costs), and presence of a low-cost carrier operating on that route. All three factors lower route profitability, reducing the incentive to operate.

Interestingly, carriers are more likely to offer flights at airports with hybrid contracts than ones with residual agreements and less likely than ones with compensatory agreements. These findings are consistent with the relative mobility of airport facilities across contract types. Resources are most and least mobile under compensatory and residual agreements, respectively, and with hybrid contracts somewhere in between. Thus, one should expect more route offerings at airports with compensatory agreements and fewer offerings at airports with residual agreements where airlines have more control over airport operations.

These coefficients also shed light on the expected market effects from the recent shift toward using hybrid agreements. Flight offerings will be reduced, or at least there will be a slower growth in flight offerings, at airports that switch from compensatory agreements. This reduction in flights is observed even after controlling for flight demand and peak airport capacity usage, two factors that constrain route offering decisions. On the other hand, flight options will increase for those fliers who patron airports that switch from residual agreements. Fliers will benefit from the signatory airlines' decreased ability from blocking entry or expansion of rivals.

In summary, construction of additional gates or reduction of the percentage of gates granted for exclusive use will increase the profits a carrier expects to earn on a route, thereby increasing its incentive to operate it. But, focusing solely on capacity expansion is not a sufficient way to address congestion concerns or encourage flight operations at an airport. One must also examine the terms in which airport operators use to grant access to their facilities. The recent trend toward using hybrid agreements to foster airport competition will increase or decrease flight options depending on the contract type currently used by an airport operator.

8   FUTURE WORK

This paper gives policymakers insights on how changes in contractual agreements between airlines and airport operators affect routing decisions and pricing behavior. These findings are based on an analysis of carrier operations of nonstop flights. The type of contractual arrangement used also can influence the path flown between endpoints. For instance, one can fly directly between Minneapolis and Boston or have a layover in Pittsburgh. The next step in analyzing the impact of contract type on market competition is to develop a structural model of carriers choosing a network of routes and prices simultaneously. This would allow one to explicitly endogenize price, take into account

Pels, Eric, Peter Nijkamp, and Piet Rietveld. (2000) "Airport and Airline Competition for Passengers Departing from a Large Metropolitan Area." *Journal of Urban Economics.* 48(1): 29–45.

Pels, Eric, Peter Nijkamp, and Piet Rietveld. (2001) "Airport and Airline Choice in a Multiple Airport Region: An Empirical Analysis for the San Francisco Bay Area." *Regional Studies.* 35(1): 1–9.

Pels, Eric, Peter Nijkamp, and Piet Rietveld. (2003) "Access to and Competition between Airports: a Case Study for the San Francisco Bay Area." *Transportation Research A.* 37(1): 71–83.

Reiss, Peter and Pablo Spiller. (1989) "Competition and Entry in Small Airline Markets." *Journal of Law and Economics.* 32(2): 179–202.

Yuen, Andrew and Anming Zhang. (2005) "Airport Congestion and Market Structure: The Case of Variable Passenger Time Costs." Working Paper, University of British Columbia.

Index